CASES ILLUSTRATIVE OF ORIENTAL LIFE

CASES ILLUSTRATIVE OF ORIENTAL LIFE

Decided in H.M. Supreme Court at Bombay

THE APPLICATION OF
ENGLISH LAW TO INDIA

ERSKINE PERRY

MANOHAR
2020

First published 1853
Reprinted 2020

ISBN 978-93-90035-28-1

Published by
Ajay Kumar Jain *for*
Manohar Publishers & Distributors
4753/23 Ansari Road, Daryaganj
New Delhi 110 002

Printed at
Replika Press Pvt. Ltd.

CONTENTS.

PART I. LAW OF PERSONS.

PART II. LAW OF THINGS.

* See Case on same subject, p. 516.

PART III. CONFLICT OF LAWS.

PART IV. MISCELLANEOUS.

PREFACE.

DURING the last few months of holding office in India I employed some leisure hours in collecting and revising a few cases of general interest that had come before me in the Supreme Court of Bombay, and I now venture to lay them before the public. The insight into human life afforded by transactions in a Court of Justice had always appeared to me to give peculiar opportunities to an observer for studying national character; but it is especially to a class like the English in India that such opportunities are most valuable. For the chief administrators in our vast Indian empire are so completely severed from the bulk of the population by colour, race, language, religion, and material interests, that they are often, if not habitually, in complete ignorance of the most patent facts occurring around them (*a*). But in courts of justice the veil which shrouds the privacy of Oriental life is necessarily drawn aside, the strong ties which at other times bind together cast and family in pursuit ot a common object are loosendc under the pressure of stronger individual interests, and there, amidst masses of conflicting testimony, and with

(*a*) A remarkable instance of this will be found in a case (*post*, p. 547), in which it appeared that a confederacy of more than forty persons had existed in the island of Bombay for very many years for the receipt of stolen goods, with profits said to amount to 60,000*l*. a year, but, although they had conducted their trade in the most open manner, and the facts were all well known to the native population, not a glimmering of the truth had ever reached the English authorities.

subtler intellects to deal with than usually appear before European tribunals, the motives, reasonings, and actions of the native population of India are displayed in broad light and may be traced with inestimable advantage. In proportion, however, as the knowledge of native manners increases do the difficulties which impede an English official in the administration of justice become embarassing. The weight due to testimony—the operation of motives familiar to every one in Court—the influence of circumstances derived from a common religion, a common mother tongue, and a unity of race—the national opinions and prejudices, with the knowledge of an infinite number of facts which are too familiar to all present to form subject of remark—are seen in an English Court of Justice to point conclusively to the decision, which the audience as well as the Bench are irresistibly led to adopt; but these guides to the judgment are either wholly wanting or are transfigured to the Anglo-Saxon who is dispensing justice to Hindus, Musalmáns, and Parsis. Moreover, rules of law which are applicable both in letter and in spirit to an English community are often felt to be grievously unjust if enforced strictly amidst Asiatic litigants, and hence most difficult questions arise as to the extent to which the letter of the English law may be departed from. For these reasons I had frequently experienced the urgent want of some authentic guide to the decisions of my predecessors, and inquired often, but in vain, how men like Sir JAMES MACINTOSH and Sir EDWARD WEST (*a*) had applied the English law to controverted questions amongst the natives of India. In default, therefore, of any better authority I have been led to think that a collection of cases on the chief subjects that come before an Indian Court of Justice, and

(*a*) Author of the celebrated Essay on Rent so often cited in the literature of Political Economy.

which presumes to boast of industry and close attention to local details in their decision, may not be unacceptable to the administrators of justice in India both in the Supreme Courts and in those of the Honourable Company, and to Natives as well as Europeans.

For although the Supreme Courts of India, from their administration of English law, would at first sight appear to be exceptional, and to have but little in common with the local Courts of the Provinces, yet the fact cannot be too broadly noted, that, so far as the suitors are concerned, the former are essentially Native Courts of Justice, and the proportion of Europeans to Native litigants and witnesses does not probably exceed one per cent. Moreover, on many of the most complicated questions, such as—Hindu and Mahomedan succession—the extent of parental authority —disputes arising out of conversion to Christianity (*a*)— native customs—the conflict of laws—the exposition of acts of the Legislative Council, &c., &c.—the Supreme Courts, and Courts of the Company, are, or ought to be, governed by the same rules. And, as I have had occasion to point out elsewhere (*b*), the fact of the English nation being the rulers of India leads to the necessary diffusion of English notions on law and morality, so as to make the study of them a necessary ingredient in the education of all who desire to be associated with Indian administration.

The principle by which I have been chiefly governed in the selection of cases is to admit those only of Indian or Colonial interest, on which the English books have not been found to furnish forth a clear authority; and it is remarkable, on how many important questions,—

(*a*) See a very important case as to the respective rights of husband and wife, after conversion of the former, p. 516, and which ought to have appeared in Part I., p. 91, with other cases on the same subject.

(*b*) Letter to Lord Campbell on Law Reform, *Ridgway*, 1851.

such as the legal relations of the East India Company as a corporation, the foundation of the sovereign power exercised by them in India, the administration of military law independent of Acts of Parliament, the liability of judicial and executive functionaries to Her Majesty's Courts of justice, the extent of legislative authority vested in the Government of India, and the conflict of Courts,—an Indian Tribunal is often called upon to decide, according to the spirit of English jurisprudence, without any very clear guide in our law literature.

Another class of Cases had been selected by me with the view of exhibiting the ruinous consequences produced by the procedure of the Master's Office in Equity suits (*a*), and as I had tested, by an experience of some years, the facility, speed and economy with which an Equity Judge can conduct inquiries under his own decrees in person, and thus wholly supersede the Master even where long accounts are in question, I was in hopes, as an old law reformer, that the testimony might be useful in the hands of Lord Brougham and others, who were seeking to advance Chancery Reform in England. But, after the cases were in print, the bill, which has subsequently become law, was brought forward, by which the greatest legal grievance of the day—the Master's Office—has been abolished, and the practice, which I am proud to say had been previously adopted at Bombay, of the Judges working their own decrees has been enjoined.

I have thus stated some of the reasons which have induced me to venture before the world with the present publication, and, I trust, they may be deemed sufficient to guard me from the charge of presumption in overestimating the value of a volume of my own decisions.

(*a*) See the two first cases in the Volume, Part I., pp. 1 & 42, and subsequent cases, pp. 158 & 162.

But the principal motive which has operated with me in preparing this work for the press has been the desire to foster the study of English law in India. In a progressive age, and in a highly advanced stage of civilization, it will probably be recognised as one of the highest duties in those whose age, position and experience have taught them any useful lessons in life to impart their knowledge to the rising generation. For many years past it has been my ambition to produce an elementary work on jurisprudence and English law, which might serve as a handbook to the studious youth both of England and of India. It has only been the difficulty of the task, and a sense of my own incompetence, that have hitherto deterred me, but I trust, if my health is spared, even yet by industry and zeal to take the first step towards supplying a want which all connected with legal education have experienced. In the meantime, it occurred to me that the very wide jurisdiction of the Supreme Court, comprising not only the whole *corpus juris* of the English law, but also the Hindu and Musalmán Codes, afforded scope for a selection of decisions by which first principles might be elucidated, and which by touching on questions of daily occurrence in Eastern life would prove a useful work in the hands of the Native as well as of the English student of Indian law. Another reason has co-operated to make a judicious selection of Oriental Cases appropriate for the end I am designating. The great function of a well organised legal tribunal is, not only to administer justice but, to administer it in a form that shall appear to be justice in the eyes of an intelligent audience. When a Court in England disposes of a case on "the rule in *Crogate's case*," on "the *scintilla juris*," or on a late decision in A. and E., the high respect in which English Courts of justice are held, the unbiassed opinion of a large independent Bar, the sympathy and support afforded by the governing classes to the judicial body, all combine to produce a general opinion that the decree of the Court is right, and to silence hostile criticism. But the Supreme Courts of India are located in the midst of a foreign but very acute population to whom technical reasoning is unmeaning gibberish, the governing classes of India are not sympathetic with her Majesty's Judges but rather prone to criticism, while the amusing gibes of Bentham and the more vehement strictures of James Mill on English law and lawyers have led to a sort of presumption in India that the decisions of these Courts must be founded on technical grounds, and therefore be opposed to justice. For these reasons it always appeared to me expedient to explain fully in simple language the grounds on which the doctrines of the law were founded, and hence a fuller treatment of the subject has been adopted than is usual, or than would be deemed appropriate, in the judgments of a Court in England. The end then in view was, I think, chiefly accomplished by the elementary and didactic exposition which I allude to, but for the purpose now more immediately before me, there can, I presume, be little doubt of its fitness. In order to make the work more useful in the rising law schools of India, I have attempted a classification of cases, which though imperfect as all such classifications must be (*a*), will still, I think, be found useful to the student.

A word or two remains to be said on the much vexed question of the orthography of Indian names. I fear that my work will be found as objectionable in this respect as those of most writers on the East. The per-

(*a*) The two first cases, for example, under Law of Persons might probably have been more appropriately placed under Law of Things, but in all systems it will be found that great variances occur as to the class in which different rights should be placed.

fection of a written character seems to be that it should convey through the eye an accurate idea of the pronunciation of each word; and this attribute is fully possessed by the Dévanágri in which Sanscrit is written, and by all the best native alphabets (*a*). The orthography used by Oriental scholars in Europe is almost universally that first propounded by Sir William Jones, somewhat modified, in which vowels are written according to their pronunciation in Italian, while each consonant has a fixed invariable sound, and this mode I always endeavour to adopt. But the genius of English orthography prefers the double *ee* and double *oo* to denote the Indian and Italian vowels *i* and *u*, and hence in a legal publication like the present, in which documents written by others necessarily appear, and wherein faithful transcription is rigorously expected, both modes of spelling have unavoidably crept in, to the confusion of the English reader, and much to the annoyance of the editor.

E. P.

London, March 4th, 1853.

(*a*) The value of this characteristic is tested by the fact that Hindu children are able to read directly they have learnt the value of each letter, so that an accomplishment, for which years are often needed in Europe, is acquired in India in three months.

RECORDERS OF BOMBAY,

UNDER 37 GEO. 3, c. 132.

Sworn in.		*Vacated Office.*
8 Oct. 1798.	Sir WILLIAM SYER.	Died 7 Oct. 1802.
28 May, 1804.	Sir JAMES MACKINTOSH.	Left India 5 Nov. 1811.
10 March, 1814.	Sir ALEXANDER ANSTRUTHER.	Died 16 July, 1819.
24 Oct. 1820.	Sir W. D. EVANS. [*Translator of Pothier on Obligations.*]	Died 5 Dec. 1821.
3 Feb. 1823.	Sir EDWARD WEST. [*Author of Essay on Rent, Treatise on Extents.*]	Created C. J.

CHIEF JUSTICES,

UNDER 4 GEO. 4, c. 71.

8 May, 1824.	Sir EDWARD WEST.	Died 18 Aug. 1828.
11 Sept. 1829.	Sir JAMES DEWAR.	Died 25 Nov. 1830.
1 Dec. 1831.	Sir HERBERT A. D. COMPTON.	Left India 2 Jan. 1839.
29 Jan. 1839.	Sir JOHN W. AWDREY.	Ditto 2 March, 1841.
16 March, 1841.	Sir HENRY ROPER.	Ditto 2 Nov. 1846.
3 Nov. 1846.	Sir DAVID POLLOCK.	Died 22 May, 1847.
22 May, 1847.	Sir T. ERSKINE PERRY.	Left India 17 Nov. 1852.
5 Dec. 1852.	Sir WILLIAM YARDLEY.	

PUISNE JUSTICES.

8 May, 1824.	Sir CHARLES H. CHAMBERS.	Died 13 Oct. 1824.
27 Oct. 1824.	Sir RALPH RICE.	Left India 27 Nov. 1827.
9 Feb. 1828.	Sir J. PETER GRANT.	Resigned 10 Sept. 1830.
11 Sept. 1829.	Sir WILLIAM SEYMOUR.	Died 24 Dec. 1829.
31 Dec. 1830.	Sir JOHN W. AWDREY.	Promoted C. J.
30 Oct. 1839.	Sir HENRY ROPER.	Promoted C. J.
10 April, 1841.	Sir T. ERSKINE PERRY.	Promoted C. J.
9 Nov. 1847.	Sir WILLIAM YARDLEY.	Promoted C. J.
— Feb. 1853.	Sir CHARLES JACKSON.	

CASES

ILLUSTRATIVE OF ORIENTAL MANNERS,

&c. &c.

PART I.

AGA MAHOMED RAHIM'S CASE.

1843.

Sept. 15th, 16th, 19th, 20th, 21st, 25th, Nov. 17th.

AGA MAHOMED RAHIM
v.
MIRZA ALI MAHOMED, BIBI MARIAM BIGUM,
MAHOMED SALAY KHAN;

and

MIRZA ALI MAHOMED AND OTHERS
v.
AGA MAHOMED RAHIM.

[*Coram* PERRY, J.]

Dealings of Mahomedan executors with a large estate; and mode of succession to a mercantile firm described.

Fraudulent attempts to defeat the execution of the judgment of the Court frustrated.

Power of the Court enforced to prevent an accounting party from leaving the jurisdiction surreptitiously.

Under very special circumstances sworn to on affidavits, and which set up a *primâ facie* case of mistake in admissions made on oath by a defendant in an answer, and in an inventory filed in the Ecclesiastical Court, the Court, contrary to the general rule, allowed a supplemental bill to be filed in order to correct these mistakes and to prove how they arose.

On a protracted inquiry, with evidence collected from numerous parts of Asia: *Held*, that the evidence to prove that mistakes had been made completely failed.

THIS case, which was tried before PERRY, J., sitting alone, in September, 1843, (Sir H. ROPER, C. J., having been engaged as counsel whilst at the local Bar), gives such a curious insight into native manners, is so remarkable for the amount of inquiry it involved, and, above all, from the ruin it

1843.

AGA MAHOMED RAHIM'S Case.

brought down on the defendant Aga Mahomed Rahim, a merchant prince of Bombay (*a*), it reads such an instructive moral as to the consequences which executors entail upon themselves by the disregard of truth when called upon to account for the estate, that it appears worth publishing, although it contains but little of legal principle.

The litigation in the case commenced by Mirza Ali and his mother filing a suit in 1833, for an account of the estate of the father of Mirza, Mahomed Ali Khan, of whom one Aga Mahomed Shustri was executor.

Suit filed in 1833 against an executor to account.

Aga Mahomed Shustri put in an answer in that year, by which he admitted a balance in hand of Rs. 57,000, and filed accounts which shewed assets of about eight laks, (80,000*l.*), besides various outstanding debts were due to the estate, but alleged reasons why these sums could not be collected. Shortly after putting in this answer he died, having left a will, by which he constituted his son-in-law, Aga Mahomed Rahim, the present defendant, his executor, and he left to him one-third of his property.

Assets admitted.

The suit was revived against Aga Mahomed Rahim, and went to the Master's Office under the usual decree to account. The plaintiffs carried in their charge, by which they established a claim to eight laks, founded on various admissions in the answer, and on an inventory filed with the Ecclesiastical Registrar, and other signed accounts of Aga Shustri, but disputes arising on three or four items relating to the ownership of two ships, and the outstanding debts, litigation respecting them went on in the Master's Office for two years.

1836. Assets formerly admitted claimed to belong to executor.

At the end of that period, *viz.*, in 1836, Aga Rahim brought in a claim to the Master's Office, in which he stated that he had discovered that his testator, Aga Shustri had made a great mistake in his accounts by charging himself with eight laks due to the original testator, for that, in fact, these eight laks belonged to Shustri himself in respect of the mercantile

(*a*) See note (*a*) at end of case, *post*, p. 41.

business he had carried on for many years past, and which his clerks, by ignorance or fraud, had set down as belonging to the original testator.

1843.

AGA MAHOMED RAHIM'S Case.

The Master, of course, refused to hear any evidence on this point to contradict the solemn admissions on oath by Aga Shustri without an order of the Court; and, in 1838, on a large amount of evidence being presented to the Court, raising a *primâ facie* case, that Shustri had, in fact, inadvertently made admissions contrary to his own interest, and that he was only prevented from correcting them by his death, the Judges, (COMPTON, C. J., and AWDREY, J.), though with considerable reluctance, gave Aga Rahim leave to file a supplemental bill, so as to get rid of the admissions previously made by himself and by Aga Shustri.

1838. The Court allowed evidence to be adduced to contradict former admissions.

Aga Rahim accordingly filed a bill, setting out the circumstances on which he claimed relief, as to the allegations in which evidence was collected from Calcutta, Bombay, Hydrabad, Bussora, Bushire, and other parts of Asia, and on which the principal subject of inquiry was, whether a mercantile firm, or Khoti, which carried on business at Bombay, Calcutta, Hydrabad, and elsewhere, from 1804 to 1820, belonged to the original testator, Aga Mahomed Khan, or to his executor, Aga Mahomed Shustri.

The principal facts in dispute will appear from the arguments of counsel, and from the judgment which follows,—but the following brief summary may be useful.

At the beginning of the century, one Abdúl Latif, a Seyad (*a*), and a man of great influence, had a large mercantile firm, with establishments, amongst other places, at Calcutta and Bombay. The great question at the Bar was, whether the Bombay Khoti descended on his death, in 1804, to Mahomed Khan, or to Mahomed Shustri. The two latter appear to have been originally fellow clerks to Abdúl Latif in the Calcutta house; but the former accompanied his master to Bombay some time before he died, which occurred in the

Evidence collected from numerous parts of Asia.

(*a*) Descendant of the Prophet.

1843.

Aga Mahomed Rahim's Case.

latter place. By Abdul Latif's will, he constitutes Mahomed Khan his executor, calls him his partner, and leaves him a third of his property, which was estimated at nearly ten laks (100,000*l.*) Mohamed Khan, soon after the death of his benefactor, married one of his widows, and from that time till his death, in 1820, all the evidence in the case concurred in representing him as a man of princely habits, the leader of his community in Western India, as exercising great hospitality, and on terms of intimacy with all the leading Europeans of the place. The complainants in the original suit were his widow and his son, Mirza Mahomed Ali. On the Khan's (*a*) death in 1820, he constituted Aga Mohamed Shustri his executor; he bequeathed to him one-third of his property, admitted a debt to him of Rs. 50,000, but said nothing respecting the Khoti.

For many years previous to Aga Khan's death, Mahomed Shustri had managed the Khoti in question. He had come round from Calcutta in 1808. He had deposited about eight laks of rupees in the house of Bruce, Fawcett and Co. in 1811, in his own name, and many other acts were shewn to indicate that Aga Shustri alone was the owner of this firm.

Aga Shustri by his will, dated 1834, constituted his son-in-law, Aga Rahim, his executor, and this latter from that period took possession of the Khoti, and carried on business on his own account as one of the most enterprising merchants and shipbuilders in the East.

The inquiry which had to be made, therefore, in the present case, related to a state of facts that commenced more than forty years previously, and which extended over nearly twenty years. The case occupied six days with the evidence and arguments of counsel.

(*a*) The Persian titles of Khan and Aga seem to be freely bestowed by the Sovereign of Persia on successful merchants. Thus we find, in the present case, both of the executors are styled Aga; the original testator bears the higher title of Khan. The hierarchy of Persian titles seems to be—Mir, or Amir, Beg, Khan, Aga, Mirza; the son of the Mir being a Beg, of the Beg a Khan, &c.

1843.

AGA MAHOMED RAHIM'S Case.

Cochrane, Herrick, and *Crawford,* for Aga Rahim.

Argument for executor, that by mistake the original executor had sworn away al his property.

Our case is, that Aga Shustri by clear mistake, which was possibly created by the fraud of his own clerks, has made erroneous admissions in his answer, by which he has sworn away his whole estate, and which, if the Court will not allow to be corrected now, will have the effect of reducing one of the most respectable and wealthy families in India to complete beggary. By the answer he put in to the original suit in 1834, he only admitted that Rs. 57,000 were due to the widow and Mirza; but by the accounts attached about eight laks appear to be due, if the Khoti belonged to Aga Khan. But this enormous discrepancy clearly demonstrates the mistake. The widow and son now say that all this belongs to them; but their suit in 1834 shews that they never made any such claim. They merely claimed an account of the real and personal estate left by their relative Ali Khan, and demand nothing in respect of any mercantile business. The fact is, that Mahomed Khan, whom we admit to be a man of princely magnificence, and who by his fortunate marriage came into a considerable fortune, and held a great position here as political agent for divers Mussalman Powers, never carried on business at all as a merchant, except in a very small way, and this business Aga Shustri transacted for him. All the evidence is conclusive to shew that Shustri alone was the merchant. He brought round eight laks of money from Calcutta, which he deposited in his own name with respectable European houses. By his energy and ability he created an immense business; and the fact that the representatives of Mahomed Ali Khan, on his death, never claimed the least interest in the Khoti, is conclusive to shew that Mohamed Ali Khan had nothing to do with it.

Much stress is put by the other side on the use of the word *Khadyagani,* which occurs in Aga Shustri's books, when the account of Mahomed Ali Khan is mentioned; and it is argued, that this is a word denoting such excessive respect, that it could only be used by an inferior to a superior, and, therefore, it conclusively shews that Mahomed Khan was the owner,

1843.

AGA MAHOMED RAHIM'S Case.

not a constituent, of the firm. The word is impure Persian, from the noun Khad (Lord), and it seems it has three different meanings, but the fact is, no argument can be based on its employment, as it is only an example of the inflated style so frequently found in Persian documents (*a*).

Lastly, it is true, that Aga Shustri filed his inventory with the Ecclesiastical Registrar, in which he admits that these balances belong to Ali Khan, as he also does in the accounts scheduled to his answer in 1834, but both the inventory and accounts were in English, which he did not understand at all, and they were interpreted to him in Hindustani, which he understood very imperfectly.

Howard and *Dickinson*, contra.

Argument for widow and child.

Immense injustice has been done to the widow and son by the course which this litigation has taken.

No evidence admissible against solemn admissions on oath.

The admissions made on oath in the solemn manner which have recurred in this case, and on so many different occasions, cannot be gainsaid in a Court of justice. (*Sheffield* v. *Duchess of Buckingham*, 1 Atk.; *Pierce* v. *George*, 3 Atk.; *Strange* v. *Collins*, 2 Ves. & Bea.)

PERRY, J.—No argument as to the binding force of admissions arises now; as the Court, under the circumstances in 1838, made an exception to the rule, and gave Aga Rahim an opportunity of shewing that a mistake had been made. That is the issue now before the Court.

Howard. In consequence of that permission a most ruinous search after evidence through half Asia has been made neces-

And no mistake made.

sary, and the result is, that not the least iota of testimony is forthcoming to shew that any mistake has been made. It is true that a *primâ facie* case of ownership in Aga Shustri to this

(*a*) It was stated at the Bar that one of the counsel in the case had devoted himself to the study of Persian for six months, in order to deal with the Persian documents on which so much discussion took place.

Khoti is shewn, but we answer it by the admissions of a whole life, and we will place the whole life of Aga Shustri before the Court. [They then went through the evidence minutely, describing and explaining the various transactions of this large business during a series of years, and the conduct of the different members of the family.]

1843.

AGA MAHOMED RAHIM'S Case.

The only plausible point in the case in favour of Shustri, is the fact that the widow laid no claim to the Khoti in her bill in 1833. But she never did claim any interest in it. Perhaps it passed to Aga Shustri on Mahomed Khan's death; Mahomed Khan took it in the same manner, as it were tacitly, under Abdúl Latif's will; for our evidence shews clearly that he was not a partner in his lifetime. And the fact seems to be, that with these Mahomedan merchants, a faithful manager is rewarded by allowing the business to descend to him, when there are no sons old enough, or willing, to carry it on. The Mahomedans as a race are not much addicted to commerce, and if a sufficient fortune is accumulated, they may be seen willingly to abandon business, and to enter on the more agreeable occupation of spending it.

Cochrane replied.

Cur. adv. vult.

November 17.

Judgment.

Only difficulty in cases arises from mass of evidence.

PERRY, J.—If the difficulty of the question raised in this suit were in any degree proportionable to the length of time during which litigation has prevailed, or to the enormous mass of evidence which has been accumulated on either side, I confess that I should shrink from the responsibility which a decision in such a complicated inquiry would involve. But fortunately for the ends of justice, the difficulty in this suit is one which any ordinary capacity may surmount, for it arises only from the great length of time and patience which are necessary to disembowel the facts from the voluminous proceedings in which they are contained, and when these are once known, the question to be decided, as it seems to me, is simple and unambiguous.

1843.

AGA MAHOMED RAHIM'S Case.

In order to state what that question is, the best course probably will be to recapitulate, with as much brevity as is consistent with clearness, the history of the litigation which has accrued between these parties or those whom they represent, and for this purpose it is sufficient to commence with the death of Mahomed Ali Khan, in May, 1820.

History of the litigation.

That gentleman was an eminent Mogul (*a*) merchant, established for many years in this island, and the agent of several Mahomedan Potentates, such as the Imam of Muscat, the Pacha of Egypt, and others.

M. A. Khan, a great Mogul merchant in Bombay, died 1820.

By his will, dated 19th October, 1819, he appointed Aga Mahomed Shustri his executor, and, after several legacies, bequeathed to him one-third of his residuary estate. Shustri proved the will shortly after Mahomed Ali Khan's death, and paid several legacies therein mentioned, such as Rs. 20,000 to Halima Bibi, the first widow of the deceased, Rs. 50,000 to Mariam Bigum, the second widow, and he otherwise took upon himself the burden of the executorship.

Halima Bibi had one son by Mahomed Ali Khan, who was living at the time of his death, namely, Hadji Mahomed Salay, one of the defendants, and who was then upwards of forty years of age; and Mariam Bigum had two sons and a daughter, Mirza Mahomed (the plaintiff in the main suit), being the eldest, and then aged nine years, and two younger children who have since died, and the remaining two-thirds of his residuary estate were to be divided amongst those children in certain proportions.

A. M. Shustri, his executor, proved will, and in 1823 filed inventory.

Aga Mahomed Shustri having, as before mentioned, proved the will of Mahomed Ali Khan, in the Recorder's Court of Bombay, in the year 1823, in pursuance of his duty as exe-

(*a*) In Western India the term "Mogul" is used for Persian, though the latter belongs as little to the Mongolian race as to the English or Hindu. The reason of this strange application of the term is to be found in the fact that the first fair Mussalmans whom the Hindu became acquainted with, were Moguls, and the term has been subsequently applied to all Western Mussalmans, who are usually much fairer than the Mahomedans of India. See 2 *Elph. India*, p. 94.

1843.

AGA MAHOMED RAHIM'S Case.

cutor, he filed an inventory of the estate of Mahomed Ali Khan, on the ecclesiastical side of the Court, which is thus headed, "The Particulars of account of his Excellency, Mahomed Ali Khan Shustri, up to the day of his death, &c." On the credit side of the account appear entries of payment of legacies and debts amounting, in the whole, to Rs. 7,00,501, and on the debit side, the amount of all the debts due to Mahomed Ali Khan's estate, stated to consist of "landed property, ships, goods, recoverable and irrecoverable, debts, &c., excepting landed property in Persia," is Rs. 18,86,471.

Several accounts of Aga Mahomed Khan's estate, up to 6th May, 1823, were also filed by Aga Mahomed Shustri, at the same time as the inventory, by which he shewed further receipts and payments on behalf of Mahomed Ali Khan's estate, and several divisions of the residue which he had made, from time to time, between himself and the parties entitled under the will, and, on the 21st of June, 1826, he filed a further account, bringing down the accounts to 31st of December, 1825.

1833. Widow and son filed a bill against executor Shustri.

In the year 1827, the widow, Mariam Bigum, went to Calcutta with her young son, the defendant, Mirza Ali Mahomed, and did not return to Bombay, till March, 1831. At the latter period, the defendant, Mirza Ali Mahomed having attained his majority, according to Mahomedan Law, a communication appears to have taken place between himself and the executor, Aga Mahomed Shustri, as to the division of the residue, and the latter having given to Mirza Ali Mahomed duplicate copies of the accounts filed on the ecclesiastical side of the Court, offered to pay him a balance of Rs. 32,300, on receiving from him a release in full of all demands. The young man refused to accept this sum as his share of the residue, or to sign the release, upon which a very hostile course of litigation commenced between Mariam Bigum and her son, Mirza Ali Mahomed, on the one side, and Aga Mahomed Shustri on the other.

The original bill in that suit, to which also the son of the first widow, Hadji Mahomed Salay Khan, was joined as a

1843.

AGA MAHOMED RAHIM'S Case.

defendant, was filed on the 7th of June, 1833, and it prayed, with the amended bill on the 11th of December, 1833, an account of Mahomed Ali Khan's estate, and a division of the residue amongst the parties entitled. The defendant, Aga Mahomed Shustri, in his answer, admitted sufficient assets, and that a large balance remained in his hands, and set out, in the schedule to his answer, accounts corresponding in every respect with those which he had formerly filed on the ecclesiastical side of the Court, but on the ground of the impossibility of collecting certain outstanding debts, he stated the balance in his hands due to the complainants, to amount only to Rs. 59,333.

Feb. 1834. Shustri answered, admitting assets.

March, 1834. Shustri died, appointing by will A. Rahim executor.

This last answer, to which the accounts were appended, was filed on the 28th of February, 1834, and in the March following Aga Mahomed Shustri died.

By his will, dated the 7th of March, 1834, Aga Mahomed Shustri constituted his son in law, Aga Mahomed Rahim, the present defendant, his sole executor, stated that Aga Mahomed Rahim only was interested (or at all events had any power) in his Khoti or house of business, and left all his property to his children. He also in this will gives a sort of *précis* of his affairs, and, amongst other things, states that about Rs. 57,000 remained unpaid to the heirs of Mahomed Ali Khan, "the detailed account of which I have filed in the Supreme Court."

May, 1834. Bill revived against A. Rahim, who answered, admitting assets.

Aga Mahomed Rahim having proved the will of Aga Mahomed Shustri in the Supreme Court, the suit against the latter, which had abated by the death of the Khan, was revived against Aga Mahomed Rahim by a bill filed in May, 1834, and Aga Mahomed Rahim having put in his answer admitting the will of Aga Mahomed Shustri and sufficient assets, a decree was made by consent in November, 1834, for a reference to the Master to take an account of the estate of Mahomed Ali Khan, and Aga Mahomed Rahim, was ordered to pay the admitted balance, Rs. 59,333, into Court.

I have mentioned that the litigation between Aga Mahomed Shustri and Mahomed Ali Khan's representatives, was of a

1843.

AGA MAHOMED RAHIM'S Case.

very hostile character; Aga Mahomed Shustri having indicted the Bigum Mariam for perjury in one of her answers in a bill which the grand jury ignored, and having also brought against her a cross suit for the discovery of assets retained by her belonging to the estate of Mahomed Ali Khan.

This latter suit was revived by Aga Mahomed Rahim on Aga Mahomed Shustri's death, and found its way into the Master's Office, with the reference in the other suit.

1835. Reference to Master to take the accounts.

The Master commenced his inquiry on the 25th of January, 1835, and between that day and the June in the following year, there appears to have been between thirty and forty meetings, which were attended for the most part by the parties and their solicitors. On the 16th of April, 1835, the solicitor for the complainants having brought in their charge against Aga Mahomed Rahim, Mr. Larkins, as solicitor for the latter, stated that he had objections to some of the items; the principal of which appears to have been as to the item charged for the value of the ship Travancore, *viz.* Rs. 98,773, and the item charged for the ship Harriet, *viz.* Rs. 33,387. Aga Mahomed Rahim appears to have claimed the ship Travancore as belonging to the separate estate of Aga Mahomed Shustri, though this does not very distinctly appear by the Master's book; and as to the ship Harriet, he claimed one-fourth as belonging to himself, and the other three-fourths as belonging to Aratoon Apcar, an Armenian at Calcutta. In support of the charge the inventory and accounts of Aga Mahomed Shustri were produced, in which he debited himself both in 1823 and 1834 with the value of these ships, as belonging to the estate of Mahomed Ali Khan. With the exception of these items which stood over, the whole of the charge brought in by the complainants against Aga Mahomed Rahim was allowed by the Master, on the footing of its having been already solemnly admitted by the party interested in disputing it, namely, Aga Mahomed Shustri; but as the explanations given by Aga Mahomed Rahim as to the outstanding debts were not satisfactory, and as the books of the Khoti or business which contained the entries of the transactions referred to in the

Charge against executor allowed.

1843.

AGA MAHOMED RAHIM'S Case.

inventory and accounts of Mahomed Ali Khan's estate were required, Aga Mahomed Rahim was examined upon interrogatories.

In pursuance of this examination, and of the demand upon Aga Mahomed Rahim to produce the books of the Khoti, a number of books was deposited with the Master. In one of these, which is an index to the book for the year of Hejira 1235 (1819-20), there is a list of the parties connected or corresponding with the House or Khoti, and it commences thus:—

Description of the accounts.

"His Highness of High Dignity my Lord Mahomed Ali Khan, sahib; may he always be prosperous!" p. 1.

In the ledger book of that year, p. 1, the account is headed, "Account in the name of my Master of High Dignity, Mahomed Ali Khan, sahib; may his illustrious fortune be perpetual!" and the first item on the credit side is as follows, "Balance of an account brought over from the last book, p. 2, Rs. 4,51,484;" several items to the credit of Mahomed Ali Khan then follow, among which, is one on the 5th of February, 1820, of Rs. 10,000, on account of damage to the ship Harriet, received from Nurseedass Purshotumdass, and down to the 15th of May, 1820, the total to the credit of Mahomed Ali Khan, appears to be Rs. 4,70,979." An entry then appears as follows:—

"Receipts after the death of my late master."

And several entries to the credit of Mahomed Ali Khan are made, coming down to the 24th of October, 1820.

The next account in the ledger stands thus, "Account in the name of Aga Mahomed Sahib Shustri," and under it, there is only one entry, *viz.*, of a receipt of interest from Government upon Rs. 18,900, which is stated to be "carried over to a new book."

The amount in the ledger for Hejira year 1233, (A. D. 1818), is headed,

"Account in the name of the dignified, my Lord; may his fortune be perpetual!" and the first item on the credit side is, "Balance of an account per preceding book, p. 1, Rs. 2,13,153;" and amongst other items on the same side is

1843.

AGA MAHOMED RAHIM'S Case.

one "Profit upon his Excellency's goods, commission and interest, &c., as per Mir Ekram Ali's writing, Rs. 68,892."

Amongst the entries on the debit side are;—Expenses of the office at Calcutta, Rs. 6,829; payments made there by Mir Ekram Ali; house expenses of Aga Sahib, Rs. 542; expenses of the office at Bombay, Rs. 7,153; expenses of his Excellency's garden, Rs. 25,041; leaving on the whole debits and credits of the year, a balance due to his Excellency of Rs. 4,51,484; and this sum, it will be seen, corresponds with the balance for which Mahomed Ali Khan is given credit in the ledger of the following year.

A number of other accounts of the Khoti, carried on in Bombay for different years, back to the year 1811, have also been before the Court, where, under the headings:—"Particulars of the account of his Excellency;"—"Particulars of my Master's account;"—"Particulars of the account of his Excellency, my master,"—a balance is credited in his favour, in each year; entries of profits appear from the Calcutta house, and from other foreign agencies; entries of the monthly salary paid by Government to Mahomed Ali Khan; entries of the receipts of interest on government securities which, though standing in different names, (some being in Mahomed Ali Khan's, some in Aga Mahomed Shustri's), were always received by one person, and then entered under one account, &c., &c., and, on the other side of the account are different items of charge for the Calcutta Khoti, the Bombay Khoti, and the private expenses of Mahomed Ali Khan, Aga Mahomed Shustri, and other persons employed in the house.

Thus stood affairs in the month of June, 1836.

June, 1836. Executor set up claim that mistakes had been made in the admissions of assets.

Aga Mahomed Rahim, as before mentioned, was met in the Master's Office with the admissions which had been made, from time to time, by his testator, Aga Mahomed Shustri, and was called upon, again and again, for satisfactory explanations; at last, interrogatories were exhibited to him, and the production of books was demanded. In his answer to these interrogatories, which were filed on the 23rd of June, 1836, an entirely new phase in the case was presented by Aga Mahomed Rahim, which I will give in his own words:—

1843.

Aga Mahomed Rahim's Case.

"This examinant saith, that he is informed, and believes that Aga Mahomed Shustri, in order to file his inventory and account of the estate of the said Mahomed Ali Khan, on the ecclesiastical side of the Court, employed one, Mirza Mohamed Mahidee Miskay, a Persian writer, in the service of the said Aga Mahomed Shustri, and who is now at Calcutta, and one Mussoba, who wrote in the English language, to prepare an inventory and account of the said Mahomed Ali Khan's estate. That the said Aga Mahomed Shustri placing every reliance on the integrity of the said Mirza Mahomed Mahidee Miskay and Mussoba, did not examine the said inventory or account when completed, and that the said inventory and account were filed or made out by the said Mirza Mahomed Mahidee Miskay and Mussoba, that on the said Aga Mahomed Shustri being called upon to put in his answer to the bill of complaint, filed by the said Mirza Ali Mahomed and Bibi Mariam Bigum, against the said Aga Mahomed Shustri, as executor of Mahomed Ali Khan, he examined the books from which the accounts filed on the ecclesiastical side of the Court had been taken, and he found that the accounts filed were wrong, and that, instead of belonging to the estate of Mahomed Ali Khan, the accounts mostly belonged to the estate of him, the said Aga Mahomed Shustri; that, notwithstanding, he, the said Aga Mahomed Shustri, annexed to the answer filed by him to the said bill of complaint, a schedule agreeing with the inventory and account so filed on the ecclesiastical side of the Court: and that his reason for doing so was, that he did not like to contradict himself, but he believed that the schedule might be rectified on taking the accounts of the estate in the Master's Office;" and Aga Mahomed Rahim proceeded to annex a schedule, professing to be a true account of the estate of Mahomed Ali Khan, by which instead of a balance being due, of nearly twelve laks of rupees, as formerly admitted by Shustri, a balance is claimed as due to Shustri's estate of upward of two laks of rupees."

Extraordinary and improbable statement.

Now undoubtedly this tale, on the first blush of it, is one of the most extraordinary that ever was presented to the consideration of a Court of justice; and before we proceed to test

1843.

AGA MAHOMED RAHIM'S Case.

its veracity, it is good to observe what sort of person it was to whom such gross errors and disregard of self interest were imputed, and whose conduct, on discovery of the mistake, was so little like what might have been expected from any rational individual. But if any one fact stands out more clearly than another in the present case, it is that of the capacity for business, the acuteness and attention to his own interests, which distinguished Aga Mahomed Shustri. He seems to have ingratiated himself so much in the favour of Mahomed Ali Khan, either by his personal attention, or by his skill in carrying on business, that the latter not only left him an entire third of his property, but also a legacy of Rs. 50,000; for, although that sum is expressed in Mahomed Ali Khan's will to be in payment of a debt due, I have little doubt (from the whole character of the case, and from the total absence of any evidence to be found in the books of money having been advanced by Aga Mahomed Shustri), that that form of giving a legacy was adopted to meet the Mahomedan rule of law, which forbids a testator to will away more than one-third of his property from his natural heirs; 4 *Hedaya*, p. 482. Independently however of, and in addition to these large bequests, we find Aga Mahomed Shustri claiming commission or per centage as executor to the amount of many thousand rupees (upwards of 55,000), most improperly indeed, as it appears to me, but still affording a clear indication that he was not a person to part with a single rupee to which he could lay any claim or title; so also we find him during the period between Mahomed Ali Khan's death and his own, attended by solicitors, counsel, and English friends, at each stage of his proceedings, using every weapon which the law afforded to protect himself and to silence his opponents, carrying on for his own account, and apparently with great success, a large mercantile business in Bombay, which was managed exclusively by himself, and presenting on the whole a character of which it seems as difficult to predicate a liability to fall into gross errors in his own concerns, or a sentimental hesitation to rectify those errors when discovered, as of any man in existence, the most noted for ability and worldly wisdom.

Mode adopted by Mahomedans to counteract the rule of law which forbids more than one-third from being devised by will away from the heirs.

1843.

AGA MAHOMED RAHIM'S Case.

Still, in June, 1836, Aga Mahomed Rahim swore that he had been informed, and that he believed the information to be true, of Aga Mahomed Shustri having committed those extraordinary mistakes, and of his having neglected, for the reason alleged, to take any steps to correct them, and as it is the business of Courts of justice to hear the case of each party fully, and to reject no story merely from its improbability, for experience proves that many stories most incredible on a *primâ facie* statement have often been established by an overwhelming mass of evidence, it is necessary to go further, and see what testimony was producible in support of this account, and what shape the litigation assumed.

Statement rejected by Master.

On this case being brought forward by Aga Mahomed Rahim, the Master was naturally unwilling to hear any evidence to contradict the solemn admissions on oath of the party whom Aga Mahomed Rahim represented, and for this reason application to the Court became necessary; accordingly, in January, 1837, Aga Mahomed Rahim made an affidavit of the facts, in which he gives a somewhat different account of the mode in which the mistake committed by Aga Mahomed Shustri flashed upon his mind. For, he states, that having been called upon in 1835, by the Master to give explanation of certain items in the account of Aga Mahomed Shustri relating to Mahomed Ali Khan's estate, he was led to examine very minutely the books of Aga Mahomed Shustri; and from such examination he was "made to believe that some mistake had been committed, and that the books deposited in the (Master's) Office as aforesaid were not wholly belonging to the said Mahomed Ali Khan's estate."

In the former account it will be remembered, that the discovery of Aga Mahomed Shustri's errors is attributed to information received *aliunde*, but here it seems to have arisen from the internal evidence afforded by a minute examination of Aga Mahomed Shustri's books. According to Aga Mahomed Rahim's affidavit, however, it appears that, whilst the inspection of Aga Mahomed Shustri's book had left him in this state of mind, one Aga Mahomed Esmail, the paternal uncle of Aga Mahomed Rahim, came to Bombay, *viz.*, in April,

1836, where he remained for three months, and he informed the deponent, Aga Mahomed Rahim, that Aga Mahomed Shustri had made the mistake, which Aga Mahomed Rahim had suspected, according to the manner stated above.

1843.

AGA MAHOMED RAHIM'S Case.

Undoubtedly nothing could be more felicitous or opportune than the appearance of a witness in Bombay at this conjuncture. There was a *dignus vindice nodus* which nothing but the direct testimony of some one or other acquainted with the facts could solve, and when it presented itself, it appeared to make out, in connection with the strong internal evidence afforded by Aga Mahomed Shustri's books, a somewhat plausible *primâ facie* case.

So at least thought the Judges of this Court in 1838, for upon a petition of Aga Mahomed Rahim, embodying the above statements, and praying for an opportunity to be allowed to bring forward evidence which should establish that Aga Mahomed Shustri had, through error, sworn away his whole property, Sir HERBERT COMPTON and Sir JOHN AWDREY yielded, though most reluctantly as it would seem, to the application, and the permission so granted was the origin of the bill which forms the subject-matter of the present suit.

But on strong *primâ facie* case in 1838, Court allowed evidence to be adduced against admissions.

The case, however, which was laid before those learned Judges, and which induced them to depart in some degree from first principles, was undoubtedly very strong; for a mass of evidence was brought forward to shew that the Khoti, or house of business, in Bombay, which had been previously admitted to be Mahomed Ali Khan's, had ever since 1809, at least, been conducted solely by Aga Mahomed Shustri; large deposits of money were shewn to have been placed in the Bombay house of Bruce, Fawcett and Co. by Aga Mahomed Shustri in his own name; conveyances of property, which had been previously assumed to belong to Mahomed Ali Khan, were shewn to have been made to Aga Mahomed Shustri; and an extensive correspondence was referred to from the foreign agencies, all of which recognised Aga Mahomed Shustri only as the principal in the Khoti. In pursuance of this permission, Aga Mahomed Rahim brought forward his case by way of supplemental bill, on the ground that, since the decree of 1834, he had discovered that the inventories and accounts

1843.

AGA MAHOMED RAHIM'S Case.

set forth by his testator, Aga Mahomed Shustri, were erroneous. He proceeds thereon to set out what the error is, and alleges that the Khoti, which was carried on by Aga Mahomed Shustri for upwards of twenty years before the death of Mahomed Ali Khan, belonged exclusively to the former, and that all the connection of the Khan with the house was in respect of certain petty business, which Aga Mahomed Shustri, as the friend of Mahomed Ali Khan, allowed to be transacted there; that, only one set of books being kept for the Khoti, it was not apparent from the books alone what particular items belonged to Mohamed Ali Khan's interest or estate, but that such information was obtainable from the vouchers in each case, and that the error which ran through the whole accounts consisted in attributing to Mahomed Ali Khan, as proprietor, the whole of the debits and credits of the Khoti. The bill then charges, that the entry in the ledger for the year 1819, crediting Mahomed Ali Khan with a large balance, was another mistake, and that it was improperly made by Mirza Mussoba, a private friend or dependent of Mahomed Ali Khan (in point of fact, however, a mere clerk in the Khoti), and that such last mentioned account appears to be the origin or commencement which caused the mistaken admissions of Aga Mahomed Shustri's; the bill also stated that the inventory and accounts of 1823 were made out by Mirza Mahidee Miskay, the brother-in-law of Shustri, and by Mussoba, and that they were filed and signed by Aga Mahomed Shustri without having been examined by him; and he imputes to Mirza Mahidee Miskay a hostility against Aga Mahomed Shustri, commencing in 1820 and continuing until 1823, when he left the Khoti,—and which arose from a refusal by Aga Mahomed Shustri to comply with certain pecuniary demands. With respect to the accounts filed in 1826, the bill alleges that they were made out by Mussoba, and were also not examined by, or interpreted to, Shustri; and as to the corresponding accounts which were filed with Aga Mahomed Shustri's answer in February, 1834, it states that Aga Mahomed Shustri at the time was upwards of seventy years of age and very infirm, and that they were only interpreted to him in the Hindustani language, with which he was very imperfectly acquainted. Aga Mahomed Rahim then adds this remarkable statement,

1843.

AGA MAHOMED RAHIM'S Case.

namely, "that Shustri never communicated to him" (although he—Shustri's son-in-law—had been engaged in the Khoti for eight years previous to Aga Mahomed Shustri's death), "nor to his legal advisers, the mistake which had been committed, but that he was in the habit of referring generally to errors and injuries to his estate which had been committed by Mirza Mahidee Miskay.

Aga Mahomed Rahim's bill then states that he had discovered the error by means of the strict investigation which he had been compelled to make of the books of the Khoti, and he refers for evidence of the mistake to a letter of Aga Mahomed Esmail, though in the last edition of his bill, this evidence is alluded to very gingerly, and the letter itself does not appear on the face, or in the course, of the proceedings.

The bill ends with a prayer that it may be declared that the Khoti at Bombay, conducted by Aga Mahomed Shustri during the lifetime of Mahomed Ali Khan did not belong to the latter, and that the schedule filed by Aga Mahomed Rahim attributing the major portion of the property in it to Aga Mahomed Shustri may be affirmed, and that the proceedings in the Master's Office under the decretal order of 1834 be annulled and declared void.

Evidence collected at great expense from 1838 to 1843.

This voluminous bill, of course, called forth very full answers, and, on the different questions raised, a mass of evidence became necessary, and was collected, in Persia, in Calcutta, in Hydrabad, and in Bombay, as to the history of the parties connected with the Khoti established in this island, during the last forty years.

The above recapitulation of facts, however lengthy, has been indispensable, in order to enable the precise question to be stated which arises in the present case. That question, according to the learned counsel for Aga Mahomed Rahim, simply is, whether the Khoti carried on at Bombay up to 1820 was the Khoti of Mahomed Ali Khan, or of Aga Mahomed Shustri; and, on the ground of the discussion of such a question bearing so directly on the interests of Aga Mahomed Shustri's heirs, application was made to postpone the hearing, in order to enable those parties to be brought into the suit, for the purpose of protecting their own interests. In the same

1843.

AGA MAHOMED RAHIM'S Case.

view of the question a number of ingenious arguments, and a long chain of reasoning was adduced, to shew that the Khoti never could have belonged to the Khan, and urgent appeals were made to the Court to put this question, which was simply one of fact, upon which so much imperfect contradictory evidence had been brought to bear, in train for a more satisfactory decision, by directing an issue to be framed, on which *vivâ voce* evidence could be taken.

Question arising out of the evidence stated.

This statement of the question, however, as it appears to me, is not the true one. It will be recollected that the case first urged upon the Court by Aga Mahomed Rahim in 1836, was, that Aga Mahomed Shustri had discovered the erroneous admissions which he had made from the year 1820 to 1826, and that although he had repeated those errors in 1834, he did so for certain specific reasons. And notwithstanding that this story, as I have before remarked, was a most incredible one upon the face of it, still it is within the bounds of imagination that it should be proveable by evidence. The parties who gave the information as to Aga Mahomed Shustri's discovery of the mistake he had made were not named in the original disclosure of Rahim's case, and it certainly is conceivable that proof might have been obtained as to every portion of the story from the numerous friends, law advisers, constituents, accounts and documents of Aga Mahomed Shustri; and it must have been on such a view of the case that the permission of the Judges to allow the point being raised proceeded.

Not whether the firm belonged to Shustri from 1808 to 1820;

The question, therefore, is not whether the Khoti belonged to Mahomed Ali Khan or to Aga Mahomed Shustri,—a question which, as involving a series of facts that took place from twenty to forty years ago, would necessarily lead to a most protracted inquiry, if it were to be treated as an open question; but the true question is, whether the admissions made by the latter during a period of fourteen years, that the Khoti did not belong to him, were made under such circumstances of inadvertence and error as to be set at naught and passed over entirely, and whether, moreover, Aga Mahomed Shustri gave any indication in his lifetime that he was conscious of having made such gross and unheard of blunders.

1843.

AGA MAHOMED RAHIM'S Case.

The two questions, although similar in their bearing, and pointing ultimately at the same result, are by no means identical, for it is evident that the latter is a preliminary inquiry to the first, and that unless it be answered satisfactorily, there can be no occasion to enter upon the first question at all. In a discussion whether certain property belongs to A. B., if A. B. is shewn to have admitted over and over again that it does not belong to him, it is evidently unnecessary to go further in the inquiry, such evidence, as an admission against self interest, is, and according to the principles of human nature always must be, most conclusive. If, indeed, A. B. alleges that the admissions were made by him inadvertently, that he had been led into them by the fraud of his agents, and that he had let them pass through the carelessness of his own nature, a Court of justice will not turn altogether a deaf ear, but it will undoubtedly assume during the recital a degree of scepticism proportionable to the strangeness of the story. A. B. in such case would have the labouring oar cast upon him to make out in every respect how it was that the mistake originated, what was the fraudulent motive which induced his servant to lead him into error, what it was that led him to be so negligent, and what was his conduct upon the discovery. But if this onus is thrown upon A. B., in what degree is it lightened when a friend of A. B. comes forward and alleges that these mistakes had been made?

But whether Shustri made a mistake in admitting the firm belonged to M. A. Khan.

So far from being lightened, it is evidently increased by the task, which arises, of shewing how it was that A. B. himself did not seek to rectify these mistakes, and it becomes magnified beyond all proportion when it is proved that A. B. never once affirmed or pretended that any such mistakes had been committed by him.

In the present case, therefore, directly it appeared from the opening speech of the learned counsel for Aga Mahomed Rahim that no evidence was to be offered as to how the mistake originated, nor of the fraudulent motives of the servants to whom it was imputed, nor of the mode in which it was discovered, nor to explain the supine lethargy of Aga Mahomed Shustri on the discovery, and that, on the contrary, the ground formerly taken of Shustri's having discovered the mistake at all

Burden of proof lies on those who assert a mistake had been made.

1843.

AGA MAHOMED RAHIM'S Case.

was distinctly abandoned, it seemed to me that the whole case of Aga Mahomed Rahim fell to the ground.

It will be observed, indeed, that Rahim brings forward the discovery of the mistake in three different ways: first of all he is informed (informant not being named) that Shustri had made these erroneous admissions, and had discovered that he had made them; secondly, Rahim is led to believe, by examination of the books, that a mistake had been made, and, at that moment, a witness (his own uncle) appears in Bombay, who informs him of the mistake, and of Shustri's conduct upon it: and, lastly, the discovery of the error is made by the "strict investigation of the books," which Aga Mahomed Rahim himself, "was induced to make."

This changing of the ground looks very unlike the consistent and self-explaining bearing of a true story, but one fact is very apparent throughout all these various readings, *viz.*, that the only informant whom Aga Mahomed Rahim has ever been able to vouch on the subject is Aga Mahomed Esmail. What then does this witness, the battle-horse of the plaintiff's whole case, depose to, when he is examined in the suit? on being asked whether the information he had given, respecting Aga Mahomed Shustri's discovery of the mistake, had not given rise to the suit by Rahim, he deposes as follows:—"In the beginning I did not occasion this cause, but it was written to me, by Aga Mahomed Rahim, that such and such disputes had arisen, and that it was about to be referred to the Court; I, the deponent, wrote in answer to it, that occurrence of such a dispute or quarrels between merchants was not proper, and that they should settle it amicably; and in the Hejira year 1252, (1836), when I was at Bombay, I persuaded Aga Mahomed Rahim and Ali Mahomed Khan that it was not proper to dispute with each other, and that, if they wished, I, the deponent, would hold a meeting with some people and decide it, and Aga Mahomed Rahim agreed, but Ali Mahomed Khan did not do so."

Can any thing be conceived more colourless, insignificant and vague, than this testimony, dealing wholly in generalities, and without any reference whatever to the story formerly set up as to the mistake committed by Shustri, and his conduct

1843.

AGA MAHOMED RAHIM'S Case.

thereupon, and which story is clearly proved to have been attributed to alleged information from this witness?

But what says Aga Esmail, on cross-examination, as to the mistake in the accounts? "I learned it, at first, by a letter from Aga Mahomed Shustri, written to me from Bombay, that a great mistake had occurred in the account, and that he had thereby sustained a considerable loss, through the negligence and mistake of the clerk and other managers of the business. I was at Hyderabad when I received such letter; there may be a letter or letters of the said Aga in this respect; a search should be made, and if it or they shall be found, I will produce it or them to you." (This witness, it should be observed, was examined at Hyderabad, the place of his residence, and of the receipt of the alleged letter, and no such letter was ever produced).

Proof entirely fails that any mistake had been made.

So, therefore, neither in chief nor in cross-examination, is one word said as to *the* mistake committed of attributing the whole of the Khoti accounts to Khan's estate, of the hostility of Shustri's relative, the clerk Miskay, or of Shustri's extraordinary silence and demeanour when he discovered the blunder. In point of fact, not one word of evidence is produced as to all those important matters, and all the various assertions formerly put forward which tended to raise a favourable view of the plaintiff's case, have been sustained by no proof whatever; and, therefore, as I said before, when I discovered that after all this length of years and vast expenditure employed in collecting evidence on the point, nothing whatever was forthcoming on the part of the complainant, his case appeared to me completely to break down.

Still, in a question of this magnitude, which has been litigated with such extraordinary pertinacity, and where such a multiplicity of facts is involved, as it is desirable to take away from litigants any pretence for imputing the decision against them to hastiness or imperfect consideration of all they might have to allege, I heard the whole case out and all the evidence that could be adduced on both sides, during a sitting which lasted six days, and since the hearing I have carefully gone through all the papers that were then laid before me.

I have, therefore, most attentively considered the question

1843.

Aga Mamomed Rahim's Case.

But clear also on evidence that firm never did belong to Shustri.

as framed by the counsel for Aga Mahomed Rahim, and taking up the question from the point of view in which it is presented by the complainant, I have no hesitation in expressing my clear conviction, upon the whole of the evidence, that the Khoti in question never did belong to Aga Mahomed Shustri during Khan's lifetime, that Shustri never did make any claim to it, and that he admitted again and again, up to the very last solemn act of his existence,—I mean the making of his will a fortnight before his death, and under circumstances which preclude any possibility of mistake,—that the Khoti did belong to Mahomed Ali Khan only, and that no mistake whatever was ever suggested by him to have been made in this respect.

One fact, undoubtedly, does stand out very broadly on this inquiry, namely, that the Khoti in question, from 1808 or 1809 to Mahomed Ali Khan's death in 1820, was conducted solely by Aga Mahomed Shustri, and that Mahomed Ali Khan, who seems to have lived from his first arrival at Bombay in a state of princely magnificence, never, or but very rarely, interfered in the management of the mercantile business. Khan succeeded to this Khoti, which had branches at Hydrabad and Calcutta, on the death of another Mogul merchant, Mir Abdul Latif Khan, in whose service he appears to have been employed, and whose widow, the Bigum Mariam, he afterwards married; and Aga Mahomed Shustri, in his turn, appears to have succeeded to the Khoti on the death of Mahomed Ali Khan, either by virtue of some arrangement tacitly understood between the parties, and therefore never brought into question, or by an easy occupancy of a vacant possession, which the death of Khan left open to the managing Gomashter, and which, from the sex and ages of the claimants who might have asserted some derivative right to it through the first proprietor, Abdúl Latif Khan, *viz.*, the Bigum and her infant sons, was undisturbed by any hostile title. The latter explanation of the mode in which the Khoti vested in Aga Mahomed Shustri seems the most probable, as it would appear by the books which I have already cited, that for six months after the death of Mahomed Ali Khan, *viz.*, up to the Diwalli of 1820, the business was carried on on the testator's

1843.

AGA MAHOMED RAHIM'S Case.

account, and it was only then that accounts were opened in the name of Aga Mahomed Shustri.

With this fact kept in view of the exclusive management of the estate being in Shustri's hands, the whole of the evidence brought forward by Rahim is intelligible, and easily reconcilable with the case of Khan's representatives, and the admissions made by Shustri.

Indeed, it is quite sufficient to disprove the case now set up by Rahim to read the depositions which he obtained from several of the highly respectable witnesses whom he himself called. Mr. Crawford, the Member of Council, Sir Roger de Faria, and other long established merchants in this island speak to their recollection of facts which took place twenty or thirty years ago, and which produce the irresistible conclusion that the only probable solution of the case is, that which common experience would dictate to be the truth, namely, that the story told and admissions made against self-interest by Aga Mahomed Shustri, the party who knew most about the facts, contain the true history of the case

Defendant's case suggested by fraud or by self-delusion.

When, on the other hand, one turns to the host of witnesses who have been produced for the defendants, it is found that every doubtful point is cleared up, every transaction which was originally calculated to bolster up the case of Aga Mahomed Rahim is satisfactorily explained, and a conviction is left upon the mind, either that the whole story put forward by him is a skilful weaving up of certain ambiguous facts, which, in the course of examination in the Master's Office, he perceived might be made to bear a favourable construction for himself and his connections, or that it is another instance of the gross credulity of the human mind, and of its proneness to deceive itself by far fetched and subtle reasonings when any thing is to be got by believing a tale however absurd or improbable.

However this may be, and it is unnecessary to decide, in the view I take of the whole case, the plaintiff has failed to make out any ground for relief; he has failed to persuade me that any of the questions he has brought forward requires further investigation; and, as I think that the story which he has thus made the subject of litigation at such a vast and unnecessary

1843.

AGA MAHOMED RAHIM'S Case.

expense, was (to take the most charitable view of it) either founded on some idle tale or derived from some specious self-deluding reasoning fostered and adhered to through the dictates of self-interest, I am unable to make any other decree than that the bill be dismissed, with costs.

1844.

Feb. 26.

AGA MAHOMED RAHIM'S CASE (*a*).

[*Coram* PERRY, J.]

Native executors are not entitled to 5*l.* per cent. commission under the practice of the Court granting such commission to European executors.

HOWARD, on a previous day, had moved that the defendant should pay into Court the sum of Rs. 26,000, which he had retained by way of commission on the estate of Mahomed Ali Khan, and which he admitted by his answer was in his hands.

Cur. adv. vult.

PERRY, J., on this day, delivered the judgment of the Court.—

I have communicated with Sir HENRY ROPER, and he entertains so clear an opinion that the order prayed for is a proper one to be made, under the circumstances of this case, that I can have no hesitation in making it.

I was always of opinion, that if the decisions warranted such an order in any case, the ends of justice warranted it in this, but I rather doubted whether the principle on which the orders for payment into Court rests, *viz.*, the clear admission of the defendant that such a sum is in his hands, and that the plaintiff has an interest, would include a case like the present. When the admission of a fund in hand is accompanied with a claim to retain it, an order to pay the sum into Court might frequently deprive the party so setting up the claim, of the only means he possessed of proceeding to establish it. But the case of *Domville* v. *Solly*, (2 Russ. 372), which was not cited in the argument, shews that the mere assertion of a claim by the defendant is not sufficient to protect him from paying the money into Court, if the Court can gather from his answer that the plaintiff has an interest in it.

Payment of money into Court *pendente lite.*

(*a*) See last case.

1844.

AGA MAHOMED RAHIM'S Case.

Now, I look upon it as completely established law in this Court, that a native executor has no right or title to claim commission. The Master has supplied me with a decision where the point was solemnly ruled on an exception to his report; and Sir HENRY ROPER states that several decisions in Sir H. COMPTON's time, and since, have settled the question.

Reason why native executors are not allowed commission.

The principle of refusing this commission does not rest upon the distinction between a dark and fair skin, as was suggested in argument, but on the ground that the only reason for allowing five per cent. commission to Europeans, was that thereby when a man died away from his native country, and from his friends or relations, strangers might be induced to step in to protect his property, and that as this could not apply, or only in exceptional cases to natives, *cessante ratione cessat et ipsa lex*.

On the face of the answer, therefore, it appears most clearly that the plaintiffs have an interest in this sum so retained as commission; and there does not appear the least reason to suppose that the defendant has any interest in it at all. An order, therefore, must be drawn up directing the defendant to pay into Court the several sums mentioned in the accounts rendered in his schedule to have been retained as commission (*a*).

(*a*) See next case.

AGA MAHOMED RAHIM'S CASE.

1845.

10th Nov.

[*Coram* ROPER, C. J., and PERRY, J.]

A writ of *ne exeat jurisdictionem*, issued to prevent a Bombay merchant leaving the island against whom the report of the Master was just about to be presented, finding a balance against him of nearly eight laks of rupees.

The affidavits on which the writ was obtained stated that the defendant was loading a ship for Bushire, and was putting on board all his household furniture, with the view, as it was believed, of leaving Bombay entirely; the affidavits, in answer, stated that the defendant was only sending his family on a pilgrimage to Karbala, and denied that he had any intention of leaving the island. The Court, notwithstanding the general rule that the defendant's approaching departure must be sworn to as a fact, and not on belief, under the circumstances of suspicion, granted the writ.

HOWARD, on a previous day, had obtained a writ to prevent the defendant Aga Mahomed Rahim from leaving the island until this suit had been disposed of.

The affidavits on which the writ was obtained stat d, that in

1845.

Aga Mahomed Rahim's Case.

pursuance of the decision, (*ante*, p. 26), the Master had been engaged in taking the accounts of the testator's estate, and that his report was just about to be presented to the Court, by which a balance was found due to the estate by Aga Mahomed Rahim of Rs. 7,81,352 (£78,135). It was further sworn that Agar Mahomed Rahim was lading a vessel of his, called the Haidri, with a valuable cargo; that he was placing all his furniture on board, and that in the belief of the deponents he was about to withdraw himself from Bombay, and the statements of members of his family were quoted in support of this belief, in order to defeat the final decree which he knew was so soon about to be pronounced against him.

Cochrane now moved, on notice, to discharge this writ, and produced an affidavit of Aga Mahomed Rahim in reply, in which he swore positively that he was not about to leave the island; that his family was going on a pilgrimage to Karbala, in Arabia, and that the chandeliers, &c., put on board the Haidri were shipped on a commission for Persian noblemen at Bushire.

Cochrane contended strongly that a writ of this kind was a high prerogative writ, and never to be issued except upon positive and undeniable evidence that the defendant is going abroad. Mere information and belief, which is all that is sworn to here, is not sufficient; *Jones* v. *Aleptsin*, (16 Ves. 470). The defendant had large landed estates and property in the island, and had no intention of leaving Bombay, and, if he had wished to do so, he might have left long ago.

Howard, contra, relied on *Russell* v. *Ashby*, (5 Ves.); *Etches* v. *Lance*, (7 Ves.); and *Hyde* v. *Whitfield*, (19 Ves.)

The Court thought that the circumstances were so suspicious of furniture, &c., being shipped on board the Haidri, and of the defendant's family being avowedly about to leave the island, that it was safer for the ends of justice to prevent Aga Mahomed Rahim from departing from Bombay, *Cochrane* accordingly took nothing, and the writ *ne exeat* was marked for bail, with the amount mentioned in the Master's report.

EXECUTION OF DECREE IN AGA MAHOMED RAHIM'S CASE (*a*).

1848.
August 1.

THE Master in this case having made his final report, and found a balance of upwards of eleven laks against Aga Mahomed Rahim, and a decree having been pronounced for payment, after the decree pronounced, Aga Mahomed Rahim petitioned the Insolvent Court for his discharge under the Insolvent Debtors' Act; but instead of giving up any property, he alleged that he possessed none, and he did not make over a rupee to the official assignee.

As it was notorious that he was possessed of very large landed property in Bombay, houses, a dockyard, besides all the estate and effects belonging to a successful mercantile business, the petition was of course dismissed, and the plaintiffs in the equity suit proceeded to sequester his various properties.

Claimants, however, arose up on every side, and various trials took place before the Court, who on application heard the inquiries of the claimants *pro interesse suo*, with witnesses *vivâ voce*, in open Court, instead of sending them before the Master.

The conveyances were nearly all set aside on the evidence, and the two following cases are selected as specimens of the proceedings.

1. A party against whom a suit was pending in equity perceiving that a decree was about to be made against him, made several conveyances of his property in order to prevent the plaintiff in the equity suit from obtaining the fruits of the decree; on inquiry before the Court, these conveyances were set aside as fraudulent, no valid consideration appearing to have passed.

2. On parties coming in under a sequestration of a defendant's property, applying to be heard *pro interesse suo*, the Court framed issues and heard witnesses *vivâ voce*.

(*a*) See the last case.

MIRZA MUTALIF'S CLAIM.

1849.
August 1.

[*Coram* PERRY, C. J., and YARDLEY, J.]

IN this case the claimant was the son-in-law of Aga Mahomed Rahim, and he claimed the property in the family

Where a suit had been commenced, in 1833, against an executor, in which it appeared probable that a decree for a very large amount would be pronounced against him, the Court set aside as fraudulent conveyances two deeds, by which the executor conveyed to his son-in-law two houses for alleged valuable consideration, in 1842, although the decree was not made against the executor for some years afterwards.

For other fraudulent conveyances see next case.

1848.

AGA MAHOMED RAHIM'S Case.

house, and one adjoining to it, under conveyances in 1842 from Aga Mahomed Rahim to his wife, Bunnoo. for valuable consideration, it being alleged that the houses had been made over to the wife of defendant in right of dower.

After a long inquiry at the Bar, the Court set aside the conveyances as fraudulent; but as the suit had lasted so long, as new Judges and new counsel had intervened in the litigation which had lasted since 1833, it was necessary to take a careful retrospect of the previous facts of the case, in order to arrive at a just conclusion. And as it was supposed that the defendant would endeavour to stave off the ultimate decision by appeal to the Privy Council, the Chief Justice thought it desirable to preface his decision by a recapitulation of the principal facts, so as to bring the matter fully before the attention of their Lordships in the Privy Council.

Cur. adv. vult.

PERRY, C. J.—The question to be decided in this case is, whether two deeds, conveying houses at the Baboola Tank, purporting to be made in March and July, 1842, by Aga Mahomed Rahim, and his wife, Bunnoo, respectively, to their son-in-law, Mirza Mutalif, are valid documents sufficient to pass the property; and if it were my duty now to sum up the case to the jury, I should tell them that the broad question for their consideration was, whether Mirza Mutalif actually bought and paid for the property at that period, or whether the whole transaction was a mere family arrangement to protect Aga Mahomed Rahim from the demands of his creditor, Mirza Ali Khan.

In order to enable the question in this broad view to be disposed of, it is essential to keep the position of these parties, and especially of Aga Mahomed Rahim, vividly before our eyes. It is sufficient, now, to state, that Mirza Ali, so long ago as 1833, sued Mahomed Shustri, who was the executor of his father, Mahomed Khan, for an account of Mahomed Khan's estate. Shustri answered this claim, and admitted that there was a large balance, amounting to several laks, due to the estate, but professed an inability to get in the debts,

1849.

AGA MAHOMED RAHIM'S Case.

&c., and alleged that he had only between Rs. 50,000 and Rs. 60,000 available for the plaintiffs. He neglected to furnish any accounts however, by which the truth of his assertions could be tested, and, before he could be compelled to do so by the process of the Court, he died. This executor was Aga Mahomed Rahim, and the suit was continued against him; and he also, for the first year or two, pursued the same line of defence as Shustri, admitting a balance due to the estate, but producing no accounts to explain why or wherefore no assets were forthcoming.

About two years after the death of Shustri, however, Aga Mahomed Rahim set up an entirely new defence, for he asserted that he had discovered a great mistake in the accounts, which had been rendered by Shustri, who had admitted that the large property, I have before spoken of, belonged to Ali Khan, whereas, in truth and in fact, it all belonged to Shustri himself. And he brought forward a tolerably plausible account of how the mistake originated, and vouched a good number of witnesses to prove all the assertions he had made.

An opportunity was, therefore, given him by the Court, although against all precedent and principle, to disprove the solemn statements on oath of his testator and father-in-law, Mahomed Shustri.

This inquiry, conducted at vast expense, lasted from 1838 to 1843. Agar Mahomed Rahim sent commissions to Hydrabad, to Calcutta, and to many parts of Persia to obtain evidence; a most voluminous mass was collected; but on a solemn inquiry, which lasted six days in this Court, it turned out that there was not the least proof or presumption to be drawn in favour of the very improbable story told of Shustri swearing away eight or ten laks of property *by mistake.*

From the day of that decision, it was apparent that the evil hour which Aga Mahomed Shustri and Aga Mahomed Rahim had been so long endeavouring to postpone, was approaching, and that a satisfactory account must be given of this large property which Ali Khan had left behind, or that those into whose hands it had come, must be held personally responsible.

The slow procedure in the Master's Office, however, when long accounts have to be gone through, gave Aga Mahomed

1849.

Aga Mahomed Rahim's Case.

Rahim two years longer time, and it was not till October, 1845, that a report from the Master was ripe, charging Aga Mahomed Shustri's estate with the divers large sums admitted to belong to Ali Khan.

At this period, the fact occurred, which is now undisputed by all parties, that Aga Mahomed Rahim freighted the ship Haidri with all the property he could collect for the fraudulent purpose of withdrawing himself and family from the jurisdiction of this Court, and of preventing his creditor, Mirza Ali, from getting one rupee of his claim.

The Court, however, on application made to it, thought this transaction was so suspicious, that, although Rahim swore he was not going to leave the island, and would have had the Court to believe that he was worth ten or twelve laks of rupees —this Court, I say, issued its fiat for an arrest, on a writ *ne exeat jurisdictionem.*

The person of Aga Rahim was thereupon secured, but the ship Haidri sailed to Persia with, as there is every reason to believe, a very valuable freight on board. Subsequently to this the dreaded report from the Master made its appearance; it was confirmed by the Court, and a decree was pronounced against Rahim for eleven laks of rupees.

The plaintiff thereupon proceeded to sequester the valuable landed property, such as dockyard, houses, &c., which were well known throughout Bombay to belong to Aga Mahomed Rahim, and at which he used to collect all the notabilities of the island to witness his worldly prosperity, and to inaugurate his different adventures; and Aga Mahomed Rahim, on his part, applied for the benefit of the Insolvent Act.

But to all this property so sequestered, claimants rise up on every side under conveyances from Aga Mahomed Rahim, and he himself, in his petition to the Insolvent Court, although he described himself in 1845, and previously in 1843, as worth from ten to twelve laks of rupees; now professes himself to be wholly destitute, and does not give up, I believe, one single rupee to the common assignee.

This is a general statement of the facts, which I have thought it right to set down, as being a necessary preliminary to be borne in mind during any inquiry as to the validity of those

1849.

AGA MAHOMED RAHIM'S Case.

conveyances, which profess to have transferred his property to other parties.

It is quite notorious, therefore, that Aga Mahomed Rahim has committed a great fraud and which, up to the present time, has been wholly successful. The large property which we know him, from his own statements and from evidence *aliunde,* to have been master of, has disappeared,—such of it as was moveable has gone by the ship Haidri to Persia, and such as was fixed has passed by conveyances, sales, and assignments to different parties in Bombay; and the only penalty which appears to attend Aga Mahomed Rahim, if these facts are established against him, would be an imprisonment under the penal clauses of the Insolvent Act, which, perhaps, would be willingly submitted to, if thereby an opponent could be defeated and a large sum of money secured.

I cannot deny that this state of facts, present in my mind, leads me to regard with the utmost suspicion the genuineness of the various conveyances, which are relied upon to prove that Aga Rahim has now no property. All the motives which ordinarily operate to produce false testimony in this Court, appear to me to be present in this case with great force. A very large sum of money is at issue, and I need not observe that the most fruitful source of perjury in this Court, arises on disputed claims to money. Amongst individuals given up to gain, and with whom no counterbalancing influences arising out of free institutions, public opinion, or cultivated training exist, this addiction to lucre is often found so soul-engrossing as to make no sacrifice too great to attain it. But a still more powerful motive, as it appears to me, is at work in this case, for I conceive that the exquisite gratification of baffling an opponent, with whom for fifteen long years the most hostile litigation has existed, would be sufficient in a native mind to overpower even the desire of self aggrandizement, and that if a course were seen open to success, even at the risk of involving its deviser in ruin, it would be willingly adopted, so as to avert the hated triumph which his adversary would otherwise secure.

These being the general grounds of suspicion which I find

1849.

Aga Mahomed Rahim's Case.

my mind occupied with, on regarding the genuineness of these different conveyances, I confess also, that they are much enhanced with respect to the particular conveyance now before the Court. For these conveyances belong to a class which always must be viewed with the greatest caution when they are brought before an Indian Court of justice. Nothing is more frequent than to have conveyances, and transfers, and assignments, from one member of a family to another, from a father to his infant child, and so on, produced in Court, of which the world knows nothing, and of which the general effect is to defraud creditors. In the present inquiry, for instance, we hear of the infant sons of Aga Mahomed Rahim, one not more than ten years of age, building the ship Haidri. And undoubtedly it must be confessed, that if Rahim were so minded as to make fraudulent conveyances for thepurpose of defeating his creditors, the members of his family, who, with any plausibility, could be selected, would be the most obvious grantees for him to fix upon.

Such are the general grounds of suspicion which attend the plaintiff's case, and his counsel, Mr. *Crawford*, very candidly admits them, and puts them forward as forcibly as I do. He admits too, I think, to the same extent with myself, the character of Aga Mahomed Rahim's conduct, but he cautions the Court not to be led away by natural feelings of indignation on the evidence of fraud in one party, so as to involve others, who are innocent, in its consequences. And, rejecting the evidence of Rahim, he refers us to the testimony of others unimpeached, and apparently uninfluenced, in the transaction, who support the genuineness of the plaintiff's case.

The caution is a just one, and is not to be lost sight of. A story may be extremely improbable, and yet it may true. Aga Mahomed Rahim may have had every motive to defraud; but his son-in-law, Mirza Mutalif, may have acted innocently, and merely in pursuit of his interests.

It is necessary, therefore to examine the evidence dispassionately, and I will now proceed to do so to the best of my powers.

[After analysis of the evidence the Court pronounced against the claim.]

MUSHEDY KAZIM'S CLAIM.

1849. May 17.

[*Coram* Perry, C. J. and Yardley, J.]

Fraudulent conveyance of property in order to defeat the creditors, set aside. Solemn decision of a Court, although on summary procedure, if unappealed against, operates as *res judicata* to prevent further litigation.

This was another of the cases in which, on sequestration of Aga Mahomed Rahim's property, the claimant asserted his title, as purchaser, to the half of Mazagon Dockyard, valued at Rs. 300,000 (30,000*l.*), and applied on affidavit to be allowed to go in before the Master, and to examine *pro interesse suo.*

The Court, on hearing the parties, consented to take the inquiry themselves, with examination of witnesses *vivâ voce*, and by consent issues were raised to try the question.

After a trial, lasting several days, the Court decided against the validity of the claim, on the following grounds:—

Perry, C. J.—This trial has lasted so many days, and has made us so familiar with the facts, that the conclusions in our minds are altogether clear and distinct, and it is unnecessary to defer giving judgment in order to put them in better language, or in a more logical order. The question to be determined in this case is, whether the conveyance of a moiety of Aga Mahomed Rahim's dockyard in December, 1845, to Mushedy Kazim was a *bonâ fide* sale, or whether it was a simulated transaction between these parties for the purpose of defeating Rahim's creditors, and particularly his old opponent Mirza Ali. In order to be in a condition to form an accurate judgment on this question it is necessary to have a distinct picture before our eyes of the position of the principal actors in the transaction at the period when it occurred. And for this purpose it is only necessary, so far as the Profession here is concerned, before whom this suit has been travelling its slow course during the whole of the career of nearly every practitioner now at the Bar, to point out that in November, 1845, the suit against Aga Rahim had reached its *dénouement.* But if it is desired to take up this inquiry to another tribunal,

1849.

Aga Mahomed Rahim's Case.

I should wish that the introductory remarks I made on another suit akin to the present, should be considered to be incorporated in the present judgment, as they are just as applicable to this case, as to the one in which they were delivered.

All, therefore, that it is now necessary to remark is, that in November, 1845, a decree against Aga Mahomed Rahim, for very many laks of rupees was about to be given; that in the same month he was charged before this Court with an attempt to abscond and to withdraw all his moveable property from the jurisdiction, in order to defeat the decree; that the Court believed the charge, and ordered his arrest, although the Aga gave the Court to understand that it was wholly untrue, and that he was a man of very large property, and quite equal and willing to satisfy the claims of his creditor in the case. It is also necessary to observe, that when this decree came on subsequently to be enforced, all the property which the Aga previously had sworn to, disappeared; and when execution issued against the greatest Mogul merchant of Bombay, one who had been the host of previous Governors, Judges, and all the society of the island, who had been for many years the agent of the great Mussalman Princes of Western Asia, and whose large possessions in landed property, in ships, and other substantial *indicia* of wealth, were patent to the eyes of all, not one single rupee was forthcoming, or voluntarily paid by him in satisfaction of the claim of the young man, whose property had been in his hands for years, and which had been the foundation of all his prosperity.

On legal inquiry, it turns out that the landed and other property, which was well known to belong to Aga Mahomed Rahim, has all been conveyed to other parties, and the question therefore arises on every such conveyance, whether there really was a *bonâ fide* transfer of property for good consideration, or whether a deep laid scheme was concocted, for the purpose of defeating the course of law, for cheating the claimant, whom he had been keeping at arms' length for a course of years by harassing litigation, and by using those provisions in the English law, which are intended for the relief of honest but unfortunate debtors, to withdraw all his property which could be realized from without the jurisdiction of the Court, and himself finally, so soon as he should have got his discharge under the Insolvent Act.

This being the statement of the question before the Court, it is obvious that any claimant to property conveyed by Aga Mahomed Rahim, at the period of his difficulties, labours under the onus of having to maintain a case which is open to the gravest suspicions. The probabilities are all against the genuineness of such a transaction, for it does not require a very long experience in this Court, to be aware that fraudulent tortuous courses, skilful deeplaid schemes, and most unblushing perjury, are constantly resorted to by persons in difficulty, whereas the same prudence in *bonâ fide* transactions, and the same care to make good bargains, and not to part with hard cash till a valid equivalent is obtained, are undoubtedly to be found amongst the natives of India, to quite as great an extent as with any nation in the world.

The conclusion which I desire to draw from this observation is, that as the plaintiff's case is necessary tainted with suspicion, it lies upon him, if the transaction be really a genuine one, to bring more than an ordinary amount of evidence to support it, and to rebut by unimpeachable testimony the *primâ facie* incredibility which accompanies his tale. The large sum of money involved in this case (at least four laks, according to the plaintiff, but probably not amounting even with the arrears of rent, to more than two), affords quite sufficient motive to the plaintiff, to make every exertion to bring forward all the evidence which is capable of being given; and I have no doubt whatever in my own mind, that the plaintiff *has* brought forward all the evidence which was calculated to support his claim.

Having thus stated the question for inquiry, and the positions of the parties at the period of the transaction, and having pointed out how extremely suspicious a case the plaintiff was coming forward to support, and the consequent burden upon him of furnishing the Court with a mass of irrefragable evidence, I make no hesitation in avowing that, directly I heard the speech of the learned counsel for the plaintiff, and ascer-

1849.

Aga Mahomed Rahim's Case.

tained that a case in itself suspicious was accompanied with the most improbable details, and that these details had absolutely no witnesses at all to prove them, I felt no doubt whatever that the defendant was entitled to a verdict, and that the conveyance was altogether simulative and fraudulent. Indeed the impression on both our minds was so strong, that if it had not been intimated that an appeal to the Privy Council was intended, we should have probably thought it necessary for the ends of justice to have cut the matter short by pronouncing our conclusions at once, that a tale so improbable and supported by no evidence ought not to be allowed to take up any further time in a Court of justice. But as the impressions on our minds were formed on previous facts connected with the suit, the knowledge of which was necessary to enable any tribunal to form an accurate judgment, but which would not appear to the Privy Council unless given in evidence, it was essential to undergo the tedious inquiry of getting these different facts, so well known to all of us, on the records of the Court in this particular suit.

These facts being now recorded, it is sufficient to say of them, that all those which make for the plaintiff (except, perhaps, one) are neutral, or irrelevant, or capable of easy explanation; that several facts are proved which throw the gravest suspicion on the plaintiff's title, and above all, that proof of those facts which were essential to the plaintiff's claim is altogether wanting.

I will briefly touch upon the most salient points of the evidence.

[After minute examination of the evidence, the Court pronounced their decision against the claim of Mushedy Kazim.]

In a subsequent term, Mushedy Kazim filed a bill against Mirza Ali, in which he founded his claim to a moiety of the dockyard, on grounds similar to those urged in the above inquiry before the Court.

The defendants demurred to the bill, on the ground that it was *res judicata*.

Jenkins, for the complainant, strongly urged that he was at

1849.

AGA MAHOMED RAHIM'S Case.

May 17.

liberty to raise the question in solemn form before the Court in the shape of a bill.

Howard and *Dickinson, contra.*

Cur. adv. vult.

PERRY, C. J.—This case stood over to enable me to look into the books, to discover whether, by the reference in the plaintiff's bill to the proceedings in this Court on his claim to be examined *pro interesse suo*, it was competent to the Court to look into those proceedings as if they were incorporated in the bill. I do not think it is necessary to determine this question, because, upon the face of the plaintiff's bill, it appears to me that his claim has already been disposed of by the Court, and is, therefore, *res judicata*.

The plaintiff's case is, that he was the *bonâ fide* purchaser, and, as such, that he possesses the legal conveyance of a moiety of the Mazagon Dockyard, and on his title, adding to it circumstances which I may almost call inappreciable, he founds his equitable claim for relief, but he admits, in his bill, that on a previous inquiry his claim was disallowed by the Court. Now as a Court of equity on an inquiry into a man's right, title, claim, and interest, or, as it is briefly called, *interesse suum*, is fettered by no form, and may give effect to the claim whether legal or equitable, whether the whole or a part, the allegation in the plaintiff's bill that he has got good title is wholly repugnant to the former decision of the Court, and, therefore, cannot be taken to be admitted by the demurrer on the principle laid down in *Arundel* v. *Arundel*, (Cro. Jac.), that "a demurrer in law is never a confession of a thing against the record, but only of that which may stand with the record; for otherwise his confession would be vain, and should not bind the Court."

The Court, therefore, is able to see on this record that the plaintiff's claim has already been disallowed by a Court of competent jurisdiction. If the decision was then objected to, two courses were open to the plaintiff, either to apply for a new trial, or to appeal to the Privy Council. The plaintiff did neither, and therefore the decision was final.

1849.

Aga Mahomed Rahim's Case.

In point of fact, it was intimated at the former trial that it was intended to appeal to the Privy Council if the decision should be adverse to the plaintiff, and for this reason, in order to facilitate such a course to the plaintiff, the Court went into the evidence at very great (and otherwise unnecessary) length, in order to get all the facts of the case upon their notes, so as to enable their Lordships in the Privy Council to be fully possessed of the question. And this is so obviously the proper mode of reviewing the solemn decision of a Court, which was given unanimously, after a trial of many days, and on a thorough ventilation of the question, that I have no hesitation in allowing this demurrer; and I think it better to place my decision on the broad ground that this is an attempt to re-agitate the same questions between (in effect) the same parties, and before the same Judges, which no system of jurisprudence allows,—than on the special grounds advanced that the plaintiff's main case, by his own shewing, is a legal and not an equitable title.

Indeed I cannot but think, that if Mr. *Jenkins* had been aware of the grounds on which this Court decided in the former case, a note of which I read during the argument, this bill would never have been filed.

Bill dismissed (*a*).

(*a*) The end of Aga Mahomed Rahim, after all the litigation recorded above, was most melancholy. After lying in gaol for some years, obstinately refusing to give up any property to the son of his benefactor, and failing in all his schemes to convey his property to other parties, he was at length allowed by his creditor, the plaintiff, to leave gaol, and he slunk out of Bombay to join his family in exile.

The following extract, from a local newspaper, gives such a glowing picture of a successful Bombay native merchant under the British Government, and offers such a startling contrast to the results above recorded, that it seems worth while to subjoin it:—

"The launch of the frigate belonging to his Highness the Imaum of Muscat, took place last night, in honour of which event numerous invitations had been issued by Aga Mahomed Rahim.

"At ten o clock his Excellency the Governor, Sir George Arthur, arrived, accompanied by his Lady, attended by his staff, &c. The house prepared for the ball was appropriately decorated and well lighted. A fine large room was laid out for dancing, which was soon commenced. The number of ladies and gentlemen was considerable;

1849.

AGA MAHOMED RAHIM'S Case.

many had relinquished other parties in order to witness the novel scene of a launch by torchlight.

" A short distance from the ball room the frigate appeared in bold relief, decorated with lamps; great eagerness prevailed, not only amongst those who were invited, but also amongst the crowds who thronged from the fort, and from the native town, to see the unusual sight.

" Shortly before midnight, Lady Arthur, leaning on the arm of Sir Robert Oliver, the Superintendent of the Indian Navy, came forward, and the ceremony of breaking a bottle and of naming the ship was gone through.—The name is 'Queen Victoria.'

" Soon afterwards, when every care was taken to prevent any accident occurring to the surrounding crowds, the signal was given by Cursetjee Rustomjee, the well known ship-builder of the dockyard, who was then assisting his brother the constructor of the frigate, and she glided straight as an arrow and buoyant as an eagle into the harbour of Bombay. The gracefulness of the motion gave great pleasure to the spectators, who loudly cheered the vessel as she swam swanlike away.

" The party then retired to a plentiful supper, at which covers were laid for two hundred persons. Sir George and Lady Arthur sat near Aga Mahomed Rahim. At the close Sir George Arthur rose and addressed the company, stating that he was unexpectedly called on to give a toast, which he nevertheless felt great pleasure in proposing. It was, 'The health of his Highness the Imaum of Muscat, the steady ally of Great Britain; and may the gallant vessel which they had seen gracefully gliding into the deep, sail long on the ocean in amity and union with the glorious flag that has braved the battle and the breeze during upwards of a thousand years.

" The toast was drunk with long and loud applause. Aga Jaffer rose shortly afterwards, and said, Ladies and gentlemen, I am now commissioned by my brother-in-law, Aga Mahomed Rahim, to return you his most sincere thanks for the honour you have done him in coming here this evening. That honour he highly prizes, and proving to him your friendly feelings to his Highness the Imaum.. Ladies and gentlemen, in his name I thank you. . . . . . I shall now conclude with proposing a toast, in which I am sure you will all join.—I propose the health of Lady Arthur and the ladies.'

" The toast was drunk with enthusiasm. The company returned to the ball room, where dancing was continued till a late hour.

" Thus terminated the launch of the frigate 'Queen Victoria,' at midnight. The calmness of the night, the stillness of the sea, of which the waves were but ripples on the shore, the illuminated ball room, the festoons of lamps hanging in the grounds, and the ship itself with lights on both decks, and at every port hole, looking, as it were, triumphant in the distance, and the full satisfaction experienced by all present, gave an interest to that scene which will not soon be forgotten."—*Gentleman's Gazette, Dec.* 23, 1843.

1846.

March 10.
July 2.

1847.

Feb. 22.

NATHUBHAI RAMDASS AND OTHERS *v.* MANMOHANDASS DAVIDASS AND OTHERS.

A HINDU FAMILY ESTATE.

[*Coram* PERRY, C. J.]

Where a bill was filed for an account by a member of a Hindu family against his cousin, who was executor of the complainant's father, the defendant set up a claim of partnership with the father, and a right to retain the assets in his hands for liquidation of the partnership claims. In the course of a long litigation which ensued, it became necessary to inquire into the validity of a release which had been made between the defendant and the testator, who were uncle and nephew, nearly forty years before, and which respected transactions sixty-five years before; this release was impeached for fraud, and for want of consideration, but the Court upheld it as a family compromise, and as an ancient transaction that had been sanctioned by time, and by each party having acted under it, although it was of opinion that neither party had been perfectly straightforward, and that tricky conduct was imputable to them both.

Effects of equity procedure in stimulating and keeping alive ruinous litigation, exemplified.

THE merchants of Western India, called Banyans, Bunneas, Wanis, or Vanyos (from the sanscrit word Banik, a trader), belong to Gujarát, from which country they have issued from time immemorial to all the ports on the neighbouring coasts, both of Africa and Asia, in pursuit of their calling (*a*).

Towards the end of the last century, one Manordass Rupjí was considered the leading Banyan merchant in Bombay, and he died possessed of considerable wealth, leaving behind him five sons, constituting an undivided Hindu family (*b*).

From soon after his death up to the present year (1852), litigation has been proceeding amongst different members of

(*a*) The Portuguese found them on the east coast of Africa, when they first doubled the Cape; the Indians described in the Periplus undoubtedly belonged to the same cast, and Sir William Harris, in his last expedition to Abyssinia, found these same industrious Hindus conducting the trade at the different towns of the African shore where no Europeans had previously touched.

(*b*) The relations belonging to an *undivided* family constitute one of the most important institutes in Hindu law. As a rule, every family is undivided; the members of it *inter se* forming a quasi partnership; a *divided* family is created by one brother or other member severing himself from the joint stock by some act of public notoriety, and his children again constitute an undivided family with himself. See *post*, pp. 129 and 133.

1846.

RAMDASS and Others v. DAVIDASS and Others.

his family, and the case here reported forms but an incident amongst the many controverted matters between different members which has been brought before the Court.

The demand in the principal, or family suit, as it was called, required an examination and scrutiny of accounts of a partnership which had been carried on between Manordass and his five sons, which extended over upwards of forty years, and in which inquiries had to be made into transactions so far back as 1770. But after many years of litigation, and after the cause had got into the Master's Office, it became abundantly clear that to take this account minutely, and with the accuracy which judicial procedure required, in a case where the property was so large, and the claimants so numerous, was beyond the powers of any Court of justice. During the course of so long a litigation, the angry feelings of the parties were of course excited, several ugly charges against one another had been brought forward, a large sum of money, from first to last (150.000*l.* and upwards), was locked up in Court, a receiver had been appointed to collect the rents of the extensive family estates, until at length the cause was brought to a dead lock. Each party was afraid to take a step for fear of the criminations and recriminations that might be excited, and each was willing to hope that by pursuing a Fabian system he might weary out the patience, or exhaust the pecuniary resources, necessary to keep up the litigation on the part of his opponents.

Inquiry in Master's Office as to accounts of a partnership, extending over forty years, and commencing more than seventy years ago.

Ultimately, the Court having made many previous attempts to bring the cause to a close, and so to prevent all the parties from being involved in inevitable ruin, succeeded by what almost amounted to personal entreaty in persuading the family to sell the family estate, and to divide the property amongst them.

This course having been pursued under the direction of the Master, a final report was announced, (August 11, 1851), on which the remaining money now in Court (70,000*l.* odd) will be divisible among the family.

The following case is only one of the many incidental disputes which have arisen between various members of the family.

The head of the family, Manordass, had five sons, with

1846.

Ramdass and Others. v. Davidass and Others.

whom, as above stated, he carried on a partnership, and the principal suit was chiefly in reference to the accounts of that partnership.

But two of his sons, Rama and Hurjeevan, carried on a separate partnership for six years, from 1776 to 1782, and it was as to that partnership that the litigation, in the following case, between the son of one brother and the grandson of the other, took place.

For an earlier stage of the proceedings on appeal to the Privy Council, see *Nathoobhoy Ramdass* v. *Moolja Madordass* (*a*).

This suit was filed by Nathoobhoy in 1832, against his cousin Davidass and another, executors of, his father, Rama's will; and the bill, after stating that a partnership had formerly existed between Rama and the defendant Davidass, but which had been put an end to, when mutual releases were executed, in 1808, prayed the usual account.

The defendant Davidass, and in the revived suit his son Manmohandass, denied that any such release had been executed, and claimed to retain the assets in his hands, as surviving partner, to liquidate the balance due to him as such partner.

There was much litigation in this country from 1834 to 1838, and the case got into the Privy Council on appeal in 1840, but the decision there proceeding on technicalities, the case was sent back to this country to be tried on its merits.

The Privy Council, by their decision, having allowed the plaintiff, in this case, to set up a release in the Master's Office, under the decree which had been pronounced in India, and permission being also given to the defendant to impeach the release, the matter was vigorously contested before the Master, and his report was presented early in 1846, by which it appeared that he rejected the release as fraudulent.

The matter came on for argument on a former day (*b*), *cor.* Perry, J. (Sir H. Roper, C. J., having been engaged as counsel in the cause), on exceptions to the Master's report.

(*a*) 3 Moore's P. C. C. 87.
(*b*) 10th March, 1846.

1846.

RAMDASS and Others v. DAVIDASS and Others.

Herrick and *Dickinson*, in support of the exceptions.

It was not necessary for us to do more in the Master's Office than produce this release; it lay on the other side to impeach it; but we went further, and proved that the release was perfectly fair. It was not so much a release as a family compromise, and Lord COTTENHAM has laid down, solemnly, in *Wedderburn* v. *Wedderburn*, (4 M. & Cr.), that on these disputed questions on partnership, when death occurs, a compromise is often the most beneficial arrangement that can be made. If a family compromise, that took place thirty-eight years ago, on matters that occurred upwards of sixty years ago, is now to be set aside, dissension and discord will be introduced into every Hindu family.

Le Messurier, A. G., and *Howard, contra.*

It is a fallacy to call this release a compromise; the latter only occurs where some doubtful point of law exists; if the facts are in dispute there must be a full examination, and a knowledge by each party of his rights, before a valid compromise can be made. Here the knowledge was all on one side, and Davidass, therefore, was persuaded to release all his rights without consideration. It is exactly like the case, cited in 1 *Story's Equity Jur.*, s. 117, of the girl who gave up her orphanage claim, not knowing she was entitled to an account.

Secondly, Rama obtained this release by downright fraud. It recites as facts clear falsehoods, which Rama knew to be false, but on the strength of which, as true, Davidass gave up his rights.

Herrick replied.

Cur. adv. vult.

July 2.

Disputed question in suit as to vali-

PERRY J.—In this suit, which has been pending for fourteen years, and which has given rise to such expensive and anxious litigation, both in this Court and in the Privy Council at home, the question which has all along been perceived, to use the words of Chief Justice COMPTON, "to be the only

1846.

RAMDASS and Others v. DAVIDASS and Others.

substantial question between the parties," comes now, for the first time, to be decided, upon an exception taken to the Master's Report. That question is, whether an agreement executed by Davidass Hurjeevandass, in January, 1808, is to be considered a valid and binding instrument, or not.

dity of family agreement, drawn up in 1808.

By what mischance or miscarriage it has been, that this point has been so long pending for decision, it may not be very easy, and it is no part of my present duty, to determine. But, in order to make clear the views I have formed upon the character of a transaction, which took place nearly forty years ago, it is necessary to recapitulate, briefly, some leading facts relating to the actors engaged in it.

1776. Two brothers, Rama and Hurjeevan, go into partnership.

1782. Hurjeevan dies.

1808. Rama dies.

It seems that, in the year 1776, there was an undivided Hindu family, residing in Bombay, consisting of Manordass, Roopjee, and his five sons. In that year, two of his sons, namely, Rama and Hurjeevan, formed a partnership, under the style of Ramdass Hurjevandass, and in the same or following year (for it does not distinctly appear which), the father, with all the five sons, created another firm, under the name of Kessordass Ransordass. Rama and Hurjeevan carried on the first-mentioned firm from 1776 to 1782, when Hurjeevan died, and from that date, Rama continued to carry on the firm alone, but in the old name, until his death in 1808. When Hurjeevan died, he left a son of a year old, named Davidass; and, it seems, that some short time previous to Ramdass' death (for no claim previous to this period appears), Davidass set up a claim to be a partner with Rama by virtue of his heirship to his father Hurjeevan. The uncle, Rama, resisted this claim, but being then on the point of death, and being desirous to appoint his nephew, Davidass, one of his executors, who also, it would seem, was anxious to obtain this appointment, the uncle and nephew agreed to refer the settlement of their disputed claim to two other members of the family, who were accordingly called in; the parties to whom this settlement was referred were, Kessordass, a brother of Rama, and Madow, his nephew, who were, therefore, respectively, uncle and first cousin of the claimant, Davidass; and the agreement which was then drawn up, in consequence

1808. Hurjeevan's son, Davidass, claims to be a partner with his uncle, Rama.

Claim referred to family arbitrators, and

of the interposition of these two relations, is the one which gives rise to the present question. It is as follows:—

1846.

RAMDASS and Others v. DAVIDASS and Others.

(Agreement.)

agreement in question drawn up.

"To Shet Ramdass Manordass, written by Shet Davidass Hurjeevandass, to wit, you and Bhy Hurjeevandass Manordass had a partnership concern: that concern was in the name of Shet Ramdass Hurjeevandass. In it the shares were equal, half and half; that in Sumwut year one thousand eight hundred and thirty-eight, (one thousand seven hundred and eighty-one, and eighty-two, A. D.), Bhy Hurjeevandass departed this life, when the profit of Bhy Hurjeevandass' share came to rupees one thousand one hundred and ten, and eighty-eight reas, which Bhy Hurjeevandass has received from you in full; afterwards you yourself did carry on your own concern from Sumwut year one thousand eight hundred and thirty-eight (one thousand seven hundred and eighty-one and eighty-two, A. D.), up to this day. I asserted, however, that I had a share thereof, to which you replied, that after the death of my father there is no share nor part retained for me; regarding this you and I had a discussion; then on your behalf and mine, we gave our authority to Bhy Keshoredass Manordass and Bhy Madowdass Runsordass, and had the matter settled at rupees thirteen thousand. Now respecting the concern of Bhy Ramdass Hurjeevandass, I have nothing to pay or receive respecting this concern; I have not the least claim whatever; any debit or credit whatever there may be belonging to Shet Ramdass Hurjeevandass is wholly yours; I have not anything whatever to do respecting this concern; I have of my free will and pleasure, sound sense and judgment, given this acquittance in writing for the same; I do agree to abide by; This Sumwut year one thousand eight hundred and sixty-four, Maha Soodh first, and Wednesday twenty-seventh January, A. D. one thousand eight hundred and eight."

After this agreement Rama appoints his nephew, Davidass, his executor.

Upon this agreement having been signed by Davidass Ramo, the uncle, who was then lying on his death-bed, carried out his intention of appointing Davidass co-executor to his

1846.

RAMDASS and Others v. DAVIDASS and Others.

last will, and died some three weeks afterwards. Davidass, with the other executor Madow, proved this will, though not without much litigation with Ramcooverboye, the widow of the deceased testator, and he proceeded to gather in the assets.

He also seems, in some way which has not been clearly explained, to have gradually become the sole acting executor of his uncle Ramdass.

1832. Rama's widow sues Davidass for an account.

In 1832, that is to say, twenty-four years after the decease of Rama, the widow and her only son Nathoobhoy, who were the legatees of Ramdass, sued the executors, praying that his will might be established, and that an account might be taken of his estate, and of the rents and profits received by the defendants. Davidass upon this set up as an answer, that although he had received certain large sums as executor of Rama, he claimed to retain them, on account of his interest in the partnership which his father Hurjeevan had formed with Rama, and to which he succeeded on the death of Hurjeevan.

Davidass claims as a partner of Rama to retain the assets in his hands for partnership claims.

This defence of Davidass was met by the complainants in two ways; first, they said, "You never were partner with Ramdass; secondly, if you were, you released and gave up all claims for the sake of being appointed his executor by your agreement of January, 1808."

The first question substantially has formed the subject of litigation up to the present time, and the Judges of this Court decided, that by the Hindu law the rights of Hurjeevan in the partnership of Ramdass Hurjeevandass did descend at his death upon his son Davidass.

Release of the partnership claims held by Master to be fraudulent.

The second question which, as I observed before, had always been perceived to be the main one in the case, was, somehow or other, withdrawn from the pleadings at an early stage of the suit, and it is only now raised by a special order of the Privy Council, for the purpose of doing justice in the case.

The Master, upon the agreement of January 1808, being brought before him, has decided that it ought not to be maintained or established, but as he has not assigned his reasons

1846.

RAMDASS and Others v. DAVIDASS and Others.

for this finding, I can only gather them from the arguments urged at the Bar in behalf of his report.

Examination of the grounds for setting aside such a release.

Now, the only grounds, as it appeared to me, on which this agreement of Davidass, a man, in 1808, of twenty-seven years of age, and of competent understanding, can be impeached, are, either that it was entered into by him in ignorance of facts which it imported him to be acquainted with, or that it was procured from him by the fraud or undue exercise of influence by his uncle Rama.

Ignorance of facts;

With regard to the first ground, however, I cannot perceive the slightest reason for holding that the agreement should be set aside. If at the time the agreement was made, it had been recognised by all parties as an undisputed fact that Davidass had an interest in the partnership, and the question was merely as to the amount to which he was entitled, undoubtedly it would have been the duty of Rama to allow his partner full inspection of the partnership books, and except such inspection was waived by Davidass, it probably would be difficult to uphold the agreement as a release of all claims, if it should turn out that the information contained in these books shewed that the sum of Rs. 13,000, agreed to be paid as consideration for the release, was grossly inadequate to the rights thereby given up. But it is impossible not to perceive here that it really was a doubtful point of Hindu law whether a child of a year old succeeded to the partnership formed by his father, which had only existed six years, and which was not a family partnership. The decision pronounced by the Judges, some thirty years afterwards, that the partnership did descend, appears to me to be unimpeachable, and to flow logically from other principles of Hindu law; but, to say the least of it, it was received as novel by some of the practitioners at the Bar; no previous decision of the point appears to have been made by the Courts, and the Hindu law books do not contain any proposition as to this particular point. The law, therefore, being thus doubtful, the parties concerned being relatives, the object sought for being peace and concord in the family, I cannot think, under the circumstances, that it was in any way necessary that the books of Rama should have been laid before

1846.

RAMDASS and Others v. DAVIDASS and Others.

Davidass for inspection, and even assuming that his interests in the partnership fund should have amounted to the large sum which he claims, namely, Rs. 1,50,000, I do not think, when one recollects the expensive process to be gone through before this could be established, and the great doubt which must have existed whether such a claim could ever be established, that there was anything grossly inadequate or inequitable in the sum awarded by the relatives as the price of peace.

This agreement, therefore, having been voluntarily entered into by Davidass, who, as I before observed, was a man of mature age, and who evidently had a purpose of his own to serve by it, namely, to get appointed executor to his uncle; I think that it is only to be set aside by shewing that he was induced to enter into it through the fraud or undue representations of Ramdass.

or fraud.

Fraud not to be presumed lightly.

Now, it need not be observed, that fraud is not to be assumed upon any light surmises.

Upon transactions of the present day, where ample evidence is procurable, a Court of justice never decides that fraud has existed, unless upon full conviction; and when the balance is even between an honest and dishonest version of a transaction, the presumption of law is in favour of the former, and rightly so, for in all countries, and amongst all races of men with whom civil polity exists, honesty and veracity must greatly preponderate over fraud and mendacity, or the business of life could not proceed atall. But if this is the rule with regard to facts of yesterday, how much more forcibly must it prevail in reference to an occurrence of forty years ago, wherein points of difficulty once easily explainable, and obscure transactions that might have been made clear by a single word, are now buried in impenetrable night?

I must say, however, that I have not the least suspicion in my mind, that Ramdass intended to perpetrate any fraud on his nephew, for I do not perceive any indication that he believed Davidass to have any claim whatever on the partnership; and I am quite convinced that the latter was not induced to enter into the agreement through any misrepresentation of Rama. Indeed, the grounds whereon to rest an imputation of

1846.

RAMDASS and Others v. DAVIDASS and Others.

fraud are so weak, that one of the two learned counsel who appeared for Davidass, expressly disavowed it, but, as it has been broadly charged in another part of the defence, it is necessary to examine the point.

Inquiry as to allegation of fraud.

The agreement of January, 1808, was drawn up by the mettah (*a*) of Ramdass, upon the instructions of Rama and Davidass; and, perhaps it may not be too much to assume, that the instructions came chiefly from Ramdass. In it Davidass is made to assert, that on the death of Hurjeevandass, the profit of Hurjeevandass' share in the partnership came to Rs. 1110: 88, which Hurjeevandas had received from Ramdass in full, and that the business was then carried on by Ramdass alone. Now it is alleged, that inasmuch as the Court afterwards decided, that the partnership between Rama and Hurjeevan did not terminate at the death of the latter; and as they also held, that no settlement of accounts in full had ever been made in respect of Hurjeevan's share, therefore Rama must have deceived Davidass, and induced him to sign this agreement by persuading him that such partnership had terminated, and that such settlement of accounts had taken place. I do not think, however, that this is by any means the correct reading of the agreement, and I cannot look upon the statement as to the death of Hurjeevan, and the payment in full to him, as anything more than the statement of Ramdass' case, in the controversy which was pending between him and his nephew; this statement of his case is immediately followed by the statement of Davidass' case, namely, that notwithstanding these assertions of Rama's, he still claimed a share in the partnership, and upon these counter-claims thus set forth, the arbitrators decide between them, by awarding Rs. 13,000 to the nephew. I am happy to find that Mr. Justice AWDREY agrees with me in the version I put upon this agreement, for he makes the very pertinent remark, that if Davidass had admitted that the partnership had been terminated and the balance paid in full, the arbitrators never would have awarded him any compensation for a claim, which he confessed to be worthless.

(*a*) A clerk.

1846.

RAMDASS and Others v. DAVIDASS and Others.

Further fraud has been suggested against Ramdass in this, that when Davidass signed the agreement, the amount to be received by him as compensation was left in blank to be filled up by subsequent computation, and that the inadequate sum of Rs. 13,000 was afterwards fraudulently inserted. But this statement is unsupported by any proof, except the mere assertion of Davidass himself, and it is expressly contradicted by the *vivâ voce* testimony of the arbitrator Madowdass. It is true that Madow's testimony was not wholly believed by the Judges at the former hearing, and they thought he was in some degree biassed against Davidass, though, I must observe that his testimony against Ramcooverboye, exposing her fraudulent conduct, was much more positive and strong than any he gave against Davidass, and Mr. Justice AWDREY states, that the witness, though "clearly unfriendly in fact (to Davidass), and at personal variance with him, was perfectly calm and decent in his demeanor."

Extraordinary disappearance of evidence.

But without balancing this contradictory evidence, there were contemporaneous documents which might have thrown light on the point in question, yet both of these documents, singularly enough, have disappeared from the kingdom of things. First of these is the agreement, which was produced at the trial of the issues in 1835, and was filed with the prothonotary, but which is now no longer forthcoming, and secondly, was the contemporaneous order for Rs. 13,000, which was delivered to Davidass, but which it appears has fallen a victim, every portion of it,—date, amount, &c., to the voracity of white ants! If these papers were before the Court, the argument as to the fraudulent insertion of the sum of Rs. 13,000 might have received either corroboration or disproof, from the appearence of the instruments, of the ink, marks, &c., and these not being forthcoming on the present occasion is certainly a remarkable fact, as remarkable perhaps as the cause which has been brought forward to account for the disappearance of one of them. If any doubt still environs this point, (though I profess to feel none myself upon it), the person to suffer by it should undoubtedly be he, who has allowed so long a time to pass by without bringing the question forward for

1846.

RAMDASS and Others v. DAVIDASS and Others.

judicial investigation, as it was his duty to do if justice were upon his side, namely, Davidass.

Conclusion. Trickiness on each side, but not sufficient fraud to set aside such an ancient document.

In thus coming to the conclusion that no fraud or misrepresentation of Ramdass induced Davidass to sign the agreement in question, and, therefore, that the finding of the Master must be set aside, I am happy to find that I coincide in opinion with the two Judges who have already dealt with the case, and with whose judgments, indeed, in every material point, I feel disposed to concur. For upon the second issue which was raised between the parties in 1832 as to when the partnership terminated, the Advocate General, as I gather from Mr. Justice AWDREY's judgment, addressed himself solely to the question that it was not terminated by the agreement of January, 1808, "because that instrument was fraudulent, or, at least, was given without his being allowed that knowledge of his (Davidass') rights to which he was entitled before he could bind them."

The Judges, however, decided that the partnership was terminated by that agreement, and, therefore, expressly negative that the instrument was obtained by fraud; for fraud would have vitiated the agreement at law just as much as in equity. There was much in the case on both sides to call for reprobation from the Bench;—spoliation of documents, falsification of documents, intercession with official people, a desire, perhaps, in both Ramdass and Davidass, to overreach the other; but upon the question of fraud we have the deliberate opinion of Mr. Justice AWDREY, expressed after hearing all the evidence that has been laid before me, and hearing it in a much more satisfactory form than I have done, namely, from the mouths of witnesses.

In his judgment on the second issue, Mr. Justice AWDREY stated, "I do not believe the transaction of January 29th, 1808, to have been a perfectly fair one on either side; Davidass wished, by a feigned acquiescence, to get that access to the documents and power over the estate which the executorship would give him, Ramdass wished to obtain a bar to all future claims before he gave that information on which alone such a bar could be fairly asked for. However, the fact of

1846.

Ramdass and Others v. Davidass and Others.

making Davidass executor, and thereby giving him the power of ripping up any fraud, satisfies me that the attempt by Ramdass to obtain an unfair advantage did not go the length of such wilful fraud as would totally vitiate every thing at law."

According to this view, Davidass attempted to defraud Ramdass, and Ramdass did not exhibit the same high moral tone and regard to the interests of the other contracting party which sound ethics demand. I quite agree that this is the correct view with respect to Davidass, and I think it is very probably correct with respect to Ramdass. But I feel clear that no suspicions, or even certitude, of this sort with respect to Ramdass, can justify the Court in deciding that an agreement thus made between two natives thirty-eight years ago, and of which one party has received the full benefit, can be now set aside and nullified. I am of opinion, therefore, that the exception must be allowed.

This case was afterwards reheard, in the November Term subsequently, before Pollock, C. J., and Perry, J., when the above decision was confirmed (*a*).

(*a*) See next case.

1851.

February 16.

DAVIDASS HURJEEVANDASS
v.
MANMOHANDASS DAVIDASS.

[*Coram* Perry, C. J., and Yardley, J.]

Rate of interest chargeable on legacies.

Where a legatee voluntarily hung up her suit to recover her legacy, the Court refused to allow her compound interest.

The rule of law, which enables English executors to make a profit by the legacies in their hands for the first year, does not extend to the Administrator General, who is obliged to account for every farthing received.

Another question raised in these family quarrels, respected the interests to be charged on a legacy of Rs. 5000, which was left to a female in the family, named Nandi. The

1851.

HURJEEVANDASS
v.
DAVIDASS.

testator died in 1811,* and the suit for the legacy was filed in 1833, when the ordinary decree was pronounced.

The judgment following sufficiently describes the character of the litigation.

PERRY, C. J.—A decree in this suit was made in 1833, by which it was declared that the plaintiff was entitled to a legacy of Rs. 5000, with six per cent. interest, from the death of the testator up to the period of plaintiff's coming of age, which was in 1841, and it was referred to the Master to compute the amount of interest up to that period, the question as to the amount of interest, subsequent to 1811, being reserved for further directions. But although the plaintiff was declared entitled to this, the payment of it was to be postponed till the accounts of the testator's estate were taken, so as to ascertain whether the defendant had assets or not.

Another suit was then pending against the defendant, in which the accounts of the testator had also to be taken, and the counsel for the plaintiff (Mr. *Roper*), advised his client not to proceed further in his suit, but to await till the accounts in the other suit were taken, and the consequence has been that the plaintiff ever since 1833, till some time in the present y ear, has laindorman t.

The accounts in the other suit have not been taken, but the defendant having consented to admit assets in this suit, the Master has been enabled to make his report as to the amount of interest which was due in 1811, and which, with principal then due, amounted to Rs. 6150.

The question brought before us on Saturday was, 1st, what rate of interest was to be charged on the legacy since 1811; 2nd, whether annual rests were to be made, that is, whether compound interest was chargeable; 3rd, whether interest was to be charged on the principal sum, or on the principal plus the interest, due in 1811.

The argument having been very desultory, having been brought before us as it were piecemeal, and no cases having been cited on either side except *Raphael* v. *Boehm*, we decided that interest at 6*l.* per cent. was the proper sum to be charged;

1851.

HURJEEVANDASS v. DAVIDASS.

that it should be simple interest only, and that it should be charged on the principal sum of Rs. 5000.

Considerable dissatisfaction was expressed by Mr. *Jenkins* at this decision, (a feeling not uncommon with the losing side everywhere), but which, perhaps, at a small Bar like this, is apt to be evinced in somewhat too lively a form, and I have been induced accordingly to search the books and discover whether there are any authorities which militate against our decision. I am happy to state that I cannot find a single case to such effect; the form of decree in Mr. Seton's work directs simple interest only; an old case, *Perkyns* v. *Baynton*, (1 Brown's C.C.), states that the interest is to be calculated merely upon the principal; and a modern case, *Donovan* v. *Newham*, (9 Beavan), shews that the interest on a legacy is only given for delay of payment, and, therefore, like that on a bill of exchange should be merely simple interest.

A contrary decision, might, in fact, be attended with the deepest injustice; for the delay which has attended the prosecution of this case, having arisen from the advice of the plaintiff's legal advisers, we must take it that her own interests were furthered by it, and that possibly, if those long accounts which she forebore to exact had been gone into, it might have turned out that there were no assets out of which even the principal of her legacy was payable.

But to make that very delay the ground work of enabling her to swell up her small legacy into the large sum which compound interest during the last thirty-eight years would produce, seems opposed to every sound principle.

Connected with this question of the amount of interest chargeable against executors, a remark occurs which is of considerable importance to the English in India, and therefore I may take the opportunity of throwing it out.

Indirect effect of English rule enables executors to make a profit on assets during the first year;

By the rule of English law, executors and administrators are not chargeable with interest until the expiration of one year from the testator's death; the reason of which rule is, that the estate is frequently outstanding, and it was necessary to fix some arbitrary period from which the executor was to be

1851.

HURJEEVANDASS *v.* DAVIDASS.

charged. But the collateral effect of this rule is, that executors are thus often enabled to make a profit of the money which comes to their hands during the year. And as the assets of testators in India are usually invested in securities bearing interest, the interest accrues from the death of the testator.

Such profit cannot be made by Administrator General.

Whether private administrators in India profit by this rule or not, I am unable to say, but my belief is that they do, and I know that the general belief is, that the Administrator General, as public administrator, does so likewise. Now this is a mistake; and it is right that the public should know that the Administrator General accounts for all the interest which accrues from the day of the testator's death, and the rules of this Court prevent him from making any profit on the assets which come to his hand, exclusive of his fixed commission.

PEROZEBOYE *v.* ARDASEER CURSETJEE.

1843. September 21.

[*Coram* Sir E. PERRY, J.]

Ecclesiastical side.

Account of the legal establishments in Bombay since the cession of the island by the Portuguese.

The Supreme Court has ecclesiastical jurisdiction over Parsees and other natives domiciled in the island, so far as respects their matrimonial contracts.

Meaning of the term *British subjects.*

SUIT by the wife (a Parsí) for restitution of conjugal rights. The impugnant entered a protest to the jurisdiction of the Court, and the case was argued at great length on the 12th, 13th, and 14th of September.

Crawford, Howard, and *Holland,* for the impugnant.

The Court has only ecclesiastical jurisdiction, under the charter, over *British subjects;* but Parsís are not included under that term in any one of the statutes where it occurs; see *Sir C. Grey's Letter to Government, 5th Appendix to House of Commons' Report on East India Affairs,* 1831, p. 68. The Ecclesiastical Courts only proceed by spiritual censures,—by excommunication, which, of course, is inapplicable to a race who are

1843.

PEROZEBOYE v. ARDASEER CURSETJEE.

not Christians; and although the Courts Christian in England have taken cognizance of the marriages of Jews (*Lindo* v. *Belisario*), that is an anomaly. If Parsís are to be considered as British subjects, and so within the ecclesiastical jurisdiction clause, Parsís in every part of India may be made amenable to the Supreme Court, which clearly was never intended.

Le Messurier, A. G., *Cochrane*, and *Dickinson*, *contra*.

The term British subjects is a most ambiguous one, and its meaning is only to be ascertained by reference to the particular act where it is used. When the charter was first granted to the Supreme Court at Calcutta, it gave jurisdiction over all the King's subjects, whether European or native; but when the Court extended its process to Benares, Allahabad, &c., and great mischief ensued, it became necessary to restrain the jurisdiction, and the 21 Geo. 3 was passed, which first drew the distinction between British subjects and natives. But that statute never was intended to exempt the native inhabitants of the Presidency from the jurisdiction of the Supreme Court, and Sir CHARLES GREY expressed a clear opinion to such effect, (*5th Appendix Commons' Report*, 1831, p. 45). The charter of the Recorder's Court in Bombay extends ecclesiastical jurisdiction to all British subjects, and undoubtedly Parsís, and all other persons born in Bombay, are, and ever have been, since the cession of the island, British subjects. The point, indeed, has been decided, for in *Bebee Muttra's case*, (Clarke's Calcutta Reports), the Court held that it had ecclesiastical jurisdiction over native inhabitants; and in this Court Sir JAMES M'INTOSH entertained a suit between Armenians for the restitution of conjugal rights.

The objections as to the procedure of a Court Christian not being applicable to Parsís, are completely met by the cases of *Lindo* v. *Belisario*, and *D'Aguilar* v. *D'Aguilar*, (1 Hagg. Ecc. Rep.), relative to Jewish marriages.

Cur. adv. vult.

September 21.

PERRY, J.—This suit has been instituted by a Parsí lady against her husband for the restitution of conjugal rights. It

1843.

PEROZEBOYE *v.* ARDASEER CURSETJEE.

appears by the libel, that the marriage was solemnized between the parties in 1830, according to the rites and usages of the Parsí religion, the age of the promovent being thirteen, and of the impugnant fifteen years.

Customs of Parsís with respect to marriage.

The lady, on account of her tender age, and in accordance with the general custom of the cast, did not, upon her marriage, quit her father's roof, but remained with him till February, 1833, in which month she joined her husband, and from thenceforward they lived and cohabited together as man and wife, till some time in the year 1836. In that year the lady went, with the consent of her husband, on a visit to her father, but shortly afterwards returned to her husband's roof, where she was received and treated by him as before. She subsequently, in the same year, paid another visit to her father with the like consent of her husband, but since that time the latter has always refused to receive her back, and lately, that is to say in the present year, when she went back to her husband, with a request to be restored to the *consortium*, he forcibly expelled her from his house.

Assumption by husband of power to divorce.

The libel then states that Ardaseer has lately entered into a contract for a second marriage, and that he intends to repudiate his wife without just cause, and contrary to the laws and usages of Parsís; and prays, thereupon, that he may be ordered to take back the promovent as his lawful wife, and that in the meantime he be interdicted from performing his contract for a second marriage.

Complaint to this Court by wife.

To this libel the proctor for the impugnant has replied by entering a protest against the jurisdiction of the Court, on the ground that the ecclesiastical jurisdiction under which this suit is instituted, extends only to British subjects; and that the parties to this suit are not persons intended to be described or distinguished by that term in the charters of the Recorder's Court, or of the Supreme Court, having been born, both of them, in the island of Bombay, and being descended respectively from the race of Parsís, inhabiting Gujarat in India, and natives of India, and not being descended from persons born within any of her Majesty's dominions other than the territories under the government of the East India Company. The peculiar word-

Jurisdiction of Court denied by husband.

1843.

PEROZEBOYE v. ARDASEER CURSETJEE.

ing of this non-liability to jurisdiction is referable to a speculative opinion of Sir CHARLES GREY, to which I shall have occasion to refer hereafter; but, passing it over for the present, it is manifest that the broad question which is raised on the present pleadings is, whether the government of the Crown or of the Legislature, or of the Company acting under their authority, have afforded any tribunal whatever to that numerous class of her Majesty's subjects settled in Bombay, comprising Parsís, Portuguese, native Christians, Jews, &c., for the settlement of difficulties and disputes arising out of the marriage contract. Indeed, to this large class, who are exclusively governed by English law, (in all cases, at least where their contracts are not based upon a rule of their religion), the bulk of the population, consisting of Hindus and Mahomedans, must be added, because, although these casts have secured to them by charter their peculiarities as to succession and inheritance, still their right to the assistance of the Supreme Court as to controversies upon the subject now under discussion, stands exactly upon the same ground as that of the parties to the present suit.

Parsís alleged not to be *British subjects* within the meaning of the Charter.

The impugnant contends, that all these classes are excluded from amenability to the Court on these questions, by the use of the term, British subject, in that clause of the Charter where the ecclesiastical jurisdiction of the Court is mentioned; and that even if the term is large enough, *per se*, to include the native subjects of Bombay, it was the clear intention of the Crown, and of the Legislature, to exclude them by the use of it.

The proposition is, undoubtedly, startling, and it requires strong evidence to produce conviction that such was the intention of the authorities in England, from whom our jurisdiction has proceeded; more especially when it is observed that the impugnant suggests no other tribunal by which the question can be decided, and in point of fact, there is no other tribunal, at Bombay or elsewhere, which has any authority on the subject. It is also to be observed, that questions like the present, between Parsís and others are, undoubtedly, within the jurisdiction of the Company's Courts in the Mofussil; and we have some valuable printed reports on the very question sought to be raised in the present suit. Still, I fully accede to the reasoning of Sir WM. RUSSEL, C. J., in *Bebee Muttra's case* (Clarke's Rules, 119), that no arguments, as to the necessity for such a jurisdiction, can give the Court any power to exercise it, if the Charter of Justice and acts of Parliament have either expressly, or by necessary implication, withheld it. It is necessary, therefore, in order to ascertain the intention of the Legislature, to observe what the course has been, which the Crown and Legislature of England have adopted, with respect to the laws and judicial establishments of this island; and it is the more expedient to trace, from the commencement, the origin of English law and rights in this island, because, 1st. The acquisition of this portion of British India has been obtained in a different manner from the rest of the Company's dominions. 2ndly. Because in relation to the *vexata quæstio*, of who are British subjects, the island of Bombay, and its inhabitants, have always been made an exception, in any conclusions drawn by the eminent Judges who have reasoned upon the matter.

Mode of introducing English law into Bombay traced.

Bombay, as is well known, came into the possession of the British Crown as part of the marriage portion of the Infanta of Portugal with Charles II., in 1661, and, by the cession, the inhabitants, whether Portuguese or natives, became thereupon, by operation of English law, the subjects of the King. The island, however, being found by that monarch to entail more burden than advantages on the Crown, his Majesty, in a very few years, namely, in 1669, dispossessed himself of it entirely, by granting it in fee to the East India Company.

1661. Bombay granted by Crown of Portugal to Charles II.

The charter, by which this grant was made, contains so many provisions relating to the government of the island, and on which both the rights and powers of the local authorities, and the rights and obligations of the inhabitants depend, that I will state them pretty fully.

1669. Grant by Charles II. to E. I. Company.

The Charter first of all recites the Treaty with Portugal of 1661, by which the island was ceded in full and perpetual sovereignty to the Crown ("the inhabitants of the said island as our liege people, and subject to our imperial Crown, &c., being permitted to remain there, and enjoy the free exercise

1843.

PEROZEBOYE v. ARDASEER CURSETJEE.

of the Roman Catholic Religion in the same manner as they then did"), and then grants to the East India Company, the said island and port, with all and singular the royalties, &c., in as large a manner as the same came to the Crown by the grant from Portugal, saving to us our heirs, &c., the faith and allegiance to us due, and our royal power and sovereignty over all our subjects and inhabitants there, to have, hold, and possess the same, to be holden of us and our heirs as of the manor of East Greenwich, in free and common socage, at a rent of ten pounds in gold payable yearly.

Charter of Charles II. analysed.

The insertion of which latter clause, was for the purpose of maintaining the sovereignty in the Crown, as indicated by the feudal tenure, and to secure the Crown's rights of escheat, in case of the dissolution of the company or otherwise. (See *Rex* v. *Cowle*, 2 Burr. 834). The charter then contains a proviso, "that the inhabitants of the island as our liege people, and subject to our imperial Crown and dignity, jurisdiction and government, shall be permitted to remain there and enjoy the free exercise of the Roman Catholic Religion (referring to the Portuguese inhabitants); and further also, that the said inhabitants and other our subjects (including all other inhabitants), shall and may peaceably and quietly have, hold, possess and enjoy their several and respective properties, privileges and advantages whatsoever, which they or any of them lawfully had and enjoyed at the time of the surrender of the port and island." It then recites, that as the island is granted to the Company as aforesaid, "it is therefore needful that such powers, privileges and jurisdictions, be granted unto them as be requisite, for the good government and safety thereof; and therefore enables the Company, at a general Court, to establish under their common seal, any laws whatsoever for the good government of Bombay, and the inhabitants thereof, and the same to revoke as they think fit" . . . . "and to impose and provide such pains and punishments by fines, amercements, imprisonment of the body, and, when the quality of the offence shall require, by taking away life and member, as to the said Court shall seem fit." Provided, "that the said laws, pains, penalties, &c., be consonant to reason, and not repugnant or

1843.

PEROZEBOYE *v.* ARDASEER CURSETJEE.

contrary, but, as near as may be, agreeable to the laws of this our realm of England (*a*), "subject to the provisos and savings hereinbefore contained," (referring to the proviso securing the free exercise of the Roman Catholic Religion to his Portuguese subjects, and which, though repugnant to the then law of England, the Company was thus disenabled from repealing).

Charter of Charles II.

The Charter then authorized the appointment of governors, officers, &c., and goes on to enable the Company, "by themselves or by their governors, &c., according to the natures and limits of their respective offices within the said port and island, the territories and precincts thereof, to correct, punish, govern, and rule, all and every the subjects of us, &c., that now do or at any time hereafter, shall inhabit within the said port and island, according to the laws as by the said Court shall be established, and to do all and every other thing and things, which unto the complete establishment of justice do belong, by Courts, sessions, forms of judicature, and manner of proceedings therein, like unto those established and used in this our realm of England, although in these presents express mention be not made thereof, and by Judges, &c., by them the governor of the said Company, or by the chief governor of the port and island to be delegated."

The extent of jurisdiction is then described to extend to all actions, suits and causes whatsoever, and the laws to govern them are to be, as near as may be, agreeable to the laws, statutes, government, and policy of England.

The only other clause which need be mentioned, is one which provides, "that all and every the persons being our subjects," (excluding, therefore, mere sojourners or aliens), "which do or shall inhabit within the said port and island, and every of their children and posterity, which shall happen to be born within the precincts and limits thereof, shall have and enjoy all liberties, franchises, immunities, capacities, and abilities, of free denizens and natural subjects within any of

(*a*) The effect of these words is to introduce the law of England, in all cases not specially provided for. See *Clark's Colonial Law*, p. 7, n. (*q*). And as to the introduction of English law into India, see *post*, pp. 84, 89.

1843.

Perozeboye v. Ardaseer Cursetjee.

our dominions, to all intents and purposes, as if they had been abiding and born within this our kingdom of England."

This clause, it will be observed, expressly confers the rights of denizenship on all his Majesty's subjects, which do or shall inhabit, and the rights of natural subjects on all who shall be born, within the island of Bombay.

Charter of Charles II.

I may also perhaps mention, that the large powers hereby conferred upon the Company, were to extend to all such places as they should subsequently acquire within the limits of their Charter; and, undoubtedly, they form a sufficient foundation on which to rest any legislation that may have been exercised by them as to the Mofussil, up to the 13 Geo. 3, c. 63. That statute, however, proposing to grant to the local Government in India powers of legislation over the immense territories they had acquired; but, intending probably, at the same time, to make the dependence of the Company upon the Legislature more direct, grants these powers in exactly the same terms that are used to enable a corporation of master bakers, to make rules and regulations for the government of their trade, and actually the Governor General in council had no authority to pass a law with the penalty of corporal punishment, extending even to a whipping, till twenty-six years afterwards, *viz.*, till the 39 & 40 Geo. 3, c. 79, when authority was granted for enforcing their rules and regulations, by moderate and reasonable corporal punishment, *i. e.* by public or private whipping, or otherwise.

Legal source of legislative power exercised by E. I. Company pointed out.

Limited by subsequent acts.

The charter, then, of Charles II., is thus shewn to contain the fullest powers for governing the island, which any form of words could convey: it concedes *imperium* and *jurisdictio*, and although it indicates the model on which the legal establishments and law should be framed, it does not fetter the grantees with any technical rules derived from English judicature, which might prove wholly unsuitable to a mixed community in the East. Indeed, it displays such comprehensive views of the powers which should be necessarily conferred for the government of a distant, already peopled, dependency, and contrasts so favourably with the obscure language of some of the later charters of justice. that I think we should do right in ascribing to the pen of Sir L. Jenkins, or some other of the eminent civilians of that day.

1843.

PEROZEBOYE v. ARDATEER CURSETJEE.

What sort of Courts the Company established under this charter, and what law they dispensed, I have not been able to discover (*a*), though it is clear that no other judicial authority, except what was derived from the charter, existed in the island. I have indeed obtained the record of one criminal trial in 1720, from the secretary's office; by which it appears that one Rama Comattee was indicted for high treason against the East India Company, for conspiring with Angria, with whom the Company was then at war; and the principal overt act alleged was, an invitation sent by him to Angria to land a body of men on the island, and seize the person of the Governor at Parell, where he was attended by none but his chamber servants.

Charter of Charles II.

The trial was carried on by the President in Council and five or six of the principal inhabitants, and the proceedings appear to have been conducted with as much attention to the substantial forms of justice as circumstances would permit, although I observe one fact which may afford an illustration for the next edition of Mr. Jardine's work; for during the trial, the president informed the Court of the method he had found it necessary to pursue with one of the witnesses to make him confess any thing, *viz.*, "irons were screwed upon his thumbs, the smart whereof brought him to a confession."

The indictment charged the offence to be against the peace of the East India Company, which I apprehend is quite correct, as in the case of all grantees of jurisdiction with *jura regalia;* and the prisoner being found guilty of a high crime and misdemeanor, was sentenced to imprisonment for life.

The next interposition by the Crown in respect to judicature at Bombay, which it is necessary to mention, is the grant

(*a*) In 1683 the King, by letters patent, authorized the company to exercise Admiralty jurisdiction in the countries within their limits, and the President of Surat was appointed Judge Advocate *pro tempore;* and by royal commission, dated 6th February, 1683-4, and another of the Court, dated 7th April, 1684, Dr. St. John was appointed Judge of the Court of Admiralty, to be erected in the East Indies, and the Court was to be held at Bombay. See *Warden's Report to Government, printed by the Geog. Soc. of Bombay, June* 1839.

1843.

PEROZEBOYE
v.
ARDATEER
CURSETJEE.

of a Mayor's Court, in 1726; for some previous grants to the Company of a power to erect a Court for causes maritime to be presided over by two merchants and a civilian (*a*) never appear to have been acted on, and indeed, from the comprehensiveness of the previous grant, were never necessary, at Bombay.

1726. Mayor's Courts established by George I.

In 1726, however, George I., on a petition of the East India Company suggesting that further powers were required by them for the punishing of crime, and administering of justice, in their different factories and settlements, determined, for the furtherance of the same, to establish proper Courts of justice, and for that purpose erected three corporations, at Bombay, Madras, and Calcutta, with various jurisdictions, civil and criminal, the power of which is described to extend "over all civil suits, actions and pleas that shall arise within the factory." Whether these terms are sufficiently large to comprehend all civil jurisdiction whatever, as in the previous grant to the local government of Bombay, is a question that has never been raised, but if they are not, I apprehend that the powers granted to the Company of establishing Courts at Bombay for the complete administration of justice still remained in them, and that if any power swere wanting to the Mayor's Court, they might have been attributed to it as a Court of the Company, in addition to its authority as a Court of the Crown.

1753. Charter surrendered, and Mayor's Courts re-established by George II.

However this may be, in 1753 the corporation at Madras, having been dissolved by the recent capture of Fort St. George by the French, and by the death or dispersal of the mayor and aldermen, the Company petitioned for another grant of incorporation at their settlements at Bombay, Madras, and Calcutta, which was accordingly granted them on a surrender of the previous charter, and, in the specification of the civil jurisdiction of the Mayor's Court at Madras, it was provided, that it should extend to all civil suits, actions, and pleas, between party and party, with an exception of "such suits and actions as should be between the Indian natives of Madraspatnam only; in which case we will, that the same be determined among

(*a*) *Quære* this, however? for I have since seen traces of a civilian having been appointed to Calcutta, I think, but I have mislaid the reference. See last note.

1843.

PEROZEBOYE v. ARDATEER CURSETJEE.

themselves, unless both parties shall, by consent, submit the same to the determination of the said Mayor's Court."

The civil jurisdiction of the Court of Bombay is not defined at length, but is expressed to extend to "all civil suits, actions, and pleas, between party and party, that shall or may arise or happen, &c., within the said town or factory of Bombay, or in the like manner, and under the like restrictions, as the Mayor's Court at Madras is hereinbefore empowered to do."

Bombay not a factory, like Madras or Surat;

An inaccuracy of language is here introduced as to Bombay in styling it a factory, which, unlike the first settlement at Surat, Calcutta, and elsewhere, it undoubtedly never was, and a question might have arisen, whether, under the restrictive words as to the Madras Court limiting jurisdiction over natives to voluntary contests, the rights of the King's native subjects at Bombay, to sue in the Courts of the Crown, were thereby taken away. Sir CHARLES GREY has shewn very satisfactorily what was the probable origin of the clause as to Calcutta and Madras, *viz.*, a hesitation to assert any territorial dominion in India, and the want of any necessity as to those two settlements may be also pointed out. The natives at that time in Bengal were, at all events, nominally, subjects of the Mogul, and the native Courts were administered in his name, and, in Madras, a morning's walk was sufficient to carry any native, who might desire to implead his adversary, out of the precincts of the factory.

but British territory from the first.

But as a very different state of facts existed at Bombay; as no doub tcould ever have arisen here as to whom the inhabitants of the island were subject; as no other tribunal was at hand to which they could refer their complaints; and as there are no express words taking away from the natives of Bombay their rights of British subjects, (even if any such words could have been operative), I take it that the true construction of the charter is, that the restrictive words in the charter did not apply to the inhabitants of this island, and that they are to be referred to the clauses relative to suing the mayor or magistrate. Certain it is that the Mayor's Court here dispensed justice to such inhabitants, and, amongst other matters, exercised ecclesiastical jurisdiction.

1843.

PEROZEBOYE v. ARDATEER CURSETJEE.

The next step taken in England as to Bombay, was the establishment by the Legislature and the Crown of a Recorder's Court.

37 Geo. 3, c. 142.

The 37 Geo. 3, c. 142, s. 9, after reciting the previous charters of justice, enables his Majesty to erect Courts of judicature at Madras and Bombay, "which said Courts shall have, and the same are hereby declared to have, full power and authority to exercise and perform all civil, criminal, and ecclesiastical and admiralty jurisdiction, &c., &c., &c., and to do all such other things as shall be necessary for the administration of justice."

Section 10 expresses that the jurisdiction shall extend to all British subjects who shall reside within any of the factories subject to Madras and Bombay; and section 11 declares that the Courts may try all manner of suits and actions, civil and criminal, which by the authority of any act or acts of Parliament may now be tried in the Mayor's Courts at Madras or Bombay (a clause, I believe, of surplusage; for I have never yet heard of any act of Parliament attributing jurisdiction to the Mayor's Court); and it then goes on to exclude from jurisdiction certain persons and matters, in accordance with the previous statute passed relatively to the Supreme Court at Calcutta, 21 Geo. 3, c. 71.

Section 13 gives the jurisdiction as to all suits and actions that may be brought against the inhabitants of Bombay, and, undoubtedly, a distinction is drawn in this act as to the jurisdiction over British subjects and natives.

1798. Recorder's Court established by charter of George III.

The charter of the King given under this act is dated February, 1798, and, incorporating the previous provision, erects the Recorder's Court at the two Presidencies; but it is unnecessary to mention the terms in which jurisdiction is parcelled out, as they seem to be precisely the same with those afterward used in the charter of the Supreme Court, and which I will state presently.

The next step was the erection of the Supreme Court at Bombay by 4 Geo. 4, c. 71, ss. 7, 8 and 9, and the charter granted in pursuance thereof. Section 7 of that act empowers his Majesty to establish a Supreme Court at Bombay, with full

1843.

PEROZEBOYE v. ARDATEER CURSETJEE.

power to exercise such civil, criminal, admiralty, and ecclesiastical jurisdiction, both as to natives and British subjects, and to be invested with such powers and authorities for the better administration of the same, and subject to the same limitations, &c., as the Supreme Court of Fort William in Bengal is invested with. The charter of George IV. of December, 1823, under which the Court is at present sitting, describes the jurisdiction of the Court to extend "to all such persons as have been heretofore described and distinguished in our charters for Bombay by the appellation of British subjects," and also gives power "to hear and determine all suits and actions that may be brought against the inhabitants of Bombay."

1823. Supreme Court established by charter of George IV.

The criminal jurisdiction is declared to extend "to all our subjects" in any of the territories subject to the Presidency, and the ecclesiastical jurisdiction is to be executed "towards and upon all persons so described or distinguished by the appellation of British subjects as aforesaid," "so far as the circumstances and occasion of the said town, island, territories, and people shall admit or require, and to grant probate of their wills, &c." So far copying the Calcutta charter, but containing an additional clause, allowing the Court to grant probate to the last wills of all persons (whether subjects or not) who shall die within the Presidency, leaving personal effects there.

Intention of all these charters to create complete judicial establishment.

Upon an attentive perusal of these charters and statutes, there appears to me to be a clear and well expressed intention to afford to all who may be subject to the jurisdiction of the Court—a tribunal before which every difference, that could arise in civilized society, might be adjusted—power, in the words of the first charter of Charles, "to do all things which unto the complete establishment of justice do belong, although in these presents express mention be not made thereof;" power, in the words of the first statute, relating to Bombay, 37 Geo. 3, c. 142, s. 9, to perform all civil, criminal, and ecclesiastical and admiralty jurisdiction, "and to do all such other things as shall be necessary for the administration of justice;" power, in the terms of the 4 Geo. 4, c. 71, s. 7, under which this Court was established, to exercise such civil,

1843.

Perozeboye v. Ardateer Cursetjee.

criminal, admiralty and ecclesiastical jurisdiction, both as to native and British subjects, as the Supreme Court at Calcutta, is invested with; and, lastly, power, under the charter, to determine all matters which might have been disposed of in the Mayor's Court, or in the Court of the Recorder. In opposition to these authorities, largely conceived as they are, I do not see the least indication to restrict the jurisdiction, on any side of the Court, as to any class of persons who are, in other respects, amenable to it, (the origin of the restrictive clause, as to natives, in the charter of 1753, having been already pointed out.)

And this course which is now seen to have been adopted by the Government of England, with respect to the jurisdiction which it established in this island, is exactly what might have been predicated of any enlightened government with a dependency at such a distance; and is, in fact, exactly what did take place in a very parellel instance, namely, when Asia, reduced into a province, fell under the Roman sway; for we learn from the Digest, that immediately on the acquisition of any such important conquest by the Republic, the administrative officers, sent there by the Senate, were invested with all powers of jurisdiction whatever, as exercised at Rome. "*Cum plenissimam autem jurisdictionem Proconsul habeat, omnium partes, qui Romæ vel quasi magistratus, vel extra ordinem jus dicunt, ad ipsum pertinent.*" Dig. lib. i. tit. 16, l. 7, s. 2; and I cite this passage the more pointedly, because it appears to me to afford a happier analogy to the case under discussion, than the illustrations which have been drawn from the condition of an infant colony, settling themselves on an uninhabited shore.

Similar practice of Romans with their Asiatic colonies.

The only argument which the counsel for the impugnant addresses against the existence of this jurisdiction is, the use of the term "British subjects," in the ecclesiastical clause of the charter; and a series of statutes is cited, which will be found collected by Sir Charles Grey, in his letter to Government, in the Fifth Appendix to the Commons' Report on East India Affairs in 1831, page 68, and which undoubtedly shew that, however ambiguous and difficult to define the

1843.

Perozeboye v. Ardaseer Cursetjee.

term may be, still, in those statutes, it never does comprehend native subjects. Sir Charles Grey himself attempts a definition of the expression, and it is upon his views, as there stated, that the present protest is founded. But it seems to me unnecessary to come to any decision on the present occasion as to whether the parties to this suit are comprehended under that term, in the ecclesiastical clause, or not. Undoubtedly, wherever the phrase, "British subjects," is used in an act of Parliament, passed with a view of affording protection to natives against European aggression, and wherever a favourable interpretation to natives would require their exclusion, it seems a most fit canon of construction that they should be so excluded; but if the present question were to be decided on the interpretation of a clause, under which inhabitants of Bombay could only secure the protection of Courts of law, by putting forth their titles as British subjects, I should be, I must confess, most unwilling to hold that any rule intervened to deny them that protection to which every subject of the Crown is entitled. But, as I said before, it is unnecessary to determine this point for on the distinct grounds taken by the Supreme Court, at Calcutta, in 1832, in *Bebee Muttra's case* (Clarke's Rules, 119), I am of opinion that, even if the term "British subjects," in the charter, does not include natives, the general ecclesiastical jurisdiction of the Court, which extends to them under the act of Parliament, as inhabitants, exists in full force, and is equally extensive with the civil, criminal and admiralty jurisdictions, which are all grouped together in the same clause. The insertion of the clause in the charter as to ecclesiastical jurisdiction over British subjects, I apprehend, proceeded *ex majori cautelâ*; for it having been previously expressed that the jurisdiction of the Court (comprehending everything) should extend to British subjects, it was possibly thought, that doubts might arise whether the exemption of settlers in colonies from ecclesiastical jurisdiction, as mentioned by *Blackstone* (Com. i. 108), might not be deemed to extend also to the British in India: and hence the repetition, in particular terms, of what had been previously granted generally. But in the clause of

Meaning of "British subject" in acts of Parliament relating to India.

1843.

PEROZEBOYE v. ARDATEER CURSETJEE.

jurisdiction as to inhabitants, the terms used are "all suits and actions that may be brought against the inhabitants of Bombay," and most undoubtedly these terms are quite large enough, with the intention already expressed, to include an ecclesiastical suit like the present.

Conclusion, natives subject to jurisdiction of Court on disputes arising out of marriage contract.

I have thus, at wearisome length, traced out from the commencement, the jurisdiction which has existed at Bombay, and which has been continued down to the present day, and I have done so, not because my mind was left in any doubt at the close of the argument, that the ecclesiastical jurisdiction as to natives (which, by-the-by, has nothing ecclesiastical about it but the name), and which has been successively exercised in this Court, both by the Mayors, the Recorders, and by previous Judges on this Bench, was illegal, but because an intimation was expressed, on the part of the impugnant, to carry this case home on appeal, if the decision should be against him; and I, therefore, thought it desirable, for the sake of both parties, to set out the materials fully, on which my judgment proceeded, so as to enable their Lordships in the Privy Council to decide, at once, on its sufficiency, or otherwise.

I ought to add that although the Chief Justice, from illness, was unable to attend on the argument in this case, he fully concurs in the conclusion that the ecclesiastical jurisdiction does extend to Parsís. The result is, that this protest must be discharged.

BUCHABOYE
v.
MERWANGEE NASSERWANGEE.

1844.
August 8.

[*Coram* PERRY, J.]

Ecclesiastical side.

1. Alimony awarded *pendente lite* to a Parsí female claiming restitution of conjugal rights, although the husband, by his responsive allegation, asserted that the marriage was void for want of consummation.

2. Claim asserted by Parsí husband to divorce his wife at pleasure.

SUIT for the restitution of conjugal rights.

The impugnant put in a responsive allegation admitting the *factum* of the marriage, but alleging that the promovent had refused to allow him to consummate the marriage, whereupon he had divorced her, and married another wife.

Dickinson now, upon an affidavit of faculties, applied for alimony *pendente lite.*

Le Messurier, A. G., *contrà*, contended, that the principles which govern English alimony are not applicable to this country. Women here are not *sui juris*, but are supported by their families. Again, though this *factum* of the marriage is admitted, it is alleged to be void, because there has been no consummation, which circumstance, in a Jewish marriage, Lord STOWELL held to invalidate it; *Lindo* v. *Belisario* (1 Hagg. Cons. Rep.)

Dickinson, contrà. Females on their marriage in this country, become disannexed from the family of their parents, and, therefore, have an especial claim to alimony. The *factum* of the marriage being admitted, it is attempted to be set aside by matter *ex post facto*, and a claim to exercise polygamy is set up.

Cur. adv. vult.

PERRY, J.—This is a suit brought by a Parsí female for the restitution of conjugal rights; and an interlocutory application

1844.

Buchaboye v. Nasserwanjee.

has been made by her after the coming in of the impugnant's answer for temporary alimony. . . . . Before examining into the faculties, on which the affidavits are conflicting, an objection which the impugnant alleges against the jurisdiction of the Court must be disposed of. For he contends, first, that the principles which prevail in England as to granting alimony in Christian's marriages, do not apply to Parsís and native females. This objection, however, was so faintly urged, that it is not necessary to expend time upon it. The case of *Perozeboye* v. *Ardaseer Cursetjee* (*a*), having decided that the Court is open to natives for the settlement of disputes arising out of the marriage contract, and Parsís being subject to the English law generally, it follows that as a Parsí husband is liable for the debts of his wife, and absorbs her property, a Parsí wife is entitled to alimony on exactly the same principles as an English wife would be if she claimed it in this Court.

The second objection is, that the marriage between the parties, though admitted by the impugnant to have taken place, is alleged by him to be no longer subsisting, and, therefore, that the obligation to grant alimony ceases. The grounds which he puts forward for invalidating the marriage are two; first, want of consummation, owing to refusal on the part of the wife; and, second, the divorce, which he assumes to himself, and as he asserts lawfully, the power to pronounce.

In *Lindo* v. *Belisario*, it was held by Lord Stowell, after a long inquiry, that a betrothment between Jews, without consummation, did not constitute the *vinculum conjugale*, and that case is referred to in order to shew that the bar set up by the impugnant may well be looked upon as an invalidation of the marriage asserted to exist here.

Now, this is a point upon which I do not intend to express any opinion. The Parsí law may accord with the Jewish, or it may not; or, according with the Jewish law, the facts alleged in this case may not bring it within the same predicament as that upon which Lord Stowell pronounced his judgment;

(*a*) *Ante*, p. 57.

1844. BUCHABOYE v. NASSERWANJEE.

or, lastly, the facts which the impugnant alleges, and which are altogether contradictory to those set up by the promovent, may not be capable of proof. But as all these are questions which the promovent has the right to have decided by this Court, and as the *factum* of a marriage is admitted by the impugnant, I think the wife is entitled to alimony in the meantime until the final decision of the Court be obtained.

Alimony of Rs. 20 a month decreed (*a*).

(*a*) The case was never afterwards brought before the Court.

MACLEAN *v.* CRISTALL.

1849. September 19.

[*Coram* PERRY, C. J., and YARDLEY, J.]

The common law of England, as to marriage, introduced into India, has not imported with it the provisions which make the presence of a minister in holy orders essential.

CASE, to recover damages from the defendant for criminal conversation with the plaintiff's wife, Mary Lewis.

The defendant pleaded that the said Mary Lewis was not, at the said times when, &c., the wife of the plaintiff; and issue having been joined thereon by consent, and by the order of the Honourable the Chief Justice, the following case was stated for the opinion of the Court:—

On the 6th of November, 1834, a ceremony of marriage was performed between the plaintiff and Miss Mary Lewis Pelly, spinster, at the city of Surat, in the East Indies.

The plaintiff was then of full age, and was a captain in the 8th Regiment of Native Infantry of the Bombay Army; Miss Pelly, at the time of the marriage, was under age. She had for some time previously been residing with her father, James Hinde Pelly, Esq., at Surat aforesaid, and the marriage took place with his consent, and was performed at his private residence in the city.

1849.

Maclean v. Cristall.

Both parties to the marriage were members of the Church of England.

The ceremony was performed according to the rites of the Church of England, by Mr. William Fyire, a missionary then residing at Surat.

Mr. Fyire had not been episcopally ordained; he belonged to a religious sect calling themselves Congregationists, or Independents, and signed the register in which the marriage was entered as "Minister of the Gospel and Missionary;" a true extract from the register of the entry of this marriage is hereunto annexed.

No person in holy orders was present at the marriage.

The city of Surat, and the country round about, did then, and do now, form a part of the territories of the East India Company, subject to the government of Bombay. Several British subjects, being civil and military servants of the East India Company, and their families, reside there. There was a small military force there under the command of Captain Tredall; a part of the force was stationed at the Castle inside the city, and the remainder were cantoned near the village of Otway, outside the walls. The town was not a garrison town, nor under military regulations, but the military force was subject to military regulations. Several civil functionaries resided there. For many years previous to the marriage there had been a Protestant church erected at Surat, to which a Chaplain of the East India Company, being a clergyman of the Church of England, was regularly appointed to do duty.

The last chaplain at Surat previously to the marriage, was the Rev. R. Y. Keays, who was removed from that appointment in December, 1831; and at the time of the marriage there were Protestant clergymen residing at Ahmedabad, at Poona, and at Bombay, but none nearer.

There was a Roman Catholic Chapel then existing in Surat and a Roman Catholic priest attached to it, and there were Roman Catholic priests residing at Demaun, a Portuguese city on the coast, about forty miles from Surat.

On the 7th November, one thousand eight hundred and

thirty-four, being the day after the marriage, the Reverend James Jackson, a clergyman of the Church of England, and one of the Chaplains of the East India Company, was duly appointed by the Government of Bombay, to the said church at Surat. Mr. Jackson joined his appointment on the first of December, 1834.

The marriage had previously been entered in the form and manner shewn in the appendix, in the register of marriages kept at the Church of Surat, and shortly after Mr. Jackson's arrival at Surat, he countersigned the entry in the presence, and under the attestation of Francis Sheane, the clerk of the church, in the manner appearing in the appendix hereto, but no ceremony of marriage was performed before him, nor did the parties appear before him for any such purpose. After the marriage the parties cohabited as man and wife, and were received as such by their relatives and friends; there are no children alive, the fruits of this union.

The Court to be at liberty to draw any inference, which, in their judgment, a jury would be at liberty to draw from the preceding facts.

The question for the opinion of the Court is, whether the preceding facts constitute a valid marriage, as stated in the plaint. If the Court shall be of opinion in the affirmative, a verdict is to be entered for the plaintiff, and a writ of inquiry shall be issued, to assess the damages to which he is entitled. If in the negative, a verdict is to be entered for the defendant, but, without prejudice in either case to the right of either party to appeal from the decision of the Court to her Majesty in council.

On this case coming on for argument,

Dickinson, in support of the plea, relied on *Regina* v. *Millis*, (10 Cl. & Fin.), and *Catherwood* v. *Caslon*, (13 Mee. & W. 126).

Howard, contrà, intimated to the Court that the plaintiff was not interested in controverting the plea, but all that he

1849.

MACLEAN
v.
CRISTALL.

required was a distinct decision as to the law. If this Court pronounced the present marriage void, which the state of the authorities seemed to require, and if the decision was confirmed by the Privy Council, then the object of the plaintiff in getting rid of the obligation, created by this marriage would be effected. On the other hand, if this marriage were pronounced valid, it would be necessary to proceed with the action, in order to obtaining a divorce in the House of Lords. Under these circumstances, he considered it his duty merely to assist the Court in bringing all the authorities before it. And he cited *Catterall* v. *Catterall*, (1 Robertson), where Dr. LUSHINGTON apparently refused to act on *Regina* v. *Millis*, and the following passage from Lord STOWELL's judgment in *Reeding* v. *Smith*, (2 Hagg. 385), "What is the law of marriage in all foreign establishments, settled in countries professing a religion essentially different? In the English factories at Lisbon, Leghorn, Oporto, Cadiz; and in the factories in the East—Smyrna, Aleppo, and others? In all of which (some of these establishments, existing by authorities under treaties, and others under indulgence and toleration), marriages are regulated by the law of the original country to which they are still considered to belong An English resident at St. Petersburgh does not look to the ritual of the Greek Church, but to the rubric of the Church of England, when he contracts a marriage with an English woman. Nobody can suppose that while the Mogul empire existed, an Englishman was bound to consult the Koran for the celebration of his marriage. Even where no foreign connection can be ascribed, a respect is shewn to the opinions and practice of a distinct people. The validity of a Greek marriage in the extensive dominions of Turkey, is left to depend, I presume, upon their own canons, without any reference to Mahomedan ceremonies."

Dickinson, in reply, contended that the marriage was clearly invalid by the authorities: but, he suggested as *amicus curiæ*, that in conformity with many decisions, in which it had been held that only so much of English law had been introduced as was suitable to the condition of India, it was worthy of consideration, whether this portion of the common law was suitable to the circumstances of the country.

Cur. adv. vult.

On this day the Judges gave their judgment orally, that the marriage was valid, but being requested to reduce their arguments to writing, the following judgment was afterwards handed down to the parties.

PERRY, C. J.---The question which has been raised in this case respecting the validity of the marriage of Major Maclean to Miss Pelly, the daughter of a gentleman in the Bombay Civil Service, is one which has been foreseen by jurists, ever since the decision of *The Queen* v. *Millis,* as certain to arise in this country sooner or later. The argument raised at the Bar was, that the above decision has established that, by the common law of England, a valid marriage can only be solemnized in the presence and by the intervention of a minister in holy orders; that the common law of England is the law of this country, so far as respects Europeans; and that, as the marriage in question had been celebrated at Surat by a missionary minister, who had not received Episcopal ordination, it necessarily followed that the marriage was null and void. And, if the premises in the above argument are valid, the conclusion urged upon the Court appears irresistible.

But as the effect of such a conclusion would be to pronounce a vast number of marriages that have taken place in India, during the last 250 years, invalid,—to extend the stain of illegitimacy to many a pedigree hitherto deemed spotless,—and, above all, to carry terror and dismay into numerous innocent and unsuspecting households, it behoved the Court to be very well assured in their convictions before they could venture to emit a decision fraught with such stupendous and deplorable effects. To motives such as these for investigating deeply into the principles of English law, it may be added, that a love for the science, and a regard for the credit of English

1849.

MACLEAN v. CRISTALL.

jurisprudence, which may be avowed without reserve by its professors, has led to a more anxious and painstaking inquiry on the part of my learned Brother and myself, than I ever recollect to have applied to any judicial inquiry; for it must not be omitted to state that the question, which has arisen now, could not have arisen if the jurisprudence of any other nation of Europe had been applied to India. With respect to our European predecessors in this country, if our present empire had been possessed by the Catholic Portuguese, the canon law of Europe would have declared this marriage legal. And so also with the civil law, which the Protestant Dutch introduced into all their conquests. Indeed, if another member of the British Islands, Scotland, instead of England, had given its personal laws to India, the present difficulty never would have occurred.

The consequence in question, therefore, if it flows from the principles of English law, is evidently attributable to some unbending peculiar institute, not traceable in other systems of jurisprudence. After the most careful research through our juridical records, I have completely satisfied myself that the English law, however insular in its character and unplastic in its powers of adaptation to extended empire, as compared with other systems, contains no such rigid doctrine; and that, on the contrary, the fund of good sense which is contained in the most valuable collection of jurisprudence in the world—I mean the English Law Reports—furnishes forth ample authority for denying a rule so inconvenient to mankind as has been alleged at our Bar to exist.

It must be assumed, however, in this argument, that the major proposition enunciated above, as to the invalidity of a marriage by the common law without the interposition of a priest, is incontrovertible. But even on this point the state of the law is so remarkable, and stands, if I may be allowed the expression, on such *unstable* foundations, that it is impossible to avoid briefly adverting to it.

From the year 1754, the common law of England, as to marriages, was abrogated in England itself; and the municipal regulations introduced by Lord Hardwicke's Act from that time constitute the law of England. The common lawyers of England therefore, during the last ninety years, have had very rare occasions for considering what the common or ancient law as to marriage was; although, as the common law still prevailed in Ireland, in America, in numerous colonies, and in India, it sometimes became necessary to pronounce opinions on the subject. But during the whole of the last century, and the greater portion of the present, the opinion almost universally prevailed amongst the Profession, as well as amongst the public, that although marriage was not merely a civil contract, still, when the natural and civil contract had been formed, it contained the full essence of matrimony, without the intervention of a priest; and Lord STOWELL, in 1811, embalmed this doctrine in decision, when he delivered his profound and masterly judgment in the case of the Dalrymples, which apparently settled the law on the subject for all time to come. But in 1826, an ingenious Barrister, in editing a new edition of a law treatise, appended a very able note to the Chapter on Marriage, in which he contended that, by English law, the presence of a minister in holy orders was absolutely essential to constitute a marriage. The speculation remained unheeded in practice till the year 1842, when a man named Millis being indicted for bigamy at the Antrim assizes, his counsel took the objection that the first marriage was void; for that Millis, being a member of the Church of England, had been married in Ireland by a dissenting minister, *viz.* by a Presbyterian. The objection was solemnly argued before the Irish Court of Queen's Bench, when two Judges thought the first marriage a good one, and the other two thought it bad: but in order to pronounce a decision, and thus to allow an appeal to the House of Lords, one of the Judges who deemed the marriage good, withdrew his opinion *pro formâ*, and thus, a majority of the Judges having been obtained, the objection prevailed, and the prisoner was acquitted. The appeal to the House of Lords having been lodged, the opinions of the English Judges were requested; and they, after considerable fluctuation in the minds of some of them, finally gave their unanimous opinion, that, by the

1849.

MACLEAN v. CRISTALL.

common law of England, a marriage was not full and complete unless made in the presence, and with the intervention, of a minister in holy orders. But, as the learned Judges were about to leave London for their circuits, they were not able to write out the reasons of their judgment *seriatim*, or to notify to the superior tribunal, the mode in which their doubts had been surmounted, with the exception of Chief Justice TINDAL, who, in delivering the joint opinion, subjoined the reasons which had operated on his own mind.

With this instruction, the case came on for argument at the bar of the House of Lords, and it may safely be alleged that no case of modern times has called forth a similar display of legal acumen, deep research, and philosophical argument, both at the Bar and at the Bench. When the period arrived for giving judgment, Lords BROUGHAM, CAMPBELL and DENMAN pronounced most elaborate judgments in favour of the marriage; Lords COTTENHAM and LYNDHURST pronounced equally elaborate judgments against it; and Lord ABINGER (the only other Law Lord present) voted in conformity with the opinions of the English Judges. These noble Lords being thus equally divided in opinion, the decision of the House of Lords, by a technical rule was held to be in favour of the Court below, and that Court, as has already been shewn, had only come to any conclusion at all by way of arrangement.

In this extraordinary conflict of opinions, it would be extremely unbecoming in an inferior tribunal to attempt to hold a balance between such distinguished living authorities, although, with posterity, it is an office which any *Dupondius* may assume without presumption. But on reading the admirable judgments of Lords BROUGHAM and CAMPBELL, on one side, and of Lords COTTENHAM and Chief Justice TINDAL, on the other, it is impossible to help perceiving, amid such nicely balanced arguments, that a sufficient legal basis existed for a conclusion on either side. And it is, perhaps, permissible to express a regret that, when the Chancellor and Lord Chief Justice felt themselves compelled, by the rigour of their logic, to adopt a principle which they recognised with regret, and the mischief of which they did not fail to acknowledge, they had not adverted to the example of their great masters in law, the classical Roman Jurists, who, when they found that propositions and dicta, laid down in early times, led to conclusions opposed to the best interests of the Commonwealth, vigorously appealed to the foundation of all human law—common sense, and—on the well received maxims *utilitatis causâ* and *jus singulare ad consequentia non producitur*—they rejected the consequence, and promulged a rule in harmony with the welfare of mankind.

The termination of the case in the House of Lords, however, in the manner above noted,—although possibly that noble tribunal may still consider the question open, if it should be again brought before them,—in the meantime, and for all inferior Courts, appears to impose the rule as to marriage in the terms laid down by me above. It should, at the same time, be observed, that a great ecclesiastical Judge, Dr. LUSHINGTON, who is profoundly versed in matrimonial law, has treated the decision of *The Queen* v. *Millis*, as if the law deducible from that case was not yet to be considered thoroughly established (*a*).

Upon this rapid review of the authorities as to the state of the common law at the present day on the question of marriage, it cannot be denied that the rule which must now be considered to be in force has extremely little about it of the characteristics which ought to distinguish a law that comes home so closely to the business and bosom of mankind. The difficulty of applying such a rule therefore to India, where on nearly every occasion the applicability of English law in all its terms is beset with thorns, becomes considerably enhanced. As a general principle, it may be taken that the British in India are all deemed to have an English domicile. The authorities for this position are collected in Mr. Jacob's note, (2 *Roper*, 460); and in the Supreme Courts of this country the doctrine is always acted on. By the rule also which applies to Europeans visiting the factory of another European power, in which case the stranger takes his legal character from

(*a*) Catherall *v*. Catherall, 1 Robertson.

1849.

MACLEAN v. CRISTALL.

that of the power to which the factory belongs, or by the more general rule which prevails amongst European nations as to *lex loci*, the English law generally is the law of all Europeans who come within the British dominions in India. But with respect to the introduction of English law generally into this country,—the time when, the mode how, and the extent to which, it has been imported, all these form questions of the greatest legal difficulty, and they have afforded subjects of continual controversy in all the Courts of the Crown since their first establishment (*a*). The difficulty has chiefly arisen from the anomalous character of the British settlements in the East. The common law of England lays down ample rules with relation to factories in foreign countries, to plantations in uninhabited countries, to cessions or conquests from European powers. But the British possessions in India are none of these, but an Eastern, densely peopled, empire, subordinate to a distant Christian power, and accordingly the rules derivable from relations between the metropolis and her colonies, or even from the international law of Europe, are often found wholly inapplicable to this new great fact in the world's history. In the slow and sometimes imperceptible process by which the British power in India has attained its present magnitude, it may be observed that all the various modes by which a foreign country becomes predominant abroad, have co-operated to create our present empire;—and that factories permitted by the Mogul; settlements connived at by subordinate rulers; and cessions and conquests from European as well as native powers, have all afforded centres from which British dominion has been enabled to radiate. Such a wonderful phenomenon as this state of circumstances presents could, of course, not be foreseen by legislation; and the natural result has been, as in all cases unprovided for by law, that institutions sprung up and became established as they were severally called for by the exigencies of the case. It is the business of lawyers, in after times, (and their industry and astuteness can never be more beneficially employed), to bring all the facts, institutions, and regulations, which they find thus established, within the domain of law; and, by applying the

Introduction of English law into India.

Imperceptible growth of British empire.

(*a*) See *ante*, p. 63

1849.

MACLEAN v. CRISTALL.

various principles which they find scattered through their jurisprudence, to place on a legal basis all such as they ascertain to have been demanded by necessity, and to be warranted by reason. The broad fact, with respect to English law at the present day, is, that however variously introduced into India, and at whatever periods, it is now the dominant law throughout the British possessions for all those inhabitants who belong to the European family of nations. For reasons which I have given at length in the case of the Kojahs and Memons, *post*, as to the European character of the doctrine of *lex loci*, I feel compelled to state the proposition in the above qualified form.

Law of England how far introduced into India.

But the next step of the reasoning as to the extent to which the English law has been introduced into India, is the point on which the judgment in the present case must depend. The rule on this subject is afforded by the doctrine of the common law with respect to colonies, which, though not strictly analogous, is more in point than any of the other rules in our law books. The rule in such case is, that although colonists take the law of England with them to their new home, they only take so much of it as is applicable to their situation and condition. In many cases no question will arise as to the inapplicability of several provisions of English law, which are clearly seen to be merely municipal; but whenever a question does spring up, it must be decided like other disputed points of law, in the law Courts of the country. Blackstone lays down the rule very authoritatively on this subject: "What shall be admitted and what rejected, at what times, and under what restrictions, must, in case of dispute, be decided in the first instance by their (the colonists') own provincial judicature, subject to the revision and control of the King in Council" (*a*).

Judge-made law.

Nor with all the sarcasms which in later days have been thrown (and in one sense justly thrown) on what is called Judge-made law, can it, I think, be denied, that within these limits the discretionary power here adverted to, when exercised under the checks of public opinion, mature deliberation, an independent highly educated profession, and a conscientious

(*a*) 1 Comm. 108.

1849.

MACLEAN v. CRISTALL.

desire on the part of experienced men to educe the rule of law most consonant with the welfare of society, is the true source from which the better as well as the greater part of English law has proceeded?

This rule has been continually and necessarily acted upon by the Judges in India since the first establishment of the Crown Courts; and with the fluctuation of opinion which was necessarily to be expected, and which it is indeed desirable should exist, whilst the slow process of argumentation founded on wide views of facts is going on, the Indian law books will be found full of reports in which judicial determinations have been obtained as to the applicability or otherwise of numerous portions of the English laws to India. But more recently the same question has been raised in the highest tribunals in England, and the Profession in India has the satisfaction now of knowing that they are proceeding on the sound doctrine when they seek to apply the rule in question.

Those great Judges, Sir WILLIAM GRANT, Sir THOMAS PLUMER, and Lord LYNDHURST, have all recognised the validity of the principle, but the greatest authority on the subject is Lord BROUGHAM, for in his judgment in the case of the *Mayor of Lyons*, he has gone into the subject of English law in India more profoundly than any of his predecessors, and he has laid down conclusively, that only such portions of the common law have been introduced into India as were suitable to the condition of the country.

The question, therefore, which now remains for inquiry, is, whether that portion of the English law, which required the presence of a minister in holy orders at the celebration of a marriage, was suitable to India at the time when English law was introduced into the country.

It clearly appears, from the discussions in the House of Lords, that in the opinion of those learned Judges who established the rule in question, the source to which such rule is traceable, is a law or institute of one of our Anglo-Saxon Kings. Not so much by way of literary curiosity, as for the immense importance attributable to this law, I prefer to cite it in its original language, and not in the Latin translation which was used in the Lords, and which I believe is due to Wilkins. King Edmund's law, which dates from A. D. 940, is as follows:—

"Æt tham giftan sceal Massepreost beon. Mid rihte se scheal mid Godes bletsunge heora gesomnunge gederian on earle gesund fulnesse." The word for word translation of which is, "At the giving (betrothal) shall a mass-priest be. With right (*de jure*) he shall with God's blessing their union bind in all sound fullness."

Now, on giving the fullest effect to the words of this law, and holding, as has been done, that they are compulsory, and not directory, it is evident that the state of circumstances to which they apply, is that where a mass-priest is available to any couple minding to be married,—to the condition, in fact, of Christendom at the period when the law was passed. And so, when the Reformation occurred in England, and when, by some process not explained, but the difficulty as to which has been pointed out by Lord CAMPBELL, the law was changed, and a deacon in holy orders was substituted for a mass-priest, the law was completely suitable to every portion of the realm where the Church of England was established. But to countries where the common law extended, yet in which there was no church establishment, or parochial divisions, the law in its terms was never capable of being applied; and, therefore, it results clearly, that that portion of the law requiring the presence of a minister, was wholly local in its character, and a mere municipal regulation. This argument is completely confirmed by a consideration of the Council of Trent. That Council, for the same reason, no doubt, as actuated the Anglo-Saxon Monarch—*viz.*, for the purpose of preventing clandestine marriages, and for securing the testimony of the most revered functionaries in society,—required the presence of the parish priest (*parochus*) at the celebration of a marriage. But the Council has always been held to be of local application only, exactly like the English Marriage Act of 1754.

It may be said, however, that at the first establishment of English law in India, the rule imposed by King Edmund, as modified at the Reformation, was capable of being complied with in terms. This, however, is completely contradicted by

1849.

MACLEAN v. CRISTALL.

history. The first establishment of the English in India was at this very place, Surat, and dates from the year 1611, and previous to that time we had establishments in Sumatra, and in Java, as well as in other of the Southern islands.

In a very few years our settlements extended themselves to Ahmedabad, Gogo, Cambay, and Broach. Factories were stationed on different parts of the Coromandel coast, and presidencies created at several different parts of the East, which were all made subordinate to the chief settlement at Surat, (1 *Mill*, 80). But it was not till near a century later that any provision was made for chaplains, and even then in the most modest proportion; and up to living memory I believe the number of chaplains assigned to this presidency, which contains many millions of inhabitants, was only three.

Marriages in India before the appointment of chaplains.

The state of the inhabitants, therefore, on Pitcairn's Island who were desirous of entering into holy wedlock, was not more forlorn or more a case of necessity than that of the English in India during the first century of their settlement.

Neither can it be alleged that in those times it was the policy or practice to encourage celibacy. On the contrary, Mr. Ovington, the chaplain to the ship-of-war which conveyed to India the intelligence of the accession of William of Orange, informs us that it was the policy of the East India Company to encourage marriages at their different factories; and he gives rather a piquant account of the ship-loads of young ladies who came out to India accordingly, and of the various hazards which beset them during the voyage.

This being the state of facts as to our early settlements in India, the practice which has existed so far back as any trace can be discovered has been to celebrate marriages in the absence of a clergyman in as solemn a manner as the nature of the case permitted. Every European in India who has been any time in the country, is able to enumerate many of his friends amongst whom, or amongst whose connections, such marriages have taken place; and if, for the reasoning suggested, the presence of a minister in deacon's orders is an institution local in its nature, and having reference only to countries such as England and Ireland, where the Church of England is established by law, it follows that the common law of England introduced into India accords with the rule which both the civil and canon law would pronounce, as well as with the dictates of reason which a dispassionate view of the subject seems to suggest. It need only be added, that if the common law was thus introduced with the qualification here mentioned, then, as there has been no alteration of the law by statutory provision since, the common law remains entire as it was first established in the country.

And to prevent any misconception which might arise as to the period when English law was introduced on this side of India, I will point out that, as to Europeans, the period in question cannot be placed at a later period than the year 1661, when Charles II. granted the island of Bombay to the Company, and empowered them to make acquisitions of other territories, and govern them all by laws "consonant to reason, and not repugnant or contrary, but *as near as may be* agreeable to the laws of this our realm of England."

The question has been hitherto viewed, however, in a much more limited sense than belongs to it, and solely with reference to British subjects, who may be sojourners for a brief period within the Company's dominions in India.

But the common law of England applicable in India is called upon for a rule of much wider scope. The general Marriage Law is not a *personal* law, in the sense in which the later civilians use the term, and in the sense in which the Marriage Law relating to members of the royal family has lately been construed. The provisions, therefore, which the English law prescribes for the celebration of a marriage do not follow the person into whatever country he may go, but he is at liberty to enter into the contract according to the law of the country where he may happen to be. On this principle, which belongs to universal jurisprudence, European Protestants, to whatever country they may belong, who find themselves in British India, are entitled, in respect of the comity between nations, to ask for the legal sanction of the country to the matrimonial engagements which they may wish to form. But it is not only in respect of European or American foreigners that this claim arises. There are, perhaps, hun-

1849. — MACLEAN *v.* CRISTALL.

dreds of thousands of Protestant Christians in different parts of India who are subject to our law. By acquisitions of various kinds, the settlements of the Protestant Dutch and Danes have come into our hands. The missionary Schwartz made converts to the Confession of Augsburg by thousands in the south of India; and our missionaries in other parts of the empire, though not, perhaps, equally successful, have nevertheless congregated large circles of native converts around them. With respect to all these widely extended classes, neither religious belief, nor their national jurisprudence, nor the regulations of the English Government, have ever suggested the idea that the presence of an ordained priest was required at their nuptials. But if, in the train of British conquest, and of the praiseworthy efforts of our zealous missionaries, one of the consequences has been to spread concubinage and bastardy throughout the land, it must cause every lawyer, I think, to blush that the system which he professes should contain a rule pregnant with such consequences, and so unsuitable to the dearest interests of mankind.

For the reasons which I have given, I am thoroughly satisfied that the second premiss on which the invalidity of this marriage is based completely fails, and that that portion of the common law requiring the presence of an ordained minister at a marriage was never introduced, and does not now exist, in India.

I ought in candour to mention, in conclusion, the only argument which appears to me to militate against the above reasoning. It is founded on the proviso in the 58 Geo. 3, c. 84, which was a declaratory act relating to marriages in India by Presbyterian ministers. For it may be contended that the effect of that proviso is to render all such marriages, except when performed in the way pointed out by the statute, illegal in future. But looking at the studious way in which the Legislature, both in this statute, and in all other statutes relating to marriages beyond the seas, has abstained from passing more than a declaratory statute,—on attending to the accurate definition by Lord CAMPBELL, in the House of Lords, as to the purport of a declaratory statute, that it is a positive announcement, by the Legislature, that the law (so) declared, existed before the passing of the statute,—and on adverting to the occasion which produced this special legislation, I am convinced that the sound construction to be given to this proviso is, that it contains no new enactment as to the general law, but special directions only as to Presbyterian ministers, the breach of which would be no doubt penal, but which, as in the case of other directory provisions in the Marriage Act, might not make the marriage so performed wholly invalid (a).

(a) Major M'Lean subsequently obtained his divorce by act of Parliament, and the validity of the above decision establishing the marriage was not questioned in the House of Lords. A subsequent statute has been since passed for marriages in India, but the common law question on marriages in other parts of the world may still occur.

1843. February 28.

THE QUEEN v. SHAPURJI BEZONJI AND BEZANJI EDALJI.

THE PARSI CONVERT'S CASE (a).

[*Coram* ROPER, C. J., and PERRY, J.]

Where a Parsi family detained an infant child from its father, on the ground of the latter having embraced the Christian religion, the Court ordered the child to be given up to the father on *habeas corpus*.

Where a writ of *habeas corpus* issued to bring up an infant child, and the parties having custody of the child, after the issue of the writ, settled Rs. 3000 upon it, and then petitioned the Court, on its equity side, to make the child a ward of Court, to appoint a guardian to it, and to enjoin the proceedings at law; the Court refused the latter application, on the ground that the settlement was fraudulent in order to defeat the common law right of the father to the custody.

DICKINSON, on a former day, had obtained a writ of *habeas corpus* to bring up the body of an infant child, aged five years, who was detained by her father-in-law, the defendant Shapurjí.

It appeared by the affidavits on which the rule was obtained, that Hormazjí Pestonjí, the father of the child, was

(a) This Report is an abridgment of a very voluminous report of the case in *The Oriental Christian Spectator*, April, 1843.

1843.

The Queen v. Bezonji and Edalji.

converted to Christianity in 1839. Before his conversion, Hormazjí used to live with his father-in-law, the defendant, but after that event he took up his abode at the house of the mission of the Church of Scotland, leaving his wife and child at her old residence; and he swore that he abstained from going to his father-in-law's house, through fear of ill treatment on account of his change of religion. He frequently applied, however, to Shapurjí, that his wife and child should be given up to him, but the defendant refused, on the ground that his conversion to Christianity was a dissolution of the marriage; and in January of this year the defendant and his family married Hormazjí's wife to another Parsí. It was also sworn, that the defendant was about to betroth Hamazjí's daughter, according to the custom of the Parsís, that he had refused to give her up to him, and that he believed the child would be removed out of the jurisdiction if the writ of *habeas corpus* did not issue.

Much difficulty was experienced in obtaining a return to the writ. First of all, the defendant Shapurjí made an affidavit, which was afterwards taken as a return, that the child was not in his custody or under his control, but was then living with its mother Ruttonbae and her new husband Bezonjí. A counter affidavit was made, that at the time of serving the writ the child was in the room with Shapurjí. Other writs of *habeas corpus* were then ordered to issue against the husband Bezonjí and his wife Ruttonbae, and subsequently writs of attachment were issued against Shapurjí, Bezonjí, and others, on its appearing that they were taking steps to defeat the process of the Court.

During these proceedings, *Howard*, on the part of the defendants, presented a petition, in a suit which had been instituted on the equity side of the Court, for the purpose of making the child a ward of Court, and for an injunction to stay the proceedings at law. It appeared that after the writ of *habeas corpus* had issued, a sum of Rs. 3000 had been settled on the child; and it was contended that the Court of equity was the proper forum for determining the proper guardianship of an infant.

1843.

The QUEEN v. BEZONJI and EDALJI.

ROPER, C. J.—The Court was at first indisposed to listen to this application, but it was well that they had done so, for the circumstances shewed that it was part of the machinery which had been adopted to defeat the process of the Court It came precisely to this: the attorney for the parties said to the Court, I shall not allow you to take cognizance of this matter in the way you want, I shall compel you to take cognizance of it by a bill in equity. The whole was a trick, cunning enough, but shallow and easily seen through.

PERRY, J.—The simple question is, whether a Court of law will allow its power to be set at defiance, and whether any man, having money at his command, is to set aside the most important process of the English law (*a*). The settlement was fraudulent, and the family were evidently conspiring to set aside the authority of the law.

After a fortnight had been thus consumed in endeavouring to enforce the writ, the child was produced this day in Court; and in the affidavits filed by the defendants, in answer to the motion for an attachment, it was sworn that Hormazjí had consented to the betrothment of his child, that the Parsí Punchayat had considered that, in consequence of Hormazjí's conversion, his marriage with Ruttonbae had been dissolved, and that they had sanctioned her subsequent marriage.

The return to the writ stated that after Hormazjí became a Christian, he deserted his wife and child, and that his father Pestonjí as the head of the family, and as having, according to the domestic usages of the Parsís, the parental control (Hormazjí being at that time himself an infant), had formally betrothed the child to its cousin; and that Hormazjí, on being made acquainted with the fact, had acquiesced in it for the space of four years.

Dickinson moved that the return should be filed, and that the Court should order the child to be given up to its father.

(*a*) So per Lord ELDON, C. "Nobody can doubt that if I give a provision to your child. it does not give me, or any one else, a right to control your care of her; not at all, &c." *Jacob.* 258.

1843.

The QUEEN v. BEZONJI and EDALJI.

It is probably intended to be argued that Hormazjí has acquiesced in the child being brought up in the Parsí faith, and in its residence with the family of its mother, and the passage in the return is relied upon, which states his assent to the child's betrothal. But his acquiescence and assent are not supported by affidavits, and they are wholly denied by Hormazjí and by the facts in the case. If Hormazjí is sincere in his embracing of Christianity, it is impossible that he could ever consent to his child being educated in a faith which he believes to be false. And his quiescence during the last four years is completely explained by the belief which he constantly entertained that he should recover the possession of his wife and child, but when the family proceeded to marry her to another, such hopes were of course destroyed, and he found himself obliged to seek the protection of the law. The cases in which a father has been held to have waived his right of custody of his children, all shew either gross immorality on the part of the father or a distinct assent on his part to a separate custody, in which case, when arrangements have been made on the strength of such assent, the Court will not allow the father capriciously to interfere; *Lyons* v. *Blenkin*, (Jacob, 245). But here the whole conduct of the father shews distinctly that he has always been desirous to have his wife and child restored to him. *Rex* v. *Greenhill*, (6 Nev. & Mann. 244), is a clear decision that the proper custody of an infant child is with the father.

Howard, contrà. The observations made by the Court on the *ex parte* affidavits of the party applying for the writ were uncalled for and much too strong. If the defendants thought that the question of guardianship could be better decided in a Court of equity than in a Court of law, they were at perfect liberty to seek the protection of the former Court, and were justified in endeavouring to avoid the service of legal process, and neither they, nor the attorney who advised this course, were blameable. The question on a writ of *habeas corpus* is purely one of illegal restraint, and if that does not appear on the face of the return, the Court is not bound to exercise any discretion by making an order; *Rex* v. *Greenhill*, (6 Nev. &

M. 244); *Rex* v. *Delaval*, (Ib. 1434). Where nice questions have to be discussed respecting guardianship, the proper mode of raising them is by a bill in equity, and the interests of the infant can be properly discussed there only; *Wellesley* v. *Wellesley*, (2 Russ.); *De Manneville* v. *De Manneville*, (10 Ves. 52); *Rex* v. *Isley*, (10 Ad. & Ell.)

The contents of the return must be taken as true, and by them it appears that Hormazjí has consented to the residence of the child with her grandfather's family, that he has consented to its marriage, and as it is contrary to Parsí usages and customs that a Parsí should have social and domestic intercourse with Christians, it follows that Hormazjí must have assented to the child being brought up in the Parsí faith. At all events, as a suit is pending respecting the settlement of the child, the Court will not run the risk, on the imperfect information now before the Court, of pronouncing any decision by which the marriage would be put an end to, and much mischief might be done.

ROPER, C. J.—I certainly am of opinion, that if the property which has been settled on this child, had been given before the writ of *habeas corpus* was issued, the question of the guardianship of the child, she being already possessed of property, would have come before the Court under a very different aspect from the questions now before us. But the vesting the money in trustees, took place after the service of the writ, and a bill was filed at the same time, to carry the case into another Court. All along, every effort has been made to set at nought the process of the Court, and I cannot regard this giving the child a few paltry rupees, as anything else than a part of that machinery which has been employed to defeat and thwart the process of the law. If there were any matters of delicacy mingled in the case, I should be disposed to remit the question, but as the case comes before us, it is, *bonâ fide*, a question before the Court.

[His Lordship here stated the return and the affidavits, comparing one with the other, and continued as follows]:—

Here I find that the man, who has married the wife of

1843.

The QUEEN v. BEZONJI and EDALJI.

Hormazjí, makes the statement that Hormazjí "deserted his wife and child." In Hormazjí's affidavit it is said he "quitted" them. Here is a vital difference, and the facts of the case bear out the latter term. If a man finds that he cannot, with any comfort or security, live in his own home, and on that account leaves it, is it to be said he *deserts*, he *repudiates*, his family? Prove that he did desert or repudiate them, and you prove a most important item on your side; but it is wholly unproved. Again, if it appeared to me that there were those delicate matters mixed up, as has been said, in this question, I should have thought it necessary to postpone judgment, and I came into the Court with the impression that it could not now be decided; but after hearing everything, I am now clearly of opinion that we can settle it on the plea side, and at once.

There is a statement on this return that bears improbability on the face of it. The child was betrothed, it is said, a month after the baptism of the father. She must then have been betrothed at the age of one year. Is it in accordance with the custom of the Parsís to betroth so early? I believe it is not; let me be corrected if I am mistaken. Say it was betrothed; it was plainly done to annoy the father. Done by whom? By the grandfather; but the grandfather had not the smallest right to do so. If he betrothed the child, the father not consenting, then that betrothment was decidedly an illegal act. The man had embraced Christianity, and, therefore, he is to be deprived of his natural right as a father. I can only say, if the Parsís set up such a claim as that, they will find they are grossly mistaken. If the father had really betrothed the child to a Parsí, I do not say the father could still have recovered the child back into his own custody; I do not positively say, whether or not the father's natural rights would in such case have been set aside; the question would have been a fair question for a Court of equity; and, I merely state the present impression of my mind, that the father could not have recovered his child. But the case before us is widely different from that supposed: the father repeatedly endeavoured to get back his wife and child. He left them in no other or stronger sense, than ceasing to live in the same house with them. He never gave his consent to the child being brought up as a Parsí.

[His Lordship then noticed the facts relating to the settlement.]

Looking then at all these circumstances, it is to my mind perfectly clear that the sole intention of this extraordinary line of conduct was to take the jurisdiction from the plea side. Were we to attach the slightest weight to this sum of money given under such circumstances, it would be precisely equivalent to sanctioning the purchase of a man's child, and so depriving him of it. Any poor man might thus be robbed of his child. When he tried to obtain his child, any rich man might step forward with a hundred or two hundred pounds, and keep the child from the parent. Can such a thing be listened to?

Then as to the point of Hormazjí having become a Christian, we cannot for one moment listen to the argument, that because a man has changed his religion, therefore his natural rights are held to be forfeited. I am, then, fully of opinion that the child must be given up to the father.

Perry, J.—I am of the same opinion. The question, as it appears to me, presents such a clear case of common law right on one side, and of illegal restraint on the other, and its consideration involves the discussion of first principles so important to all the members of the community, that the Court is called upon to pronounce its opinion immediately, and not to allow it to be supposed that any doubts exist on so plain a question. It has been strongly urged upon the Court, that we are not in a condition to decide the question in the present application, because we have already expressed strong opinions as to the conduct of the parties detaining the child, and that we have done this on what is said to be an *ex parte* view of the case. But protesting against this description of the facts, for I refer my own former expressions of blame entirely to the statements and letters of the parties themselves, I feel wholly uninfluenced by the argument, because I am

1843.

The QUEEN v. BEZONJI and EDALJI.

prepared to decide this case entirely on the facts as they appear on the writ and return, without reference to any other proceedings that have been before the Court.

Inquiry as to power of Parsí Panchayat over a convert to Christianity.

The case then, upon such facts, resolves itself into this simple question;—does a Parsí of mature age, who has conscientiously (as far as all appearances go) embraced Christianity, thereby forfeit the dearest rights of citizenship, and expose himself to the being deprived of his wife and children? Above all, does the cast to which he originally belonged possess the right of divorcing him from his wife, reference not being had, so far as appears in the case, to the wishes of either party? and does the father of the wife, or the divorced wife herself, possess the power of depriving the father of any intercourse whatever with his own offspring?

Parsí law of marriage.

On entering upon such questions, the first point to be determined is as to what law they are to be governed by; and this is a point that usually presents a greater difficulty in Parsí cases than in any other that comes before this Court; for although undoubtedly, as to general law, the Parsís, like any other body of strangers who settle in a country not their own, are to be governed by the laws of that country, still the institution of marriage is with them, as with most races of Asiatic origin, so mixed up with, and incorporated in, their religious ordinances, that the Court, having regard to the circumstances in which it is placed in this country, would never think of applying to their established practices any mere municipal regulation of English law. Still, when the proposition is broadly put forward that a body of men, styling themselves the Panchayat, lawfully may, and in this case lawfully have proceeded to divorce a man from his wife, and deprive him of his child, without the consent, it appears, of either party to the marriage contract, and without any moral stain on either, the proposition assumes so startling an aspect, and appears so opposed to the first principles of natural law on which all municipal systems are more or less founded, that undoubtedly the *onus* of establishing such a practice to be within the competence of the Parsís or their Panchayat, is thrown upon those who are here to advocate their cause.

1843.

The QUEEN v. BEZONJI and EDALJI.

Mr. *Howard* has wholly failed to make out his case on this point. He has cited no authority, and referred to no books to prove that such a power as to marriage and divorce is sanctioned by the system peculiar to the Parsís.

If any question respecting marriage were raised here between two Hindus or Mussalmans, we should have to refer to their law books for authorities on the subject, and so also, I take it, if Parsís claim to have peculiar rights, distinct and different from the rest of the community, we must look into the books which they recognise as authentic, to see whether the rights claimed are there conceded to them.

I must here say, that it is with very great reluctance I express any opinion on questions mixed up with the religious views or practices of natives, and especially with respect to marriage; but still this matter is now forced upon us by the conduct of the parties themselves, indirectly, as respects the power of divorce assumed by the Panchayat, but directly and broadly, as to the power of a family to deprive a father of the custody of his child.

Little to be found on marriage in the Zend-Avesta.

As I observed before, the learned counsel for the Parsís has cited no authority from the Parsí sacred books to support the position they have taken up; and according to the best examination of the Zend-Avesta, in M. Anquetil's translation, which I have been enabled to make, with reference to these points, I believe so far from any authority being to be found there which would have availed them now, the doctrine and the precepts are quite the other way.

In the absence then of any authority or usages founded in Parsí law, the simple question we have to decide is, whether a Parsí, having changed his religion, can therefore be legally deprived of his child by his relations? No such penalty being made out to exist in Parsí law, I have no hesitation in deciding, on the first principles of law, which aim at giving each citizen all possible full and undisturbed liberty in the enjoyment of such natural rights as are compatible with the safety of the state, that no such penalty exists in the English law either, on the exercise of one of those rights, *viz.*, that of conscience.

1843.

The QUEEN v. BEZONJI and EDALJI.

For the sake of the numerous natives whom I see around me, I may put the case thus:—Suppose a European, domiciled in Bombay, to go up to Poona for a few months, and in the course of that period to embrace, from conscientious motives the Mussalman faith, a case quite supposable, because it is believed to have actually occurred with the learned Sale, the translator of the Koran. Suppose then that during his absence a body of Christians, zealous missionaries for instance, got hold of his children, and withheld them from him on his return by violence; can it be supposed for a moment, that on application to this Court for a *habeas corpus*, the order would not be made for the delivery up of the children to the parent? And if the writ was issued out to such parties to bring up the body of the child, would the Court allow its peremptory order to be trifled with and defeated, by some little subscription being got up on the spot to make the children wards of Court, for the purpose of bringing them up in doctrines different from the father's? But if the Court would not allow the natural rights of the father to be thus displaced in the case of a European who had embraced Islam, is it to be so weak as to deny that protection to its own creed which it grants to every other?

Right of father to the custody of his children indisputable.

So far then, I think, a clear case of legal right in the father to have the custody of his child at the time of issuing the writ, is made out.

The next question is as to the illegal restraint, as to which all difficulty vanishes, when we recollect the facts as to the mode in which the father was driven from the house when he sought to have intercourse with his child.

This being so, and the common law right of the father being thus apparent, the ground on which the delivery up of the child to him is resisted, is that a settlement has been made upon the infant who is now a ward of Court, and that in all such cases a Court of equity, and not a Court of common law, is the fitting tribunal to decide upon the question of guardianship. And in behalf of this argument, the different cases in the books have been cited, where, on the one hand, Courts of equity have interfered with the custody of the father; and, on

1843.

The Queen v. Bezonji and Edalji.

the other, Courts of law have refused to enforce the legal rights of the father, till the decision of a Court of equity as to proper guardianship should be obtained.

But I do not think that it has been made to appear to the Court that any question exists for a Court of equity in this case, so as to interfere with the common law right of the father, at any rate in the meantime, to the custody of his child. With respect to the cases cited on the very delicate jurisdiction of the Court in interfering with parental control, I believe, from a perusal of them which I made with reference to this case, that the distinction drawn by Mr. *Dickinson* is perfectly correct, and that they are all divisible into two classes; first, where the father has shewn such gross immorality as to induce the Court to take his children from him; secondly, where the father has allowed his children to be separated from him, and, in consequence, pecuniary advantages are dedicated to them, of which they would be deprived if the father were allowed to assert his legal rights. Now, of these two sets of cases, it cannot be for a moment contended that a man's changing his religion, conscientiously, is immoral conduct, nor is it even pretended that the father has assented to any pecuniary arrangement by which the child is to be benefitted independently of his control.

Cases where Court interferes with parental control. 1st. Immorality of father: 2nd. Pecuniary benefit of children, and previous consent of father.

The latter point, however, appears to me to furnish a still stronger answer to the argument, and one upon which the case may be easily disposed of. For I look upon this paltry settlement of three thousand rupees, made upon this child as it was after the issuing of the writ, to be so entirely fictitious, so evidently part of a subtle scheme to defeat the course of the common law,—a scheme adopted, I must say, on most injudicious advice, that I entirely dismiss it from any bearing on the question.

Another point urged is, as to the assent which the father is said to have given to the marriage of his child, and which assent, it is contended, must therefore have contained within it his permission that the child should be brought up in the religion of its forefathers. But I think that no such conclusion is to be drawn. The assent of the father to the marriage is

1843.

The QUEEN v. BEZONJI and EDALJI.

very faintly stated, and he appears indeed to have had but little to say to it; but even if he had been most active in promoting such a contract, I cannot see why he is, therefore, to be deprived of the custody of his child during the period of infancy, and before it arrives at the age when married couples in this country commence their *consortium*.

It is possible, and most probable, that he may desire to bring up his child in the faith he has himself adopted, but it is also possible that he may not choose to interfere, and, at all events, I do not see that it follows because he has assented to what he may consider a beneficial advancement in life for his child, namely, marriage, that he has thereby renounced any other legal rights which he possesses as to his care and custody of it.

However this may be, the parties making a return to this writ have not stated any such assent on the father's part to part with the custody of his child, as to make the Court see that a question remains to be decided by a Court of equity.

I think therefore, on all these grounds, that the common law right of the father to the custody of his child stands out broadly in the midst of all these facts, and that the Court would do wrong if it hesitated to enforce it on the present application (*a*).

(*a*) See the next case.

THE QUEEN
v.
REV. ROBERT NESBITT.

1843.
November 3.

THE BRAMIN CONVERT'S CASE.

[*Coram* ROPER, C. J., and PERRY, J.]

Rights of fathers to the custody of their children.

The Court, on *habeas corpus*, ordered a Hindu boy, of twelve years of age, to be delivered up to his father, and refused to examine the boy as to his capacity and knowledge of the Christian religion, or as to his wishes to remain with his Christian instructors.

Conflicting decisions of the Supreme Court at Calcutta on these points.

HOWARD had obtained a *habeas corpus*, directed to the defendant, ordering him to bring up the body of one Shrípat Shreshadri.

The writ was issued on the affidavit of Govinda, the father of Shrípat, who stated that the latter was in his twelfth year, and was forcibly detained from him by the defendant.

Mr. Nesbitt made return to the writ, that Narayan, the brother of Shrípat, had been educated at the Missionary School of the Church of Scotland, of which the defendant was the head, since 1838, and that in 1841 Shrípat had also been placed at the same school with consent of his father. That Narayan and Shrípat were now both living at the house of the defendant, voluntarily, and that the defendant exercised no detention over Shrípat, but that at his request Shrípat was now present in Court.

By the affidavits of Narayan and others, it appeared that Narayan had embraced the Christian religion in September of this year, and that his brother Shrípat had not for fifteen months past joined in the worship of Hindu deities, or attended the ceremonies of the Hindu religion, except by putting the usual Hindu marks upon his forehead; that since they had been living at Mr. Nesbitt's, Shrípat had eaten with Narayan and others of the family, and had taken food not lawful to Hindus to eat, and had thereby made himself an outcast; and

1843.

The QUEEN v. NESBITT.

that if he returned to his father's house he would suffer much hardship and persecution.

It also appeared that Govinda, the father, was a person of no means, and that he had been chiefly, and, for the last few months entirely, supported by Narayan out of his salary as a teacher at the Mission School. By the affidavit of Narayan it was also stated that Shrípat was upwards of twelve years of age.

The boy was produced in Court this day, and appeared extremely juvenile for a lad of twelve years old.

Howard moved that the above return should be filed, and that the Court should order the child to be given over to his father.

Dickinson, contrà. On a writ of *habeas corpus*, the Court has no other duty to perform than to see that no illegal restraint is exercised. In *Rex* v. *Johnson* (1 Str. 579), a child of nine was brought up in the custody of its nurse, and the Court ordered that it should be delivered to its uncle, whom the father had constituted guardian by will; but in *Rex* v. *Smith* (2 Str. 282), the Court overruled that decision, and held, that all they could do was to relieve the party from illegal restraint, and they allowed the boy there (who was between thirteen and fourteen years of age), to choose his own custody. So in *Rex* v. *Delaval* (3 Burr. 1434), Lord MANSFIELD would not order the girl, who was eighteen years of age, to be given up to her father, and he laid down the rule, that "the Court is to judge upon the circumstances of the particular case, and give their direction accordingly." But the leading case is *Rex* v. *Greenhill* (4 Ad. & Ell. 624), where Lord DENMAN pronounced this rule, "When an infant is brought before the Court by *habeas corpus*, if he be of an age to exercise a choice, the Court leaves him to elect where he will go."

It results from all these cases, that the Court must exercise a discretion in every case, whether the youth is capable of exercising a choice; and for this purpose the Court will examine into the capacity of the child. It appears by the

1843.

The QUEEN v. NESBITT.

affidavits that Shripat has been studying English and the elements of the Christian religion, and the Court will be able to judge by his answers whether he is of a capacity to exercise his choice sufficiently. Nor can it be said that he is too young to be capable of entertaining fixed opinions on these subjects. If he were tendered as a witness, his testimony would be available if the Court were satisfied with his capacity; if he committed crime, he would be amenable to the laws; then why should he be denied the dearest privilege of citizenship,—the right of conscience, and of providing for his own happiness in this world and in the world to come?

The results of this decision are so important to the whole interests of this boy, that the Court cannot safely pronounce it without examining the boy's attainments themselves.

Roper, C. J. (a)—It is contended that the father has no right to the possession of the child—that the boy is of sufficient intelligence to choose for himself, and that the Court accordingly ought to make no order, but allow him to exercise his own discretion in choosing his place of residence. Now it is obvious that the boy is of very tender age—but it is contended that it is the duty of the Court to examine him, and so be enabled to decide on his competency to form a judgment. I am quite prepared to believe all that has been urged in reference to his intelligence; but even were he much further advanced than he is, I could not interfere with the father's rights. The proposal that we should undertake an examination of the child is entirely out of the question. Very probably such an examination would end in a theological examination between us and the boy—a thing that would be quite preposterous: the question of religion must be entirely set aside, it is one with which we can have nothing to do.

Were I to allow these considerations to come in, and permit my own views and feelings on these matters to influence me in the least, I would say that it were much better for the happiness and interests of the boy that he remained where he

(a) Condensed from *The Oriental Christian Spectator*, December, 1843

1843.

The Queen v. Nesbitt.

is, under the care of the gentleman whose protection he has sought. But we must not forget that it is not competent to this Court now to enter into the consideration of religious questions and interests. But as the greater part of the argument was founded on the religious basis, directly that is removed, there is scarcely anything more to be noticed.

The poverty of the father has been insisted on, but that surely is no reason for depriving him of his parental rights, he has done nothing whatever to forfeit them; and, whatever our feelings or predilections might be, his child must be restored to him.

Perry, J.—I quite agree. There is a general rule which prevails in this Court, by steady attention to which it is clear that only one decision can be arrived at. The Court is not at liberty to draw any distinctions between the different religious creeds existing in this country, or to favour one more than another. The impartiality of decision should be such, that a Hindu or Mussalman coming before the Court, should put the same confidence in a just determination being arrived at, as if he were appealing to a Judge of his own creed and colour. But if the course that is suggested should be adopted, and the child were examined as to its proficiency in the Christian religion, the natives never could feel confidence that the inquiry had been conducted on the strict principles of judicial impartiality.

Duty of English Judges in India on religious questions.

Nor do I put any value on what the opinions of a child of twelve years of age might be on such a subject as religion. It is the nature of children to imbibe the opinions of those with whom they live, and to whom they are accustomed to look up with reverence and regard. The question now raised is a question affecting all fathers, and it might easily occur to a European in this country to place his children at a seminary in Europe where different religious opinions to his own were taught, and where, if a system of proselytism were adopted, and ordinary kindness exhibited, there is little doubt but that in a few years the tender minds of the children might be made to imbibe the peculiar doctrines of their teacher. Yet

Opinions of children on religious questions not to be attended to.

1843.

The QUEEN v. NESBITT.

a Protestant father, when he claimed his children, would be astonished to hear that, if his children lisped forth their wishes to remain with their Roman Catholic instructors, such infantine accents could form the rule of law.

Common sense seems to shew that, although the choice of a religion is the most important act in life, still the paternal authority must prevail, and the father's choice govern, up to a certain period of life. What that period is, is not very well fixed in the English law. For some purposes a man is considered *sui juris* at twenty-one, though for others he is not considered emancipated from paternal control till he is married, or has a separate abode. In India the period of majority is earlier for many purposes, and eighteen is called the legal age. But it is sufficient to say that this child of twelve years of age is not of an age to throw off his father's control; and as nothing can be urged against the conduct of the latter, I think the boy should be given up to him, exactly as, in the case of the Parsí father, we enforced his civil rights, although his family asserted that he had lost them by embracing the Christian religion (*a*).

Up to a certain age the child must obey the will of the father as to religion.

(*a*) The Supreme Court at Calcutta arrived at a different conclusion in a case much similar to the above, a short time after the above decision; and the Supreme Court at Madras on one occasion during the last few years, after a lengthened examination into the Christian knowledge of a young convert, refused to make an order on *habeas corpus* to give him up to his father; but as the youth afterwards reverted to the Hindu faith, his father subsequently got possession of him on a fresh *habeas corpus*.

The principle on which the Supreme Court of Calcutta decided was, that the writ of *habeas corpus* was only intended to prevent illegal restraint, and that if the child, on being brought into Court, did not appear to be under illegal restraint, and was of an age to choose for himself, the Court would allow him to exercise his own discretion where he would go. And as the boy in this case, who had been a pupil in Dr. Duff's school, and was a convert to the Christian religion, was about fourteen years of age, and expressed his wish to remain with Dr. Duff and not to go to his father, the Court allowed him to do so. And in 1847 the Supreme Court at Calcutta pronounced a similar decision.

There is, therefore, a direct conflict of opinion between the Supreme Courts of Calcutta and Bombay: and as the subject is one of extreme importance, I will venture to make a few observations upon it.

The laws of most nations invest the father of a family with great power over his children. Amongst

1843.

The Queen v. Nesbitt.

the Romans this power, at first absolute over life and death, became restricted subsequently within closer limits; and these later rules have been adopted by nearly all the continental nations of Europe. Thus the Code Civil places children under the absolute authority of the father till majority or emancipation (Art. 372); and Thibaut expressly lays it down to be the right of the father to educate his child in his own religion; 1 *Pandekten Rechts*, § 247. The Roman writ of *habeas corpus* (*de libero homine exhibendo*) also issued in favour of parents, whenever the child was out of their custody, although in other cases it was necessary to shew illegal restraint; *Dig.* 43. 30. 1. § 2.

But the Hindu law gives even more power to the father than the Roman Code, and therefore it is that the course of procedure amongst civilians is well worthy of being consulted when a question of Hindu *patria potestas* arises, for by 21 Geo. 3, c. 70, s. 18, the rights of Hindu and Mussalman fathers are expressly guaranteed to them.

I conceive also that the English law equally maintains the rights of parents to the custody of their children, and that a Court of common law will enforce them by *habeas corpus*, unless it appears that there are strong moral objections to the custody of the father. On this latter ground Lord Eldon refused to Mr. Shelley and Long Wellesley respectively the custody of their children,—to the former on the ground of his opinions on religion, to the latter on the ground of his profligate life; but these decisions have not been generally approved of, and they appear to partake too much of an inquisitorial character to warrant their being safely used as precedents.

But the Supreme Court at Calcutta has proceeded on the doctrine that *habeas corpus* is only intended to remove illegal restraint, and if the restraint is not illegal, the Court cannot, under this process, enforce the right of the father to the guardianship of the child, which must be brought forward either by suit in equity, or by some of the ancient actions of the common law mentioned in *Rex* v. *Smith* (2 Str. 982). But in that case, as was pointed out by Lord Mansfield in *Rex* v. *Delaval* (3 Burr.), the boy wanted only six weeks of being fourteen, and the reason why the Court refused to order the child to be given up to the father was, "because they had a bad opinion of his (the father's) design in applying for the custody." And so in *Rex* v. *Delaval*, Lord Mansfield held, in his discretion, that there was no occasion to deliver the daughter, who was eighteen years of age, to her father, as he had ill used her, and his conduct seemed suspicious. It would appear, therefore, that the law is correctly laid down in *Rex* v. *De Manneville* (5 East), that "the father is entitled by law to the custody of his child;" that the law of England has not marked out in precise terms at what period the parental authority ceases, although Lord Mansfield clearly did not think that the age of eighteen, *per se*, was the age of emancipation, but that the common law Judges must exercise a sound discretion in every case whether they will order on *habeas corpus* the child to be given up to the father; and that such order ought to be made, unless the father is seeking the possession of his child for purposes of mischief, or unless questions of property are involved which require the interference of a Court of

1843.

The QUEEN *v.* NESBITT.

equity. Indeed, if this were not so, there would be a denial of justice to all such fathers as were too poor and helpless to encounter the expenses of a suit in equity.

As the question contained in the above two cases is likely often to recur in the Courts in India, I submitted the above views, soon after the conflicting decisions at Calcutta, to one of the most eminent Judges on the English Bench, and I subjoin his reply. "I cannot doubt that you were quite right in holding that the father was entitled to the custody of his child, and enforcing it by writ of *habeas corpus*. The general law is clearly so, and even after the age of fourteen, whereas this boy (Shrípat) was only twelve. The right may indeed be forfeited by misconduct of a very gross nature, but nothing of that kind appears to have been brought forward. It may have been an act of imprudence originally in the father to place his boys with persons who were likely to bring them up in religious opinions and faith contrary to their father; I suppose he made some stipulations for avoiding this; but whether he did or not, I do not think that the law would be affected thereby. Even if he had changed his mind on that subject, as well as on the education of his boys in other respects, I know of no law which forbids him to do so, or binds him to the arrangement which he had at first made."

THE QUEEN *v.* REV. W. FLETCHER.

1849.

[*Coram* PERRY, C. J., and YARDLEY, J]

Where a European officer had left directions in his will that his natural children, by a native woman, should be brought up as Christians; *Held*, on *habeas corpus*, that the mother of these children was entitled to the custody.

DICKINSON, on affidavits, shewed cause against a writ of *habeas corpus* issuing to the directors of the Byculla school, to bring up the bodies of some young children.

It appeared that these children were illegitimate, and were the daughters of a European officer and native female. The officer was dead, and the mother now demanded the custody of the children. It appeared that the father desired that these children should be brought up as Christians; and it appeared that some small provision was made for their schooling on the part of the father's friends; but

1849.

The QUEEN v. FLETCHER.

PER CURIAM.—The law gives the custody of illegitimate children to the mother, and there is no property here, or suit instituted, by which the Court, on its equity side, can interfere with the ordinary legal custody.

Rule absolute.

1847.

June 19, 20, September 15, October 11.

CASE OF THE KOJAHS.

HIRBAE AND OTHERS v. SONABAE.

GUNGBAE v. SONABAE.

CASE OF THE MEMONS.

RAHIMATBAE v. HADJI JUSSAP AND OTHERS.

[*Coram* PERRY, C. J.]

1. Right of succession amongst Mussalman dissenters.

2. If a custom, as to succession, is found to prevail amongst a sect of Mahomedans, and be valid in other respects, the Court will give effect to it, although it differs from the rule of succession laid down in the Koran.

3. Discussion, as to the true source of customary law. Conflicting opinions of jurists compared.

4. Validity of a law at variance with a text believed to be divine discussed.

5. Monogamy of the Jews introduced by a law of the Roman Emperors, and not observed by Jews settled in India.

AN interesting question was raised in these two cases, namely, whether a rule of succession amongst particular sects of Mahomedans at variance with the rule laid down in the Koran could be given effect to in this Court.

At the trial at the Bar of these equity suits on *vivâ voce* evidence, both the Kojahs and the Memon Cutchees were proved to be settled for the most part in Hindu countries, principally Cutch and Kattiawar, and the belief amongst themselves was, that they had been converted from Hinduism about three or four hundred years ago. The rule of succession, which prevailed amongst them, was nearly analogous to the Hindu rule of succession.

1847.

Kojahs and Memons' Case.

The *Kojah case* was argued by *Howard* and *Wallace* for the plaintiffs, who attacked the custom, and by *Dickinson* and *Holland*, in support of it, on the 19th of June, 1847.

The *Memon case* was argued the 15th of September, 1847, *Crawford* and *Howard*, in support of the custom, and by *Le Mesurier*, A. G., and *Wallace*, against it.

Cur. adv. vult.

Perry, C. J.—The question which has arisen in the cases of the Kojahs and of the Memon Cutchees is founded on such similar states of facts, and depends so entirely on the same principles of law, that it may be conveniently disposed of in one judgment.

The facts in the Kojah case are as follows:—The plaintiff Hirbae, and her infant sister, were the only children of Hadjibhae Mir Ali, late a merchant in Bombay, who died intestate, leaving behind him a widow, Sonabae, and property consisting of land and moveables, said to be worth three laks of rupees. He had carried on trade at this place with his brother, Sajum Mir Ali, and the latter, on his brother's death, took possession of his property, which he retained till he himself died in 1843, when he left a will appointing his sister-in-law Sonabae, and his wife Rahimatbae his executrixes.

The plaintiff now files her bill against these executrixes, the object of which bill is to obtain a declaration from the Court that she, as a Mahomedan female, is entitled to the share in distribution of her father's property which is ordained in the Koran. The defendants meet this demand by a plea that all the parties to the suit belong to a certain exclusive sect or cast of Mahomedans called Kojahs, which has existed from time immemorial, separate and distinct from other bodies or sects of Mahomedans, and under the government of divers laws and customs peculiar to themselves, and differing in many respects from the laws and customs of the Mahomedans: and the plea then avers a custom in the cast by which females are not entitled to any share of their father's property at his decease, nor to any benefit whatever except, if they should be unmarried to maintenance out of the estate, and to a sufficient sum

1847.

Kojahs and Memons Case.

to defray the expenses of their marriage according to their condition in life.

A replication having been put in to this plea, application was made to the Court, in pursuance of a very general feeling amongst the Profession at Bombay as to the superiority of *vivâ voce* testimony over evidence obtained in the Examiner's Office, to grant issues for the purpose of testing the plea; and, accordingly, three issues were directed, which in substance raised the question, whether a good and valid custom existed amongst the Kojahs to the effect stated in the plea.

History of the Kojahs.

These issues came on for trial before me on the 19th and 20th of June last, and a great many witnesses, comprising the chief and most intelligent members of the Kojah cast were examined, who told us all that they appeared to know themselves respecting their origin, history, habits, and religious opinions. It turned out that there was little or no conflicting testimony as to the existence of a custom such as is stated in the plea, and as the principal question then arose, whether such custom was valid or not, I thought it best, at the conclusion of the trial, to deliver no opinions on the law of the case, but to leave that open for discussion at a future stage of the inquiry on the facts which had been proved before me on that occasion, and of which the following is a sketch :—

Converted from Hinduism.

The Kojahs are a small cast in Western India, who appear to have originally come from Sindh or Cutch, and who, by their own traditions, which are probably correct, were converted from Hinduism about four hundred years ago by a Pír named Sadr Dín. Their language is Cutchí; their religion Mahomedan; their dress, appearance, and manners, for the most part, Hindu. These latter facts, however, do not warrant the conclusion being drawn, if such conclusion is necessary for decision of the case (and I think it is not) that the Kojahs were originally Hindu, for such is the influence of Hindu manners and opinions on all casts and colours who come into connection with them, that gradually all assume an unmistakeable Hindu tint. Parsís, Moguls, Afghans, Israelites, and Christians, who have been long settled in India, are seen to have exchanged much of their ancient patrimony of ideas for Hindu tones of thought; and, in observing this phenomenon, I have been often led to compare it with one somewhat similar in the black soil in the Deccan, which geologists tell us possesses the property of converting all foreign substances brought into contact with it into its own material.

1847.

KOJAHS and MEMONS' Case.

However, this may be, the Kojahs are now settled principally amongst Hindu communities, such as Cutch, Kattiawar, and Bombay, which latter place probably is their head quarters. They constitute, at this place, apparently about two thousand souls, and their occupations, for the most part, are confined to the more subordinate departments of trade. Indeed the cast never seems to have emerged from the obscurity which attends their present history, and the almost total ignorance of letters, of the principles of their religion, and of their own *status*, which they now evince, is probably the same as has always existed among them since they first embraced the precepts of Mahomed.

Although they call themselves Mussalmans, they evidently know but little of their Prophet and of the Koran; and their chief reverence at the present time is reserved for Agha Khan, a Persian nobleman, well known in contemporaneous Indian history, and whom they believe to be a *descendant of the Pír*, who converted them to Islam (*a*). But even to the blood of their saint they adhere by a frail tenure; for it was proved, that when the grandmother of Agha Khan made her appearance in Bombay some years ago, and claimed tithes from the faithful, they repudiated their allegiance, commenced litigation in this Court, and professed to the Kazí of Bombay their

(*a*) This is a mistake, I think; from an instructive note I have seen by Lt. Col. Rawlinson, it appears that Agha Khan is a lineal descendant of the sixth Imám, and that a large section of Mussalmans believe this sixth Imam is again to appear on the earth. It is probable that the Pír, who converted these Kojahs, belonged to this Imamy sect of Persia, and hence the reverence for Agha Khan, which is shewn by numbers in Persia, and which induced the late King to bestow on him his daughter in marriage. "The peculiar doctrine of the Ismaillies, as this section of Mahomedans is called in Persia, is that they believe each successive Imám from Ali to Ismail was an incarnation of the Divine Essence, and further that the incarnation is hereditary in the direct male line; hence Agha Khan is worshipped as a God by all true Ismaillies."—*Col. Rawlinson's Rep. to Gov. of India.*

1847. Kojahs and Memons' Case.

intention to incorporate themselves with the general body of Mussalmans in this island. To use the words of one of themselves, they call themselves Shías to a Shía, and Sunniys to a Sunníy, and they probably neither know nor care any thing as to the distinctive doctrines of either of these great divisions of the Mussalman world. They have, moreover, no translation of the Koran into their vernacular language, or into Guzaratí their language of business, which is remarkable when we recollect the long succession of pious Mussalman kings who reigned in Guzarat, and in the countries in which the Kojahs have been located. Nor have they any scholars or men of learning among them, as not a Kojah could be quoted who was acquainted with Arabic or Persian, the two great languages of Mahomedan literature and theology; and the only religious work of which we heard as being current amongst them was one called the Das Avatar, in the Sindhí character and Cutchi language, of which Narayan the interpreter has procured me some translated passages, and which, as professing to give a history of the tenth incarnation in the person of their Saint, Sudr Dín, appears to be a strong combination of Hindu articles of faith with the tenets of Islam.

No other fact of any material bearing on the case was proved; but the defendants brought forward evidence to shew that Hirbae, the complainant in one case, and her cousin Gungbae, the complainant in the other, had received jewels from the executrixes of Sajun Mir Ali, which, it was contended, amounted to a recognition and confirmation of the will of the latter, according to the rules of Mahomedan law. But as I was clearly of opinion, on looking at the sex, the tender age, and the helpless condition of these young women, that the simple act of receiving jewels tendered to them by their elders in the family amounted to no compromise of their just and legal rights, the fact may be passed over without further notice

When this case was standing over for judgment, a suit was instituted in relation to the Memon Cutchi cast, in which it was intimated that exactly the same question arose.

In this case, also, a suit was instituted by Memon Cutchi females, praying for a distribution of the paternal property in accordance with the text in the Koran, and a plea of exactly the same import as in the Kojah case, of a peculiar custom existing amongst the Memon Cutchis, was filed, upon which *vivâ voce* evidence was taken before me, by consent, in the last term.

1847.

KOJAHS and MEMONS' Case.

Amongst the Memon Cutchis it was also clearly proved that the custom of excluding females from the inheritance prevailed amongst them exactly as it does amongst Hindus. The Memons were originally, and still are, seated in Cutch, from which they have spread themselves into many of the adjoining countries in Western India, and, by their own account, even into Malabar and Bengal. By their traditions they were originally Loannas, a Hindu commercial cast in Cutch; but they are not able, and no records are forthcoming, to indicate the period of their conversion, although there is every reason to believe it must have been some hundreds of years ago. They may be characterized as being more orthodox Mahomedans than the Kojahs, and in being in every way their superiors, so far as wealth, numbers, and learning are concerned. They make the pilgrimage to Mecca, which is unknown amongst the Kojahs; and a branch of the cast, the Hala Memons, who are settled in Kattiwar, are said to observe every portion of the Mahomedan law, including the injunctions as to the division of an inheritance.

Origin of the Memons.

These facts having been established, the first question which arises is, whether this peculiar custom of succession which has prevailed from time that may be called immemorial amongst these casts, can be sanctioned in a British Court of justice? and secondly, it has been made matter of grave argument, whether any customs conflicting with the express text of the Koran can be valid amongst a Mahomedan sect. The importance of these questions, both to the casts themselves, from the large pecuniary as well as social interests involved, and as regards other casts and Courts in the interior, from the universality of the principles involved in the argument, has caused me to apply myself to the inquiry with more than usual anxiety, and as it is unlikely, from the magnitude of the stakes at issue, that the parties against whom I have formed a conclusion will be satisfied with my decision, I am studious

1847.

Kojahs and Memons' Case.

to set out the grounds of it fully, so as to enable a superior Court to judge of its validity.

1. Rules of succession usually founded on custom.

1. It may be perhaps laid down, that it is a matter of comparatively little interest to the Commonwealth how the affairs of private individuals are conducted among themselves. So long as the public interests do not require a uniform line of conduct to be observed or refrained from, or that the heedlessness of individuals, in the regulation of their own affairs, does not make it expedient to lay down some arbitrary rule to govern contingencies, which they themselves have not foreseen, a wise Legislature is slow to interfere. In every well ordered community it is essential to its peace that clear and certain rules should exist as to the various relations of domestic life, and in every early history it will be found, that as to most of these, such as marriage, succession, adoptions, as well as to the various occupations, agricultural, pastoral or mercantile, which may happen to prevail in such society, the exigencies of man have framed rules long before written laws existed. A considerable body of law thus arises in every state, and the legislator, when he is required to enter upon his task, rarely seeks to interfere with regulations which the habits and manners of the people have spontaneously adopted. In the English system two arbitrary rules arose, partly from this source and partly from judicial decision, for the division of property, in order to provide for the contingency of an individual, dying either without children or with more than one. But the mere fact of two completely different rules being in existence for the division of real and personal property (a difference traceable to historical causes), clearly shews that no principle of public policy has called forth any universal law The same proposition is demonstrable by the various local customs of succession which have always been allowed by the English law, but still more by the provision which has existed from very early times, whereby every individual is allowed to make a law, a *privilegium*, for himself, by which the succession to his property, after his death, is absolutely governed. allude to the power of making that instrument called a will, to which, if formally authenticated and prepared, the Courts

English rules arbitrary and accidental.

1847.

KOJAHS and MEMONS' Case.

of justice will attribute the same dispositive power over property as to an act of Parliament.

Principles such as these will, in great part, account for the large share which customary law, as it is called, *mores majorum*, or *jus consuetudinarium*, may be found to hold in most codes. In some cases the wisdom, but in most the indifference or want of skill, of the legislator, has left mankind to frame their own rules for the conduct of daily life, and when such rules grow up into a custom, we may see by the present cases that it is often more difficult to change it than even the peculiar religion out of which it perhaps arose. A considerable difference of opinion exists amongst jurists as to what the foundation of this customary law is. The Roman lawyers, and Sir WILLIAM BLACKSTONE following them, hold that the common consent of the people, or of any particular class of the people, gives to any custom the validity of a law *per se*, and the Romans held this with much apparent logic, for as a *plebiscitum* in the time of the Republic formed a valid law, they argued "*quid interest, suffragio populus voluntatem suam declaret, an rebus ipsis et factis.*" Dig. lib. 1, tit. 3, l. 32, § 1. Other great lawyers hold, and I think with juster views, that a custom is not valid as a law until it is recognised by the established tribunals of the country. And as it is very important in the present controversy to ascertain whether the custom in question can be based upon any recognised legal foundation, I think it is worth while to cite the ablest expositions I am acquainted with of the two conflicting doctrines.

Source of customary law.

A great modern civilian writes as follows:—

Conflicting opinions of jurists.

"Where a class of persons by common consent have followed a rule intentionally, whether by positive or negative acts, a law arises out of this public common consent for each person belonging to the class, provided that the custom is not unreasonable, and applies to matters which the written law has left undetermined. Customs conflicting with the law are not valid in the Roman system, unless they have been recognised by the ruling authority, or have been in use from time immemorial, and this whether their effect may be to repeal a law by disuse (*desuetudo*), or to introduce a new principle at

1847.

Kojahs and Memons' Case.

Thibaut and Blackstone.

variance with the law; and their being confirmed even by judicial authority does not give them validity in the latter case." (On this point, however, I may observe there is much conflicting opinion amongst civilians). "A custom, therefore, to hold good in law, requires, besides the above negative conditions, the following positive condition, namely, that the majority at least of any given class of persons look upon the rule as binding, and it must be established by a series of well-known, concordant, and, on the whole, continuous instances. How many examples are necessary to prove a custom cannot be laid down beforehand, neither is the number to be left to the arbitrary discretion of the Judge,—but the point in each case is, whether the common consent of the class in question is clearly demonstrated by the number of instances proved.

"A custom complying with the above conditions is binding in itself, and does not require either the special recognition of the ruling power, or its confirmation in Courts of law, or the efflux of any long period of time, definite or indefinite,—least of all does it require prescription, although either of these latter tend very much to prove the existence of the common consent; and from a uniform series of decisions common consent may be inferred." (1 *Thibaut System des Pandekten Rechts*, p. 15).

Austin's opinion.

Professor Austin, on the other hand, in his work on Jurisprudence, thus expresses himself:—

"Every positive law, or rule of positive law, exists *as such* by the pleasure of the Sovereign. *As such* it is made immediately by the Sovereign, or by a party in a state of subjection to the Sovereign, in one of the two modes which are indicated by the foregoing article. *As such* it flows from one or another of those sources."

"But by the classical Roman jurists, by Sir William Blackstone, and by numerous other writers on particular or general jurisprudence, the occasions of laws, or the motives to their establishment, are frequently confounded with their sources or fountains.

"The following examples will shew the nature of the error to which I have now adverted:—

"The prevalence of a custom amongst the governed may

1847.

KOJAHS and MEMONS Case.

determine the Sovereign, or some political superior in subjection to the Sovereign, to transmute the custom into positive law. Respect for a law writer whose works have gotten reputation, may determine the legislator or judge to adopt his opinions, or to turn the speculative opinions of a private man into actually binding rules. The prevalence of a practice amongst private practitioners of the law may determine the legislator or judge to impart the force of law to the practice which they observe spontaneously. Now till the legislator or judge impress them with the character of law, the custom is nothing more than a rule of positive morality; the conclusions are the speculative conclusions of a private or unauthorized writer; and the practice is the spontaneous practice of private practitioners. But the classical Roman jurists, and a host of other writers, fancy that a rule of law, made by judicial exposition on a pre-existing custom, exists as positive law, apart from the legislator or judge, by the institution of the private persons who observed it in its customary state. And the classical Roman jurists have the same or the like conceit with regard to the rules of law which are fashioned by judicial decisions on the conclusions or practices of private writers or practitioners. They ascribe their existence as law to the authority of the writers or practitioners, and not to the Sovereign, or the representatives of the Sovereign, who clothed them with the legal sanction." (*Austin on Jurisprudence*, App. p. xi. *London*, 1832).

According to the Roman law, therefore, this custom of the Kojahs and Memons would be held to be valid in itself without any sanction by the Court, provided that it were reasonable, and that it did not conflict with any written law of the ruling authority.

English law as to customs.

According to the English law, as I conceive it, and to the sound principle of universal law, the custom would require the sanction of the Court, as representing the sovereign authority, before it obtained any legal validity. Both these theories, however, agree in this, that the custom must be reasonable, or rather not unreasonable, and that its reasonableness must be tested in a Court of justice. In the present

1847.

Kojahs and Memons' Case.

instance accordingly it has been stoutly argued, that this Hindu custom of disinheriting daughters, which has been adopted by these Mahomedan sectarians, is most unreasonable, and that public policy would dictate the adoption of the wiser rule laid down in the Koran, by which daughters are allowed a defined share in the succession. A contrast is then drawn between the relative positions which females hold in the Hindu and Mussalman systems, and it is argued, that the policy of the latter is so much more enlarged and beneficial, that it is the duty of the Court to give it effect when the two come in collision. But I have often disclaimed in this Court any desire to decide private rights with reference to political results. "Public policy," in the words of Mr. Justice Burroughs, "is an unruly horse, and if a Judge gets upon it he is very apt to be run away with." Where public policy accords with the well-recognised track of morality, it is the duty of the Judge to make every decision conform to it, if the letter of the law permits; but wherever public policy is a matter of controversy, a lawyer should be the last to express any opinion upon it: and I hardly know any question connected with the East on which so much might be said on either side as on the different characteristics of the marriage state between Hindus and Mussalmans, and on the *status* in life and influence in domestic circles which Hindu and Mussalman females respectively enjoy. It is sufficient, however, to say, that a custom for females to take no share in the inheritance is not unreasonable in the eyes of the English law; for it accords in great part with the universal custom as to real estates where there are any male issue, and entirely with some local customs mentioned in Blackstone, by which, in certain manors, females are excluded in all cases.

But this custom has not only been attacked on the score of unreasonableness, but it has been tested by every one of the seven requisites which Blackstone has laid down for the validity of an English custom. It may be asked, however,— and I did ask,—why the various special rules which have been laid down in any particular system, and some of which clearly have no general applicability, should be transferred to a state of things to which they have no relation? Why, for instance, the municipal rules of the English law are to govern a Mahomedan custom any more than the municipal rules of the Roman law. I apprehend that the true rules to govern such a custom are rules of universal applicability, and that it is simply absurd to test a Mahomedan custom by considerations whether it existed when Richard I. returned from the Holy Land, which is the English epoch for dating the commencement of time immemorial, or by cases, such as that cited from 3 *T. R.* 371, to shew that it is a bad custom at Southampton to sell butter by the pound weighing eighteen ounces. Least of all does the English rule which limits a custom to a particular locality apply to a cast custom in this country. The English rule is founded most probably on the various local laws which the different monarchies in the Heptarchy, or the different races of conquerors, left behind them; but the customs of casts are all eminently personal, and are as clearly traceable and distinct in one locality as another. But even in England the custom of London with regard to succession follows the person. (2 *Vern.* 82).

1847.

KOJAHS and MEMONS' Case.

Incidents of a valid customary law.

It appears to me that if a custom has been proved to exist from time whereof the memory of man runneth not to the contrary, if it is not injurious to the public interests, and if it does not conflict with any express law of the ruling power, such custom is entitled to receive the sanction of a Court of law.

2. Law of Mussalmans conflicting with Koran.

2. This brings us to the second question in the case; for it has been contended, and indeed the main stress of the argument has rested on this point, that however valid this custom might be in other respects, it can never have validity with respect to the Mahomedans, as it is in conflict with the Divine law as revealed to them by the Koran; that in this respect it is equivalent to a custom in England which conflicts with a subsequent act of Parliament: and the passage from *Thibaut* also shews that the Roman law allowed of no custom if the *lex scripta* had laid down a rule on the subject.

This view of the question, as bringing the binding effect of Divine law into discussion, opens up a very interesting field of inquiry, and one on which it becomes difficult to express oneself

1847

KOJAHS and MEMONS' Case.

Conflict of divine law (so called) and human law.

Duty of jurists and Courts of justice.

clearly, if any regard to conciseness is to be maintained. But in a juridical point of view I apprehend there is no difficulty in stating what the sound conclusions are.

A jurist *quâ* jurist has only to deal with human laws: he recognises the existence of divine laws, and their validity *in foro conscientiæ* with those to whom they are addressed, or who believe in the revelation containing them; but he does not recognise them as enforceable in Courts of justice any further than the secular power has ordained. Under a government such as that of England, which has established the principle of universal toleration as to religious belief, it is no doubt the duty of a secular Judge to pay the utmost respect to the religious opinions of every suitor who comes before the Court; and his judicial impartiality should be preserved within such inflexible limits, that on every controversy which is capable of arising within the bosom of society, the opinion should be universally diffused that a calm and just decision between the litigant parties would as surely issue from the judgment-seat as if it were occupied by a Judge of their own creed and colour. But the question on every such occasion for the Judge would be, what the law was which had been delivered to him for administration by his Sovereign.

When India fell to the arms of the British it was competent to the Legislature to have repealed the whole of the law which the greater part of the inhabitants considered Divine. It might have been very intolerant and tyrannical to have done so, and most probably such laws would have had no operation on the customs and habits of the people, though a very singular example to the contrary is to be found among the Jews of Europe. By the Jewish law, as it is clearly shewn by Selden and Lightfoot, polygamy on a very large scale was permissible; but the Roman Emperors Theodosius and Arcadius, repealed the Jewish law of marriage, and thereby introduced the Roman law of monogamy, which has prevailed amongst the Jews, as amongst the Christians, of Europe, ever since. (*Cod.* lib. 1, tit. 9, l. 7 (*a*)).

(*a*) And, remarkably enough, the Jews settled in India, or Ben-Israel, as they are called, and who, according to the best authorities,

1847.

KOJAHS and MEMONS' Case.

But whether an act of Parliament, introducing the English law of marriage and primogeniture, would have succeeded in exterminating the practices of polygamy and division of property, now prevalent in India: there is no doubt that if a question arose upon them before an English Judge, the rule laid down in the act of Parliament would have to be enforced.

Wherever, therefore, a question arises as to the binding effect of a law believed to be Divine by any peculiar cast, the true inquiry for a Court of justice is, how far that law has been recognised, or sanctioned, or adopted by the ruling power. In the present instance this question depends on the true construction to be placed on the following clause of our charter, which contains the expression of the legislator's will:—

Personal laws secured to the Mahomedans and Hindus under the British rule.

"In the case of Mahomedans or Gentoos, their inheritance and succession . . . . shall be determined, in the case of the Mahomedans, by the laws and usages of the Mahomedans, and where the parties are Gentoos, by the laws and usages of the Gentoos, or by such laws and usages as the same would have been determined by if the suit had been brought and the action commenced in a native Court."

Now if the meaning of this clause is that it is an absolute enactment or adoption of the Koran, as of a positive unchangeable law, without regard to what the usages of the Mahomedans of India, whether Shías, Sunníys, or sectarians, might have been, undoubtedly the custom set up in conflict with the text of the Koran cannot be sustained. But I think it is quite clear that the clause in question was framed solely on political views, and without any reference to orthodoxy, or the purity of any particular religious belief.

It was believed erroneously that the population of India might be classified under the two great heads of Mahomedan and Gentoo; and the use of the latter term as a *nomen generalissimum*, which is unknown, by-the-bye, in any Eastern tongue, or even in colloquial use, except in the presidency of

have been established here for two thousand years, do not confine themselves to one wife: in this, however, as in many other customs, they may have merely imitated their Hindu hosts.

1847.

KOJAHS and MEMONS' CASE.

Madras, shews that the main object was to retain to the whole people lately conquered their ancient usages and laws, on the principle of *uti possidetis.* It may be questioned whether one individual in the Legislature,—with the exception, perhaps, of Mr. Burke,—was aware of the sectarian differences which distinguished Shía from Sunníy; and not even that great man, we may be assured, was at all conscious that there were millions of inhabitants in India, such as Sikhs, Jains, Parsís, Israelites and others, who had nothing, or next to nothing, in common with Brahminical worship. But the policy which led to the clause proceeded upon the broad, easily recognisable basis of allowing the newly-conquered people to retain their domestic usages.

Just as the Gothic conquerors preserved the personal laws of the Romans.

And it is remarkable that an exactly similar precedent is to be found for the course adopted by the English Legislature at that very interesting period of history which was referred to in argument, though for a different purpose, by Mr. *Wallace.* When the northern nations successively overran the declining Roman empire, and conflicts of laws were consequently arising every day with each new race of conquerors and those coming under their command, our rude Gothic ancestors had sufficient political wisdom to establish, as a fundamental principle, the same doctrine which is to be found in our English legislation. Marculfus, as cited by von Savigny, 1 G. R. R. 127, has preserved a Charter of Justice which a Frank conqueror laid down for a provincial ruler, and which, in its broad comprehensive terms and intelligible principles, evinces that we have not learnt much in the language of legislation during the last twelve centuries. The Frank ordains as follows:—"*Et omnis populus ibidem commanentes, tam Franci, Romani, Burgundiones, quam reliquas nationes sub tuo regimine et gubernatione degant et moderentur, et eos recto tramite secundum legem et consuetudinem eorum regas.*"

I am clearly, therefore, of opinion, that the effect of the clause in the charter is not to adopt the text of the Koran as law, any further than it has been adopted in the laws and usages of the Mahomedans who came under our sway; and if any class of Mahomedans—Mahomedan dissenters, as they may be called—are found to be in possession of any usage which is otherwise valid as a legal custom, and which does not conflict with any express law of the English Government, they are just as much entitled to the protection of this clause as the most orthodox Sunníy who can come before the Court. It may be observed, that express authority for this view is to be found in the decisions of the Company's Courts in Bengal, in their exposition of the clause as to Gentoos; and those Courts have held, that where any custom has been clearly proved to exist, even in a single family, although at variance with the general Hindu law, such custom, if otherwise valid, is supportable. And in a case in this Presidency, in 2 *Bor.* 33, the text of the Koran, in a case of inheritance, was also set aside in favour of a different prevailing custom, on the ground that during the previous Brahmin Government the Mahomedan law had fallen into disuse, and had given way to the custom of the country (*a*).

1847.

KOJAHS and MEMONS' Case.

Ancient usage, not the text of Koran, must govern the succession amongst Mahomedans.

It should also be further observed, that these Mahomedan sectarians have lived chiefly in countries reigned over by Hindu princes, and I can have no doubts whatever on the evidence, and on what we know of the manner in which native Courts dispose of the controversies of their subjects, that if the present suit had been brought before the Rao of Cutch, or any of the Rajput Rajahs of Kattiwar, upon payment of the dues of office, the twenty-five per cent., or whatever the exaction might be, the decision would have been in conformity to that which is reverenced by all mankind, but by Hindus, perhaps, more than any other portion of mankind, —ancient usage. If this be the true exposition of the rule which would be meted out to these people in their own country, it would be a monstrous thing that an English Court

(*a*) So also in Central India, Hindus, who have been converted to Mahomedanism, perhaps forcibly, retain the greater part of Hindu observances. Thus in Caunpoor, a class called Neer Mussalmans, "wear the garb of the Hindus, and observe their fasts and religious observances, but their marriage ceremonies are after the manner of Mussalmans The mode of inheritance is according to the Shastrees, not the Koran." *Statistical Report of Caunpoor*, p. 102, *drawn up by Mr. Montgomery.*

1847.

Kojahs and Memons' Case.

of justice should be obliged to reverse such a time-honoured custom, and almost to revolutionise the internal economy of two whole casts, out of some supposed obligatory force in a text called Divine, which neither the Judge nor the parties to the suit believe in.

3. *Lex loci.*

3. But there is another view in which the question may be placed, and although it was not taken during the argument, its extent is so much wider and more important than any of the principles above discussed, that I am desirous to make a few remarks upon it. It was admitted on both sides at the Bar, that if the Memons and Kojahs could not support their custom as a valid Mahomedan custom, their successions must be governed either by the Koran, as if they were orthodox Mussalmans, or by the law of England, as the *lex loci.* I think that this latter conclusion is erroneous, although I admit that some decisions, in former years, of this Court, and even an act of the Legislative Council relating to the Parsís, would seem to demand it. But as the opinion of the Privy Council will very likely be taken in this case, it seems desirable to call the attention of their Lordships to this point.

European doctrine of *lex loci* peculiar to Christendom.

The doctrine of *lex loci* seems to be one of altogether modern growth, and peculiar to Christendom. The early Roman law did not recognise it, but administered their own municipal regulations to Roman citizens, and appointed a *prætor peregrinus* for strangers. I have before alluded to the intermixture of the Gothic nations with the Romans, and it is easy to see from thence how the *lex loci* arose. At first each nation had its own personal laws preserved to it; but when Lombards, Visigoths, Franks, and Romans became amalgamated into one mass, fighting in one field by each other's side, or struggling in the cities to achieve a common freedom, marrying and intermarrying in social life, and communicating at the same altar in religious rites, it is not wonderful that personal laws, among other national characteristics, should disappear, nor even that the laws of the conquering race should give way to the more comprehensive and refined code of their conquered subjects.

Thus was introduced, gradually, a common law, and at the

same time a common language, into those countries. But the nations of Europe have such a family character from this similarity of race, institutions, and religion, that the municipal laws of any one Christian country are, without any violence, applicable to every Christian stranger who comes within its jurisdiction; and consequently the manifest advantages which the doctrine of *lex loci* presents, has gained for it admission into the codes of modern Europe. But directly a Christian and non-Christian nation come in contact, the foundation of the doctrine of *lex loci* altogether disappears. Lord STOWELL, though without any local experience to guide him, observed this distinction with his usual profundity, and expressed it in a passage of more than ordinary beauty.

In the case of the *Indian Chief*, he said, "Wherever a mere factory is founded in the eastern parts of the world, European persons trading under the shelter and protection of those establishments, are conceived to take their national character from that association under which they live and carry on their commerce. It is a rule of the law of nations, applying peculiarly to those countries, and is different from what prevails ordinarily in Europe and the western parts of the world, in which men take their present national character, from the general character of the country in which they are resident; and this distinction arises from the nature and habit of the countries. In the western parts of the world, alien merchants mix in the society of the natives; access and intermixture are permitted, and they become incorporated almost to the full extent. But in the East, from the oldest times, an immiscible character has been kept up; foreigners are not admitted into the general body and mass of the society of the natives; they continue strangers and sojourners, as all their fathers were. *Doris amara suam non intermiscuit undam.*" (3 Rob. Adm. R. 29).

And not applicable in its whole extent to Asiatics.

By the comity of nations, therefore, as existing between princes of Christian and non-Christian faith, the *lex loci*, to its whole extent, is held not to apply to Europeans placing themselves under the government of the latter. But if this is the case as regards Christian aliens in a foreign state, there

1847.

Kojahs and Memon's Case.

can be no doubt that a similar comity requires a similar rule to be observed, where a Mussalman or Hindu seeks a domicile in a Christian country. How far the peculiar laws of such non-Christian aliens would be recognised it may not be very easy, nor is it necessary, to define beforehand. On each occasion it would afford matter for judicial discussion and determination when the question arose. But on very many questions, such as marriage, divorce, succession, and, possibly, adoption, there seems no reason to doubt that the proper law to be referred to for the decision of any controversy would not be the law of the Christian community, but the law and usage of the peculiar non-Christian class. That this was the opinion of the great jurist whom I last cited, is not left a matter of doubt, for he has stated it expressly in many of his judgments with respect both to Jews and that other singular oriental race, the Gypsies. (See 3 *Rob.* 32; *Ruding* v. *Smith*, 2 Hagg. Com. 384; *Lindo* v. *Belisario*, 1 Hagg. 216).

Examples.

Jews; Gypsies

The case of the Jews in Europe is, indeed, a case completely in point as to the extent of the *lex loci* over a race not professing the Christian faith. Unfortunately, from the smallness of their numbers in England, we gain but little assistance from our law books as to the mode in which a British Court of justice would dispose of their controversies, although, indeed, the principles laid down by Lord Stowell, when carried to their legitimate consequences, seem sufficient for all practical purposes. But we have ample information as to other European countries, and *Selden*, in his *Prolegomena* to the *Uxor Ebraica*, tells us, that throughout Europe this race has always had their own law administered to them in every case, "*ubi aut expressæ principum Christianorum sanctiones contrarium de eis non statuerint, aut mores adversi sanctionum vim sortiti, neutiquam involverint.*"

Selden, as to legal status of Jews in Europe.

Conclusion as to validity of custom.

The conclusion I draw is, that if a custom otherwise valid is found to prevail amongst a race of Eastern origin and non-Christian faith, a British Court of justice will give effect to it, if it does not conflict with any express act of the Legislature. And, as I have before shewn, that the succession to an inheritance is one of those subject-matters in which the English

1847.

KOJAH and MEMON'S Case.

Legislature has not thought it fit to speak by any general enactment, it follows that the particular custom of these Kojahs and Memon Cutchees ought to be supported.

On all the above grounds, I think that the attempt of these young women to disturb the course of succession which has prevailed among their ancestors for many hundred years has failed, and, as a price of an unsuccessful experiment, that their bills must be dismissed with costs, so far as the defendants seek to recover them.

DOE *d.* SACARAM SADASEWSETT *v.* LAXUMABAI AND OTHERS.

1844. July 14.

[*Coram* PERRY, J.]

THE title of the lessor of the plaintiff in this case depended on what is ordinarily called a Bengal mortgage.

The instrument in question, dated 26th of February, 1836, consisted of a money bond given by one Parshotam Wittoba, by Moroba Bhao, and Laxuman Sacaram, in the penal sum of Rs. 16,000, with a defeasance on the payment of Rs. 8000, and interest four years after the date of the bond, and after reciting that the obligors had borrowed the sum of Rs. 8000, to be repaid at certain dates, proceeded for the purpose of securing the repayment of the same, to transfer and assign over, by way of mortgage, the premises in question.

At the trial, it appeared that the premises in question belonged to an undivided Hindu family, of which Parshotam was the manager. That the mortgage bond was given as a security for sums of money borrowed for family purposes, and

The manager of a Hindu undivided family is entitled to dispose of the family estate for urgent wants affecting the family interests. Where, therefore, a conveyance was made by the manager of an undivided property, which all the members of the family who were adult executed, but there were infants who did not join, on its being shewn that the conveyance was made as a security for advances which have been expended on necessary family expenses, such as marriages and the thread ceremony, the conveyance was held valid, although it was not expressed on the face of the deed that the money was raised for family purposes.

1844.

Doe v. Laxumabai.

that out of the proceeds, the expenses of the funeral rites of Sacaram, the father of the defendants, had been defrayed, as also of the thread ceremony necessary to be performed in the case of Bramins, and of their marriages.

The defendants were the widow, and two of the sons of Sacaram, the latter of whom were infants at the time of the above conveyance, but which was executed by their brother Laxuman Sacaram.

Crawford, for the lessor of the plaintiff.

Holland, for the defendants, contended, that by Hindu law, a deed did not bind the infant members of an undivided family, unless the deed states on its face that the money was raised for family purposes. (1 *Strange's Hindu Law*, 177).

There was no evidence in this case that the mortgagee knew that the money was to be applied for family purposes; and the fact of all the adult members of the family joining in the conveyance, shews that the mortgagee was well aware that the interest of a member of an undivided family could not be transferred, without his joining in the conveyance.

Cur. adv. vult.

Perry, J.—In this case an action of ejectment has been brought to recover the possession of some lands and houses which appear to have belonged to an undivided Hindu family (*a*). The deed, upon which the lessors of the plaintiff found their title, is one of those instruments peculiar to this country, called Bengal mortgages, and which seem to be considered now, though after some doubt, as legal conveyances and part of the common assurances of the country. At all events, no question has been raised as to the validity of the instrument in this case, I am, therefore, at liberty to treat it as perfectly legal.

Powers of manager of a Hindu family over family estate.

The case, however, raises a question of peculiar interest to the Hindu community, namely, how far and under what forms the manager of an undivided family can dispose of the family

(*a*) As to undivided family, see *ante*, p. 42, note (*b*), and *post*, p. 133.

estate, and especially of the immoveable property, where there are infants who are entitled to a coparcenary interest.

It was but faintly disputed at the trial, and indeed it seems indisputable that there are certain cases in the Hindu law which authorizes the manager of an undivided family to dispose of the ancestral estate, notwithstanding the minor brothers who, from their age, would be incompetent to join in the conveyance. The Mitàcsharà, ch. 1, sect. 1, §§ 28, 29, both text and commentary, is express in this point, and a decision in Bombay in 1811, reported in 2 *Strange Hind. Law*, p. 282, proceeds expressly in conformity with it.

The cases allowing the disposal of family property comprise urgent wants affecting the whole family, and indispensable duties incumbent upon the family at large; and the lessors of the plaintiff put forth, as the ground work of their case, that the money which was lent by them, and for which they obtained the mortgage deed in question was borrowed for, and applied in discharge of, such indispensable duties touching the whole family.

The defence did not apply itself seriously to contradicting this view of the plaintiff's case, but relied on certain technical points, belonging to the nature of the action which the lessors of the plaintiff have adopted, and to the English rules of evidence having in view the shutting out of certain facts, and as I disposed of these at the time, giving the defendants leave to bring the objections forward again, if they should turn out to amount to more than I conceived at the time they were worth, there remained for me at the close of the trial scarcely any question of disputed fact to decide.

But as this case is apparently novel, and embraces considerations of great interest to an Indian commercial community, I will state shortly the facts as they were proved at the trial, with my conclusions upon them, and this will facilitate any further consideration being given to the case which may be thought desirable.

The Hindu undivided family in question descends from two brothers, Narron and Wittoba, who were living in 1802. Wittoba, though the youngest of the two, was the manager of

1844.

Doe v. Laxumabai.

the family, and was succeeded by his son Parshotam, who had continued in the management of the family property up to the present day. The other brother, Narron, is represented by his great grandson Luxamon, whose mother and infant brothers are the defendants in this suit.

The lessors of the plaintiff claim under a conveyance which was made to them in February, 1836, by Parshotam, by Moroba his nephew, (a grandson of Wittoba), and by Luxamon, and these it would seem were all the members of the family who were adult at the time of the transaction.

The mother of Luxamon now objects that, as her infant sons were equally entitled with Luxamon to a share in the property, the security is void from their not being parties thereto.

But the plaintiff has shewn, and I think most satisfactorily, that the money was borrowed by different members of the family, and was applied by them, and especially by Parshotam, in the discharge of indispensable family duties, in the burial of Sacaram the father of the infant defendants, in the marriage of the sons of Parshotam, and in the thread ceremony (*a*) of one of the infant defendants themselves; and all these appear most clearly from the Mitàcsharà, ch. 1, sect. 7, §§ 3, 4, to be charges upon the whole family estate.

It results, therefore, from the principle cited at the commencement, that the case has clearly arisen in which a member of an undivided Hindu family may dispose of an estate in which infants are concerned. It further appears, that Parshotam has fully maintained and supported all the members of this family, including the widow and the infant defendants, who required his assistance, and, therefore, not the slightest equitable consideration interposes in their behalf to defeat an instrument which, according to Hindu notions, was given expressly for their benefit and advancement.

Unless, therefore, there is something in the form of this deed which disables it from operating as a legal conveyance of the property, the verdict must be for the plaintiff. Very

(*a*) The thread ceremony, or investiture of the young Hindu with the sacred string, is one of the most important ceremonies in the life of the three higher casts.

little argument has been raised upon this point, and, therefore, I will say nothing upon it, except that, as at present advised, I see no reason why a Hindu, under the circumstances in this case, should not be able to make such a conveyance.

The verdict, therefore, will be for the plaintiff.

Holland subsequently obtained a rule *nisi* for a new trial, on the ground that the manager of an undivided family could not bind the rest by his bond, except it appeared on the bond that the money was raised for family purposes; citing another case, 2 *Str. Hind. Law*, 269, against which *Crawford* shewed cause, and *Dickinson* and *Holland* were heard in support.

SED PER CURIAM.

Rule discharged (*a*).

(*a*) See next case.

DOE *d.* NARRAYEN BHAU *v.* GANPAT HURRICHUND.

1849. September 11.

[*Coram* PERRY, C. J., and YARDLEY, J.]

Where a Hindu widow of one seised of a separate estate, made a deed of gift of the property to her daughter's son, who died in her lifetime, leaving a son, held on the death of the widow that the latter succeeded to the property in preference to the nephews of her husband, who had not given their assent to the gift by the widow.

On a point of Hindu succession, where there was a conflict between the authorities, and the Shastrees of the Sudr Adalut, on a reference to them, also differed; the Supreme Court decided the case, in conformity to what the English law, and the rule of natural succession would seem to dictate.

EJECTMENT for a house and premises in the island of Bombay.

In this case, it appeared that the two brothers of the Purvoe or Khetri cast were established, the one in Bombay, the other at Chowl, on the main land, and they were separated in estate. The Bombay brother having acquired by his own industry certain property, moveable and immoveable, died in 1823, leaving a widow and daughter, who was married and

1849.

DOE *v.* GANPAT.

had a son. The daughter died in 1833, and the widow, by a deed of gift, in 1839, assigned the property she took from her husband to her grandson, the daughter's son. This son died in 1843, leaving a son, (the defendant), and the widow died in 1848. On her death the question arose, whether the sons of the Chowl brother, or the great grandson of the Bombay brother were entitled to the property.

The pedigree will appear more clearly by the following sketch :—

Brothers.

A. — NARRAYEN BHAU, *lessor of plaintiff.*

B., *ob.* 1823.

- Widow, *ob.* 1848.
- Daughter, *ob.* 1833. — Son, *ob.* 1843. — GANPAT, *defendant.*

Rights of widow to her husband's estate, when divided from family.

Howard, for the lessor of plaintiff, contended, that the widow took the estate for life only, and that her gift to her grandson was void, for although the widow of a party seised of separate estate may, with the assent of the next heirs, make a gift of the property: the lessor of the plaintiff was the heir, and he had not assented. And he cited *Mayuk* and *M'Naghten* to this effect. He contended further, on the authority of a passage in 1 *Strange's Hindu Law*, 160, that the defendant could not be heir, as the succession in the descending line proceeds no further than the daughter's son, and that the son's son was too remote.

Conflict of Hindu law.

Dickinson, contrà, contended that the authority cited by Sir *T. Strange* was contradicted by the Mitàcsharà.

The Court, on this conflict of Hindu law, suggested that a case should be stated raising the point for the opinion of the Judges of the Sudr Adalut, and accordingly a reference was made, which elicited the following opinions :—

Shastree's first Answer.

1849.

DOE *v.* GANPAT.

Having perused the questions relating to the Hindu Law of inheritance put by the Judges of her Majesty's Supreme Court, and the several opinions already obtained from the Shastrees of the Zilla Courts, as referred for my opinion, I beg to submit the following answer,—

A Hindu Pandit's opinion on a disputed point of law.

It is not clear from the question, whether A. B., after receiving his share of the ancestral property, and otherwise formally separated, came to live in Bombay; or whether he was still a member of an undivided family, though living separate.

If, however, A. B. had (formally) separated, and he expended money from his own share; or if unseparated, while living in Bombay, he appropriated no portion of the undivided ancestral property, but with money acquired by his own industry, bought ground and built a house, and lived therein; in neither case can his brothers or kindred have any claim to it; it is exclusively his own, according to the texts of Yádnyawalkya and Manu, as quoted in the section of Daya Bhága (Partition of Heritage) in the books of Mitakshurà and others.

A. B. died in 1823, without male issue; and his widow, by right of inheritance, succeeded to his property, according to the texts above mentioned. In 1833, A. B.'s daughter died, leaving a son who would be A. B.'s heir in the absence of A. B.'s widow. A. B. s widow, therefore, executed a deed of gift in his favour, and he being her grandson by her daughter, the grant made to him from affection cannot be nullified, as stated by Yádnyawalkya in Mitakshurà and other works. The deed of gift was executed without the consent of the sons of A. B.'s brother, and without any intimation to them,—on which circumstances they found their claim to the house; but the declaration in the Shastra (*a*), that a widow has no right, without the consent of her husband's kindred, to bestow in gift any immoveable property, applies to improper gifts for dancing and diversion, and not to such gifts as are made to

(*a*) Shástras, in the plural, are the Scriptures of the Hindus, and when used generally mean all the works on law and religion considered by them to be sacred. The Shástris are the expounders of such works. See *Horace Wilson's Dict. ad voc.*

1849. — Doe v. Ganpat.

secure happiness in a future state, as mentioned in Mayook, p. 135, line 6, and also in Veermetroduga; and it is laid down in these books, after weighing opposite texts, that a woman is not subject to control in making a gift to secure happiness in another world.

Though the deed of gift has been executed without the consent of the sons of A. B.'s brother, this is not sufficient to invalidate it; because the injunction of the law, to take the consent of the kindred in the case of giving away immoveable property, is intended to impart that formality to the transactions which will leave no doubt as to whether the persons concerned in it belong to a divided or undivided family; when kindred are separate in interest, gifts, &c., made without their consent, are valid, according to Mitakshurà and other works on law.

The widow having given the house to her daughter's son under a deed of gift, she forfeited her proprietary right in it, and it became his; and when he died in 1843, his son, by right of inheritance, succeeded to it. Therefore, the son of A. B.'s daughter's son has, on the authority of Hindu law, the strongest title to the house. The texts in Sanskrit to support the above exposition are as follows.

Dated 12th June, 1849.

(Signed) Soorujram Wullubrham Shastree.

Translation of the Shastree's second Answer.

If heirs or brothers have not divided their ancestral property, or become separate, and if one of them die without male issue, his share in such undivided property, and in that acquired by his own exertions through the use of it, can be claimed under the right of inheritance by his (the deceased's) brother's, &c., according to the Mitakshurà, Mayook, &c., where they treat of the right of inheritance. Therefore, as regards the question, if A. B., being unseparated from C. D., die without male issue, his whole share in the undivided property can be claimed under the Hindu law of inheritance by the heirs of C. D., I am of this opinion from the text of Yadneavulkya, as quoted in the Mitakshurà regarding the right of inheritance.

I have perused the answers from the Zillah Shastrees; they are given upon the supposition that a separation had taken place. All of them seem to agree in the main point. As to the answer of the late acting Shastree of the Sudr Adalut, it assumes that a separation had taken place, and he gave it as his opinion, that if a person separate in interest die without male issue, his widow has no right to assign away in gift, or by mortgage or sale, his (the deceased husband's) immoveable property without the consent of his heirs, as laid down in the Shastras; and that, therefore, the grant of the house passed by the widow to her daughter's son ought to have borne the attestation of the kindred of her husband, without which it would be invalid, and that the daughter's son's son could not claim the house. This opinion is opposed to those of the Zillah Shastrees, and the one already given by me. Dated, 2nd July, 1849.

(Signed) SOORUJRAM WALLUBHRAM SHASTREE.

On the cause coming on again this day for argument,

Howard pointed out the groundlessness of the doubt which existed in the mind of the Shastrees as to the Bombay family being separate in estate, and contended, that as it was quite clear they made the title of the defendant depend entirely on the validity of the gift from the widow, they repudiated any title of the defendant as heir. But the gift of the widow was clearly not valid, because the consent of those persons who were proved to be heirs at the time of her death had not been given, although her grandson was heir at the time of the gift. And he cited *W. M'Naghten* (*a*), to shew that the period of the widow's death was that which determined who were the heirs whose assent was necessary.

SED PER CURIAM.—The opinion of the Shastree of the Sudr Adalut ought to prevail. The conclusion which English law and which natural reason would dictate was, that the great grandson of the acquirer of the property should inherit it in preference to the nephew; and it could only be

(*a*) Principles of Hindu Law, by Sir W. Macnaghten, Bart., 2 vols., 8vo, Calcutta, 1829.

1849.

Doe v. Ganpat.

on some strict rule of Hindu law that such natural succession should be interrupted. It was competent to the Court therefore, in the conflict of authority between the Shastrees, to give their adhesion to that view which seemed most consonant to reason and to Hindu feelings. The title of the defendant might be based on two grounds;—first, on the gift of the widow to his father, which the father, as heir apparent, assented to; secondly, on his own descent,—for the passage cited by *Sir T. Strange*, as to succession stopping with the daughter's son, seems not to have been corroborated by any decision, and the reason given altogether fails, as in fact the funeral cake (*a*) had been administered here by the defendant.

Judgment for Defendant.

(*a*) As to offering the funeral cake to the deceased, see *Crustnarao's case, post*, p. 151.

1850. June 27.

BHAI KILLABHAI,

(BY HIS NEXT FRIEND PURMANUNDASS),

v.

HURGOVIND DEWJEE AND OTHERS.

[*Coram* Perry, C. J.]

Contest between the next of kin of the husband and the executors of a Hindu widow for the management of an infant's estate.

The ordinary practice of sending a long inquiry into the Master's Office departed from, and the inquiry disposed of at one sitting by the Judge, on examination of witnesses in open Court.

Where an infant's estate amounted to Rs. 30,000, held that an expenditure of Rs. 50, a month was a proper allowance to the administrator, although it appeared that such sum included his own expenses.

The present case is an example of a numerous class which occur in Bombay, wherein a struggle arises between the relatives of a Hindu widow and of the deceased husband, as to the enjoyment of the property left by the latter. The facts are sufficiently fully stated in the following judgment:—

Perry, C. J.—In this case, which was argued before me yesterday, as the proceedings adopted were of a novel character, and by way of experiment, to obviate the very heavy expenditure which attends proceedings in the Master's Office, I have thought it better to put my judgment in writing. 1850.

BHAI KILLABHAI'S Case.

The facts which have given rise to the litigation are shortly as follows. One Rajaram, a small trader in Bombay, died about four years ago, leaving behind him property to the amount of Rs. 30,000, a wife, Gunga Vuhow, and some infant children, of whom Killabhai, the plaintiff, was the only son. By his will he left his property in terms apparently to his wife, but, according to Hindu law, and, in fact, according to the true construction of his language when all the terms of his will are taken together, to his wife for life only, and at her death to his son. The wife however, as is frequently the case in Hindu society, finding herself undisputed mistress of the property during her lifetime, assumed a disposing power over it after her death; and she framed a will, wherein, according to the methodical and useful practice observed by Hindus in such documents, she enumerated her property *seriatim*, and, bequeathing it very much as the Hindu law itself would have distributed the property, she constituted four parties, not relatives of her husband, executors.

But as the widow had only a life estate, and as, at her death, it descended entirely to the infant Killabhai, it is obvious that she had no power to make any disposition of the property; and the parties to whom the law assigns the administration of Rajaram's estate, during the infancy of Killabhai, are the next of kin of Rajaram.

Accordingly, an application was made to this Court that administration of the estate of Rajaram should be granted to such next of kin, *viz.*, to Hurgovind, the present defendant,— and to him were joined Virzbhurean, Ransordass, and Jamnadass Hurri, who had been appointed by Rajaram himself the managers for his widow.

Now, as the administration of an infant's estate gives considerable advantages to poor relatives—in the power over expenditure, in family importance, and in other respects, even where the most rigid and honest administration is observed, it is not to be wondered at that, in the state of facts I have described, a most active contest should take place between the executors of the widow and the next of kin of the husband

1850.

BHAI KILLABHAI'S Case.

for the prize in question. The next of kin opposed the will of Gunga Vuhow, and the bill of costs for one side only, as it transpired yesterday, amounted to no less than Rs. 1700 odd, although there was no regular suit, and the proceedings were what is called in England summary. The executors opposed the grant of administration to the next of kin,—the costs no doubt coming out of the widow's estate, which equally belonged to Killabhai; and for two or three years past nothing but litigation has been going on between them.

The Court, however, granted the administration to the next of kin, and one of the first steps taken by them was, to bring actions against two of the executors for monies owing by them to the estate, and which, after a trial in this Court, they recovered.

One of these actions was against Purmanundass, who has now instituted the present suit, as the next friend of Killabhai, against the administrators; and he charges them with being improper persons to administer the estate—from their poverty, from their undue expenditure of the income, and from other suspicious conduct; and he prays that the Court should take steps to secure the estate, which he suggests is in great danger of being, according to Hindu idiom, eaten up. On leave being granted to file this bill, the administrators come to the Court and deny, on affidavit, all the allegations that have been made against them, giving an account of the estate come to their hands, and averring that all the family and relatives are perfectly satisfied with the mode in which they perform their duties; and they represent this suit as a great hardship, and as certain to entail great expenditure upon the estate of the infant.

The ordinary practice on this state of facts would have been, to refer the case to the Master to inquire, first, whether the suit which has been instituted would be for the benefit of the infant, and, if so, secondly, whether Purmanundass would be a proper person to conduct it.

It is obvious from the facts which I have stated, that, whilst there is no dispute whatever as to the right to the property in question, whilst both parties represent that it is only the interest of the infant which they have in view, there is, in reality, great and imminent danger of the estate being swallowed up, not by either of the parties, but by the litigation they have resorted to.

And if the ordinary practice of the Court had been observed, and the reference had been made to the Master,—as the inquiries to be conducted before him would have involved the personal misconduct of the administrators on the one side, and the personal misconduct of the next friend Purmanundass on the other, the vicious procedure which unfortunately characterizes the Master's Office in all English Courts of equity, would have enabled dishonest or vindictive, or mutually exasperated suitors, to protract litigation thereby, as we occasionally observe it, at an expenditure of time and money much to the discredit of the Court, and to the detriment of the community.

The Court therefore, in pursuance of their determination to seize every opportunity to make the paths of justice accessible, willingly listened to a suggestion thrown out at the Bar, not to make the reference to the Master, but to conduct the inquiry themselves in open Court, and accordingly, as a matter of convenience, it was arranged that the inquiry should come on before me after the sittings for small causes yesterday.

The parties accordingly appeared by their counsel; the administrators were examined *vivâ voce;* other witnesses were called, and a very close judicial inquiry, lasting above three hours, was gone into.

The charges made against the administrators were fourfold:—

1. That they are in insolvent circumstances.
2. That, by their own accounts, they had made away with Rs. 7000.
3. That their outlay of Rs. 50 a month on the infant was unwarrantable.
4. That Jamnadass, one of the administrators, had been partner with the testator, and, therefore, that it was for the interest of the estate that the accounts should be taken at once.

But at the close of the argument I was fully satisfied, and

1850.

Bhai Killabhai's Case.

on reflection I am confirmed in my opinion, that no ground had been made out for the propriety of instituting this suit.

The managing administrator is poor, but not insolvent; and no charge whatever, nor any suspicious fact, has been made out against him. He left his employment at Tanna, where he earned from Rs. 100 to Rs. 150 a year, to manage the estate of his young relative in Bombay. And it is very probable that the Rs. 50 a month, expended in household expenses, have constituted the fund from which his *viaticum* has been wholly defrayed. But I see nothing wrong in this. The family consists of three females, the child, and a female servant; and he, as the nearest male relative invested with authority, is the proper person to be at the head of such establishment. It would be extremely harsh, I think, if a Court of justice should interpose to break up the arrangements of a Hindu family, merely because the head of it is not a man of fortune.

Next, he has accounted satisfactorily *primâ facie* for the administration of the Rs. 7000. The expenditure of Rs. 50 monthly for the maintenance of the infant, is, as it occurred to my learned Brother and myself at the hearing, quite suitable to his condition in life: and the partnership between Rajaram and Jamnadass seems only to have lasted for sixteen months; and during Gunga Vuhow's career no question ever appears to have been made, as if any inquiry whatever was necessary on the subject.

On the other hand, I am quite satisfied that Purmanundass has instituted this suit from mere personal motives, and without any of that *bona fides* which Lord Brougham so justly laid down as essential in a *prochein amy*. (*Nalder* v. *Hawkins*, 2 M. & K. 243).

I therefore think the suit ought to be dismissed.

But as the English practice opens a very wide door to the institution of suits on behalf of infants, and as the practice, which has occurred here for the first time, will be a very wholesome one for the imposition of checks on the undue administration of estates, I think that I ought to make no order as to costs.

WIDOW OF MACCUNDASS VALUBDASS

v.

GANPATRAO GOPINATH, DOWLUTRAO GOPINATH, BALCHRISHNA GOPINATH.

1850.
December 2.

[*Coram* PERRY, C. J., and YARDLEY, J.]

THIS was a rehearing of a suit for the partition of a landed estate belonging to three Hindu brothers. At the first hearing the Court pronounced a decree, which, for the reasons subsequently given, appeared to be untenable.

According to the new practice adopted in Bombay, by which equity suits are heard on *vivâ voce* evidence, a question arose whether a rehearing was a matter of course. This point was disposed of in the following judgment; and the important point in Hindu society, of the power of joint members of a Hindu family over the undivided property, will be found fully discussed.

The member of an undivided Hindu family cannot mortgage his share of the family property, except subject to the claims which the other members may have upon it in respect of family disbursements.

Where a Hindu family, on account of differences, agreed to divide the family property, except as to one portion; *Held*, that as to that portion they were to be considered an undivided family.

A Hindu, by will, directed that the family property bequeathed by him to his grandsons should never be sold: *Held*, that this was merely precatory, and did not operate as a strict settlement.

By Bombay equity practice, evidence is heard *vivâ voce*: *Held*, that a rehearing is still a matter of course, if no fresh evidence is required.

Decree worked by the Judge instead of the Master.

Jenkins, for complainant.

Howard and *Dickinson*, for defendant Dowlutrao.

Cur. adv. vult.

PERRY, C. J., now delivered judgment.—The complainant in this case is the widow of a money lender, who filed a bill in 1849 to compel the partition of a landed estate in Bombay

1850. MACCUNDASS v. GANPATRAO.

belonging to three brothers, two-thirds of which had been mortgaged to him by two of them. The case has been argued before us twice; and as it appears to the Court that a different decree should be pronounced to that which seemed correct at the first hearing, and more especially as some nice questions touching the power to charge undivided Hindu property have been discussed, it is necessary to state the facts with precision and in some detail.

But before I proceed to the case, I will notice a discussion that arose at the Bar on an important rule of practice. By the old equity rules, a party dissatisfied with a decree, who could obtain a certificate of counsel pledging his professional reputation that the cause was a proper one to be reheard, was able to obtain a rehearing as a matter of course. On the introduction of the common law practice of taking evidence *vivâ voce*, it was necessary to frame a new rule, in order to meet the case of dissatisfaction with the evidence—on the ground of surprise or perjury, and it was thought advisable to proceed in analogy to the common law, and not to allow a rehearing with fresh evidence, except upon good cause shewn. The question has now arisen as to the mode of proceeding where a party, dissatisfied with a decree, did not desire to call fresh evidence, but to present different conclusions arising out of the facts already in evidence, from those which the Court had arrived at. On the one side it was contended, that a rehearing was no longer of course; on the other, that the old rule remained in force except when fresh evidence was required.

Now, in the interesting experiment which is being conducted in this Court, of adapting the better parts of common law practice to equity proceedings, it has been the desire of the Judges not to lay down too many rules *à priori*, but to proceed gradually, with the benefit of practical experience on the new system at each step. The object being to combine the speed, comparative economy, and finality which characterize proceedings at common law, with the completeness of equity procedure, which enables the whole case of the parties to be brought forward and disposed of on its merits, it is

1850.

MACCUNDASS *v.* GANPATRAO.

obvious that, whilst every unnecessary step entailing delay and expense on the suitor should be abolished, no practice should be interfered with which tends to secure correct decision on the part of the Court. But the advantages of a rehearing of a complicated cause are very great. Sometimes by the fault of the Bar, sometimes by the fault of the Court, the discussion and decision at the first hearing proceed on points which are afterwards discovered to be collateral; and the true bearing of the case is occasionally not made patent until after a determination has been arrived at. I think it is probable that, by the introduction of *vivâ voce* evidence, this evil will increase, and that, in the ardor of a *nisi prius* discussion on disputed facts and the trustworthiness of witnesses, the attention of both Bench and Bar will occasionally be directed too exclusively to the points in immediate contest, in neglect of more important portions of the case; and it has occurred to me, that it may possibly be found desirable, at the first hearing of a complicated cause, where witnesses are to be examined, to confine the attention of the Court to the facts only in dispute, and when these have been decided upon, the case is ripe for coming on at a subsequent day with all the evidence belonging to it. It is clear, however, that the value of a rehearing is not diminished by the introduction of the new equity rules. And Rule 4 of September, 1849, seems accurately to provide that no change shall be made in the existing practice, except when it is desired to bring forward fresh evidence. It is a matter for consideration, whether, instead of the long, expensive, and unnecessary petition, which is now required for a rehearing, it should not be competent to the parties to obtain it as a matter of course, by a hand motion, accompanied by the certificate of counsel, and, possibly, a statement of the grounds on which the decree is impeached, as in the case of an award.

Practice, and advantages, of rehearing a cause.

Suggestion as, to precedence where evidence in equity suit is taken *vivâ voce*.

The original bill in this suit was filed by Maccundass Valubdass on the 1st May, 1849, and the general scope of it is as follows: One Súndar Bawajee, who died in 1830, left all his property to his three grandsons, Dowlutrao, Ganpat, and Balchrishna, cutting off his son Gopinath with a legacy

1850.

MACCUNDASS v. GANPATRAO.

Dealings by Hindu family, partly divided partly not.

of Rs. 5000, and enjoining his grandsons to live as an undivided family, with an imprecation upon them of a most severe Hindu curse—the curse of parricide committed at Benares,—if they allowed the wife of Gopinath to meddle with the produce of the immoveable estate. The three brothers, however, not living in concord, determined upon a partition of the estate, and entered into an agreement for this purpose on the 19th of February, 1838. But as they found it impossible to divide the real estate exactly, they agreed that the family house and premises should be retained for their joint residence and property, and that certain other property, dedicated to religious purposes, should also be held by them in common. The remainder of the property, consisting of houses and land, was valued by them at Rs. 40,000, and, estimating that the debts and legacies due from the inheritance amounted to Rs. 10,000, they agreed that the whole of this property should be made over to Ganpatrao, who should take upon himself the payment of the debts, and who should pay to each of his brothers Rs. 10,000.

It further appeared, that jewels had been pledged to secure the debts due from the inheritance, and Ganpat bound himself to redeem these jewels, and to make over one-third of them to each of his brothers. It was also specified that all the rents and profits to be derived from the remaining undivided property should be deposited in a common chest, and should only be liable to the charges on that property.

In 1843 Ganpat mortgaged his one-third share of the family dwelling-house to Maccuudass for Rs. 5100; and on the 22nd of March, 1843, having paid off a portion of that money, and borrowed more, he granted a fresh mortgage for Rs. 3600, which sum included all that was then owing to Maccundass.

On the 31st May, 1847, he granted a new mortgage for Rs. 10,000, on two-thirds of the property, namely, his own third, and his brother Balchrishna's; and Maccundass succeeded in procuring from both these brothers, at this period, several instruments of conveyance to strengthen his title.

On these facts the complainant prayed that, for the payment of the Rs. 10,000, and interest due on the last mortgage, the

1850.

MACCUNDASS v. GANPATRAO.

mortgaged premises should be sold, and his charge paid out of the proceeds.

The principal defendant was the remaining brother Dowlutrao, who, at the first hearing, relied upon several defences for dismissing the complainant's bill. First of all he shewed that, prior to the second mortgage of March, 1843, *viz.*, on the 7th of February, 1843, Ganpat filed a bill against his two brothers to enforce the agreement of 1838, and that he, Dowlutrao, had filed a cross bill, which suit proceeded to a hearing, and that finally, by consent, an award had been made, shewing that Rs. 12,674 was due from the two brothers to Dowlutrao. It was contended, that this suit operated as *lis pendens* to bar any mortgage of Ganpat's which might affect prejudicially the claim of Dowlutrao. But we did not think that a suit instituted by Ganpat himself, and which he might have dismissed at any time, could be considered to operate as *lis pendens* in preventing him from disposing of his own share.

Lis pendens.

It was then strongly argued, that a passage in the testator's will operated as a strict settlement of the family house, and disenabled the sons from mortgaging or disposing of the same. But as the artificial right in a testator to tie up property for generations after his death is novel in Hindu law, and has not been introduced by English decisions, we stoutly resisted these views.

Power of Hindus to create a strict entail.

It was contended, finally, that Dowlutrao was a prior mortgagee from Ganpat by virtue of a Mahratta document, dated the 12th of November, 1838; but this claim was also disallowed, as it appeared to us, upon the evidence, that this document had been lying dormant, not having been brought forward in the previous litigation between the parties, and, therefore, was not entitled to the character of a valid mortgage.

These views of the Court entitled the complainant to the relief she sought.

But on the further argument which has been addressed to us, in which the case has been much more fully gone into, it has been contended that, even supposing all the above views are sound, Ganpatrow could not mortgage his share of the

1850.

MACCUNDASS v. GANPATRAO.

A Hindu brother can only mortgage his undivided share, subject to the claims of his family on the inheritance.

undivided estate except subject to the claims of his brother on the inheritance. We think this is undoubtedly sound law with respect to pure undivided property; the English law distinctly recognises, in cases of partition, the claims of the party in possession for monies expended on the premises as a *quasi* lien; *Swan* v. *Price* (8 Price); and the Hindu law, according to Sir *T. Strange*, only makes partition on "accounts being previously settled, and debts and other charges provided for." (Vol. 1, p. 199).

It is contended, however, that this family has become a divided family by the agreement of 1838, under which the greater part of the property has been divided, and that whatever claims Dowlutrao may have on his brothers, except in respect of monies laid out on the family house, they are mere personal claims against them individually, and constitute no charge on the undivided estate.

On investigating the facts we think this argument does not hold. It appears that the agreement has never been fully carried out, and that Dowlutrao has been compelled to pay legacies for which the inheritance was liable, and otherwise he has not received the benefits which he was entitled to under the agreement. As then Ganpat could not compel a partition in this Court against Dowlutrao, without recognising all the equitable charges against the inheritance possessed by the latter, so neither could he confer on Maccundass a better or larger title than he himself possessed. And we feel no embarassment in coming to this conclusion, for the case is not like one of those where a party has been induced to part with his money, on the security of property with all the *indicia* of title being handed over to him. The money lender in this case has consented to lend his money on a mere equitable title. He bases his case on the agreement of 1838, by which he had full notice that Ganpatrao had duties to discharge with respect to the inheritance, and it was matter of the most obvious and ordinary prudence for him, whilst dealing with a Hindu brother for a share of undivided property, to inquire whether the other brothers had any claim against the inheritance.

1850.

MACCUNDASS *v.* GANPATRAO.

It now remains to discuss the form of the decree. The defendant Dowlutrao being entitled, according to the above views, to charge in account all his *bonâ fide* charges in respect of the inheritance, there would be probably little difficulty in pronouncing a final decree if the complainant is to be deemed bound by the proceedings in the suit of Ganpatrao against his brothers; for an account has been there taken by a Hindu arbitrator, to which all three brothers have assented.

There seems much valid argument for contending that Maccundass should be deemed so bound; but the case has not been sufficiently argued on this point to warrant us in coming to a decision upon it. Still, if an account is to be taken afresh, such an opening would be given to additional and expensive litigation, should the case be sent before the Master, that the Court would willingly exert itself to discover a speedier termination. I have before stated from this Bench, that I think it is the duty of the Court to recur to the ancient practice of the Court of Chancery, (see *Wyatt's Pr. Reg.* 360), and work their own decrees whenever they have time so to do, and it is only a diffidence of my own competency in matters of account that has withheld me on many occasions from making the offer.

Recurrence to ancient practise of Judge taking accounts.

In this case, however, I think it is so probable, that a single day's sitting before a Judge in Chambers will terminate the litigation between the parties, that I am quite willing to undertake the task directly these sittings are closed (*a*).

(*a*) The case accordingly came on in Chambers before PERRY, C. J., and on the award of the arbitrator being tendered as evidence by Dowlutrao, it was objected to by the counsel for complainant as *res inter alios;* it was admitted, however, as *primâ facie* evidence of the state of the family accounts, with liberty to the complainant to impeach it for error or fraud. As she was unable to bring any objections on either of these grounds, the effect of the award was conclusive, and the inquiry terminated, as predicted, with one sitting.

1851.
January 29.

CRASTNARAO WASSADEWJI,
(BY HIS NEXT FRIEND),
v.
RAGHUNATH HARICHANDARJI AND ANOTHER.

[*Coram* PERRY, C. J., and YARDLEY, J.]

Spiritual and worldly motives, which lead to the adoption of a son by childless Hindus, described.
Question as to the validity of an adoption.
Discussion as to the acts which constitute misconduct on the part of executors so as to justify the appointment of a receiver.
Inquiries under a decree taken by the Court instead of the Master.

THIS was a suit, in which the validity of an adoption by a Hindu widow was brought in question.

The conduct of the executors, in dealing with the estate for their (alleged) own purposes, was also brought before the Court.

The facts and arguments appear sufficiently stated in the judgment.

Cur. adv. vult.

PERRY, C. J.—This is a bill praying for an account from the executors of Raghunath Dadaji of the estate come to their hands of one Wassadew Wittaji, and for a receiver on account of their alleged misconduct, and praying also for certain inquiries with respect to litigation said to have been vexatiously and wrongfully conducted by the executors, by which the estate has been much diminished. On the argument before us last week, the main question discussed at the Bar respected the validity of the adoption of the infant plaintiff Crastnarao as the son of Wassadeo; and as this discussion involved a consideration of one of the most important rites of Hindu social life, and as the estate was said to be considerable (ten laks of rupees in the statement of the bill, though this is probably the exaggerated language of a claimant out of possession), the arguments at the Bar necessarily ran to great length.

1851.

CRASTNA-RAO'S Case.

Importance of a son to a Hindu.

The importance attributed to a son, whether natural or adopted, according to the Hindu system, for procuring the happiness of the father in a future state, is well known, and is clearly laid down in the Hindu law books. Such beatitude depends, according to the authorities cited by Sir *Thomas Strange*, "on the performance of the father's obsequies and the payment of his debts by a son, as the means of redeeming him from an instant place of suffering after death. The dread is of a place called Pút, a place of horror, to which the manes of the childless are supposed to be doomed, there to be tormented with hunger and thirst, for want of those oblations of food and libations of water, at prescribed periods, which it is the pious and indeed indispensable duty of a son (*puttra*) to offer." In addition to these spiritual motives which impel a childless Hindu to adopt a son, we may observe also the operation of a more secular feeling, very familiar to us in Europe, namely, the desire to preserve and perpetuate the name of one who has possessed a notable position in life. Under the influence of motives such as these, Wassadeo Wittaji expressed a strong desire in his will that a son should be adopted to him; and as we find it indisputably proved that the widow did in fact solemnly adopt the infant plaintiff, in the presence of a great many Bramins, Purvoes, and relatives; that all the more important ceremonies were observed,—the Ganputty Púja, or worship of the god Ganput, the Púja Wachan, or reverence to the Ganges, the Hóm, or sacrifice of fire,—we were inclined to think that even if other observances had been disregarded, still, the essence of the ceremony having been adhered to, the adoption was good for every legal purpose, "according to the maxim of the civil law, prevailing, perhaps, in no code more than in that of the Hindus,—*factum valet, quod fieri non debuit*," (1 Str. 75). And see a very similar case to the present, which was decided at this Presidency, after much discussion, in 1826; *Bhasker Buchajee* v. *Warroo Ragornath*, (1 Morley's Digest, 25). But we were also strongly disposed to think, on the evidence before us, that even in point of form the ceremonial was unimpeachable. As the documentary evidence, however, was very voluminous, and in parts con-

Ceremonials observed on Hindu adoptions.

1851.

CRASTNA-RAO'S Case.

flicting, we thought it right to go through it all carefully a second time, before pronouncing our decree.

The principal facts undisputed in this case are as follows:—One Wittoba Canoba, who was of the Purbhoo cast, and apparently a man of much wealth, adopted one Wassadeo, and died. This Wassadeo Wittoba was also childless, and by his will, which he executed a few days before his death, he expressed himself as follows:—

Hindu will directing adoption.

"I hereby direct that a male child, either from my own family, or others, may be adopted as my son, to continue my and my father's name, in order to carry the wish of my late father into execution; and such child is to be chosen by my executors, and not by any other person whatever; and to such adopted son I hereby will and bequeath all my wealth, after payment of the legacies hereinafter mentioned.

"I hereby further direct, that if my executors refuse to adopt a son for me, in such case I authorize and empower my wife Luxamee to adopt a child from my own family, or others, under the consent and discretion of four respectable persons of the Purvoe cast therein named, *viz.*: Luxamond Hurrichunderjee, Gunpatrow Jadowji, Wassoden Wiswanathji, and Wassodeo Cannoba, who are empowered hereby to select a male child and adopt him to be my son, provided my executor refuses to do so himself, and such child is to be brought up under the care and instruction of Ragoonath Dadojee, who I appoint as the guardian of that child; and to such child I hereby give and bequeath all my property, both moveable and immoveable, which property is to be given by my executors to the charge of such adopted child when he arrives at the age of twenty-one years, and until then it shall remain in the possession of my executor, who is authorized to defray such expense therefrom as may be required to bring up the child, and to perform all ceremonies provided for by the Hindu religion in a suitable manner."

The will then contained a bequest of the whole residue of his property to Ragoonath Dadojee in the event of all efforts failing to procure a son in adoption, and continued as follows:—

1851.

CRASTNA-RAO's Case.

"I further direct, that should a son be adopted as I have above directed, and I hope there will be one, Rs. 40,000 be given to my wife as her own property, to be placed under some secure hands, to run at interest, and to be enjoyed and disposed by her pleasure, in addition to the jewels which I have bestowed upon her, and which I bequeath her.

"I further direct, that my wife shall remain in my dwelling-house as if it were her own property, and also enjoy the benefit and profit accruing from my Cocoanut ort in Girgaum during her lifetime, and after her death I give and bequeath to my adopted son both the house and ort (*a*) as part of my property.

"I further direct, that my wife shall be provided with the necessaries of life in a respectable manner by Ragoonath Dadajee and the adopted son, if one be adopted, from my estate should she behave well and remain with them in one house, otherwise she may maintain herself with the interest from the legacy of Rs. 40,000."

Interests of relatives to prevent adoption.

He then bequeathed many legacies, and amongst them a legacy of Rs. 1,50,000 to Ragoonath Dadajee, whom he constituted his sole executor.

Wassadeo Wittaji died in December, 1837, and Ragunath, the executor, after much litigation with the widow Luxamee, proved the will in the Supreme Court. Ragunath, it seems, was living in the house of Wassadeo at the time of the death of the latter, and disputes immediately arising between him and the widow respecting the succession to the property left by Wassadeo, the widow quitted the house of her deceased husband sixteen or seventeen days after the death, and left Ragunath in possession. The disputes between these two continued to rage for some years, and much money having been spent in litigation on the will, in August, 1841, Ragunath sent one Pandurung Dadajee to the widow to see if a compromise could not be effected; she, on her part, employed one Harichund Narronjee, who appears to have been a lawyer's clerk, and who is now the managing clerk of the defendant's attorney, and through their intervention, and that of another

(*a*) The local word for an inclosure or garden, derived, no doubt, from the Portuguese word *Horta*.

1851.

CRASTNARAO'S Case.

Litigation between widow and executor.

person named Anundtraô Vencají, a compromise between the widow and the executor was effected. The widow withdrew her petition of appeal to the Privy Council in August, 1841, and went back to reside in the family house of her late husband, then in the occupation of Ragonath, and it also does not seem to be disputed that she took with her the child Crastnarao, whom she afterwards adopted. She continued to live with Ragonath for some months, probably till December, 1841, when she left him to reside with her own relations.

In the month of August, 1842, the widow adopted the infant plaintiff, with the ceremonies above described, in a house of her late husband's, but which was not the family house occupied by Ragonath, and neither Ragonath, nor any one of the four leading members of the Purbhoo cast mentioned in Wassadeo's will, was present. In the December following Luchshumibae filed a bill against Ragonath for her legacy of Rs. 40,000, and for her jewels; and in the same month Ragonath made his will, by which he willed away the whole of Wassadeo's property to his own children in case no adoption should be made.

This litigation between Luxumi and Ragonath was referred to an eminent member of the Purbhoo cast, Luxuman Harichunderjí, better known perhaps under his familiar name of Bhaú Russel, and who was the leading member of the cast selected by Wassadeo in his will. Before this arbitrator the question of the validity of the adoption by the widow was solemnly raised, the inquiry appears to have extended over more than three years; thirty witnesses, Shastries and Pundits, were examined, and the arbitrator finally decided that the plaintiff Crastnarao had been *duly adopted*, and he awarded specifically the sums due to the widow.

Ragonath died before the award was made, *viz.*, in October, 1843, and he appointed, by his will, the present defendants as executors.

The defendants now allege, in answer to the claims of the adopted son of Wassadeo, that the estate of Wassadeo has been fully administered, and without broadly resting their defence on the alleged invalidity of the adoption, the point having been already decided against them by a competent authority,

1851.

CRASTNARAO'S Case.

they limit themselves to stating facts which they contend shew that the adoption was void in law, and, therefore, that the plaintiff has no title whereupon to sue them for an account. This mode of defence, by which an obstacle is merely, as it were, brought into Court, and prominently pointed out to attention, without being pleaded as a bar, is probably resorted to, in order to avoid the objection that the point as to *them* was *res judicata*.

The defendants contend, that by the terms of Wassadeo's will, it was indispensably necessary to the validity of an adoption, either that the executor Ragonath should select a child for the widow to adopt, or that he should expressly refuse to do so, in which case the selection would fall on other parties; and they allege that Ragonath never did assent to the infant plaintiff being adopted, or refuse generally to make any selection.

The plaintiff contends, that it clearly appears, by the evidence, that Ragonath did assent to the adoption made by the widow.

The widow wishing to adopt, and the executor to resist an adoption, a compromise occurs.

It is evident, from the facts previously stated, that the assent, or dissent (whichever it was) of Ragonath to the adoption, must have occurred about August, 1841, when the compromise between himself and the widow took place. Now the plaintiff produces a pregnant piece of evidence as to the terms of this compromise, in the shape of an affidavit which, though not sworn, was assented to, as indicated by their indorsement, in December, 1843, by the three parties who effected the compromise, *viz.*, Pandurung, Harichund, and Anundtraô, and which clearly shews that the principal inducement to the widow to listen to the compromise was Ragonath's consent to her adopting the boy Crastnarao, who was his own grandson. This evidence is confirmed by a number of small circumstances, by the mother of the child as well as the father attending at the negotiation between Ragonath and Luxumibai, by the child being from that period given up by its own natural parents, by its going to reside with the widow in Ragonath's house, by Ragonath taking upon himself the payment of its schooling in lieu of its natural father, but still more from the inherent proba-

1851.

CRASTNA-RAO'S Case.

bilities of the case as to how a woman placed like Luxumibai would act when under the guidance of a skilful lawyer's clerk.

If a Hindu child is adopted, he ceases to be (in law) the son of his natural father.

To appreciate this point it is necessary to pay close attention to the relations between Ragonath and Wassadeo, and to the special character of the latter's will, as affecting the interests of Ragonath and Luxumibai. It was scarcely noticed at the Bar that Ragonath was the father of Wassadeo, and although, by Hindu law, when Ragonath gave over his son to be adopted by Wittoba, the legal relation of father and son entirely ceased between himself and Wassadeo, it clearly appears that the ties of Nature were more powerful than those of law, and Ragonath continued to be in the closest connection with his former son. He lived with Wassadeo, and the paternal influence in the long will, which Wassadeo executed three days before he died, is very perceptible. By this will, Wassadeo leaves to Ragonath who, in law, was a mere stranger, Rs. 1,50,000, and he gives to him the power of adopting a child. He appears to have considerable fears that there will be difficulties in obtaining an adoption, and nevertheless he constitutes Ragonath the residuary legatee of all his wealth in case no adoption should be made. We may see, therefore, by the contents of this will, that the widow was not undertaking a desperate litigation when she opposed a document that not only disinherited herself, but also savored so strongly of undue influence.

Motives of each party analyzed.

The interest created in Ragonath, under the will, was first, to set up the will and so obtain the large legacy bequeathed to him by Wassadeo, second, to stave off the adoption by all possible means so as to secure the residue of the fortune for himself. The interest of the widow, if she could not set aside the will, was, to obtain the adoption of a son to her deceased husband and herself as speedily as possible, not only from the potent spiritual motives mentioned above, but also because she thereby became immediately entitled to the legacy of Rs. 40,000, and to all the advantages of position which accrue to the mother of a well endowed infant heir.

Compromise effected by lawyer's clerk.

It was under these circumstances that the parties met to effect a compromise in 1841, and when we see that this attorney's clerk was the adviser of the widow throughout, it is

1851.

CRASTNA-RAO'S Case.

impossible to doubt that the leading interest of the widow was prominently put forward and insisted upon.

Now what have we to oppose this chain of facts, and the intrinsic probability of the plaintiff's story? We have, first of all, this same attorney's clerk coming forward in 1850 to swear that Ragonath did not consent to, but dissented from, the adoption in 1841; this Hurrichund Narranjee, who, being taunted with having gone round to the other side, denies that he is assisting the defendants, *otherwise* than as the clerk to the defendants' attorney! This evidence is contradicted by Anundtraô, and also by the statements which Harichund evidently either dictated or assented to in 1843, and which it is clear he also repeated before the arbitrator in 1845-6. We have next the statements of Ragonath in 1843, that he did not assent to the adoption, at the time that he is making a will leaving all Wassadeo's fortune to his own son. And, lastly, we have the statement of the arbitrator, Bhaú Russel, in 1850, that he decided on the adoption of the plaintiff, as being partly in accordance with the will, but partly not so; of which evidence it is sufficient to state, that we very much prefer his solemn decision in 1846, after hearing thirty Pundits and Shastries, and all the witnesses available, that the plaintiff was "duly adopted in pursuance of the directions in that behalf contained in the will." On the whole, we think it is abundantly clear, either that Ragonath expressly assented to the adoption of the plaintiff, or that he made the widow believe he assented thereto, which for the validity of the adoption we consider completely equivalent. His subsequent statements of dissent are so clearly motived by the desire to leave the property to his own son, that they may be dismissed without further notice.

Evidence of lawyer's clerk, who had changed sides, sifted.

The validity of the adoption being therefore clear, the question arises as to the form of the decree.

The plaintiff, among other things, asks for a receiver, and very strong grounds exist for thinking that the demand is proper. The first broad fact is, that the testator, who died so long back as 1837, has been thwarted, so far as lay in the power of Ragonath and the present defendants, in nearly all his wishes. The litigation raised by the present defendants in denying the plaintiff's title is in itself strong evidence of

Misconduct of executors.

1851.

CRASTNA-RAO'S Case.

misconduct; for, as amongst Hindus, what could be a more solemn or deliberate decision of the question than that which was delivered by the Judge of their own religion and cast selected by themselves? Second, the numerous suits which the defendants have defended unsuccessfully, in attempting to resist compliance with the will, give the Court reason to suspect a wrongful waste of the testator's estate. Lastly, there is evidence in the cause, which does not seem to be contradicted, that one of the defendants has applied to his own purposes a large sum of money belonging to the estate.

Still it may be said that this question has not been discussed sufficiently fully at the Bar to warrant the Court in pronouncing decisively that the defendants have been guilty of misconduct, and that the further inquiries which have been prayed must be first gone into.

The plaintiff contends that the defendants ought not to be allowed to charge against the estate the costs of defending an action and various suits which had been brought against them; and an inquiry as to the grounds on which the defendants did enter into these defences is certainly the due of the plaintiff; for, *primâ facie*, the motives of the defendants in defending the four suits and one action are open to grave suspicion. Still the inquiry as to each of these suits must necessarily be very minute, and the discussion, if conducted in the Master's Office, even at the new and accelerated rate of procedure, may be made most harassing and protracted by defendants who desire, above all things, to postpone the fatal day of reckoning.

Harassing procedure of Master's Office.

This Court has thrown out, on several occasions, their willingness to aid suitors on inquiries of this nature. Unlike the Courts of equity in England, the Judges here have ample time to conduct a judicial inquiry without a reference, and they have also the will to do so; it lies, therefore, with suitors who seek to obtain a speedy termination of their suit to act upon the present intimation. And as the inquiries now asked for are eminently fit for being conducted before a single Judge, I will, if the plaintiff desires it, take the inquiries in person, and adjourn the cause for that purpose to some day after the present sittings. If, on the other hand, the suitor thinks it more to his interest to go to the Master's Office, the plaintiff may take a reference as to the various points urged in his prayer (*a*).

1851.

CRASTNA-RAO'S Case.

(*a*) The inquiry accordingly came on in Chambers before PERRY, C. J., and at the first hearing application was made for an order on Ragonath to pay Rs. 50,000, which was admitted by his schedules, into Court: the order was opposed, but made, and it had the effect of stopping any further proceedings in the suit; for it turned out that Ragonath was insolvent, and he soon after applied for the benefit of the Insolvent Act; when it appeared that he had lent upwards of 10,000*l.* of the infant's money to a Maratha Sirdar, or nobleman in the Deccan, and, at the time of writing this note (May, 1852), it appears still uncertain whether there is any Court in the Honorable Company's territories in which this claim against the Sirdar can be enforced.

A. B. COLLETT *v.* HUBBARD AND CURSETJI MERWANJI PATEL (*a*).

1851.

February 18.

PROCEDURE IN MASTER'S OFFICE.

[*Coram* PERRY, C. J., and YARDLEY, J.]

Power afforded by vicious procedure in Master's Office for hostile litigants to ruin each other.

When an inquiry between partners had been proceeding for two years and a half in the Master's Office, and the warrants alone had cost 800*l.*, but not a single step had been made towards deciding the suit, the Court took upon itself the inquiry, and terminated the litigation in two or three meetings (*b*).

A BILL had been filed in this case by the plaintiff under the following circumstances.

In 1844-5, a partnership had been entered into between Hubbard and Collett to carry on business as merchants, and especially in connection with the firm of Hubbard and Co. in London, one of the members of which firm was father of the Hubbard in Bombay. The other defendant, Cursetji, was to

(*a*) This case is inserted here from its connection with the three preceding cases, in respect to inquiries in the Master's Office.

(*b*) See the two preceding cases.

1851.

COLLETT v. HUBBARD.

be the broker of the firm, and, according to the custom of Bombay was to supply cash for purchases at 9*l.* per cent. interest, neither Collett nor Hubbard having any capital of their own.

Soon after the deed of partnership was entered into, Collett, in order to push the business of the firm, went in April, 1845, to England, and there entered into disputes with the London firm of Hubbard and Co., whom he accused of defrauding the firm of Hubbard and Collett in Bombay by various overpriced consignments and otherwise.

On his return to Bombay in November, 1846, it appeared that the firm of Hubbard and Collett was in difficulties, and the defendant Cursetji claimed of Collett Rs. 60,000, for his share of the advances made to the firm.

Hubbard and Cursetji, in the mean time, had got into difficulties with the Government as to the supply of coals, and on being indicted for fraud in September, 1847, they were sentenced to two years' imprisonment.

Before the criminal trial took place, Collett filed his bill against Cursetji to restrain him from bringing his action at law, and requiring an account of the partnership dealings in the firm of Hubbard and Collett, alleging frauds on the part of Hubbard and Cursetji in order to cheat himself, Collett.

The answer imputed to Collett an attempt to wipe out the debt due by him to Cursetji by making use of the difficulties into which Cursetji had fallen in other transactions; and it was suggested that the criminal charge had been brought against Cursetji through information supplied by Collett.

February 18, 1851.

A decree having been pronounced for the usual account on February 3rd, 1848, a motion was this day made to the Court, that one of the Judges would take the inquiry out of the Master's Office and conduct it either in Court or in person.

The affidavits on which the motion was made stated that in pursuance of the decree the defendant Cursetji brought in his accounts in June, 1848, but that being at the time of the decree and up to October, 1849, confined in gaol, he was not able to attend to his interests with effect; and that on getting out of gaol he made every effort to get his account taken, but was met with every species of frivolous opposition on the part of the plaintiff Collett, who raised all kinds of frivolous objections, and that he was unable to get a decision from the Master on any one point that had been raised before him, up to the date of the affidavit (January 21st, 1851), although no fewer than three hundred and twenty warrants had been taken out, "the costs alone of issuing and attending which amounted to Rs. 8000, or thereabouts."

The affidavits in answer denied that the Master was in anywise to blame for not having decided on the items brought before him, and imputed to Cursetji fraud and concealment in withholding the information necessary for the account.

Howard, on these facts, urged on the Court the cruel injustice that the defendant Cursetji was undergoing, and suggested that if one of the Judges would take the inquiry, the whole litigation would probably be terminated at three sittings.

Dickinson, contrà, opposed the application, and contended that such an inquiry could only be taken fitly before the Master, and the fault lay wholly with the defendant Cursetji.

The Court held that it was their duty to afford the relief prayed. Without seeking to ascertain where the blame lay, it was not denied that the inquiry had been going on for more than two years and a half in the Master's Office, that the warrants for attendance alone had cost 800*l*., and *that not a single step towards progress in the cause had been made.* Under these circumstances, if the Court could render any assistance by taking the inquiry from the Master's Office, it would willingly do so.

It was arranged that the inquiry should come on before the Chief Justice in Chambers after the sittings were concluded.

At the end of the first sitting, which lasted two hours, and at which much hostile feeling was displayed, charges of incrimination and recrimination being freely indulged in, it was plainly apparent, that whatever Cursetji's claim might ultimately turn out to amount to against Collett, the latter was in

1851.

COLLETT *v.* HUBBARD.

no condition to pay more than a very small sum, being a man avowedly without capital; it was also clear, that as Collett was entitled to an account of the partnership transactions, he was able to harass his opponent by a very protracted inquiry if the accounts should be gone into; and it was also sufficiently manifest, that at the end of the inquiry a considerable balance would be found due to Cursetji.

On these facts appearing, the Chief Justice threw out that it would be for the interest of both parties to terminate the litigation by Cursetji agreeing to accept a small sum, such as Collett could afford to pay, and by the latter waiving the account. If this arrangement were not acceded to, then it would be the duty of the Chief Justice to take the account, and he would sit *de die in diem* for that purpose till it was concluded. The parties separated to consider the proposal.

At the second meeting the compromise was assented to, and after two or three meetings, at which some subsidiary points were discussed and settled, a final decree was pronounced on the 28th of March following, by which Collett paid to C. Merwanji Rs. 4000, and made over to him all the assets of the partnership, receiving from Cursetji Merwanji a guarantee against all claims.

ON THE PETITION OF

EBENEZER ALEXANDER.

1851.

February 25.

[*Coram* PERRY, C. J., and YARDLEY, J.]

By the Bombay regulations the Accountant General is charged with the duty of accepting funds deposited for the benefit of infants.

By the English Trustee Act, the Court is empowered to make an order on petition for the payment of dividends, on funds standing in the name of infants, to their *guardians* for maintenance; on the joint petition of the mother and father-in-law of the infants that such an order should be made: *Held*, that as the latter had been appointed by the Court of Session in Scotland factor *in loco tutoris*, he came within the meaning of the word "guardian" in the English act.

LE MESSURIER, A. G., moved on the joint petition of Mrs. Alexander and her husband, that the dividends on a sum of Rs. 3300 which Mrs. Alexander had deposited, whilst a widow, with the Accountant General, in the names of her three children by her first husband, should be paid over to the petitioners as they accrued, for the maintenance of the children.

A doubt arising on the power of the Court to make this summary order, the Court took time to look into the act.

Cur. adv. vult.

PERRY, C. J., now delivered judgment.

This is an application under 11 Geo. 4 & 1 Wm. 4, c. 65, s. 32, (extended to this country by act 24 of 1841), to order dividends on funds standing in the names of the infants to be paid to their guardians for their maintenance.

By some regulation of Government, which we have not seen, but which is evidently very beneficial for the public, the Accountant General is charged with the duty of accepting funds deposited for the benefit of infants; and in the year 1845, the widow of Mr. M'Bean deposited accordingly Rs. 3300 with that officer, in the names of her three children, and with directions to invest the interest, as it accrued due, in Government Securities on their account. This sum has now increased to nearly five thousand rupees, and Mrs. M'Bean having remarried, her husband and herself now petition for an order that the dividends on this stock should be paid to them for the maintenance of the infants.

The English statute authorizes this order to be made upon the petition of the guardian of the infants, and as the husband, in this case, has been appointed by the Court of Session a factor *in loco tutoris*, which is a species of guardianship known to the Scotch law, and as the mother joins in the petition, we think we are justified in putting a liberal construction on the act, and in holding that the petitioners come within the meaning of the clause.

The order, therefore, may be that the Accountant General do pay to the petitioner Ebenezer Alexander, or to his attorney, the dividends due and as they become due during the respective minorities of the infants, and the costs of the application may be defrayed out of the accumulations in the savings bank, so far as the sum extend to defray the same.

1842.

July 28.

KARSONDASS HUNSRAZ *v.* RAMDASS HURRIDASS AND OTHERS.

[*Coram* Perry, J.]

Native executors are not entitled to a commission on the administration of their testator's estate, and the Court will set aside an agreement between an executor and the devisee, by which the latter binds himself to pay a sum of money in respect of commission.

This bill was filed to set aside an agreement which had been entered into by the complainant on the ground of fraud. The defendant had absconded after appearance, and *Crawford* now prayed that the bill should be taken *pro confesso*, and such a decree be pronounced as the statements in the will warranted.

Cur. adv. vult.

Perry, J.—When the bill in this case was read the other day, in order that such a decree might be pronounced upon it as the plaintiff could shew himself entitled to, I rather doubted whether any circumstances of fraud were alleged, which would warrant the Court in setting aside the agreement of July, 1840. For as the plaintiff Karsondass is of mature age, appears to have entered into the agreement with his eyes open, and to have conceived it upon the whole to be for his advantage, his folly and weakness in entering into it would scarcely form grounds for equitable relief (*a*).

However, upon considering the case more attentively, I do not think that the fraudulent nature of the agreement is the proper basis upon which to rest the decision: but that the Court is bound to take a higher position, and declare on grounds of public policy, that an agreement such as this, obtained by an executor from the next of kin entitled to the residue, is not such a contract between two independent parties as the Court will sanction or enforce. The parties are

(*a*) See Milnes *v.* Cowley, 8 Price, 620.

1842.

KARSONDASS v. RAMDASS.

in litigation, first, with respect to the representative character which Ramdass Hurridass enjoys by the decision of a competent Court; second, with respect to the possession of the assets which Ramdass had obtained by virtue of that character; Ramdass being in this position, therefore, and having all the funds in his disposal, either to distribute to the next of kin, or to make away with, as the case may be, enters into an agreement with Karsondass, the sole next of kin, but then an insolvent, to pay him over the residue on receiving Rs. 30,000.

The statement of the facts is enough to shew that one of the contracting parties had such means of undue influence over the other, by the relations existing between them, as to make all contracts between them, whilst that relation existed, however otherwise unexceptionable, void. (*Hylton* v. *Hylton*, 2 Ves. Sen. 549; *Wright* v. *Prond*, 13 Ves. 136; *Ward* v. *Downes*, 18 Ves. 120).

In this case, however, it clearly appears that the Rs. 30,000 were to be paid by Karsondass, not as a voluntary gift and to buy peace, but to satisfy the *claim* made by the executor for his commission, and this by itself would be sufficient to warrant this Court in setting aside this agreement.

The evidence of this fact is contained in a letter from Messrs. Patch and Bainbridge, the solicitors of Ramdass (fo. 86). The prayer of this bill, however, does not pray that the agreement should be set aside probably on the grounds that the plaintiff having agreed in the breach of trust which Ramdass, as executor, seemed willing to commit, he is not entitled to ask for relief upon that matter (*a*). It may be sufficient, therefore, to pronounce a decree as prayed.

(*a*) See *per* Lord ELDON, C., 3 Swanst. 64.

1843.
January 19.

IN THE GOODS OF JAMES TANT.

[*Coram* PERRY, J.]

Administration of the estate of an officer in the Company's service dying in camp and quarters, granted to the Ecclesiastical Registrar for the sake of creditors, notwithstanding the provision in the Mutiny Act, 3 & 4 Vict. c. 37, s. 52.

HOWARD moved, on the affidavit and petition of a creditor residing at Deesa, that administration should be committed to the Ecclesiastical Registrar. The New Mutiny Act enacts, that the Ecclesiastical Registrar shall not be entitled to take out administration in cases where, on a military man dying in camp and quarters, the surplus, after payment of regimental debts, is remitted to the military secretary at Bombay. The consequence is, that creditors, not knowing where to apply, frequently lose their money, the surplus being remitted home after the expiration of twelve months by the military secretary.

Cur. adv. vult.

PERRY, J.—This is an application, on the part of a creditor at Deesa, that administration may be granted to the Ecclesiastical Registrar, the deceased having died in camp and quarters, and the surplus of his effects, to the amount of upwards of Rs. 500 having been remitted to the military secretary at Bombay. The last Mutiny Act (3 & 4 Vict. c. 37, s. 52) directs, that the military secretary, on receipt of such surplus, is to pay the same to the executor or legal representative (if in India) of the deceased, or, if not in India, to remit it at the end of twelve months to the representative in Europe; and also enacts, that the Ecclesiastical Registrar shall not be required or entitled to take out administration in respect of such surplus.

In cases, therefore, where the surplus is thus remitted, and where creditors exist, an obvious difficulty arises as to the mode of getting their debts paid, a difficulty, of course, much increased where they happen to reside at any distance from the Presidency, and almost insurmountable if, with the procrasti-

1843.

Re TANT.

nation we are often accustomed to see in India, they allow twelve months to pass over their heads.

The Registrar obviously is not entitled to apply. A creditor absent from the Presidency, and being out of the ordinary jurisdiction of the Court, is certainly not a fit person to entrust the estate to, and I do not find any case in which such a party has been enabled to appoint an attorney to take out administration for him. Under these circumstances I think the Court may exercise its discretion by committing the administration to the Registrar, under act 39 & 40 Geo. 3, c. 79, s. 21, and the clause in the charter; just as the Ordinary in England will grant it to some discreet person, though without interest, where legal representatives are not forthcoming. (See *In the Goods of Keane*, 1 Hagg. Eccl. R. 692, and 3 Bac. Abr. 482).

MUCCONDASS VULLUBDASS *v.* VANS KENNEDY.

1846.

February 27.

[*Coram* PERRY, J.]

An assignment by an officer in the Company's service of his pay, is invalid, as being against public policy, although the India Insolvent Act enables the Court to make a stop order on a portion of such pay, and although the pay itself is seizable in execution from month to month, by virtue of the charter of justice.

Where a general officer took the benefit of the Insolvent Act, the Court made an order deducting two-thirds of his total pay, by which an income was left him of Rs. 7375 a year.

GENERAL KENNEDY having obtained the benefit of the Act for the relief of Insolvent Debtors, a question arose between certain of his creditors, who had obtained from him assignments of his pay, on which the Paymaster General had been in the habit, under General Kennedy's order, of paying them from month to month as they became due. When the General petitioned for the benefit of the act, the Paymaster refused to pay over any more instalments.

1846.

MUCCONDASS v. KENNEDY.

Howard now appeared for certain of the creditors.

Herrick, for other creditors.

Dickinson, for the common assignees.

The points raised are fully stated in the judgment.

Cur. adv. vult.

PERRY, J.—In this case Major General Kennedy petitioned the Court for his discharge, under the act passed for the relief of insolvent debtors, upon the 11th of November last, and he obtained his discharge in the month of January following.

He had previously to his petition, namely, upon the 25th of July, 1843, assigned to one Balcrustna Gungadher Shastry, in trust for a creditor, the monthly sum of Rs. 595 out of his pay as oriental translator, and the further sum of Rs. 304 out of his military pay, as such sums should successively become due, and General Kennedy also wrote an order to the General Paymaster, to the effect that the sum of Rs. 595 was to be so paid, under which order payments were regularly made from October, 1843, to August, 1845.

On the 1st of September, 1845, and the 1st of October, and 3rd of November following, the sheriff, under a writ of *fi. fa.*, at the suit of the plaintiff, who is a judgment creditor, attached the arrears of pay due to General Kennedy, as oriental translator, amounting to Rs. 5086 : 2, and as there are now three claimants to this fund, *viz.*, the common assignee, Gungadher Shastry, and the judgment creditor, the Paymaster has very properly refused to pay the money over without the order of this Court.

Upon these facts, two questions arise; First, what is the effect of an assignment for a valuable consideration by an officer of a portion of his pay, (and I do not think it is necessary, to discriminate, in this case, between the pay which an officer may receive in a civil or military capacity); and second, what is the effect of a seizure by the sheriff, at the suit of a judgment

1846.

MUCCONDASS *v.* KENNEDY.

creditor, of the arrears of pay due to such officer in the hands of the Paymaster General.

When the question first arose in England, whether the pay of an officer, in the service of the Crown, could be assigned, Lord HARDWICKE, in 1742, and Lord MANSFIELD, in 1770, decided that it could, and Chief Justice DE GREY, in 1777, adopted their decisions at law; (*Stuart* v. *Tucker*, Sir W. Bl. 1137); subsequent decisions, however, have established that such pay being given for the public service, it was against public policy to allow of its being alienated, and this principle, as laid down by Lord KENYON, in *Flurty* v. *Dy Mentrose*, in 1791, and a similar decision, it would appear, had been previously come to by the House of Lords, in 1765, in the case of *Cathcart* v. *Blackwood*, (Cooke's B. L. 306, 6th ed.).

On grounds of public policy, officers pay not assignable.

Officers in this country, however, whether in the service of the Crown or of the East India Company, do not stand exactly in the same position as officers in England, for the Insolvent Act, which has been passed for India, enables the Supreme Court to order such proportion of the receipts of such officers' pay as they shall think fit to be paid to the common assignee; whereas no such power belongs to the Insolvent Courts in England. And as under this power, the Court is in the habit of making orders for the deduction of a portion of the pay of any insolvent officer, in proportion to his rank, station, and other circumstances, that is to say, increasing the proportion as the pay is higher, it is clear, that to a certain extent, the above mentioned principle of public policy has been infringed by the enactment in question.

But attachable in India under Insolvent Act.

It seems, therefore, to be open to argument whether, as the Legislature itself has sanctioned the assignment of a portion of an officer's pay to his creditors, there is any longer any objection to his doing so of his own authority and for the same purposes, namely, for the payment of his debts. It is admitted that the assignment can have no effect unless it is recognised and admitted by the officer of Government who is entrusted with the distribution of pay, and it is obvious that it is in the power of Government at any moment to put a stop to such assignments if the public service is found to receive any

1846. MucCondass v. Kennedy.

detriment from them. I confess that I can see no objection to the validity of such assignments, except upon the grounds of public policy, for although the future pay of an officer is not a debt due from the Government, nor a *chose in action* capable of being sued for, yet it appears to me to be a valuable interest or possibility, as Lord Hardwicke called it in *Whitfield* v. *Tangset,* (1 Ves. 391), of sufficient certainty and character to obtain a price in the market, and, therefore, as a species of property which it may suit the convenience of mankind to deal with, entitled to the same recognition in Courts of justice where it has been made the subject of a conveyance for valuable consideration as other future and contingent interests, such, for instance, as assignments of probable profits, freight not yet earned, &c. (*a*).

In this view of the subject I was for some time inclined to think that the assent of the General Paymaster to the assignment in question, coupled with the clause in the Insolvent Act, got rid of the objection that is founded upon public policy Further consideration, however, has led me to conclude that the above proposition gives undue weight to the assent of the paymaster. His acceptance of the order to appropriate pay of officers to particular creditors, probably arises only from a consideration due to the convenience of such officers, and not with regard to the public service at all.

The order which the Court may make upon the receipts of an insolvent only extends to a proportion, not to the whole of them, and the discretion of the Court, of course, has to be exercised with reference to the position of the officer and the duties he has to discharge; but if we were to allow the assent of the paymaster to be sufficient to validate the assignment of an officer's pay, it clearly might extend to the whole of the pay, and thus be more stringent than any order which the Court is enabled to make. But as it is clearly against public policy that the whole of an officer's pay should be thus disposed of,—for although a remedy might in some cases be

(*a*) See the cases collected in Story's Equity Jurisprudence, and the same principle in the Pandects with respect to future possible profits, or even a mere hope. . Lib 18. 1. 8., *proem.*, and § 1.

obtained by removing a spendthrift from employment, still it is easy to conceive that, occasionally, the services of such a man could not be dispensed with,—I am of opinion, that the principle which prevails in England to forbid the assignment by an officer of his future pay must rule over decisions in this country also.

1846.

MUCCONDASS *v.* KENNEDY.

The second question is, whether the seizure by the sheriff at the suit of a judgment creditor of the arrears of General Kennedy's pay in the hands of the paymaster, although such seizure has not been returned into this Court, or, at all events, no order has been made by this Court to sell the debt, is sufficient to entitle such creditor to the amount against the common assignee, who claims it by virtue of the assignment which was made posterior to the seizure.

Attachment by sheriff of arrears of pay in the hands of paymaster, transfers the title to the creditor.

The judgment creditor's claim is resisted on two grounds; first, that the writ of execution under the charter only operates to extend debts *eo nomine*, and that pay is not a debt due to an officer; and, second, that such extent does not bind the debt by the act of seizure, nor until the debt is returned to this Court and an order is made upon it.

In support of the first proposition, *Gidley* v. *Lord Palmerston*, (3 B. & B.), is relied upon; but I am clearly of opinion, that where the pay due to an officer of Government has been placed in the hands of the proper distributing officer for payment, an action will lie against him if he refuses to pay the money to the officer or those claiming under him; see *Priddy* v. *Rose*, (3 Mer. 102); *Row* v. *Dawson*, (1 Ves. Sen.), and *Allen* v. *Dundas*, (8 T. R. 125); all of them being cases in which the right to sue public officers for moneys in their hands, admitted to be due to subordinate servants of Government, was recognised. With respect to the time when a debt becomes bound by a writ of execution, I think it is also clear, that the moment it is extended, that is, as soon as the debtor has notice of the claim, it is placed in *custodia legis*, according to the language of *Giles* v. *Grover*, and that the subsequent order of the Court is not necessary to prevent its passing to the common assignee as an "interest" belonging to the insolvent, under the 26th section of the Insolvent Act.

1846.

Muccondass v. Kennedy.

The result is, that the claims of Mr. *Herrick's* client and of the common assignee must be disallowed, and an order must be made upon the paymaster to pay over to the judgment creditor these arrears of pay belonging to General Kennedy, which were attached in his hand previous to General Kennedy's petition and assignment.

I will add, that although the above decision appears to me to be dictated by the authority of the cases in England, and by the clause of our charter which permits of debts being extended by judgment creditors, I cannot view it with any satisfaction, because there is no distinct principle to which I am capable of referring it. The law in England is consistent, it forbids the assignment of an officer's pay; and as the debts of a debtor cannot be seized in execution, the arrears of pay due to an officer cannot be laid hold of by the creditor, except he happens to find it in the debtor's own possession. But we are unable to carry out this policy here, except by halves; for although we may and do hold ourselves bound by the English authorities to the effect of denying the validity of an assignment of future pay, yet as the arrears of pay are seizable *de mense in mensem* under the charter, it is obvious that the officer has as much power, or almost as much power, of disposing of his future pay, by giving a warrant of attorney to enter up judgment to the party with whom he is dealing, as if he were enabled to assign the pay absolutely (*a*).

Except for its inconsistency, however, I see no evil in the above decision, as it never can be against public policy that officers should be compellable to pay their debts out of moneys due to them (*b*).

(*a*) Maud's case, 7 Rep. 182. Gerrard *v.* Boder, 2 Ves. 518. York *v.* Twinean, 5 Jur. 78. Allen *v.* Allen, 3 Term R. 126. Row *v.* Dawson, 1 Ves. 331.

(*b*) See the next case.

IN THE INSOLVENCY OF

MAJOR GENERAL VANS KENNEDY (*a*).

1848.

April 14.

[*Coram* PERRY, C. J.]

A general officer in receipt of emoluments to the amount of Rs. 22,128 per annum, having obtained the benefit of the Insolvent Act, two-thirds of his pay and allowances were ordered to be deducted.

THE insolvent having obtained the benefit of the Act for the relief of Insolvent Debtors, the Chief Justice, after communications with the Judges at Madras as to the amount of deductions made by that Court on officers in the receipt of large pay, made an order that two-thirds of the pay and allowances should be stopped for the creditors. General Kennedy having presented a petition against this order, the following was the decision.

PERRY, C. J.—I do not see anything urged in General Kennedy's petition that should induce the Court to vary the order, as all the circumstances therein set forth were fully brought before me when the case was heard.

It appears to me that a general officer, who, on receipts of Rs. 22,128 per annum, has been driven by improvidence into the Insolvent Court, is exceedingly well off when he is left with a clear allowance of Rs. 7376 a year; that to give him more would be to give him a much larger allowance than is made to insolvents of lower rank, from whom a smaller proportion of their actual receipts is deducted; and further, that it would be of very bad example if the penalty was made less than it is on an officer of high rank and large emoluments obtaining the benefit of the Insolvent Act.

It is an error in General Kennedy to suppose that the Court laid down a general rule as to major generals when it ordered two-thirds to be deducted from his receipts. To the credit of the service, no major general had previously, at any of the Presidencies, obtained the benefit of the act, and,

(*a*) See the last case.

1848.

Re Kennedy.

therefore, no decision was applicable to General Kennedy's case; but the sound principle seemed to be laid down in the communication from Madras, that, in every case of extraordinary occurrence, the peculiar circumstances would be considered. I attended to these in General Kennedy's case, and came to the conclusion that to an unmarried man of scholastic habits, and not addicted to society, the allowance of Rs. 7376 a year would be ample.

It is urged now, as it was urged before me in Court, that no particular favor should be shewn to General Kennedy's creditors, on account of the great usury that had been exercised; but as none of these creditors appeared in Court, I was not able to form an opinion of any of their claims, or whether the interest they exacted was more than proportioned to the risk they encountered, or whether they have been losers or otherwise in their dealings with the insolvent. I made the order, therefore, on the footing of their being *bonâ fide* creditors.

END OF PART I.

PART II.

LAW OF THINGS.

THE OPIUM CASES.

1847 to 1852.

For marginal notes, see *post*, p. 178.

THESE cases, which occupied the Indian Courts of law for years, on which the widest differences of opinion existed on the Indian Bench, which were carried home twice on appeal to the Privy Council, which are still under discussion in the Supreme Court at Calcutta, and which were said to involve sums almost fabulous in amount (*a*), caused so much legal discussion on the essentials of a valid contract, that a report of them may well head a collection of cases on this branch of the law.

As the first case here reported came on upon demurrer, it may be well to premise with a few local facts for the sake of non-Indian readers.

It has been a practice, for many years past, with the wealthy native merchants of India, to speculate on the price which the opium to be sold by Government, at their first periodical sale of the season, would produce. These speculations, as will be seen hereafter, were, in substance, exactly similar, and, in form, frequently identical with time bargains on the Stock Exchange; and they appear to have been carried on to an

(*a*) It was said that from one million to two millions sterling was at stake on the decisions in the Privy Council, which follow.

1847-52.

The Opium Cases.

immense extent, and as an ordinary branch of business, by most of the great banking houses in India.

The plaintiff Ramlal was the representative, at Bombay, of a very wealthy banking firm established at Muttra, on the Jumna, which had ramifications at most of the commercial cities in India. This firm, it seems, had sustained great losses in previous years, the speculators throughout India forming themselves into large parties, equivalent to the *Bulls* and *Bears* of London, and the powers of combination between Hindus being sufficiently developed to carry out pecuniary operations requiring capital and numbers to an extent unknown in Europe. For the purpose of making up previous losses Ramlal's party entered into large time bargain operations in the year 1846, for the first sale of the season 1846-7, to take place in the November following. For some weeks previous to this sale Ramlal, and his agents throughout India, continued to make their wagers, offering the opposite party a very high price as the sum at which the opium would sell, and as these prices were much above the market price of opium, and much larger than opium had ever been sold at before, his wagers were accepted greedily.

When the period for the auction sale approached, Ramlal gave out that he intended to purchase the whole of the opium that should be offered at Rs. 1800 a chest, which is above 50*l.* a chest above its market value.

The consternation which this news excited amongst all the commercial cities of India will be well remembered by the inhabitants of India at that period, and of Bombay particularly; when the news of the auction sale from Calcutta was expected, nearly all the population was on the *qui vive* for the arrival of the expresses with the intelligence, and the excitement pervaded all circles.

At the auction sale, however, at Calcutta, the opposite party having learned the intentions of Ramlal to bid so highly, contrived to defeat his plan by an ingenious manœuvre. On the first chest of opium being put up by the auctioneer, the *Bears*, in order to prevent any sale from taking place, bid against one another till twelve o'clock at night, when the price for the first lot amounted to above 15,000*l.*, and the auctioneer, finding himself gulled, postponed the sale.

Ramlal thereupon, through the medium of some respectable firms at Calcutta, offered to buy the whole of the opium at Rs. 1800 a chest; but the Government declined the offer, and gave notice of a public auction on a future day, with new conditions, so as to defeat any such trick as had been practised at the last.

At the adjourned auction Ramlal, by himself and agents, bought nearly the whole of the opium at prices averaging Rs. 1793 per chest.

Having won his wagers, the parties throughout India who had bet with him refused to pay.

Numerous actions were thereupon commenced on these wagers in the Supreme Court of Bombay, but before they were ripe for trial, an action on a similar wager, but for a previous opium sale, had been brought in the Supreme Court at Calcutta, in which, after the plaintiff had obtained a verdict, the Court arrested the judgment; Peel, C. J., assigning as a reason, that these wagers had an injurious tendency towards the public, as they created an interest in one of the parties to diminish the amount of revenue payable to Government on the sale of that commodity (*a*).

The defendants in the several actions (of which the following is the representative) armed with such a decision in their favour, withdrew their pleas, and filed a demurrer.

The report of the following case will probably be now intelligible.

(*a*) See 1 Taylor's Calcutta Reports, p. 1.

1847.

March 5.

RAMLAL THAKURSIDAS *v.* SUJANMAL DHONDMAL.

[*Coram* POLLOCK, C. J., and PERRY, J.]

Wagers respecting the average price of opium at the Government sales at Calcutta, held to be illegal by the Supreme Courts of Calcutta and Bombay, as being against public policy, *dissentiente* PERRY, J.; but the decisions overruled on appeal to the Privy Council.

Gigantic operations having been entered into by the parties speculating for a high price, wagers were made by them and their agents at all the commercial towns in India, in which the price named was notoriously far above the market or selling price of the drug; before the day of auction occurred, the party (represented by the plaintiff) speculating for the high price, gave out publicly that he should buy the whole of the opium at the auction at his own price; and accordingly, by himself and his agents, he purchased the whole of the opium at a very high price, and by great outlay of money, and thus won his wager. Under these circumstances the Supreme Court at Calcutta held that the wager had been won fraudulently; the Supreme Court at Bombay held that there was no fraud, as it was an understood term in the contract that the plaintiff would run up the price, if possible, by speculation; and the Privy Council, on appeal, affirmed the judgment of the Bombay Court.

For other points decided in these cases, see *post*.

ASSUMPSIT to recover differences on a contract respecting the average price of opium at the first ensuing public sale of the Government at Calcutta.

General demurrer.

Crawford, in support of the demurrer. The Supreme Court at Calcutta has just decided in a similar case that these contracts are illegal, because they tend to injure the Government, by diminishing the revenue to be obtained from a public sale. (*Tomauram* v. *Hormazjee Bazonjee*, Taylor's Calcutta Rep.) [PERRY, J.—That ground seems difficult to maintain, for unless the whole world enters into a conspiracy, an article cannot well be sold at a public auction under the market price. These contracts may have the effect of unduly enhancing the price, and so be injurious to the public, but they cannot be otherwise than beneficial to the Government, who are always secure of the market value, and who may also obtain the exaggerated value which speculators have created]. The latter is the sound objection to these contracts. The entering into this contract gives the plaintiff, and all those who act with him, a tendency to operate against the public interest.

It is immaterial whether that tendency actually leads to crime or misdemeanors, it is sufficient if the tendency be created. Now, a party entering into this wager would be interested in entering into conspiracies to enhance the price of this opium, to create fictitious prices, to interfere altogether with the *boná fide* value of the commodity, and if that be the tendency of this contract, it is the policy of the law to disallow it. This is the true conclusion to be drawn from the numerous decisions on the subject. (*Jones* v. *Randall*, Cowp.; *Allen* v. *Yearn*, 1 T. R. 56; *Good* v. *Elliot*, 3 T. R. 693; *La Caussade* v. *White*, 7 T. R.; *Gilbert* v. *Sykes*, 16 East, 151; *Shirley* v. *Sankey*, 2 B. & P. 130; *Evans* v. *Jones*, 5 Mee. & W. 80; *Hartley* v. *Price*, 10 East, 22).

It is moreover an object of interest with the law to maintain the integrity of sales at public auctions, and *uberrima fides* is required; 1 *Sugd. Vend. and Pur.* 23, 9th ed.; and *Levi* v. *Levi*, (6 C. & P. 239), shews how severely the criminal law punishes any interference with the genuine prices to be obtained by auction. A trial of this case might also necessitate the investigation of public accounts, and on that ground also the contract is invalid. (*Atherfold* v. *Beard*, 2 T. R. 600).

It is true that *Hibblewhite* v. *M'Morine*, (5 M. & W. 462), has held that time bargains are legal, but the evil public tendency was not considered there.

Herrick, contrà. By the law of England, all wagers are legal, except, 1, where they involve disclosures prejudicial to third parties; or, 2, where they are opposed to morality or to the public interest. All the cases which have been cited fall within one or other of these classes. Now the decisions in England that time bargains are legal are quite in point, unless it be made out that opium can be distinguished from any other commodity. If the effect of these speculations is to create an evil tendency, they should be all void; but this ground being not sufficiently tangible for the Courts to proceed upon, their legality, like every other contract against which no specific evil can be established, is unimpeachable.

Atherfold v. *Beard* has no application here, because *non*

1847.

RAMLAL v. SUJANMAL.

constat the Government books will ever be required, and the fact of the price obtained at a public sale can be ascertained by any bystander.

Cur. adv. vult.

The Judges not agreeing in opinion, now delivered their judgments *seriatim.*

March 5.

Judgment of PERRY, J. Question stated, whether a gambling contract can be sued on in an English Court of justice.

PERRY, J.—The broad question which has been argued in this case is, whether a time bargain in the nature of a wager on the future price of opium at one of the Government public sales at Calcutta is a valid contract according to the law of England.

A few facts not strictly contained within the record have been imported into the argument, but as they were of public notoriety—such as the sale being by public auction, and the proceeds being a branch of the Government revenue,—the Court, with a view of saving expense, was not unwilling to hear them assumed as if apparent on the face of the pleadings.

By English law money lost on a wager may be recovered by action; except in certain specified cases.

Now the nature of the contract being such as I have stated, it is obviously a mere gambling transaction, and, as such, fraught with all the evil consequences to society which that vice engenders. But in considering the validity of a gambling contract from a legal point of view, all these evil consequences attached to gambling generally must be kept out of sight; because the common law of England, unlike the Code Civil, and most other European codes founded on the Roman law, allows gambling contracts to be sued upon, except in certain special cases, where considerations of a public nature—such as are sufficient to invalidate all contracts—intervene, or where the rights or interests of third parties would be injuriously brought into discussion; for although the British Legislature, by a statute passed two years ago (8 & 9 Vict. c. 109), has assimilated the law of England to the civil law by making all wagers and gambling contracts null and void, that statute has not interfered with the English common law prevailing in other parts of the British empire.

It is, I think, to be deplored, that the common law has

taken this course, and I have always regretted that the fine juridical arguments which Mr. Justice BULLER brought forward in *Goode* v. *Elliot*, against the validity of wagers generally, were not allowed to prevail, and that the Judges are compelled, as a general rule, to devote the public time and to lend all the powerful machinery of Courts of justice to the enforcement of the contracts of mere gamblers.

To be desired that time of Courts of justice should not be occupied with discussions on such matters.

Still such is the law, and however much Judges, as grave moralists, may be disposed to frown upon gambling, and to find astute reasons in each particular case for disallowing the contract under discussion, I think the mischief which is produced by the Court permitting to itself this large discretion, confounding thereby the provinces of legislation and judicature, and rendering it impossible for the Profession or the public to predicate in any case what the law on the subject is; I say, I think these consequences are so grave, that it is our bounden duty to follow out the law which has been laid down into all its logical conclusions, and not to endeavour to give it the go by, by inventing subtle and artificial distinctions.

Still the law should be enforced, and not evaded by judicial subtleties.

Accordingly as the decisions in England have laid down most distinctly, that time bargains, whether in the public stocks, or in goods, are valid at common law, it appears to me that the Courts have no longer any discretion to exercise on the subject, but that they must humbly follow the current of authorities, and pronounce this time bargain in opinion to be valid.

This, indeed, has been the conclusion, which this Court has arrived at, and acted upon, for some years past, and in the many opium cases, which have come before us, it had never been suggested that there was any thing to distinguish a time bargain in that drug, from the time bargains on other commodities which had been sanctioned by the Courts at Westminister Hall.

And as previous decisions have sanctioned contracts like this, they should be followed.

The decisions I refer to, however, have not made the same impressions upon his Lordship here, nor, as I understand, upon the Supreme Court at Calcutta, which they have upon myself, it is, therefore, incumbent upon me, and indeed it is due to the public, who have been influenced by our previous decisions,

But this position being doubted, necessary to examine the principle of former decisions.

1847.

Ramlal v. Sujanmal.

Perry, J.

to state my reasons, why I think those decisions were sound, and ought now to be upheld.

It is conceded by those who maintain the invalidity of this contract, that a wager, *per se*, is legal, and that it lies upon the party, who resists the enforcement of it, to bring forward distinct legal grounds for its nullification. I have alluded briefly to the excepted cases wherein wagers are illegal. Statutory provision, immorality, injury to third parties, and tendency to affect the public interest, or public policy, comprise, I believe, the whole of the grounds on which the illegality can be based. In the present case, the illegality of this wager is rested on its alleged evil tendency as respects public policy. A direct motive, it is said, is given to the contracting parties, on the one hand to lower the prices of Government opium, and so to diminish the public revenue, on the other hand unduly to enhance prices, and so to injure the consumer by raising the fair market value of the commodity.

Conditions which vitiate a contract: 1. *Lex scripta.* 2. Immorality. 3. Injury to third parties. 4. Injury to public.

Now before examining this argument in detail, some general observations may be made which seem to me to shew that the inquiry ought not to be gone intc at all.

These contracts impeached on grounds of public policy.

It is obvious that a consideration of this argument necessitates an investigation into the various causes which influence prices. In order to ascertain what the tendency of speculations upon prices may be, an extensive knowledge is required of the doctrines relating to supply and demand, to monopoly and competition, besides a large induction from the facts connected with the particular commodity in question. I hold that these inquiries are wholly foreign to the province of a Court of justice. It is possible, certainly, that a Judge may be a great political economist, and a distinguished predecessor (*a*) of ours happened to be one of the first of his day, but no one would think of deferring to the opinion of the Bench on a question of political economy any more than on a disputed point in geology or agricultural chemistry. The answer to arguments founded on this basis therefore is, that these are not considerations for lawyers to entertain. Their province is to give effect to the rights and

But Judges have nothing to do with public policy; the Legislature alone is competent to judge of that.

(*a*) Sir Edward West, author of the celebrated Essay on Rent.

1847.

RAMLAL v. SUJANMAL.

PERRY, J.

obligations which individuals create amongst one another by their private contracts and agreements. On broad legal principles, and as a general rule, individuals have a right to enter into whatever contracts they please, and it is the office of Courts of justice to enforce fidelity to such engagements, except in certain specified cases, where the exceptions are as well known as the rule. The Legislature has often seen reason to interfere with such contracts wherever it finds or considers that the public interests are injured by any particular class of dealings, and full notice is given to the world of what the forbidden contracts are. But Judges have not the same materials before them as the Legislature for forming sound notions on public policy, and fortunately we have the light of experience to guide us in pointing out the extreme danger which is incurred when Courts of law go out of their path, and found their decisions not on solid juridical grounds, but on their own imperfect notions of what public policy requires. The common law can scarcely boast of two abler men within its own particular sphere than Lords KENYON and TENTERDEN, and yet, when they assumed to apply their notions of public policy to the contracts between man and man, they laid down doctrines that made the whole commercial world tremble, and which the veriest tyro in political science would now repudiate. In *Rex* v. *Waddington*, (1 East), Lord KENYON condemned a respectable merchant to four months' imprisonment and 1000*l*. fine for certain mercantile operations which are now carried on every day by every individual in commerce, and which, indeed, it is the peculiar and beneficial province of a merchant to undertake. Mr. Waddington, it seems, was an extensive merchant, and having a quantity of hops on hand, he considered, on what appears to have been sound mercantile reasoning, that the prices were ruinously low; he calculated the amount of stock in the hands of the brewers with the forthcoming supply, and came to the conclusion that the prices must speedily rise, and that undue causes had depressed them. He acted upon his convictions, stated openly in the market his reasons, and bought hops largely, with the avowed object of raising the market price. For these

Office of Courts of justice to enforce fidelity to engagements.

Evil of Judges interposing their own views of public policy.

1847.

RAMLAL
v.
SUJANMAL.

PERRY, J.

acts he received the punishment I have before mentioned; and Lord KENYON laid down the following doctrine: "It has been said, that if practices such as these with which the defendant stands charged are to be deemed criminal and punishable, the metropolis would be starved, as it could not be supplied by any other means. I by no means subscribe to that position. I know not whether it be supplied from day to day, from week to week, or how otherwise; but this is to me most evident, that in whatever manner a supply is made, if a number of rich persons are to buy up the whole, or a considerable part, of the produce from whence such supply is derived, in order to make their own private and exorbitant advantage of it to the public detriment, it will be found to be an evil of the greatest magnitude, and I am warranted in saying that *it is a most heinous offence against religion and morality, and against the established law of the country.*"

Here then is a doctrine which would bring within the pale of the criminal law nearly every merchant in the realm, and yet Lord KENYON tells us, in the same judgment, that he had read through Adam Smith's work in order to form sound views upon the subject. Lord TENTERDEN went equally far wrong in a case to be mentioned presently, by his speculations founded on his own particular views of public policy. When, therefore, we have such flagrant examples as these before our eyes, I accede most cordially to the observations urged at the Bar against the impropriety of Courts of law founding their judgments on considerations of public policy upon which the Legislature has not thought fit to pronounce; and I had considered the strong observations made on this point by such distinguished living Judges as Barons PARKE, ALDERSON, and MAULE, in a case (*Hibblewhite* v. *McMorine*) very parallel to the present as having completely disposed of any argument to be raised on that score.

But this case turning upon it, the question of public policy examined.

The argument, however, has been strongly urged at the Bar, and the present case, it would seem, is to be disposed of upon it. It behoves me, therefore, to consider it somewhat closely.

These time bargains, it is said, are contrary to public policy, because they have a tendency to stimulate the contracting parties to commit offences with regard to prices. The party who has an interest in a low price ruling has a direct motive supplied him to prevent persons, by any illegal means he may devise, from becoming purchasers; the other party has a motive equally direct to rm illegal combinations, to raise prices, and it is quite immaterial whether such results follow or not, as it is sufficient for the argument that such is the tendency of the contracts in question.

I cannot help observing, that I always suspect a fallacy is lurking in the ratiocination where I see some particular word introduced and harped upon, and twisted into every possible shape. Reasoning is so apt to degenerate into verbal disputation that the greatest care is necessary to prevent oneself losing sight of sense and ideas, in vain discussions upon the mere counters of thought. Thus, the present argument resorts to the word *tendency* at every step, and indeed does not seem to be able to frame any distinct proposition without the employment of the term. But as tendency is not a technical law term of conventional value, it must represent a distinct idea as applicable to this argument, which if it has any precise and uniform meaning, is capable of being translated into other language. Let us see then what this idea is. If the contracts in question are adverse to public policy, it must be either because the effect of them upon the whole is to lower prices and so to diminish the public revenue, or to raise prices and so to injure the consumer.

It is quite clear that the contracts cannot produce both these results, though it is quite possible they may produce neither, and yet both these results are pointed at as proofs of their evil *tendency*. The argument in question also draws a distinction between public policy and public interest, which is notable, and indeed novel; but the argument does not pause to explain the apparent collision, but contents itself with simply alleging, that if prices are lowered, the first is affected, if they are raised, the latter.

Now, with respect to the public revenue, it is so obvious that the general results of these contracts may be to raise the

1847. Ramlal v. Sujanmal. Perry, J.

revenue, and that they cannot cause the article to be sold under its fair market price; that it is impossible when the argument is carefully analysed, to say they are injurious to public policy on that score, and, accordingly, this branch of the argument was very faintly insisted upon at this Bar.

With regard then to the public interests, the question is, whether the consumer, in point of fact, is injured by these speculations; for if, on the whole, these contracts should turn out to have no operation on his interests, or to have even a beneficial operation by steadying prices, it would seem a monstrous conclusion to arrive at, that these contracts are void on public policy, on account of their evil tendency to produce all sorts of possible or impossible offences. Now, the effect of speculation on the market is a very difficult question to decide. Say that prices are ultimately governed by the relation between supply and demand, the adjustment between these two is no doubt regulated by the opinion of the day, and on this opinion every idle rumour and immaterial event operates more or less strongly. A large portion of mankind is credulous, weak-minded, and desponding, and when these persons happen to be holders of saleable commodities, a rush is made into the market to sell on the slightest cause that may appear to them portentous. Another class comprises the sanguine and the headstrong, who never lose confidence in their star, and whose tendency is to operate exactly in the contrary direction. And then a third class, perhaps, the select few of the community, stands by and profits by the faults of either. Thus speculation, and even time bargains, may on the whole operate to prevent prices from being unduly affected by either needless fears or exaggerated hopes.

Beneficial effects of speculation to the public.

The defendant, however, contends that it is immaterial for him to point out what the probable results of these time bargains may be, and that it is sufficient for him to shew that they have a *tendency* to produce illegal and improper acts on the part of the contracting parties; and he relies on *Evans* v. *Jones*, (5 Mees. & Wels.), and *Gilbert* v. *Sykes*, (16 East). But the answer to these two cases is simple,—in each of them the Court was able to see its way to the conclusion that the

Previous decisions on public policy examined.

1847.

RAMLAL *v.* SUJANMAL.

PERRY, J.

particular contract was injurious to the public interests; in this case the Court does not possess materials for forming such a conclusion. No lawyer will doubt, I think, that *Evans* v. *Jones*, which was a bet relating to the conviction of a third party, was properly decided. None are more fitted than Judges to decide what acts are likely to induce witnesses to commit perjury, and to interfere with the due administration of justice. I think that the bet on the life of Napoleon was, perhaps, also well decided, though I doubt whether the reasons of the learned Judges are not somewhat far fetched and unsatisfactory. One Judge, for instance, held the bet to be void, on the ground that the Yorkshire baronet who made it had an interest to assassinate Napoleon; another Judge assigned as his reason, that the other betting party, the clergyman, had an interest not to kill Napoleon, in case of his invading the country as an enemy; and a third Judge held that the bet was bad on neither of these grounds, and, indeed, that it was a valid contract. Still, in both these cases the majority of the Court found their way to a conclusion based on public policy. But in the present case, as I said before, the Court is not able to see what the evil tendency of these time bargains is, and I say this on the authority of *Hibblewhite* v. *M'Morine*, *Wells* v. *Porter*, *Oakley* v. *Rigby*, and *Morgan* v. *Pelver*.

Reasoning of them unsatisfactory.

Express decisions in point.

I do not forget the able arguments which Mr. *Crawford* addressed to the Court as to the evil consequences to trade which these contracts might produce, and the frauds, such as that committed in *Levi* v. *Levi* and Lord Cochrane's Stock Exchange transaction, to which they might give rise. These possible results were eloquently pointed out, and I do not think they could have been placed more forcibly before the Court; but they have all been addressed in equally forcible terms to the Courts at home, and in vain.

Lord TENTERDEN held that time bargains were attended with the most mischievous consequences, and in *Bryan* v. *Lewis* and other cases disallowed them; but his decisions have been expressly overruled. Mr. *Tomlinson* before the Court of Exchequer, and others before the Court of Common Pleas, placed the subject in every possible view, and scarcely

1847.

RAMLAL v. SUJANMAL.

PERRY, J.

any question of the day has received more judicial consideration. I therefore think I am justified in holding that the Courts of law are unable to pronounce judicially that time bargains are injurious to public policy.

Time bargains and these wagers identical in principle.

It only remains for me to observe, that throughout this discussion I have treated time argains and wagers such as that now before us as identical. Any considerations of public policy which would make the one invalid apply with equal force to the other; and it was, therefore, with the soundest logic that Lord TENTERDEN classed them under the same category in *Bryan* v. *Lewis.* But, moreover, the identity of the two contracts has been specially brought to the notice of the Court in *Wells* v. *Porter* and *Oakley* v. *Rigby*, where the defence was, that the time bargains for the delivery of stock were, in fact, mere wagers, and it was held to be an immaterial distinction. And it is quite obvious to any one who knows anything of Stock Exchange transactions, that these operations at Bombay are, in fact, exactly the same as those which take place in London. The same wants, the same passions, the same occupations, lead men both in the East and West into similar transactions, although a different garb and form may clothe their contracts as well as their persons,—

Springs of action the same in Hindu and in European transactions.

"facies non omnibus una
Nec diversa tamen;"

as we have constantly occasion to observe, when we come to compare native with European transactions. And thus, in the present case, the contract to pay seventy-five times the difference on a fixed price of one chest of opium, and the price at a future day, is, in substance, the same contract as a purchase of seventy-five chests at that price, where the delivery is to be made at a future day. And so also the paying of a sum of money down on the promise of the other party to pay five times the difference on one chest if it exceeds so much, is the common stock-jobbing operation of paying a premium for the liberty of calling for so many chests on a certain day if the price should attain the amount agreed upon. And lastly, if a

1847.

RAMLAL v. SUJANMAL.

PERRY, J.

distinction were to be taken between this wager and an ordinary time bargain, it would be at once evaded by speculators throwing all their wagers into the form of the latter.

I regret the great length into which I have been led unavoidably, to set out the grounds which have compelled me to differ from the Chief Justice, and it is a great satisfaction to me to think that if they are erroneous they can do no harm, whereas, if they are sound, they may facilitate the parties in their endeavours to get them confirmed by a higher tribunal.

Judgment of POLLOCK, C. J.

POLLOCK, C. J.—This is the case of a wager of a very peculiar description, on the price of opium, to be determined at the Government sale of Patna opium, which should take place next after the making of the wager. I have considered the question raised upon the demurrer, in all its bearings, and the numerous cases which are to be found applicable to the subject; and the result in my mind is, that the wager in question is void, in consequence of its being contrary to the principles of sound policy, and that, therefore, there ought to be judgment for the defendant. I regret that my opinion should not coincide with that of my learned Brother; but I cannot but think that unless it is to be considered, that in the case of time bargains, where the Courts have upheld them, although in some cases, argued upon as wagers, and admitted so to be, the decisions are to be taken as having concluded all arguments on such matter, (as my learned Brother has very broadly thrown out), this case is so distinguishable in its tendency from all that have preceded it, as to leave it open to the Court to adopt a contrary decision in perfect conformity with the general principles which all the Courts have dwelt upon very strongly, and have been disposed to uphold in every practicable instance. It is undeniable that wagers have been uniformly discouraged by our Courts in England. But as the legality of wagers, unless brought within the exceptions which have been raised from time to time, has been too often recognised to be now successfully questioned: it remains to be considered whether the present wager, from its very nature and obvious tendency, is not so completely against the public

Wagers are valid by English law, unless they contain terms opposed to public policy.

1847.

RAMLAL v. SUJANMAL.

POLLOCK, C. J.

interest as to bring it within the exception of being contrary to sound policy. It is unnecessary to consider the various objections which have led the Courts to declare certain wagers illegal; except, perhaps, for the purpose of proving that the decisions have proceeded upon the tendency of the wagers themselves, quite irrespective of the parties to them; but that, however improbable it might be that any illegal act would be committed by the parties to secure a victory, yet if the wager had a tendency to produce the commission of such acts, it was held sufficient to avoid it. Thus, in the case of *Gilbert* v. *Sykes*, (16 East, 50), which was a wager upon the duration of the life of Napoleon Bonaparte, and was held to be illegal and void, as tending to the assassination or other violent death of the subject of it; the Court never could have acted upon the idea that either the plaintiff, who was a clergyman, or the defendant, a well known and honorable person, could be suspected of promoting such a mode of terminating their engagement to each other. But this, and all the other similar cases, have been decided entirely upon the consideration of the consequences to which such a wager tends. It was upon the same principle that the decisions took place in *Cole* v. *Gower*, (6 East, 110), and *Hartley* v. *Rice*, (10 East, 22). I also pass by the decisions upon gambling in the funds, because that was the subject of an act of Parliament, and the act being silent on the subject of foreign funds, it followed, of course, that any transactions respecting them were not within the statute.

Cases of illegal wagers discussed.

The cases on which the plaintiff's counsel have mainly relied, are those in which the *dictum* of Lord TENTERDEN, at *Nisi Prius*, in *Bryan* v. *Lewis*, (Ry. & M. 386), has been questioned, and overruled, and a principle established, that time bargains for goods may be enforced, even if they are admitted by the parties to be mere wagers; provided they do not come within the established exceptions. The strong cases upon this point are those of *Hibblewhite* v. *McMorine*, (5 Mees. & W. 462), and the cases there quoted; and it must be admitted, that the decision in *Hibblewhite* v. *McMorine*, has settled that a time bargain for goods, or even a wager respecting their price,

1847.

RAMLAL *v.* SUJANMAL.

POLLOCK, C. J.

is not illegal; unless brought within the exceptions, one of which is, that it is contrary to sound policy. I am of opinion that by the numerous wagers laid by the plaintiffs with various parties, two of which only have been argued before the Court, the natural consequence or tendency in the plaintiffs was, to influence the next Government sale of opium, upon which the decision of the wager depended, by some contrivance, by which the price should be enhanced beyond the marketable price, and the higher the sum at which opium should be sold, the better would it be for the plaintiffs, as the interest they had created by the wager was, that they were to receive in one case, five, and in the other case, seventy-five times the amount of the difference between the current or real value of the opium, and the price at which it should be sold at such Government sale. Was, therefore, such an interest contrary to sound policy or not? The extent to which cupidity will go to secure an advantage, was strongly evidenced in a case that has not been quoted at the Bar, but which, I think, furnishes in the judgment of the Court, composed of very able Judges, a guide to the decision of the present case, upon the broad principles of public policy. I allude to the case of *Rex* v. *De Beranger and Others* (3 Maule & Sel. 67). The defendants were indicted and convicted of a conspiracy to occasion, without any just or true cause, a great increase and rise of the public Government Funds and Government Securities of this Kingdom; and in the judgment of the Court upon a motion in arrest of judgment, Lord ELLENBOROUGH says, "the purpose itself is mischievous—it strikes at the price of a vendible commodity in the market;" and although the gist of the offence of which the defendants stood convicted, was effecting their mischievous object by spreading false rumours, yet the Court appears to have entertained no doubt as to the mischievous effects of interfering improperly with the price of a vendible commodity in the market, as being contrary to sound policy; and in his judgment, DAMPIER, J., says, "the means used are wrong—they were false rumours: the object is wrong,—it was to give a false value to a commodity in the public market, which was injurious to those

If these wagers are opposed to sound policy, they are void.

Natural tendency of these contracts stated.

1847.

Ramlal v. Sujanmal.

Pollock, C. J.

who had to purchase." This case, therefore, completely establishes the principle, that to give a false price, by raising it, is contrary to sound policy; while the decision of *Levi* v. *Levi* (6 Car. & P. 239), affords a similar decision with regard to the illegality of an interference with the free course of an auction, by a combination to lower the prices. Now, to apply these principles to the present cases, which the Court is entitled to consider as two of a large number pending before us, in which the same plaintiffs appear in all. The large interest thus created, almost in an infinite number of times of the difference between the price of opium fixed in the wager, and that at which the declaration alleges the average price per chest to be upon the first Government sale, clearly shews that so large a pecuniary interest is created in the plaintiffs to raise the price, that the tendency would naturally be to impel them to adopt measures for raising the price very extensively. This appears to have been effected, by some means or other; for it cannot be presumed to have occurred naturally. Such a consequence, by creating so high and fictitious a price, might, and in many instances would, inevitably have the effect of paralysing the market,—of creating a convulsion in the opium trade generally, which would disable many from completing those engagements which, in the management of commercial concerns, those who deal in opium would have been justified in entering into,—relying upon the fair competition, which usually takes place, at such public sales as that in question, with *bonâ fide* biddings by merchants engaged in that branch of trade, and unaffected by the adventitious, though extensive interest, created by a gambling wager. It appears to me that such consequences are too probable to be doubted about; and might produce all the pernicious effects of bankruptcy, insolvency, or ruinous loss among the members of the opium trade. The plaintiffs (if the wager could be enforced) would be perfectly secure; even if they, in order to win the wager, became the purchasers of all the opium; for the receipt of the multiples of the difference from the various parties, with whom they have betted, would indemnify them for such an infringement (as I think it) of the

The tendency of the wagers, being to create ruinous loss and to disturb the opium trade, makes them void as opposed to public policy.

rights of the public. Upon the ground, therefore, that the natural tendency of these wagers is contrary to sound policy I am of opinion that they are illegal, and cannot be supported.

I have refrained from referring to many of the cases cited at the Bar; such as *Da Costa* v. *Jones* (2 Cowp. 729); *Evans* v. *Jones* (5 Mees. & W. 77), and others; as having been decided upon points of objections, which do not arise here; but which serve to shew how ready the Courts have always been to repress wagers when they could legally do so. And I may also remark, that the reasoning of Mr. Justice BULLER, in the case of *Good* v. *Elliott* (3 Term Rep. 693), although overruled by the majority of the Court, has been largely imported into the grounds on which subsequent cases have been decided; and it has been, among lawyers, a subject of general regret, that the case of *Good* v. *Elliott* had not been decided the other way.

There will, therefore, be judgment for the Defendant (*a*).

(*a*) Judgment reversed by Privy Council, see next case.

1848.
Feb. 22.

RAMLAL, APPELLANT,
v.
SUJANMAL, RESPONDENT.

In the Privy Council, on appeal.

THIS case having been carried home on an appeal to the Privy Council was argued before Lord LANGDALE, M. R., Lord CAMPBELL, Dr. LUSHINGTON, and Mr. PEMBERTON LEIGH.

Sir F. Kelly, and *Peacock*, for the appellants.

1848.

RAMLAL v. SUJANMAL.

Channell, Serjt., and *Smirke*, for the respondents.

Cur. adv. vult.

Feb. 22.

Lord CAMPBELL, on this day delivered judgment:—

This was an appeal from a judgment of the Supreme Court of Judicature at Bombay, holding, on a demurrer to a declaration, that the contract therein set out was illegal, and could not be enforced in a Court of justice. The contract amounts to a wager upon the average price which opium should fetch at the next Government sale at *Calcutta*, the plaintiffs having to pay the defendants the difference between this price, and a sum named, per chest, if this price should be below that sum; and the defendants having to pay the plaintiffs the difference between this price and that sum, if this price should be above the sum.

We are of opinion that we must take judicial notice, that the opium to be sold was the property of the Government of India, and that the produce was to form part of the public revenue.

Evil of Judges attempting to avoid a bad law by legal subterfuges.

I regret to say that we are bound to consider the common law of England to be, that an action may be maintained on a wager, although the parties had no previous interest in the question on which it is laid, if it be not against the interests or feelings of third persons, and does not lead to indecent evidence, and is not contrary to public policy. I look with concern, and almost with shame, on the subterfuges and contrivances, and evasions to which Judges in England long resorted, in struggling against this rule, and I rejoice that it is at last constitutionally abrogated by the Legislature, an event which probably would have happened much sooner without the abortive attempts to accomplish the object by judicial decision.

The statute, 8 & 9 Vict. c. 109, does not extend to India, and although both parties on the record are Hindus, no peculiar Hindu law is alleged to exist upon the subject; therefore, this case must be decided by the common law of England.

On the part of the defendants, the general rule, as I have stated it, is admitted; but they contend that this wager is illegal, on the ground of public policy, as it concerns the public revenue, and it gives the defendants an interest unduly to lower the price, whereby individuals dealing in opium, and the East India Company, may be injured.

We are of opinion, that the mere circumstance that this wager refers to the public revenue does not establish its illegality. The cases about the hop duties, *Atherfold* v. *Beard*, (2 Term Rep. 610), and *Shirley* v. *Sankey*, (2 Bos. & Pul. 130), proceed on the ground, that the wagers could not be determined without calling, as witnesses, officers of the Government, and making them disclose what had been the amount of a tax within a particular district. A wager on the amount received for a tax, as it shall appear, in a return published by the authority of the House of Commons, I think, would have been free from legal objection.

But the great question here is, whether the wager gave either party an interest, which is to be considered injurious to individuals or to the Government. We are of opinion that, although to a certain degree it might create a temptation to do what was wrong, we are not to presume that the parties would commit a crime; and as it did not interfere with the performance of any duty, and as, if the parties were not induced by it to commit a crime, neither the interests of individuals nor of the Government could be affected by it, we cannot say that it is contrary to public policy.

Presumptions are not to be made in a Court of law that parties will commit crime.

Suppose the wager had been laid in England within a month before the sale was to take place at Calcutta, I see no valid objection to its legality; for it could not by possibility have affected the result of the sale; and I can see no difference, in point of law, from the fact that they were residing at Calcutta, where the wager was laid, and the sale took place.

The defendant's counsel mainly relied upon the case of *Evans* v. *Jones*, (5 Mees. & W. 77), in which it was held that a wager upon the result of a criminal trial was illegal: but this proceeded upon the ground, that it gave the parties an interest

Previous decisions examined.

1848.

RAMLAL v. SUJANMAL.

at variance with duties they might have to perform as witnesses, or prejudice, in the same manner as a wager, upon the event of a law suit, would be illegal with the Judge who had to decide it, or a wager on the result of a parliamentary election with one of the electors.

Had the case of *Gilbert* v. *Sykes*, (16 East, 150), respecting the life of Napoleon, been decided on demurrer, or in arrest of judgment, it would have been an authority of great weight in support of the doctrine, that a wager that has any tendency to tempt a man to offend against the law is illegal. But we must recollect that it was discussed on a motion for a new trial, after a verdict for the defendant against evidence, and that the Court was mainly influenced in refusing a new trial, by the consideration, that according to the evidence, the wager arose out of a conversation respecting the probability of Napoleon being assassinated, so that it was considered tantamount to a wager that he would be assassinated within one hundred days. It is likewise remarkable, that Mr. Justice GROSE, who, when he differed with the rest of the Court, was generally thought by the Profession to be right, was of opinion that this wager, under all the circumstances, was lawful, although he concurred in refusing the new trial.

The doctrine contended for is disproved by the consideration that time bargains in English funds were not unlawful till the Stock-Jobbing Acts, although such bargains gave an interest to raise or to depress the funds, injuriously to individuals and to the state: by the consideration that, before the 19 Geo. 2, an insurance on a British ship was lawful, although the party assured had no interest in the ship, and had a temptation to contrive her destruction before she reached her destination; and by the consideration, that, before the statute 14 Geo. 3, insurances on lives were lawful, without any interest in the life insured, although as soon as the policy was executed, the party who had paid the premium had a temptation to commit murder.

The danger of such speculations is illustrated by Lord TENTERDEN's ruling, that a contract for the sale of goods, the seller not having any such goods at the time of sale was void; whereas it must now be considered as settled, that not only such a mercantile contract is valid, but that there was no illegality at common law in a time-bargain for goods at home, any more than in a time-bargain for foreign securities; *Hibblewhite* v. *McMorine*, (5 Mees. & W. 462).

We were referred to the case of *The King* v. *De Berenger*, (3 Maul. & Sel. 67), to shew the frauds which may be attempted from the desire of gain in such speculations; but the defendant's counsel might as well cite the murders supposed to have been committed a few years ago, which have been made the subject of a popular novel, to shew that insurance on lives ought to be entirely prohibited. If the doctrine contended for were established, it ought to be followed up with an enactment, that the life of the Queen (whom God long preserve!) should never be introduced into a lease, because, by its introduction, her sacred person is endangered. But the law believes that the awful penalties which it provides, to enforce the dictates of conscience and religion, will outweigh the temptation to commit spontaneous crimes, for the sake of gain, where no conflict is introduced with a positive duty.

It is for the Legislative Council at Calcutta to consider how far it may be conducive to the benefit of our Indian empire, to introduce into it the provisions of the statute 8 & 9 Vict. c. 109 (*a*).

We think that, by the common law of England, the wager in question is not illegal, and may be enforced in a Court of justice; and, agreeing with Mr. Justice PERRY, we shall report to Her Majesty that, in our opinion, the judgment appealed against ought to be reversed.

Wagers in question legal, and views of PERRY, J., confirmed.

(*a*) An act of the Legislative Council of India was accordingly passed, 10th October, 1848; see *post*, p. 221.

1849.
April 5.

RAMLAL THAKURSIDAS AND OTHERS
v.
DULABDAS PITAMBER.

[*Coram* Sir E. PERRY, C. J., and Sir W. YARDLEY, J.]

Plaintiff and defendant having entered into several wagers on the average price to be obtained for opium at the ensuing Government public sale at Calcutta, on its appearing that the practice of speculating on such average prevailed very extensively in India, that the price speculated on was not the market price, but a price to be operated on by speculation, and that the speculators for a high price used all the means in their power to raise prices, while the speculators for a low price endeavoured to depress them: *Held*, that under these circumstances it was not fraudulent in the plaintiff to buy up all the opium at the auction at a price much exceeding the market price, *dissentiente* YARDLEY, J.

Held, also, that such wagers, by the usage at Bombay, carried interest.

Held, also, that a verdict for the plaintiff, where the Judges differ, ought to carry costs, although the practice had usually been otherwise, *dissentiente*, YARDLEY, J.

Held, also, that a difference in the conditions of sale by Government shortly prior to the auction did not affect the contract, as the parties did not appear to have contracted with any reference to the conditions before published.

The above decisions all confirmed on appeal.

See further points arising out of these opium contracts, *post*, pp. 221, 224.

AFTER the above decision, the next opium cause came on in the first Term of 1849, for trial on the following pleas.

Assumpsit on forty-six different time bargains on the average price of the Patna opium at the first Government sale at Calcutta, for the season 1846-7.

Pleas, 1. Non assumpsit.

2. That defendant was induced to enter into the contract by the fraud and covin of plaintiffs and their agents.

3. That the average price at the sale was enhanced by the fraud of plaintiffs and others in collusion with them.

4. That the government sales at Calcutta were held periodically according to certain conditions, and that it was a practice at Bombay to speculate by way of wager upon the chances or contingency of the prices to be obtained at such sales; that the contracts entered into by the defendant were made subject to such conditions: averment, that no sale according to such conditions had taken place, the conditions having been materially altered.

It appeared at the trial, that a practice had existed all over India for many years past, of speculating upon the average price to be obtained for opium at the first of the periodical sales advertised by Government in each year; those speculating for a high price, or *Bulls*, being called Téjiwallahs, the *Bears* being called Mundiwallahs. Government, having the monopoly of the sale of opium in their hands, were from time to time in the habit of publishing in the Government *Gazette*, a notice as to the number of sales appointed for each year, the quantity of opium to be brought forward, and the conditions of sale; and, on the 26th of August, 1846, Government published that the first sale for the season would take place on the 30th of November following, and that 1690 chests of Patna opium would be brought forward.

The first wager entered into between the plaintiffs and defendant was on the 20th of October, 1846, the price then fixed on being Rs. 1386 per chest, and from that day to the 23rd of November following, a series of other wagers was made by them, with a gradual rise in prices, till the sum was run up to Rs. 1775. The market price of Patna opium during these periods fluctuated between Rs. 1250 and Rs. 1400 per chest.

Before the day fixed for the sale at Calcutta arrived, a rumour had gained ground that Ramlal and his party, having speculated for a very high price, had determined to run up the whole of the opium that was to be offered for sale to exorbitant prices, and to buy it himself. To thwart this plan, when the auction commenced the Mundiwallahs, for the purpose of preventing any sale taking place, kept continually bidding up the first lot of opium till near twelve o'clock at night, when the auctioneer, not having been able to effect any sale, left the room.

The Government thereupon issued a fresh notification that the sale would take place on the 7th of December following, but altered the conditions of sale, by introducing some clauses for the purpose of preventing fictitious biddings. After the interruption of the first sale, and before the appointment of the second, four or five mercantile firms in Calcutta, who, it was admitted at the trial represented the plaintiffs, offered to purchase the whole of the Patna opium at Rs. 1800 per chest, but the offer was declined.

At the sale, on the 7th December, several parties attended

1849.

RAMLAL *v.* DULABDAS.

on the part of the plaintiffs, and they purchased the greater part of the opium at different prices, but averaging on the whole Rs. 1795 per chest. There was some conflict in the evidence whether these parties bid against one another; but it appeared to be notorious in the auction room that the purchasers were nearly all agents of the plaintiffs.

The speculative bargains at Bombay were divided into three classes,—Paty, Téji, and Téji Mundi; but it does not seem necessary to describe the minute differences between them. The wagers were ordinarily made by parole by the brokers of the parties, and, when made, an entry by the broker employed was made in the books of each principal.

The following is the entry of the first wager, a Paty contract, declared upon:—

Kartik Wud 15th (20th Oct., 1846), 5 chests, at Rs. 1386, purchased of Doolubdas Pitamberdass, by the means of the broker, Hurgovind Hurrivulubdass.

The signature of Hurgovind Hurrivulubdass.

Howard, Dickinson, and *Holland,* for the plaintiffs, having proved these facts, claimed a verdict.

Defendant's argument.

Montriou, for the defendants, who had come round on a special retainer from Calcutta, addressed an argument to the Court, which lasted two days, and of which the following is a sketch:—

1. The event betted upon has not come to pass.

1. The main answer to the plaintiff's case is, that *the event* on which the defendant betted has never come to pass. The civil law must be referred to in order to ascertain exactly the essence of a contract. It appears there (Inst. III. 16), that all promises to perform an act are either absolute or conditional. And the civilians divide conditions into *conditio casualis* and *conditio potestativa.* The condition in this contract was *casualis,* that is, one depending on chance; but the plaintiff, by his acts, has converted it into a *conditio potestativa,* by bringing about, by his own acts, the event which was speculated upon, and that he had no right to do. [Sir E. PERRY, C. J. The division of conditions into *casuales* and *potestativæ* is clearly

Essentials of a contract examined.

Conditions in a wagering contract are either casual, *i. e.* depending on chance, or potential, *i. e.* depending on spontaneous acts.

imperfect, because many conditions may depend both on chance and on the faculties of the party; a jockey, for instance, may bet that he will win a race, the event will depend very much on the chances of there being a better horse in the race, or of a horse falling, &c.; but it will also depend in some degree on his own skill and horsemanship. And if you assume that the condition here was solely *casualis*, you assume the whole question] (*a*). The essence of a bet is the uncertainty of the event, and if a party has the event in his own hands, the bet is simply void; *Fisher* v. *Waltham* (*b*). But here, by the course adopted by the plaintiff, he had it in his power to make the prices anything he pleased. [Sir E. PERRY, C. J. Surely it was not a certainty that plaintiff should be able to bring from 20 to 30 laks of ready money to the auction three or four months subsequently, or that it would be his interest to do so, or that he would be alive, or that the Company would bring forward only a limited number of chests. But if all these were matters of uncertainty, they might well be speculated upon.] It is clear by the evidence that this rich firm of the plaintiffs, ramified all over India, was enabled to bring any sum of money they chose to the auction.

The plaintiff here has converted a *casual* condition into one to be effected by himself, and that vitiates the contract.

2. On another view of this case, the defendants are entitled to succeed on the pleas of fraud. This may be put in two lights. If the fraud was in the mind of Ramlal at the time of entering into the contract, and was carried out by him, the defendants are entitled to a verdict on both the pleas of fraud. If the fraud was only subsequently adopted by him, then we are entitled to a verdict on the 3rd issue only. The best definition of fraud is also to be found in the civil law: *dolus* is there defined as "calliditas, fallacia, machinatio ad circumveniendum, decipendium, fallendum alterum, adhibita!" The tactics of the plaintiff here were a *machinatio ad decipiendum*. His bidding against himself by the different agents he employed at the sale, was clearly fraudulent. [Sir E. PERRY, C. J. Do you contend that it would also have been fraudulent if Ramlal

2. These wagers fraudulent.

Fraud defined by the Roman lawyers.

(*a*) And see Cod. VI. 51, § 7, by which it appears that the civilians divided conditions into *casuales*, *potestativæ*, and *mixtæ*.

(*b*) 4 Q. B. 889.

1849.

RAMLAL v. DULABDAS.

had bid Rs. 1800 for the opium in one bid?] It is necessary, perhaps, to go that length. The bet was on the *average* to be obtained at the sale; a preposterous bidding by Ramlal to any amount does not determine the average in the sense in which it was contemplated by the parties. Even if the acts of Ramlal come within the terms of the contract, they are in themselves illegal, and fall within the class of cases in which it has been laid down that no one shall profit by a wrongful act, even of a third party; *Robson* v. *Calze* (*a*).

3. Government having altered conditions of sale, subject-matter of contract gone.

3. The conditions of sale were altered by the Government which entitles defendant to a verdict on the last plea; and as no average was obtained at the *first* sale, the plaintiff has not proved his contract, and defendant, therefore, is entitled on that ground also to a verdict on non assumpsit.

[Sir W. YARDLEY, J., observed, that the question between the parties appeared to be one rather of morality than of law, and he read the Chapter in *Paley on Contracts of Hazard* (*b*) as peculiarly applicable.]

Reply for the plaintiff.

Howard, in reply, was desired to confine himself to the issues of fraud. These pleas are not proved. The first rests exclusively on the evidence adduced to sustain the second, and that is simply that Ramlal purchased nearly all the opium at prices sufficient to win the wagers in the plaint. This act, it is argued, has made a drawn bet, the event on which the wagers turned not having occurred. But if Ramlal was entitled to buy the opium at all, which is a question depending on the construction of the contract, he has not exercised this right in a fraudulent manner, for he has done nothing which might not have been more simply accomplished by one bid, in his own name, of Rs. 1800 for each lot of opium. It is admitted that he was not excluded by the contracts from the sale; but, if it was competent to him to bid at the auction, he was at liberty to buy the opium at any price which his own interests dictated, and it is not legitimate to inquire what those

(*a*) 1 Dougl. 228. (*b*) Moral Philosophy, c. 8.

1849.

RAMLAL v. DULABDAS.

were. Ramlal's bet was, that it would be worth the while of some person or persons, possibly worth his own while, to buy the opium at the auction at the price mentioned in each wager. The defendant bet that it would not. Ramlal was not bound to declare what his own intentions were or what influence he had reason to believe would be brought to bear on the sale in question to bring the average price up to the sum he named. Wagers are not contracts of reciprocal benefit, one party only can win, and each backs his own knowledge, skill, acumen, and resources against those of the other. It is very conceivable, however, that if Ramlal, in this case, had openly told the defendant what he meant to do, the latter would, nevertheless, have made all the wagers in the plaint, the difficulties and risks of the scheme being so great, it not being incumbent on either party to a wager to unveil his mind to his opponent. When the loser, under this peculiar description of contract, affirms that something has happened, which was not within the chances betted upon, the question always must be was it a legitimate subject for him to have included amongst the risks of the speculation. Now the wagers in question do not affect to be upon the value of Patna opium, as an article of merchandize on a particular day, but they are on the result of a public sale, and they necessarily comprehend all the contingencies which influence one of these sales.

It is proved, in the cause, that wagers of this description are, and have been for years past, largely entered into throughout India, and that the parties interested in the rise and fall of the average openly influence the average to the utmost of their power. The wagers, in this case, therefore, necessarily comprehended the influence of this class of spectators, including, of course, Ramlal himself, and as the operations of the wager market are no more a matter of secresy than those of the sale market, it must have been obvious to every one, when the price in the former had risen above the value of the drug for exportation, that those who were backing a high and at last an extravagant average were the only persons who could purchase at that price, their contracts in the wager market being the manifest explanation of the profit they looked to. And latterly the wagers plainly became questions whether

1849.

RAMLAL v. DULABDAS.

Ramlal had the resources to buy the opium at so high an average, and whether it would be worth his while to do so, in other words, whether he could make a sufficient number of wagers with respectable and solvent persons to remunerate him, and every rise of Rs. 100, in the price backed by him, greatly increased the difficulties. It is assumed that it was his intent to secure a high average. It is clear, however, that the defendant must have tempted him to bet on in the hope of making it impossible for him to win. There were 1690 chests to be brought forward for sale. Every rise of Rs. 100, in the price to be paid for them, involved an additional outlay of Rs. 169,000, or nearly 17,000*l.*, and, when the average backed rose above the market value of the drug, every additional Rs. 100 per chest, involved a certain loss to him of the above sum, only to be recompensed by a sufficient number of wagers. And it is extremely doubtful, on the whole, whether Ramlal has been any great gainer after all, as he certainly would have been if the average had been kept lower. The only difference between this case and any former sale is one of degree, and the defendant who has made the wager with his eyes open cannot complain of this. He never repudiated them at a time when it became notorious that Ramlal intended to purchase. On the contrary, he betted on, and the proceedings of the Mundiwallahs, at the sale of the 30th November, are the best evidence of the view which they took of Ramlal's rights and of their own liabilities.

Cur. adv. vult.

April 5.

Judgment of YARDLEY, J.

The Court not being unanimous, the Judges on this day delivered their judgments *seriatim*.

YARDLEY, J. This action is brought to recover a large sum of money from the defendants on forty-six different wager contracts as to the average price of Patna opium at the first Government sale at Calcutta, in the year 1846-7. There are four issues raised on these pleadings:—

First. That the defendants did not make the contracts.

Secondly. That the defendants were induced to enter into the contracts by the fraud of the plaintiffs.

Thirdly. That the average price of the Patna opium sold at

the said Government sale was an average price, enhanced by the fraud and collusion of the plaintiffs and others.

Fourthly. An issue on a long special plea, to the effect that the conditions of the sale which took place were different from the usual conditions of the Government sales, and from those in reference to which the contracts were made.

I am of opinion that the first and fourth issues must be found for the plaintiffs.

General evidence has been given that the defendant made, through different brokers, a great number of opium bargains with the plaintiffs for the first Government sale of the season of 1846-7, and that those bargains were such as are declared upon in this action, being of three different kinds, each well understood by those who are in the habit of entering into these speculations; and the admissions of the entries in the books of the respective parties will be resorted to for the purpose, if it should become necessary, of computing the amount of loss or gain upon these transactions.

With regard to the issue on the fourth plea, I think it has been satisfactorily proved that the Government has long been in the habit of making alterations in the conditions of sale, and that the bargains of speculators have never been affected by such alterations, and, therefore, in the present instance, we must take it that the bargains were made with the full knowledge on both sides that the conditions of sale might be at any time varied, and with the understanding that the bargains should not be affected thereby.

The main question in the cause, however, arises upon the second and third pleas, or one of them, and it is necessary to enter upon rather a full consideration of the facts proved under the commission at Calcutta, and by the witnesses who have been called before us here before we can arrive at a satisfactory determination of that question; and I should wish, in the first place, to state distinctly what material facts I have taken as proved, and then to state the conclusions I draw from those facts, in order that if I have fallen into error, either from misapprehension of the evidence, or in the deductions I have drawn from it, such error may at once be detected, and the argument grounded thereupon at once confuted.

1849.

RAMLAL v. DULABDAS.

YARDLEY, J.

The plaintiffs are members of a co-partnership which, under various styles, carries on extensive business in many of the principal cities of India. Ramlal Thakursidas is the representative of the firm at Bombay, and Luckmeechund Radakissen at Calcutta.

For many years previous and up to the end of the year 1846 the plaintiffs have entered largely into speculations on the average price of Patna opium at the Government sales at Calcutta; the average price at the first Government sale of each season being that to which those speculations chiefly had reference.

Previously to the season of 1846–7 it had been customary to hold five Government sales of opium in each year. The number of sales was in that season increased to nine, in consequence of which increase in the number of sales the opium offered at each was reduced in quantity.

The first Government sale of the season of 1846–7 was, on the 26th of August, 1846, advertised for the 30th of November in the same year.

The whole quantity of Patna opium for sale on that occasion was 1690 chests.

Of this quantity the French government has, by convention with the government of India, the right to claim 300 chests to be withdrawn from the sale, and to be taken by the French government at the average price fetched by the rest.

This claim must, of course, be made before the sale.

Previously to the sale the plaintiffs made an enormous number of what are called time bargains at Bombay, Calcutta, and other great cities in India, and in these bargains the average named ranged from 1300 or 1400 rupees a chest up to nearly 1800.

In the contracts declared upon in this action the lowest average named was 1387 rupees, and the highest 1775 rupees.

In the great majority of instances of which we have any account the plaintiffs were buyers, or, in other words, speculated on the rise in the price; but it has also been proved that in some instances they were sellers, and speculated on the fall. I do not think it is in proof at what price or to what extent they speculated on the fall. Nor indeed have we any precise evidence as to the extent to which they speculated on the rise of price, but most of the witnesses describe it as something very great, and we have on the records of the Court upwards of forty plaints in which the plaintiffs seek to recover from different parties the difference between the price at which they (the plaintiffs) bought, and the average price at the first Government sale. There was, in the months of October and November, great excitement in the Bazaars of Bombay and Calcutta on the subject of these opium transactions, and it is certainly proved that a rumour prevailed in Bombay that Ramlal (one of the plaintiffs) intended to buy up all the opium, or to influence the average at the sale in such a manner as would make the buyers great gainers and the sellers great losers. The precise time when this rumour arose is not in evidence, nor, in my view of the case, is it of much importance to ascertain when it arose: but I mention it because it is a good deal insisted upon by the learned counsel for the plaintiffs in his argument.

The sale, as before stated, was advertised for the 30th of November, and upon that occasion representatives of the firms of Oswald, Seal and Company, Macintyre and Company, Luckmeechund Radakissen, and Mutty Lall Seal, all of Calcutta, attended the sale to bid on behalf of the plaintiffs.

On that day, however, no sale of Patna opium took place, owing to some parties keeping up the biddings for the first lot all through the day, and running it up to a preposterously extravagant price; and the Government agent, finding that those parties were determined to keep up the biddings until night, was obliged to abandon the design of selling at all on that day; so that there was no sale whatever on the 30th of November.

Immediately after the failure of the intended sale, the letter (A.) offering Rs. 1800 per chest for the opium was written by the parties above named to Mr. Torrens, the secretary to the Board of Opium.

The sale was again advertised for the 7th of December with some new conditions introduced, chiefly with the view of preventing a recurrence of the interruption which had taken place on the previous occasion. I have already said that I do not think the contracts made upon the average of the first

1849.

RAMLAL v. DULABDAS.

YARDLEY, J.

Government sale were affected by the change in the conditions of sale. The sale of the 7th of December was also attended by representatives of the before mentioned five firms, and also by Cassinath Day and Nancy All on behalf of the plaintiffs.

Mutty Lall Seal expressly says, that it was arranged and agreed between these parties that they should bid against each other, and not suffer the average of the sale to be less than Rs. 1800, or a sum very little short of that amount. Mr. Fergusson and Mr. Ashburner (of the firm of Macintyre and Company) deny that there was such a previous arrangement; and I do not know that, for the purpose of this cause, it is necessary to decide whether there were such a previous arrangement or not. One fact is beyond dispute, and that is, that all those parties whom I have mentioned were commissioned by Luckmechund Radakissen to attend the sale and to bid up to Rs. 1800, or thereabouts, per chest for the Patna opium.

Before the sale, also, Mutty Lall Seal, on behalf of Luckmechund Radakissen, induced the agent of the French government, by the payment of Rs. 30,000, to claim the 300 chests on behalf of his government, whereby the whole quantity of Patna opium offered for sale was reduced to 1390 chests.

On the 7th of December the sale took place, and it appears from a list furnished by the Government agent, and admitted on both sides, that with the exception of seventy-five chests purchased by a Mr. Pereira, at the rate of Rs. 1750 per chest, the whole of the Patna opium was purchased by the plaintiffs and their agents at prices which made the average price amount to rather more than Rs. 1793 per chest. It is also positively stated by Mutty Lall Seal, by Dadabhoy Hormusjee Cama, and, if I mistake not, by other witnesses, and is not, that I remember, positively denied by the witnesses for the defendants, that this result was brought about by the parties commissioned by the plaintiffs bidding against each other for some lots, and putting up others at the first bidding at a very high rate.

True it is, that certain witnesses for the defendants examined under the commission at Calcutta, say that they made biddings to the amount of Rs. 1700, and one, I think, even higher;

but the impression made on my mind by the whole evidence is strongly to the effect that the average price at the sale was greatly enhanced by the efforts of the plaintiff's agents, and that they did, to accomplish that object, advance upon each other's biddings. And I think it right to state my opinion distinctly upon this fact, because I consider it extremely material to the decision of the case.

Mr. Pereira, it appears, had orders from China to buy, and was unlimited as to price. He considered it his duty to buy at any rate, and says, that for those seventy-five chests he would have gone to Rs. 2000 a chest, though he considered the price very high at which he did purchase.

Assuming that the plaintiffs acted from the motive imputed to them by the defendants, it would have answered their purpose a great deal better if other parties had been the purchasers of the whole of the drug, provided the average had been forced up to a sufficient height to make the speculators upon a high average the gainers.

Luckmeechund Radakissen paid the Government for the whole of the opium except that purchased by Pereira, and it certainly required an immense command of capital to enable the plaintiffs to operate as they did upon the market, for the sum paid by them to the Government exceeded twenty-four laks of rupees.

Soon after the sale this very opium, or, at least, a portion of it, was sold by them at Rs. 1200 and 1300 per chest, so that to gain by such a transaction, the number and extent of their wager contracts must have been prodigious.

I believe I have now given a general statement of the material facts of the case. At least these are the facts upon which I form my judgment. And if any of them are not borne out by the evidence, I am, to that extent, in error in my estimate of the evidence.

I shall proceed now, as briefly as possible, to state the conclusion I draw from these facts. There are three classes of contracts in the plaint in this action declared upon; and it is not necessary to enter into the distinction between these three classes. They may all be described as wagers upon the

1849.

RAMLAL *v.* DULABDAS.

YARDLEY, J.

average price of one chest of Patna opium, of the Patna opium to be sold at the first public Government sale of opium to take place at Calcutta next after the making of the contract. And the question really is, whether it was in the contemplation of the parties to this contract, that one of them should be at liberty, if he could acquire a sufficient command of capital, and effect a sufficient combination of influences to force up by his own acts the price at such sale to such a height, as materially to affect one of the conditions of the contract into which he had so entered. And it must be maintained by the plaintiffs before they can make out their right to recover upon these contracts, that if they had been able to command sufficient capital to force up the average price to ten times the height it actually reached, they would have been entitled to recover the difference between the price at which they purchased under the wager contracts and such exaggerated average. And, indeed, Mr. *Howard* has most ably contended that the plaintiffs would have been so entitled to recover; and that the average named in the wager was the average of the price which it would be worth the while of the plaintiffs or any one else, for any purpose whatever, to give for the opium at the sale. But I do not think that is the meaning of the contract declared upon. If what the civilians call the *conditio casualis* were that the plaintiffs should be able to command such an amount of capital and effect such combinations as would raise the average price of the article above a certain height, then such a condition ought to have been expressed in the wager contract, and could not, I think, be implied by the terms of these contracts. We must not suffer ourselves to be confounded by the magnitude and complexity of these operations. If a party to a wager concerning an event requiring great means and extensive combinations before it could be brought about, be at liberty himself to use those means and effect those combinations, it would be equally lawful for him to do so, if the event were of the same nature, but of a more simple character, and more easily brought about. And if the plaintiffs in this case were at liberty, for the purpose of winning money upon these

1849.

RAMLAL *v.* DULABDAS.

YARDLEY, J.

wagers, and to do that which it is in proof they have done, any man laying a wager upon the price a horse or any other ordinary chattel would fetch at an auction, might himself, by his own act, win the wager, by bidding that very sum, though perhaps much more than the real value of the thing sold. The learned counsel for the plaintiffs says he might do so unless forbidden by the terms of the contract. I think it would not be lawful for him to do so unless enabled by the words of the contract, if then. Indeed, according to the decision of the Court of Queen's Bench in *Fisher* v. *Waltham*, (reported in 4 Q. B. Rep.), and cited by the learned counsel for the defendants, such a wager as would enable him to insure his own success would be void altogether, *ab initio*, and could not be made valid, although in the event he did not avail himself of such power. The judgment of the Queen's Bench is not very elaborate in that case, the Court evidently having felt a perfectly intelligible distaste for questions of that nature; but the principle I have referred to is, I think, plainly deducible from that decision. That wager was what is called "a bubble bet," because one of the parties had the event in his own hands.

I think it a sufficient misfortune that Courts of justice ever recognised contracts of hazard entered into neither for the benefit of commerce nor for the purpose of providing in some measure against the uncertainty of life, or against the destruction of property by fire; but I know not any principle of law or morals which calls upon us to give effect to practices and contrivances such as those resorted to by the plaintiffs in this case. It has been argued, that the success of such practices and contrivances entered into the chances upon which both parties speculated, because the intention to resort to them was openly avowed.

There is in the case some evidence of a vague rumour that the plaintiff Ramlal intended to operate upon the opium market in some manner that would have the effect of raising the average at the sale, but there is no evidence to shew when that rumour arose, by whom it was promulgated, to whom known, nor whether it was founded on any express declaration

1849.

Ramlal v. Dulabdas.

Yardley, J.

of such intention by the plaintiffs, or any of them, or suggested by the apprehensions of those who had speculated for the lower average, when the extent to which the plaintiffs had engaged in these transactions became generally known. But, assuming for the moment that the belief was general that the plaintiffs intended, if they could do so, to puff up the opium at the sale to an unnaturally high price, and assuming, also, that of which there is some evidence that speculators have been in the habit of influencing prices at the sales, my view of the case would not be materially altered. Persons might be found reckless enough to play with professed gamblers, though it were more than suspected that they were in the habit of packing the cards, or loading the dice, and who even had the hardihood to avow such practices; but, if it became necessary to resort to a Court of justice for the purpose of enforcing contracts of hazard on the result of such games, if otherwise lawful, I suppose it would hardly be contended that Courts should recognise the legality of such devices and stratagems.

On the whole, then, I am of opinion, that the plaintiffs having, at the time of the making of these bargains, cherished the design of forcing up the prices by the expenditure of a very large sum of money in the purchase of the opium at a price very much higher than it would have otherwise fetched, in order that they might win a much larger sum of money on the wagers they had made; and having, in pursuance of such design, by themselves and agents, attended the sale, and by advancing on their own biddings actually forced up the price to a fictitious and delusive height, and thus greatly enhanced the average price, the second and third pleas on this record have been proved, and that, consequently, there ought to be a verdict for the defendants, upon the issues raised by those pleas.

Perry, C. J., after stating the pleadings, proceeded as follows:—

Judgment of Perry, C. J.

The plaintiff having launched his case by proof that the contracts in question were made, that the average price at the sale was Rs. 1793, and that the defendant has not paid his bets, the defendant entered upon a most elaborate defence, and by his counsel, Mr. *Montriou*, took a very discursive range over provinces not often touched upon in this Court, and cited a variety of authors from Cicero and Justinian down to *Frazer's Magazine*.

Court unanimous in disposing of technical objections.

The earlier part of his defence was directed to the making of the contracts, to the explanation of their language, and to the alleged breach of the defendant. But, after hearing a great deal of ingenious argument on the meaning of the terms *first, average, sale, auction*, we had not the least hesitation at the close of it in coming to the conclusion, that there was no ambiguity whatever in any of the terms used between the parties, and that the exposition of them on the record by the plaintiff was correct, and was established by evidence.

The contracts having thus been shewn to have been made, and the breach proved, it was necessary for the defendant to make out the defences set up by the second and third pleas, *viz.*, either that he was induced to enter into the wagers by the fraud of the plaintiff, or that the plaintiff fraudulently enhanced the average price at the sale.

No ground for suggesting that plaintiff induced defendant by fraud to enter into the contract.

Of the first allegation of fraud there is not the slightest evidence, and it is quite as probable to my mind that the plaintiff entered into these different wagers at the solicitation of the defendant,—as his counsel, Mr. *Howard*, suggests on very plausible arguments,—as that the plaintiff persuaded the defendant to accept them.

The only question at issue is, whether the purchase by Ramlal of the whole of the opium is fraudulent.

The defendant's case, therefore, rests entirely on the third plea, and it appears to me to raise a very simple as well as a very short question. The point is, whether, the plaintiff and defendant having entered into wagering contracts on a future event, it was fraudulent on the part of the plaintiff to bring about that event by acts of his own, such acts being admitted to be not otherwise illegal; or, if this abstract mode of stating the question should be objected to, it may be put concretely, whether it was a fraud in the plaintiff, after having made these bets, to buy up all the opium at the auction, by himself and his agents, at three or four hundred rupees per chest above the market price.

This question appears to me, both in sound morality and

1849.

RAMLAL v. DULABDAS.

PERRY, C. J.

sound law, to turn entirely on one point;—was it understood by the parties, at the time the bets were made, that it was competent to the plaintiff to enter the market as a speculator and to endeavour to raise the price at the auction by his own biddings? If it were not so competent to him, and the event on which the two parties in Bombay were speculating was the market price as it should be governed by the ordinary causes of supply and demand, or as it should be governed by the contests between other speculators wholly unconnected with the plaintiff, then undoubtedly the plaintiff, by the course he has adopted, has taken an unfair and fraudulent advantage of the defendant, and the event which has been brought about by his own agency is not the event which was contemplated in the contract of hazard entered into between the parties.

Question entirely of fact as to the understanding of the parties, of what acts were permissible on either side.

But the fact stands out in this case as clearly established as anything I have ever seen proved by evidence in a Court of justice, that the defendant knew full well, when he made the wagers, that the plaintiff would use all the means in his power, which his command of capital allowed him, to run up the prices at the sale, and the defendant contracted with him on such terms; and I look upon the bets as nothing more than one speculator backing his own opinion against the opinion of another, on an event to be operated upon by the wealth, faculties, and judgment of each party. The elements of calculation were equally patent to either party; the resources of the plaintiff—the number of bets he should be able to make—the facility of bringing 300,000*l.* to bear on one spot within a few weeks,—were all matters of uncertainty, on which the two parties might well entertain different opinions; and if, in the result, it turns out that the plaintiff has taken a more correct view of one element of the calculation than the defendant, *viz.* of the facility of buying up the whole of the quantity to be offered at this sale, which was smaller than on previous occasions,—this, in the language of the moral writer cited by my learned Brother during the argument, is a fair advantage, because it results from the superior judgment exercised on the facts which were equally within the reach of, although they may not have been equally attended to by, both parties.

Fact clearly proved, that each party was to be at liberty to operate upon prices.

Paley's moral view referred to.

In point of fact, for aught that appears to the Court on the

1849.

RAMLAL v. DULABDAS.

PERRY, C. J.

evidence before it, the wagers which the defendant made may have been exceedingly advantageous to him. The plaintiff, having been charged with fraud, has very wisely allowed all kinds of evidence to be gone into, and has not endeavoured to keep out of sight any part of his transactions. But, I repeat, it nowhere appears in evidence that the defendant did not enter into a very safe speculation at the time when he made the contracts in question, and it is quite certain that, if the contracts on the record were the only ones which the plaintiff was enabled to effect, the advantages would have been wholly on the side of the defendant. A witness called by the defendant, a gentleman whom we all know and respect, Mr. M'Culloch, explained in a few pregnant words the principle which guided each party on entering into these operations, and the practices by which the Téjiwallahs or *Bulls* had been accustomed to raise, and the Mundiwallahs or *Bears* to depress, the prices at the auction sales; and during the three or four weeks while the speculations were going on between the parties, the Mundiwallahs were evidently pursuing the same operations which had been successful on previous occasions.

Solemn contracts made by a man of mature years, with his eyes open, and not forbidden by law, must be enforced.

On the simple ground then that, when a man of mature years enters into a contract which the law permits and with his eyes open, the law imposes upon him the obligation of performing that contract, I think that the plaintiff is entitled to recover, and that the defendant is no more at liberty now to obtain the assistance of this Court to annul the solemn contracts which he has made, on the plea that he has been defrauded, than he or another defendant was at liberty two years ago to shelter himself under the plea of fraud upon the Government or of fraud upon the public.

Provinces of law and morals compared.

I am not insensible to the strong appeals made to the Court to regard the dictates of pure morality in this case, and I trust I have never been found wanting in my exertions to make the provinces of law and ethics coincide, in so far as the nature of things, and the useful interference of Courts of justice, may permit. But I have always viewed it as a fundamental rule in morals that a man should keep his promises, and so soon as

1849.

RAMLAL v. DULLABDAS.

PERRY, C. J.

I can clearly see what the promise made is, I listen with the greatest reluctance both in this Court and out of it to any casuistry which seeks to relieve a party from the solemn obligation of his word.

Shock to morality when a Court of justice assists a man to avoid his own contracts.

That a Court of justice is a great instructor in morals I gladly recognize, and I see every day that to large classes of mankind it is the only school in which efficient lessons of morality are likely to be taught. But the legal doctrine enforcing sound morality, which this Court should keep more steadily in view than any other, accords with that fundamental rule in ethics which I have just adverted to, and which is laid down most emphatically in that system of law on which the learned counsel has bestowed so much eulogy, as the governing rule which the Court must observe when contracts are brought before it. *Pacta conventa servabo, ait Prætor,* is the rule I allude to, or as it is neatly put in the recent able work of Muhlenbruch, *Universim autem conventionum vis eo continetur præcepto: esse servanda pacta* (*a*).

And when the moral duties of the Court are brought under discussion, I for one must express my long-formed opinion, that the deepest shock to morality is occasioned by Courts of justice when solemn engagements between parties are set aside upon some subtle and fanciful ground. It may be injurious to the public interests that bets should take place on the hop duties,—it may tend to produce the crime of murder that a man should lay a wager on the lifeof Napoleon,—it may be of evil operation to compel the seducer to perform the engagement of maintenance which he has entered into with the victim of his arts. All these may be, or they may not be, valid public grounds for the refusal of Courts of justice to enforce solemn engagements; but in all these cases it is quite clear that, whatever the rule of law may enforce, the moral obligation is obvious and decisive, and every one must wish, who does not desire to see craft and roguery prevail, that the occasions on which the moral and legal rule diverge should be as few as possible.

Main duty of Courts of justice to enforce contracts, and to make law and morality coincide.

In deference to my learned Brother, who, I regret to find,

(*a*) *Doctrina Pandectarum*, Vol. II., p. 230, *Halle*, 1831.

arrives at a different conclusion from mine, although we both start from the same principles, and differ, I believe, very little as to the facts; and, in explanation of an expression of mine, as to the difference between the provinces of law and morality, I think it right to add a qualification, which may, perhaps, prevent misconstruction, and may, possibly, account for the difference in our views.

I have expressed my clear and unhesitating opinion, that the moral obligation in this case on the defendant to pay his bets is indubitable.

I have also stated by implication that the plaintiff has committed no illegal act, by which his moral right has been defeated. But I have not stated, and am not of opinion, that a very enlarged and refined view of morals would have allowed either the plaintiff or the defendant to enter into operations which are extremely injurious by way of example, and which do not appear in any way to be beneficial to mankind. On the contrary, I think very obvious ethical considerations dictate that the whole of these gambling contracts should have been abstained from altogether, and the learned counsel for the plaintiff, in his able argument, admitted that on the first contemplation of these facts, an unfavourable view of the plaintiffs' case might be taken.

Refined morality condemns gambling.

What I am now solicitous to point out is, that although sound and enlarged morality may condemn the whole of these gambling transactions, the law, which only seeks to lay down broad rules for the government of human conduct generally, is not able, nor ought it, in my opinion to attempt, to set aside the transactions of mankind, because they may not square in all minute particulars with what the most enlightened ethics demand.

But law can only lay down general rules for large classes.

My learned Brother may disapprove of the acts of the plaintiff, and of what has been termed the outrageous prices which he gave at the auction; but, if it was open to the plaintiff to bid up the prices at all, sound jurisprudence, with its known objections to the arbitrary, cannot lay down any line or limits beyond which the plaintiff was not authorized to dispose of his own money.

And jurisprudence disapproves of distinctions depending on the arbitrary will of the Judge.

1849.

RAMLAL v. DULABDAS.

PERRY, C. J.

Legal principle of commercial contracts stated.

The principle which the law has adopted is, that in commercial transactions, and the ordinary dealings between party and party, each individual must trust to his own acumen for discovering the facts connected with the case, and that it is not incumbent on the other side to disclose the circumstances which, in his opinion, make the contract advantageous for himself. Refined speculations in ethics might possibly dictate another rule; but the prevailing opinion, even amongst moralists, is, that the legal rule is right. The case which I mentioned, during the argument, of the corn merchant selling at a famine price during a period of scarcity at Rhodes, and not disclosing circumstances which he alone knew of, and which would have brought down the prices immediately, is fully discussed by Dr. Whewell in his recent work on Morality (*a*), and the legal rule is shewn to coincide with the moral obligation. But, whatever the reasonings of moralists may be on very speculative questions, the rule of law is clear, and throughout our whole system it will be found that the doctrine of *caveat emptor*, i. e., of each party trusting to his own resources and skill when he acts upon his opinion and judgment in dealings with another, is the only practical doctrine for disposing of the daily transactions of life.

Rule of morals open to much discussion, but on the whole coincides with the legal rule.

The law is able to interpose with effect between parties when any crime or obvious fraud has occurred, such as is capable of being made apparent in broad distinct traits to the minds of a jury, but all the more delicate obligations of morality, which are subjects rather of feeling than of reason, must be left to a different tribunal, to the powerful voice of a high-toned social circle, or the more solemn dictates of religion and conscience.

Morality enforces a wider and higher class of duties than law.

The plaintiff, in my opinion, was not bound by any rule of law, nor by the rules of morality received amongst mankind at large, to disclose to the defendant that he intended to make larger purchases now than on former occasions; it was his interest and his tactics to raise the price as high as he could on this as on all former occasions; and it was the defendant's own fault that he did not perceive that circumstances in the

Conclusion; Ramlal's conduct did not vitiate the contract either in law or morals.

(*a*) Elements of Morality, vol. 1, pp. 97, 260.

present case enabled the plaintiff to do so with effect. The plaintiff, therefore, must have judgment for the differences on the several contracts in the declaration, and as this is a mere matter of calculation, it can be ascertained at once.

Verdict for the Plaintiffs.

On a petition of appeal being transmitted, Sir E. PERRY, C. J., forwarded to the Privy Council the following additional reasons, which, as they notice one or two points not mentioned in the judgment, are here given :—

In compliance with the orders of Council, which directs the Judges below in all cases of appeal to transmit the reasons of their judgment, I beg to subjoin a copy of the decision I pronounced at the trial, and to refer to the reasons therein stated.

With respect to these reasons, there is only one fact in the case, as to which I think it necessary to make any remark, or to explain the impression on my mind concerning it. The fact I allude to is, the alleged bidding by the plaintiffs' agents, one against another, at the sale at Calcutta. One or two witnesses speak to this on the part of the defendant, and it is denied on the part of the plaintiff. As a juror I am satisfied that the fact is wholly immaterial; that, if it happened, it did not at all contribute to the high price which the opium obtained at the sale, that the employment of agents was not attributable to any attempt or desire on the part of the plaintiff to conceal his object; that no one at the sale was deceived thereby, and that the employment was attributable to many causes, all of which were consistent with good faith and every day's transactions in the East. This was so strongly felt by the counsel for the defendant, that he admitted he was bound to contend that a single bid for each lot by the plaintiff, without any agents, to the amount of Rs. 1800, would, under the circumstances, have been fraudulent.

There are two other points mentioned in the petition to

1849.

RAMLAL v. DULABDAS.

PERRY, C. J.

appeal, (the award of interest, and the granting of costs), on which it is necessary to make a remark.

The Court allows interest in their judgments on all mercantile contracts, although there may be no count for interest.

1st. Interest. It is the universal practice amongst the trading classes of India to charge and allow one another interest (at this Presidency nine per cent.) on all book debts, and the practice of this Court is to carry out the contracts made by the parties, by awarding interest, unless some special reason intervene to prevent it.

On pronouncing the verdict, application being made by the plaintiff for interest, we were unanimously of opinion that the contract was one of those in which the payment of interest was understood to be a term between the parties, and we accordingly awarded it as damages.

Reasons for giving the successful party his costs, although the Judges may differ.

2ndly. Costs. The awarding of costs in this Court is in the discretion of the Judges, but the rule which I have always endeavoured to follow since I have been on the Bench, is derived from the analogy of the Statute of Gloster. But, in cases where the two Judges are divided in their opinions, although the charter directs that the judgment shall follow the opinion of the Chief Justice, the ordinary practice has been that in such cases no costs have been awarded. This practice has always appeared to me to be injurious to the interests of justice, and to have been adopted rather from a feeling of delicacy between colleagues, than from a sense of what rigorous logic demands.

Where two Judges are sitting on the Bench it may be taken *a priori* that the opinions of one Judge are just as likely to be right as the opinions of the other, and the opinions of the Chief Justice are entitled to no preponderance, except such as may be due to his (in most cases) longer experience in India. But, if the interests of justice require a rule to be laid down that in such cases the opinion of the Chief Justice shall prevail, it appears to me that the judgment should be treated as an ordinary judgment of the Court; and although, I am quite alive to the evils which ensue (especially in colonial Courts) where the Bench is equally divided, I do not think the evil will be increased, but, on the contrary, that it is likely to be diminished, by adding the responsibility which is thrown on the Chief Justice, when the costs of the cause, as well as the judgment, are made to follow his decision.

1849.

RAMLAL v. DULABDAS.

PERRY, C. J.

As I have expressed opinions to the above effect more than once, both as a puisne Judge and as Chief Justice, and have never heard any argument against them, I thought the present case, which was going home on appeal, a fit opportunity for pronouncing what appeared to me to be the sound rule.

E. PERRY (*a*).

(*a*) Judgment confirmed on appeal, see *post*, p. 252.

OPIUM CASES.

1849.

September.

1. The act of the Indian Legislature, xxi. of 1848, for avoiding wagers is not retrospective, *dubitante*, YARDLEY, J.

2. *Query*, as to extent of legislative authority possessed by the Government of India:

Unlimited powers attributed to it by legislative member of Council, but denied by Governor General.

IN the September Term of the same year, several causes on similar opium contracts to those in the last case having been brought to trial, two new points were brought forward for the defendants; first, that act XXI. of 1848, had annulled all existing contracts; second, that by Hindu law all gambling contracts were void, and the case in question being between Hindus was governed by Hindu law (*a*).

Holland, for the defendant, on the first point, pointed out the distinctions between the English act, 8 & 9 Vict. c. 109, and the Indian act, and he contended, that as the decision in *Moon* v. *Durden* (*b*), was pronounced February 18th, 1848, and the Indian act was passed 10th of October in the same year, it must be taken that the Indian Legislature had that decision before their eyes, and that, as the effect of that case was to shew that the English act was not retrospective, the alterations which the Indian Legislature have introduced clearly prove their intention to make *their* act retrospective. The word " made, introduced by the Indian Legislature was a very

(*a*) As to this point, see *post*, p. 224.
(*b*) 2 Exch. 22.

1849.

RAMLAL v. DULABDAS.

marked distinction, and the use of that word has been held to shew that a retrospective operation is intended; *Freeman* v. *Moyes* (*a*); *Towler* v. *Chatterton* (*b*).

Howard, contrà. There is not the least difference in meaning between the English and the Indian act: *Moon* v. *Durden* is, therefore, conclusive.

The cases relied upon by the defendant, if they are not overruled by *Moon* v. *Durden,* are distinguishable. Both decisions relate to mere procedure, and do not affect vested rights. The decisions on Lord Tenterden's act are supportable on the ground that the Legislature pointed out a future period when the act was to come into operation, and gave eight months to parties to proceed according to the old law. And in *Freeman* v. *Moyes,* which was as to the liability of an executor to pay costs, LITTLEDALE, J. dissented from the justice of the decision even there.

Cur. adv. vult.

Sir E. PERRY, C. J.—The new point made in the opium cases is that the act of the Indian legislature has annulled all wagers in existence at the time of the act's passing. A similar point as to the retrospective effect of the English statute, from which this act has been taken, was also raised in the Court of Exchequer, but without effect.

The Indian act departs needlessly, and as it turns out mischievously, from the language of the English statute, in one or two minute particulars; but the principle laid down in the Exchequer decision is so broad, and the distinction now relied on so subtle, that I am convinced it would be a very unsound decision to depart from the one and give effect to the other.

Besides which, on applying the strictest grammatical construction to the words of this act in the clause relied upon, I am of opinion that there is no difference of meaning whatever between the two following forms of expression,—"all agreements, whether by parol or in writing, by way of gaming shall be

(*a*) 1 A. & E. 338. (*b*) 6 Bing. 258.

void," and "all agreements, whether *made* in speaking, writing or otherwise, by way of gaming shall be void."

I also think it would be opposed to sound principle and to precedent for any legislature to annul a class of contracts as to which litigation was going on, and which had been pronounced by the highest authority to be legal; and I agree with the Governor General in some views of his which have been lately laid before Parliament (*a*), that it would savour of much impropriety, and be opposed to all constitutional doctrines, for a body like the Legislative Council, with its limited powers and very peculiar composition, to attempt to give a retrospective operation to a statute of this kind.

For these reasons I am of opinion that the statute only

(*a*) On the discovery of some defalcations in the office of the Ecclesiastical Registrar, at Calcutta, Mr. Bethune, the Legislative Member of Council, proposed to enact a retrospective bill of pains and penalties, by which the defaulting member should be subjected to transportation for fourteen years. The Marquess of Dalhousie recorded the following minute on the subject:—"I am by no means confident that the power of the Council of India to pass a retrospective act, inflicting punishment on an individual for conduct which the statute law of England had not recognised to be a crime, and thus exercising an authority which the Imperial Parliament itself does not put forth except on the rarest occasions, and at distant intervals, would be received as indisputable, either by legal authorities in England, or by the Honorable Court of Directors under whom we serve. The Honorable Court has of late, on more occasions than one, evinced an inclination to hold that the legislative powers of the Council of India, on other points than those which are specially regulated by the Charter Act, are anything but co-extensive with the powers of other legislatures; while it is very certain, that if the highest legal authorities of her Majesty's Government and of the Honorable Company should be of opinion that the Council of India, in passing an act of pains and penalties had exceeded its powers, or had even exercised a power that was questionable, their opinion would of necessity prevail, and very embarrassing results might be produced."

To this view of the Governor General Mr. BETHUNE thus replied:

"I hold the legislative power conferred by Parliament on the Governor General in Council to be as large within the sphere of its operation as that of Parliament itself for the whole of her Majesty's dominions, subject only to these express exceptions, made by the act by which this power was created, and I think it right to assert this opinion as plainly and broadly as possible, when the observations of the Governor General appear in some degree to countenance a different doctrine."

1849.

RAMLAL v. DULABDAS.

applies to actions on future contracts, and that the Legislative Council never intended it should have any further effect (*a*).

Sir W. YARDLEY.—I thought that it was a doubtful point whether the introduction of the past participle "made" did not give a retrospective effect to the statute, as the two cases, *Freeman* v. *Moyes* and *Towler* v. *Chatterton*, were so strongly in point.

Objection overruled.

(*a*) And see *Hitchcock* v. *Way*, 1 Nev. & Perr. 72.

1849.

September.

1. Speculations, by way of wager, on the price of opium at the periodical Government sales are not invalid by the Hindu law.

2. *Query*, whether the reported cases of decisions of the Sudr Adalut, are authorities which can be cited on a point of Hindu law.

3. On Hindu contracts at the Presidencies the English law is the practical rule by which they are expounded, although the charter of justice preserves the Hindu law as to contracts between Hindus.

OPIUM CASES.

CRAWFORD, in the same term in another case, took an objection that, as the parties to the suit were both Hindus, the decision in the case under the clause in the charter must be governed by Hindu law. Now, by Hindu law, as manifested by a decision of the Sudr Adalut (reported 2 Borrodaile, 621), a contract such as this cannot be sued upon, and from the time when that decision was passed, in 1822, not an instance can be found of a similar action having been brought. At p. 415 of Mr. Borrodaile's second volume, a note is inserted, explaining the nature of these gambling contracts as they are entered into at Ahmedabad and at Bombay. He says:— "Waida Vyapar is precisely the illegal gambling in the funds called stockjobbing in England, except that it is only upon the price of merchandize, and the settling day is determined by the bargain. It has been put a stop to at Ahmedabad by proclamation, and the merchants there have lately agreed to abolish dealing in aut." (*i. e.* differences).

In the case before the Zillah Judge at Ahmedabad on one of these contracts, it appears that the Judge below had passed a decree in favour of the contract; but on appeal the Judge, Mr. IRONSIDE, pronounced this decision:—"Many people in

Ahmedabad carried on the Waida Vyapar, and in it many had failed. It was just like gambling, neither *bonâ fide* paying nor receiving, but depending entirely on word of mouth, on which thousands of rupees were often won and lost. It was proper to discover whether such transactions were not contrary to the Shastr, and a question was proposed to the Shastri, who declared that the Adalut was not at liberty to decree the amount of such transactions, as they were improper and contrary to the Shastr." The decree of the Judge below was accordingly reversed, and on appeal to the Sudr Adalut, "that Court entirely agreed with the lower Courts in the view they had taken of this kind of transaction, and dismissed the appeal."

Sir E. PERRY, C. J. As this is the first time I have ever heard the reports of cases in the Zillah Courts cited to prove a point of Hindu law, I think it right to say that I have great doubts whether they can be cited as authority at all. As collections of native customs, they are often valuable, and when they contain passages of native law, they may, of course, be referred to; but, as decisions of Judges delivering out the Hindu law as the English Judges pronounce the English law when the occasion occurs, they appear to me to have no weight whatever. In the East, the provinces of legislation and judicature have not been divided as in Europe, and a declaration by the Judge has always been submitted to as the will of the ruling power, even though it be thought by the community to be unjust. And in the case before us, I see clear evidence, by the terms used, of the authorities framing a new law to put down what they conceived (possibly rightly) to be a pernicious practice.

Besides which, it is impossible to close one's eyes to the fact, that the English gentlemen administering Hindu law have no special knowledge of the subject, and reports of their decisions, therefore, are entitled to less weight than the decisions of the country gentlemen at quarter sessions in England would be deemed to be, since the latter have the advantages of having the body of English law accessible to them in their

1849. RAMLAL v. DULABDAS.

mother tongue, and of having a body of highly educated practitioners before them.

In this case, as in all other cases where Hindu law is in question, the proper course is to bring before the Court the law as laid down in those Hindu authorities which are recognised by all, and which are just as accessible to the practitioners of this Court as to the Judges of the Sudr Adalut.

Crawford thereupon craved time to refer to such authorities, and on a subsequent day he renewed the argument.

The decision of the Zillah Court, or even of the Sudr Adalut, is not referred to as authority *per se*, although in the Privy Council Mr. Borrodaile's reports have been noticed with the greatest respect; but its authority depends on its proceeding on the opinion of the Shastri, which is the source this Court refers to when a disputed point of Hindu law arises. [Sir E. PERRY, C. J. The opinions of the Shastri are used legitimately when there is no text of the law available to the Court in a language which it can understand, or when the language of the law is ambiguous. But, if the law itself appears in an English dress, this Court does not refer to Shastris for their opinion but puts its own construction on the language used. Now, in the highest authority on Hindu law, (Menu), it is laid down, that matters arising out of gaming with dice, form the 18th title of the causes to be disposed of by the Judge. And at s. 159, where the liabilities of a son to pay his father's debts are discussed, it is said, "But money due by a surety, or idly promised to musicians and actresses, or lost at play, or due for spirituous liquors, or what remains unpaid of a fine or toll, the son of the surety or debtor shall not in general be obliged to pay." It is for you to meet passages so express as this, with something still more express in point]. I think I can. In Chapter 9, Menu lays down the strongest denunciation of gambling. He says, s. 221: "Gaming, either with inanimate or with animated things, let the King exclude wholly from his realm: both these modes of play cause destruction to princes. Such play with dice and the like, or by matches between rams and cocks, amounts to open theft; and the King must ever be vigilant in suppressing both modes of theft." Again, s. 225: "Gamesters, public dancers and singers, revilers of Scripture, open hereticks, men who perform not the duty of their several classes, and sellers of spirituous liquors, let him instantly banish the town." The same denunciations are to be found in all the Hindu law writers.

Howard and *Dickinson contrà*, were not called upon by the Court.

Hindu law of contracts not referred to by Hindus at the Presidencies.

Sir E. PERRY, C. J.—Although the clause in the charter directs that matters of contract between Hindus shall be decided by the laws and usages of the Hindus, in point of fact, on every question that arises, it is the English law of contract which is alone referred to (*a*); the reason of which, no doubt, is, that both laws are founded upon the same broad principles of good faith, and that very little difference exists between them. And, if on any contract some peculiar institute should be found to exist in Hindu law which would nullify a contract good in English law, this clause in the charter would operate strangely, for it would probably put a construction on the contract which neither of the parties, accustomed to English law, contemplated. Still, if the Hindu law does forbid contracts of this kind, I am of opinion that it must prevail.

It appears to me, however, quite plain, that the Hindu law does not forbid wagering contracts, but, on the contrary, recognises them. The passages in the ninth chapter of Menu appear to refer to certain well known instances of gambling, which it denounces as matters of police regulation. And the passages in the eighth book shew that certain kinds of gaming contract could be sued upon (*b*). Besides which, it is not

(*a*) So also at Calcutta, Sir Francis M'Naghten, C. J., observes, "I never knew or heard of an instance in which the Supreme Court was called upon in a case of contract to decide by such laws and usages."

(*b*) See also Halhed's Gentoo Laws, c. 21, and Vyuvaharu Muyookhu, c. xxi.

1849.

RAMLAL v. DULABDAS.

sound construction to hold that the term *gambling* includes all wagers. A Legislature may think fit on large views of expediency to refuse the aid of their Courts to recover monies lost on a wager, but a wager is often an innocent thing, and even beneficial in society, as the mode of visiting with a pecuniary penalty the man who dogmatises and advances his opinions in an offensive manner.

Use of native law officer in Company's Courts.

With respect to the opinion of the Shastri in the case relied on, it is of no weight whatever, because it is the office of a Shastri to bring forward texts of the law not otherwise known to the Court. And when the text is cited, it can be compared with other texts of the Hindu law, and its due weight will be assigned to it. In the case at Armedabad, all that seems to have occurred is, that a picture of the pernicious effects of opium gambling is drawn by the European Judge, and the Shastri was asked whether such transactions were not contrary to the Shastr. The Shastri of course answered that all transactions which were immoral and pernicious were contrary to the Shastr. It is a peculiarity of the Hindu character that a leading question from a superior will nearly always elicit the answer expected.

Effect of leading questions on Hindu witnesses.

Sir W. YARDLEY, J.—It is the duty of the defendant to make out that the contract in question is invalid by Hindu law. In my opinion he has failed to do so.

Objection overruled.

In all these opium cases (and upwards of a hundred had been brought), execution was stayed on paying the amount into Court, until the decision of the Privy Council in the two cases appealed home should be obtained.

OPIUM CASES.

1849.

Nov. 16.

1. Law as to cancelling of contracts before breach and after breach.
2. Difference of opinion between the Judges.

In another case, a question arose whether the wager had not been rescinded, under the particular facts mentioned in the following judgment.

Howard and *Dickinson* for the plaintiffs, *Crawford* for the defendant.

Cur. adv. vult.

Nov. 16.

Perry, C. J.—These opium cases have preserved their original character to the last, for on nearly every question that has arisen upon them in this Court, whether of law or fact, the Judges have differed, and the present case forms no exception.

The question which has arisen now is, whether the wager which was made between the plaintiff and defendant was cancelled by mutual consent before breach. There is a technical distinction in the English law as to the cancelling of contracts after breach, for, in the latter case, something more than mutual consent is required, but, according to the principles which I always endeavour to apply to the construction of native contracts, I have kept this technicality out of sight, and have directed my attention solely to what the intention of the parties really was amongst one another. For it certainly would appear to be very unjust, if the parties deliberately intended to cancel these contracts, and expressed such intention in unambiguous language, that the Court should treat their agreement as waste paper, merely because the formality of affixing a seal or wafer to it had not been complied with.

On looking at the whole of the evidence, much of which is suspicious on either side, at the facts which are admitted on either side, on the authentic written document which was signed by both parties, and throwing aside the suspicious evidence, but coupling only the admitted facts with the probabilities of the case, I have not the slightest doubt that

1849.

RAMLAL v. DULABDAS.

the plaintiff never agreed to release the defendant from the obligation of his wager.

The evidence relied on by the defendant, on whom the burthen of proof rested, is, that the paper signed by the parties on the 12th of December, 1846, declared the contracts to be null and void, and that the earnest money was accordingly refunded. The language of the agreement, after reciting that an opium sale had been advertised at Calcutta for the 30th of November, and that time bargains upon it had been made at Bombay, proceeds as follows. "But although the sale by auction commenced at Calcutta on the 30th of November, no average thereof was made; consequently the claims, debts, and mutual dealings connected with these time bargain speculations have become null; therefore the claims and debts relating to it are not to be paid or received by any one, for this speculation relates to Calcutta. We are, therefore, to act according to what the majority of the merchants at Calcutta may determine respecting the payment and receipt of the claims and debts." And the agreement thereupon binds the undersigned "to assist one another, and in case any one should sue any one of us the undersigned, he is to be assisted, and the expenses to be paid by all proportionably."

This agreement was entered into on the 12th of December, when the news of the abortive sale at Calcutta had reached Bombay; and on the 16th, when the news of the average at the sale on the 7th of December had also reached Bombay, the defendant paid back to the plaintiff Rs. 163, which he had received as earnest money on the wagers which are now sued on.

The defendant's counsel contends that the clear conclusion from these facts is, that the contracts were wholly rescinded between the parties.

The plaintiff, however, replies, that the meeting on the 12th of December was a meeting of the losing party or Mundiwallahs only, as it undoubtedly was, and that the sole object of the agreement was to enter into a league for mutual protection against the Tejiwallahs or winners, that the whole language of the agreement has reference to them and to them only, and that there is not one word which has reference to a cancelling of the subordinate contracts which might have been

1849.

RAMLAL v. DULABDAS.

contracted between the Mundiwallahs. I feel satisfied that this is the true construction, and that the plaintiff, who as well as the defendant was a Mundiwallah or loser on the whole, although he was entering into a joint combination with the endeavour to cancel the wagers generally, never intended to cancel his own wagers on which he had won, absolutely, unless those on which he lost were cancelled also. And this construction, which appears to me to be the only one reconcileable with the acute, prudent character in money matters of the classes whose acts we are considering, is admitted to be the true intention of the parties who signed the agreement by one of the defendant's own witnesses, who also signed, and who nevertheless has compelled this very plaintiff to pay him the amount of his wagers. I, therefore, look upon the agreement as nothing more than a general vote by the losing parties that the wagers were void, being an endeavour by them to procure their cancellation, and thereupon a contract was entered into with one another for mutual protection against the common enemy. I should further add, that if this agreement had been entered into at a general meeting of Mundis and Tejis, instead of Mundis only, I do not think that clause declaring the contracts void would have been operative, for it proceeds entirely on the statement of a fact as to the average, which turns out to be wholly erroneous.

If then this agreement does not cancel the contracts, we have next to consider the effect of the repayment of the earnest money, which took place on the 16th of December. Here, unfortunately, some very untrustworthy evidence presents itself. The entry in the plaintiff's cash book states most clearly that the contracts are only to be rescinded in the event of the authorities pronouncing them to be illegal. The defendant's entry, on the other hand, states that they are rescinded absolutely. But I must say that, so much suspicion attaches to either set of books, I am unable to base any conclusion on the one or the other. The same observation attaches to much of the *vivâ voce* evidence in the cause, for it is clear that large pecuniary interests are involved in the inquiry, and I therefore weigh every statement with great distrust. But, on looking again at the probabilities of the case,

1849.

RAMLAL v. DULABDAS.

and still more at the conduct of other parties connected with this agreement, I am satisfied that the earnest money was received back on the terms mentioned by the plaintiff's witnesses; and the evidence given by the Munim of the plaintiff as to what occurred at the meeting at Amerchund's on the 14th or 15th December is so plausible, that it is probably, on the whole, a faithful representation of the facts.

YARDLEY, J., gave his reasons for thinking that the contract had been rescinded.

Verdict for the Plaintiff.

1850.

Dec. 9.

DULUBDAS PITAMBARDASS, APPELLANT, *v.* RAMLAL THAKURSIDAS AND OTHERS, RESPONDENTS.

OPIUM CASES IN APPEAL.

In the Privy Council.

The above case having been carried by appeal to the Privy Council, was argued by *Bethell* and *Leith* for the appellants, and by Sir *Fitzroy Kelly* and *Peacock* for the respondents (*a*).

Cur. adv. vult.

Judgment of Privy Council. Decisions of PERRY, C. J. affirmed. Objections raised by Supreme Court of Calcutta.

PARKE, B., now delivered the judgment of the Court:—

This case was fully argued before us at the sittings after last Trinity Term. [His Lordship then stated the pleadings.]

The plaintiffs traversed each special plea by the general replication *de injuria;* and the cause came on to be tried in

(*a*) Before this case came on for hearing in the Privy Council, a similar action was tried at Calcutta to which similar pleas of fraud were pleaded; at the trial the Judges gave a verdict for the plaintiff; but on a subsequent motion to enter the verdict for the defendant, the Court set aside their former decision, and the Judges (PEEL, C. J., BULLER, J., and COLVILE, J.) gave elaborate judgments in favour of the pleas of fraud set up by defendant.

1850.

DULUBDAS v. RAMLAL.

March, 1849, before Chief Justice ERSKINE PERRY, and Mr. Justice YARDLEY, who, after time taken to consider, differed in opinion, and pronounced their verdict on the 2nd of April. 1849. Both agreed in finding a verdict for the plaintiffs on the first and last issues, but on the second and third the Chief Justice was in favour of the plaintiffs, Mr. Justice YARDLEY of the defendants; but, as provided for in such a case, the judgment was given according to the opinion of the Chief Justice, and, the sum recovered was given with interest and costs, and against that judgment there is an appeal.

Technical objections of the defendants overruled.

In the argument before us, the objections, which we collect from the papers were taken in the Court below, were renewed, and additional objections urged to the plaintiffs' right to recover. I will shortly recapitulate those objections, and it will then be found that the main question to be decided is a mere question of fact. One of those objections which were taken at the trial was, that the contracts were not proved to have been made by the defendants' authority, and that, if proved, they were not properly described, being contracts, as they were in form, for the purchase and delivery of opium, not wagers, or contracts, for the payments of differences as alleged. Their Lordships were of opinion, and expressed that opinion in the course of the argument, that there was ample evidence of the authority of the defendants' brokers to make the contracts, and also that the real nature of these nominal purchases was, that they were contracts to pay differences, so that the unanimous decision of the Court on these points must be deemed quite satisfactory.

Another objection also was taken on the trial arising on the fourth plea. It appeared that the course was, that all sales of opium, of which the East India Company had the monopoly, took place at stated periods, which were advertised; and at the time of the contracts the first sale of opium was advertised for November 30th, 1846, subject to certain conditions. This sale turned out to be abortive, as the whole day was spent in bidding up the opium to an extravagant price, and the Company's agents would not allow the sale to take place. The sale intended for the 30th of November was postponed

1850.

DULUBDAS v. RAMLAL.

till the 7th of December, and fresh conditions were presented for that sale, which took place then; all the opium was sold; and the average price of a chest exceeded that which the plaintiffs and the defendants had fixed upon in their wagers.

Technical objections overruled.

It was contended, for the defendants, that the first sale mentioned in their contracts was meant to be a first sale, subject to the then usual conditions, and as there had been no such sale, the event contemplated had never occurred, and, therefore, the wager had not been lost. If the additional qualification, that the first Government sale should be a sale subject to the same conditions as were then imposed, could be imported into the contract by parole, (which we need not decide), the evidence, as the Court has already intimated, did not prove any usage of trade to that effect. Indeed, there is evidence to the contrary. (Appendix, p. 41). That objection therefore fails.

But it was also contended, that the exposure to sale on the 30th of November was the first sale meant by the contract, and that on that sale there was no difference between the price fixed and that actually realized, because no price was obtained, and, therefore, the wager had not been lost; and though this had not been made the subject of a plea, yet that it was an available objection in reduction of damages, and that only nominal damages should be recovered, as there was in effect no difference to be paid. We, however, think that, according to the true construction of the contract, the price of the first actual sale was the object of the wager, and the intended sale on the 30th of November was not a sale, but the sale on the 7th of December was the first sale. This objection, therefore, also fails. Two other objections, one of which could not be, and the other was not, urged in the Court below, were also taken, on both of which their Lordships intimated their opinion in favour of the respondents, and they see no reason now to alter it.

Objection that contract was avoided by legislative act overruled.

The first was, that since the contracts were entered into, and since the commencement of the trial in the Court at Bombay, these contracts were rendered invalid by the act of the Governor General in Council of the 10th of October, 1848, entitled "An Act for Avoiding Wagers," and, therefore, the plaintiffs could not have judgment, and this judgment ought to be reversed.

That act provides, "That all agreements whether made in speaking, writing or otherwise, by way of gaming or wagering, shall be null and void. And no suit shall be allowed in any Court of law or equity for recovering any sum of money or valuable thing alleged to be won on any wager, or entrusted to any person to abide the event of any game, or on which any wager is made."

Their Lordships are of opinion that this legislative act is not to be construed as affecting existing contracts,—at all events not those contracts,—on which actions have already been commenced, for statutes are *primâ facie* deemed to be prospective only, *nova constitutio futuris formam imponere debet, non præteritis* (2nd Institute, 392), and there are no words in this act sufficient to shew the intention of the Legislature to affect existing rights. Their Lordships agree in the judgment of the majority of the Court of Exchequer on the construction of the corresponding act of the Parliament of the United Kingdom in *Moore* v. *Durden*, (1 Exch. Rep. 22).

Also that it was void by Hindu law.

In the next place it was contended, that by the Hindu law such contracts were void, and that this objection was open to the appellants, the declaration being, on the face of it, bad.

Their Lordships have already said that they are not satisfied, from the authorities referred to, that such is the law amongst the Hindus, and supposing that, *primâ facie*, the contracts are to be taken to be between persons of that nation (a point on which we need say nothing), we think we cannot say that the contracts were illegal, especially as the point was not made in the Court below, which had better means of deciding that question than we have.

It remains therefore for us to consider the other, and the main objections to the right of the plaintiffs to recover, arising on the second and third pleas, which have been most relied upon in the argument before us.

For the appellants, the defendants below, it was contended,

1850.

DULUBDAS v. RAMLAL.

that it was a fraud on the defendants, on such wagers as these, to bring about the event by which each wager could be won by acts of their own—that such fraud was meditated and prepared by the plaintiffs before the contracts were entered into, and therefore, the defendants meditating no such acts on the part of the plaintiffs, the contract was void on the ground of fraud on them, and the second plea should have been found for the defendants; or if not, that at all events the meditated fraud having been carried into effect and the prices raised by the acts of the plaintiffs, and their agents, those prices were fraudulently raised as against the defendants, and therefore the third plea ought to have been found for the defendants.

Main objection as to fraud depends on a question of fact.

This point appears to their Lordships to be purely a question of fact depending on the evidence. It may be conceded that there was evidence, not that any steps were taken to enhance the price, by employing persons to bid at the intended sale prior to the date of the contracts, but to raise a reasonable inference that the plaintiffs at that time meant by their own acts to raise the market, and then the question would be whether this intention would enable the defendants to avoid the contract under the second plea. Further, there was no doubt ample evidence that the plaintiffs did try to raise the price at the sale by their own acts and did succeed in so doing; and the question is, whether those acts are a fraud on the defendants within the meaning of the third plea.

This, the main point in the case and which applies to both pleas, depends entirely on the question of fact, what was the understanding of the parties to the contract when it was made? Both the learned Judges of the Court below appear to have agreed on this being the question.

The Chief Justice, in his very able judgment, most correctly states, that if the event on which both parties were speculating was the market price as it should be governed by the ordinary cases of supply and demand, or as it should be governed by the contests of speculators wholly unconnected with the plaintiffs, then, undoubtedly, the plaintiffs would have taken a fraudulent advantage, and the event brought about by their own agency is not the event which was contemplated in the

1850.

DULUBDAS v. RAMLAL.

contract of hazard entered into by the parties; and Mr. Justice YARDLEY agrees in that position, and illustrates it by a simple supposed case, in which it would be manifestly a fraud in one of the contracting parties against the other himself by his own act to win the wager, as where a man bets that a horse would fetch a certain price at an auction, he could not win the wager by bidding that very sum, and there can be no doubt upon that proposition.

Chief Justice's view of the evidence correct.

But the true question is stated most correctly by the Chief Justice to turn on one point. Was it understood by the parties, at the time the bets were made, that it was competent to the plaintiffs to enter into the market as speculators and endeavour to raise the price by their own biddings, and this is the question of fact on which the two learned Judges differed, Mr. Justice YARDLEY thinking that the evidence did not prove any such understanding, indeed going so far as to intimate an opinion that nothing short of the expression of that understanding in the contract itself would be sufficient. The Chief Justice being of opinion that the understanding was most clearly proved, that the defendants knew well when they made the wagers that the plaintiffs would use all their efforts and all the power which their command of capital gave them, to run up the prices at the sale, and that the defendants contracted with them on those terms, and that the wagers were, in fact, nothing more than one speculator backing his own opinion against that of another on an event to be operated upon by the wealth, faculties, and judgment of both parties; that according to their mutual understanding, each, therefore, had a right to use the means in his power, and to elevate the market price by bidding, and inducing others to bid, the others to depress it by persuading persons not to bid, always supposing that such means were otherwise legal.

Upon a full consideration of the evidence, their Lordships are of opinion that the view taken of it by the Chief Justice is the correct one, and think his decision as to the matter of fact fully warranted and called for by the evidence set out in pages 40, 41, 52, 55, 78, 82, 84, 88 of the Joint Appendix.

The plaintiffs had entered into a great speculation, the

1850.

DULUBDAS v. RAMLAL.

success of which was very doubtful, and depended on the amount of capital they could produce, when the opium was to be paid for, and the number of wagering contracts they could make upon the price of it in the meantime, and also upon the greater activity of themselves and their agents in bidding to raise the price than that of the defendants or their agents in endeavouring to lower it. This we think clearly proved.

It is true that some of the witnesses use the expression that it was the practice for the speculators for a rise to attend themselves and bid at the sale, and an argument is used that the evidence shews only an understanding that the contracting party should himself bid, but the witnesses do not state negatively that another or others might not attend on his behalf, and one of the witnesses, as Dadabhoy Rustomjee, gives evidence that speculators for a rise influence the market, and that a large purchaser always bought through several hands. So far as relates to the understanding between the parties as to what it is competent for either to do, we think that the evidence does not shew that the parties were to be confined to their own personal efforts by bidding themselves, or inducing others not to bid, but that they are at liberty to employ agents, and not one agent only, for these purposes, without breaking the contract between them. Whether the employing of more agents than one will render the act of bidding illegal, as to third persons, is another point which will afterwards be considered, between the parties we think it was clearly no violation of their mutual understanding so to do.

Conclusion, the plaintiff's acts not fraudulent *quoad* defendant.

Their Lordships think, therefore, that the efforts made to raise the market by the plaintiffs by bidding by themselves and agents were no fraud on the defendants, as such course was, according to the understanding of both parties, to be pursued, and, consequently, that the intention to use those efforts was not a fraud which rendered the contract voidable by the defendants. But it was further argued, that, even admitting that there was no fraud on the defendants by pursuing that course, the acts done by the plaintiffs and their agents were a fraud on third persons, and, therefore, illegal, and that the contract might be avoided by reason of that

Further objections raised by Calcutta Supreme Court.

1850.

DULUBDAS v. RAMLAL.

intended fraud, or at all events that the plaintiffs could not recover damages which they were only entitled to do by reason of that fraud on third persons. It would seem from the report of the judgment in the Court below that this view of the case was not pressed on the learned Judges. Both consider only whether this conduct would be a fraud on the contracting parties, and the Chief Justice states that the acts were admitted to be "not otherwise illegal."

1. Acts of plaintiff fraudulent on third parties.

But on the hearing of this appeal, this further objection is brought forward, and we are bound to dispose of it. The objection is, that the means used by bidding merely to enhance the price was a fraud on those who were intending to purchase *bonâ fide*, and especially when others conspired with the plaintiffs to bid for the same purpose, and, further, that the act of giving to the French Consul the sum of Rs. 30,000 to induce him to exercise the option given by treaty to the King of the French to buy 300 chests, was also a fraud on the East India Company, and the average price having been raised by these acts conjointly, the plaintiffs could not recover if either was illegal.

It was argued on behalf of the respondents that this species of fraud, and consequent illegality, did not fall within the meaning of the third plea, and so their Lordships are disposed to think, but, being unwilling to dispose of so great a case upon a point of pleading, they proceed to consider whether the defendants are entitled to succeed on the merits.

With respect to the bidding by one of the plaintiffs himself, said to be done merely to enhance the price, their Lordships think it was no fraud on any one. There is no law which prevents any person buying any quantity of a commodity at any price that he likes, whether to use himself, or to sell again in gross or by retail, or to give away, or to prevent another having it, provided always that he does not commit the common law offence of forestalling or regrating, which this is not, or engrossing, which the authorities shew can be committed only with respect to the necessaries of life, provided also that he makes no false representation in order to effect the purchase.

1850.

DULUBDAS v. RAMLAL.

In all these cases, the buying of any commodity when the purchaser does not want it, necessarily raises the price, and so causes a damage to all others who do, and who buy for the purpose of using it, but the purchase is not on that account a fraud on them. The market is open to all who buy, whatever their object may be. Whether the plaintiffs meant to buy to sell again at a profit, or to make their profits by the collateral contracts that they have entered into with others, appears to their Lordships to make no difference.

2. Employing agents said to be a conspiracy.

But it is said that the fact of employing several agents who were all cognisant of the purpose, as well as the plaintiffs, constituted an illegal conspiracy, an indictable offence, and the plaintiffs cannot, therefore, recover a difference of price created by that illegal conspiracy. But, as far as the doctrine of conspiracy has been extended, we do not find that there is any satisfactory authority that this would be an indictable offence where there was no *crimen falsi* committed, when the commodity is not a necessary of life, to which only, as has been said, the offence of engrossing or regrating applies, a charge of a description which certainly ought not to be extended, and which itself would not meet with much countenance in these times when the true principles of trade and commerce are better and more generally understood.

3. Frauds on *boná fide* sale by auction.

The dictum of Baron GURNEY, in the case of *Levi* v. *Levi*, was much relied upon, to shew that an agreement of several not to bid at an auction was an indictable offence, but this was a mere dictum in a Nisi Prius case, and cannot, we think, be relied upon.

It is argued, however, that this proceeding by bidding by the plaintiffs themselves, or in conjunction with others, is analogous to "puffing," and is illegal on the same principle. But the distinction is in our judgment plain—a puffer is not a real bidder, by arrangement between him and the vendor his bid is to go for nothing, but, as to the competing bidders it appears to be what it is not, a real bidding, and the vendor, by authorizing it, is guilty of a fraud on them, and cannot profit by it.

Here the plaintiffs and their agents are all real bidders.

He whose bid is the highest is bound to pay the price, and no false colours have been held out to other intended buyers.

Another point insisted upon before us was, that the purchase of the option reserved to the French government was illegal.

By the 6th article of the convention between Great Britain and France there is reserved to the French government, or those employed by them, the right to request a reserve of not exceeding 300 chests a-year, and if the quantity required is not taken and paid for in the agreed period, the quantity required is to go in reduction of the 300 chests. The plaintiffs purchased from the French consul this option for Rs. 30,000, meaning not to exercise the right of purchase, but to cause that quantity to be retained, and so to diminish the quantity of opium to be sold at the sale. The requisition was accordingly made, and the quantity offered for sale at that sale diminished by 300 chests.

4. Fraud on E. I. Company.

It was argued that this was a fraud against the East India Company, the vendors—who were thereby prevented from selling the 300 chests at that sale, which they would have done if the French government had been left to itself. But their Lordships do not think that this is a fraud on the Company. By the treaty, the French government has an unlimited power of exercising the option, and may do so for any reason they think fit, and the East India Company have no right, which is infringed upon by the exercise of the option for a collateral pecuniary advantage. It was, indeed, insinuated that this sum was given as a bribe to the French consul, and was, therefore, a fraud on his government, but it is not proved that the money was given as a bribe—but it must be intended that it was given for the use of the French government. Their Lordships, therefore, think that none of these objections are sustained, and that the plaintiff's conduct does not appear to have been illegal. However much they disapprove of these wagering transactions (which happily are now put an end to) however disreputable and unbecoming in men of a nice sense of honor, or of high mercantile character, the means adopted by the plaintiffs to win their wager may

But all these objections overruled by Privy Council.

1850.

DULUBDAS v. RAMLAL.

be, still we cannot pronounce them to be fraudulent in contemplation of law, which only seeks to lay down broad rules for the government of human conduct, applicable to all classes of persons, and does not exonerate parties from their contracts (which it is its primary duty to enforce) on the ground of fraud, except where they are distinctly shewn to be in violation of the ordinary rules of morality. Our attention was called to the decision of the learned Judges of the Supreme Court of Calcutta in a similar case. The Judges of that Court on the trial considered the conduct of the plaintiffs as not fraudulent, and gave their verdict for the plaintiffs at Nisi Prius. That opinion they subsequently changed. What the particular facts in evidence were, to shew that it was the understanding of the contracting parties as to using all means to raise or depress the prices, does not appear, and, therefore, we are not in a condition to say what the verdict ought to have been. But the opinion delivered by those learned Judges, on the supposition that there was such an understanding, that the bidding was a fraud on third parties, we cannot think to be well founded.

We are of opinion, therefore, that the plaintiffs were entitled to recover in this action. Two subordinate points remain for consideration. First, as to interest, we think the Court below were warranted in giving it, for it appears that interest was accustomed to be paid on such pecuniary transactions.

Conclusion, judgment for plaintiff, and views of PERRY, C. J. as to granting costs confirmed.

Lastly, as to costs, we concur in the opinion of the Chief Justice that the general rule should be, that they follow the event of the verdict, and, in this case, as the verdict for the plaintiffs was in the judgment of their Lordship's right, they ought to have their costs.

We shall, therefore, recommend to Her Majesty that the judgment should be affirmed.

Sir *F. Kelly*. And the appeal is dismissed with costs.

PARKE, B.—Yes.

Bethell. I do not know whether your Lordships would not

think, that as there was a difference of opinion with the two learned Judges in the Court below, there should be no costs.

PARKE, B.—No, we think the costs ought to follow the event.

Bethell. Then your Lordships give the costs of the appeal.

PARKE, B.—Yes.

POTTER v. B. AND A. HORMAZJI.

1844. Feb. 23.

[*Coram* PERRY, J.]

An agent in Bombay, who ships goods in his own name for an undiscovered principal in England, is liable for freight, although the bill of lading expressed that the freight was to be paid, "customary after the ship's arrival," and it was proved that the custom at Liverpool, which was the ship's destination, was to deliver the goods to the consignee, with sixty days' credit for payment of freight.

INDEBITATUS assumpsit for freight. Plea, non assumpsit.

At the trial, it appeared that the plaintiff was master and part owner of the William Shand, which had been chartered by Messrs. Boggs, Taylor and Co., of London, for a voyage to India and back, and was consigned by them to the defendants to procure a return freight. The defendants were also agents for other parties in England, and, amongst others, for Gardner Boggs, of Liverpool, to procure consignments of merchandize; and accordingly, the defendants shipped on board the William Shand 410 bales of cotton, to be delivered at Liverpool to ——— or order, or to assigns; freight for the said goods customary after the ship's arrival, as "per memorandum indorsed."

On the ship's arrival at Liverpool, Gardner Boggs received the goods in question under a bill of lading indorsed by defendants, but failed before payment of the freight, it being proved to be the custom at Liverpool to deliver India freights to any consignee not known to be insolvent, and to give sixty

1844.

POTTER *v.* HORMAZJI.

days' credit for the freight, but it was not shewn that by this custom the shipper was relieved of his liability.

It was also proved that, in the freight list sent by the defendants, in some cases they had stated that the goods were shipped by them as agents, but not in the present instance.

It was contended for the plaintiff, that the defendants being agents for merchants living in a foreign country, as England must be considered to be with reference to Bombay, the credit must be held to be given exclusively to them, and *Story on Agency*, 228, and *Domett* v. *Beckford*, (5 B. & Ad.), were relied on.

It was contended for the defendants, that as they were known to be agents for principals in England, there was no authority to warrant the proposition that the English shipowner gave credit to the Bombay agent, and that it must be taken that the credit was given to the consignee with the lien on the goods.

PERRY, J., inclined to this view, and cited a passage in 2 *Molloy*, 331, which lays down that an agent shipping goods in a foreign country is not liable, but the goods only and the consignee; but he reserved the point, and gave a verdict for the defendants.

A rule nisi having been obtained accordingly,

Le Messurier, A. G., and *Holland* shewed cause. When an agent at home does not disclose his principal he is liable; *Ex parte Hartopp*, (12 Ves.); *a fortiori* abroad. Bombay, with respect to England, is as much a foreign country as any other. They further cited *Story on Agency*, 251; 2 *Smith's Leading Cases*, 198, and *Shee's Abbott*, 290.

Dickinson, contrà. The defendants here were agents both for the plaintiff and his co-shipowners, and for Gardner Boggs. Being such agents for the plaintiff, the latter had constructive notice that they were shipping these goods for Gardner Boggs. The contract for freight is not like a contract of sale, for the shipowner has always the possession of the goods as his security; and in a shipment from Bombay to his own country it must be taken, unless there is an express contract to the contrary, that he looks to the goods and consignees only; 2 *Molloy*, 331.

1844.

POTTER *v.* HORMAZJI.

Cur. adv. vult.

June 21.

PERRY, J.—This is an action of *indebitatus assumpsit* for freight.

The plaintiff is the master and part owner of the "Wm. Shand," and the defendants are agents at Bombay. In order to prove the contract with the defendants, the plaintiff puts in and relies solely on the bill of lading, which is to the following effect:

"Shipped, &c. by Messrs. Bomanjee and Ardaseer Hormusjee, of Bombay, in and upon the 'Wm. Shand,' &c., 410 bales of cotton, &c., to be delivered in good order at Liverpool, or unto order or to assigns. Freight for the said goods customary after the said ship's arrival, as per memorandum indorsed;"—and the indorsement mentioned the amount of goods laden and the freight payable, *viz.* 385*l.* 17*s.* 6*d.*

The plaintiff further proved that, on arrival of the ship at Liverpool, the goods were claimed by one Gardner Boggs, under an indorsement of the bill of lading, and the custom being at Liverpool to deliver India freights to the consignee with sixty days' credit for the freight, the goods were delivered; but before the expiration of such sixty days Gardner Boggs failed, and the freight was unpaid. The plaintiff thereupon comes upon the original shipper for the amount.

The defendants proved that they were only agents for the shipment of this cargo, and that the plaintiff knew that fact, although he did not know who their principal was in England for this particular lot of cotton. They also proved that there were relations of a very intimate nature between them and the plaintiff, which arose as follows: Messrs. Boggs and Taylor, of London, had chartered the "Wm. Shand" for an Indian voyage, and they insisted upon the ship being consigned to the defendants at Bombay. The defendants thereupon became

1844.

POTTER v. HORMAZJI.

agents for the ship on its arrival at this port; and it became their duty to collect freight, &c. for the homeward voyage. The defendants were also agents to make shipments for different principals in England: and, under these circumstances, the defendants being agents of the plaintiff and his co-owners for the ship, and also agents of other parties in England, their counsel contended, that the true contract between them was not that they should pay the freight on this cotton, but that the principal in England should do so on delivery.

I was of opinion at the trial that such, in point of fact, was the true contract, that the defendants never intended to bind themselves to pay the freight on this cotton, and that the plaintiff, who, with his co-owners, were all domiciled in England, looked solely to the unknown principal in England as the party from whom he was to get his freight.

A rule has now been obtained, according to leave reserved, to enter a verdict for the plaintiff for a misdirection, or for a new trial, if the presumption drawn from the whole of the facts is not the correct one.

With regard to the first point, if the legal effect of a bill of lading is at once to throw upon the shipper the obligation of paying the freight, there was an undoubted misdirection, and there is no occasion to go further. But no case has yet decided this point; there is a passage in *Molloy*, vol. 2, p. 331, and in *Beawes' Lex Mercatoria*, p. 114, which lays down that an agent shipping goods is not liable for the freight, but the goods only, and the consignee receiving them under the bill of lading; and there is a decision of Lord TENTERDEN, that a mere shipper is not liable solely by virtue of a bill of lading; *Drew* v. *Bird*. An American decision, however, which seems to be approved of by our Courts, has held that the shipper is liable if he is the owner of the goods; and *Domett* v. *Beckford*, (2 Nev. & Man.), and *Tobin* v. *Crawford*, (5 M. & W.), also hold that the owner is liable under the bill of lading, although the bill of lading expressed in each case that the consignee was to pay freight on delivery. The point, therefore, under discussion has not yet received a decision, *viz.*, whether, when a party ships as agent only, he is liable under the bill of lading without more; and it is made a subject of *quære* by several writers. See notes of the reporters to *Drew* v. *Bird*, (2 M. & W. 156); *Smith's Mercantile Law*.

I think, therefore, that it would not have been a misdirection to tell the jury that the bill of lading did not absolutely bind the defendants, but that they were at liberty to look *aliunde*, and see from the other facts in the case what the true contract was. The question, therefore, upon this point is, whether those facts were sufficient to warrant the presumption that the defendants never did contract to pay the freight.

Contract of freight analysed.

Now, in inquiring into the nature of the contract which takes place between the shipowner and the merchant at the time of the shipment of goods, it cannot be denied, I think, that the former is much favoured by the law merchant. The contract which arises between such parties, contains in its essence an engagement to pay freight by the shipper; if the contract is reduced to writing, such obligation appears as an express term in the charter-party: if the contract is tacit, it is still an implied term as an essential part of the species of contract entered into. *Pothier*, treating of charter-parties, and of the *Ordonnance Maritime*, which has always been regarded with much respect in our commercial law, and which has been followed closely in the *Code de Commerce*, says, that "if a party loads goods on board with the consent of the master, but nothing is said about the freight, the contract is still a valid one, and they will be deemed to have agreed tacitly as to the freight, according to the current rate of the day." *Charter Parties*, Part 1, Act 1, *Du Fret*.

Construction of clause as to delivery of goods only on payment of freight.

The liability in law thus lying upon the shipper to pay freight, our Courts seem to have carried out the principle by leaning against any attempts to shift the liability. There can be little doubt, I think, that when the clause was first introduced into the bill of lading, of making the goods deliverable only on the payment of the freight, it was the intention of the consignor to rid himself of the obligation; and so thought Lord KENYON, and he ruled accordingly when the point first came before him at Nisi Prius. The Court above, however, thought otherwise; and it is clear law now, that such a clause

1844.

POTTER v. HORMAZJI.

is only for the benefit of the shipowner, although it may be observed that the shipowner did not require any such clause, having already a lien upon the goods for his freight. The decisions upon this point have been made where the contract between shipper and merchant has been expressly stated in the charter-party, but it is evident that the same law must apply to the contract, whether it is express or implied; and this brings me to the point upon which I think this case must be decided. The contract between the parties in this case was an implied contract, or at all events we have to gather from the circumstances what the contract was. But it has been shewn, that in an ordinary contract for freight it is a term that the shipper shall pay freight. If, therefore, in this particular case the defendants seek to make out that they did not enter into the usual contract which the law recognises, I think it is for them to establish that fact, and that in the absence of any evidence more positive than that which has been given, the defendants must be looked upon as shippers generally, and we are bound to presume that the ordinary contract of law was entered into by the parties.

The defendants have shewn that they were agents only in this shipment; but an agent who does not disclose the name of his principal, is to be looked upon, to all intents, as the principal himself. This is undoubted law as to principal and agents generally in other cases of contract, and I do not think, upon reflection, that there is anything in the contract of affreightment to warrant a different conclusion, or to allow, in this case the presumption being drawn that credit was given to the unknown principal in England from the mere facts that the freight was to be paid by the consignee on delivery, and that England was the domicile both of the unknown principal, and of the shipowner. The result is, that the defendants are to be looked upon as shippers generally, and the ordinary incidents of the contract arise.

It is with regret that I have come to this conclusion, because I have a strong conviction that at the time of entering into the contract neither party considered that the defendants were ever to be held liable for the freight. Still if the mercantile law does make the shipper generally liable for the freight, and the parties do not enter into any express contract so as to vary the ordinary obligations raised by the law, the presumption of the law must, I think, prevail over any faint presumption to be gathered from the facts of the case.

There ought, therefore, to be a new trial, or, if we have already all the facts before us which the defendants are capable of proving, no further expense need be gone to, but the verdict should be entered for the plaintiff.

JUSSUF BALADINA *v.* HOLDERNESS.

1843.

June 17.

[*Coram* ROPER, C. J., and PERRY, J.]

Where a charter party on a voyage from Bombay to Calcutta and back expressed that half the freight should be paid on delivery of the cargo at C., and the remaining half after delivery of the homeward cargo at B., and it was also covenanted that the freighter should make advances for the ordinary disbursements which were to be deducted from the amount due for freight at the completion of the voyage: *Held*, that advances so made were not in payment of freight, and therefore that they might be recovered back on the ship being burnt during the performance of the outward voyage.

ASSUMPSIT on the money counts to recover back Rs. 3900, which the plaintiff had advanced to the defendant as master of the ship Eleanor, for the ordinary disbursements of the ship.

At the trial it appeared that the plaintiff had chartered the vessel on a voyage from Bombay to Calcutta, and from thence back to Bombay; and that during her outward voyage the ship had been burnt (under somewhat suspicious circumstances (*a*)) off Alleppee, on the Malabar coast.

The clause in the charterparty as to freight was as follows:—"And also that they the said freighters shall and will truly pay, &c., unto the said master, &c., three days after the said vessel shall have delivered her cargo at Calcutta, half of whatever amount shall be found on calculation to be due for freight . . . . . . and the remaining half three days after the delivery of the homeward cargo at Bombay."

(*a*) See *post*, Reg. *v.* Alu Páru.

1843.

Jussuf v. Holderness.

Then followed several covenants on behalf of the freighters and, lastly, the following covenant:—

"And it is also covenanted and agreed by and between the said parties that the said freighters, their agents, correspondents, or assigns, shall and will advance to the said master, free of commission and interest, such sums as may be necessary for the ordinary disbursements of the said vessel, which amount is to be deducted from the amount that may be due for freight at the completion of the homeward voyage.

The plaintiff loaded a cargo on board the Eleanor, and prior to her departure from Bombay made an advance to the defendant of Rs. 3900, who gave him the following receipt:—

"Received from Jussuff Balladina Rs. 3900 on account of freight."

Howard, for the plaintiff, contended, that the advance made in this case was not in payment of freight, but as a loan without interest, and, therefore, that it was recoverable back, and he cited *Mashiter* v. *Buller*, (1 Cowp.)

Dickinson, contrà, relied on *Da Silva* v. *Kendall*, (4 Maule & Sel.); *Anon.*, (2 Show. 291); and cited *Mansfield* v. *Maitland*, (4 B. & Ald.), and *Saunders* v. *Drew*, (3 B. & Ad.)

Cur. adv. vult.

June 20.

By law freight is not payable till voyage is safely performed, and advances may be recovered back if voyage is not performed.

Perry, J.—The principle of law is fully assented to on either side that the freighter generally is not liable for freight unless the voyage is safely performed, and that, unless he has bound himself by express agreement to pay freight in advance, any sum he may have paid as freight before the commencement of the voyage, may be recovered back, if through any disaster the ship does not reach her port of destination. These two points are neatly put in *Roccus De Nav.*, not. 80:—"Naulum seu vectura non debetur si locator navis propter amissam navem, vel alium casum in eam contingentem, iter non fecerit, immo, si solutum fuerit, repetitur," and they are implicitly received in our law. See per Lord Ellenborough,

C. J., in 1 Camp. 85, and per Lord ABINGER, C. B., in 8 Carr. & Pay. 393.

By attention to this principle we are enabled to clear the case of any question that might otherwise arise on the form of the receipt on the bill of lading. The contract for the payment of freight is wholly governed by the terms of the charterparty; if, in that instrument, the freighter has bound himself to pay freight in advance, the advances cannot be received back; if he did not so bind himself, the advance was either a voluntary payment without consideration which may be sued for as money had and received, or it was a payment according to the charterparty, that is a loan without interest.

But in practice parties usually contract and pay freight in advance.

The whole question, therefore, is, whether the freighter has so bound himself, to pay freight before the completion of the voyage by way of advances, and, I think, that the true construction of the contract is, that he has not. The policy of the law and the interests of the merchant both require that freight should not be payable till the service to be rendered for it is performed. This maxim, of very old reception in the marine code, seems best fitted to secure faithful service and remove temptation to fraud from those persons entrusted with ships, and I do not think that there is anything in the present state of society to shew that the reasoning on which the maxim is founded, has become less operative. Parties undoubtedly, by special contract, may subject themselves to what obligations they please, and may voluntarily throw aside the protection which the law would otherwise have afforded them.

But in every contract of such nature it appears to me that the true rule of construction is,—the party who is alleged to have voluntarily given up certain rights shall not be taken to give up more than he has expressly stipulated. The covenant in question was introduced for the benefit of the master; it was his duty to have the point made clear as to whether the advances were to be made *quâ* freight; if such were the intention,—if he has left this point ambiguous, *verba fortissimé accipiuntur contra proferentem*, and the policy of the law supplies the deficiency by construing the omission in favour of the freighter.

1843.

JUSSUF v. HOLDERNESS.

The decided cases which have recognised the payment of advances as payment of freight appear to bear out this construction entirely. In all of them it is said that the stipulation must be to pay advances as freight, *eo nomine.* Thus, in 2 *Shower*, it is said, "Advance money paid before, in part of freight, *and named so in the charterparty,*" is a good payment of freight. So, in *De Silva* v. *Kendall,* Lord ELLENBOROUGH, after laying down the general principle, says, "But if the parties have chosen to stipulate by express words, or by words not express but sufficiently intelligible to that end, that a part of the freight (*using the word freight*) should be paid by anticipation,—may they not so stipulate?" So also in *Saunders* v. *Drew,* (3 B. & Ad. 445), the freighter, after hiring the vessel at so much a ton per month, agreed to pay four months of such monthly hire in advance, hire and freight being of course interchangeable terms.

The principle which governs our construction of this charterparty seems to me to be further confirmed by *Mansfield* v. *Maitland,* (4 B. & Ald. 582). For in that case where the charterparty, after expressing that freight was to be paid on delivery, half in cash and half in bills, contained a covenant that "the captain was to be supplied with cash for the ship's use," it would have been very easy for the Court to act upon the previous decision of *De Silva* v. *Kendall.* The mercantile transaction was in both exactly the same. The shipowner, foreseeing that he might need advances for the ship's use, required a stipulation from the owner that he would make them. A very easy construction therefore would have enabled the Court to say that the advances in both instances were made as freight; that the mere circumstance of the clauses as to payment of freight and advances being separate, was immaterial, and that they must be construed together according to the clear intention of the parties. But the Court refused to carry that case further, or to act on its analogy. ABBOTT, C. J. said, "It is undoubtedly competent for the owner to make such a stipulation as that in *De Silva* v. *Kendall.* But if he does so, it is his duty to take care that it is inserted in *clear and explicit words in the charterparty*, that the money advanced shall be an *advance in part payment of the freight*."

The Court, therefore, refused to extend the principle of decision in *De Silva* v. *Kendall* beyond its express terms. But the present case is confessedly an extension of that decision. The stipulation by the freighter is not nearly so clear and explicit, being unconnected with the clause as to payment of freight, and yet it is sought to be construed much more unfavourably for him than even that in *De Silva* v. *Kendall*. For if these advances are to be construed as a payment of freight, they are not advances which the freighter could recoup on the first amount of freight becoming due. The advances are to be repaid out of the homeward freight, but half of the entire freight is to be paid at Calcutta, and I feel no doubt that by this charterparty the master could demand and retain, on receipt of it at Calcutta, the whole of such freight, irrespective of whatever advances had been made at Bombay.

But this very unfavourable construction of the rights of the freighter undoubtedly demands most clear and unambiguous expressions to warrant it, and I confess I am quite unable to find them.

The case, indeed, would be entirely within the terms of *Mansfield* v. *Maitland*, if it were not that the clause as to advances contained a stipulation that no interest or commission should be allowed upon them, and this circumstance was undoubtedly much relied upon in *De Silva* v. *Kendall*, to shew that the transaction was not a loan, but a payment of freight in advance. We may easily understand, however, why a freighter, in his desire to get his cargo dispatched, should consent to advance money without interest, and this is all the express terms of the covenant convey. Then the decided cases shew that when the freighter also binds himself to make the payment as freight, the stipulation must be express as to that provision also. I therefore think, that the true construction of this charterparty is, that the freighter has only stipulated to make advances, without interest, for the use of the ship, which, in case of the safe prosecution of the voyage,

1843.

JUSSUF v. HOLDERNESS.

were not recoverable till the return to port of the vessel, but which, on her destruction, were recoverable absolutely (*a*).

(*a*) The defendant in this case was afterwards tried for wilfully burning the ship "Eleano," but was acquitted: by evidence subsequently obtained, however, it appeared that one Alu Páru, a wealthy merchant in Bombay, had shipped various packages of rubbish on board the vessel on which he effected very large insurances, having, by previous agreement with Holderness determined on the burning of the ship. After the acquittal of Holderness the underwriters paid the insurances. But the subsequent evidence coming to light Alu Páru was tried and transported for life. Holderness absconded.

1842. June 14.

KHIMCHUND MOTICHUND *v.* STRUTHERS AND OTHERS

[*Coram* ROPER, C. J., PERRY, J.]

Where a merchant in Bombay directed his agent at Macao to invest the proceeds of a cargo of opium in sycee silver, bills, &c., and the agent sold the opium to H. M. Plenipotentiary in China, and took his bill for the amount in his own favour, on the Lords of the Treasury, which he indorsed in blank, and remitted to defendants on account of the plaintiff, advising the plaintiff thereof, but at the same time directing the defendants privately not to part with the bill, but remit it to London for realization: *Held*, that the property in the bill had vested in the plaintiff so as to enable him to bring trover, either in respect of the bill specifically representing the plaintiff's opium, or that a sufficient delivery of it had been made to plaintiff by the agent in China.

TROVER for a bill of exchange, drawn by Capt. Elliot on the Lords of the Treasury, in favour of Messrs. Dent and Co. for 5385*l*., and indorsed by them in blank.

Pleas. 1st. Not guilty. 2nd. Not possessed.

The case came on for argument on admissions, by which it appeared that in January, 1839, the plaintiff, who was a merchant in Bombay, being about to make a shipment of opium to China, the defendants, as the agents of Messrs. Dent and Co. at Macao, advanced the plaintiff 72,115 dollars, on the security of the opium which was to be consigned to Dent and Co. for sale. The plaintiff accordingly, on the 15th of January, 1839, wrote to Dent and Co., inclosing the bill of lading, invoice, and policies of insurance for 200 chests of opium, and informing them of his draft in favour of themselves, in payment of the amount he had received from the defendants, *viz.*, 72,115 dollars. And as to the surplus he directed them as follows: "any surplus which may remain of the sale proceeds, after paying this draft, you will be pleased to invest in Sycee silver, Mexican dollars, or bills drawn by the Court of Directors on this Government, or by the Company's agent on the Government of India, or in such manner as in your opinion will pay better, protected by insurances."

On the 17th of July, 1839, Dent and Co. wrote to the plaintiff, referring to a message they had sent him through the defendants in the previous month, and they informed him that they had sold his opium to H. M. Chief Superintendent, Capt. Elliot, for 94,400 dollars, which, after deducting the draft in his favour, left a balance of 22,282 dollars, 5,385*l.*, in favour of plaintiff, for which sum they write, "we have sent Capt. Elliot's bill on the Lords of the Treasury, No. 9, dated Macao, 3rd of July, 1839, at twelve months in our favour, and indorsed to Messrs. Ritchie, Stewart and Co. (*a*) on your account. These gentlemen will arrange with you as to the best means of making the money available, either by procuring a remittance from England, or negotiating the bills in Bombay." The plaintiff, on the receipt of this letter, on the 14th of October, enclosed an extract from it to the defendants, requesting them to indorse and forward them the bill as soon as convenient. The defendants replied, "we shall not indorse the bill, nor send it to you; but in compliance with the instructions of Dent and Co., who indorsed it to us in their letter of 16th of July, we shall forward it to London, and, if paid, the proceeds will be returned to you in due course." The plaintiff made a similar demand on the 14th of October, threatening to hold the defendants responsible if they withheld the bill, and the defendants made a similar reply; the fact being that fears were entertained that this bill, which was one of those given by Capt. Elliot in respect of the opium handed over to the Chinese authorities, would not be honored by the British Government, and that Messrs. Dent might render themselves personally liable, if the bill got into circulation with their acceptance upon it.

(*a*) The defendant's firm.

1842.

KHIMCHUND v. STRUTHERS.

Certain other facts appeared, which are stated in the following judgment:—

Howard and *Burgass* for the plaintiff, contended that this bill of exchange represented his opium, and, therefore, that he was entitled to claim it, and they cited *Story on Agency*, 194; *Taylor* v. *Plumer*, (3 Mau. & S. 562); *Jackson* v. *Clark*, (1 You. & J.)

Le Messurier, A. G., and *Dickinson*, *contrà*. The cases cited are inapplicable, as the property there was earmarked, and, as there was no delivery of the bill to the plaintiff, the property remained in Dent and Co. If the defendants had assented to hold the bill on plaintiff's account, they might have made themselves liable, but they never did so. *Williams* v. *Everett*, (14 East, 582); *Westlake* v. *Harley*, (1 C. & J. 83); *Yates* v. *Bell*, (3 B. & Ald. 643); *Fisher* v. *Miller*, (1 Bingh. 150); *Brind* v. *Hampshire*, (1 M. & W. 365); *Scott* v. *Porcher*, (3 Mer. 652).

Moreover, even if the property was in the plaintiff, there has been nò conversion.

Cur. adv. vult.

PERRY, J., after stating the principal facts as above, continued as follows:—The defendants claim no interest whatever in this bill, they are the mere agents of Dent and Co., and having taken the bill with knowledge of all the circumstances of the case, they can set up no title whatever to the instrument, except such as their principals, Dent and Co., could confer; for the purposes, therefore, of this action, Dent and Co. may be looked upon as the true defendants.

Attempt by sub-agent to prefer the interests of agent to those of principal.

If the case then stood here, I must confess that I should require very strong authorities in point of law to convince me that an agent who has held goods on behalf of his principal, and taken a bill for the amount, and who confessedly has no claim of any kind against his principal, shall be permitted on any pretence to withhold that bill from his principal after he has demanded it from him. Here is a valuable instrument drawn upon the Lords of the Treasury by Her Majesty's Plenipotentiary in China, having several months' currency upon it, which, by the avowal of Dent and Co., might be negotiated in Bombay, and the proceeds of which indisputably belong to the plaintiff; and yet it is contended that an agent who has received this bill for his principal has a right to withdraw it from circulation, and to withhold it from him till it is due.

There are, however, other facts in the case, for it seems that, on the 28th of October, 1839, plaintiff writes to the defendants, or rather signs a letter written by the defendants, in which he requests them, as they decline delivering up the bill received from Messrs. Dent and Co., to forward the same to London for recovery.

On the 4th of January, 1840, Finlay, Hodgson and Co., who are the agents for the defendants in London, write to the plaintiff to inform him that they have received from the defendants Capt. Elliot's draft on the Lords of the Treasury on the plaintiff's account, and that it had been refused acceptance. They also enclosed the protest for non acceptance.

On the 23rd of February, 1840, the plaintiff encloses a copy of this letter to the defendants, and requests that the original bill should be sent to him, if in their possession. The defendants write back on the following day, stating that one copy of the bill had been sent to them by Finlay, Hodgson and Co., (the bill having been drawn in sets), and after referring to instructions they had received from Dent and Co., they conclude "under these circumstances, we would suggest your consenting that we should forward the bill to Dent and Co., as requested by them."

The plaintiff, however, refused to give such consent, and again demanded the bill, which the defendants refused to give up without an indemnity, whereupon this action has been brought.

Upon this statement of the case it would seem, that the defendants had acted either with extraordinary zeal for the interests of Dent and Co., or from some other motive not so apparent, in withholding this bill from the plaintiff, for, as

1842.

KHIMCHUND v. STRUTHERS.

they knew that the proceeds of the bill belonged to the plaintiff, and as they had their principal's own letter to the plaintiff of the 17th of July laid before them, in which the bill is stated to be sent to them on the plaintiff's account, it could only be as agent of the plaintiff that they could be entitled to perform any act with respect to it. It seems that the former supposition is the true solution of their conduct. For, by a letter of the 16th of July, 1839, to the defendants, Messrs. Dent and Co. state "that they think it best, for several reasons, to enclose this bill, with others of a similar nature, to the defendants, on account of the respective parties," and you, they continue, "will arrange with them as to the best mode of realizing the amount, either by getting the money remitted from England, or by negotiation of the drafts themselves in Bombay." By a letter of the following day, they write with reference to the opium given up to the Chinese, "As we are already under very heavy liabilities for this opium, and are uncertain of the means of the parties concerned, it might not be desirable to negotiate the bills with our names on them, should there be the least shadow of ground for fearing that course of proceeding might involve us in further risk of any kind."

They therefore direct these defendants, under certain circumstances, not to negotiate the bill in question in Bombay, but to forward it to England for recovery of the amount.

Here, then, we have Messrs. Dent and Co., of Macao, writing to the plaintiff on the 17th of July, informing him of the sale of his opium, of the balance due to him, and that they had sent a bill for the amount to the defendants, who would arrange with the plaintiff as to the best mode of making the money available, either by procuring a remittance from England, or *negotiating the bills in Bombay*, and on the very same day they write to their own agents, the defendants, directing them *not to negotiate the bill in Bombay*, if they think that the interests of Dent and Co. will be in any way affected by it. This is a species of dealing on the part of Messrs. Dent and Co. which, I must say, by no means recommends the case of the defendants to the favour of the Court.

1842.

KHIMCHUND v. STRUTHERS.

Upon these facts the plaintiff contends, that, as his opium is clearly represented by this bill of exchange, he is entitled to demand and have it, either from his agent, or from any person who has received it from his agent with notice; and he has referred the Court to *Taylor* v. *Plumer*, (3 Maul. & Sel.), and *Jackson* v. *Clarke*, (1 You. & Jer.) The defendants, on the other hand, base their defence not on any claim or title, but entirely on the technical nature of the action of trover, and of the character of a bill of exchange. One of the learned counsel for the defendants admits, that in some other form of action (though he does not say what) the plaintiff might have recovered the bill, and that, on the equity side of the Court, the defendants might perhaps have been compelled to indorse the bill over to the plaintiff.

To technical objections of this kind the Court must be always reluctant to give ear, more especially as we are directed by our charter "to give judgment and sentence according to justice and right." Undoubtedly, however, if the objections of the defendants shew that the plaintiff does not possess the right to bring this action of trover, the objection must prevail. I therefore proceed to examine them. The first objection appears to be, that the plaintiff is not entitled to recover this bill of exchange, because there has been no delivery of it to him, as a bill of exchange requires delivery as well as indorsement to pass the property in it. Undoubtedly, in a certain sense, delivery is required as well as an indorsement, and, if the bill belonged to Dent and Co., their indorsement and delivery of it would have been necessary to convey the property in it to a third party. But the plaintiff contends that the bill never did belong to Dent and Co., that directly they purchased with his opium this bill of exchange, it became *ipso facto* his, and that he has the right to claim it at their hands. I am of opinion that this reasoning is correct, and that it is fully borne out by *Taylor* v. *Plumer*. It is unnecessary, however, to dispose of the objection on this point, because if any delivery of the bill to the plaintiff was necessary to complete his title to it, I think that there was a sufficient delivery. Dent and Co. indorsed the bill in blank, and

1842.

KHIMCHUND v. STRUTHERS.

enclosed it to the defendants for the use of the plaintiff, and gave him notice to that effect. It is clear that the defendants, upon this advice from Dent and Co., had no power over the bill, that any general indorsement of it by them would have been a fraud, and that their indorsement was not necessary to make it available for the plaintiff. But the property in a bill so sent (not being fettered by any special indorsement) vests in the party for whose use it is remitted; *Sargent* v. *Morris*, (3 B. & Ad. 277); *Evans* v. *Marlott*, (1 Ld. Raym. 271).

It may be said that Dent and Co. never did deliver the bill to the plaintiff, and did not intend that the bill should be given up to him, as fully appears by their letter of the 17th of July to the defendants; but after Dent and Co. had written the letter to the plaintiff, telling him that they had sent the bill for him, how can they be listened to in a Court of justice to contradict their own statement?

The defendants however contend, that their consent to hold the bill for the plaintiff was necessary in order to give the plaintiff a title to it, and they cite the class of cases of which *Williams* v. *Everett*, (14 East), is the representative; but in my opinion those cases are wholly inapplicable.

This bill is not indorsed to the defendants, as their counsel would contend; they did not become, on the receipt of it, debtors to Dent and Co. to that amount; but they hold it, and had exactly the same right over it as Dent and Co., and no other.

The question, therefore, is entirely as to the property in this bill of exchange, and if that be in the plaintiff he has a right to maintain trover for it.

It is contended, however, that if the plaintiff adopts the act of his agents in taking the bill of Capt. Elliott, he must also adopt all their subsequent proceedings in regard to the bill.

But this proposition, which is so clearly repugnant to common sense, has no foundation in the law. Undoubtedly, if the act of an agent is made the foundation of an action against a third party, the whole of the act of the agent on that particular occasion is adopted; and so if, on the tortious act of an agent, the tort is waived, and an action for money had and received is brought against him, the defendant is let into any set-off he may have, but even then no other recognition of his conduct is made; *Hunter* v. *Prinsep*, (10 East, 378). The plaintiff, by this form of action, recognizes the propriety of Dent and Co. selling his opium for a bill of exchange. By such a ratification would he have been also held to have ratified Dent and Co. passing away the bill for their own private purposes? But in point of right, what greater power did Dent and Co. possess to withhold the bill from the plaintiff than to pay it away to their own creditors?

It is also contended, though faintly, that the bill does not represent the plaintiff's opium. I am of opinion, however, that in the account given by Dent and Co., in which they take credit for their own balance, and get Capt. Elliot to draw in their favour for the exact balance due to the plaintiff, it is impossible to conceive goods more specifically represented by a bill of exchange than in the present instance.

The last point insisted on is, that there is no proof of conversion. I think, however, there is sufficient proof. If the effect of the refusal to deliver up the bill when demanded on the 11th of October, is obviated by the letter written by the plaintiff on the 28th of October (and which I think, under the circumstances, is somewhat doubtful), I think the refusal to deliver up the bill in February, 1840, is ample evidence of a conversion. On the whole, I am of opinion that all the objections made by the defendants fail, and that the plaintiff is entitled to a verdict for 5385*l.* 9*s.*

Judgment for the Plaintiff.

1846.

Nov. 13.

CASSIM NATHA
v.
G. V. G. FARRAND, ESQ., AFTERWARDS JAIRAZ BALU.

Coram POLLOCK, C. J., and PERRY, J.]

1. Where a merchant buys goods, and pays for them by a forged cheque on bankers, *quære* whether a subsequent *bonâ fide* purchaser for value can hold them against the original vendor. Per PERRY, J.—He can so retain them, for, although the original vendor was imposed upon, and the contract he made was rescindible, still the property passed from him by the sale.
Per ROPER, C. J., he cannot do so.
Per POLLOCK, C. J., *quære.*
2. Conflict between ancient rule of law and exigencies of commerce; how treated by the Dutch law, by the French law, by the American, by the English.
3. Decisions in English civil and criminal law on subject reconciled.

TROVER for ivory. Plea. Not guilty.

The facts proved on the trial were as follows:

On Sunday morning in February last, one Hírjí Jetsy, a petty merchant in Bombay, bargained with the plaintiff for the purchase of a lot of ivory. The ivory was weighed, an entry of the sale was made, in the books of the plaintiff, as of a sale at two months' credit, with a rebate for ready money; and everything was settled but the taking away and paying for the goods. It was agreed however, at the trial, that although the sale was expressed to be made on credit, it was a ready money transaction, and the term of two months was inserted, with the two per cent. rebate, as a mode of ascertaining the ready money price.

On the Monday following, Hírjí sent his servant with a cheque for Rs. 5000, which was something under the amount due on the ivory. The cheque, which was in English, purported to be drawn on the Bank of Bombay by Manockji Nasserwanjí, a well known merchant, and was delivered to a partner of the plaintiff, who, although unable to read English, saw that the figures were for the sum of Rs. 5000, and therefore he delivered the ivory.

On that same Sunday Hírjí applied to the defendant Jairaz, who was a respectable merchant, for an advance on ivory, and the defendant, who had been in the habit previously of making him advances on merchandize, consented to do so. The ivory accordingly, which was taken away from the plaintiff's warehouse about 4 P. M. on the Monday, was brought to the defendant Jairaz's warehouse about 5 P. M., and a sum of Rs. 3000 was advanced. 1846.

CASSIM v. FARRAND.

The cheque, having been given so late in the day, was not presented at the bank till the next day at eleven or twelve o'clock, when it was discovered to be a forgery. Search was immediately made after Hírjí, but he had absconded. It was then discovered that Hírjí had pledged the goods with the defendant Jairaz; proceedings took place at the police office, when the ivory was impounded by the magistrate, and this action was brought against the magistrate on his refusing to give up the ivory to the plaintiff.

At the trial of this action before ROPER, C. J., and PERRY, J., the Chief Justice, being of opinion that the magistrate had no right to detain the ivory, and that it belonged to the plaintiff, gave a verdict accordingly, *dissentiente* PERRY, J. (*a*).

ROPER, C. J., having afterwards thought that a new trial ought to be had, a rule *nisi* was granted accordingly, against which cause was now shewn, (*Cor.* POLLOCK, C. J., and PERRY, J.), and, as the facts were undisputed, it was agreed that the decision should be governed by the disposal of this rule.

The three points made by *Le Messurier*, A. G., in moving for his rule, were: 1st, that by the sale the property in the ivory, to the extent of Rs. 3000, passed to Hírjí Jetsy: 2ndly, that the contract having been made by Hírjí, who was to be considered a broker of the plaintiff, even if the broker committed fraud, the plaintiff was bound by it as principal: 3rdly, that even if the sale were fraudulent, and no property passed under it, the plaintiff was estopped by his own negligence to recover from an innocent purchaser.

Howard shewed cause. This rule was obtained on the

(*a*) PERRY, J., held that a charge of felony, for obtaining goods by false pretences, having been made, the magistrate was justified in impounding the property till the charge was disposed of and that a simple refusal to give them up to the plaintiff was no conversion on his part. It was subsequently agreed to drop the proceedings against the magistrate, and to substitute Jairaz as the defendant.

1846. CASSIM v. FARRAND.

authority of *Parke's case,* (2 Leach Cr. Ca. 614), but that is quite inconsistent with the principles of law that a man cannot convey more title and property than he himself possesses; *Chitty on Contracts,* 406, 3rd. ed.; and a long string of decisions. It is a universal proposition, that where there is fraud no property passes, and Hírjí accordingly having got possession of these goods by fraud, if not by felony, could pass no property in them. Formerly, it was held, that where goods were obtained by false pretences, a *bonâ fide* purchaser could retain them against the owner; *Parker* v. *Patrick,* (5 T. R. 175); but that case has been overruled; *Peer* v. *Humfrey,* (2 A. & E. 495); 2 *Wms. Saund,* 47, note (*p*).

Several cases shew that, where goods have been obtained by fraud, trover will lie by the owner; *Noble* v. *Adams,* (7 Taunt. 59); *Earl of Bristol* v. *Wilsmore,* (1 B. & C. 514); *Fergusson* v. *Carrington,* (9 B. & C. 59); *Keable* v. *Payne,* (8 A. & E. 555); *Irving* v. *Motley,* (7 Bing. 543).

Nor is it necessary that Hírjí should have been convicted in order to recover the property, for *White* v. *Spettigue,* (13 Mees. & W. 603), shews that that is not necessary, even when felony has been committed, and as Peel's Act establishes that the property is to be restored on a conviction for false pretences, just as upon a conviction for felony, the analogy is made complete.

As to the negligence which the plaintiff is said to have been guilty of in taking the cheque, it was the ordinary dealing of the bazaar.

Le Messurier, A. G., *contrà.* This is a case of great importance to the mercantile world. In none of the cases which have been cited does there appear to have been a *bonâ fide* purchaser for value. The distinction between goods obtained by fraud and by felony is very great; in the latter case, there is no consent by the owner, in the former, there is; and, if it subsequently happens that through this fraud one of the two innocent parties is to suffer, it is more fitting that the man who has not had his wits about him should be the party to ose. In *Kent's Commentaries,* vol. 2, p. 497, he enters into

1846.

CASSIM *v.* FARRAND.

the subject at length, and after citing the Roman law, and *Ross on Sales*, he quotes two cases before the American tribunals, which held that, in cases like the present, the *bonâ fide* purchaser is entitled to retain the property. Then *Parke's case* is a solemn decision by the twelve Judges, that in a case like this the property does pass, and Lord ABINGER, C. B., carried out the principle in *Sheppard* v. *Shoobred*, (Carr. & Marsh. 61), which is quite in point for this case.

The late provision of the criminal law as to the restitution of property on a conviction for false pretences cannot be taken to have altered the law of property, but must be construed to extend only to those cases where the goods are in the hands of the fraudulent party.

Cur. adv. vult.

POLLOCK, C. J., on a later day, delivered judgment for the defendant, on the ground that the property passed to Hírjí by the contract on the Sunday, and that the subsequent fraud of giving the false cheque on the Monday did not affect the original contract (*a*).

PERRY, J.—The question to be decided in this case is, on which of the two innocent parties the loss occasioned by the fraud of Hírjí is to fall.

Where loss has to fall on one of two innocent parties rule of law more or less arbitrary.

Whenever such a case arises the rule which selects one or other of the parties to bear the burthen must proceed on grounds more or less arbitrary, and, in the present case, abundance of argument is available on either side to guide the judgment of the Court in favour either of the plaintiff or defendant.

The point to be decided on is, whether a *bonâ fide* purchaser who obtains goods from a party who has got possession of them by a fraudulent contract is entitled to hold them against the original holder, and the state of the decisions in the English law is such, that it appears to me that it is very much open to the discretion of the Court to decide either way.

(*a*) See his judgment, 2 Morley's Digest, 406.

1846. CASSIM v. FARRAND.

This, indeed, is always the case in the English system when a new point arises, and it is the boast of the common law, that it is able to mould itself to the growing exigencies and ever changing events of a commercial and progressing society without recurrence to the Legislature, as is necessary in some other countries.

Mode of growth of English law, so as to meet the exigencies of time.

The theory is, that our system of jurisprudence contains within it principles capable of being applied to all the varied relations of life according to the soundest views of justice and expediency. But it follows from this view, that, where any case arises to which the rule applicable is not very readily perceptible, the inquiry takes the direction as to what the principles of sound reasoning demand, and the proper answer to what the law is, may often readily be determined by ascertaining what the law ought to be.

In the present case two conflicting principles meet us at the onset; it is one of the first axioms of jurisprudence that a sale of goods belonging to a third party confers no title on the purchaser; on the other hand, the exigencies of commerce require that the transfer of merchandize should be made in the readiest manner, and that *bonâ fide* possession should be protected But, as the difficulty raised by this conflict must have occurred in other countries besides our own, it becomes important to see what principle other commercial codes have established on the subject, and to ascertain whether the rule, which experience and the wants of mankind have suggested elsewhere, can be made to accord with the principles of our law.

Principle as to transfer of property in Roman law.

Now, the Roman law, it is said, gave a valid title to a *bonâ fide* possession, even in the case of stolen property, and the owner had only a remedy against the thief; 2 *Kent's Commentaries*, 320; *Ross on Sales*, 187. But the American Chancellor, and our own countryman, are, undoubtedly, wrong in their statement of the law, for it is most clear, that by the early Roman law a man could gain no title by prescription to property, either stolen or obtained by violence; see *Inst.* 2. 6. §. 1, 2, and *Vinnius ad eund. tit.*, except, indeed, by the prescription of thirty years, and even in the later law, when trade began to arise under the emperors, there is a very pithy constitution in the code, rebuking some merchants who had bought stolen goods *bonâ fide*, and who applied to have their advances paid by the owner before they gave them up—*Code*, lib. vi., tit. 2, "Incivilem rem desideratis," &c.

1846.

CASSIM *v.* FARRAND.

The Roman law, therefore, made the rights of property paramount. *Res furtiva* could be claimed by the owner wherever he found it, and every moveable which had been aliened improperly was considered *res furtiva;* see 4 *Hugo's Civ. Cur.* p. 102, 3; and the *condictio furtiva*, which *Kent* speaks of, was only an additional remedy against the thief and his heirs, if the owner could not recover his goods elsewhere. But in the countries where the Roman law was adopted, a relaxation of the rule was required in favour of commerce, and *I. Voet* has collected a quantity of statutes of the Low Countries in which he wrote, by which the Roman law was altered in favour of *bonâ fide* purchasers. He also discusses the question whether goods obtained by fraud are to be considered in the same light as goods obtained by larceny, and he thinks they are, though he cites the opinions of other civilians who differ on the point. But the practical conclusion to which those commercial countries appear generally to have arrived at is, that a *bonâ fide* purchaser of goods in market overt ("*in publicis nundinis*,") whether they were obtained by felony or fraud, obtained a good title; *I. Voet. Pand.* 419, et s. 99.

Altered in favour of commerce in Dutch law.

The Scotch law, as I had occasion to mention during the argument, allows the owner of stolen goods to recover them any where, even though bought in market overt; but, as to goods obtained by a fraudulent contract, it enables a *bonâ fide* purchaser to retain them; see the note in *Erskine's Institutes*, p. 666-7, ed. 1838.

Also in Scotch law.

In the French law exactly the same question has arisen, and the same arguments have been used, as in the present case. The French, like the English, law enables the owner of stolen property to recover it from a *bonâ fide* purchaser (though under more restrictions than our law imposes); and in a case where goods had been obtained under a fraudulent contract, and sold to a *bonâ fide* purchaser, it was contended that they

Also in French law.

1846.

CASSIM v. FARRAND.

were exactly in the same category as goods obtained by theft: that to pass a property in goods the consent of the owner was required: and that consent obtained by fraud was equivalent to no consent at all. The Cour Royale of Paris assented to these arguments, and held that the original owner might recover, but the Court of Cassation reversed the decision on this, amongst other grounds, and the reasoning proceeding on general principles is so applicable to this case, that I venture to translate the passage:—"Larceny must not be confounded with obtaining goods by false pretences (*escroquerie*), as in the latter case the party defrauded accepts the credit of the rogue, *and by the sale he makes to him he confers upon him a title wholly independent of the possession,* whereas in larceny there is neither sale nor voluntary delivery." *Arrêt du* 20 *mai.*, 1835, *Ch. Civ. Dall.* 1835, 1338; *Rogron's Code Civ.* 1445.

Also in American law.

Finally, in the American law, two decisions are cited in the note to the last edition of *Kent's Commentaries*, vol. 2, p. 325, 4th ed., which shew that a *bonâ fide* purchaser may retain goods which have been obtained from the original owner under a fraudulent contract, and those decisions are the more in point, because that law, following the tendency of the English law as to sales in market overt but going much further, wholly disallows a change in the title to property to be effected by public sale.

According to all those codes of law, therefore, it would seem that the defendant, under circumstances such as have arisen in the present case, would be entitled to hold the goods, and, I think, the English law affords the same rule.

English criminal law accords.

The principle seems to me quite indisputable in our criminal law, that where the owner of goods parts with the possession of goods, intending to part with the property at the same time, the property passes, however fraudulent the means may have been by which his will has been determined. *Parke's case,* and many others collected in 2 Russ., established this proposition, and I am unable to distinguish them from the present case.

On the other hand, there are many cases on the civil side of the Court in which it has been held, that where goods are obtained by fraud no property passes. It is our duty to

1846.

CASSIM v. FARRAND.

reconcile these apparent *antinomiæ*, if possible, and to draw from them a harmonious rule which shall bring our decision within the principles of all the previous authorities. I think that this may be done, and that all the cases, in which the general expressions alluded to were employed, may be explained on grounds which leave the principles recognised in the criminal law entire.

Conflicting decisions in English civil law explained and reconciled.

In *Noble* v. *Adams*, (7 Taunt. 59), for instance, which is one of the first cases where no property was said to pass in goods obtained by false pretences, it was the plaintiff himself who was suing on the fraudulent contract. And it obviously would be monstrous to allow a party who had obtained goods under a fraudulent contract to set up his title to them as on a valid contract. So in *Irving* v. *Motley*, (5 M. & P. 380; 7 Bingh. 543), which has been so much discussed here, the defendant had got possession of the goods by the fraud of his agent, and that evidently is the true ground of the decision as it was put by Mr. Justice GASELEE.

Then, in *Earl of Bristol* v. *Wilsmore*, (1 B. & C. 514), the party who obtained the goods by fraud made them over on the same day to his sister-in-law, who was a creditor, and that circumstance might very well prevent any title passing to her, as it would in the Scotch law, where creditors are not allowed to avail themselves of the title of goods which their debtor has acquired under a fraudulent contract, but I admit that that circumstance was not adverted to in the arguments or judgment.

Keable v. *Payne*, (3 Nev. & P. 531), at first sight appears a very strong authority for the plaintiff, as it seems to proceed on the conceded point of law, that a *bonâ fide* purchaser gains no title where the goods are obtained by fraud. On first reading the case, and adverting to the state of the authorities, I was surprised to find that the very able counsel for the defendant had not made the point which has been argued in this case, but, on looking at it again, I think it is fully explained by the note of the reporters, namely, that the jury found that the defendant was not a *bonâ fide* purchaser.

In addition to those authorities apparently making for the plaintiff, there must be added the remarks which have from

1846.

CASSIM *v.* FARRAND.

time to time been thrown out on *Parker* v. *Patrick*, (5 T. R. 175). Lord KENYON's decision undoubtedly has been much shaken, and especially by Lord DENMAN's observations in *Peer* v. *Humfrey*, (2 Ad. & Ell. 495; 1 Har. & Woll. 28); still, the latter were in some degree *obiter*, the former was a decision *in rem;* and a decision by Lord KENYON, on the principles of property and its modes of transfer, can never be overruled except with the greatest deliberation.

Principle of English law;

If it be true, that by the law of England the property passes in goods which the owner is induced by fraud to sell, the decision in *Parker* v. *Patrick* was right, and should be adhered to; and it appears to me that that is the principle of the law, although as against the fraudulent contractor, and those claiming under him as volunteers or even creditors, it may be perfectly true to say that no property passes.

It may, perhaps, seem a contradiction in terms to say that cases can be reconciled, some of which hold that the property passes in such a case, some that it does not; but this contradiction is only superficial. In the civil cases in which the latter form of expression is to be found, it was not necessary to consider what the rights of a *bonâ fide* purchaser might be, and therefore perfect accuracy of definition was not required. No one doubts that such a fraudulent contract is invalid, and that the innocent seller has the right, as against the fraudulent purchaser and those claiming in privity with him, to treat it as altogether null, and therefore the compendious forms of speech fully justify the use of the phrase in the civil cases referred to. But *Parke's case*, which was a decision by the twelve Judges, and the other cases of the same class, decide the very point under discussion, namely, that the property does pass.

accords with doctrine laid down by Pothier.

I think it is right to add, that a very great authority on the nature of contracts, the President Pothier, gives exactly the same exposition of a fraudulent contract as the decisions in our law seem to suggest, namely, that, although the contract is vicious, and may be rescinded by the innocent party, still it is a contract, and the property passes under it. "Lorsqu'une partie a été engagée à contracter par le dol de l'autre, le contrat n'est pas absolument et essentiellement nul, parce qu'un consentement quoique surpris ne laisse pas d'être consentement, mais le contrat est vicieux," &c. Traité des Obligations, part. 1, sec. 1, art. 3, du Dol. It follows, that if the property in such case gets into the hands of a *bonâ fide* purchaser, he is entitled to retain, though neither the fraudulent contractor nor those claiming in privity with him would be enabled to do so (*a*).

1846.

CASSIM *v.* FARRAND.

Judgment for defendant.

(*a*) Compare with this the law in the Code, 4. 44. 18, *viz.*, that, where fraud has taken place in a contract on the part of the purchaser, the vendee cannot bring trover (*rei vindicatio*) against a third party, who derives title from the purchaser, but must resort to the fraudulent purchaser. So Bac. Ab. Trover (*c*) lays down, if a bailee gives goods (*à fortiori*, if he sells) to a stranger, bailor cannot maintain trover. But see Story on Bailments, c. 2, § 105, and Cooper *v.* Willmott, 1 C. B. 683.

SYERS, LIVINGSTONE AND CO. *v.* DADABHAI PESTONJI.

1849.

Nov. 28.

[*Coram* PERRY, C. J., and YARDLEY, J.]

Rules of the English law as to stoppage *in transitu*, and rules of other commercial codes on the same subject discussed.

Course of business of Bombay brokers.

TROVER to recover a large quantity of cotton which the defendant had purchased as broker for the plaintiffs, and which, on the insolvency of the latter, the defendant had obtained possession of under a claim of stoppage in transitu. The case was tried on the 26th and 28th of November, and, at the close of the trial, the Court pronounced judgment in favour of the plaintiffs; but, as the sum at stake was very large (said to be 35,000*l.*), the Chief Justice, at the request of the parties, afterwards reduced to writing the reasons he had assigned for the decision of the Court.

PERRY, C. J.—This is an action of trover for the recovery of a quantity of cotton, which it is agreed between

1849.

SYERS & Co. v. DADABHAI.

Mode of business between Bombay English merchant and native broker

the parties that the Captain's receipts represent, and which, it would seem, amounts in value to upwards of three laks and a half of rupees, or, at least, that sum is involved in the present decision.

On the evidence before us I think it clearly results that the defendant purchased this cotton on his own credit for the plaintiffs, to whom he was broker, and that the cotton was actually delivered to the latter. I think it also appears that the mode of doing business between the parties was, that the plaintiffs should pay for the cotton delivered to them, from time to time, so soon as they could negotiate bills in Bombay to be drawn on London against the consignments; and as, at the period in question, when these large purchases were made, the paper of the plaintiffs was not negotiable, either from the unfavourable state of the exchange, or from the commercial panic consequent upon the failures of Reid, Irving and Co., and other great London houses, I think it must be taken as a clear fact in the case, that the defendant delivered the cotton to the plaintiffs on their personal credit. On the 29th of November, 1847, after the delivery of the cotton, the news arrived at Bombay that a firm in Liverpool, with which the plaintiffs were closely connected, had stopped payment, whereupon the plaintiffs determined to suspend also, and having informed the defendant of their intention, the latter, on the refusal by the plaintiffs to deliver over the Captain's receipts, made himself master of them, not, probably, as is alleged by one witness, by any surreptitious act, but by demanding them from the servants of the plaintiffs, who gave them up.

The defendant by this act being, as it were, now in possession of the cotton, is sued nominally by the plaintiffs, but, in fact, by the trustees of the firm, which is winding up under inspection, on behalf of the other creditors.

The question in the case principally involves the right to stoppage *in transitu* by the English law, as it is alleged that the relation between defendant and plaintiffs was, that of vendor and purchaser, and, although I do not exactly assent to the correctness of this proposition, I admit that for the purposes of stoppage *in transitu*, the cases of *Feise* v. *Wray*, and

1849.

SYERS & CO. *v.* DADABHAI.

Hawker v. *Dann*, shew that a broker buying on his own credit may be looked upon as a *quasi* vendor. Now, there is no doctrine better settled in the law merchant than that the right of an unpaid vendor to recover possession of goods which have not been paid for only exists so long as the goods are in a state of transit to the purchaser. Directly these goods come to the actual possession of the buyer, the property and possession are vested indefeasibly in him, and the seller must look to the purchaser for payment, like any other creditor. In all rules which govern the transfer of property, there must be something more or less arbitrary in the provisions which regulate the mode how, or the precise period when, the property passes from one individual to another, and it is not so material what this arbitrary rule should be, as that, when once established, it should be inflexibly adhered to. In nearly every case of insolvency, as in the present instance, there are two innocent and meritorious parties before the Court, each of whom has trusted to the credit of the insolvent, and each of whom, therefore, has, in most cases, equal claims to the favourable considerations of the Court. What, therefore, is to be desired in such cases, especially in a commercial community, is a clear and precise rule of law, defining which of the two innocent parties is to bear the loss, so that parties may at once know their rights, and a further sacrifice of property in ruinous litigation may be avoided. The rule of English law in this case, and the doctrine on which the right to stoppage *in transitu* is founded, is, as I said before, completely settled, and, as I think, on a very intelligible and satisfactory basis.

Rule of law as to partition of loss between two innocent parties an arbitrary rule, in first instance.

By the English law, on a contract of sale, when nothing remains to be done by the seller, such as weighing, separation from the bulk, &c., the property in goods sold vests at once in the purchaser, but the seller retains a lien on the possession for payment of the price. And, if before delivery the purchaser becomes insolvent, the seller may refuse to deliver the goods, unless payment is made to him, even although the original contract of sale was on credit. On the other hand, if the goods are delivered to the purchaser, the right of possession and right of property have coalesced in the latter, and all

Transfer of property on sale, when it occurs.

1849.

Syers & Co. *v.* Dadabhai.

right to these specific goods, on the part of the seller, is gone. These two propositions only embrace the cases of the goods remaining in the possession of the vendor, or of their coming to the possession of the purchaser; but it is obvious that there is a third case, where the goods are not in the actual possession of either party, but are in the custody of a third person, for the purpose of being delivered to the purchaser. In such case, it is clear that the law may treat this third person's custody as the possession of either the vendor or the purchaser; in many cases, by a convenient fiction, and for the purposes of justice, the law treats it as the possession of the purchaser, and he may bring possessory actions in respect of the goods; but in stoppage *in transitu*, the English law treats this custody as the possession of the seller, and then it follows, most logically, that his lien on the possession still exists. Lord Kenyon called this right, on the part of the seller, an equitable lien; but, if the above view is just, it might be better called a legal lien, on the ground, that the *custody* of a servant, in nearly all cases, amounts to *possession* by the master, and *quoad hoc* the carrier of an unpaid vendor may be considered as his servant.

Right of possession, right of property, distinct.

The objections urged on the part of the defendant rest chiefly on the broad and natural equity which, it is asserted, exists on the side of the vendor to retake possession of goods which have not been paid for. The conclusive answer to such arguments is the clear rule of law which I have already stated. But even on equitable principles it is evidently open to an almost endless argument as to what would be the expedient rule to lay down if the question were *res integra*; for, as in most cases, it is plainly an accident whether the goods remain in the possession of the purchaser or not, if the vendor has once parted with them, trusting to the credit of the purchaser, there seems no good reason why he should be preferred to any other creditor. There is, however, *primâ facie* an apparent equitable claim on the part of an unpaid vendor, which may easily lead to different conclusions being drawn. This is manifested by the conflicting rules which have been adopted by various commercial nations. Thus, the English Court of Chancery has established a rule, by which the unpaid vendor

Stoppage *in transitu* founded on right of possession.

1849.

SYERS & Co. v. DADABHAI.

of landed estate may follow it in the hands of even a third purchaser with notice, but the doctrine gives rise to such nice distinctions and expensive inquiries, that the most accomplished equity Judge in modern times regretted its existence. Lord ELDON, in *Mackrell* v. *Symonds*, (15 Ves.), and *Story* points out how far it departs from the simple and logical doctrine of the Roman law. So by the old Dutch law, as we learn from *I. Voet*, the vendor might seize his goods whilst in the possession of an unpaid purchaser, if the latter became insolvent; but this was placed on the manifestly unsatisfactory ground that a purchaser by such insolvency is fraudulent, and, therefore, the contract was void; and, I believe, in the modern law, the rule no longer exists. Again, in the French law, the vendor of goods unpaid for may reclaim them by the action of revendication, whilst they remain in the possession of the purchaser, provided he institutes his proceedings within eight days of the delivery. In this conflict of authority it is clear that no universal opinion has been arrived at in the most civilised commercial nations as to what the wisest rule on the subject is.

French modern law accords with English.

But it is satisfactory to find that, as to the present case, the French law affords exactly the same rule as our own. In the case of insolvency the *Code de Commerce* lays down that the right of an unpaid vendor to reclaim possession no longer exists, but the right to stoppage *in transitu* is given him so long as the goods have not come to the possession of the purchaser, and the definition of the period during which this right exists might be transferred in terms to our own law. Art. 577 of the original *Code* lays it down:—"La revendication ne pourra avoir lieu que pendant que les marchandises expédiés seront encore en route, soit par terre, soit par eau, et avant qu'elles soient entrées dans les magasins du failli," &c.

In fact, the universal right of stoppage *in transitu*, which Lord ABINGER points out to exist throughout Europe, is always limited by the fact of the possession not having yet arrived at the hands of the purchaser, and, although I have been desirous to give to this case additional consideration from the large amount involved in the decision, directly the fact became established in evidence that the possession

1849.

Syers & Co. v. Dadabhai.

had vested in the plaintiffs, it did not appear to me that there was any question left on which a Court of English law could entertain discussion.

Technical objection.

Another argument has been urged more particularly to-day, when the equitable doctrine, which was urged so strongly on Tuesday last, has not been so much referred to, namely, that although, in a case of bankruptcy, the assignees might be entitled to recover in circumstances like the present, the case of an insolvent suing in his own name stands altogether on different ground, and that he ought not to be listened to in a Court of justice when he sets up such an inequitable claim.

Trustees of an insolvent are treated by the Court like assignees of a bankrupt.

But I am unable to draw any distinction between the assignees of a bankrupt suing in their own names, and the trustees of an insolvent suing in the name of the latter. They both sue on behalf of the creditors at large, and whatever rights pass to the one ought, in consistent reasoning, to pass to the other also. But supposing that a Court of law is not enabled to take notice that this action is brought on behalf of the trustees, and that the plaintiffs on the record only are to be looked at, still if the legal right is in those plaintiffs, they are entitled to the verdict of the Court; and the only ground for relieving the defendant from payment of the damages would be, that in equity neither the plaintiffs nor their trustees are entitled to hold them. But in equity it is quite manifest that the title of the assignees elected under the Bankrupt Act, and of trustees elected out of Court by the creditors at large, stands precisely on the same footing.

There being therefore, as it appears to us, no doubt as to the rule of law which entitles the plaintiffs to a verdict, we have thought it right not to delay our judgment, but to pronounce it at once, so as to enable the parties who may be affected by it to take any proceedings they may think their interests require, in England, at the earliest possible period.

MIRZA ALI MAHOMED SHIRAZI
v.
AGA MAHOMED RAHIM (*a*).

1847.
Nov. 4.

Where a purchaser bought a share in a ship at sea under a sequestration in an equity suit, he was ordered to pay the purchase-money into Court, as there was no dispute as to title, on the purchaser being indemnified against any claim for lien by the ship's husband in respect of disbursements previously made.

In this case a question arose as to the right to compel the purchaser of part of a ship at sea under a sequestration to pay the money into Court. The ship's husband having a lien on the produce of the voyage for all disbursements made by him, it became a question how on a sale this claim could be guarded against. The facts appear from the following judgment:—

Perry, C. J.—In the case of the *Sir Herbert Compton*, which was sold under a sequestration by order of this Court, the question is, whether the purchaser should be ordered to pay the purchase money into Court. The ship was sold whilst on a voyage to China, and the contract was for ready money. I take it to be clear, that, if any question were raised as to the power of the sequestrator to give a good title, the order now asked for could not be made. But although an objection as to title was once raised, it is now abandoned, and the only question is, whether the part owners have got any lien on the ship, which ought to be satisfied before the purchaser can be ordered to pay in the money.

The purchaser bought a moiety of the ship from the 30th of March last; up to that time all the profits, if there were any, belonged to Aga Mahomed Rahim, and any lien which might exist on the part of the ship's husband against him in respect of those profits would, even supposing this case to fall within *Holderness* v. *Shackels*, (8 B. & C.), attach only to the freight or produce of the voyage. On the other hand, any disbursements which the ship's husband may have made since the 30th of March form a charge against the purchaser, and may or may not constitute a lien on the produce of the voyage, but they are not matters with which the vendor, the sequestrator, has anything to do.

(*a*) See *ante*, p. 1, Aga Mahomed Rahim's case.

1847.

MIRZA v. RAHIM.

This case, however, may possibly occur, the purchaser is to have all the profits subsequent to the 30th of March, Aga Mahomed Rahim is liable for half the disbursements up to that period; and, as the voyage commenced on the 30th of March, it is possible that the ship's husband may have made disbursements for the purpose of that voyage, the half of which he may be enabled to obtain by virtue of the lien on the produce of the voyage. If this is so, the purchaser ought to be secured that the ship's husband's claim against Aga Mahomed Rahim shall not be satisfied out of the results of the voyage, so as to drive the purchaser to a personal claim against Aga Mahomed Rahim.

I express no opinion whether, under the circumstances, the ship's husband possesses such a lien or not, but as it appears that the claim for lien only amounts to Rs. 6000 or Rs. 7000, which is much less than the purchase money, I see no objection to the order that the latter should be paid into Court, and that the Master should ascertain whether any and what claims exist upon it, and, if any advances were made previous to the voyage, that he should suggest a proper mode of indemnifying the purchaser against the same.

The other objection which was urged that the purchaser should not be compelled to pay the money till registry is obtained, and that registry cannot be obtained because the ship is at sea, is, I think, not tenable, because the purchaser agreed to purchase for ready money with full knowledge of the circumstances.

PEEL, CASSELL AND CO. *v.* PEARSON.

1851. April 7.

[*In the Small Cause Court. Coram* PERRY, C. J.]

1. Where goods have been delivered on board well packed, and in good condition, and on delivery they turn out to be damaged, chafed, and iron-moulded, the *onus probandi* of showing that the damage has not arisen from improper stowage lies on the captain.

2. Practice at Lloyd's as to petty damage by breakage and leakage.

3. *Quære*, as to the power of agents for sale in Bombay to sue the captain on a bill of lading for negligence.

QUESTIONS having frequently arisen in the port of Bombay as to the liability on the part of captains of vessels to make good petty damages to cargo sustained during the voyage, the above action was brought to try the point.

It will be perceived that the whole difficulty in the case arises from the circumstances which frequently make it impossible to say from what cause the damage has arisen.

Howard for plaintiffs.

Jenkins for defendant.

Cur. adv. vult.

Question where the loss on petty damage to goods on sea voyage is to fall.

PERRY, C. J.—In this case six bales of canvass, consigned to the plaintiffs from Liverpool were brought out by the defendant in *The Rubena,* and delivered in a damaged state, chafed and iron moulded, so as to be pronounced on survey unmerchantable, and the question is, on whom the loss is to fall?

It is clear that the loss may fall either on the underwriters as a particular average by perils of the sea, or on the shipowner by reason of his negligence in stowage, or on the merchant by its being an inevitable incident, or one attributable to the ordinary wear and tear of a long sea voyage.

If the evidence in such cases were full so as to point out with distinctness the cause of damage, there would be no difficulty in applying the rule of law. It is clear, for example, that the underwriters are not liable for damage incurred without any extraordinary cause, such as for canvass broken or chafed, sails and yards carried away in the ordinary service of the ship, &c.—for these are attributable to ordinary wear and tear. So, also, the shipowner is not liable if he has furnished a good ship, and has stowed the cargo properly. In some cases, therefore, as when the ship's bottom was eaten through by rats, and the cargo thereby damaged, the loss would fall on the merchant alone; *Hunter* v. *Potts* (4 Campb. 203.) The risk insured against by the office had not occurred; the contract entered into by the carrier had not been broken.

But the difficulty in these cases arises from the deficiency of evidence, and when it is recollected what the subject-matter of inquiry is, and the small value at stake, it is not

1851.

PEEL & Co. *v.* PEARSON.

wonderful that the cause of loss should be usually left very obscure at the trial.

The question then which arises is, on whom the burthen of proof should fall if an action be brought in respect of damaged goods. If the action were against underwriters, it would undoubtedly be incumbent on the merchant to prove that the loss was occasioned by perils of the seas, and I observe that according to the custom at Lloyd's underwriters are only liable for breakage, when the vessel strikes the ground with sufficient force to derange the stowage. (*Benecke: Marine Insurance*, p. 474.) This must proceed on the principle that the damage in such cases is usually attributable to bad stowage.

The rule applicable in cases like the present, I think, is, if goods are delivered from the ship in a damaged state, it lies with the captain to prove by what cause the damage has been sustained. The goods have been received by him according to his own admission in good condition, the damage has happened while they were in his exclusive custody, and it is much more reasonable to expect evidence of facts which have occurred during such custody from him, than from the merchant who can know nothing of the incidents of the voyage. In this case, the evidence given by the mate has failed to convince me either that the goods were well stowed, or, which is nearly the same thing, that any perils of the sea occurred during the voyage, such as a ship well found should not have been able to surmount without injury to the cargo.

Another point was taken from the defendant, viz. that the plaintiffs being only agents are not entitled to sue in this case, and *Sargent* v. *Morris,* (2 B. & Ald.) which was not cited in the argument, is certainly a strong authority to this effect.

But as this point was not fully argued at the Bar, and was only thrown in as a make-weight, I am unwilling to consider it now, for if it should turn out that the action was wrongfully brought, the plaintiffs could immediately commence a new one in the names of their principals.

There must, therefore, be a verdict for the plaintiffs for Rs. 120.

ORIENTAL BANK
v.
FRAMJEE COWASJEE.

1849.
March 12.

[*Coram* PERRY, C. J.]

THE construction of guarantee bonds to joint stock banks often coming into question the following case is given:—

Construction of a guarantee bond to a bank for a cash credit.

PERRY, C. J.—This is an action on a bond, which was given by the defendant to secure the balance of an account opened at the Hong Kong branch of the Oriental Bank by Dadabhoy Rustumjee, and in which the bank had agreed to grant the latter a credit for a lak of dollars.

The defendant pleads, 1st, *non est factum;* and secondly, that no demand in writing had been made for the balance: as to which pleas no question arises.

In his third plea he alleges, that the parties representing the bank at Hong Kong had closed the account opened in Dadabhoy Rustumjee's name before action brought, and that thereupon Dadabhoy Rustumjee paid all that was due on such account,—and this plea raises the question in issue between the parties.

On looking at the bond there can be no doubt, I think, on the whole, that what was contemplated by the parties was, that a cash credit should be afforded at Hong Kong to the extent of one lak of dollars, and that Framjee Cowasjee should be liable for any balance on that account, within such limits, but the words which describe the species of accommodation to be afforded by the bank are very large, and undoubtedly include fixed loans, or any other mode of lending money which might be agreed upon between the parties.

Now it seems that at the end of 1847, the Hong Kong branch was dissatisfied with the mode in which Dadabhoy Rustumjee had worked the cash credit account, and pointed out to him that the operations were unfavourable to the bank, and in consequence of these representations, Dadabhoy Rus-

1849.

ORIENTAL BANK v. FRAMJEE.

tumjee took a fixed loan from the bank of one lak of dollars. On the 24th of April following, and before any part of the loan was paid off, he, or rather his agents, discounted a bill drawn on himself at Bombay for Rs. 21,500, and, on the 18th of July subsequently, another bill for Rs. 86,000, with which he also gave shipping documents covering the greater part of the amount.

The fixed loan for a lak of dollars having been paid off by Dadabhoy Rustumjee on the 4th of July, and Mr. Dunlop, the agent of the bank, having then given up to him the letter from his principals, containing the terms of the cash credit, as a closed account, the question is, whether Framjee Cowasjee can be made liable for the balance due on these bills of exchange, which have not been paid in consequence of Dadabhoy Rustumjee's failure.

This question depends entirely on the true meaning to be placed on the language of the condition of the bond wherein Framjee Cowasjee binds himself to pay any balance on the account current between Dadabhoy and Rustumjee and the bank. If the amounts due on bills discounted justly form an item in such account current it is clear he is liable, otherwise not. Now it would seem that the words of the recitals of the bond are large enough to include such an operation, if it took place in respect of this cash credit, but, as Mr. Stuart, of the bank of Bombay, observes, it is unusual in practice that such an operation occurs; and, on consideration, it appears clear that if a party has a cash credit of a limited amount in his favour, and wanted money, it would be wholly against his interest to exhaust that credit by discounting his own bills with the bank, as he might get the whole amount from the bank without a bill, and might get further funds by discounting his bill elsewhere. The inference, therefore, is very strong that when Dadabhoy Rustumjee did discount his bill with the bank, it was not in respect of his cash credit account at all, but a wholly independent transaction. And, I confess, I agree entirely with Mr. Stuart in thinking that when the loan of 100,000 dollars was made and running, the cash credit was exhausted, and subsequent transactions must be attributed to a different credit.

1849.

ORIENTAL BANK v. FRAMJEE.

But this opinion is rendered conclusive by the evidence of Mr. Dunlop, who was the manager of the bank at Hong Kong. Whether the bill transactions formed items in the account current was a matter of fact best known to Mr. Dunlop, who kept that account on behalf of the bank, and we find by his evidence, and still more by his conduct, that the bills never did enter into such account. It is said that the bank ought not to be prejudiced by the act of Mr. Dunlop, and that his admissions cannot get over the obligations imposed by a bond. But the acts of an agent acting within the scope of his authority cannot be severed from those of a principal; this account was placed by the bank in the hands of Mr. Dunlop, to be worked for them by him, and his admission that the bill transactions do not form an item of that account is equivalent to an admission by themselves. The verdict, therefore, must be entered for the defendant.

ORIENTAL BANK
v.
WISWANATH BALCHRISHNA.

1851.

July 27.

[*Coram* PERRY, C. J., and YARDLEY, J.]

ACTION on a bond in the penal sum of Rs. 50,000.

Plea, after craving oyer, *non damnificatus*.

The replication assigned four breaches.

Construction of a guarantee bond to a bank.

Where a cashier or head shrof of a bank had the sole appointment and controul over the petty shrofs in his department, and bound himself with two sureties in a penal bond for his own good conduct and obedience as cashier, and against all losses from the petty shrofs taking bad notes or bad money: *Held*, that the word "misconduct," in a subsequent part of the bond, did not include the felonious acts of the petty shrofs whilst not on duty, so as to make the cashier liable if one of the petty shrofs stole money from the bank.

Various forged hoondies were discounted at the bank, and passed through the cashier's office: *Held*, that, if it was a special duty imposed on the cashier to ascertain the genuineness of the hoondies, negligence in such respect did not come within the terms of the bond, it not being the duty of a cashier or head shrof to ascertain the genuineness of acceptances.

Held also, that, as the principal negligence appeared to have occurred on the part of the superior officers of the bank, the inferior officer, who was acting under their orders and surveillance could not be sued for negligence or misconduct.

Facilities to fraud from the imperfect character of Marwadi writing pointed out.

1851.

ORIENTAL BANK v. WISWANATH.

The cause was set down for trial at the sittings after June Term, 1851, but as one Dorabji, who was mentioned in the plea to have stolen the notes from the bank, was to take his trial for larceny at the ensuing July sessions, the Court, on the application of Dorabji's counsel, put off the trial until the sessions were over.

At the sessions, *cor.* YARDLEY, J., Dorabji was convicted of the larceny, and also one Láldás, a petty shrof in the employment of the defendant.

When the cause was called on at the adjourned sittings in July, *Howard* for the plaintiffs applied to amend the record by inserting an averment in the second breach, that the notes had been stolen by Láldás, a servant of the defendant.

Le Messurier, A. G., opposed; but the Court, on ascertaining that notice of the amendment had been given, and that the Advocate General did not desire time to consider whether he should alter his defence, allowed the amendment to be made.

The case was tried on the 22nd and 23rd of July, on which day the Court gave a verdict on the facts, but reserved all discussion on the construction of the agreement to a further day.

On the 25th of July accordingly, *Le Messurier*, A. G., moved to enter up judgment for the plaintiff.

Howard and *Dickinson*, *contrà*.

Cur. adv. vult.

On the Monday following, the judgment of the Court was delivered by

PERRY, C. J.—This is an action on a surety bond, by which Wiswanath, Moroba, and Wittoba have bound themselves jointly and severally to the Oriental Bank, in the sum of Rs. 50,000, for the performance of certain duties by Wiswanath and his subordinates.

1851.

ORIENTAL BANK v. WISWANATH.

What these duties are must be gathered from the terms of the bond, which, leaving out the verbiage, are as follows:—

"Whereas the directors of the bank have appointed Wiswanath to hold the situation of cashier, or head shrof, and whereas Moroba and Wittoba have agreed to become bound for the good conduct and obedience of Wiswanath while he shall hold such situation, and to indemnify the bank against any loss or damage it may sustain by reason of Wiswanath being appointed to such situation, or by reason of Wiswanath or his subordinates (for whom he is liable to the bank) taking bad notes or bad money;"

Conditions of surety bond.

Now, the condition is (and I break it up into paragraphs for distinctness),

(1). That if Wiswanath do and shall at all times during which he shall hold such situation of cashier, or head shrof, faithfully, honestly, diligently, and carefully execute, perform, and discharge the duties of his said situation;

(2). And do and shall whenever thereunto required give a just and true account of all monies and other things that shall come to his hands, or which he shall be entrusted with, in such situation as aforesaid, and do on demand deliver the same up to the bank;

(3). And do make good to the bank all losses which may occur by reason of Wiswanath or any of his subordinates taking any bad notes or bad money;

(4). And do and shall keep secret all the business and transactions of the bank;

(5). And do and shall indemnify and save harmless the bank from and against all manner of loss or damage whatsoever, which may be sustained by the bank, by, from, or through, or by means of the neglect, failure, insolvency, omission or misconduct of Wiswanath, or by any person in his immediate employ, in anywise relating to the said situation, or being his subordinates in the bank, or which shall in anywise be occupied by him or such person or persons as last aforesaid:

"Then the said obligation to be void, otherwise to remain in full force."

1851.

ORIENTAL BANK v. WISWANATH.

Breaches alleged.

The plaintiffs, in their replication, have assigned four distinct breaches of the condition in this bond:

1st. That bank notes to the value of Rs. 95,915 having come to the hands of Wiswanath, he did not deliver them up on demand;

2nd. That whilst the said bank notes were in his hands, they were stolen by one Dorabji, and by one Láldás, the said Láldás being a subordinate of Wiswanath.

3rd. That it was the duty of Wiswanath, as cashier or shrof, when notes or hoondies, purporting to be drawn by persons in Bombay, or other parts of India, on persons or firms in Bombay when presented for discount to the bank, to ascertain by himself, or his subordinates, that the signatures on the said notes or hoondies of the drawers or acceptors, and holders or discounters, were their genuine signatures, and that by the neglect, omission, carelessness and misconduct of Wiswanath and his subordinates, Wiswanath received as genuine, divers forged hoondies, whereby a loss accrued to the bank, amounting, in the whole, to Rs. 1,09,300, (or 10,000*l.*)

4th. That the defendant and his subordinates took divers bad notes for the payment of money, whereby a loss is averred generally of two laks.

The defendant by his rejoinder, which is objected to as informal, in effect denies that any breach of the conditions in the bond has occurred.

If the construction put upon this bond by the Advocate General for the defendant be the correct one, the facts which are necessary to be kept in consideration for disposing of the question are not numerous, and are wholly undisputed. It may, therefore, be desirable to set them forth in a compendious form, in order to facilitate a reference to a superior tribunal, if the decision of this Court should be objected to.

Wiswanath, the cashier of the Oriental Bank, appears to have held his situation from the commencement of the bank, about ten years ago, when he gave a bond to them similar to the present, as a security for himself and his subordinates. But the bond on which this action is brought is dated in Feb-

1851.

ORIENTAL BANK v. WISWANATH.

ruary, 1849, and was given, it is said, in consequence of the style of the bank being then changed.

Wiswanath's salary amounts to about 20*l.* a month, but he receives from the bank 45*l.*, out of which he has to defray the salaries of his subordinates, three of whom are petty shrofs in the office, and altogether the shrof's department consists of about twelve persons.

The system adopted by Wiswanath for checking his petty shrofs in the details of his office is altogether left to himself, and it is not necessary to describe more of it than to say, that on arriving at the bank every morning he was accustomed to distribute the cash and bank notes among his three subordinates, and to receive from them the balance at the end of the day. This balance he was accustomed, at the close of business, to deposit in a tin box secured by a Chubb lock; and this box, after being properly locked, was deposited in the iron safe of the bank, which was secured by five keys in the custody of different officers. The keys of this box he used to deposit in the desk of his office, the key of which he always took home with him at night.

On Saturday evening, the 8th of February last, the three subordinates brought as usual to the defendant the balance of notes in their hands, amounting to Rs. 95,910, which the defendant deposited in the tin box, and, having locked it, sent it by one of the servants of the bank to the strong room, where it was safely secured in the presence of the proper officers. On the return of the defendant to the bank on Monday morning at twenty minutes past ten, which was a little after office hours had commenced, he found the tin box placed as usual in its place at his desk, the strong room having been opened by the proper officers, one of whom was Babaji, a subordinate of defendant, who had unlocked that lock to the iron safe, of which the key was entrusted to him by Wiswanath. And it would seem from the evidence, that it was the ordinary practice for the box to be thus taken out of the iron safe before the defendant came to the office.

On examining the box the defendant found it unlocked, and all the notes missing, and he immediately communicated the fact to his three subordinates who were present.

1851.

ORIENTAL BANK v. WISWANATH.

No clear conclusion can be formed on the evidence whether this theft took place on the Saturday evening or on the Monday morning. The impression of my learned colleague on the evidence given at the criminal trial held before him, was that it took place on the Monday morning; and the counsel for the plaintiff as well as the defendant in this case, both point out that as the probable period. The evidence given of the facts at this trial by the plaintiffs, consisted in putting in the depositions as to the robbery given by the defendant in the Police Office, but, as it was not to the interest of either party to shut out any evidence in the case, the defendant himself was examined by consent. And I must say, by parenthesis, that this defendant's examination in this case was eminently conducive to the ends of truth, for whilst his admissions on the one hand considerably strengthened the plaintiff's case against him, his assertion of facts shewing non-liability were all made in the presence of the bank officers, and, therefore, could have been contradicted on the spot, if false.

Now, from the evidence given by the defendant in this trial, it clearly appears that ample opportunity was afforded, both on the Saturday evening and on the Monday morning, to the three subordinates in the office, if they were rogues enough, either to open the desk with a false key on the Monday morning, or to seize the occasion of the defendant's back being turned for five minutes, on the Saturday evening, to take the Chubb key out of the drawer.

But probably it is not material on which of these two occasions the stealing of the bank notes took place.

With respect to the forged hoondies, it appears that thirty-one hoondies, or bills of exchange in the native character, and two English bills of exchange, *bonâ fide* accepted by a respectable firm in Bombay, amounting altogether in value to about 10,000*l.*, have been discounted at the bank, all of which turn out to be forgeries either in whole or in part, and the forged signatures to which are attested by the petty shrofs in the employment of the defendant. The plaintiff's case is not based on the ground that the defendant's subordinates were accessary to these forgeries; and it certainly is possible that

1851.

ORIENTAL BANK v. WISWANATH.

these bills passed through the shrof's office without any guilty knowledge on the part of the subordinates there employed. The probabilities of the case, however, very strongly point to one of these subordinates—Babaji, who absconded immediately on the frauds being discovered, and to a Marwadi broker, who also absconded, as the authors or part-authors of these forgeries. It was not material, however, to the case made either by the plaintiff or defendant, to push the inquiry on this subject further.

On these facts the defendant contends, that no breach of the condition of the bond has occurred, for that the true meaning of the instrument is, that he and his co-sureties only guaranteed in substance two things, first, the good conduct, fidelity, and obedience of himself in his office of cashier: secondly, an indemnity against any loss from the subordinates taking bad notes or bad money. He argues, that the loss as to the notes occurred through the felony of one of the subordinates and of a stranger, which was a responsibility that the sureties never intended to incur; and that the loss as to the forged hoondies also did not come within the terms or meaning of the bond, for that the looking after the genuineness of acceptances was no part of the duty of a cashier, even if it were a special duty imposed on Wiswanath, which, however, was denied.

The plaintiff, on the other hand, contends that the defendant has contracted absolutely to deliver up the notes that had come to his hands, whatever contingency might have happened to prevent his doing so, and that it is his own fault not to have protected himself by more guarded language: further, that the general words at the end of the condition make him responsible for any misconduct whatever, or, at all events, for the misconduct that has occurred on the part of his subordinates.

On full consideration, we are satisfied that the construction put by the defendant on the instrument is the true one.

The rules of law which require to be principally kept in view for the construction of this document are as follows:

1851. ORIENTAL BANK v. WISWANATH.

Rules for the construction of bonds.

1. "That the construction should be favourable, and as near to the minds and apparent interests of the parties, as possible it may be, and the law will permit" (*a*).

2. That general words following well-defined limited clauses, shall be controlled by the specific declarations of the parties' intentions—which precede.

3. That if general words in the condition are ambiguous, they shall be controlled by the recital.

4. That the condition of the bond, when doubtful, is always taken most favourably for the defendant, and against the plaintiff (*b*).

5. That all these rules apply *a fortiori* in favour of defendants, when they are sureties.

Lastly, 6. A rule which we may venture to lay down as applicable to this country, that where a document is in question between parties speaking different languages, *e. g.* between Europeans and natives, the benefit of any doubt on the language should be given to that party to whom the language is that of his opponent.

Principal rule.

Of all these rules the first is unquestionably the most important, and it overrides the rest. *The Touchstone*, which is the great authority on this subject, places it at the head of its canons, and it is clearly in accordance with the grand duty of Courts of justice to give effect to the contracts of parties according to their plain meaning. However stringent on the defendant the terms may be, however much the condition may transcend the recital, if the language of the condition is clear, unambiguous, and precise, the Court must discard all considerations as to hardship, and enforce the letter of the bond according to the expressed intention of the parties. But the other rules are, I think, characterised by equal wisdom, where any doubt arises on the language. The plaintiffs, as representing a powerful monied establishment, were dealing with a humble individual seeking their service, they were able to dictate their own terms, and were, in the language of the Roman lawyers, "masters of the contract." It is probable that, if they had insisted on a clause guaranteeing against all

(*a*) 1 Touchst. 86. (*b*) 2 Shep. Touch. 376 a.

acts of embezzlement or felony on the part of the subordinates, or for the faithful and careful performance by Wiswanath of *all* banking duties whatsoever as well as those of cashier, the defendant and his co-sureties would have assented. But it is quite possible that they would not. And it is sufficient for Wiswanath to say, that they had not done so. The defendant and his co-sureties might have been well willing to bind themselves in a heavy penalty for the honesty and care of Wiswanath himself in discharging his duties as cashier, and for the due performance of the specific duties belonging to the subordinates. The honesty of Wiswanath they might have had a firm reliance on, and the duties of the cashier or head shrof and of the petty shrofs were well known to them, but before they can be made liable for the due performance of other duties not belonging to a cashier, and for the honesty of other persons whom they knew nothing about, the rules of justice require the language imposing this liability to be distinctly expressed.

Now it being clear that the liability of Wiswanath depends entirely on the language used in the bond, the four corners of which contain the whole controversy, it is instructive to observe the mode in which the bank have framed their claims against him.

With respect to the stolen notes, the plaintiffs base their case mainly on the covenant to account for the notes come to the hands of defendant, and *to deliver them over on demand.* The second breach, in which the facts are stated specially as to the theft, is said to be merely an expansion of the first; and it is only by the accident of the trial being postponed, that the allegation as to the theft having been committed by a subordinate of Wiswanath has found its way on to the record. It is argued that this covenant is absolute on the part of Wiswanath, and that he must perform it whatever may have become of the notes; and it is likened to a covenant to pay rent, which is still binding, it is said, although the premises are burnt down. According to this doctrine, Wiswanath would be liable if a fire broke out at the bank and the cash and notes entrusted to him were all either stolen or burnt; or if a stranger in the

1851.

ORIENTAL BANK v. WISWANATH.

course of the day, or even the manager of the bank (for defendant is no more responsible for Dorabji than he is for the manager), insinuated himself into the cashier's department and robbed the till. These absurd consequences are arrested by the common sense view that such is not the meaning of the contract. There is not a word used in the covenant to account which differs from the ordinary contract that arises wherever money is placed with an accounting party; and such a contract does not bind the depositee to pay over the money deposited at *all events*, and under *all* circumstances.

So with respect to the forged hoondies, the fourth breach assigns the loss on this score to that clause of the condition which indemnifies against "taking bad notes or bad money." But, on referring to the bond, the word "notes," there used so clearly, denotes bank notes in opposition to cash, that though faintly suggested in the witness box to include hoondies, that construction of the word was promptly surrendered by the counsel for the plaintiffs.

There remain, then, only two breaches on which any question can arise, and on examination it will be found that the sole language in the bond on which liability can be asserted against Wiswanath, in respect either of the stolen notes or of the forged hoondies, is the word "misconduct," at the close, and the concluding words of the condition, "or (losses) which shall or may in anywise be occasioned by him (Wiswanath), or such person or persons as last aforesaid." The question is, whether the expression "all losses by misconduct of the subordinates" is to be taken in the most extensive signification which they may bear by logical construction, in which case they would include losses occasioned by the arson, burglary, or felony of the subordinates, or whether a more limited construction must be put upon them, and if so, what.

We are clearly of opinion that these general words must be limited and controlled by the specific expressions of the parties' intentions which precede. Full effect is given to the word "misconduct," by referring it to the "good conduct" which the sureties had agreed to guarantee, *viz.*, the good conduct of Wiswanath in his situation as cashier. It possibly also includes any misconduct by the subordinates in the discharge of their specific duties, but it is not necessary to decide this point, as to which many decided cases are applicable. And even if on ultimate analysis it should appear that the term "misconduct" is ambiguous, and may mean either one thing or another, then, according to the rule of law above cited, the more favourable construction must be put on it on behalf of the defendant.

If, however, this construction of the bond is unsound, and the terms of it include every breach of duty or negligence on the part of the defendant, whether such duty belongs to the office of cashier or not, then another question on disputed facts arises, and it becomes necessary to review the evidence given at the trial to decide between the conflicting testimony as to whose duty it was to ascertain the genuineness of indorsements.

For this purpose I will read the principal evidence on the point by the conflicting parties. [The C. J. read the evidence].

On balancing this evidence, and comparing it with the other circumstances of the case, we are satisfied that it was not the special duty of Wiswanath to ascertain the genuineness of the acceptances and indorsements. It is admitted that such is not the ordinary duty of a cashier, nor is it of a shrof. There is no evidence of any special orders to Wiswanath; no single instance in which Wiswanath is found having anything to do with these indorsements, and, what is more forcible, no one occasion on which any communication takes place between the officers of the bank and Wiswanath respecting them. The bank deed requiring two names on every bill discounted, and the practice as to native hoondies being that they are not accepted in writing, unless held by a bank, the probability is that when the practice first arose of presenting these up-country hoondies for discount, the rule was laid down that they should be sent to the acceptor to get his signature, and there is nothing to shew that this practice has not been always observed. It also seems probable that originally the rule was that inquiries should be made as to the genuineness of the acceptances when they were left for discount with the ac-

1851.

ORIENTAL BANK v. WISWANATH.

ceptance on them. But it is evident to us that this rule has been long relaxed, and that no one in the bank for years past has enforced the duty of sending hoondies accepted in writing to the acceptors to ascertain whether the acceptance was genuine. If this is so, and if it is proved that the communications on this subject took place between Babaji and the bank, and that he received all his orders from them, and not from the defendant, it does not lie in the mouths of the bank to say that the forgeries have occurred through the negligence of the defendant, for we are satisfied the negligence is much more clearly traceable to their own door. All the evidence at the bar in fact shewing that Babaji throughout, as to these hoondies, was acting under the special orders of the manager, and not under the defendant. The fact seems to be, the English officers of the bank were not aware, and by their evidence they do not even now appear to be aware, of all the circumstances in the case which made these forgeries comparatively facile. Nor have bank officers the same experience for forming sound conclusions on the subject as we who are sitting in Courts of justice daily, and daily investigating native documents.

Imperfection of Hindu mercantile writing.

To a banking officer fresh from England all documents in the native character seem pretty much alike, and the Nagari, with its long and short vowels distinctly marked, is possibly as perfect a written character as any in the world. But the Marwaddi character, which is used by the indefatigable class of money dealers, who are to be found all over India from the cities on the Indus to the most eastern parts of Assam, is most defective and illegible. The words are all written into one another, and the vowel marks are omitted. The characters in different districts differs. The consequence is, that their documents are most difficult to decipher, and even in our translator's office they often cannot be read without the assistance of the writer. I may mention, as an example, a case that lately occurred there. The Marwaddi word expressing the numbers 25, 50, and 500, contains the three same consonants, p, ch, s; a Marwaddi document being brought to the office with the word (pchs) in it, the translator interpreted

1851.

ORIENTAL BANK v. WISWANATH.

it pachís (25), but the party, on getting the translation, remonstrated strongly, and insisted it was pachás (50), and it was altered accordingly; but when the case was brought into Court, the Marwaddi's partner, who professed to be the writer, declared it was pachso, or panchso (500), the mark for the nasal n being omitted like the vowels. I do not think these facilities for fraud were apparent to the bank, for they seem to have taken for granted that there were persons in the shrof's office who could read Marwaddi, which I certainly do not believe was the case.

Lastly, the fact of the bank not having made any demand on the defendant in respect of these forged hoondies till five months after the discovery, although they commenced an action against him immediately in respect of the stolen notes, raises a presumption almost impossible to surmount, that the practical men in the bank parlour did not consider that it was the special duty of Wiswanath to ascertain the genuineness of these acceptances.

On the whole case, therefore, both on the legal construction of the documents as Judges, and on a review of all the facts as a jury, we are satisfied that the verdict ought to be entered for the defendant.

I may add, in conclusion, that to avoid all technical objections, it was agreed that this case should be argued throughout on its merits.

1850.

June 7.

MAHOMED TUCKAY
v.
SUNDA NANJI.

"GENERAL WOOD" INSURANCE CASE.

[*Coram* Perry, C. J., and Yardley, J.]

A policy having been effected on goods from Sincapore to Bombay, it appeared that the ship had sailed from Hong Kong to Sincapore, with ninety-four Chinese convicts on board, and a guard of only six water police. After the ship left Sincapore, on her voyage to Bombay, the convicts rose upon the crew, murdered the master, and made off with the ship towards China, when she struck upon a rock and became a total wreck:

Held, 1. That the loss was within the terms of the policy;

2. That the taking on board so large a cargo of dangerous characters did not constitute unseaworthiness;

3. That, even if the master had been negligent in taking such a cargo without a proper guard, his negligence did not affect a subsequent shipper;

4. That, where facts are equally within the knowledge of the shipper and the insurance office, there is no obligation on the former to communicate them.

Action on a policy of insurance on goods shipped on board the *General Wood* on a voyage from Sincapore to Bombay.

Pleas. Non assumpsit; deviation; unseaworthiness, and other pleas.

At the trial, it appeared that the ship had sailed from Hong Kong with a party of Chinese convicts on board, ninety-four in number, under a guard of six water police; and it appears that, during the month the ship remained in harbour at Sincapore, the convicts were employed in loading the cargo. A day or two after the ship sailed for Sincapore the convicts rose upon the crew, murdered the master, and made off with the ship towards China, when, after beating on and off the coast for some days, she struck upon a rock and became a total wreck.

Under these circumstances, it was argued that the fact of a cargo of convicts being on board, who were imperfectly guarded, either vitiated the policy, or that the loss accrued from a risk not insured against.

Cur. adv. vult.

Perry, C. J., after stating the facts, proceeded as follows:

1850.

MAHOMED *v.* SUNDA.

The question arises whether, under circumstances, the underwriters are liable.

The first point to be considered is, whether the loss of the ship is ascribable to any of the risks mentioned in the policy. It is not denied that the immediate cause of the loss was a peril of the sea; but it is argued that, as that loss did not occur during the prosecution of the voyage insured, but on a deviation which was occasioned by the misconduct of the convicts,—it was not a loss, properly speaking, by the perils of the sea, but by such misconduct, for which the underwriters are not liable. We are of opinion, however, that the words of the policy are sufficiently large to include the risk that has occurred; they are so large as to embrace almost every imaginable risk that may happen, and being the language of the underwriters, the rule of construction is, that if any ambiguity arises as to the extent of the risk covered, the words of the policy are to be taken most strongly against the party who used them, and who had the power of introducing any qualifications in his own behalf which he chose. This being so, the cases shew that it is immaterial whether the loss is ascribed to the perils of the sea, or to the preceding piratical seizure. But if it be necessary to give an opinion on the point that has been raised as to the non-liability of underwriters for *thefts* committed on board, by parties not coming from without,—a point which has been mooted by *Roccus* and other early writers on insurance,—I should not hesitate to hold that the acts here committed amounted to piracy (*a*), and fall, therefore, within one of the risks specially insured against.

Acts of crew amounting to piracy.

The loss being thus proved to have occurred within the terms of the policy, there are only two grounds, as it appears to me, on which the underwriters can ward off their liability to pay,—1st, the unseaworthiness of the ship; 2nd, the culpa-

(*a*) "If the mariners of any ship" (and *a fortiori*, parties on board not mariners) "shall violently dispossess the master, and afterwards carry away the ship itself, or any of the goods or tackle, apparel or furniture with a felonious intention, in any place where the Lord Admiral hath jurisdiction, this is also robbery and piracy." Sir Charles Hedges to the Grand Jury at the Admiralty Sessions, 1696.

1850.

MAHOMED v. SUNDA.

bility of the party insured: and arguments under both these heads have been addressed to the Court.

But with respect to unseaworthiness, it seems to me an abuse of language to hold that the having a party of convicts on board, even unguarded, and without due means for securing them, can make a ship unseaworthy. The danger arising from such a cargo may be very great, but it is similar in degree to what would occur from stowing a large quantity of gunpowder in bulk between decks and other exposed places. Such an act would be, no doubt, extremely negligent; if any accident arose, it would make the master responsible, and it would, in all probability, prevent him from recovering on any policy he had effected; but the true description of the act would be *negligence*, and not that it made the ship unseaworthy. And, in fact, it was not strongly urged at the bar that the act in question did constitute unseaworthiness.

Effect of dangerous cargo on other policies of insurance.

But the principal argument urged before us to-day has been, that the fact of a number of convicts being on board at the time the insurance was effected, either vitiated the policy altogether, or that it created an implied exception that no risk was insured against which should be traceable to the acts of these convicts. And it has been ingeniously attempted to shew that the shipowner and the shipper of goods are entirely identical in character. If this position be true, it follows that any act of negligence which can be fastened on the master, and which would prevent him from recovering on the policy, equally attaches to the shipper. The same argument was put in another form, when it was asserted that the shipper, at the time he effects the policy, enters into an implied warranty for the acts of the master, and guarantees that he will do nothing, and ship no cargo, which shall bring about the risk insured against. But we think there is no foundation for these positions. The only implied warranty which the law lays down as attaching to the shipper, relates to the seaworthiness of the ship; on this point he and the shipowner stand in the same shoes; but it would be introducing an altogether novel doctrine to hold that he gives any guarantee for the acts of the master, or for the acts of other

1850.

MAHOMED v. SUNDA.

shippers, whose proceedings he is ignorant of, and whose conduct he cannot control.

Even assuming, then, that negligence is ascribable to the master in the imperfect guarding of these convicts,—and on this point we need not say anything,—we are clearly of opinion that such negligence does not affect the plaintiff, who was the shipper of the goods, or prejudice him in his remedy.

But it is argued, lastly, that even if the underwriters are liable under the policy for the acts of the convicts, still there was an undue concealment by the plaintiff of the fact of these convicts being on board, which vitiates the policy. But on this point we do not feel the least difficulty. I gather from the case that the facts relating to the convicts were at least equally patent to the underwriters as to the plaintiff, and we see no obligation whatever on the part of the latter to communicate matters which he had no special interest to inquire about, and which it is not even proved that he knew. On this point some observations of Lord MANSFIELD, in his judgment in *Carter* v. *Boehm* are very pertinent:—

What facts must be disclosed by insurers.

"There are many matters as to which the insured may be innocently silent; he need not mention what the underwriter knows,—*scientia utrimque par pares contrahentes facit.* An underwriter cannot insist that the policy is void, because he did not tell him what he actually knew; what way soever he came to his knowledge. The insured need not mention what the underwriter ought to know; what he takes upon himself the knowledge of; or what he waives being informed of."

On the whole, upon taking a view of this contract as it was entered into in the Bazaar, the probability is that the risk, which actually did occur, presented itself to the attention of neither party; if it had so presented itself, it is impossible for us to say whether it would have made any alteration in the premium demanded; but as the comprehensive words of the policy include the risk in question, and as it was not brought about by any negligence of the shipper, the law of insurance throws the loss upon the underwriters.

Verdict for Plaintiff for Rs. 20,460, with interest from Sept. 25, 1848.

1849.

July 14.

THE HYDROOS.

[*Coram* PERRY, C. J., and YARDLEY, J.]

Admiralty side.

A native vessel having been compelled to anchor on the Malabar coast during the south west monsoon, by distress of weather, the ship, which was full of Mecca pilgrims, being in great distress for wood and water, and being deserted by a portion of her crew, was unable to get off from a very dangerous position without assistance. The fishermen on the shore refused assistance except on the most exorbitant terms. The European collector of the district having proceeded to the spot, and by the activity of himself and his subordinates, having prevailed on the coast fishermen to supply the vessel with the requisites needed, she got away safely from the spot, and made a port some sixty miles to the southward. The collector subsequently made a large claim for salvage, but the Court rejected the claim on the grounds, first, that the salvage service, if any, had been performed by the boatmen, not by the collector and his subordinates; secondly, that the latter had undergone no personal risk; thirdly, that it was the duty of collectors and magistrates to render assistance to vessels in distress on the coast.

The Supreme Court is governed in its decisions, as to costs, by its own practice, and not by the rules of the Admiralty Court.

On appeal to the Privy Council, the appeal was dismissed, on the ground that the appellants had perempted their claim by applying for costs after the decision against them.

THIS was a claim for salvage, which was brought before the Court by act on petition. The vessel, which had a lak of rupees on board, and about 400 pilgrims, was returning from Judda, on the coast of Africa, to Bombay, when she was driven by distress of weather to a place called Konkeshwar, a wild spot on the Malabar coast, fifty or sixty miles to the northward of Goa. She cast anchor in seven fathoms water about half a mile from the shore, and the weather, which had been previously blowing strong at the commencement of the south west monsoon, moderated to a fair wind from the north west. On casting anchor, the pilgrims on board, who were in great distress for want of water and fuel, made the best of their way to the shore, by the aid of the ship's boats, and of some other boats which they procured from the shore at exorbitant prices. But many of them were drowned in their passage through the surf, from the overcrowding of the boats. A portion of the crew had also left the vessel, and some of the ship's spars had been made use of to construct a raft.

Information having been given to the European collector, Mr. Loughnan, who resided at Malwán, twenty-five miles to the southward, he gave orders to one of his deputies to proceed to the spot to render assistance; but on a subsequent day having heard that the ship was in imminent danger, and that many lives had been lost, he proceeded himself to the place. On arriving at Konkeshwar he made off in a boat to the ship, to ascertain the state of matters, and there, on finding the Nacodah (or native skipper) and crew in a state of great lassitude and depression, he recommended the former to allow him to convey the treasure on shore, so as to secure it in the meantime. The Nacodah assented to this proposal, and the treasure was accordingly landed. Mr. Loughnan and his native deputy, by much personal activity, then succeeded in inducing the boatmen on shore to take off the necessary supplies to the ship, which having been put on board, the ship, after riding at anchor for eleven days, was worked out, and safely made the port of Goa in about twenty-four hours.

A correspondence, thereupon, ensued between Mr. Loughnan and the owner, a native merchant of Bombay, in which the latter expressed his warm gratitude for the services rendered by Mr. Loughnan, and after reimbursing him for the expenses which had been incurred, accounts of which had been rendered by Mr. Loughnan, he expressed a desire to display his gratitude by contributing a donation to any local improvement in the neighbourhood.

Mr. Loughnan, in reply, disclaimed any particular merit on his part; but strongly urged on the shipowner the propriety of his bringing to the notice of Government the active services of Mr. Loughnan's native deputy, Narrain Abbajee.

The immediate superior of Mr. Loughnan also, Mr. Coles, in reporting the circumstances to Government, and in noticing the strong recommendations of Mr. Loughnan in behalf of the native officer, pointed out in his report a sum for salvage, as the source from whence this native might be remunerated.

The case was accordingly referred by Government to their legal advisers, and the present suit for salvage having been instituted, Mr. Loughnan refused to restore the lak of rupees which he had taken from the Nacodah.

The ship having subsequently come up to Bombay, proceedings were taken against her in a salvage suit, and a penal bond was entered into by the shipowner and several others to the amount of Rs. 50,000. But at a later period a bond was given

1849.

The Hydroos.

to the sheriff, authorizing the release of the ship, on security being given to the amount of Rs. 20,000. The shipowner having put in his answer to the act on petition, admitting in substance the greater part of the statements in the act, but denying that any case for salvage had occurred, application was made to the Court that evidence might be taken *vivâ voce,* and accordingly, in this Term, the cause was heard and witnesses examined on the 13th and 14th of July.

Le Messurier, A. G., and *Howard,* for the plaintiffs.

Crawford and *Dickinson,* for the defendant.

The Court, on the close of the plaintiffs' case, were unanimous in thinking that the claim had not been made out so as to call on the defendant for any defence, and they accordingly dismissed the claim.

The Advocate General, on a subsequent day, applied to the Court to grant the claim as to their costs, and he relied on several decisions of the Admiralty Courts, and especially of Dr. LUSHINGTON, to shew that, in salvage cases, the principle of the Court was to allow the salvors costs, where their services had been meritorious, even although, in strict law, the service did not amount to salvage.

But the Court thought that in adherence to their own rule of practice as to costs, which was to make them follow the event on all sides of the Court, unless some special ground interfered to prevent it, they could not govern themselves by the rule as to costs of the Admiralty Courts. The present cause of action might have been brought on the common law side of the Court, as well as on the Admiralty side, and the rule as to costs should not be subject to variation by the mere accident as to the side of the Court on which the cause was brought. Under the circumstances, they thought it fit that each party should pay his own costs.

Leave to appeal having been subsequently granted, the Judges reduced their judgments to writing under the rule of the Privy Council.

1849.

The Hydroos.

Sir E. Perry, C. J.—The ship *Hydroos* in this case was arrested for Rs. 50,000 on a claim for salvage, which was alleged to have been rendered by Mr. Loughnan, the assistant collector of Rhutnaghery, and by six others, under the following circumstances:

Facts constituting danger stated.

The vessel, which was of 460 tons burden, and which with the specie and cargo on board is valued at Rs. 1,60,000, or 16,000*l.*, sailed from Judda on the coast of Arabia, on the 17th of May last, with a large number of pilgrims (four hundred) on board, and a native Nacodah and crew, on her return voyage to Bombay. On the 19th of June, she was driven by stress of weather to a place on the Malabar coast called Konkeshwar, which is about sixty miles to the northward of Goa, where she cast anchor in seven fathoms water, having the wind at north west and an abrupt headland under her lee at the distance of three quarters of a mile. Shortly after anchoring she put off her long boat, with twenty or thirty sailors on board, and a quantity of pilgrims, but in endeavouring to get through the surf, which beats heavily on the Malabar coast at all seasons, but especially during the south west monsoon, the boat was swamped, and ten of the crew with the supercargo and several of the pilgrims were drowned. The ship continued at single anchor for ten days in this position, during which time nearly all the pilgrims (with the exception of several drowned in the attempt) made their way in some way or another to the shore, and the remainder of the crew with the Nacodah, who continued on board, were in great distress for want of wood and water; and from those circumstances, as well as from the want of hands, they were wholly unable to get out of their position and make the port of Goa without assistance. It was also affirmed by the petitioners, and (although denied by the defendants) it appears to have been the case, that nearly all the yards of the vessel had been used in making rafts to convey the passengers on shore. Mr. Loughnan, who was the only European magistrate in that district, and was stationed at Malwan on the coast about twenty-five miles to the south, having had the case reported to him on the 21st, gave orders to one of the native

1849.

The Hydroos.

officials (a Mahalkuri or district officer) to repair to the spot and render all assistance; but it having further been reported to him, on the 26th, that the vessel was in imminent danger, and that no assistance could be obtained, from the extortionate demands of the fishermen on the coast, he immediately proceeded to the place, which he reached next morning, and by the active exertions of himself and some seamen, whom he took from his own village of Malwan, and especially of his Mamlutdar (a subordinate native revenue officer), he succeeded in procuring supplies of wood, water, hands, and spars, which were conveyed to the ship on the morning of the 30th, when she was warped out about three cables' length to windward, got an offing, and fetched Goa safely in about twenty-four hours. For the services rendered under these circumstances, the Advocate General made the large claim above mentioned on behalf of the seven petitioners, whose *status* it is here necessary to describe.

The first was Mr. Loughnan, the magistrate already mentioned. The second was Narrain Abbajee, the active native officer also alluded to. The third and fourth were two peons (or running footmen) in the service of Mr. Loughnan. The fifth and sixth were privates in the Rutnaghery Rangers. The seventh was a native trader in an adjoining village. And the grounds which were advanced to govern the discretion of the Court in awarding a due remuneration were; 1, the imminent peril from which the ship had been rescued; 2, the risk of life to Mr. Loughnan and to those of the petitioners who accompanied him in two trips to the vessel; 3, the responsibility Mr. Loughnan incurred in borrowing Rs. 300 within his district for the purposes of the ship; 4, but above all the great personal hardships which Mr. Loughnan had encountered during the period in question. And a late decision of this Court in the case of the *Minerva*, where Rs. 10,000 had been awarded for a few hours' service by a powerful Government steamer, was mainly relied upon. After hearing the petitioners' case carefully, and devoting our attention almost exclusively to Mr. Loughnan's own accounts in writing of the transaction, the Court was so clearly of opinion, on weighing all the facts of the case, that if any salvage service at all had been performed, it was performed by the fishermen; that Mr. Loughnan had never incurred any personal risk at all; that the services performed by the petitioners were all performed by landsmen on land, (the only active parties besides Mr. Loughnan never having been shewn to approach even high water mark); that the personal hardships relied on were greatly exaggerated, and that the services which Mr. Loughnan had rendered, and which the Court thought very meritorious, came completely within the scope of his duties as the only influential Government officer in the district, and such as every European throughout the country would have considered it incumbent upon him to undertake: the Court, I say, taking these views, and having had occasion very lately to consider the whole law of salvage, and having the decision of Lord STOWELL in the *Aquila* present to their minds, did not think it necessary to call upon the defendant to enter upon his case, but pronounced a decision at once against the claim equivalent to a nonsuit. Leave having been granted, however, to appeal to the Privy Council, and the above conclusions being founded on several minute and local facts which are scattered through the evidence, it is due to the defendant to detail them somewhat lengthily, so as to enable the superior Court to decide on the propriety of the decision.

Two broad views occurred to this Court at the time as the result of the evidence, and as the proper grounds on which the case should be disposed of; 1st, that the service rendered by the petitioners was not salvage service at all; 2nd, that the service of Mr. Loughnan (whose claim and services were in fact alone discussed) was just such service as the officers of an enlightened and paternal government were called upon to render to their fellow subjects in distress; and that an occasion like this afforded a fine opportunity for contrasting the beneficial working of British government in the East with that which previously existed, or which now exists on many of our adjoining and semi-barbarous shores. We further indicated, that the services which Mr. Loughnan and his people had afforded, if entitled to remuneration in law at all,

1849.

The Hydroos.

being all performed on shore, did not come within the jurisdiction of the Admiralty, and on this point I beg to refer to the *Charlotte*, (reported in 12 Jur. 567).

Character of the Malabar coast, and its inhabitants.

On the main point, as to the imminent danger of the ship, it clearly appears, from the evidence, that her peril resulted from the unwillingness of the fishermen on shore to afford her any assistance. The Malabar coast, with the south west monsoon blowing, is a lee shore and beset with dangers, but with the north west wind, which blows during the greater part of the year, there is not a safer coast in the world. At the period in question the season of the south west monsoon had begun, but during the ten days the *Hydroos* was riding at single anchor, the wind was from the north west, and the weather, as Mr. Loughnan describes it, was unusually fine for the season. But during the breaks in the south west monsoon, when the wind lulls, or, as in this case, veers round to the north, the weather is as fine as at any period of the year During this season, however, the fishermen on the coast draw up their boats and betake themselves to other occupations, from which they are very unwillingly withdrawn. As another source of reluctance to render assistance, it should also be observed, that the Malabar coast, which is singularly indented with creeks (karis) and harbours of refuge for small craft, has always been notorious for piracy, which, for the first time in history, has disappeared under British government, but which has left behind it habits and dispositions, not very different from those of Cornish wreckers during the most lawless periods. It appears most clearly from the evidence, that if these coasters, who were standing on the shore with the apathy so often witnessed in the East when self-interest does not stimulate to action, augmented also probably, in this instance, by speculations on the value of the wreck should the vessel go to pieces,—if these men had chosen to supply wood, water, a few hands, and the spars of the vessel which had been taken away, she could have got safely off from her position, as she subsequently did in a couple of hours. Mr. Loughnan, in explaining in his report to Government the large amount (Rs. 700) which he was obliged to expend on behalf of the

1849.

The Hydroos.

defendant in remuneration to the fishermen and others, writes as follows :—" If the charges appear heavy, it is simply because fear and an inordinate lust of gain rendered the fishermen most untractable, and indeed I could not succeed in getting off any boats to the ship, nor could I trust to getting anything done but by going on board myself. To enable you to judge of the extent of the extortion of these fishermen, it will be sufficient to mention that two of the passengers who came on shore on one of the rafts, were compelled by them to pay Rs. 600 for two boats to bring off their families from the ship, only two days before I arrived, and after both wind and sea had subsided." Narrain also, the active Mamlutdar, describes the extortions of the coasters. He says two pilots asked Rs. 1000 each to pilot the ship to Goa; and a native crew demanded Rs. 25,000; yet Goa was only sixty miles to the south, and with the wind fair for it. Mr. Loughnan however, by his presence on the spot and by his activity, brought these fishermen to a sense of their duties, and on the morning of the 30th he succeeded in dispatching five boats, at 7 A. M., with spars, a native boat's anchor with hawsers, and wood and water; and Mr. Loughnan's own account of the mode in which the vessel then got away, will best explain to nautical men the state of the weather and sea. He says, after describing the departure of the boat, "I left people watching to make report to me of her having got out. The report was brought to me about mid-day I think. It was to the effect that she had been hauled off with the assistance of the boats' grapnel and cables (meaning I presume hawsers) so as to weather the headland to leeward of her; had then loosed her sails, and got round the point clear away. The boats afterwards came in, and I was informed that it had been necessary to haul the vessel out to the full length of the three united cables." (hawsers?)

Extortions practised by coasters.

But this successful warping out of the vessel, in the eye of the wind, and to the distance of at least 600 yards, clearly shews what very moderate weather then prevailed, and on this part of the case I entirely agreed with Mr. Loughnan in the view he formerly took of the services rendered by those

1849.

The Hydroos.

Personal hardships and risk sustained by magistrate.

fishermen, *viz.*, that they had been (to say the least) overpaid by the defendant.

The next point urged for Mr. Loughnan was the risk of life which he and the peon who accompanied him had encountered in their two trips to the vessel from the shore. But we were completely convinced by the evidence, that he encountered no other risk on these occasions than any other person who goes into a boat during the fine season, with the wind from north west, which, as is nearly always the case with this wind, and as occurred here, was tolerably fresh in the afternoon, but light in the morning, and it was in the morning that these trips were made. The evidence of a nautical witness, Captain McGregor of the *Buckinghamshire*, who was called for the petitioners, appeared to me very just. In reply to questions from the petitioner's counsel, he said: "From all which I have heard to-day, I should say if I were going on board there would have been no danger. It would not have been an imminent risk of life, but in the present instance, if bad weather had sprung up, there would have been considerable risk." The next point, which both Mr. Loughnan and his counsel seemed strongly to rely upon, was the responsibility he had incurred with his government in borrowing money within his district. The government has a very proper regulation, prohibiting their servants from borrowing from natives within their jurisdiction. But, to suppose that the borrowing of Rs. 300 by Mr. Loughnan on behalf of the ship, and in order to protect the lak of rupees which he had taken into his charge from the Nacodah, could come within the government regulation, appeared to us a most unfounded apprehension; and the point raised reminded me of the crotchet noticed by Grotius, "where a law of Amsterdam having made shedding blood in the streets a capital offence, a question was raised whether, on a man falling down suddenly on the road with apoplexy, the surgeon who was called upon to bleed him came within the penalty." But the urgent claim which was principally advanced at the trial for Mr. Loughnan was in behalf of the great personal hardships he had undergone in his adventurous journey from Malwan to the spot in question, and the discomforts which beset him during his residence there in the four or five days he was absent from home. It is difficult to preserve a suitable gravity in comparing the facts proved in evidence with the statements made in the act on petition, and more especially with the highly coloured ones in the opening speech of counsel. It may be sufficient to state that a very picturesque account of the ravines, sheet rocks, creeks, and other difficulties which beset the route was given, and almost every personal annoyance was suggested which to lawyers in Westminster Hall would appear intolerable; but the account which Mr. Loughnan himself gave at the trial describes such an ordinary Indian journey of twenty-five miles, by two easy marches, that every one in India who is acquainted with Mofussil travelling must smile at such "moving accidents by flood and field" being pressed into the balance sheet. Mr. Loughnan describing his mode of travelling, says: "I took my Doolie (a sort of palanquin) and Doolie bearers and servants, altogether about twelve persons, and I think two peons, and two or three privates of the Rutnagherry Rangers, and the Mamlutdar was to follow;" a little retinue, therefore, of about sixteen persons, with his horse and groom besides, as will afterwards appear. Not, perhaps, a very large following for an Indian officer of high rank, but certainly not so small as to put the salvor at the head of it, then going to the scene of action, altogether out of the pale of social comforts. On the first evening and half way, Mr. Loughnan continues, "I slept in my Doolie in an open part of the Temple the night I started." "While travelling, I was in the Doolie part of the time, occasionally walked, and when the road was pretty clear I rode." On the second night he slept in a native house at Deoguhr with mud walls, but which he states was not so dry as his own house, "and it was extremely damp." But dampness, during the rainy season, is the predicament of every house in India, from the Governor's palace to the humblest hut. In short, the evidence as to Mr. Loughnan's discomforts completely broke down. And indeed it appeared to the Court that Mr. Loughnan himself altogether disclaimed the idea of having undergone anything unusual, or different from what befalls every civilian who moves above his

1849.

The Hydroos.

districts, or indeed any active European who travels in India either for business or pleasure. The great stress which was laid upon this point appears to have originated from a mistaken conception which had arisen in the minds of Mr. Loughnan's legal advisers in Bombay, as to the hardships of travelling during the monsoon; and on reference to the evidence it will be seen that, under the influence of this idea, the subject was continually reverted to by Mr. Loughnan's counsel throughout the whole of that gentleman's examination, in order to elicit those statements which, it was believed, would depict a considerable case of hardship; but the real fact is, as the Court knew well from personal experience, that travelling along the coast by easy stages, during a break in the monsoon, with a cloudy sky, and the thermometer probably at 80°, and the sleeping in a palanquin placed in open huts, choultries or temples, is an adventure accompanied by no hardship whatever, and indeed is rather pleasurable than otherwise. Upon all these grounds, the Court were of opinion on the first point that no salvage service had been rendered by Mr. Loughnan and his people; that the salvage service, if any, had been rendered by the boatmen, and had been amply paid for; and I do not recollect whether on this occasion we distinguished the case of the *Minerva*, in which we had awarded a heavy salvage, but in a subsequent demand of salvage, which was also brought forward by Government officers in another case (making three cases within the year), we took occasion to point out that the reason of so large a salvage being awarded there was, that, in the opinion of the Chief Justice, the abandonment of the ship on a lee shore by the master and crew amounted to a *quasi derelict*.

The second question on which our judgment was based appears to me to be equally strong for dismissing Mr. Loughnan's claim. We felt it difficult to draw any correct analogy between the position of Mr. Loughnan and that of any high county authority in England; for no high authority in a county, wielding powers such as are possessed by Europeans in this country, is a paid officer of Government. Lords lieutenant, sheriffs, magistrates, are all unremune-

Duty of Government officers in India.

1849.

The HYDROOS.

rated, and their duties are generally circumscribed, often merely nominal. But even in the case of an unremunerated English magistrate, Lord STOWELL prescribed what the duties were on an occasion like the present, and remarked that if the services performed only amounted to the ordinary discharge of his duty, he was disposed to leave him, the magistrate, to the general reward of all good magistrates, the fair estimation of his countrymen and the consciousness of his own right conduct. The statute of 26 Geo. 2, c. 19, s. 6, expressly throws on magistrates, *unpaid* magistrates, the obligation of assisting ships in distress, and empowers them to adjust the quantum of salvage to be distributed amongst the persons they employ. A very clear indication, therefore, that the Legislature never intended that services such as Mr. Loughnan rendered should be remunerated. But these duties and obligations on magistrates, which are thus shewn to rest upon them in England, are demandable in far greater force and with a view to the public interest from European officials in India. I have already shewn what large powers are exercised by such officers: it is also well known that the pecuniary remuneration attributed to such service is commensurate with their duties. But it should also be carefully observed, in reference to this case, that all the high offices in this country are exclusively occupied by Europeans; and the consequence is, that the European officer of each district is, and ought to be, and is expected by his Government to be, the life and soul of every exertion which is required to be made on behalf of the community committed to his charge.

Considerations like these induced me at the trial to remark that I took a far higher view of the duties which are incumbent upon European officials than the Advocate General's mode of putting his client's case suggested, and that the public interests, and the high toned liberal spirit which prevailed throughout the service, did not require that a mere money reward should be awarded by law for active exertions in behalf of ships wrecked on the coast. But, in justice to Mr. Loughnan, I am bound to add, that he takes an equally large view of the responsibilities of his post, and the following statement by himself to the defendant (written some days after the lawyers,

1849.

The Hydroos.

apparently unknown to him, had advised a claim for salvage), gives, I conceive, a very correct view of the opinions of the distinguished and eminent services in India on this subject. In acknowledging the grateful thanks which the defendant addressed to Mr. Loughnan, the latter replied thus, "I am obliged to you for your expression of thanks, but I have only to say that nothing more than what my duty requires was done by me in saving your ship and cargo." Indeed we were so pleased with the conduct of this gentleman up to the time of the case coming into Court, we saw so clearly that he had never put forth a claim for salvage himself, and that all he required was that his active deputy, the Mamlutdar, should be noticed by Government, that we were extremely sorry we could not depart from our usual rule as to costs, any further in his favour, than by absolving him from paying any more than his own.

On re-perusing the evidence, I now see clearly that this desire on his part to obtain some reward from Government for the Mamlutdar, and the casual suggestion of the term salvage by his immediate superior, Mr. Cole, as a source from which this native could be remunerated, led to a reference to the legal advisers of Government, from which this great salvage claim emerged full blown, and which, for the reasons I have given, I was induced to think had no foundation in law.

Yardley, J.—My reasons for concurring in the decision that the claimants had not made out any case on the Admiralty side of the Court are all reducible to one, which is, that the services performed, though valuable and highly creditable to the claimants, were not salvage services.

Without pretending to define precisely the exact meaning of the term "salvage services," they may, I believe, be generally described as acts performed upon the sea in extricating vessels, or merchandize on board of vessels, from situations of imminent danger, and the compensation to be recovered must depend upon the circumstances under which the services were performed in each particular case, it being manifestly impossible to lay down any rule sufficiently comprehensive to be applicable to every case that may arise. The principal elements which go to constitute the claim of salvage are— 1849. The Hydroos.

First. The danger of the vessel and merchandize.

Secondly. The value of the things salved.

Thirdly. The amount of risk, labour and expense incurred by the salvors in personally rescuing the ship and cargo.

1st. I am satisfied, from the evidence in the present case, that the principal danger to the ship arose from the utter incompetence of the Nacodah and crew to perform their duties, and that the situation of the vessel was not one of imminent peril if the people on board had displayed the ordinary energy of even native sailors. I do not mean to say, that if a vessel be brought into peril by the incompetence of the captain and crew, persons rescuing her from such a situation are not entitled to compensation in the shape of salvage, but, to shew that the danger, in the present instance, arose not so much from the situation of the vessel, or the state of the weather, as from the want of skill and energy of the crew, not the slightest difficulty was experienced by the fishermen in conveying the ship to Goa.

2nd. It is unnecessary to enter upon the question of value, because

3rdly. As I have already intimated, the claimants, although they did undergo some labour and trouble, and, as regards Mr. Loughnan, the principal claimant did incur some expense (which has, however, been repaid him), they cannot, any of them, be properly said to have been personally engaged in extricating the ship from a situation of danger. True it is, they went off to the ship in a boat, and prudently landed the treasure which was on board, but none of the witnesses pretend to say that this was a service attended by any considerable danger or trouble. The actual salvors of the vessel, if any, were the fishermen whom Mr. Loughnan prevailed upon to embark and lend their assistance, for which, in his opinion, they were exorbitantly paid by a few hundred rupees, and yet this claim for heavy salvage mainly rests upon the meritorious service performed in persuading, instigating, and almost compelling the fishermen so to assist the vessel. I have no desire

1849. — The Hydroos.

to depreciate Mr. Loughnan's exertions. He did every thing that intelligence and energy, combined with power and influence could effect; but, surely, if a few hundred rupees were an exorbitant remuneration for the performance of certain services, the procuring of such services to be performed cannot constitute a salvage claim to the amount of many thousands.

On the whole, I think, that all the services rendered for the purpose of conducing to the saving of the ship having by these claimants been performed on shore, and no sort of risk or danger having been incurred in landing the treasure, the persons who actually conducted the ship safely to port having been amply remunerated, and Mr. Loughnan having been repaid the moneys advanced and expended by him for the use of the ship, no claim whatsoever for salvage has been established.

LOUGHNAN, APPELLANT,

1851. *v.*

JUSSAPH BULLADIN, RESPONDENT.

CASE OF THE HYDROOS.

In the Privy Council.

On the above case being called on in appeal, objection was taken by the respondents that Mr. Loughnan had perempted his appeal by having applied for costs after a decision in the suit had been pronounced against him, and the Court being of opinion that the objection was fatal,

Dismissed the appeal (*a*).

(*a*) I trust I may take the liberty of noting the extreme unsatisfactoriness of a decision of the Court of Appeal like the above. A Colonial Court can never be expected to be conversant with the technicalities in practice of special Courts in England. Their business is, and

1851.

should be, to deal with the merits of every cause that comes before them; and the Court of Appeal, according to the views of a great jurist, Lord KENYON, should disregard all formal objections, and look to the substantial merits of the decision only in the Court below. See Rex *v.* Suddis, 1 East, 306.

The decision in the principal case I consider to be sound, but it was much canvassed in India, and I should have been very glad to have had it reviewed in the superior Court; the parties, however, who objected to it must naturally feel much discontented on the dismissal of their appeal, because they had *perempted* their cause, a term which no practitioner in the Court knew the meaning of.

THE LORD DUFFERIN.

1849.
August 13, 14.

CASE OF SALVAGE.

[*Coram* SIR E. PERRY, C. J., and SIR W. YARDLEY, J.]

Admiralty side.

A Government steamer having been dispatched under orders of Government, to a vessel in distress, in Bombay harbour, the Court held that R. 5000 was a sufficient salvage reward, the officers and crew having undergone no personal danger, and the salvage service being in fact performed by the powerful Government steamer.

Distinction between the claims of Government officers using public property, and private sailors, as to the amount of reward.

THE act on petition presented a claim on behalf of Lieut. Rennie commanding, and for the East India Company owners, and for the other officers and crew of the steam ship *Feroze*, for salvage service to the *Lord Dufferin* on the 25th of June, 1849, then being in a state of great danger outside the harbour of Bombay.

The owner tendered Rs. 5000 for the services performed, denied that the *Lord Dufferin* was in any danger, and alleged that the master could have hired another steam vessel at a moderate charge to perform the services rendered by the *Feroze*.

By consent evidence was taken at the Bar *vivâ voce*.

Le Messurier, A. G., and *Howard* for the claimants.

1849.

The Lord Dufferin.

Crawford, for the defendant.

At the conclusion of the case on the second day, the Judges decided that the sum tendered was sufficient for the services performed, and dismissed the plaintiff's claim with costs.

Leave to appeal to the Privy Council having been afterwards granted, the Chief Justice transmitted the following reasons for his decision.

I have the honour to transmit the following reasons for my decision in the *Lord Dufferin*, the greater part of which I wrote out on the day of delivering judgment.

Vessel in distress salved by Government steamer under orders from Government.

Perry, C. J.—This is a case of salvage, claimed against the ship *Lord Dufferin*, on the part of several of the officers of the East India Company, and we intimated yesterday that it appeared to us on facts, which seemed to be undisputed, that the service performed in this case was a salvage service. Without attempting to lay down a complete definition of what salvage is, for all definitions in law are said to be dangerous, it does not seem open to objection to hold that salvage occurs wherever assistance is rendered to a ship at sea, who is in such a dangerous position that in all human probability she will not be able to extricate herself by her own unassisted efforts. We are clearly of opinion that the *Lord Dufferin* was in this condition. The loss of her rudder, her exhausted crew, her position in foul ground, the strong wind of the monsoon, and a large shoal under her lee, all rendered it highly improbable, that at the time when the *Feroze* made its appearance, she would have got out without the assistance of steam; and it is not at all unlikely, that if the strong gusty weather, which often occurs at that season of the year, had come on, she would not have been able to ride out another flood tide. All these circumstances constitute the service—which was rendered—a salvage service, nor does it, I think, detract from the character of the service, that in the weather which did actually occur, and by the means which the captain was in the act of taking for procuring assistance from the shore, he, in all probability, would have been able to get his vessel off at a comparatively small expense.

1849.

The LORD DUFFERIN.

Such considerations may affect the *quantum* of the award to be paid as salvage, but they do not alter the nature of the service rendered, which is to be determined, I conceive, by the actual danger at the moment of rendering it, and not by subsequent events which no one was capable of perceiving.

This being so, the main question in the case is, whether the sum of Rs. 5000, which has been tendered, is a sufficient remuneration for the salvors.

Question, whether salvage claimed by Government as well as by Government officer.

To determine this question it is important to ascertain who the salvors are who are claiming; for this fact certainly does not appear very clear in the meagre pleadings of this case, although owing to inquiries put by the counsel for the ship, and by certain minute facts in the case, I think a very satisfactory conclusion upon it may be arrived at.

At the first view of this case it certainly would appear that the present claim was preferred by the Government of the country; and if this were the case a number of considerations would have to be carefully weighed which have never, to my knowledge, been discussed in a Court of justice. For, although we have seen cases in the books where the Lords Commissioners of the Admiralty have preferred claims incidentally for reimbursements to Government ships whose crews had earned salvage, there is no case, that I am aware of, in which the Queen's Government, having determined to assist a merchantman in distress, have subsequently brought their demands in a Court of justice for salvage rewards. Whenever such case does occur, it will probably be held that the Government are entitled to claim salvage, though, if the act of salvage be an act of Government, there is some difficulty in understanding how it would form the basis of a civil contract, which seems to be the true foundation of a salvage claim, or what reciprocity there would be so as to give the merchantman a cross action against the Government, if the salvage was negligently performed. But, however this be, if the legal right was held to exist, undoubtedly a variety of topics would occur, which, although more fitting for discussion in the Cabinet or the Legislature, would also be perfectly legitimate in a Court of justice in order to determine the *amount* of damages which a jury or other competent tribunal ought to give. For it is

1849.

The Lord Dufferin.

impossible to avoid seeing that there are various marked distinctions between a Government and a private salvor. The latter builds and maintains his ship and crew solely for purposes of profit, he is seeking it eagerly in every port of the world—time to him is money, and he has no interest or concern in the successful ventures of his neighbour. But the public ships of a government are not kept for profit at all, but entirely for the public service; in peace, they have scarcely any duties to perform but the protection of commerce, and when they are not performing these duties, they are often lying idle in harbour, with powerful crews, ample equipments, and actually doing nothing. Moreover the private salvor has no large and abiding interest to protect the commerce of a particular port, he happens to be there for the nonce, and it is wholly indifferent to him, except so far as his individual interests are concerned, that large, generous principles of protection to commerce should be extended to the mercantile world generally. But an enlightened government, especially a British government, has such motives always acting upon it most forcibly, and in every British dominion in the world I will not scruple to say that the most large protection and assistance to British commerce which can be afforded by the Government without disparagement to other public duties is regarded as among their paramount obligations: and I was rather surprised, I confess, to hear in this Court the light, not to say contemptuous, tone with which "cotton bales" were spoken of. It appears to me that the interests of commerce, such as I have been referring to, should always be kept broadly in view by civil Courts of justice; and if in the highest tribunal of the kingdom a woolpack was placed to remind the authorities of the great staple of the country, so a maritime Court, sitting in dominions won by the energy and enterprise of a company of merchants trading to the East Indies, should not be slow to recognise that one of its most important offices is the protection of British trade.

But it does not appear to me that, in fact, the government have preferred a distinct claim here for salvage remuneration, and although the act on petition professes to be made for Lieut. Rennie, the officer commanding, for the East India

1849.

The LORD DUFFERIN.

Company, the owners, and for the officers and crew, of the steam ship *Feroze*, still I think that the true conclusion which is to be drawn from all the facts of the case is, that the Government has no further interposed than to allow Lieut. Rennie to use their name, in order to enable him to make the best of it he can for his own purposes. And I found this opinion on the three following considerations, which are corroborative of the conclusion I draw in my own mind as to the enlarged views of policy entertained by the Bombay government: 1st. The government, acting through its military department, sent in its charge for the expenditure of coal, &c. in the two steamers employed, and made no mention of any other demand; 2nd. The government have not preferred any distinct claim as to the amount to which they may be entitled in respect of a per centage or interest on the valuable government property employed in the salvage, which is a very different matter from the claim made by Lieut. Rennie for his *personal* services; 3rd. In the nominal rule which the claimants were called upon to make, it is only the names of Lieut. Rennie, and the officers of the *Feroze*, and of the pilots, which appear. The only visible intervention of the government, therefore, in this case is traceable in the allegation, not on oath, of the act on petition, that the claim is made on behalf of government as well as on behalf of Lieut. Rennie, which allegation is explicable on the suggestion before made.

Government claims to salvage considered.

But supposing that I am altogether wrong in the conclusion of fact which I have drawn, and that the government of Bombay does not take those views of policy which I suppose to actuate them as to the duties of protecting British commerce, when in distress, and within reach of government assistance, and that they are preferring this claim in order to get as much remuneration for its services as the law awards: and supposing also that I am wrong in my legal doubts whether a government ship, lying idle in harbour, is entitled to remuneration for salvage *on the same scale* as the ship of a merchant who is seeking only his own private emolument (on which point Sir JOHN NICHOLL's observations (3 *Hagg. Adm. R.*, p. 121) support my views), still both these errors, if they be such, are innocuous

1849.

The Lord Dufferin.

on this inquiry, for I cannot possibly see how, in any view of the case, the claims of the government as salvors can be placed higher than the claims of private salvors.

The harbour of Bombay is beset with many dangers in the south west monsoon; once to the northward of the harbour, and the road back is difficult; to the southward, there is a lee shore, and at the entrance of the harbour much foul ground. Occasions, therefore, will frequently arise for assistance to merchant vessels making for the port at this period of the year. But if government enter the field as a salvage company, it must be admitted they will have great advantages over private salvors. Several government establishments, such as the Light House, the Pilot Service, &c., are kept up for other public services, through which establishments information of what is occurring in the offing will reach the government more speedily than the ears of private shipowners; and in time of peace large steamers, ready for sea at a few hours' notice, will usually be available for any salvage purpose without detriment to the public interest. When a salvage claim is made by government under such circumstances, the inquiry naturally will arise as to what a private salvor would have done the work for, if he had been enabled to make a fair start in the race. And, as it is proved to me satisfactorily in this case that a private steam company would have been glad to undertake, and well able to perform, the salvage service in question for four or five thousand rupees, it appears to me to be impossible to award a larger sum to the present claimants whoever they may be.

Claims of Government on salvage service.

The claim for salvage in this case is referable entirely to the state of danger from which the *Lord Dufferin* was rescued; and the steam-engine and the coals were, in fact, the true salvors. Of personal risk, or any extraordinary labour and skill on the part of Lieut. Rennie and his officers, I see no indication; and the few hours employed in the trip to the *Lord Dufferin* do not appear to me to have differed, so far as the equipage of the *Feroze* is concerned, from any similar amount of steaming about the harbour at that period of the year. But Lieut. Rennie's claim is based by his counsel on the responsibility which he encountered in employing a government vessel in the service of private shipowners; and the case of the *Lustre*, (3 Hagg. 154), is relied on; but there is a fallacy in arguing that responsibility on this score can exist, as the service was performed under the direct orders of government. It is true that in the examination of Lieut. Rennie he brought forward a responsibility of another kind which he confronted, by deciding to take the steamer out of the pilot's hands. But this also, on examination, appears to have been so slight a responsibility, that it is not measurable in money. For Lieut. Rennie states, and I have no doubt quite correctly, that he considered he knew the harbour quite as well as the pilot; the part of the harbour to which he was steaming was not pilot's ground, and therefore was not better known to the pilot than to himself, who has been acquainted with the harbour for twenty years; and it appears, by the evidence, that under the experienced treatment of Lieut. Rennie, long conversant with steamers and with the then state of the tide, the *Feroze* encountered no dangers whatever.

1849.

The Lord Dufferin.

The salvage claim is, therefore, limited to the due remuneration for a steamer, powerful enough to perform the requisite service, and I am satisfied, from the evidence at the Bar, that Rs. 5000 is quite enough, and that, looking at the interests of commerce on one side, and the personal services rendered by Lieut. Rennie and the crew on the other, it would be unjust and impolitic to give a larger sum.

Feeling of Court against claims by Government officers.

I have gone at greater length than I could have wished into a discussion of the principles which I have applied to the decision of this case, but I have been desirous fully to explain them because, in my opinion, unsound doctrines have been broached in this Court with respect to them. To all who are conversant with jury trial in England, it is well known that, in cases of assessment of damages, the moral feeling which is prevailing amongst the jury on the subject under discussion operates largely, and in most cases beneficially, on the amount awarded. The jury not being called on to give reasons for their decision, the exact opinion, and the grounds of it, entertained by them, cannot be made patent in black and white. But when the decision is vested in Judges, who have to give

1849.

The Lord Dufferin.

their reasons, they are usually able to explain the motives operating on their judgment, and I have no reluctance whatever to explain the temper of mind with which I regard these claims brought forward by government officers for salvage, and which have made their appearance on three several occasions during the last year. I view them with regret. I do not like to hear it suggested that what has been termed three-and-sixpenny motives are necessary to be put in action to call the distinguished Services of India into performance of public duties. I recollect reading, before I arrived in India, a glowing eulogy on the different Services made by Sir John Malcolm at the Bar of the House of Commons, describing their zeal, their public spirit, their freedom from all petty sordid motives. "*Avidi laudis, pecuniæ liberales,*" as was said of another distinguished race of administrators during their best period. My own experience of India confirms the truth of the above description, and the spirit it denotes is, in my opinion, so desirable to be encouraged, both for the renown of England and the welfare of India, that I have no doubt this impression has operated on my mind whilst engaged in estimating the pecuniary claims of members of the Service on British merchants in distress (*a*).

(*a*) The appeal was afterwards abandoned.

END OF PART II.

PART III.

CONFLICT OF LAWS.

M'INTYRE
v.
HIRJIBHAI RASTAMJI.

1842. Sept. 12.

[*Coram* PERRY, J.]

The Supreme Court at Bombay has jurisdiction to entertain a suit for setting aside a judgment of a foreign Court, on the grounds of its having been obtained by fraud, and of the defendant not being within the jurisdiction of the foreign Court.

A writ of *ne exeat regnum* granted in such a suit.

Proceedings of a Portuguese Court at Macao detailed.

Where a suit was entertained to set aside a foreign judgment, on the ground of collusion between the Judge and the plaintiff abroad, the foreign Judge happening to pass through Bombay during the examination of witnesses, was brought before the examiner to give evidence, but refused to do so, on the ground of privilege: *Held*, that he was compelled to give his evidence, *de bene esse*, and that the objection to its reception must be taken at the hearing.

Quære, whether an English Judge can be compelled to give evidence as a witness of matters that have come before him judicially.

A BILL had been filed in this case against the defendant, to recover back money which had been obtained from him under a judgment of her Portuguese Majesty's Court at Macao, and which it was charged had been obtained by the fraud and collusion of the defendant and the Judge of the Court; and on affidavits stating that the defendant was about to leave Bombay immediately for China, *Howard* obtained a rule nisi for a writ *ne exeat jurisdictionem.*

1842.

M'INTYRE v. HIRJIBHAI.

Le Messurier, A. G., shewed cause, and contended that, as the plaintiff had had a judgment against him by a Court of competent jurisdiction, it was not open to this Court to give relief; and he cited *Story's Conflict of Laws*, 492, and *Burrows* v. *Jemimo*, (2 Str. 783).

Howard, contrà, cited *Price* v. *Dewhurst*, (4 M. & Cr.); *Novelli* v. *Rossi*, (2 B. & Ad. 757), and 3 *Burge's Colonial Law*, 1069, in which latter work it is laid down distinctly that the jurisdiction to set aside the judgment of a foreign Court vitiated by fraud is undoubted.

Cur. adv. vult.

Application to restrain a defendant from leaving Bombay till he gave security to meet plaintiff's claim.

Sir E. PERRY, J.—In this case an application was made by the plaintiff for the writ *ne exeat regnum* to restrain defendant from leaving Bombay until he gave security for the amount demanded of him by the plaintiff's bill. The circumstances relied on by the plaintiff are in substance as follows:—

Plaintiff's claim stated.

In April, 1840, the plaintiff M'Intyre, being then in command of the barque *Ardaseer*, which was at anchor off the island of Macao laden with opium, went on shore, and by verbal contract agreed to sell to the defendant Hirjibhai fifty chests of opium at 450 dollars, for cash on delivery. The opium was to be delivered at Tonkkoo, which is about three or four hours sail from Macao, and on board a receiving ship there lying, belonging to Hirjibhai.

Hirjibhai accordingly gave him a sealed note to one Lyons, the captain of his receiving ship, and M'Intyre proceeded there on the same day, with the vessel and the opium on board. M'Intyre gave Hirjibhai's letter to Captain Lyons, and offered to deliver the opium also on receiving cash or securities; but the captain refused to accept the opium on such terms, having, as he alleged, received no order to that effect from Hirjibhai. M'Intyre thereupon informed him that he should remain at Tonkkoo a few days, and that the captain had better communicate with Hirjibhai. The captain wrote accordingly, but no answer having arrived from Hirjibhai, the plaintiff M'Intyre, at the end of six days, sailed back with his

1842.

M'INTYRE v. HIRJIBHAI.

opium to Macao, and there informed the defendant that he had not delivered the opium to Captain Lyons, on the ground of his declining to pay for it, and that he had given him six days to take it. M'Intyre thereupon sold the opium to other parties, and again left Macao in further prosecution of his voyage. He returned to it about the 18th of May, and having gone on shore, he was arrested at the suit of Hirjibhai for 7600 dollars, as the alleged measure of damage arising out of the non-delivery of the opium. M'Intyre gave bail for his appearance in the Portuguese Court on the Monday following, and on appearance there the Judge informed him that the matter must be settled by arbitration: and the Judge thereupon nominated Mr. W. Sprott Boyd as arbitrator for Hirjibhai, and ordered the plaintiff to select an arbitrator for himself. M'Intyre protested against the jurisdiction of the Court altogether, and he especially protested against Mr. Boyd as an arbitrator, as he believed him to be in partnership with Hirjibhai in opium transactions. The Judge, however, overruled the objection, on the ground that Hirjibhai was determined to have Mr. Boyd, and he informed the plaintiff that he could not be allowed to leave the Court till he also had named an arbitrator. The plaintiff thereupon named one of the persons present in Court, and the Judge named an umpire. M'Intyre shortly after sailed from Macao, having put in bail to stand by the award, but this also, as he alleges, upon compulsion; and on the 17th of June following, Mr. Boyd and the arbitrator named by M'Intyre made an award against him for 8700 dollars, which is equivalent to about Rs. 19,200. This sum, it appears, has been actually paid by the plaintiff's agents.

Plaintiff arrested in foreign Court on false claim, and by fraud of defendant and Judge, compelled to pay a large sum to obtain his liberty.

The plaintiff alleges that Hirjibhai had no cause of action whatever against him; that by a fraudulent conspiracy between the Portuguese Judge and Hirjibhai, to which Mr. Boyd and others became more or less parties, the moneys had been extorted from him.

The plaintiff has been engaged in several voyages since that period, and, having arrived in Bombay in August last and discovered that Hirjibhai was residing here, he immediately

1842.

M'INTYRE v. HIRJIBHAI.

took measures for proceeding against him, and on the 8th of September last, having learned that Hirjibhai was about to proceed in a couple of days to China on board the *Inglis*, he comes to this Court to ask its compulsory process in order to put the matter in a train for litigation. The question which arises on this state of facts appears to be, whether it is competent to this Court to entertain a suit, the object of which is to deprive a party of the fruits of a decision he has obtained in a foreign tribunal. By what has been termed the comity of nations the judgments of foreign Courts are undoubtedly entitled to the greatest respect: by the English law, in particular, they have more weight attributed to them than they receive in some of the codes of other civilized nations—in the French, for example. The English law presumes that foreign Courts proceed on the same fixed principles of right and justice as govern our own tribunals, and it lends itself to enforce their decisions whenever no recognised principles of the *jus gentium* appear to have been violated. Furthermore, it sturdily refuses to sit in appeal on any decision on the merits, which have been already investigated by a competent tribunal (*a*).

Question, whether it is competent to this Court to examine judgment of foreign Court.

Respect paid by English law to foreign judgments, and presumption that all done there by Judge done rightly.

Now, although in this case many of the statements made by the plaintiff are rather awakening, especially as to the mode in which he was forced into Court, and an arbitrator imposed upon him by the Judge, I think it is my duty to presume, until the contrary be shewn, that the Portuguese Court proceeded in conformity with their law. According to English jurisprudence, it is of the essence of judgment by arbitration that the litigating parties should freely consent to the matter being referred, and very large discretionary powers, both over law and facts, are therefore given to arbitrators, as being judges voluntarily selected by the parties themselves. But in examining the procedure of a foreign tribunal, it is necessary to divest one's mind of all attachment to mere technical rules; and, if the Portuguese law authorizes the Judge to drive the parties into arbitration against their consent, I cannot say that the practice is so contrary to first principles as to induce us to

Large powers of arbitrators, from their being the Judges voluntarily selected, and the plaintiff's own arbitrator decided against him.

(*a*) See *Bank of Australasia* v. *Nias*, 20 Law Journ. (N. S.) Q. B. 284, where the doctrine in the text is established in a most elaborate judgment.

consider all the proceedings, which have been based upon it, a nullity.

Plaintiff here is telling his own story, *ex parte*.

Again, it does not appear but that the plaintiff had an opportunity of stating his case in person, and urging all the facts he brings forward here before the arbitrators; and as he is telling his own story, and is silent upon the subject, it is too much to call upon the Court to presume that the arbitrators made their award without having fully heard him or his agent; but if the arbitrators did fully hear the case, and if they heard both the plaintiff and defendant and the other witnesses in the cause, with all the local advantages which must always attend a trial on the spot, I should be very unwilling to admit that their *bonâ fide* decision, however much it might clash with my own views, was examinable in this Court. And on this point it will not fail to be observed, that the arbitrator—nominated at least, if not freely chosen, by M'Intyre, joined in the award against him, and that the umpire was never called in.

On these grounds the *merits* of the decision not examinable.

There are two other distinct grounds, however, on which it is contended that this suit is maintainable; first of all, because M'Intyre was not liable to the jurisdiction of the Portuguese Court; secondly, because the judgment was obtained by fraud.

But fraud and want of jurisdiction also charged.

Undoubtedly either of these objections to the validity of a foreign judgment is sufficient to warrant an English Court in entering into an examination of it, and I am of opinion that both are sufficiently raised on the plaintiff's affidavit to entitle him to put the matter in suit. With regard to the first, it appears that the plaintiff and defendant, both British subjects, entered into a contract at Macao with respect to property out of the Portuguese jurisdiction, and that the plaintiff, M'Intyre, was undoubtedly not domiciled in that island. According to the common law, which takes but little notice of domicile, if foreign merchants come within the jurisdiction of an English Court merely for a period of time long enough to be served with process, the competence of the English Court accrues; but this is not the case in countries governed by systems founded on the civil law,—not in Scotland, for instance, where the defendant must reside forty days before jurisdiction over

Jurisdiction arises by the English law over all parties who come within its territory.

But by the civil law, a certain amount of residence is required.

1842.

M'INTYRE v. HIRJIBHAI.

Judgment pronounced by a foreign Court without jurisdiction is a nullity.

him arises; 3 *Burge*, 1017. And in this case M'Intyre alleges that the Portuguese Court had not jurisdiction over him, and we find his statement corroborated by the letter of Captain Elliot, R. N., who was the representative of British interest in those waters. But, if the Portuguese Court was not one of competent jurisdiction, its judgment was a nullity, the money obtained under it does not belong to Hirjibhai, and the matter is a fit subject for inquiry in this Court.

So also all judgments obtained by fraud may be set aside.

Again, the plaintiff distinctly alleges that the judgment was obtained by the fraud of the defendant, conjointly with the Judge and one of the arbitrators. Whether it were so or not I have not now to determine, but merely whether a party, who alleges himself to have been injured by a judgment obtained by fraud, has a right to seek relief in this Court. "If," says Lord ELDON, (2 *Ves. Jun.* 135), "a judgment at law was obtained, a bill shewing that it was obtained against conscience by concealment would open it to relief in this Court." Fraud, in the language of Lord COKE, avoids all judicial acts, ecclesiastical and temporal.

But, if the judgment of an English Court of law is thus examinable, it follows that the comity of nations cannot entitle foreign judgments to greater immunity; and the cases of *Novelli* v. *Rossi*, (2 B. & Ad.), *Price* v. *Dewhurst*, (8 Sim.), and the MS. case of *Blake* v. *Smith* there cited by the Vice Chancellor, fully shew that our Courts will examine into and set aside a foreign judgment not impartially obtained. A doubt passed through my mind during the argument, whether the plaintiff M'Intyre ought not to have appealed from the sentence of the Portuguese Court to the Court above, if there be one, or, at all events, to have shewn that no such Court existed, according to the principle which prevails in our law with regard to the judgments of the supreme Courts; but, on reference to *Rossi* v. *Novelli*, I find that no appeal was made to the Court of Cassation, and that in *Price* v. *Dewhurst*, though lodged, it was not prosecuted; and on principle it clearly cannot be requisite for a party, who has been improperly dragged into a foreign Court, and against whom judgment has been obtained by fraud, to waste his time and his

Where judgment obtained in foreign Court by fraud, English Court will afford relief, although party might have appealed to foreign Court of appeal.

money in endeavouring to procure a reversal of the decree, and he ought to be allowed to obtain his remedy against the other party whenever they may happen to come within the jurisdiction of a Court of their own country.

A formal objection was made to the issuing of the writ, which it may be necessary to notice, namely, that, if all the facts be true, there is no debt due to the plaintiff, he not having himself paid any money, and that the party entitled to sue is the agent at Macao. But I think there is nothing in the objection; "*qui solvit per alium solvit per se,*" and the plaintiff adopts, and is bound to adopt, the acts which he authorized his agent to perform for him; besides which, this is not a question as to a legal debt or an arrest at common law, but as to the equitable claim of the plaintiff to have Hirjibhai declared a trustee for the money he has received under a fraudulent judgment.

Conclusion, suit maintained, and defendant restrained from leaving Bombay.

On the two grounds, therefore, of alleged want of jurisdiction and fraud, I think the plaintiff has made out a *primâ facie* case for relief, and, under the circumstances of the defendant being about to leave the island immediately, the rule for granting the writ *ne exeat regnum* must be made absolute (*a*).

(*a*) The suit was never brought to a hearing, and I learned from the counsel in the case that the defendant satisfied the plaintiff's claim, and paid the costs of the suit. See the next case.

M'INTYRE *v.* HIRJIBHAI.

[*Coram* PERRY, J.]

Quære, whether a Judge is examinable as to the grounds of his decision.

IN consequence of the preceding decision the defendant put in his answer, and the cause being at issue evidence was taken before the examiner. Whilst the examination of witnesses was proceeding, Don ——, the Macao Judge, mentioned in the bill, happened to touch at Bombay on his route from Macao to

1841. M'INTYRE v. HIRJIBHAI.

Europe; the plaintiff subpœnaed him as a witness but he refused to attend, and, on being threatened with an attachment, he came voluntarily into Court, *coram* PERRY, J., who was sitting on the trial of small causes, and stated his objections to appear, *viz.*, that by Portuguese Law no Judge was examinable as to the reasons of his decision, or in any matter respecting the subject-matter of the suits that came before him.

Dickinson, for the complainant, urged that he should be committed, if he did not give his evidence.

PERRY, J.—It is a question of much nicety how far a Judge can be compelled to give evidence of matters that have come before him judicially; but it is a point that must be decided in this Court by English, not by Portuguese, law. I am unable to say offhand what the decision of the English law might be, but it is quite clear that the objection to give the evidence ought not to be allowed now, for, if it should turn out on argument hereafter that the evidence is admissible, the opportunity for obtaining the learned Judge's evidence will be altogether lost to the complainant. The gentleman, therefore, must give his evidence provisionally, and under protest, if he choose, before the examiner, and then at the hearing it will be rejected, if it is not admissible by law (*a*).

(*a*) At a trial for perjury committed before PLATT, B., in Chambers, during the present year (1851), *cor.* Lord CAMPBELL, C. J., the learned Baron attended the trial on a subpœna, but the Lord Chief Justice reprobated the practice of summoning Judges as witnesses, and said that the learned Baron should have taken no notice of the subpœna.

ROSA MARIA DE LIMA, (BY HER NEXT FRIEND,) *v.* FERNANDEZ.

1841.
June 11.

[*Coram* Roper, C. J., and Perry, J.]

The Vicar General of Bombay committed to gaol for contempt of Court in performing the marriage ceremony of an infant ward of Court, in express disobedience of the order of Court.

Quære, as to the right of the Portuguese inhabitants of Bombay to their own laws (*a*).

Claims of the Roman Catholic Church, in opposition to the civil law.

A bill had been filed in this case for the purpose of making the infant plaintiff a ward of Court, and on an application to Perry, J., in Chambers, on the 24th of May, on affidavits setting forth that a marriage was about to be solemnized immediately between the plaintiff and a son of the defendant, also an infant, under circumstances which seemed to shew that the interests of the plaintiff were sacrificed, an injunction to stop the marriage was awarded.

The order was served upon the mother of the plaintiff, on the defendant, and on the priest, Fré Miguel, Vicar General of Bombay; but the latter tore up the order contemptuously, and stated that he should pay no attention to it, and subsequently performed the marriage ceremony.

The Advocate General now moved on affidavits that the priest should be committed for the contempt.

The affidavit of the Vicar General set forth that he was ignorant of English, that the parties in the suit were Portuguese, and that he had bound himself by an oath not to refuse the sacrament of marriage to any parties whatsoever against whom no canonical objections could be urged, and that if he had obeyed the order of the Court he should have rendered himself liable to ecclesiastical censure.

The defendant's affidavit disclaimed all knowledge of the marriage.

(*a*) See the next case, p. 333.

1841.

Rosa v. Fernandez.

Campbell and *Crawford* shewed cause, and contended, that by the treaty granting the island of Bombay to the English, the laws of the Portuguese were guaranteed to them, and, although they could not produce the treaty or a copy of it to the Court, judicial notice of it must be taken; *Taylor* v. *Bentley*, (2 Sim. 213). If the Portuguese were to be governed by their own law, they ought not to be made subject to the consequences for contempt in not obeying the English law.

Roper, C. J., thought a gross contempt of the Court had been committed, and committed the priest to the gaol of Bombay.

Perry, J., stated the pain which he felt on putting the criminal process of the Court into execution, but the validity of the decrees of the Court depended ultimately on the power to enforce them, and, if that power was wilfully braved, it must be enforced however reluctantly.

It was impossible to conceive a grosser case of contempt. The plaintiff, as a ward, was entitled to the protection of the Court; if the marriage in question would have been beneficial to her, after due inquiry made, it would have been sanctioned; but the Vicar General had taken upon himself to decide that the Queen's Court had nothing to do with the matter, and referred to some superior ecclesiastical Court elsewhere to which he owed allegiance.

The excuse put forward that the Portuguese have separate laws of their own amounted to nothing. If they had, those laws are still to be administered by this Court, and its orders must be obeyed. But there seems no ground to suppose that the Portuguese, as they are called, in Bombay, are in any way distinguished by law from other British subjects (*a*).

(*a*) The Vicar General, after remaining some months in gaol, apologised to the Court for his contempt, and was set at large, but he first of all addressed himself to Mr. O'Connell, M.P. to ascertain whether any redress could be obtained in the House of Commons, as I ascertained from his successor, Right Rev. Bishop Whelan.

THE WARDENS OF NOSSA SENORA DA SALVACAO

v.

RIGHT. REV. BISHOP HARTMANN AND OTHERS (*a*).

1851. June.

[*Coram* PERRY, C. J., and YARDLEY, J.]

1. Jurisdiction of the Court to decide disputes involving the right of property between a Roman Catholic Bishop and the parishioners; and also as to the right in the parish to elect their vicar, maintained.
2. Relations between the Government and the Portuguese Roman Catholics of Bombay.
3. Existence of special laws affecting the Portuguese in Bombay denied.
4. Claim of Advocate General to take a bill off the file, in which public charities were involved, disallowed.
5. The East India Company not a necessary party to a suit between a Roman Catholic Bishop and the parishioners respecting the right to appoint a vicar.

THIS was a bill in which the churchwardens and other parishioners of Makin sought to restrain the Roman Catholic Bishop from interfering in the management of the parish charity funds, and from intruding a vicar upon the parish contrary to the wishes of the majority of the parishioners.

Demurrer, for want of equity.

Howard and *Dickinson*, for the complainants.

Le Messurier, A. G., and *Jenkins*, for the defendants.

Before the cause was called on, the Advocate General moved *ex parte* that the bill should be taken off the file for irregularity, as it appeared on the face of the bill that it affected a public charity, and that therefore such a suit should be brought by the Advocate General in the shape of an information, and that the sole control and conduct of the suit belonged to himself. He further stated, that he not only had

(*a*) This case, though decided ten years subsequently, may conveniently follow here.

1851.

Wardens of NOSSA SENORA v. Bishop HARTMANN.

not given his consent to an information, but had refused it on the ground that the bill stated matters which were not true.

Howard and *Dickinson*, *contrà*, denied the right claimed by the Advocate General, and asserted that it was sufficient for the ends of justice to make him a party to the suit, which had been done, though perhaps informally.

The Court reserved the point, and the case was then argued on its merits.

Cur. adv. vult.

June 25.

PERRY, C. J., now delivered the judgment of the Court. This bill is filed by the Fabriqueiro and wardens of the church of N. S. de Salvacaô at Mahim, in which they pray that the church property may be vested in trustees for the benefit of the parish, that the Rev. Braz Fernandez may be declared by the Court to be their lawful vicar, and that Bishop Hartmann may be restrained from intruding another vicar into the parish, or intermeddling with the Church property, and from deposing the said Braz Fernandez without the consent of the majority of the parishioners.

The bill states that the church in question was built about the year 1651, by subscription among the Roman Catholics residing at Mahim, and that it has been always served by a priest in holy orders, who, by virtue of his office, becomes entitled to the fees payable on performance of the Sacraments and other rites of the Roman Catholic Church. The church has also been endowed with divers gifts of lands and monies, applicable for religious and charitable purposes, to the use of the church, and for the benefit of the Roman Catholics residing in its neighbourhood.

Ecclesiastical jurisdiction over Catholics in Bombay vested in Archbishop of Goa.

The bill then states, that while the island of Bombay belonged to the Crown of Portugal all Roman Catholic priests were appointed by the Archbishop of Goa, as Primate of the East, but subject to the approbation of the majority of the parishioners, and that on the cession of the island of Bombay to the English the articles of convention reserved to the Crown

1851.

Wardens of NOSSA SENORA v. Bishop HARTMANN.

of Portugal the rights of Portuguese to all the churches of the island for ever. (I may here observe, that in all discussions as to the rights of Portuguese in this Court, we hear allusions to a convention of this kind, the legal existence or validity of which has never been established, and which certainly has never been recognised in this Court.)

Carmelite mission established in Bombay, circa 1700.

The bill proceeds to state, that spiritual jurisdiction and episcopal government being thus exercised in Bombay by the Archbishop of Goa, about the commencement of the last century a mission of Carmelite friars, sent out from Rome by the Propaganda, established themselves in the island, under the government of a Vicar Apostolic, who, after a time, succeeded in ingratiating himself with several of the Roman Catholic communions, and thereupon appointed vicars to their churches as vacancies occurred. The Crown of Portugal having been moved by remonstrances from the Archbishop of Goa to apply to the British Government on this subject, the Court of Directors wrote out to the Bombay Government, in 1786, stating that the jurisdiction of the Archbishop of Goa had been interfered with, and that it was the desire of his Majesty's Secretary of State that it should be restored, and the Honorable Court accordingly ordered the local government to restore this jurisdiction, but to reserve to themselves, as heretofore, the power of rejecting all improper persons appointed by the Archbishop.

Differences between Archbishop and Carmelite Bishop.

The execution of these orders proving very distateful to the Roman Catholics, who recognised the Carmelite jurisdiction, the Honorable Court, on application being made to them, write again on 15th September, 1790, stating their regret to find that their orders of 1786 had given great uneasiness to the Roman Catholics, and that, as they found that they were uniformly averse to the jurisdiction of the Archbishop, they were disposed to comply with their unanimous wishes, and to allow them to recognise the jurisdiction of the Carmelites.

A proclamation was accordingly made by the Governor in 1791, by which he ordered all the Catholic inhabitants of Bombay to pay due obedience in spiritual matters to the

1851.

Wardens of NOSSA SENORA v. Bishop HARTMANN.

Interference by Bombay Government.

Carmelite Bishop, under pain of incurring the severe displeasure of Government.

This order proving to be as distasteful to the Archbishop's party as the previous one had been to the Carmelites, the Court of Directors write again on the 15th December, 1793, stating that they had made their previous order under the erroneous idea that the Catholics were almost unanimous on the subject, but, as a large and respectable party adhered to the Archbishop, and it was immaterial to the Court who officiated in the churches, provided that the inhabitants were satisfied, and that the pastors conducted themselves as good citizens, they direct that steps be taken to divide equitably the churches of Bombay between the Carmelites and the Archbishop's priests. Under these orders a division accordingly was made, and the church of N. S. de Salvacaô, at Mahim, fell under the Goa jurisdiction.

But, in the year 1813, the Archbishop of Goa, attempting to remove the vicar of that church, against the wishes of the parishioners, the latter petitioned Government against the interference, and the junior magistrate of police was thereupon directed to take the votes of the parish, and ascertain on whom the choice of the parishioners fell. The parish re-electing their old vicar, the Government recognised the election, and authorized an application to be made to the rival Carmelite Bishop for the episcopal confirmation or induction, which is admitted to be necessary.

The parish being thus transferred to the Carmelite jurisdiction, it is stated that in the year 1828 the Vicar Apostolic, Bishop Fortini, procured himself to be appointed vicar of the church, and so continued to officiate till his death, in 1848. On his death a dispute arose between the new Carmelite Bishop, Fré Miguel, and the parishioners, as to the right to appoint a new vicar, the parishioners being desirous to elect the Rev. Braz Fernandez, who had been curate of the church for some years, and the Bishop claiming to nominate an Italian friar. The parishioners thereupon addressed a letter to Government, and received a reply from Mr. Lumsden, the

1851.

Wardens of Nossa Senora v. Bishop Hartmann.

secretary to government, the effect of which is stated to be, that the question as to the spiritual jurisdiction of the Carmelites was entirely for the parishioner's own consideration, that the right of pastoral election was vested in the parishioners, and that the government would confirm any unexceptionable appointment made by the majority without reference to whether the induction was made by the Carmelite Bishop or by the Archbishop of Goa. The local government thereupon appointed the junior magistrate to take the votes of the parishioners, and, Braz Fernandez having then obtained the votes of a great majority, the government confirmed the election by a letter, dated 18th October, 1848, and Braz Fernandez has since performed the duties, and is still, the bill alleges, the lawful vicar of the parish.

Bombay Government leave decision on jurisdiction to the parishioners.

The bill then alleges, that in October last Bishop Hartmann, who is now the superior of the Carmelite mission, in combination with six of the parishioners (who are made defendants) assumed to deprive Braz Fernandez of his vicarage, against the will of the majority of the parishioners, and to appoint two other priests to the charge of the church; and on the 31st October Bishop Hartmann delivered to Braz Fernandez, at the church, a Latin letter of deprivation, and, accompanied by a large police force, proceeded to the church with the view of taking forcible possession of the church and property, whereupon the parishioners, on the 1st November, 1850, petitioned the Vicar Apostolic, representing the Archbishop of Goa, praying to be admitted again within his jurisdiction, a prayer to which that prelate, of course, acceded.

The bill then states, that the priests appointed by Bishop Hartmann seek to take possession of the church, assume to act as vicars, and claim to take the fees and emoluments, and under these circumstances the relief is prayed which I have already stated.

The Bishop and the other defendants have demurred to the plaintiff's claim, principally for want of equity, and the Court was occupied for the better part of three days in hearing the elaborate arguments of the Advocate General and Mr. *Jenkins*

1857. Wardens of Nossa Sunora v. Bishop Hartmann.

as counsel for the Bishop and of Messrs. *Howard* and *Dickinson* for the churchwardens.

But, before we proceed to the arguments on the demurrer, we must notice a preliminary objection brought forward by the Advocate General, not as counsel for the Bishop, but in his own right as Advocate General representing the Crown, with respect to charities.

Claim of Advocate General to control all charities.

He argues that the present suit respects a public charity, and that it is the prerogative of the Crown, represented by its Attorney General, and in this country by the Advocate General, to bring on all suits of such nature, by way of information, and that the entire control of such suit rests with the Advocate General, and that as the parties had declined to observe the suggestions of the Advocate General, they had no right to bring their bill, for the decision of the Advocate General was binding upon them, and not subject to any control by this Court. He therefore moved that the bill should be taken off the file.

Now, on a question of exercising any extraordinary powers, as the stopping of a plaintiff's suit *in limine* unquestionably is, the wise rule for a Colonial Court to follow is to do nothing without express precedent, and the absence of any precedent for the course suggested by the Advocate General would be sufficient to ground a refusal of his motion.

But, on the merits of the question, it seems very doubtful whether this suit ought to be an information. Lord Eldon has laid down in a case not dissimilar from the present (*Davis* v. *Jenkins*, 3 V. & B. 154), that the question, what is that species of suit that must be maintained by information, and cannot proceed upon a bill is a point of "great difficulty," and that case, as well as numerous others, shews that where the right of parochial election is the object of the suit, and the charity funds are only incidental matters, as to which no scheme or regulation is prayed, the Attorney General is not a necessary party.

At all events, if he is a necessary party, and I am inclined to think that in this suit he would prove to be so at the

1851.

Wardens of NOSSA SENORA v. Bishop HARTMANN.

hearing, it is sufficient to make him a defendant, and, as at present advised, I wholly repudiate the doctrine that the right of the plaintiffs to sue in a Court of justice can be restrained by the fiat of the Advocate General, or of any other individual. And the decision of Lord ELDON, in a very analogous case (*Crowder* v. *Tinkler*, 19 Ves.), where he allowed private parties to sue, for the purpose of abating a public nuisance, although the Attorney General had refused to file an information, convinces me that the claim set up is opposed to the first principles of English law.

It is necessary, therefore, to pass on to the arguments of the Advocate General, as counsel for the Bishop, in favour of the suit being dismissed even on the facts set out by the complainants.

Jurisdiction of Court on disputes between Catholics and their Bishop,

These arguments are principally based on want of jurisdiction in the Court to entertain the suit; first of all, on the ground that the Court has no power to pronounce on a question of ecclesiastical jurisdiction; and, secondly, that by the law or usage which has prevailed in this island the Government of the East India Company is the proper authority for deciding the disputes which have arisen.

But, on the first point, the case of *Hughes* v. *Porral*, (4 Moore's Privy Council Cases), furnishes a clear authority. Bishop Hughes, in that case, in answer to the claim of the parishioners to manage their own parochial affairs without interference by the Vicar or Bishop, affirmed that, "by virtue of his office, he had in himself full right, power, and authority, to manage, govern, and direct all the concerns and affairs of the said church, and to administer the revenues thereof, according to the established rules and regulations of the Roman Catholic Church, and that no assembly of laymen had or ought to have any right to interfere in the management and government of the said church, *but that the same did wholly appertain to ecclesiastical control and jurisdiction.*" The Court below, however, overruled this claim, affirmed the right of the parishioners, and the Privy Council, in substance, confirmed the decision. It is quite true that this Court has not power, any more than any other lay tribunal, to pronounce for or

arises when property is in dispute.

1851.

Wardens of NOSSA SENORA v. Bishop HARTMANN.

against spiritual dominion asserted by a Roman Catholic prelate, but if this spiritual dominion is exercised so as to interfere with temporalities, and thereby to cause disputes as to the right of enjoyment to property, the jurisdiction of the Court, on a proper case being presented, immediately arises.

The position of a Roman Catholic communion in this island, as well as of other voluntarily associated bodies, possessive of property, very much resembles the case of dissenting congregations in England, who, when they differ amongst themselves, as to the enjoyment of the property, the mode of electing the minister, or the doctrines which ought to be propounded, resort to the Court of Chancery to compose their differences, and however difficult the matter may be the Court is compelled to undertake the task.

In the case before cited of *Davis* v. *Jenkins*, Lord ELDON observed, "it is very difficult to know what to do with these dissenting societies. The Court will certainly enforce their rights; but they must first inquire what they are," and he bases the jurisdiction of the Court on the inability of a Court of law to supply a remedy.

Claim of executive Government to jurisdiction denied.

But it is said that the proper tribunal, in a case like this, is the local government which has always interposed successfully hitherto to compose differences like the present. I should have thought *a priori* that a wise government would eschew being mixed up in any parochial controversies between a Bishop and his flock possessing a faith different from that of the government, and on perusing the eminently judicious state papers of the executive authorities which are set out in this case, and which denote the mode in which the interference of government has been exerted, I am satisfied that the view I take is that of the Bombay Government. But, even if government desired to take the jurisdiction in question into their own hands, I am at a loss to perceive how they can exercise it. If the parishioners, on the one hand, claim to elect their vicar to manage the church property, and to recognise any spiritual superior they please, and a Roman Catholic Bishop, on the other hand, claims to be their spiritual head, to appoint the vicar, and to administer the funds without

1851.

Wardens of NOSSA SENORA v. Bishop HARTMANN.

control, the local government is equally impotent with this Court to decide on the spiritual question, and has none of the machinery incidental to a Court of justice for determining the rights of property. These are the general grounds which have been alleged as to the want of equity, or want of jurisdiction in the Court to entertain the suit, but it has been further contended specially, that the suit is defective for want of parties; first, because the East India Company should have been joined, and secondly, the Advocate General, as representing the Crown. It has also been contended, that, as no relief is prayed against the six parishioners who are made defendants, the suit must, at all events, be dismissed as against them.

With respect to the East India Company we can see no ground whatever why they should be represented in the suit. No claim is set up for them as a corporation to any private rights, their interference in this parish has been solely as a government, and any rights which may belong to government in a visitorial capacity belong to the Crown, and may be exerted by the officer of the East India Company representing the Crown in this capacity, *viz.*, the Advocate General.

To the objection that the Advocate General ought to be a party, the reply is, that he appears by the record to be a party. The bill prays that, on being served with a copy of the bill, the Advocate General may be bound by all the proceedings in the cause; on which service it is unquestionably competent to the Advocate General to appear and answer, and set up any case in respect of the public interests that it may be necessary to make. A recent case in England certainly shews that the new rules for proceeding against a nominal party in this compendious and economic form do not apply to an Advocate General, but on demurrer this objection for an irregularity in the mode of service would not seem to be open to any one but the actual party as to whom the irregularity occurred, for *non constat*, on this record, but that the Advocate General has waived the irregularity, and has actually appeared* and answered.

We think that the objection as to the six parishioners has more weight in it than any of the other objections which we

1851.

Wardens of NOSSA SENORA v. Bishop HARTMANN.

have noticed, for certainly their interference in the parish dispute, and their amount of participation in the acts of the Bishop, are stated so generally, and in such vague terms, as to leave it doubtful whether any case is made out against them which calls for an answer.

But it is unnecessary to decide this question, for a defect appears on the face of the plaintiff's bill, which it appears to the Court to be impossible to get over; and although this defect was not pointed out by the counsel for the Bishop, we may well understand why silence should have been observed upon it, and why it should have been desired to get a favourable decision on other points in the case.

No ground of interference by the Court in this case; as the party complaining is quietly in possession.

The facts stated by the plaintiff's bill being admitted by the demurrer to be true, it appears that the legal right of lecting a vicar belongs to the parishioners, that the majority of the parishioners have elected Braz Fernandez, who has entered upon his office, and who has been confirmed by Government. It also appears that the parish funds are vested in trustees, and are in no danger, and it appears clearly that the Bishop's nominees are out of possession, and that no part of the church property has come into the hands of the Bishop.

If this is the case, the complainants do not require the protection of this Court. *Beati sunt possidentes*, in the language of the civil law. If they disclaim the spiritual jurisdiction of the Bishop, his spiritual thunders may be disregarded by them, and his letters and claims, whether in Latin or English, furnish no ground for the interposition of a Court of equity. It is stated that the Bishop made use of a large police force, with a view of asserting his rights; but it is not stated that the police force did anything in infringement of the rights of possession; and it is evident that with the views expressed by the government, and in deference to the general law, the executive would never lend the constabulary force of the county to determine a disputed right.

The jurisdiction of this Court to interpose at all is manifestly based on the want of power in a Court of law to afford relief. If the office in dispute were a corporate office, or involved any franchise of the Crown, the mode of determining any controversy as to the right of election would be by *mandamus*, if the office were vacant, and by *quo warranto*, if the office were full. The office is full in this case by the election of Mr. Fernandez, and if the complainants seek relief on the ground that the Bishop has appointed another person to the office, the law is quite distinct on the point that they cannot come to the Court, unless they shew not only that the new appointee has accepted the office, but also the specific acts constituting acceptance and possession. A mere claim to the office, an asserted right to take the fees, a demand to administer the parish funds, does not give the party in possession any right to come to the Court. See *Rex* v. *Whitwell*, (5 T. R. 85), which has been confirmed in many modern cases.

1851.

Wardens of NOSSA SENORA *v.* Bishop HARTMANN.

The consequence is, this demurrer must be allowed.

DHAKJI DADAJI
v.
EAST INDIA COMPANY.

1843.

Sept. 13th.

[*Coram* ROPER, C. J. and PERRY, J.]

TRESPASS for breaking and entering the plaintiff's dwelling-house and taking away papers, letters, &c.

Plea, not guilty.

At the trial it appeared that the plaintiff, who was a merchant and justice of the peace at Bombay, and who had formerly been the Dewan (or minister) of H. H. the Gaikwar at Baroda, occupied a dwelling-house without the Fort, and a mercantile office within the Fort of Bombay. In December last

The Charter Act (3 & 4 Wm. 4, c. 85) having taken away from the E. I. Company their mercantile character, and deprived them of the possibility of deriving pecuniary profit from acts of misrule, the Company, as a corporation, are not liable in trespass for any illegal acts by the Company's officers.

If any illegal acts are committed by the Company's officers, the liability falls only on the immediate actors, and on those who gave the command.

Illegal acts committed under orders of the local governments cannot be sued on in the Queen's Courts in India, but the remedy given by statute belongs to the Courts at Westminster Hall.

The liability of the E. I. Company, as a corporation, for acts done in its political character explained.

Corporate acts by the Company's officers in India do not require the corporate seal.

1843. DHAKJI v. E. I. COMPANY.

the superintendent of police, under the authority of a warrant signed by the Governor in council, took forcible possession of his dwelling-house and examined all his papers; but nothing suspicious being found at his house, he proceeded to his office in the Fort, and took possession of all the papers there found, and then sealed up the door and left the office in charge of a detachment of police. The superintendent subsequently made over the premises to the chief magistrate, who retained exclusive possession of them under orders of government from the 8th to the 14th of December, during which time a close examination was made of the plaintiff's books.

At the trial, counsel for the defendant refused to produce the warrant under which the government officers acted, but admitted that it was signed by the Governor in council, and that it did not set forth any charge of treason or felony.

At the conclusion of the case for the plaintiff, the Advocate General moved for a nonsuit, on the ground that the Bombay government was not to be identified with the East India Company, and, therefore, that the latter were not responsible for the acts of the former, unless it was shewn that they had expressly authorized them.

Argument for plaintiff. The Company liable for illegal acts of their officers.

Cochrane and *Herrick*, for the plaintiff. If the company are to be treated as a corporation, trespass will lie. The local governments of India have all the power in their own hands which is necessary for the discharge of the functions of government, and, as it is impossible for them to have a warrant under seal to perform each act as it arises, the law cannot prescribe in the case of the East India Company the necessity for any such warrant. The present case, therefore, falls completely within the principle of those English cases which hold that a corporation is liable for acts committed by their servants within the scope of their authority; *Yarborough* v. *Bank of England*, (16 East, 1); *Maund* v. *Monmouthshire Canal Company*, (20 Law Journ. 317); *Regina* v. *Birmingham Railway Company*, (2 Gale & Dav.)

If the plaintiff had committed felony, Go-

If the plaintiff here had been committing treason against the state, or any high misdemeanor by which the *salus populi* would be affected, the Bombay Government would have been quite justified in acting as they have done; and in such case they would have been compelled, *ex necessitate rei*, to act by virtue of the powers inherent in them, and it would be absurd to suggest the necessity of a reference to Leadenhall Street for an authority under the common seal.

vernment would have been justified.

Authorities in favour of action.

In *The Bank of Bengal* v. *East India Company*, (Bignold, 119), Sir C. GREY, C. J., held expressly that the Company, although in some sense sovereign, was suable as a corporation; and, if so, that decides this question. And in a case before Sir E. RYAN, C. J., he held that the act of the Governor General in council was the act of the Company. If it were otherwise, and the Company were not responsible, then under circumstances like the present the Bombay Government might employ a number of coolies to break open the office of Messrs. Forbes and Co., or any other individual, might examine their books, and when called on for redress might refer Sir Charles Forbes to an action against the coolies, as the act of Parliament prevents this Court entertaining any action against the members of Council personally.

Argument for E. I. Company.

Le Messurier, A. G., *Howard*, and *Dickinson*, *contrà*.

1. The Company not liable in trespass unless for the illegal act.

1. As no justification is pleaded in this case, it must be taken now that the trespass was wilful and malicious. On the ordinary law of principal and agent, therefore, the Company are not liable for the acts of the Bombay Government, unless it be shewn that they sanctioned, or subsequently ratified, them. On this principle Sir EDWARD WEST decided two cases in favour of the East India Company,—one an action of tort respecting the *Deccan* prize money, (2 *Morley's Digest*, 266); the other a case of contract, *Cursetjee Manockjee* v. *East India Company*. But the East India Company is not a principal at all, for it does not interfere with the local government. The government of Bombay resides principally in the local government, subordinate to the orders of the Governor General in council, subordinate to the East India Company, subordinate to the Board of Control, which again is subordinate to Parliament. *Non constat* that in the present case the act in question

Complicated character of the Indian Government.

1813.

DHAKJI v. E. I. COMPANY.

has not been strongly disapproved of by the East India Company, or it may have been in pursuance of orders sent out by the Board of Control against the express remonstrances of the Court of Directors.

2. A corporation acting for public purposes is not responsible for illegal acts of subordinates.

2. Where a corporation or public body is acting for public purposes, they are not responsible for the unlawful acts of their agents; *Hall* v. *Smith*, (2 Bing. 156); *Gidley* v. *Lord Palmerston*, (3 Bro. & B. 275). *Vin. Abr.* tit. "*Trespass*," 10, 3; *Plate Glass Company* v. *Meredith*, (4 T. R. 794); *Boulton* v. *Crowther*, (2 B. & C. 705).

3. Authorities against action.

3. The cases shewing that actions of contract, or even of tort, are maintainable against the East India Company are distinguishable. When the Company was a trading corporation, they were treated at law like any other corporation. Now they have only a public trust to perform as a government, and are not liable to actions of tort; *Gibson* v. *East India Company*, (5 New Cases, 262). The corporation *qua* corporation has no powers at all, and whatever illegal acts are performed, the only persons responsible are the parties who commit the acts. The revenues of the East India Company, moreover, by the last charter act, are all devoted to specific purposes, and there is no fund from which the damages in an action of tort can be maintained.

Cochrane replied.

Cur. adv. vult.

ROPER, C. J., delivered judgment for the defendants, (see 2 *Morley's Digest*, 307)

Judgment.

PERRY, J.—This is an action of trespass against the Honorable the East India Company for a series of illegal acts committed against the plaintiff and his property by the orders of the local Government of Bombay. The trespasses, in question, have not been attempted to be justified or palliated, and are undoubtedly of a nature to call for heavy damages if the action can be sustained. The form of procedure adopted is somewhat novel, for I cannot find a single instance, during

Illegal acts admitted, and heavy damages due if action maintainable.

1843.

DHAKJI v. E. I. COMPANY.

the 240 years existence of the Company as a corporation, (and I asked the question particularly at the Bar), of an action having been brought against the Company for the illegal acts of their Governors and Members of council. The legal mind is necessarily, therefore, on the alert so as to avoid being led astray from the safe and ancient tracks of law.

This form of action an experiment.

The novelty of the *form* of action, however, must not deter the Court from exercising its legal jurisdiction, if it shall be found to consist with the true principles of law applicable to corporations in general, and to the statutes passed in special reference to the East India Company. And, indeed, to any one who observed the decorous and abstract mode in which this case was treated at the Bar, so abstract, indeed, as to names, dates, and facts, that the Court could hardly get possession of sufficient materials for its judgment, it must occur that this mode of seeking redress from nominal defendants presents certain, not inconsiderable, advantages, in its avoidance of those asperities which actions against individuals, especially against the high functionaries of government, are pretty sure to call forth.

But if allowed by law not without its advantages.

As the plaintiff, to sustain his present action, must base his claim on the legal theory which enables him to substitute other parties than the actual tortfeasors as the defendants civilly responsible, it seems desirable to state a few of the leading principles applicable to corporations, from which this relation arises.

Principles on which a corporation is liable to be sued for acts of its officers.

It is indisputable, then, that a corporation aggregate is just as much civilly responsible for every damage which may be caused through its corporate agency, as any private individual. This responsibility always did exist, as it would seem at common law, though in the case of trespasses from the form of process (*capias*) necessary in early times to bring defendants into Court, a difficulty arose which, though frequently got over, as appears by the earliest books, gave rise to the erroneous notion that an action of tort would not lie against a corporation. That error has been completely removed by recent decisions in England, and now it is quite manifest that redress can be obtained against a corporation both by civil and criminal pro-

1843.

DHAKJI v. E. I. COMPANY.

cess for every injury which can be repaired by pecuniary charges upon them.

A corporation, being merely a legal institution, denotes its corporate acts by the corporate seal.

But as a corporation aggregate is a mere entity of law, composed, it is true, of individuals, but incompetent to act physically on any occasion, a mode has been devised, by the law, for enabling the corporate will to be expressed on every occasion.

This mode is by the use of a common seal, which, on being attached to any order expressing the will of the majority of the ruling body, gives validity to its acts, binds the corporate property, and binds also, to a certain extent, every individual corporator, whether he may have assented to the order or not.

Exceptions to the rule requiring the corporate seal, from the necessity of the case.

But, as there are certain trivial and ordinary acts which every corporation must have to discharge, and which would constantly go unperformed if an order under the common seal were required on each emergency, an exception has been made, from the earliest times, as to the necessity of attaching such seal to the orders in question. The most familiar instance on this head is that of the appointment of a bailiff to distrain for rent, which, it was long ago held, might be made by parole; *Cary* v. *Matthews*, (1 Salk. 191). The principle of this decision has been extended, in later times, to all such duties as are thrown upon corporations, whether by charter or act of parliament, and which are of such constant occurrence, or of such immediate urgency, as to render the object of incorporation wholly nugatory if the ceremony of the common seal were required on each occasion. "This principle," in the words of Lord DENMAN, adopted and confirmed by the recent decision of the Court of Exchequer in 6 *Mee. & Wels.* 822, "appears to be convenience, amounting almost to necessity. Wherever to hold the rule applicable would occasion very great inconvenience, or tend to defeat the very object for which the corporation was created, the exception has prevailed;" and on this principle the *East* India Company was made liable for the bills drawn upon it in India by parties duly authorized by parole, but who are not invested with the common seal of the Company; *Murray* v. *The East India Company*. On these grounds, then, the plaintiff

1843.

DHAKJI v. E. I. COMPANY.

launches his case, and he contends, that as the last Charter Act, 3 & 4 Wm. 4, c. 85, has vested or rather continued the Government of India in the Company, with its power of nomination to the different offices at the several presidencies, the acts of such officers in India, in the necessary conduct of Government, are the acts of the Company itself, that they are moreover acts of such daily and immediate urgency as to dispense with the necessity of any order under seal, and, therefore, if any act of local government be shewn, illegal in its character, but within the scope of the authority necessarily committed to distant agents, the Company, as a body corporate, is responsible in damages.

Acts by officers of E. I. Company in India come within the exception.

It seems to me that on the principle of corporation law these positions are perfectly well founded, and that they have not met with any sufficient answer at the Bar. For if it be conceded that the members of the local government are corporate officers, if they are placed here to carry on the government vested in the Company, it seems preposterous to suppose that any special authority, for the daily and necessary acts of Government, can be required, and, therefore, all arguments as to the necessity of an order under seal falls to the ground. The plaintiff contends, that, as a corporation cannot act by itself, the government is carried on by agents here in the only mode in which a corporation can conduct a government at a distance, that therefore the executive government on the spot is the corporation. In the words of Sir E. RYAN, "the Governor General in council does act here as the united Company, and this is not to be considered as a recognition by an agent of an agent, but an act of the united Company themselves." (*Bignell*, 180). The counsel of the defendants meet these positions with several arguments, the untenableness of which convinces me that the positions of Mr. *Cochrane* and his hypothesis are sound. First, it is alleged that the plaintiff's argument rests on the assumption that the local government here and the Company are identical, it is then shewn that the local government is one of very limited powers, amenable to orders from Calcutta, to orders from the Court of Directors, and Board of Control, to orders and inter-

First argument for E. I. Company disposed of.

1848.

Dhakji v. E. I. Company.

ference from the imperial Legislature of Great Britain, and it is, therefore, contended that the whole foundation of the argument is destroyed. But this appears to me fallacious: a bailiff duly appointed to act for a corporation undoubtedly makes the corporation responsible, and his acts are *pro tanto* the acts of the corporation itself, and may be so alleged in pleading, yet no one will contend that because the bailiff had only certain limited powers, his acts to that extent, and within the scope of the authority, are not the acts of the corporation.

Argued for Company that acts of Bombay Government were wholly wanton, and out of the scope of their authority;

The argument therefore, on this point, being felt to be somewhat clinching against the defendants, great struggle was made to shew, secondly, that the acts which form the subject-matter of the present action were in no wise within the scope of the authority committed to the local government of Bombay. It is alleged by the defendant's counsel that the acts were wholly unauthorized, unjustifiable, and—if not malicious —*wilful*, on the part of the Governor in council, and that the Company ought to be no more made responsible than if the same parties had sent so many coolies to plunder the house of a native or English banker for their own purposes. I can by no means acquiesce in the position which seeks to place the immediate actors in this transaction in such an unfavourable light. For, although I do not think it is competent to this Court to make any distinction in its presumptions with reference only to the high station and importance of the parties who may be brought before it, and although, in common justice to the plaintiff, it must be assumed on this occasion that no just cause existed for the forcible interference with his house and papers, still I do not conceive that the Court or any one is warranted, on the facts of this case, in imputing to the members of the government anything beyond an indiscreet exercise of the powers committed to them. Several cases may be suggested in which the acts in question would be perfectly justifiable,—others may be supposed where suspicions ran so high as to the safety of the state being in danger, that the award of very moderate damages would suffice for any infraction of law; and, though the Court is not at liberty to suppose that either of these two species of cases

1848.

DHAKJI v E. I. COMPANY.

had taken place on the present occasion, the utmost, I think, that can be fairly inferred against the government is, the having acted perhaps with over zeal, or easy credulity to some untrustworthy information in a verbose letter from Caprese," but with no shade of blame whatever beyond such imputations. Indeed, the plaintiff himself scarcely represents the impropriety of conduct displayed by them so strongly as I have now put it; I think, therefore, that the acts in question must be distinctly taken to come within the scope of their authority. And here I may observe that I cannot at all understand the principle on which two decisions of Sir EDWARD WEST in this Court proceeded, and which have been much relied on by the defendants. In the first of them (*Cursetjee Manockjee* v. *The East India Company*) an action was brought by the plaintiff to recover the price of sandals which had been furnished by him as a contractor to the army. It appeared that, by a contract under seal, he had engaged to supply certain articles of clothing to the troops, not specifying sandals, and that by a parol order of some officer of government, he had furnished sandals also in large quantities. The government, not conceiving that the plaintiff had any claim on this score, resisted the demand, and the counsel for the Company urged their objections in different forms; Sir EDWARD WEST, after some strong observations on the moral liability of the Company, thus notices the last objection:—"The third ground of defence is, that the contract for, and delivery of, the sandals was unauthorized on the part of the Company. This objection was not placed or argued upon the right ground for the defendants. The objection is a valid one, upon the principle that a corporation cannot be bound but by contract under seal. This objection, though not taken by counsel, of course occurred to the Court," &c. But it appears to me, I must confess, that the true objection *was* taken by the counsel, and that a fallacy is lurking in the learned Chief Justice's argument. The principle is not that a corporation cannot bind itself except by contracts under seal, and it is not the common distinction, which exists between a parol order and a deed, that comes in question in these cases, and which appears to

but not so, possibly indiscreet, but might have been justified as prudent acts of government.

Two decisions of Sir E. WEST, C. J., in Government cases commented on.

1843.

Dhakji v. E. I. Company.

have made Sir E. West distinguish between the two contracts; but the principle is, that a corporation can only bind itself under its *common corporate* seal, and a contract under seal of one of its agents is no more binding, except in the excepted cases, than a parole order by the same individual; and the contract which the learned Judge considered binding, appears to have been equally destitute of the authority of the *common* seal as the parole contract which, for that reason, he held insufficient.

The other case is *Amerchund Bedreechund* v. *The East India Company, Mr. Mount Stuart Elphinstone and Others*, which was trover for a large quantity of treasure which had been seized as booty, at the close of the last Mahratta war, by Lieut. Robertson, and which, by order of Mr. Elphinstone—then the highest civil officer at Poonah, had been paid into the government treasury. The refusal to give up this money by the officers of government was proved, and yet the Court thought the verdict ought to go against Mr. Elphinstone and Lieut. Robertson personally for the seven laks of rupees and interest, but not against the East India Company, "because no demand and refusal had been made upon them." The decision seems rather startling, and one would have conceived that the true liability lay, if anywhere, with the Company into whose treasury the money had found its way, and not with the mere agents who were the channels used by the corporation. A demand upon the Company could only be made upon the officers of the Company, and the officers acting upon the spot appear to have been the appropriate officers for that purpose, or, in the language of the counsel of the plaintiff in this case, to have been legally the Company itself. And the decision, indeed, was afterwards overruled (upon another ground) on appeal to England (1 *Knapp. Priv. Coun. Cas.*)

But it is also pressed on this head, that as no order from the Court of Directors has been shewn, and as it has been by no means proved that the acts in question have conduced to the benefit of the Company, no argument can be derived from any supposed acquiescence by the authorities at home, so as to bring the defendants within the category laid down by

Lord COKE, (4 *Inst.* 317), where the agreement to a trespass after it is committed is shewn, in certain cases, to have relation back, and to be equivalent to a previous command. But this reasoning is founded on the relation between principal and agent, which, strictly speaking, never exists in the case of a corporation, for wherever a corporation is liable at all for the acts of one of its servants acting within the scope of his authority, it is liable as principal; it is liable on the ground that it is the corporation's own act, as clearly appears from *Small* v. *Birmingham Gas Company,* (12 L. J., K. B. 165), and *Maund* v. *Monmouthshire Canal,* (20 L. J., N. S., C. 317); whereas the liability of an ordinary principal in such cases is founded on another ground, namely that laid down by Gaius in the *Digest,* "quod operâ malorum hominum utatur," (D. 44. 7. 5, § *ult.*); and as also clearly appears from Lord KENYON's judgment in *Crickett* v. *M'Manus,* (1 East). The objection, therefore, resolves itself into the former question, as to whether the officers of the corporation have been duly appointed, and whether the acts in question came within the scope of the *bonâ fide* execution of the powers committed to them.

Relation of a corporation to its servants, not that of principal and agent.

It is next insisted that an action of trespass does not lie at all, and that it never did lie, in the Supreme Court against the Company for an act done by them in their political capacity, and the decision of Lord Chief Justice TINDAL in 5 *Bing. N. C.* 562 is strongly relied upon, in which a distinction is drawn between the liability of the East India Company as to contracts made by them in their political or in their commercial character. General principle, however, independent of various statutes upon the subject, affords a ready answer to this objection. Whatever political powers were committed to the companies of merchants incorporated by Elizabeth and succeeding monarchs, they were never exonerated from the liability attaching to every subject of the Crown, *viz.* to answer the complaints of every other subject or individual wherever the Courts of the Crown were established. This liability rose up against them in India directly the Mayors' Courts were erected, *viz.* in 1726, though possibly,

Argued that Company not liable in trespass for political acts;

but refuted by principle, and by express authority.

1843.

DHAKJI v. E. I. COMPANY.

from the difficulty of bringing a corporation into Court, this liability was more nominal than real. The charter of the second Mayor's Court, however, in 1753, fully remedies any deficiency which might exist on this score, and provided that in actions against the Company the appearance in Court should be made by the Governor or President of council. A series of statutes cited by Mr. *Cochrane, viz.* 26 Geo. 3, c. 57, s. 37,—53 Geo. 3, c. 155, s. 123,—55 Geo. 3, c. 84, s. 9, and to which may be added an earlier one, the 10 Geo. 3, c. 47, ss. 4, 5, carry out the remedy already existing at common law, and most clearly provide for actions to be brought against the Company for the torts and trespass of their servants *committed* in India. And lastly, the charter of the Supreme Court, in 1774, at Calcutta, expressly mentions the action of trespass against the Company, and all of these without the slightest reference to any distinction between the political and commercial character of the corporation. The distinction drawn by TINDAL, C. J., as referred to, appears to me to have no bearing on the present point, and is wholly referrible to the subject under discussion there, *viz.* the excepted cases contemplated by the act of Parliament, in which contracts were permitted to be made without the common seal of the Company.

Argued that the Company had no funds out of which damages can be paid;

Lastly, as to this part of the case it is contended, that as the territorial revenues of the country are appropriated to certain specified legal debts and liabilities, and as the dividends of the proprietors are expressly exempted from such charge, and as, moreover, the Company have no other fund from which damages can be defrayed, this action cannot be maintained on the principles laid down in *The Banker's case,* (14 State Tri.), by Sir C. GREY in *Bank of Bengal* v. *East India Company,* (Bign.), and in *Duncan* v. *Findlater,* (6 Cl. & Fin.) But this argument appears to me to be met by the following dilemma: either the damages to which the Company have exposed themselves by a *bonâ fide,* though illegal, exercise of

but untenable.

their authority constitute "a liability lawfully incurred on account of the government of the said Company," or they do not; in the first case, the damages come within the words subjecting the territorial revenues to the charge.—in the second, the clause exempting the separate stock of the Company and the dividends of proprietors has no operation *quâcunque viâ*, therefore ample funds are available.

1843.

DHAKJI v. E. I. COMPANY.

Conclusion.

On ordinary corporation law, Company would be liable, but under last Charter Act Company are mere public trustees acting for public interests, &c.

If the question were to remain here, and were to be decided on the ordinary law relating to corporation, and on the charter of the East India Company as it has been usually recognised in our Courts of law during the last 200 years, I confess that I incline to the opinion that the action would well lie. But the Advocate General has added another line of argument, which has placed the subject in a new light to my mind, and which, after much consideration, I conceive to afford the true principle of decision applicable to the present case; for he has distinctly shewn that, under the last charter act, the character of the East India Company is completely changed; they are no longer an association of merchants trading to the East Indies, filling their coffers with the commercial results of their enterprise, or with the territorial revenues of empires gained to their hands by the skill and energy of their servants, —they are now to be considered, or at all events the governing portion of them, as a great department of the state, into whose hands, for high political purposes, the immediate patronage and government of India are confided, but wielding these great powers exclusively for the benefit of the state, and unable to apply them, except by the commission of high crimes and misdemeanors (which, of course, are not to be presumed), to their own personal advantage or that of the corporation.

The Company can derive no pecuniary profit from wrongful acts of officers.

It is true that the Company receive as dividends a large portion of the territorial revenues of India secured to them by the guarantee of the Legislature, but not an iota of profit can accrue to them extra these dividends, and the remuneration is not to be looked upon as the salary for governing India, which might engender corresponding obligations on the Company as in *Henely* v. *Mayor of Lyme Regis*, but as the fruits of a solemn Parliamentary contract, by which the Company surrendered in fee all its splendid acquisitions in the East, and received in compensation this Legislative annuity. But if this be the true view of the case, all the analogies upon which we have been hitherto reasoning, derived from the ordinary commercial or

1843.

DHAKJI v. E. I. COMPANY.

trading responsibilities of corporations, fall to the ground, and a new class of cases present themselves, holding forth much broader principles and much more striking analogies to help the mind to a decision. Indeed, whilst searching for the rule of law during the former part of this argument, one feels oneself to be embarrassed and hampered by narrow principles and petty considerations wholly incommensurate with the grave questions at issue; but directly that the character of the Company is placed in its true light, and that the governing body is seen to be simply a great engine of state, public trustees invested with all the necessary powers of government, our law books furnish us with abundant authority to shew that civil responsibility can never be brought home to them except for *personal* misconduct. If even, then, in the present case, it had been distinctly proved that the acts forming the subject of the present suit had been commanded by the Court of Directors or Board of Control, I should still have been of opinion that the plaintiff must be nonsuited; for although, undoubtedly, the members of those Boards, like every other great functionary of state, would make themselves personally responsible for every illegal act they might command, how would such misconduct affect the proprietors at large, the Company? They would be neither art nor part in the trespass, they could not control it, they could not benefit by it, and on what could their liability be made to rest? Merely on their corporate character. But the act, being one of such an extraordinary nature, unconnected with the business of the corporation, and bringing down liability upon parties merely for their *personal* misconduct in the act, never, I think, could be held to affect the proprietors at large, even if the order in question came out under the authority of the common seal. *A multo fortiori*, therefore, must their immunity from liability exist, where not even the legal participation involved in the attachment of the common seal can be alleged against them.

and, therefore, civil responsibility does not attach to them for the *personal* misconduct of individuals.

Cases and statutes relied on by plaintiff explained.

This view of the question appears to me to explain all the cases, and all the provisions in the acts of Parliament and charters, which the counsel for the plaintiff has so strongly urged upon us. So long as the Company were incorporated

1843.

DHAKJI *v.* E. I. COMPANY.

Previous liability of Company for acts of Government founded on their mercantile character, and participation in profits.

for their own benefit every addition of territory gained, every fresh port of commerce successively opened to their trade brought additional profits, or the chance of them, to the proprietary at large. The Company were, therefore, justly made responsible for the illegal acts of their agents in prosecuting the common purpose in different parts of the globe. This explains the principles of the decision of the Judges referred to in *Skinner* v. *East India Company*, as mentioned in argument, and by Lord MANSFIELD in *Mostyn* v. *Fabrigas*, (Cowp). It explains the ground on which the action in *Moodalay* v. *East India Company* (1 Brown Ch. Ca. 468) must have been deemed to be founded; and it explains also the actions of tort which we have heard of in this Court before the present charter was granted. It also accounts for the different provisions of the charters of justice and acts of Parliament, enabling actions *ex delicto* to be brought against the Company for the acts of their servants.

The only doctrine at all conflicting with the distinction now taken, is that which is said to have fallen from Sir EDWARD RYAN in 1840, in a case of *Gopee Mohun Dele* v. *East Indian Company*, and the authority of that very learned person is enforced upon us with all the weight so justly due to it. But on turning to the short note of the decision in that case, in the newspaper of the day to which we have been referred, it most clearly appears that the immediate question now under consideration, *viz.*, whether the action of tort should be brought against the Company or against the immediate actors in the business, was in no ways mooted. Any thing therefore that fell from Sir EDWARD RYAN on the point would be merely *obiter*, and would undoubtedly be instantly disclaimed by himself, as of no authority, if the point itself should hereafter come under discussion before him. But, on attending to the case itself, and to the words that fell from the Court, it appears to me most clearly, that the parties contemplated by the Judges as the proper defendants were the lottery committee who committed the wrong and not the innocent Company. The dictum, therefore, relied upon is really of no weight.

1843.

DHAKJI *v.* E. I. COMPANY.

I have thus come to the conclusion that the action, in the present case, does not lie; and although I could have wished to have been able to devote more time to the preparation of my judgment, both in respect to the very able arguments urged at the bar, and to the interesting questions involved, I confess that I put forth my opinion without much hesitation, because I feel that it is upon the safe side. For, undoubtedly, this Court, like every other tribunal, has an undue bias towards extending its jurisdiction, and is prone to grasp at any increase of powers (so dear to human frailty), more especially when urged upon it in the flattering and eloquent appeals of suitors at the bar. It is a consolation, therefore, to think that this sort of fallacious judgment has not had any place in the errors that I may have fallen into unconsciously to-day. It is, besides, a satisfaction to think, that in deciding against the plaintiff no door is opened to injustice, no great disappointment can be inflicted upon his hopes. The parliamentary remedy which holds out such eminent advantages to suitors against the Government is equally available to him, and the present action, which has been launched as an experiment, has, undoubtedly, been founded on no clear or distinct precedent which could justify any deep seated anticipation of success.

Conclusion, if wrong, on the safe side, from the natural tendency of Courts to extend jurisdiction on the prayer of suitor's asking relief.

Indeed, with reference to this view of the case, and to the 21 Geo. 3, c. 70, which affords such cogent means in this Court to aggrieved suitors in India, I confess I think the importance of our decision, in the present case, has been somewhat exaggerated by the counsel for the plaintiff. It is always of importance, of course, that the Court should deliver sound law, but it seems of very little moment to the plaintiff whether his remedy shall be obtained from one set of responsible parties or another.

Importance of the decision of this Court has been exaggerated on both sides.
The plaintiff has clearly a remedy in the Courts of England, if not here.

So also I think the counsel for the Company have magnified our decision in the case into proportions not belonging to it. For it is contended, that, if this action be held to lie, the Company will be harassed with an infinitude of suits for every petty act of trespass committed by their servants throughout their large dominions. But no such inference

And if the remedy is in this Court, not to be presumed that innumerable actions would be brought;

1843.

DHAKJI v. E. I. COMPANY.

appears to me to be justly deducible. It should be recollected that the portals of this Court are already open to suits against the servants of the Company, except against those in the very highest place; and that facilities exist for poor men to urge their complaints in the Courts of British India, in a manner far superior to any which the Courts of law in England afford, and yet I am happy to say that the records of our Court furnish few traces of any such actions having been brought, and I am still happier to think, for the honour of the British name, that those oppressions, crimes, and tyrannies, which once formed the theme of parliamentary denunciation and enactment, no longer find a place in this country.

Besides also, I must add, on behalf of this Court, that it is not to be presumed that a well organized tribunal, conscious of its duties to the public, and of its proper relation to the Government of the country, would hesitate, on behalf of that Government, to exercise the strong powers it possesses of repressing undue and vexatious litigation, powers which it is bound to exercise in favour of individuals harassed and oppressed by an abuse of legal process, but which it is no less bound to exercise in favour of Government itself.

or that the Court would fail to repress vexatious litigation.

Judgment for defendants (*a*).

(*a*) The proceedings which gave rise to this action caused great excitement amongst the mercantile community, European and native, in Bombay, since for aught that appeared to the public (and the Judges were equally in the dark), a *coup d'etát* of a very arbitrary character had been committed against one of the wealthiest citizens of the place, without any apparent ground to justify it, and certainly without any result. The judgment of the Court, accordingly, denying its jurisdiction to afford relief was not received with much satisfaction. I understand that the language of the judgments in which the legal liabilities of the Company and its officers were canvassed in something of the searching tone of inquiry which characterizes Westminster Hall, gave more than equal dissatisfaction to the local government.

The liability of the East India Company, under circumstances such as occurred above, being a point of considerable legal interest, I trust I may be pardoned for inserting the following extract of a letter from one of our most distinguished living Judges: "I read your judgment in the actions of trespass against the Company with great satisfaction. I think that you have

1843.

DHAKJI *v.* E. I. COMPANY.

put it on the right footing, for certainly the situation of the Company is materially changed by the last charter, though they were the governing power before as much as now yet they were also a trading company, and it was necessary that in that latter capacity they should be responsible for many things which in their former they might not be, and then their two characters were so blended that it would have been very difficult to say that they were in any given case liable as traders, but not as governors. Now their situation is altered, and no such diffiulty arises. *Me judice*, you are quite right in your view of the case."

As to the fears excited in the Presidency that British subjects were wholly without protection under such circumstances as occurred in the principal case they were unfounded, for if the plaintiff had commenced his action in the Queen's Bench against Sir George Arthur, as Governor or against his council, under 21 Geo. 3, c. 70, that Court would have issued a *mandamus* to the Supreme Court at Bombay to compel the production of the Government order to examine witnesses in open Court, whereupon it would have appeared what the circumstances were (if any) which extenuated the invasion of individual liberty.

For remedies against individual officers of Government, see *Hurkissondass* v. *Spooner*, *post*, p. 373.

1844. July 14.

RAMCHUND URSAMUL *v.* H. H. GLASS, ESQ.

[*Coram* ROPER C. J., and PERRY, J.]

1. Jurisdiction of the Supreme Court over acts of Custom House officer in collection of revenue under Bombay regulations.
2. Course adopted by Parliament in attributing legislative powers to the Governments of India.
3. Registration of legislative acts why required in Supreme Court.
4. Difficulties on subject from Parliament having treated E. I. Co. as a mere corporation.

TRESPASS for seizure of the plaintiff's opium. Plea to the jurisdiction of the Court. A rule was subsequently obtained, calling upon the defendant, who was the collector of customs in Bombay, to shew cause why a feigned issue should not be ordered to try whether certain opium of the plaintiff's, which had been seized by the revenue officers, had been duly imported or not.

This proceeding was adopted under Bombay Regulations XXI. of 1827, set out fully in the judgment.

Le Messurier, Attorney General, shewed cause.

1. This regulation is void, never having been registered in the Supreme Court, therefore it cannot give this Court any jurisdiction. Nor does act VII. of 1836 legalise the regulation, as the only effect of the act is to prevent acts done under any such regulation being questioned in a Court of law.

2. The subject-matter of demand relates to the revenue, and, therefore, the jurisdiction of this Court is ousted by 21 Geo. 3, c. 65.

3. The Court has only power to order feigned issues, where there are parties to a cause already in Court.

Dickinson, contrà. The regulation was not illegal. The Supreme Court had the power, before it was passed, to try such a case as this, as it is not a matter connected with land revenue. And the 53 Geo. 3, c. 155, which authorizes the Government to make regulations, expressly gives jurisdiction to this Court.

Cur. adv. vult.

PERRY, J.—This is an application framed upon Bombay Regulation XXI. of 1827 against the collector of sea customs, in order to recover sixty-one maunds of Malwa opium, which it is alleged have been illegally seized by the superintendent of police, and delivered over to the charge of the collector.

The regulation in question enables the police authorities, upon information on oath of any opium having been smuggled, to issue a search warrant, break doors, &c., and seize such opium; and after information has been given to the collector of sea customs of such seizure having been effected, the opium is to be considered as under his charge, and may be confiscated by him after a certain time, if no claim is made.

1844.

RAMCHUND v. GLASS.

This regulation goes on to provide, that if the owner make claim to the opium, and prove, by suit instituted in the Court having jurisdiction in the case, that the full amount of customs has been paid, and the opium legally imported, the articles seized shall be restored.

The subsequent clause enacts, that the proper Court of jurisdiction in such cases is, in the Mofussil, the magistrate's Court, if the opium does not exceed Rs. 500 in value, and the Zillah civil Court when it does exceed that amount: in the Presidency, the Court of petty sessions for the smaller sum, and the Supreme Court for sums of larger amount.

The regulation does not state what species of suit is to be instituted in the Supreme Court in cases within its jurisdiction; and as there is no suit at the common law by which judgment can be passed for the delivery of the specific articles claimed, the complainant has availed himself of the express provision in this regulation, and has called upon the collector to shew cause why a feigned issue shall not be ordered, to try whether the opium has been legally imported or not: and, if this Court has jurisdiction to hold plea of the matter, a feigned issue seems the most appropriate and economic form of procedure that can be adopted.

But this application is opposed altogether by the Advocate General, irrespective of the merits, on two grounds, *viz.*

1st. That this is a matter of revenue, and therefore that our jurisdiction is excluded by the terms of our charter, and by the 21 Geo. 3, c. 65, s. 8; and, 2ndly, that we have no power to order a feigned issue, because the regulation in question is void, from never having been registered in the Supreme Court.

If the first of these objections is well founded, it is unnecessary to consider the second; because, if we have no jurisdiction in revenue matters at all, it is wholly immaterial whether the regulation in which a particular species of suit or proceeding is pointed out be void or not. If, on the other hand, the clause in the 21 Geo. 3, c. 65, s. 8, is not in operation, so as to prevent this Court holding jurisdiction in a plea of this nature generally, it will become necessary to inquire whether the regulation establishing this particular form of proceeding has any validity in law.

1844.

Ramchund v. Glass.

Now, in approaching a question as to the jurisdiction of this Court, I am quite alive as to the temper of mind with which the inquiry should be conducted. The maxim, once so familiar in Westminster Hall, "*boni est judicis ampliare jurisdictionem,*" is no longer, I apprehend, generally received. And, although it must be the desire of every right-minded man that in a country governed by law the legal tribunals should afford a remedy for every wrong, still the paramount duty of the Judge consists, in every case, in strictly conforming himself to the limits which the law has set upon his jurisdiction, and not to transcend them one tittle, however grievous the outrage, and however much his interposition in the particular case may recommend itself to his notions of natural justice.

Jurisdiction of Supreme Court, why limited.

In the present instance, however, it would be a case of morbid sensibility to shrink from exercising the jurisdiction in question, on the ground that it was contrary to the intention of the Legislature; for, first of all, we know historically the reasons on which the clause in the 21 Geo. 3, c. 65, was introduced, namely, to prevent the Supreme Court of Calcutta from bringing within their jurisdiction the whole of the civil service, and their employees, for acts done in the collection of the revenue throughout Bengal, Behar, and Orissa, and thus engrossing to themselves the chief civil function of an Asiatic government; and, secondly, we see clearly that the local government never dreaded the interference of the Supreme Court in a matter like the present, because the Bombay regulation itself is a voluntary declaration that the Supreme Court is the proper tribunal where a question above Rs. 500 in value arises at the Presidency.

To me, therefore, it seems very doubtful whether the words in the 8th sect. of the 21 Geo. 3, c. 65 (which words, and not the more restrictive ones in our charter, afford the rule to our Court, according to *Vencata Runga Pillay* v. *The East India Company* (1 Strange's Madras Cases, 174), confirmed on appeal), namely, "that the Supreme Court shall not have

1844.

RAMCHUND *v.* GLASS.

jurisdiction in any matters concerning the revenue, or acts done in the collection thereof," refer to any thing more than the land revenue; and whether all that was contemplated by the Legislature would not be effected by taking "revenue" to mean only that large and main source of the national supplies, with which alone any interference by her Majesty's Courts of justice was to be deprecated. Customs revenue in India is not to be compared for a moment, in point of importance, to the corresponding branch of revenue in England, and not the least reason exists for extending further privileges to officers in this country, in the collection of such customs revenue, than exists with respect to similar officers in England.

But the decision of the present point does not turn upon any subtle distinction as to what was meant by the term "revenue" in the 21 Geo. 3, c. 65, but upon the express words of the subsequent act of the Legislature, *viz.*, the 53 Geo. 3, c. 155, s. 98. That act confers upon the local Indian government, for the first time, the power of imposing duties and taxes upon the inhabitants at the Presidencies, but at the same time that it throws these new obligations upon the British and others there residing, it also confers upon the latter the accompanying rights of suing in the Supreme Court for any illegal acts committed against them, upon any matter or thing arising out of the new revenue regulations to be imposed by the local government.

The words of clause 98 are, "That it shall be lawful for all persons whatsoever to prefer indictments, and maintain suits in the Supreme Court for enforcing such laws and regulations, or for any matter or thing whatsoever arising out of the same, any act, charter, or other thing to the contrary notwithstanding."

Jurisdiction given to Supreme Court on powers of taxation being given to Indian Government.

These words are so very general, that I have not the least doubt they give a party aggrieved a remedy against any and every revenue officer for illegal acts done under such revenue regulations, although perhaps, without such provision, the previous enactment in the 13 Geo. 3, c. 63, might have prevented the remedy from being brought in the Supreme Court

1844.

RAMCHUND v. GLASS.

If this is so, and if an action of some sort is sustainable for an illegal seizure of opium, the second question arises, whether the particular form of suit now adopted, and framed on the Bombay regulation, can be maintained. This almost wholly depends upon the validity of the Bombay regulation, either taken by itself absolutely, or as confirmed by the legislative act VII. of 1836. The Chief Justice is of opinion, on the authority of the decision in the *Stamp case* at Calcutta, in 1827, 16 *Oriental Herald*, and of a decision of Sir C. GREY in 1830, (*Bign.*, p. 1), that the regulation is invalid for want of registration in the Supreme Court; but he is inclined to think that that deficiency has been supplied by the legislative act of 1836. I regret much that I am unable to subscribe to either of these views, as I conceive that the regulation of 1827 was amply valid, in virtue of the sanction of the Court of Directors, and their approbation. But if I am wrong in this view, and if, according to law, the regulation should also have been registered in the Supreme Court, I am undoubtedly of opinion that the act of the legislative council does not amount to a rehabilitation of it, but has left the regulation with all its original infirmity upon its head, merely providing that acts done in conformity with its spirit shall not be questioned in Courts of law.

Check on legislation imposed by Parliament.

It is very difficult to say, in point of fact, what the legislative act VII. of 1836 actually does mean. It is very short, and still more obscure: it contains no preamble, nor any clue as to what the evils were which were to be provided against. It undoubtedly does not mean all that it says in terms, because it provides that the legality of acts under certain regulations (this regulation being one of them) shall not be questioned in any Court of law; and it certainly could not have been intended by the legislative council that acts of murder, or of trespass, committed by revenue officers, should receive this immunity. But if the act cannot be construed to mean all that it says, I think it is equally incompetent to us to hold that it means more than it says; and I conceive the only possible construction of it is, that it was an act passed *ex majori cautelâ*, in order to prevent any acts, properly done under the

1844. RAMCHUND v. GLASS.

various regulations, being questioned in Courts of law, certain of these regulations being open to objections on the ground of their not having been confirmed at home; and this very regulation being open to the objection which the Judges of Calcutta took in the case of the *Stamp Act,* of its requiring registration in the Supreme Court.

As, however, the Chief Justice and myself arrive at the same ultimate conclusion, though by different roads, namely, that the remedy pointed out by the Bombay regulation is open to the party grieved, it would be unnecessary to go further; and I should be unwilling to set out at length the grounds on which I have formed my opinion, if I did not think it probable that the satisfactory course would be adopted of taking the opinion of a superior tribunal, and of thus affording the Court here a clear rule for the future.

The Judges at Calcutta, *viz.*, Sir CHARLES GREY, Sir J. FRANKS, and Sir EDWARD RYAN, have undoubtedly laid down, in very strong terms, that regulations imposing duties at the Presidency, and containing the proper machinery for enforcing them, require to be registered in the Supreme Court. This decision was first made by them when the stamp duties regulation was under discussion at Calcutta, in 1827, and was again affirmed by them incidentally in 1830, in *Doe* dem. *Peareemony Dossee* v. *Bissonath Bonnerjee* (Bign., p. 1). To such an authoritative exposition of the law, in any ordinary case, it would be my duty to bow; but, on an occasion where it seems possible that the opinion of the Superior Court may be obtained, it may appear not presumptuous that I should endeavour to urge what appears to me to have been the clearly opposite intention of the Legislature, and which intention, if it can be plainly established, it is our undoubted duty to carry out, notwithstanding one or two conflicting decisions.

Registration in Supreme Court, why necessary.

In order to inquire into the necessity for the registration of a revenue regulation in the Supreme Court, it is necessary to look back to the origin of the practice. This is to be found in the 13 Geo. 3, c. 63, s. 36, which enabled the Governor General and council to make rules and regulations for the good order and civil government of the Presidency of Fort William, but the same were not to be valid until registered and published in the Supreme Court, with the consent and approbation of the said Court. This was the first delegation of any thing like legislative power to the Company by the imperial Parliament; but these powers were dealt out to them so charily, that they will be found not to exceed, in point of magnitude, those which were incidental to the incorporation of any petty company whatever. A corporation of tin-plate workers might enforce good order and government in their trade by rules and bye-laws enforceable by fine; and the Company, having undisputed government over thirty or forty millions of subjects, could do no more. (See *Clarke's case*, 5 Rep. 64.) Accordingly, some years later it was found necessary to extend the powers of the Company, and they were enabled, for the purpose of preserving good order in the settlement, to go so far as to enforce their rules and regulations "by public or private whipping;" such regulations, nevertheless, to be subject to registry in the Supreme Court. (See the 39 & 40 Geo. 3, c. 79, s. 18.) In point of fact, these narrow and wholly insufficient powers for the government of a great country were wholly framed in accordance with views of corporation law. Charters incorporating different companies will be found to contain exactly similar provisions for making bye-laws, to be enforced by fine or moderate corporal punishment; and the mode adopted of opposing a check to the establishment of bye-laws repugnant to the general law of the land is also precisely copied from a prevailing practice in England as to corporations.

Limited power of legislation originally granted by Parliament.

By early statutes (the 15 Hen. 6, c. 6, and the 19 Hen. 7, c. 7) corporations were directed to enter their bye-law of record before "justices of the peace, or chief governors," and to have them examined by the Chancellor or Judges; and it appears that the ordinary practice was for the Judges to sign such regulations, as a matter of course, on circuit, without thereby giving any legal validity to the bye-law in question. (See *Comberbach*, p. 222.) This ancient practice, therefore, of the law, as to bye-laws enforceable by fine and moderate

1844.

RAMCHUND v. GLASS.

punishment, was imported into India when a power to make similar bye-laws was first given to the Company.

Larger views subsequently applied to India by Parliament.

But when Parliament legislated for India in 1813, it will be seen that they had emancipated themselves from the narrow notions which they had previously entertained of the legal character of the Company. The draftsman who framed the provisions for the extended powers of Government conveyed by the 53 Geo. 3, c. 155, no longer betook himself to the precedents on his file applicable to ordinary corporations in England, but boldly gave the requisite powers for governing on the spot as to a distant great Government. Thus the 98th section of that statute gave the local government the power of imposing duties and taxes on all persons within the jurisdiction of the Supreme Court; but as these were large and novel powers to be exercised over British subjects by a new authority, it was requisite, in a constitutional view, that an efficient check should be placed upon the local government against any arbitrary taxation, and this check was constituted by subjecting every regulation imposing such tax to the sanction of the Court of Directors and the authority of the Board of Control: these three authorities,—the two latter, namely, the respective Governors in Council,—constituting the sole governing powers to whom the Legislature had attributed the government of India. It is scarcely to be anticipated, therefore, that in constituting an act like the one in question the Parliament should have committed the powers of legislation to any other hands than to the actual responsible government; and, accordingly those authorities only are mentioned as empowered to take any share in the establishment of laws.

Supreme Court not intended to have a share in legislation.

But the argument is, that although true it is, Parliament has given the local government the power of imposing taxes on the community at the Presidency, still, if the regulations imposing such taxes contain any provisions for enforcing the collection of the same, such provisions are regulations for the good order and civil government of the Presidency, and therefore they fall within the meaning of the earlier statute, and must be consented to, and approved of, by the Judges in the Supreme Court, before they can be passed into law.

The direct consequence of this conclusion is, that any tax regulation, which the whole united government of India might think it indispensable for the interest of the country should be established, might be defeated by any one Judge who happened to be sitting alone; for the reasoning of Sir EDWARD RYAN, in the *Stamp case*, is, I think, incontrovertible to shew that the first statute (the 13 Geo. 3, c. 63) gave legislative, and not mere ministerial powers to the Judges, and empowered them to reject an act if they did not admit of its expediency

In other words, the powers of legislation conferred by the imperial Parliament, and guarded by various checks, imposed in express terms, were all to be defeated by a construction admitting of the *veto* of a single individual, of whom no mention is made in the statute.

This conclusion seems to me so monstrous, that it at once shews that the reasoning upon which it is founded must be erroneous.

It is said that "the imposition of a tax, and the law by which it is to be enforced, are easily distinguishable from each other;" but I confess that I am unable so to distinguish them. If a tax is imposed by competent authority, it can only be by a law, and a law is not an effectual law unless it carries its own sanction with it. An enactment that the inhabitants of Bombay shall pay customs if they choose is no law at all; but a simple enactment that they shall pay customs is an imperative command, capable of being enforced by the same authority which had power to make the law. In some systems, such as the Roman, there are what is called laws of imperfect obligation, where no sanction is contained in the enactment for carrying its provisions into effect; but in the English system a much sounder principle prevails, and whenever a law enjoins a particular course of action the party is punishable if he fail to comply with the provisions.

I am quite unable, therefore, to distinguish the power of imposing a tax on a British community from the incidental powers which are necessary for carrying the first power into effect. The grant of the first necessarily involves the latter,

1844.

RAMCHUND v. GLASS.

on the well known principle that by the grant of any thing "*conceditur et id sine quo res ipsa esse non potest.*"

If, therefore, the 98th section gives the power to the local government, under the checks above mentioned, of imposing taxes on the British community, without the necessity of registration in the Supreme Court,—and so much is admitted,—it follows, from the above principle, that all the incidental powers for carrying out the legislation are inseparably bound up with the former grant, and therefore, like that, cannot require registration; and, remarkably enough, it will be seen that both Sir CHARLES GREY and Sir EDWARD RYAN make use of this argument in terms to establish that the necessary powers which they held were accorded to the local government by the grant of legislation.

Registration not necessary in Supreme Court except as to bye-laws.

It appears to me, therefore, on the above grounds, that the registration required in the Supreme Court only applied to those regulations to which express reference was made in the early statutes, *viz.*, to those simple powers of making bye-laws enjoinable by fine and moderate corporal punishment, which were accorded to the Company in common with most other corporations; but that, when larger powers of legislation were granted to them, a much more efficient check was supplied than any which could be exercised by the Judges of the Supreme Court. Sir EDWARD RYAN has shewn very forcibly that the Judges have not the requisite information before them for ascertaining what the wants of the community may be as to any particular law: their time is fully occupied in studies of a different nature; and, even if they had time to devote to inquiries of a political character, it would be most inexpedient to place them in a condition which would inevitably bring upon them the imputation, either of yielding to government solicitation on the one side, or of stooping to obtain a little transient popularity on the other. Indeed, the expediency of separating judicial and legislative functions as much as possible has been so long felt by all sound thinkers, and the evils caused by the ill-defined functions of the Supreme Court and local government at Calcutta were so immediately before the eyes of the Legislature in 1813, that I cannot bring myself to believe that they intended to subject the powers of legislation committed to the local government to the control of the Supreme Court. If they had no such intention, it is manifest that the astute reasoning and subtle distinction, by which the clause in a previous statute is made to extend to other objects, not contemplated by the Legislature, can have no place, but must be rejected.

If, then, the regulation in question was valid *ab initio*, so soon as it received the sanction of the home government, a further question, perhaps, arises (although it was not made at the Bar), whether this particular proceeding in the Supreme Court could be authorized. The proceeding enjoined is an action *in rem :* no damages would be recoverable for the improper seizure, and nothing is said about costs. I have said before that at common law we have not got such a remedy for the recovery of the article in specie (although *detinue* approaches to it) ; and it might be objected that the local government could not frame a new form of action for the jurisdiction of the Queen's Court. But, on the whole, I think this objection not sustainable. According to the view of the Chief Justice and myself, this Court has jurisdiction generally, under the 53 Geo. 3, c. 155, s. 98, for illegal acts committed under revenue regulations at the Presidency. It has been already shewn that the imperial Legislature, in delegating to the local government the power of imposing taxes, must have delegated, also, all necessary powers for carrying the object contemplated into effect; and as to afford a remedy for any injustice committed by their subordinate officers may be said to be a necessary power towards carrying the act effectually into operation, I think that the local government may be held to have had the power to establish this particular remedy in the Supreme Court. At all events, if the true construction should be that they had no power in any way to limit the jurisdiction of the Court in respect of the party aggrieved, such jurisdiction being founded on the 53 Geo. 3, c. 115, still I think it is not competent to the servant of the Company to take this objection. The proceeding is a much more beneficial

1844. RAMCHUND v. GLASS.

one for them, and the only effect of giving way to it would be to allow an action at common law to be brought, with all its incidents of arrest, cost, and vindictive damages.

Upon the whole, therefore, I am of opinion that no impediment exists towards carrying out the provisions of the Bombay Regulation XXI. of 1827, and this conclusion appears eminently in harmony with the justice of the case; for if this seizure had taken place in the Mofussil the claimant would have obtained redress there, either summarily or in the Zillah Court, the regulation being confessedly valid in the Mofussil, whether registration is required in the Presidency or not. But, if the arguments of the Advocate General are correct, if the present plaintiff cannot get redress in the Supreme Court, he can get it nowhere. It is said that another remedy is afforded by the 21 Geo. 3, c. 70, s. 22, which enables the Governor in Council to decide, as a Court, on all offences and extortions committed in the collection of the revenue. But it is needless to say that no such Court exists for this purpose now; and although, I believe, in Bombay the senior magistrate of police has some jurisdiction as a Judge in local revenue matters, it is quite clear that he could not exercise jurisdiction in cases of this nature, for he is the very party who is to originate the series of acts, the legality of which is to be determined judicially.

It is clear, therefore, that this is the only Court where justice on the subject-matter can be rendered; and this makes it quite clear why it was that the 53 Geo. 3, s. 98, enacted that "all persons whosoever might sue in the Supreme Court for any matter or thing whatsoever arising out of the laws and regulations" to be passed by the local government.

As the effect of our decision is to overrule the plea to the jurisdiction, I think that the collector should be called upon to answer the affidavits as to why a feigned issue should not be awarded.

HURKISSONDAS HURGOVINDASS
v.
SPOONER AND ANOTHER.

1847.

June 22.

[*Coram* PERRY, C. J.]

TRESPASS for breaking and entering the plaintiff's dwelling-house, and seizing and carrying away a globe lamp there being. Plea, not guilty by statute. At the trial, before PERRY, C. J., the action appeared to be one against the collector of land revenue, in the island of Bombay, and his native assistant, for a distress which had been made in the plaintiff's house for the arrears of a Government claim, called pension, amounting to six annas (9*d.*) per annum, and which had been unpaid for twenty-one years. The seizure was made under a warrant, which was directed against a former occupant of the house, and on complaint before the police magistrate, on this fact appearing, the distress was abandoned by the defendants.

Le Messurier, A. G., objected that the Court had no jurisdiction, it being a case concerning the revenue, and *Howard*, for the plaintiff, contended that this objection, not having been pleaded, was not open. Both points were reserved, and on the facts proved, a verdict was pronounced for the plaintiff, damages Rs. 250.

Le Messurier, A. G., on a subsequent day, obtained a rule nisi for a nonsuit, on the ground that the terms of 21 Geo. 3, c. 70,

1. Where the collector of land revenue in Bombay made a seizure in the house of A. for arrears of revenue, called pension, charged on the house, which had been formerly in the possession of B., and the warrant of distress was made out against B., but afterwards abandoned the distress, on the ground of the warrant being illegal; *Held*, that an action for trespass lay in the Supreme Court, but overruled on appeal to the Privy Council.

2. *Quære*, whether objection to the jurisdiction of the Court under 37 Geo. 3, c. 142, s. 11 (revenue clause), requires to be made by special plea? Not necessary, per Privy Council.

3. Where leave was refused to appeal, on the ground of the amount in dispute being exceedingly small, the Privy Council allowed the appeal to be entered on the condition of the appellants paying the costs of the other side.

4. *Quære*, where redress is to be obtained at Bombay for wrongs inflicted by revenue officers in collection of the revenue.

1847. HURKISSONDASS v. SPOONER.

s. 8, and of 37 Geo. 3, c. 142, s. 11, were so express, that it was clear the jurisdiction of the Court was taken away, and although Sir C. GREY, C. J., in *Bignell's R.*, p. 6, intimated that the action would lie if trespasses were committed by revenue officers, such observations were extra-judicial.

Howard and *Holland* shewed cause. The Advocate General is bound to contend that whatever trespasses may be committed by revenue officers no action will lie in this Court. But the Supreme Court laid down a much more intelligible and satisfactory rule in the case cited from *Bignell*, (*Doe* v. *Bissonault* v. *Bonnerjee*), and the analogy of procedure in England shews that to be the true rule.

The jurisdiction of the Court of Exchequer over matters concerning the revenue is sole and exclusive, per BLACKSTONE, J., *Scott* v. *Shearman*, (2 W. Bl. 977); but the other Courts have jurisdiction to try whether revenue officers commit trespasses or not. It must be contended, therefore, that when any revenue is due, the jurisdiction of this Court is excluded however harshly the officer behave, however much against the usages of the country or the Company's regulations. The decision in *Calder* v. *Halket*, (3 Mor. Priv. Coun. R.,) on an analogous statute, shews, however, that no such total immunity is given to revenue officers.

In this case no question occurred as to revenue being due or not. It was admitted by the defendant that their proceedings were illegal, and it was not necessary for the plaintiff to shew that no revenue was due from any one, as perhaps he might have been able to do.

Lastly, the objection as to jurisdiction should have been pleaded specially: it used to be so before the new rules, (*Smoult's Orders*, 129-30), and, *a fortiori*, should be so now.

Le Messurier, A. G., and *Herrick*, *contrà*.

It is clear that the act in question was committed in the collection of the revenue. [*Howard.* I deny that. No inquiry was gone into on that point, and it was not necessary.] There is no doubt that some revenue was due, and some of it from the plaintiff himself. In the case cited from *Bignell*, Sir C.

1847.

HURKISSON-DASS v. SPOONER.

GREY, C. J., admits that the Court is not to take notice of trivial informalities, and admits also that for cases in the Mofussil the Court has no jurisdiction; and he gets rid of the statute there on the ground of Calcutta not being within the terms of 21 Geo. 3, c. 70. But the Presidencies of Madras and Bombay are expressly excluded from revenue jurisdiction by the subsequent statute. It may be conceded, that if a collector made a seizure on a mere pretext and without any colour of claim, an action would lie here, or a criminal information; but for all informalities the proper forum is the Court established by Regulation XIX. of 1827.

The sole question to be determined, therefore, in this Court, as to whether an action lies or not, is, whether *bona fides* existed or the contrary. *Wedge* v. *Berkley*, (6 A. & E.), shews that this is the point which the Courts in England consider when an action is brought against magistrates. And it is not contended that the defendants were actuated by malice or any improper motives.

Then it is said that the objection to jurisdiction should have been pleaded specially. But this is not so; a general law exempts a revenue officer from the jurisdiction of this Court, and therefore the Court must take judicial notice of it; *Parker* v. *Edling*, (1 East, 354). Moreover the defendants are protected by 42 Geo. 3, c. 85, s. 6, and *Calder* v. *Halket* is an authority that the defence is open to them on the general issue.

Cur. adv. vult.

PERRY, C. J.—This is an action of trespass for breaking and entering the plaintiff's house, and seizing a globe lamp there being and carrying it away. The defendant pleaded not guilty by statute.

At the trial, it appeared that the action was brought against the collector of land revenue and his native agent for a distress made in the plaintiff's house, under the following circumstances:—Mr. Hutchinson, the deputy collector, having discovered by his books that a small quit rent, called pension, amounting to six annas a year, and issuing out of land occu-

1847.

HURKISSON-DASS v. SPOONER.

pied by the plaintiff, appeared to have been unpaid for a great number of years (twenty-one, I believe, was the number mentioned), he ordered his people to demand it of the occupier of the land from which the pension accrued. The servants of the collector thereupon demanded the arrears, amounting to eight or nine rupees, from the plaintiff, who is an opulent Banyan (*a*) merchant in Bombay, and who had bought the land in question, about ten years before, at a sale by the sheriff of the property of one Narrondass Takidass, and he had had the transfer made at the collector's office of the property into his own name. The plaintiff denied his liability to pay the arrears due from Narrondass, upon which the defendant issued a distress warrant against Narrondass Takidass, by virtue of which the collector's servants entered the plaintiff's house, exhibiting considerable violence, and executed the warrant by seizing a globe lamp; but by their own statements made before the magistrates, they certainly performed their duty in a very objectionable manner, for they would not allow the warrant which they were executing to be read. They then proceeded to make a complaint against the plaintiff's servants for obstructing the process of the law, but the magistrate, having heard the evidence, dismissed the charge.

Mr. Spooner, who appears to have taken but little part in the transaction up to this time, except by signing the distress warrant, appeared at the police office with his servants when they made their complaint against the plaintiff, and then, having probably, for the first time, heard the circumstances under which the distress was made, he discovered that the warrant was illegal, and informed the plaintiff that he should not persevere with it.

The plaintiff thereupon wrote, what I thought was a very proper letter, claiming some compensation for the expense he had been put to by the illegal distress, and requesting the defendant to reprimand his servants for their violent conduct. The defendant, by his legal adviser, at first seemed inclined to entertain the claim to compensation, but afterwards rejected it, and confined himself to sending back the lamp.

(*a*) As to this term, see *ante*, *Nathabhai Ramdass's case*.

At the trial of this cause, I thought the question to be left to the jury was, whether the irregularity, which had been confessedly committed by the defendants in the execution of this warrant, was a mere slip, such as might happen to the most careful revenue officer in the exercise of his duties, or whether it was a substantial breach of the law, which entitled the plaintiff to due compensation. In the first case I should have thought that the Court, acting upon the analogy of English statutes for the protection of magistrates, would have been justified in finding either a verdict for the defendants, or, at all events, a verdict for the plaintiff with such nominal damages and deprivation of costs as would discourage any similar frivolous action being brought. In the second case, I considered the rule to be applied was that also which has been laid down for English magistrates, and which decides, that where they act without jurisdiction, and without ordinary caution,—with what a learned Judge, in *Cann* v. *Clipperton*, called "a foolish imagination of jurisdiction,"—that there the rights of the subject required a verdict for substantial, though temperate, damages. And as, upon the whole case, I was of opinion that Mr. Hutchinson, who was the principal mover in the business, had, from his zeal to collect revenue, in some degree overlooked the necessary inquiries to be made as to the parties from whom the revenue was due,—as I thought advantage had not been taken of the able legal advice which is open to Company's officers in Bombay, as to the mode in which an obsolete claim should be enforced,—as I considered that the claim was prosecuted by the collector's agents with unnecessary harshness and violence, and, lastly, as the collector did not avail himself of the opportunity to make amends when he acknowledged himself to be in error, I considered that the plaintiff who, as an inhabitant of Bombay, enjoys all the rights of a British subject, was only moderately compensated by a verdict of Rs. 250 damages.

At the close of the plaintiff's case, the Advocate General, on the part of the defendants, submitted that the Court had no jurisdiction, as the case was one concerning the revenue; the counsel for the plaintiff, on the other hand, objected that

1847.

HURKISSON-DASS v. SPOONER.

the defence was not open to the defendants, as it had not been pleaded. As I was not prepared to decide offhand on either of these points, I reserved them, and they have since been argued solemnly before me.

The objection of the Advocate General is founded on the clause in the charter of justice which provides that the Court shall not "have or exercise any jurisdiction in any matter concerning the revenue under the management of the said Governor and Council of Bombay respectively, either within or beyond the limits of the said town, or the forts and factories subordinate thereto, or concerning any act done according to the usage and practice of the country, or the regulations of the Governor and Council of Bombay aforesaid."

If this clause stood by itself, and were to be construed according to the natural and apparent meaning of the terms, which is the mode of construction always to be resorted to in the first instance, I do not think any difficulty would arise. A universal jurisdiction, both civil and criminal, being first of all attributed to the Supreme Court over all the inhabitants of Bombay, such jurisdiction being to be exercised according to English law, the clause in question evidently has two objects, and cuts off from the general jurisdiction two special classes of cases. It first of all provides that the Court shall not exercise jurisdiction in revenue matters, just as all the Courts in England, except the Exchequer, are prohibited by the King's prerogative from exercising revenue jurisdiction; secondly, it provides that acts done in the collection of the revenue, according to the usage and custom of the country or the Government regulations, shall not be actionable, although they may not be warranted by the law of England. When a general jurisdiction is given, and then a special exception is made, it is obvious that the extent of that exception is to be measured solely by the terms employed. And therefore, when a question is raised as to the jurisdiction of the Court on this clause, if it arises on the first branch of it, the decision must proceed on the determination whether the revenue is immediately in question, as to which several cases in England, and especially *Cawthorne* v. *Campbell*, (1 Anstruther), supply

1847.

HURKISSON-DASS v. SPOONER.

the appropriate rule. If the question arises on the second branch of the clause, the point to be determined is, whether the act complained of is warranted by the usage of the country, or by the Government regulations. If the act falls within neither of these categories, then it is a wrongful act on which the general jurisdiction of the Court attaches. But in this case, as in every other affecting the jurisdiction of the Supreme Court, it is not sufficient to look merely to the terms of the last charter of justice. The clause upon which any particular question arises, must be traced back to its source, and a careful study must be made of the various charters, statutes, regulations, and decided cases connected with the subject; and the peculiar circumstances of the country, at the time when such special legislation was applied to it, must also be steadfastly kept in view. These materials for a correct judgment are to be found in very heterogeneous collections. Even in India we have not got all of them at hand; the best furnished law library in England would probably be found deficient in the greater part of them. On a close examination, however, of all the principal authorities which bear on the present question, I have not the least doubt that the Legislature never intended to give the Company's servants in India a total immunity from action in the Supreme Court, for wrongs committed in the collection of the revenue, any more than the 21 Geo. 3, c. 70, gave them a total immunity for wrongs committed as magistrates; *Calder* v. *Halket*, (3 Moo. Priv. Coun. Cas.)

The statute of 13 Geo. 3, establishing the Supreme Court, was founded, as is well known, on reports of a committee of the House of Commons, attributing grievous oppressions to the British officers who, after the grant of the Dewanne to the East India Company, were roaming about the province of Bengal, Bahar, and Orissa, occupied wholly in making fortunes for themselves, and equally regardless of the orders of their superiors as of the rights of the natives.

Five years after the establishment of the Supreme Court, the Chief Justice writes, in the name of his brethren, to the Secretary of State, "We are likewise unanimous in our

1847.

HURKISSON-DASS v. SPOONER.

opinion that the representations made in England of the frauds, cruelties, and extortions committed by British subjects, or by persons deriving influence from them and the Company were by no means exaggerated; but, on the contrary, that there exists at present numberless sources of fraud and rapine totally unheard of there (*i. e.* in England), and more especially in the provincial councils, which act as Adawluts or Courts of civil jurisdiction, and in the Board of Commerce at Calcutta, composed of senior servants of the Company." Warren Hastings, also, writing in 1776, says, "You will have seen many instances in the papers which I have sent home of the most glaring acts of oppression committed by the Board, which would have produced the ruin of the parties over whom they were exercised, but for the protection of the Court" (*a*).

The Legislature undertook to provide a remedy for these evils, by the establishment of a Supreme Court, which should exercise complete jurisdiction over all British subjects residing in Bengal, Bahar, and Orissa, and civil jurisdiction over all natives employed by the Company, or by British subjects, and the charter of justice emanating from the Crown in consequence of this statute extended the jurisdiction over the latter class of persons to criminal matters also. The regulating statute, however, was studiously silent on one point; it was not convenient, for many reasons, to declare in whom the sovereignty of Bengal was vested, and to this ambiguity the whole of those unfortunate dissensions between the Supreme Court and council, which nearly distracted India, may probably be traced. A year before the 13 Geo. 3 passed, Warren Hastings, of his own authority (but upon a broad legal basis, as I pointed out in a former case in this Court), established Courts of civil and criminal jurisdiction throughout the provinces, but for the interest of the Company he established the latter in the name of the Nawab. He did this, however, entirely on his own authority, and without even consulting the Nawab, as appears by the affidavit which the Governor General made in the Supreme Court of Calcutta, in the pro-

(*a*) See Life of Sir E. IMPEY, by his son.

secution against *Fowk* (20 State Trials). The royal charter of justice, on the other hand, by its grant of jurisdiction to the Supreme Court over native in Bengal, Bahar, and Orissa, clearly assumed a right of sovereignty in the Crown, which the Judges considered themselves bound to assert and vindicate on every occasion. On the question of sovereignty, as it then appeared to all parties, depended the validity of the Company's Courts, and of the proceedings under their orders. It was whilst these discussions were pending that revenue disputes were brought before the Court. Mr. Justice HYDE, who appears to have been rather pedantic in his views as to the applicability of English law throughout the whole of India, claimed for the Supreme Court the right of jurisdiction in all cases of revenue demanded by the Company. The terms of the clause giving jurisdiction possibly warranted this claim, but Sir ELIJAH IMPEY, who was evidently a more practical man, saw that it was wholly impossible for the Supreme Court, with its other business and its forms of procedure, "to determine one-hundredth part of such cases;" and he states of Justice HYDE, that he had "such very high notions of the liberty and general protection from the laws of England, in all revenue cases, that he (Sir ELIJAH) found it absolutely necessary to oppose him." It was under this state of circumstances that the Legislature enacted 21 Geo. 3, c. 70, in which the clause taking away revenue jurisdiction from the Supreme Court for the first time appeared. Looking at the preamble of that statute, I can have no doubt that the revenue referred to in sect. 8 was the revenue of Bengal and Orissa, and I quite agree with Chief Justice GREY (*Bignell's Reports*) that the clause was not intended to extend to the British factory at Calcutta, where English law only had prevailed since it first became a settlement. The statute 37 Geo. 3, c. 142, however, which provided for the better administration of justice at Madras and Bombay, carried the exception from revenue jurisdiction somewhat further, for it expressly enacted that the Courts to be thereby established should not exercise jurisdiction in any matter concerning the revenue, either within or beyond the limits of the said towns, or concerning

1847.

HURKISSONDASS v. SPOONER.

any acts done according to usage or regulations. And such extension of the clause was very appropriate to the constitution of those settlements, both of which contain what has been lately called an *arrondissement* of considerable extent, in which land revenue would have to be collected, just as in the Mofussil. On perusing the whole of these statutes, it appears to me clear that the intention of the Legislature was to erect a separate Court for the decision of revenue claims, and to allow the Company's officers to collect the revenue, either in the mode in which they had been accustomed to do so heretofore, or according to the regulations to be laid down from time to time by the local government.

Ample powers are thus given for all Governmental purposes, but it is so contrary to the spirit of British legislation to suppose that unlimited irresponsible powers were attributed as to make me require express words to shew that such was the intention.

It was said, however, that the subject would not be without remedy in any case of wrong, as the regulation of 1827 establishes the Court of a revenue Judge for the island of Bombay, to which a complaint like the present might be made. But that regulation did not receive legislative force till the year 1834, when it was confirmed by the Supreme Government, and even if it were in force from its commencement, still, from 1797 till 1827, there was no tribunal except the Supreme Court open for the redress of such grievance. And so at the present moment where is a party in the Mofussil to sue for any illegal act committed in the collection of the revenue? All cases in this presidency are, I believe, tried, in the first instance, before a native Judge, but the idea of a collector being tried before a Suder Amin for trespass presents such a ludicrous aspect that it never could be seriously entertained by any one acquainted with India.

For all these reasons, I think that the jurisdiction of this Court has not been taken away when the act complained of is not warranted by the usage of the country, or by the Company's regulations; and as I do not see the slightest trace of any authority to demand the arrears of twenty years, or of two hundred years, as claimed by the deputy collector, from any person found in occupation of the land, I think the act in question was not authorized by usage and practice, neither does the regulation of 1827 furnish any authority for the act. It was urged for the plaintiff that the mode there pointed out for executing a distress had not been followed, but this is a mistake; the warrant there spoken of does not refer to a distress for land revenue, but for other matters comprised in a different Chapter.

I am inclined to think, indeed, that the regulation does not apply to the present case at all, for the quit rent, called pension, and the revenue, called assessment, are two very different subject-matters, and the regulation only appears to refer to the latter. But however this may be, and whether the right of the collector to levy for pension depends on the usage of the country, or upon that and the regulation also, neither the one nor the other confer the right to enforce absolute claims according to the off-handed violent process observed on the present occasion.

This being the view which I have taken on the objection made by the Advocate General, it is unnecessary to consider the point of pleading raised by the plaintiff's counsel.

Rule discharged.

Application was afterwards made by the Advocate General for liberty to appeal to the Privy Council, which was refused, on the grounds mentioned in the following note, which PERRY, C. J., transmitted to the clerk of the Privy Council.

Sir E PERRY's Note.

This was an action for trespass *de bonis asportatis*, which was tried before me in the June Term of this year, when I found a verdict for the plaintiff, damages Rs. 250. On a point reserved at the trial, the question of jurisdiction was afterwards solemnly argued, and upon a review of the different authorities and statutes, I held that the jurisdiction attached.

In the September Term a motion was made before me for

1847.

HURKISSON-DASS *v.* SPOONER.

liberty to appeal to the Privy Council against the above decision. I stated my desire that the opinion of the Privy Council should be obtained, if the East India Company saw reason to be dissatisfied with the judgment; but, as the charter of justice for the Supreme Court and the orders of the Privy Council had established the rule that appeals are not to lie in cases of this small pecuniary amount, I had no power to grant the leave.

But I suggested that if the East India Company wished, on constitutional grounds, to obtain an authentic exposition of the rule as to the extent of liability of their collectors of revenue in the island of Bombay, it would seem just that they should conduct the appeal at their own charges; for that the plaintiff, a Banyan merchant, was only interested to sustain his verdict to the amount of 25*l.* and the costs of suit, and that if an appeal generally were to be permitted, it might be more advisable for him to abandon his action altogether.

This suggestion was not acceded to on the part of the Honorable Company, and it was understood that application would be made to the Privy Council for leave to appeal, notwithstanding the rule laid down by their Lordships above referred to.

Under these circumstances, I have thought it right to transmit to the Privy Council a copy of the judgment which I delivered on behalf of the plaintiff, to which I will only add, that the Supreme Court at Calcutta, in 1819, appears to have arrived at the same conclusion in a case against Sir Geo. Doyley, as appears from Sir E. H. EAST's notes, abstracted in Mr. *Morley's Digest of Reported Cases in India*, vol. 1, p. 15.

E. PERRY.

27th Sept. 1847.

SPOONER, APPELLANT,
v.
HURKISSONDASS HURGOVINDASS

In the Privy Council.

1848.

On application being made to the Privy Council by the appellants in this case to set down the cause on appeal, notwithstanding the refusal in the Court below and the smal amount at stake, on the ground of the case being one involving a point of great importance, and in which the Honorable Company felt deep interest, Lord LANGDALE, M. R., in pronouncing the decision of the Court, held that permission could only be given on the condition of the Company paying all the costs of the respondent.

The counsel for the Company assenting to these terms, the cause was accordingly set down, notification was transmitted to the Supreme Court at Bombay of the conditions on which the appeal was allowed, whereupon the Chief Justice addressed to the Privy Council the following reasons for his judgment (*a*):—

(*a*) The above judgment having been reversed on appeal, as will be seen, *post*, the present state of the law, so far as the inhabitants of Bombay are concerned, is so unsatisfactory, in respect to injuries committed by revenue officers, that it has been deemed useful to set before the Profession and the public in the text the arguments which seemed to require either a different decision to what the Privy Council has arrived at, or an alteration in the law. Criticism, by the present editor, on the arguments of so great a master of the common law as Lord CAMPBELL, would be, of course, unseemly; but it may be within the scope of scientific professional discussion to observe, that he is unable to perceive the analogy between statutes which confer a total immunity from action for certain acts and statutes which regulate how an action should be brought, in case of admitted breaches of the law. In the latter case, of course, the protection of the statutes is only required when the law has been broken. In the former a more strict construction seems necessary to guard against arbitrary conduct.

1848.

SPOONER v. HURKISSON-DASS.

Sir E. PERRY.

On jurisdiction in revenue cases.

Liberty to appeal in this case having been granted by the Judicial Committee of the Privy Council, it becomes my duty to furnish a statement of the reasons on which my judgment was founded; and if it were not for the great importance which the law officers of the East India Company, and apparently the Court of Directors, attach to the decision, I should have thought it sufficient merely to transmit a copy of the written judgment which I delivered at the time of the trial. But as the decision of the Supreme Court seems to have been considered a usurpation of authority, and extreme susceptibility is evinced as to the interference of a Court of justice in questions of this nature, I think it my duty to point out, *seriatim*, the chief arguments present to my mind when I decided the case; and I rejoice to think that the subject is to undergo investigation in a superior tribunal, for if it shall be finally decided that the Supreme Court has no jurisdiction, the Legislature will probably think it fit to provide that some legal tribunal or other should be open to afford redress when wrongs have been admittedly sustained by British subjects.

If the Supreme Court has no jurisdiction in this case, the Legislature will probably afford a remedy.

Facts stated.

The facts of the case may be stated in a few words:—The assistant to the collector of land revenue in the island of Bombay, supposing that he had a claim on the occupier of a house in the town of Bombay for twenty-one years' arrears of a small quit or ground rent (as it is usually called in legal language at Bombay), or pension (from the Portuguese word pensão, signifying rent, as it is called among the natives), and amounting to nine-pence a year, made a demand for it on the occupier of the house, a respectable Hindu merchant, who had bought the premises some eight or nine years previously. The plaintiff, it appears, was willing to pay the arrears due in his own time, but demurred to payment of the arrears due from his predecessor; upon which, as it would seem, without further inquiry, the defendant issued his warrant of distress, but made it out against the preceding occupier of the house, and seized some property of the plaintiff by force. On further inquiry arising out of this transaction before the magistrate, the latter decided that the warrant of distress was illegal, whereupon the

1848.

SPOONER v. HURKISSON-DASS.

Sir E. PERRY.

defendant restored to the plaintiff the property seized. The plaintiff then demanded some amends for the wrong he had sustained, and the solicitor to the Company first of all entertained the application, but subsequently rejected it. Under these circumstances, the plaintiff brought his action for trespass in this Court, to which the defendants pleaded not guilty by statute. And I have mentioned in my judgment at length the circumstances which influenced me at the time in assessing the damages at Rs. 250, or 25*l*.

Reasons for judgment.

I will now briefly recapitulate the legal reasons which were present to my mind when I decided in favour of the plaintiff.

1. Natives of Bombay British subjects, and entitled to protection of British law;

1. The natives of Bombay, unlike those of other parts of British India, have always been British subjects since the cession of the island to Charles II., and English law has been the *lex loci* during all that period. The Court, therefore, as it appears to me, is bound to put as strict a construction on any clause taking away the protection of Courts of justice from the inhabitants of Bombay, as if they were construing a local act for imposing a tax on the town of Liverpool. Indeed, as the law here makes no distinction between natives born and English subjects, a merchant of Liverpool or London settled in Bombay might as well have been the plaintiff in the action as this Hindu.

Consequently, statutes infringing on common law rights to be construed strictly.

2. Questionable, whether ground rents in island of Bombay come within the term "revenue" in Indian statutes.

2. I think it is a matter of great doubt whether the term 'revenue' used in 21 Geo. 3, c. 70, s. 8, and in subsequent statutes, which take away the jurisdiction of the Supreme Court in certain cases, includes a claim for ground rent in the island of Bombay. The object of the clause, as we gather from the preamble, and as we know indubitably from other sources, was to ensure the collection of the revenue according to the ancient usages and practice of the country, and the collection of the land revenue of India being founded on principles so wholly different from those which prevail in English taxation, it was quite fitting that the rules of English law should not apply to it. Sir Charles GREY, C. J., in *Bignel's Reports*, p. 6, points out the distinction between land revenue in the provinces, and rents of the Company's houses

1848.

SPOONER v. HURKISSON-DASS.

Sir E. PERRY.

in Presidency towns. But as the island of Bombay contains lands on which revenue has to be collected according to the same principles as land revenue in the provinces, the clause in the statute, applicable to Bombay, vests all the jurisdiction, relative to such revenue, in the hands of servants of the Company, who may be supposed to be conversant with the subject. But it vests such jurisdiction as to *land revenue* only, and the other different charges, which may, be imposed by law from time to time on the inhabitants of a densely peopled city, who have congregated together under the protection of English law, and which the government is enabled to claim and recover (as in the present case) solely by virtue of the English law like any other landlord, are left to be regulated by the statutes imposing the new taxes, or by the law generally.

Distinction in Bombay Regulations between ground rents and land revenue.

Regulation XIX. of 1827, which has the force of an act of Parliament, and under which the duties of the collector of land revenue in Bombay are prescribed, draws, very clearly, the distinction which I point out. The collector of land revenue, at Bombay, has to assess and collect, or to collect only, the following items:

1. The land revenue.
2. The tax called market taxes on shops, &c.
3. A house tax on houses within certain limits.
4. A tax on carriages and horses.
5. The quit or ground rents belonging to Government.

As to all these items, except the last, the regulation gives the collector summary powers of collection, attachment, and sale. As to the latter, which is a European, not an Indian, tenure, no special power is given, except when the owner of a house sells without notice. The power of distress, therefore, which is exercised by Government, must be founded on their claims as landlord, although distress for rent generally is not in use at Bombay. That which is called land revenue in the regulation, is the same land revenue as accrues to Government all over India; the assessment is to be made in the same manner; and the powers of attachment and sale are defined in a previous regulation, which prescribes rules for the assessment

1848.

SPOONER v. HURKISSON-DASS.

Sir E. PERRY.

and realization of the land revenue generally, Regulation XVII. And it is only over suits relating to this land revenue that the special jurisdiction, referred to in the petition of appeal has relation. Regulation XIX. s. 7, enacts, that the revenue Judge shall decide all suits before him, by contributors to the land revenue, at the presidency, against the collector, or any person of his establishment, *on account of land revenue.* It is clear, therefore, that this revenue Judge has no jurisdiction over other suits, and the argument appears to me a very strong one to shew that the Bombay Government, who drew the regulations in 1827, put the limited construction on the term revenue in the English statutes, which the reason of the thing, and the principles of English law, seem to require.

The Court of the Revenue Judge has only jurisdiction over suits for land revenue.

3. But assuming that this construction is incorrect, and that the clause in 21 Geo. 3, taking away jurisdiction, in revenue cases, from the Supreme Court, applies to every new tax which may be imposed by Government, and to all property, (equivalent to Crown lands in England) possessed by Government, whether within the Presidency towns where English law prevails, or without, and including the right to perpetual ground rents incapable of being raised, as in the present case, and whether any other Court exists for hearing complaints on the subject or not,—still the true construction of that clause, I conceive to be, that an action lies in the Supreme Court, against any one who is liable to its jurisdiction generally, for any outrage committed in the collection of the revenue, which is not according to the usage and practice of the country, or to the regulations of the Government. In these two cases the jurisdiction of the Court is ousted, and so, also, if the suit involves the question whether revenue is due or not. In all other cases of wrong done, the jurisdiction of the Court attaches, and any larger construction of the clause would exclude the jurisdiction of the Court in a case of murder.

3. But whether so or not, the true construction of statutes only gives immunity from actions for acts illegal by English law.

1st, where the acts of the collector are according to the usage of country;

2nd, or, according to the orders of Government;

or 3rd, where the action involves the question whether revenue is due or not.

The decisions of the Supreme Courts in India have been conformable to this view, incidentally in *Doe* v. *Bissonath*, (Bignell's Reports, p. 6), and directly, it would appear, in a case, of which I have only seen the marginal note, in Mr. *Morley's Digest*, from the notes of one of the presiding Judges, Sir E.

Indian decisions conformable to this view.

1848.

SPOONER v. HURKISSON-DASS.

Sir E. PERRY.

H. EAST. But the case of *Calder* v. *Halket*, in the Privy Council, lays down the authoritative rule in exposition of a similar clause, namely, that the immunity from jurisdiction, given to servants of the Company, is not to be carried further than reason, and the analogy of the English law would prescribe.

4. The statutable defence of defendant should have been pleaded.

4. It was argued, for the plaintiff, that it was not open to the defendant to rely on this defence without pleading it, that no statute gives the collector of land revenue the general plea, that the practice had always been, before the new rules, to plead this defence specially, as was evidenced by the precedents of pleas given in *Smoult's Orders*, and that *à fortiori*, since the establishment of the new rules, the necessity was greater; and I think these arguments are valid, for the principles laid down in *Calder* v. *Halket*, as to the general issue, do not include a collector of land revenue distraining for rent.

5. Argument *ex probabili.* If no jurisdiction in supreme Court, there is jurisdiction nowhere.

5. Lastly, if jurisdiction does not exist in the Supreme Court to correct wrongs of this kind occasioned by Europeans, it exists nowhere. I have already shewn that in Bombay a special revenue Judge has jurisdiction only in suits relating to the land revenue. But, even in Bombay, although in theory and on the face of the regulations there is such a Judge,—in practice there is none. He has no Court, its existence is unknown to the natives, the legal practitioners of Bombay would be unable to stir a step from their ignorance of the procedure,—and how then would a poor man complaining of some injury, for which fifty or a hundred rupees might be an ample compensation, be able to get redress? During the (nearly) eight years which I have been in Bombay, I have never heard of more than one suit being brought before the chief magistrate, which was a suit brought, I believe, by an intelligent Parsi, who probably, from his intercourse with the English, had the proper course pointed out to him by some one acquainted with the Government regulations, and it was a suit over which the Supreme Court had clearly no jurisdiction, as it merely raised the question whether revenue was due or not.

The Bombay Revenue Court has limited jurisdiction only, and is a Court *in nubibus.*

In the provinces, suits to try the liability to revenue demand are to be brought in the Zillah Courts against the collector; all suits in this Presidency, I believe, are brought before native Judges (Munsiffs and Sudr Amins) in the first instance, and such functionaries, I dare say, are very competent to decide questions of fact as to the liability of a particular field to Government assessment or otherwise. But on looking at the relative positions of the collector of a province, and of a Munsiff,—the former with his Rs. 3000 a month, the latter with his Rs. 100 to Rs. 150,—and the still greater inequality in social position, independence, and education, the idea of a Munsiff sitting in judgment in an action of trespass over a collector, and having to weigh the moral quality of the acts of the latter with judicial gravity and indifference to persons,—this idea it was which presented the ludicrous image to which I alluded in my judgment. Nor is the tribunal which a young European assistant Judge affords in these respects much more efficacious. The arguments under this head, however, are rather political than legal, and they only have bearing on this case in so far as they point out what the probable intention of the Legislature was, and the extent to which they proceeded in depriving the Supreme Courts of jurisdiction. They seem to me to shew, that whilst the Legislature intended to prevent the Supreme Court and the forms of the English law from offering any obstruction to the collection of Indian land revenue, according to the old usages of the country, or according to any regulations which the Executive might propound it neither intended nor desired that the collectors of revenue should be emancipated from the ordinances of law generally,—and that this remark, true of British India as a whole, is applicable with tenfold force to the inhabitants of the Presidency capitals, where all the provisions of English law in favour of the liberty of the subject exist.

In the provinces, suits against collector as to liability to revenue are brought before native Judges.

But a native Judge trying a collector as a tortfeazor and trespasser is an absurdity.

Improbability, therefore, that English Legislature intended to give a total immunity for all outrages committed in collection of revenue.

Nov. 25th, 1848. E. PERRY.

In the Privy Council.

1850.

The appeal was argued in this year by *Wigram*, for the appellants, and by *Peacock*, for the respondents.

Cur. adv. vult.

Feb. 22.

Lord CAMPBELL, on the 22nd of February, 1850, delivered the following judgment, reversing the decision of the Court below:—

The foregoing decision reversed in Privy Council, on the ground that the statute gives immunity from action, in cases of breaches of the law, if the revenue officer, *bonâ fide*, and not absurdly, believes that he is acting legally.
2. The statute giving an immunity from action need not be pleaded specially.

This is an appeal from a judgment of the Supreme Court at Bombay. The action was brought by Hurkissondass Hurgovindass deceased, the husband of the respondent, who is his executrix. The declaration complained that the defendants broke and entered the plaintiff's house within the fort walls of Bombay, and carried away a globe lamp his property, which they converted and disposed of to their own use. The defendants pleaded only "not guilty."

The trial came on before Sir T. E. PERRY, a Judge of the Supreme Court, when it appeared from the evidence of the witnesses called by the plaintiff, and documentary evidence adduced by him, that in November, 1846, he was residing in the house mentioned in the declaration; that in respect of this house there was a small annual payment in the nature of quit rent due to the East India Company; that this house had formerly belonged to one Tookaydass, in whose name it still remained registered in the collector's books; that in the year 1836 it had been sold, under an execution by the sheriff, to a person who soon after sold it to the plaintiff; that the quit rent was in arrear from the year 1827; that in October, 1846, by the authority of the defendant Spooner, the collector of the Company at Bombay, the arrears, amounting to 8 rupees, 3 annas, 8 pice, were demanded from the plaintiff; that he offered to pay the quit rent which had become due while he was owner of the house, but denied his liability for the prior arrears; that therefore the defendant Spooner, as collector, granted a warrant to distrain for the whole arrears on the goods of Tookaydass, who appeared to be the registered owner of the house, and that under this warrant the other defendant, on the 24th of November, 1846, entered the plaintiff's house and, having again demanded and been refused payment of the arrears, seized and carried away the globe lamp in satisfaction of the demand.

At the close of the plaintiff's case, the Advocate General, as counsel for the defendants, objected that, under the statutes and charters constituting the Court, this action could not be maintained, as the supposed cause of action was "a matter concerning the revenue under the management of the Governor and council at Bombay, and concerning an act done according to the usage and practice of the country and the regulations of the Governor and council of Bombay," which authorized a distress for any arrears of quit rent. The plaintiff's counsel contended that this objection could not be taken without a special plea to the jurisdiction, and that, if pleaded, it would be unavailing. The learned Judge reserved the question for future consideration.

A witness was then examined on the part of the defendants with the view of shewing that the distress under the warrant was lawful. But the learned Judge held the distress to be unlawful, and directed a verdict to be entered for the plaintiff with Rs. 250 damages.

The case was afterwards argued before the same learned Judge (who was then the only Judge of the Court), and after a very learned and elaborate judgment he decided in favour of the plaintiff.

On account of the great importance of the question, on a special application to this Court their Lordships gave leave to appeal notwithstanding the small amount of the damages, the East India Company undertaking to pay the costs of the appeal on both sides.

Two questions arise: first, whether the objection to the jurisdiction of the Court could be taken under the plea of Not Guilty, and, secondly, whether the objection be well founded.

1850.

SPOONER v. HURKISSONDASS.

Lord CAMPBELL.

On the first question we have had some difficulty, and my own opinion has varied during the argument. It appears from the books of practice cited that it has been usual to plead such a defence in the Indian Courts, and certainly the convenient course would be to put it upon the record. The issue joined seems simply to be whether the alleged trespasses were committed by the defendants, and it is urged that the necessity for a special plea is rendered more urgent by the New Rules introduced at Bombay, which provide that in actions of trespass under the plea of Not Guilty no defence shall be given in evidence which confesses and avoids.

However, looking to the statutes and charters under which this Court is constituted, and to the cases in point which have been decided in Westminster Hall, we have come to the conclusion that the Court under the plea of Not Guilty was bound to admit the objection.

His Lordship then gave his reasons for this view, which turning on a point of special pleading are omitted.

Upon the second question we have not been able to entertain any doubt. Whether the plaintiff might have redress before any other tribunal can only be material in a doubtful construction of the statutes and charters establishing the Court in which the action was brought. If by these statutes and charters its jurisdiction in this action is clearly taken away, our decision could not be influenced by the consideration that the plaintiff is left without remedy.

We are of opinion that the quit rent being part of the revenue of the East India Company, the cause of action is a matter concerning the revenue under the management of the Governor and Council of Bombay, and concerning an act done according to the Regulations of the Governor and Council of Bombay. The quit rent goes into the Treasury of the East India Company, and the defendants *bonâ fide* professed to act under Regulation XIX. of the Regulations made by the Governor and Council of Bombay giving power to the collector to distrain for all arrears of rent due to the Company. For this purpose no distinction can be taken between this quit rent and the rent due from the Rajahs or Zemindars in respect of the land which they occupy and cultivate.

1850.

SPOONER v. HURKISSON-DASS.

Lord CAMPBELL.

The point therefore is, whether the exception of jurisdiction only arises where the defendants have acted strictly according to the usage and practice of the country and the Regulations of the Governor and Council. But upon this supposition the proviso is wholly nugatory; for if the Supreme Court is to inquire whether the defendants in this matter concerning the public revenue were right in the demand made and to decide in their favour only if they acted in entire conformity to the Regulations of the Governor and Council of Bombay, they would equally be entitled to succeed if the statutes and the charters contained no exception or proviso for their protection (*a*). Our books actually swarm with decisions putting a contrary construction upon such enactments, and there can be no rule more firmly established than that if parties *bonâ fide* and not absurdly believe that they are acting in pursuance of statutes and according to law, they are entitled to the special protection which the Legislature intended for them although they have done an illegal act. In this case it may well be that the warrant against the goods of Tookaydass did not authorize the taking the goods of Hurgovindass, or even that Hurgovindass might not be liable for the arrears of quit rent which occurred before he became owner of the house. Still the collector was evidently of opinion that a distress might be made for the whole of the arrears due, and that it was sufficient to introduce into the warrant the name of Tookaydass in whose name the house continued to be registered. The other defendant never could have doubted the sufficiency of the warrant. If Indian revenue officers have fallen into a mistake, or without bad faith have been guilty of an excess in executing the duties of their office, the object of the Legislature has been that they should not be liable to be sued in a civil action before the Supreme

(*a*) With great submission, this would not be the case: the *usage and practice* of the country might comprise many acts for the collection of the revenue, which without this clause would be illegal by English law; so also if it was deemed necessary to introduce any new practice however stringent and arbitrary, it is open to the Governor and Council by new regulation to do so—but if neither ancient 'usage and practice,' nor modern regulation, authorized the act in question, then the argument is that the Legislature did not intend to except any such act from the supervision of the law.

1850.

SPOONER v. HURKISSON-DASS.

Lord CAMPBELL.

Courts. Liability to be prosecuted criminally stands upon a totally different foundation.

We must view the question of the jurisdiction of the Supreme Court of India in cases of revenue upon the supposition that there are peculiar Courts in which these questions are to be discussed and decided. In England, if such an action were brought in any other Court than the Court of Exchequer it would be a mere matter of course to remove it into that Court and to prevent any other Court taking cognizance of it. Thus in the seventh year of James I.:—"Process issued out of the Exchequer to levy an amercement of 10*l.*; the bailiff levied the amercement. I. S., the person on whom it was levied, brought trespass; and it was said by the Barons and ordered, that if I. S. will bring an action for the distraining of this amercement, be it lawfully imposed or not, yet I. S. shall be restrained to sue in any other Court but in this, and here he shall sue in the office of Pleas, for the bailiff levied it as an officer of this Court;" *Lane's Exchequer Reports, 55.*

The same doctrine is to be found in *Cawthorne* v. *Campbell,* 1 Anstr. 205, and I can testify that I myself, while I had the honor of being Attorney General to the Crown, in several instances stopped actions commenced in the Courts of King's Bench and Common Pleas by an application to the Court of Exchequer, upon an allegation that the King's revenue came in question in the subject to be discussed, without attempting to shew that the parties impleaded had acted lawfully and had a good defence.

We are therefore bound to differ from the Judge below, who says that "the jurisdiction of his Court has not been taken away when the act complained of is not warranted by the usage of the country or by the Company's Regulations." If it concerned the revenue, or was a matter concerning an act *bonâ fide* believed to be done according to the Regulations of the Governor and Council of Bombay, his jurisdiction was gone, although *primâ facie* it appeared to be a trespass over which his jurisdiction might be properly exercised.

We hope that if the plaintiff was injured he might have had redress by a different proceeding; but at any rate we are of opinion that he was not entitled to redress by suing in the Supreme Court at Bombay, and we shall humbly advise her Majesty that the judgment appealed against should be reversed.

1843.
May 8.

THE QUEEN *v.* LE GEYT.

[*Coram* PERRY, J.]

Where a prisoner who had escaped from civil custody in Mysore, (a state in alliance with the Hon. Company), and had been apprehended in Cutch, was sent down to Bombay in order to be remitted to his former custody in Mysore, the Court, on these facts appearing on a return to a *habeas corpus*, refused to discharge the prisoner, although there did not appear to be any formal warrant for his detention.

CRAWFORD had obtained a writ of habeas corpus addressed to the chief magistrate of police to bring up the body of one Hurridass Heerjee.

The return was filed this day, and set out that the prisoner was in custody on a judgment obtained in Mysore, a state in alliance with the Honorable Company, but whose civil and military jurisdiction was administered by the Honorable Company; that the prisoner escaped from custody and went to his native country, and that the Rao of Cutch, on application made to him, gave up the prisoner:

That, on requisition of the Resident of Mysore, the Resident at the Court of the Rao had forwarded the prisoner to the Government in Bombay to be remitted to Mysore to his former custody:

That Mr. Le Geyt, as chief magistrate under the orders of the Government, had kept the prisoner in custody until he could be so forwarded by the first opportunity.

Crawford and *Dickinson* contended that the return was insufficient, as the warrant on which he was detained should have been set out, and consequently the prisoner should be discharged.

PERRY, J.—*Regina* v. *Suddis,* (1 East), shews that this objection ought not to prevail in a case of this kind. *Non constat* that there was any warrant, and the Court is bound to ascertain whether there has been any violation of substantial justice before it can order a prisoner to be discharged.

Prisoner remanded.

1847.

October 11.

AGA MAHOMED JAFFER
v.
MAHOMED SADUCK.

[*Coram* PERRY, C. J.]

Conflict between the jurisdiction of the Supreme Court and Mofussil Court.

It is a contempt of the Supreme Court to arrest its officer while in execution of its process, and the officers of the Mofussil Court who effect the arrest are liable to be committed.

A party in the Mofussil who lays claim to property seized in execution by the sheriff, may be called upon by a process under the Interpleader Act to come in and support his claim.

THE plaintiff in this case, having obtained a verdict, issued out execution and seized some horses of defendant at Nassick in the Mofussil (*a*), whereupon a Nassick creditor, claiming the said horses under mortgage, filed a suit before the Sudr Amin of Nassick against the European bailiff who had made the seizure and against the plaintiff, and in this suit the bailiff was arrested and detained at Nassick.

The Advocate General thereupon applied to PERRY, C. J., to indorse the process of the Nassick Judge against the plaintiff, and contended that it was compulsory on the Judge so to do. *Wallace* made a cross motion, calling on the Nassick plaintiff to appear in this Court to maintain or abandon his claim.

Cur. adv. vult.

PERRY, C. J.—In the case of the sheriff's bailiff, who has been imprisoned at Nassick under a writ of the Sudr Amin respecting some property which he seized by virtue of a writ issuing out of this Court, and in which Mr. *Wallace* applied for a rule under the Interpleader Act calling on the Nassick creditor to shew cause here as to his claim to the property seized, I have also been applied to by the assistant Judge of Nassick to indorse his process calling upon the Bombay creditor, Aga Mahomed Jaffer, to defend the suit in the Nassick Court.

(*a*) Mofussil in India is the term opposed to Presidency, and Presidency denotes the seat of Government, as Calcutta, Madras, Bombay, so that the distinction is much equivalent to town and country. At the Presidencies English law prevails, in the Mofussil Company's law.

Questions which involve any possible collision of Courts of justice are attended with such unpleasant results that every friend of good government must deprecate seeing them raised unnecessarily, and must desire, when they are unavoidably brought forward, that a clear intelligible rule should be forthcoming by which they may be disposed of before passion and intemperance have arisen on either side.

I have thought it best, therefore, to point out at this early stage what the rule of the English law is, in order to prevent a collision between two co-ordinate Courts.

The facts in this case seem to be as follows. The Bombay plaintiff brought an action against a Bombay defendant and recovered a verdict for about Rs. 20,000. Before judgment was signed the defendant had removed his property, consisting of horses, to Nassick, where during the rains a better climate and cheaper food are procurable. The plaintiff, on discovering this fact, obtained the process of the Supreme Court and seized the defendant's horses at Nassick, and on the sheriff's bailiff having done so, a Nassick creditor comes forward with an alleged mortgage on these horses, and obtains from the Sudr Amin of that jurisdiction a warrant to arrest the bailiff in a suit to recover their value. The horses are brought to Bombay, the bailiff remains in durance, and the Nassick creditor and the Bombay creditor are now each anxious to have the question as to the right to these horses determined in the respective Courts of their own domicile.

Now on these facts there can be no doubt that if the Sudr Amin had any discretion to exercise he has acted indiscreetly in allowing this bailiff to be arrested. No complaint seems to have been made as to the mode in which the bailiff executed this writ; he was merely acting as a servant for an absent principal, and as an officer under the special authority of this Court, and he would have been punishable if he had not so acted. This is not the mode in which the officers of a Court of justice should be dealt with on a question of property by co-ordinate Courts, much less by the Court of the Sudr Amin with respect to an officer of the Supreme Court. If the Sudr Amin had the power of obtaining the opinion of the Zillah

1847.

JAFFER v. SADUCK.

Judges or of the law officers of Government in a novel case, for which no guide is to be found in the Regulations, I feel no doubt that he would have been counselled to have nothing to do with the suit. The Advocate General would have told him that the cases are numerous, clear, and specific, in England to shew that where Courts of exclusive jurisdiction exist, they have been in the habit of preventing other Courts from interfering with their jurisdiction. No Court of superior jurisdiction will allow the conduct of its officer to be canvassed in another tribunal. The Court of Exchequer, the Court of Common Pleas, the Court of Chancery, always interfere if any other Court, though of equal power with themselves, entertain a suit respecting the conduct of their officers. (See the cases collected by Lord CAMPBELL *arguendo* in *Stockdale* v. *Hansard*.)

This being, therefore, the clear principle with English law, the question is how to apply it in India. Where the Supreme Court has jurisdiction in the Mofussil, it executes its process by its own officers. Any interference with the execution of such process is a contempt of this Court, and the party so interfering may be proceeded against by attachment. To bring an action against the officer who executes the process is an interference with the process, and the party who brings the action may be committed for a contempt, and so also any parties who assist in the bringing of the action, such as the officers of the Sudr Amin who make the arrest, may be themselves imprisoned. The power of this Court, therefore, depends entirely on the exercise of physical power against those who invade the well recognised principle of law.

Thus in *Brass Crosby's case*, where the Lord Mayor of London committed an officer of the House of Commons for a trespass in executing its process, the House of Commons committed the Lord Mayor to Newgate, and four Judges of the realm, comprising Lord Chief Justice DE GREY, and Sir W. BLACKSTONE, held that the chief officer of the city of London was properly committed.

There appears to me, therefore, to be no doubt that the Nassick plaintiff might be committed by this Court for con-

1847.

JAFFER v. SADUCK.

tempt. It may be a matter of hardship that a *bonâ fide* mortgagee should have to come down to Bombay, a hundred miles distant from his home, to prosecute his right; on the other hand, it would be much greater hardship to a Bombay creditor if the process of this Court could be defeated by the mere setting up a native mortgage, which we may be sure would never be wanting if it be discovered to be an effectual instrument for frustrating the execution of the Supreme Court. The case, however, is not to be disposed of by the consideration of hardships on either side, but by the rule of law applicable.

From the principles which I have stated it is quite clear that the Supreme Court is the forum in which the Bombay plaintiff is entitled to have his rights determined. I therefore have no difficulty in determining to refuse my indorsement to the process of the assistant Judge which summons Aga Mahomed Jaffer to Nassick.

With respect to Mr. *Wallace's* application I have more difficulty. He demands that the Nassick plaintiff should be summoned to Bombay to support his claim, because the subject-matter, the horses, are in Bombay. I doubt, whether as the subject-matter is moveable property, this affords any ground for jurisdiction. But the Interpleader Act states, that if *any party* makes any claim to property seized by the sheriff, such party may be called on by the Court to maintain or abandon his claim. These words are quite large enough to include the Nassick claimant, and I do not at present see anything in the spirit of Indian legislation to prevent the words having their full effect. I think, therefore, Mr. *Wallace* may have a rule nisi, to be served at present on the Advocate General only. This will give an opportunity of considering the last question, but above all it will call the attention of Government and its law officers to the subject, and will enable them to take the course which sound discretion and the powers vested in them may warrant or dictate.

Rule Nisi.

No cause being shewn against this rule it was afterwards made absolute.

1847. Nov. 26.

KHURSETJEE MANOCKJEE *v.* DADABHAI KHURSETJEE AND ANOTHER.

[*Coram* PERRY, C. J., and YARDLEY, J.]

A suit in a Zillah Court having been confirmed on appeal by the Privy Council, who decreed that the appellant or his representatives should pay the amount awarded, and the Sudr Adalut having directed the Zillah Court to carry out such decree, the Zillah Judge issued a summons to the representatives, who were inhabitants of Bombay, to appear in the Zillah Court and shew cause why they should not obey the decree, which was laid before the Judges of the Supreme Court for indorsement, and it being a matter of doubt whether the representatives were liable to the Zillah Court or not, the Supreme Court, under the circumstances, indorsed the writ in order to enable the point to be raised below.

It is discretionary with the Judges of the Supreme Courts to indorse a Mofussil process, and they ought not to do so unless the parties are liable to the jurisdiction of the Mofussil Court.

IN this case considerable discussion took place on the point whether the Judges had any discretion to exercise in the indorsement of Mofussil process, under Act 23 of 1840: *Le Messurier*, A. G., and *Dickinson* contending strenuously that they had not, and that the practice of the other Supreme Courts in India was to indorse all process presented to them indiscriminately.

Howard, contrà.

The Chief Justice intimated that he would communicate with the Chief Justices at Calcutta and Madras to learn their practice; and afterwards delivered judgment as follows.

PERRY, C. J.—This is an application to the Court, under Act 23 of 1840, to indorse a writ of execution issued by the Judge at Surat against the property of the late Khursetjee Manockjee.

It appears by the proceedings that Dadabhai obtained a decree to account against Khursetjee in the Surat Court in 1829, which was confirmed on appeal by the Privy Council in 1837. Under that decree the Judge at Surat made an order for a jury to investigate the accounts, who found that Rs. 2,10,837 were due from Khursetjee to Dadabhai, and this sum the Surat Judge, on 10th May, 1843, decreed to be paid by Khursetjee.

1847.

KHURSETJEE v. DADABHAI.

It would seem that Khursetjee was a resident at Bombay, and after the decision of the Privy Council unsuccessful attempts were made to obtain his appearance in the Surat Court, but before any execution could be obtained of the decree of May, 1843, Khursetjee died (it does not exactly appear when, but apparently) in 1845.

Regulation 4 of 1827, sect. 100, directs that the decrees of her Majesty's Privy Council shall be enforced by the Zillah Judge acting under the directions of the Sudr Adalut; and as the Privy Council decreed that the sum of Rs. 2,10,837 should be paid by Khursetjee or his representatives, the order in question is made under the directions of the Sudr upon the representatives who are inhabitants of Bombay and subject to the jurisdiction of the Supreme Court.

When the application was first made to this Court in 1846 to allow execution of the Surat decree to be levied upon Khursetjee's representatives at Bombay, Sir HENRY ROPER and myself refused the application upon the following grounds. We thought that the intention of Act 23 of 1840 was to place creditors who had obtained judgments in the Mofussil Courts in the same position with respect to the persons and property of their debtors, which might happen to be situated in Bombay, as Bombay creditors are placed in after having obtained judgment in the Supreme Court. But as the rule of English law generally is, that execution cannot be taken out on a judgment more than a year old, or against the representatives of a party against whom the decree was obtained, without a fresh application to the Court, by which an opportunity is given to the party sought to be charged to shew cause, if he have any, why execution should not issue, we thought that the exigency of justice required that some such opportunity should be given to the Bombay executors. A Bombay creditor would clearly have been compelled to bring them before the Court, and there is nothing whatever in the act, and no possible reason can be suggested, to shew that Mofussil creditors were to be allowed greater advantage than Bombay creditors.

On this intimation of the opinion of the Court, the Mofussil creditor summoned the Bombay representatives to appear in

1847.

KHURSETJEE v. DADABHAI.

the said Court to shew why execution should not issue against them, and on their refusal to appear there, the Zillah Judge made the order which this Court is now asked to indorse.

It has been contended by the Advocate General, who applied for the indorsement of the Mofussil process, that the duty of this Court, under Act 23 of 1840, is merely ministerial, and that, as the provisions in question are made for the advancement of justice, the clause enabling such process to be enforced in the Presidency by the indorsement of the Judge is imperative upon the Judge, although the words used are that he *may*, not that he *shall*, indorse.

A different construction has been placed upon this act by the Judges of Bombay, from Chief Justice AWDREY's time to the present, and I have repeatedly refused to indorse process summoning inhabitants of Bombay to appear as defendants in a distant Court, where I could not discover from any part of the documents submitted to me that the inhabitant of Bombay was liable to the Mofussil jurisdiction.

It was suggested, however, that a different course was adopted by the Supreme Courts of Calcutta and Madras, and as it is obviously desirable that her Majesty's Courts should adopt a uniform procedure upon the same act of the Legislature, I have communicated with the Chief Justices of Calcutta and Madras in order to learn their practice.

It appears that those Courts agree with the Supreme Court at Bombay in thinking that the clause requiring the Judge's indorsement is not compulsory. This being so, the question in each case is one for the discretion of the Judge before whom the proceedings are laid; and as in every case where discretionary powers are attributed occasional differences of opinion will exist, it is eminently desirable, if possible, to lay down some principle by which that discretion shall be guided.

The plain object of the act appears to me to be to prevent the frustration of justice by the jurisdiction of the Supreme Court interfering with the execution of Mofussil process over persons and property subject to the Mofussil Courts; and I think that, to carry out this object, it is the duty of this Court to be forward in lending its assistance to

1847.

KHURSETJEE *v.* DADABHAI.

back any Mofussil process that may be presented to it, and I would therefore strive to make the act of the Judge as ministerial as possible, and would never refuse to indorse except on grounds that appear to me irresistible.

But it also seems to me quite clear that the Mofussil Process Act does not give the Mofussil Judges any extension of jurisdiction, and accordingly that if they summon defendants to their Courts, who on the face of their process appear to be liable to the Supreme Court only, it is the duty of the Judges of the Supreme Court to withhold their indorsement.

The present case stands midway between the above two positions. It appears to me to be a doubtful question whether the Bombay executors are subject to the jurisdiction of the Surat Court; and the immediate point to be decided is, whether this question should be discussed and decided in the Surat Court or here. Many arguments suggest themselves for either view of the question; on the one hand, it is clear that the Supreme Court is the *forum* to which the executors are amenable for every claim against them, and it may be hard upon them to be drawn away to another Court to discuss their liabilities. On the other hand, parties in this country may be, and often are, liable to the jurisdiction of two separate forums.

The liability of the executors depends much on the jurisdiction clauses of the Regulations, and on the expositions which have been made of them, with neither of which this Court is familiar, and which may be more fitly decided by the Mofussil and its appellate Courts.

On the whole, after discussing the matter carefully with my learned colleague, we think that the balance of conveniences requires that this process should be indorsed, and that the question of jurisdiction should be raised in the Surat Court, although possibly the same question may be also forced directly upon us by an action against the sheriff.

1849.
July 23.

CASE OF DHARWAR PROCESS.

[*Coram* PERRY, C. J., and YARDLEY, J.]

Exposition of Mofussil Process Act, No. 23 of 1840.

1. The Mofussil Judges have no jurisdiction over parties on their personal obligations, unless they are resident within the Mofussil jurisdiction. Therefore where an inhabitant of Bombay authorized his agent to enter into a security bond for a defendant in a suit pending before the Judge at Dharwar, *Held*, that such act did not bring him within the jurisdiction of the Dharwar Judge, and that therefore the Judges of the Supreme Court ought not to indorse process of the Dharwar Court to compel the attendance of the Bombay inhabitant before the Court at Dharwar, *dubitante* YARDLEY, J.

2. The act of indorsement by the Queen's Judges is judicial, not ministerial.

3. Zillah Judges have authority to summon witnesses from Bombay, although not subject to their jurisdiction; but they have no authority over Bombay residents as defendants to suits, unless their jurisdiction has already accrued, per PERRY, C. J.

A MOFUSSIL writ from the Court at Dharwar ordering the sheriff to take bail for the appearance of D. and M. Pestonjee before the Dharwar Court having been presented to the Judge in Chambers (YARDLEY, J.), was indorsed by him in the usual form. But the liability of these parties to the Dharwar jurisdiction having been disputed, the writ was brought before the full Court on a former day, when

Howard moved that the indorsement should be cancelled on two grounds; first, that the Pestonjees, being inhabitants of Bombay, were not liable to the jurisdiction of the Dharwar Judge; secondly, that the Dharwar Judge had not proceeded according to the Regulations, and that he had taken a security bond from the agent, which he had no authority to exact.

Le Messurier, A. G., *contrà*, contended that this Court had no jurisdiction to exercise under Act 23 of 1840, but were bound to indorse all such Mofussil process as should be brought before it, and if such process were irregular or void the proper tribunal for correcting it was the Sudr Adalut. In support of these views he relied strongly on a written opinion in a letter from Sir L. PEEL, Chief Justice at Calcutta, and on a former decision of this Court in the *Surat case* (*ante*, p. 402). He further contended that the act of the Pestonjees in giving a security bond through their agent clearly made them liable to the Dharwar Court.

1849.

Case of DHARWAR PROCESS.

THE COURT held that they were bound to exercise a discretion as to what process was indorsable under Act 23 of 1840, and that if a mere ministerial act were required the interposition of the Queen's Judges would not have been required; and they animadverted on the impropriety of reading the private opinions of Judges of other Courts as being contrary to sound practice. The Court also held that it ought to appear on the face of the Mofussil process in what way the inhabitants of Bombay sued in a Zillah Court were liable to its jurisdiction, and as this fact did not appear on the face of the writ, it was remanded back to the Judge at Dharwar to state in what manner the jurisdiction arose.

The writ in its amended form was in substance as follows:—

"Whereas a decree was passed by W. E. FRERE, Esq., Judge of Zillah of Dharwar, to the effect that defendant should pay to plaintiff Rs. 98,125, and whereas plaintiff has petitioned that the decree should be enforced against the defendant's securities, D. and M. Pestonjee, who stood security for the defendant in Rs. 48,742 to produce certain property of the defendant, or part thereof, sufficient to satisfy the judgment that should be passed against him provided the defendant should not have fulfilled the decree; and whereas the defendant has not fulfilled the decree; therefore the securities D. and M. Pestonjee, now residing in Bombay, are required to produce the aforesaid property before the said Judge within sixty days from the date of this process, or in default to pay the sum of Rs. 48,742 to the person directed to execute this process within the limits of the Supreme Court, and on the said securities failing, &c. to take their bodies, so that they may be before the said Court at Dharwar within sixty days from the date hereof."

The indorsement on the writ was in the usual form, ordering the sheriff to execute the within process according to the tenor thereof.

Le Messurier, A. G., and *Crawford* now moved for the indorsement of the writ.

Howard, *contrà*. There are two objections; first, that

1849.

Case of DHARWAR PROCESS.

which was argued before, that a Mofussil Court has no jurisdiction over inhabitants of Bombay; secondly, that the writ is incapable of being executed. The sheriff is a mere ministerial officer, and only does what he is told. But he is ordered here to arrest the parties and to take them to Dharwar unless they perform the agreement. But the agreement is to produce the property of the defendant mentioned in a schedule, when required, or to pay such amount as the property not produced is there valued at. How is the sheriff to ascertain whether the property has been produced or not, or how much has been produced, or what the value is? It is clear that there ought to have been two processes, the Pestonjees should have been summoned to produce the property, and on their failure the Judge should have issued his writ against them for a sum certain.

Le Messurier, A. G., in reply. It is unnecessary to re-argue the point as to jurisdiction. As to the second point, if the writ is not so regular or so formal as those known in English practice, the remedy is not here, but the parties should go to the Sudr Adalut. The whole question, therefore, is whether the Dharwar Judge had jurisdiction or not.

PERRY, C. J., observed, that after the former argument he had looked carefully into the question of jurisdiction, and had written down his views at length, and as his opinion was quite clear against the jurisdiction, he would read the judgment he then prepared, which, with a few alterations, entirely met the present argument.

In the case of the Mofussil process from the Court of Dharwar the writ recites that the Judge there having decreed that one of the parties in a suit before him should pay Rs. 98,125, and the successful party having applied to the Judge to enforce this decree against the securities of the defendant, *viz.*, Dadabhai and Muncherjee Pestonjee, who are inhabitants of Bombay, and who had been securities for the Dharwar defendant to the extent of Rs. 48,742, the Judge accordingly issues his writ, requiring Dadabhai and Muncherjee Pestonjee, now residing

Case of DHARWAR PROCESS.

in Bombay, to produce the property of the Dharwàr defendant before the Dharwar Judge within sixty days, or in default the sheriff is to arrest them and to take them to Dharwar unless they pay the sum of Rs. 48,742 forthwith.

As Dharwar is nearly 400 miles from Bombay, and with the ordinary facilities for travel in this country at least twenty days journey distant, it is not at all surprising that the Bombay securities should make vigorous attempts to resist being sued out of their own forum.

The case was brought before the Court on a former occasion, and on its appearing on the face of the writ that the Pestonjees were inhabitants of Bombay, and as such only subject on their personal obligations to the Bombay Court, the process was referred back to the Zillah Judge to state in what mode they had made themselves liable to the Dharwar jurisdiction.

The Judge makes a return, by which it appeared that the Pestonjees in Bombay authorized by letter a Parsee at Dharwar to sign their names to what is called in the letter of authority a security bond; and the main question now is, whether this act of the Pestonjees in Bombay makes them liable to the Dharwar jurisdiction.

Construction of Mofussil Process Act, 23 of 1840.

The question turns mainly on the Mofussil Process Act, No. 23 of 1840, which has given rise to so much discussion, and its due construction appears to be still a matter of so much doubt, that it is eminently desirable to take this opportunity of pointing out what the duty of the Judges of the Supreme Court is when Mofussil process is presented to them for indorsement.

By the enactment in the first clause any writ or other process issued by any Court or magistrate in the Mofussil may be executed within the limits of the Supreme Court, on its being presented to a Judge of the Supreme Court and receiving his indorsement directing the sheriff to execute it.

The generality of the words used in the enactment is such that it is not at all surprising to find that many Mofussil Judges have construed it as giving them power to issue their process to apprehend an inhabitant of Bombay whenever the interests of justice appear to them to require it. But all jurists

1849.

Case of DHARWAR PROCESS.

Axiom of jurisprudence: a defendant should be sued in the forum of his residence.

are aware, that although some nice questions exist in certain cases as to what the proper forum is in which a defendant should be called upon to answer, it is a fundamental axiom in all systems that a defendant is entitled to be sued in the Courts where he himself resides on all personal liabilities. And it may be laid down as a universal rule, that, with respect to personal obligations, no Court possesses a jurisdiction over the person unless the defendant happens to be present within the local limits of that jurisdiction.

Now, as the act in question does not contain one word expressive of any intention to alter fundamental rules as to jurisdiction, and as it would be open to much argument whether the Legislative Council possesses authority to extend the jurisdiction of the Zillah Courts over the Presidency towns, it is clear that the general words in the first enactment must be restricted, and applied, to carry out the intentions which are very clearly expressed in the preamble.

The preamble recites that inconvenience has been experienced in consequence of the difficulty of procuring inhabitants of the Presidency to attend as witnesses before the Mofussil authorities, and in consequence of justice being often frustrated by reason of persons and property within such limits being exempted from process issued by such authorities.

For the ends of justice all parties should be compelled to attend Court as witnesses:

Two different subject-matters are here referred to, and they must be carefully distinguished. The first is the attendance of witnesses; and as it is a recognised duty in every citizen, according to English notions, to give his evidence in Courts of justice when the interests of the state or of private individuals require it, and as the inhabitants of the Mofussil and the Presidency are so much intermingled, it seems very desirable that process to compel the attendance of necessary witnesses should follow them into whatever jurisdiction they may happen to be; and I conceive that the true construction of the act is to give the Zillah authorities power to issue their process in all such cases.

the act gives Zillah Judge power to enforce such attendance.

I may, however, remark, that although the same sort of exigency exists between adjoining counties in England and Scotland, the difficulties inherent in the subject have apparently prevented the Imperial Legislature from passing any act similar to the present.

1849.

Case of DHARWAR PROCESS.

The second object aimed at by the act is to prevent justice being frustrated by reason of persons and property within the Presidency limits being exempted from process issued by the Mofussil authorities. The key note to this clause is to be found in the words "frustration of justice," and whenever it can be made appear to a Judge of the Supreme Court that justice will be frustrated unless he indorse the Mofussil process, I conceive that in his judicial discretion he will be, generally speaking, at liberty to do so.

Subjects of the same Government should not be allowed to defeat justice by flitting from one jurisdiction to another.

Act prevents this evil.

But, for the reasons I have before given, I cannot believe that this clause was intended to extend the jurisdiction of the Zillah Courts over suitors not otherwise amenable to their jurisdiction. On the contrary, it appears to me quite plain that the only object in view by the Legislature in this behalf was to prevent the already existing jurisdiction of the Zillah Court being defeated by a temporary removal of the person or property to the Presidency jurisdiction. And if this is, as I conceive it to be, the true meaning of the act, it follows that the Zillah Judges have not authority to summon inhabitants of the Presidency to answer suits in their Courts, unless their jurisdiction over them has already accrued.

But does not give Zillah Judges an increased jurisdiction.

Whenever, therefore, Mofussil process is presented to a Judge of the Supreme Court for indorsement, it behoves him to satisfy himself that the inhabitant of Bombay, who is sought to be made a defendant in a distant Court, is subject to the jurisdiction of the Zillah Court; and the practice of the Madras Judges, which in fact corresponds with our own, appears to afford the correct rule, for the Judges there always require that the Mofussil writ should shew that the Presidency defendant is amenable to the Mofussil jurisdiction.

Now the Regulation which defines the jurisdiction of the Zillah Courts in the Bombay Presidency, is Reg. II., s. 21, and it points out three cases in which the Zillah Judges has jurisdiction.

Jurisdiction of Zillah Courts defined, Reg. II. 21.

1. When immoveable property within the limits is in controversy.
2. When the cause of action arises there.

1849.

Case of DHARWAR PROCESS.

3. When the defendant is a *fixed inhabitant.*

In order to understand the meaning of this clause, and especially of the term *fixed inhabitant,* it is necessary to note a distinction which exists between the English and civil law as to jurisdiction, for it will be seen that the Bombay Regulations follow the doctrine of the latter, and I believe, in fact, that they were chiefly drawn up by a gentleman educated at the Scottish Bar (*a*).

Residence required for jurisdiction to arise varies in different codes.

By the English Law jurisdiction arises over a man, as to all his personal obligations, the instant he sets his foot within the territory, and if during that period he can be served with the process of the Court, he cannot plead that he is sued in a wrong forum. But by the civil law and the general rule a man can only be sued on personal liabilities in the forum of his domicile, and if he comes into a foreign jurisdiction as a mere sojourner it is a good answer to the jurisdiction of the Court, see *Erskine's Institutes,* B. 1, tit. 2. As this rule, however, must often operate evilly in defeating plaintiffs, for a man, though domiciled in one country, may be often sojourning in another, most civil law countries have engrafted an exception or supplement on the rule, and have laid down that a defendant may also be sued in the place where the contract was made, or where it was to be performed, and this is styled, in the language of the civilians, the forum *ratione contractus.* But to enable this jurisdiction to arise the personal presence of the defendant within the jurisdiction is an indispensable element; the authorities are cited by *Story* in his *Conflict of Laws,* and the following passage from *Huber* is conclusive, "*Sed contractus ita forum tribuit, si contrahens in eo loco reperiatur* (*b*)."

Regulations follow the civil, not the English law.

The meaning, therefore, of the Regulation clearly is that in respect of real property, and possibly, in all cases where the *action* is *in rem,* the jurisdiction attaches.

So, likewise, it does when the defendant is a fixed inhabitant. And so also when the defendant is a temporary

(*a*) The late Mr. Erskine, the distinguished orientalist, and prothonotary of the Recorder's Court, at Bombay, under his father in law Sir James Macintosh, and succeeding Judges.

(*b*) See also 3 Burge, 1018.

1849. Case of DHARWAR PROCESS.

inhabitant, provided that the cause of action arose within the particular Zillah. What length of time is necessary to bring a defendant within the second category as a fixed inhabitant, whether forty days as are required by the Scotch Courts, or longer, need not now be discussed.

To apply these principles to the present case, it is quite clear that Messrs. Dadabhai and Muncherjee do not come within any of these classes.

The suit against them is not to recover immoveable property, but a sum of money, they are not, therefore, within the first class; nor is it contended that they are fixed inhabitants of Dharwar so as to bring them within the third. The only pretence, therefore, which can be made for bringing them within the jurisdiction of the Dharwar Court is, that the cause of action arose there, but, as has been already shown, jurisdiction does not arise in such case unless the defendant can be found within that jurisdiction, and to cite the same writer (*Huber*) whom I before quoted, jurisdiction over defendants arises, first of all in the forum of a defendant's domicile; 2ndly, in cases of real property in the Court of the place where that property is situated; and 3rdly, in the place of the contract (*or res gesta*) if the defendant can be found there, otherwise not, *alias secus; Story, Conflict of Laws*, s. 537.

YARDLEY, J., observed, that on the former argument, as to jurisdiction, he was inclined to think that the Dharwar Judge had jurisdiction and he retained that opinion still. The jurisdiction appeared to come within the second category mentioned by the Chief Justice, the "cause of action having arisen at Dharwar." Where a party becomes security on a bail bond in the Supreme Court, it is true that he indorses upon the bail piece his assent to be sued in the Supreme Court if necessary, but he (Sir W. YARDLEY) considered that the authority given by the Pestonjees to their agent to execute this security bond was equivalent to express consent to be sued in the Dharwar Court. He stated, however, that he had not looked into this question so carefully as the Chief Justice who had often had to consider these points before;

1849.

Case of DHARWAR PROCESS.

and he added that he should feel great difficulty in imposing on the sheriff the difficulty of executing such a writ as the present.

Indorsement refused.

1844. March 14.

MARK PORRET'S CASE.

[*Coram* PERRY, J.]

1. Introduction of military law into India traced.
2. The Indian Mutiny Acts are modelled on the English acts, but they recognise three distinct armies, and three commanders-in-chief.
3. Where a prisoner is in custody under sentence of a Court martial, it is no ground for his discharge that the gaoler has received no *warrant* for his detention.
4. Defects in procedure at a Court martial are not cognizable by the Supreme Court, as the procedure is not governed by the Mutiny Act, but by the usages and customs of war, and by ancient practice in the army: but all constructions of the Mutiny Act and Articles of War constituting the powers of Courts martial may be called in question in the Supreme Court, if jurisdiction is denied.
5. Whenever any forces of the line are employed at the Presidency, the commander in-chief has the exclusive power of convening Courts martial; if none are employed, the Crown may authorize the Court of Directors to arm local governments with such power.
6. Where soldiers of one Presidency are serving in another Presidency, or out of the Company's territories, the authority to hold Courts martial over them must emanate from the commander-in-chief of their own Presidency, not of the army in which they may temporarily be serving.
7. If a portion of the Bombay army is serving in another Presidency, there is nothing in the Mutiny Act or Articles of War to prevent the commander-in-chief of the Bombay army delegating the authority to hold Courts martial over the Bombay army to any officer above the rank of a field officer, though not under his own command.
8. The Governor of Sindh commanding portions of the Bengal, Madras, and Bombay armies has no power to hold Courts martial over Bombay troops, except by virtue of the warrant he holds from the Bombay commander-in-chief: when, therefore, he confirmed the sentence of a Court martial which sentenced a European to seven years' transportation, and the warrant under which he had authority to convene Courts martial, directed all such sentences to be forwarded to the commander-in-chief for confirmation, *held*, that the imprisonment was illegal; and the prisoner was discharged (*a*).

CRAWFORD, on the 15th of November last, obtained a writ of *habeas corpus* to bring up the body of Mark Porret, who had been sent down from Sindh under sentence of a Court martial held by Major General Sir Charles Napier, Governor of Sindh, and awarding him seven years' transportation for embezzlement.

The return merely stated these facts, and did not set out under what authority Sir Charles Napier held the Court martial.

(*a*) In consequence of this decision the 6 & 7 Vict. was passed in order to guard against the difficulty in a similar case, but the difference between the Indian and the English armies, and the few cases reported on Courts martial will perhaps make the above discussion useful, more especially as the tendency to oppose one authority to another is so common where double jurisdictions exists, and cases may occur where the jurisdiction of the Supreme Courts over Courts martial will come in question.

1844. — PORRETT'S Case.

Crawford moved that the prisoner should be discharged, as the sentence was disproportioned to the offence, and as it did not appear that Sir Charles Napier had any authority to hold and confirm Courts martial; for although Governors of colonies have power to do so under the English Mutiny Act, the appointment of Sir Charles Napier as Governor of an Indian province could not give him any such authority.

Le Messurier, A. G. The Court will not discharge the prisoner on this application. The Government of Bombay is not in possession of the facts as to what authority Sir Charles Napier is acting under. Sir Charles Napier may have ample authority, and therefore it would be highly inconvenient to discharge the prisoner. The Supreme Government may have conferred upon him the power to hold Courts martial (*a*).

Sir ERSKINE PERRY, J., held that the prisoner could not be discharged on the present return, as it might turn out that the Governor of Sindh had ample authority; but he doubted whether the Governor General in Council had any power to enable him to hold Courts martial.

The prisoner was accordingly remanded.

Crawford, in February last, renewed his application, and moved for a rule nisi for a *habeas corpus*, on affidavits of the prisoner and his attorney that the prisoner was on the strength of the Bombay army, and that he was tried under a warrant granted by Lt. Gen. Sir T. M'Mahon, commander-in-chief of the Bombay army, which warrant required all such sentences to be confirmed by the commander-in-chief, and the present sentence had not been so confirmed.

Le Messurier, A. G., shewed cause, and contended that it was very dangerous to act on such affidavits. The Bombay Government have applied to the Bengal Government and to the commander-in chief in Bengal, to ascertain under whose authority Sir Charles Napier had acted, and no answer had yet been returned.

(*a*) See note at end of this case, *post*.

1844.

PORRETT'S Case.

PERRY, J. enlarged the rule for making the return until sufficient time for obtaining an answer from Bengal had elapsed.

On the 11th of March following the return was filed, by which it appeared that the Court martial had been held under the warrant of Sir Thomas M'Mahon, and had not been confirmed by him.

Le Messurier, A. G., now contended that confirmation was not necessary. The prisoner had been tried for embezzlement under sect. 16 of the Indian Mutiny Act, 3 & 4 Vict. c. 37, and that section does not say a word as to the necessity for confirmation. Article 67 of the Articles of War specifies the necessity for confirming a general Court martial, but if the articles and the act clash, the former must give way. If this is not the true construction the man must be discharged.

Crawford, contrà. The prisoner is a soldier of the Bombay army, and, therefore, he is entitled to the provisions in the Mutiny Act which are in his favour.

Cur. adv. vult.

March 14th.

PERRY, J.—In the case of Mark Porrett, who was brought before me by *habeas corpus* on Monday last, the return states that the prisoner is in the custody of the marshal of the gaol under sentence of a Court martial, which was held under a warrant granted by his Excellency Lieutenant General Sir Thomas M'Mahon to his Excellency Major General Sir Charles Napier, and as the proceedings on the former return and in the former rule are referred to, they may be taken as before the Court on the present occasion, though, in strict procedure, possibly, the return should have been amended by inserting them.

By these proceedings it appears that at a Court martial held at Karachi on the 23rd of August last, Mark Porrett, being a sub-conductor belonging to the Bombay army, was tried upon two charges, the first of which in substance was, the having, on a sale of unserviceable Government stores, altered the figures in a sale list with the fraudulent intention

1844.

PORRETT'S Case.

of appropriating the difference: the second, the having embezzled and fraudulently misapplied money of the Government amounting to Rs. 170, or thereabouts.

The Court upon the first charge found him guilty, with a slight exception not necessary to be noticed here, and upon the second they likewise found him guilty in these terms: "Guilty of substituting the amount of 159 rupees and 9 annas for 170 rupees, or thereabouts, such conduct being most disgraceful and unbecoming the character of a warrant officer. The sentence of the Court was that the prisoner should be transported as a felon for seven years.

This sentence was confirmed by Sir Charles Napier in the following manner: "Approved and confirmed by C. J. Napier, Governor;" and the prisoner was sent down under a military escort to Bombay, for the purpose of being forwarded to his destination.

The prisoner was brought before the Court on a *habeas corpus* in last November Term, when the above facts appeared, with the further one, that no warrant authorizing his detention in gaol had accompanied him, but this latter point had been urged unsuccessfully as an objection in cases of prisoners in England, for instance, in *The King* v. *Suddis*, (1 East), and in the late case of the Canadian prisoners. It may be perhaps considered as settled law, that it is not absolutely necessary that a warrant should accompany a prisoner in the course of his detention under sentence of a Court of competent jurisdiction. But various other objections were then urged as to the adequacy of the sentence, as to the deficiency of the proceedings in point of form, and, above all, as to the power of Sir Charles Napier to hold and confirm Courts martial, most of which were of an important character and fit to be considered somewhere, but serious questions arose as to how far it was competent to this Court to entertain them.

Some of these objections, however, were disposed of at the time; but as to others there was a deficiency of facts, in the absence of which the Court did not think it fit to pronounce any decision, more especially as nice points of military law were involved, on which very little assistance was to be derived from the usual sources of legal information.

1844. The case has come twice before the Court since November

Porrett's Case. Term last, on the first of which occasions a copy of the warrant granted by the commander-in-chief of Bombay to Sir Charles Napier was set out; and now on the face of the present return it is stated that the Court martial was held by virtue of that warrant.

Whether in point of fact it was so or not, and whether the Court is in possession of all the circumstances which have raised the difficulty in the present case so as to enable it to apply a solution, may perhaps be doubted (*a*).

At the first argument in this case much reliance was placed by the counsel for the prisoner on the objection arising out of what was termed the disproportionate punishment awarded to him in reference to the offence committed; but it was clear that this Court had no jurisdiction whatever to interfere on any such ground. The power of awarding punishment for military offences is left entirely to the discretion of Courts martial, and of the authorities by whom they are appointed; and when a discretionary power is thus vested, the Queen's superior Courts have no power to control it, even in the case of subordinate civil Courts. It is equally clear that all objections made to want of due formality on the face of the proceedings in the Court martial could not be listened to by this Court. It has been laid down over and over again that the superior Courts are not Courts of review for a Court martial. In *Sergeant Grant's case* (2 H. B. 107), there was an undoubted informality in the finding of the Court martial, but Lord Loughborough disposed of it in these terms: "It would be extremely absurd to comment upon it, as if it were a conviction before magistrates, which was to be discussed in a Court where that conviction could be reviewed." Lord Denman adopted the same language in a case in 5 *B. & Adol.* p. 688. So also in *Rex* v. *Suddis* (1 East), where an imperfect finding of a Court martial came before the Court of King's Bench, Lord Kenyon said, in answer to the objections made by the counsel of the prisoner: "We are not now sitting as a Court of error to review the regularity of these proceedings, nor are we to hunt after possible objections."

(*a*) See note (*a*) *post*, p. 433.

1844.

PORRETT'S Case.

The objection made in that case was indeed very like the objection made in the present, namely that, although under certain circumstances the Court martial might have had jurisdiction to award the punishment they had ordered, still those circumstances did not appear on the face of the proceedings: but Mr. Justice GROSE, after stating the objection, answered it thus: "That, however, is an objection in error, and we do not now sit as a Court of error. It is enough that we find such a sentence pronounced by a Court of competent jurisdiction to inquire into the offence, and with power to inflict such a sentence; as to the rest, we must presume *omnia rite acta.*"

Procedure of Courts martial founded on old usages, and regulations of the Crown not prescribed by statute law.

And the principle of the non-interference of the Courts of law with the procedure of Courts martial is clear and obvious. The groundwork of the jurisdiction, and the extent of the powers of Courts martial, are to be found in the Mutiny Act and the Articles of War, and upon all questions arising upon these her Majesty's Judges are competent to decide; but the Mutiny Act and Articles of War do not alone constitute the military code, for they are, for the most part, silent upon all that relates to the procedure of the military tribunals to be erected under them. Now this procedure is founded upon the usages and customs of war, upon the regulations issued by the Sovereign, and upon old practice in the army, as to all which points common law Judges have no opportunity, either from their law books or from the course of their experience, to inform themselves. It would therefore be most illogical, to say nothing of the impediments to military discipline which would thereby be interposed, to apply to the procedure of Courts martial those rules which are applicable to another and different course of practice.

The objections, therefore, which were founded on the informality of the sentence, and its want of finding distinctly whether an act of embezzlement had been committed, were not urged by the counsel subsequently to the first argument. But although the principle of non-interference was thus distinctly laid down by the Court, and the inclination to presume every thing in favour of the tribunals established by the Le-

1844.

PORRETT'S Case.

gislature was strongly manifested, still the grounds on which it is the bounden duty of this Court to interfere, on the demand of any British subject, to have the protection of the law extended to him, were equally present to our minds. Lord LOUGHBOROUGH, in a case where the sentence of a Court martial was in question, laid down the law on this point thus: "Naval Courts martial, military Courts martial, Courts of Admiralty, Courts of prize, are all liable to the controlling authority which the Courts of Westminster Hall have from time to time exercised for the purpose of preventing them from exceeding the jurisdiction given to them." A Court martial sits under the authority of the Mutiny Act and of the Articles of War; its constitution and powers, as to all the graver offences, are strictly defined by their express provisions, and if any parties but those contemplated by the Legislature assume to wield the powers therein defined, their proceedings are altogether void and, in law language, *coram non judice*; or, if the Court being duly constituted in the first instance, a procedure is adopted or sentence awarded contrary to the enactments of the Legislature, such sentence is wholly illegal Again, if any question arises as to what the proper construction of the statute upon the matters contained in it is, and any difference of opinion takes place amongst those who have to carry out its provisions, the competent tribunal—and the only competent tribunal to decide the difficulty—is that with which the construction of all the acts of the Legislature ultimately rests, namely, her Majesty's Courts of law.

Extent of jurisdiction over Courts martial, &c., by civil Courts.

It is impossible to help perceiving that such a difficulty exists in the present case, and however much indisposed the Court may be to pronounce any decision upon a statute which has but rarely formed the subject of legal controversy, and under which some divaricating practice may perhaps have occurred, still it is impossible to advert to the different positions on which the authority to hold Courts martial has been grounded on the one side, and to those on which it has been attacked on the other, without recognising the fact that the greatest uncertainty prevails upon the subject, and that no clear rule has been advanced by either party towards a

Differences of opinion amongst officers of Government.

1844.

PORRETT'S Case.

solution of the difficulty. But as, in the words of that great Judge, Lord STOWELL, it is the office of the Court to dispose of difficulties when they arise—not to state them, to send into the world decisions—not doubts, I will endeavour to lay down as briefly as possible what, upon a review of all the Mutiny Acts relating to this country and of the military code in England, I conceive to be the true exposition of the law with reference to the points raised in the present case.

Difficulties surrounding the question as to the authority to hold Courts martial over Company's forces.

The chief questions of difficulty which have arisen may, I conceive, be stated as follows: first, in whom has the Legislature vested the power of authorizing Courts martial over the Company's forces in India? second, in what mode is the power so granted to be delegated? It is evident that these two questions are essentially distinct; the Legislature may have defined very clearly the authorities from whom the power is to proceed, but in pointing out the mode in which the delegation of authority is to be made, expressions may have been used, and unforeseen cases may arise, which may render it very difficult to say how that power is to be put in exercise. Again, as provisions would have to be expressed in the act to embrace these two different objects, it may occasionally occur that the terms so used with respect to the one subject-matter will apparently clash with those previously laid down with respect to the other, and then the question arises (which is a question of construction), how are these several provisions to be reconciled so as to carry out the intention of the Legislature?

Now, as the sole end of all rules of construction with respect to written instruments, and more especially with respect to acts of Parliament, is to ascertain what the true intent and meaning of the language used amounts to, it is evident that no approach to any accurate conclusion on the subject can be made, without a careful survey of the circumstances which existed at the time when the Legislature interposed its authority, and of the objects which were chiefly in view in exercising legislation at all. So soon as these are distinctly ascertained a clue is provided by which any ambiguity that may arise on particular expressions can be solved.

1844.

PORRETT'S Case.

The objects of the Mutiny Act are very easily stated: the first and main object is clearly expressed, in the preamble to the English Mutiny Act, to be the maintenance of military discipline by the erection of summary tribunals unknown to and unauthorized by the common law; the second object, which is only subordinate to the first, and which, though not expressed in terms, is equally apparent on the face of the act, is to interpose in favour of the individuals necessarily subjected to such anomalous Courts a variety of checks and limitations calculated to guard against misdecision, and to rectify it when arrived at.

Objects of English Mutiny Act, 1st, maintenance of discipline, 2nd, protection of the soldier.

The circumstances of the country, that is to say, the state of the army to which the Indian Mutiny Act was to be applied, require a few, and but a few, more words. Powers of martial law appear to have been first committed to the Company by one of the earlier charters. At that period, which was before the Revolution of 1688, such powers were supposed by the Crown to appertain to it, and were undoubtedly exercised by it as the head of a feudal monarchy; but how far such powers could be delegated to one set of British subjects over another may perhaps be a question, though it is one of no interest in the present inquiry. For when the collisions between the French and English Companies, under Dupleix and Lawrence, produced the effect of introducing into India European troops in greater numbers than theretofore, and when, moreover, royal regiments began to be sent out in aid of the slender forces then in the pay of the Company, it was found necessary to base the military power over these latter troops on a better defined and more undoubted authority, and accordingly the 27 Geo. 2, c. 9, was passed. That statute introduced the same principles, couched in nearly the same language, with respect to the Government of the Company's forces, as the English Mutiny Acts contained with respect to the forces of the Crown. The act in all its main provisions corresponds with the act now in force; the same power is vested in Her Majesty to issue her warrants and to frame articles of war, and the same power of authorizing Courts martial is attributed to the commander-in-chief of the

When introduced into India; 27 Geo. 2, c. 9.

1844.

PORRETT'S Case.

forces of the Crown as exists at present, and nearly all the clauses on which any difficulty now arises will be found to exist almost *in terminis* there. It is therefore most important for the purpose of ascertaining the meaning of any expressions in the act now in existence to look back to the first statute and see how they were used then. This statute, with a slight addition in the 1 Geo. 3, continued to be the law of the army for nearly seventy years, namely till 1823, when the 4 Geo. 4, c. 81, was passed. That statute, which has been since supplanted by 3 & 4 Vict. c. 37, contains an expanded enactment of the various provisions comprised in the first Indian Mutiny Act, with the addition of such provisions as it had been found necessary to introduce from time to time into the English Mutiny Acts. And this leads me to note the source of the difficulties which occur on the construction of the Indian act; for whereas the Mutiny Acts relating to Her Majesty's forces recognise but one army, one commander-in-chief, and one Judge Advocate General, the Mutiny Act for the Company's forces recognises quite as distinctly the fact, as it exists, of three separate armies belonging to the several Presidencies, three commanders-in-chief, and three Judge Advocates General; nevertheless, in various passages of the Indian act, it will be found that this essential distinction between the two forces has been occasionally lost sight of, or not clearly marked, and language referring to the one English army, and the one commander-in-chief, has been transferred verbatim to the Indian statute, from whence the ambiguity arises as to which of the three armies and commanders-in-chief the singular term used has reference.

Indian Mutiny Act copies English Act, which relates to one army and one commander-in-chief, whereas in India there are three.

Having thus stated the objects of the Legislature in passing the Mutiny Act, and the state of the forces to which it was applicable, namely, their division into three distinct armies, it now becomes easy to proceed to the first question to be considered, namely, in whom has the Legislature vested the power of authorizing Courts martial over the Company's forces in India.

1st question: in whom is the power vested to authorize Courts martial over Company's army?

This question depends upon the true meaning which is to be attributed to section 9 of 3 & 4 Vict. c. 37, or rather to the

1844.

PORRETT'S Case.

proviso at the end of it. That section enables Her Majesty to authorize the Court of Directors to empower the Indian Governments and their commanding field officers to appoint Courts martial, but this only in certain cases, namely, wherever none of her Majesty's forces are employed under the Company's Presidencies. In this latter case the power over Courts martial is absolutely and exclusively vested in the commander-in-chief of the Presidencies where such Queen's forces are employed. The terms of the proviso are these: "provided that whenever any of her Majesty's forces shall be employed to act under the authority of any of the said Company's Presidencies in the East Indies, the power of appointing Courts martial, or authorizing the appointment of Courts martial for the trial of any officer or soldier of the said Company of or belonging to such Presidencies shall be in the officer for the time being commanding in chief at such Presidency."

Exclusive authority is vested in commander-in-chief of Presidency if her Majesty's forces are employed there.

These words therefore give an absolute statutory power to the commanders-in-chief to institute Courts martial, and that they also vest this power in such officers exclusively, so long as her Majesty's forces are employed at the Presidency, is apparent from the consideration that if it were also competent to the Crown to issue its warrants concurrently to the other authorities mentioned in the previous section, two different authorities would be enabled to convene Courts martial for the same offences, two different Courts might be held, and two different sentences pronounced, which is absurd, or at all events, a collision of authorities would be rendered possible, which, it must be presumed, could not have been in the contemplation of the Legislature.

The question therefore is considerably narrowed at the outset by showing that the only parties in India who are authorized to institute General Courts martial (certain excepted cases excepted) are the three commanders-in-chief at the different Presidencies. This being so, there is no difficulty whatever in understanding the meaning of the terms used in the proviso, as to the different jurisdictions to be exercised by the three commanders-in-chief in the great majority of cases

1844.

PORRETT'S Case.

likely to arise. It is quite clear that the jurisdiction is given to each commander-in-chief respectively, and to each exclusively over his own army, and this whether the army be employed "in the territories of the Company or elsewhere," as it is expressed in section 10. A Bengal commander-in-chief never would assume, under this clause, to hold Courts martial over Bombay soldiers under the command of the Bombay commander-in-chief, nor *vice versa*. So long, therefore, as the army of the Presidency remains under the orders of its own commander-in-chief, no possible question of jurisdiction can arise. But it is evident that the supreme Government, in the exigence of the public service, may withdraw any portion of the army of one Presidency and place it temporarily under the authority of the commander-in chief of another Presidency; or it may place a combined army composed of portions of the three Presidency armies under the separate command of an officer, not a commander-in-chief, and this army may be employed, either in foreign service, or in territories unannexed to any of the Presidencies. The question then arises as to how the soldiers, composing this combined army are to be tried, and how the proviso in section 9 is to be applied to this new set of circumstances. To take the last case first, that of a portion of a Presidency army, say the Bombay army, put under the separate command of an officer, not a commander-in-chief, and sent on service *extra fines* of any of the Presidencies. From what has been said above it is clear that the authority to try the soldiers of this army can only emanate from one of the three commanders-in-chief; it is also clear that as the army, by the hypothesis, is not within the local jurisdiction of any Presidency at all, the authority of no other commander-in-chief but that of the commander-in-chief of the Presidency to which the portion of the army belongs can be referred to as a legal source for instituting a Court martial; and the conclusion follows, that the commander-in-chief of that Presidency is the only authority designated by the Legislature.

Question as to respective authority of the three commanders-in-chief when portions of the three armies are combined.

The second supposed case was, that a portion of the

1844.

PORRETT'S Case.

Bombay army is placed temporarily under the command of the Bengal commander-in-chief, and the question then arises as to which of these two commanders-in-chief is to institute the Court martial. This will be found to depend upon the meaning to be given to the words in sect. 9, "Officer or soldier of the said Company of or belonging to such Presidencies," or to any such Presidency, as it is expressed more clearly in the previous act 4 Geo. 4.

If the words "of and belonging to the Presidency" designate the Presidency to which the army in fact belongs, the authority to convene the Court martial is vested in the commander-in-chief of that Presidency; if on the other hand they mean the Presidency where the army happens temporarily to be serving, the authority is vested in the commander-in-chief of the latter Presidency. The terms used cannot comprise both commanders-in-chief, so as to give them a concurrent jurisdiction, as is evident from the reasons alleged above in a similar case, and from other provisions which I will mention presently; and upon a careful survey of all the provisions of the act, and of the various objects in view, I conceive that the Legislature has clearly denoted that the commander-in-chief of the Presidency to which the offender belongs is the exclusive authority to institute a Court martial for his trial.

For, in the first place, the act itself (sect. 3), has taken the clear distinction between the Presidency to which the offender actually belongs, and that in which he is temporarily serving, and therefore gives a legislative explanation of the terms "of and belonging to the Presidency."

Secondly, it is evident that the main object of the act, *viz.* the maintenance of military discipline can be effectually secured, in whichever of the two commanders-in-chief the authority is vested, but a variety of provisions seem to show that the secondary object of the act, *viz.* the security intended for prisoners at their various trials can only be attained by construing the words in question according to their ordinary and natural import, and not by giving them any strained extension. Thus sect. 13 provides, that when

1844.

PORRETT'S Case.

prisoners are sentenced to death by a Court martial the commander-in-chief of the Presidency to which the offender shall belong, instead of causing such sentence to be carried into execution, may order the offender to be transported as a felon.

Power of commuting punishment, where lodged.

Here we see a power of commuting punishment, the power residing exclusively with the prerogative in England, delegated to the commander-in-chief of the army to which the prisoner belongs. This power is the peculiar function of such commander-in-chief confessedly in the great majority of cases. By what construction then can it be made to appear that this delegated authority is transferable to another? It is evident that this transfer of the power to remit punishment might operate very injuriously to the offender; in the army to which he belongs, and where he may have been serving for a number of years, circumstances may be known and brought forward which might have great weight with his commander-in-chief towards commutation of a sentence, but if the temporary service of a few days in another Presidency is to place his fate in the hands of another officer, to whom the same grounds for exercising a merciful discretion are not readily presentable or available, it might make all the difference between life and death to the prisoner.

Again, by sect. 26, another provision on behalf of prisoners is laid down to the effect that the original proceedings, sentence, &c., of all general Courts martial shall be transmitted to the Judge Advocate General of the army in which such Court martial is held, and the offender on demand is entitled to a copy. How important an enactment this is for the benefit of prisoners is readily apparent, and the present case affords an apt illustration of the desirableness of a clear rule being established as to what Judge Advocate General and what army the clause applies. For although it now appears on the return that the general Court martial was held under the authority of the Bombay commander-in-chief, the prisoner was never able to obtain from the office of the Bombay Judge Advocate General a copy of the proceedings.

For these reasons I am of opinion that the Legislature has

1844.

PORRETT'S Case.

clearly denoted its intention to vest the jurisdiction over the Company's armies in the commanders-in-chief of those armies respectively, that the commanders-in-chief with respect to those armies being invested with the functions exercised by the Crown in England over the English army, in such wise as to render them incapable of being mutually interchangeable, these functions, which are created for the benefit of prisoners, are not to be construed as transferable on any temporary change of service which the members of the army of any one of the Presidencies may be called upon to undergo. The Legislature indeed seems to me to have spoken so strongly on this point, that I should not have thought much question could have been made upon it, if I were not aware that a learned opinion had been given in England putting forth a different construction.

That opinion, it is true, proceeds upon the interpretation of another clause, sect. 2, which contemplates a special class of crimes, and as to which a different construction may be applicable. But even in that case, I should conceive that the same construction should be applied as is applicable to sect. 9, and it is impossible to help perceiving that in the opinion alluded to, a most important provision in sect. 3 is altogether thrown aside, which is a mode of construction never permissible except on a total failure to reconcile the rejected clause with the other provisions in the act. And it is possible that if that opinion should ever form the subject of judicial consideration, it may be held that the words there relied on "under his command," as so positively denoting the commander-in-chief of the Presidency where the offender happened to be serving, are not necessarily applicable to that officer, but to the immediate antecedent in the clause, *viz.*, the officer to whom the warrant is to be directed; and in point of fact, in the precedents of the warrants of the Crown to commanders-in-chief authorizing them to delegate their power to hold Courts martial, and from which such words appear to have been introduced into this act, it will be seen that the words "under his command" do not refer to the commander-in-chief issuing the warrant but to the officer to whom it is directed. (See the Warrant to Major General Dundas from his late Majesty Geo. 3, Treatise on Military Law, 306.)

If then the conclusion as to the first question be, that the Legislature has placed the commander-in-chief of the armies of the several Presidencies in the same position with respect to jurisdiction over those armies that the Crown exercises over the British forces, and that this jurisdiction so vested in each commander-in-chief attaches upon the members of his army, wherever they may be temporarily serving, it remains to be considered in what mode the power of delegating the authority to convene Courts martial is to be exercised.

Mode of delegating authority to hold Courts martial.

Now as to this mode, nothing appears to be laid down in the act, or in the articles of war, and no question appears to have been raised upon it except as to the officer to whom the commander-in-chief should direct his warrant; sect. 9 contains the authority to delegate, but expresses no mode whatever; it simply says that the commander-in-chief shall have the power of appointing or authorizing the appointment of Courts martial for the trial of any officer or soldier, &c. With respect to the class of cases mentioned in sect. 2, it is expressed that the officer to whom the warrant is to be addressed must not be below the rank of a field officer, and as this provision occurs so frequently in military documents, it may be taken possibly to exist as a restriction on the authority to delegate which is conveyed absolutely in sect. 9. It has been before shown that the commander-in-chief under sect. 2, is not, by the strict grammatical meaning of the words there used, restricted to addressing his warrant to officers who are under his command. There are no fetters therefore constituted by the act or the articles of war, as to the mode in which the commander-in-chief should delegate his authority; to effectuate the objects of the act he is called upon to do it in some way or other, and in a well-regulated harmoniously conducted service like that of the East India Company, it would seem to depend on mutual arrangement, and the rules of military etiquette, to ascertain the mode in which the three commanders-in-chief should severally delegate their

To whom authority must be delegated.

1844.

Porrett's Case.

powers. It possibly was not contemplated by the act that the contingency raising these questions as to clashing jurisdictions would arise, or that portions of the army of any of the Presidencies would be transferred temporarily from one to another. But when the public service calls for such an arrangement, it lies with the military authorities to expedite it, by enabling the provisions of the law to be carried into execution, in the most available manner.

It is true that sect. 10 points out that "for bringing offenders to justice it shall be lawful for her Majesty to grant her warrant to the persons hereinbefore mentioned (commanders-in-chief being amongst those persons) for convening and authorizing any officer under their respective commands not below the rank of a field officer," to convene Courts martial; and as this section follows the provision which vests the authority to hold Courts martial in the commanders-in chief it would seem at first sight to indicate that the commanders-in-chief could only delegate their authority to officers under their actual command, and therefore that the mode of delegating their authority is specifically pointed out and limited.

But on examining this clause more closely, it seems clearly to result that it does not apply to commanders-in-chief at all, and that it only refers to those cases wherein her Majesty is competent to issue a commission or warrant, which cases have been already pointed out. The clause itself will be found to exist almost in terms in the original act 27 Geo. 2, c. 9, s. 2, and it clearly does not apply to commanders-in-chief there, for the authority is vested in the latter officers absolutely, in a clause subsequent to that pointing out those to whom the king may direct his warrant, and the term "respective commands" which has run through the different statutes clearly refers in the original to the governments of the different Presidencies. In the course of transcribing the different sections, on new acts being passed, the original proviso has been dislocated from its original position where the meaning of the Legislature is obvious; or rather in the later acts the proviso has been followed by an amplification of the preceding clause in a manner not uncommon in English lawmaking, in which additional words do not always aid in explaining the sense, and thus the original independence of the clause to the proviso has become obscured. It would appear that the view I take of the power of the commander-in-chief over Courts martial of the Company's forces resting solely on the parliamentary enactment, and not on any warrant derived from her Majesty, is confirmed by the course adopted by those whose duty it is to advise the Crown at home on those matters, for in point of fact, I believe, the commander-in-chief holds no warrant from her Majesty for holding Courts over the Company's forces, but only over those of the Crown.

In practice delegation only made to field officers.

There is nothing therefore in the act to prevent the commander-in-chief of the Presidency from delegating the jurisdiction vested in him over the Presidency's army, wherever that army or a portion of it goes, to any officer whatever, whether under his command or not. If it is necessary, according to the rules of the army, that the officer to whom a commander-in-chief directs his warrant should be under his command, possibly an officer put into temporary command of a portion of such Presidency's army may be considered with reference to the provisions in the Mutiny Act to be so far under the command of the commander-in-chief of the Presidency, as to authorize the latter to delegate to him his warrant. If, however, the rules of the military service present any invincible obstacle to the delegation being made in the manner here indicated, and if the case in question is a *casus improvisus* by the Legislature, the remedy is to be found by new regulations amongst the military authorities themselves, or by a new act of Parliament.

Application of principles to present case.

It now remains to apply the conclusions which have been arrived at to the facts of the present case, and it will be evident that whatever difficulties may exist as to the details in carrying the act into execution in certain special cases, difficulties having reference more to the rules of the army than to ambiguities raised by the statute itself, a clear rule presents itself for deciding on the validity of the several grounds on

1844.

PORRETT'S Case.

which the authority of the Governor of Scinde to hold and confirm this Court martial has been based.

First of all, it was contended that Sir Charles Napier, as Governor of Sindh had power to confirm this Court martial, and sect. 2 and the 92nd article of war were referred to. But it was seen early in the discussion that those clauses had reference only to a special class of crimes, namely, to crimes not of a military nature, and accordingly, as the crime in question was a military crime, under section 16, the above mentioned clauses were wholly inapplicable. The incautious use of the word "governor" in article 92 is very probably the cause of the error that has been committed in this case, and may be very well conceived to have misled a military man, when we find even lawyers puzzled at it. The term itself does not occur in the corresponding section of the act, sect. 2, and no conceivable case can exist in India wherein a governor could have authority to hold such a Court martial. If none of her Majesty's forces were employed in the Presidency, then indeed a different authority than the commander-in-chief might be invested with power to institute Courts martial, but it would not be the governor, but the governor in council under section 9. The truth is, that the word governor has been inconsiderately copied from the corresponding section of the English Articles of War, in which it is significant and effective.

Governor of Sindh had no power to confirm Courts martial,

It was then suggested that Sir Charles Napier might hold a separate warrant from her Majesty, but this it has been shewn it is not competent to her Majesty to grant, except by virtue of a fresh act of Parliament.

and the Crown could not grant warrant containing such power.

Another basis for Sir Charles Napier's authority might be conceived to exist in article 91, which enables the commander-in-chief of an army in the field, "for the prompt and instant suppression of all irregularities and crimes committed by the troops," to deal with the case summarily on the spot; but this article so clearly refers to crimes demanding instant punishment and example, and what is termed, I believe, in the army drum head Courts martial, that no lawyer for an instant could

1844.

PORRETT'S Case.

refer proceedings on a crime like the present to that article, and, accordingly, it was not even mentioned in Court.

I have thus disposed of all the different authorities to which Sir Charles Napier's power can be referred exclusive of the warrant derived from the commander-in-chief of the Bombay Presidency; and I have done so, because it would appear from these proceedings that one or other of such authorities was relied on in point of fact; and it therefore was highly desirable, with a view to the future, to lay down the undoubted rule with respect to them.

But when the question is looked at solely in reference to Sir Thomas M'Mahon's warrant, it is evident that the power there delegated has not been pursued, and that the sentence pronounced without the confirmation required by the warrant, was not a legal sentence on which execution could pass. Directly this fact appeared on the face of the proceedings, it only remained to be considered whether the prisoner should be discharged at once, or remanded for the purpose of his being made forthcoming at a new trial, as he might be when a miscarriage of the first had taken place through irregularity, or for the purpose of enabling the commander-in-chief of the Presidency to deal with and confirm the sentence if he should think fit to do so. The latter, however, it was intimated, was not in the contemplation of the commander-in-chief, and, under the circumstances of the case, as the prisoner is on the strength of the Bombay army, and therefore amenable to the military authorities, no end of justice seems to be attained by keeping him any longer in custody; he may therefore be discharged (*a*).

Power to confirm in commander-in-chief only, and his refusal.

Prisoner discharged.

(*a*) After the conquest of Sindh it was not formally annexed to any Presidency, but Major General Sir C. J. Napier then commanding a division of the Bombay army was appointed Governor, and a large force from all three Presidencies was placed under his orders. Sir C. J. Napier, whilst previously serving in Sindh, had the usual warrant to hold Courts martial over the Bombay forces from Lieutenant General Sir Thomas Macmahon, commander-in-chief of the Bombay army, but it would seem that some of the military authorities were of opinion that Sir C. Napier, in his new character of Governor, had independent authority to hold Courts martial. Hence all these difficulties, which, as suggested in the above judgment, nothing but an act of Parliament could solve.

1846.
August 13.

REGINA *v.* SHAIK BOODIN.

[*Coram* PERRY, J.]

1. Principles of the responsibility of Judges to civil action reviewed, and application of the municipal rules of English law to Indian Mofussil Judges discussed.
2. Ground of jurisdiction in Queen's Bench to issue writs of *habeas corpus*.
3. Jurisdiction of Supreme Court to issue *habeas corpus* to Mofussil.
4. The Supreme Court has no jurisdiction over a native Court martial, and will not grant a *habeas corpus* to bring up a native prisoner in execution, on the ground that the Court below had no jurisdiction.
5. *Semble*, that the jurisdiction of the Court over wrongs committed by Europeans does not give jurisdiction to review judicial proceedings in Mofussil Courts.
6. Legislative acts of the East India Company's Government, and other acts of sovereignty, traced to legal basis.
7. Explanation of limited powers of legislation conferred by the earlier acts of Parliament.
8. Dicta of PARKE, B. and Lord MANSFIELD, C. J., and their inapplicability to India, noticed.

HOWARD had obtained a rule to show cause why a writ of habeas corpus should not issue to the Judge at Ahmednuggur to bring up the body of Shaikh Mahomed Boodin, late Kotwal of Poona, who was confined in prison there under a sentence of a Native Court martial, on charges of extortion, and which sentence it was alleged was not in conformity with the regulations.

The motion was made before PERRY J. during the criminal sessions, and a rule *nisi* was granted for the purpose of having the question discussed.

Howard in support of the writ argued in substance as follows:—

Assuming the affidavit to be true has the Court jurisdiction to issue the writ?

The Supreme Courts in India issue the writ by virtue of the clauses of their charter giving them the powers of the Judges of the Queen's Bench.

GREY and RYAN, both Chief Justices, writing to the Board of Control in 1830, and after the decision on the petition of Sir J. P. GRANT was known to them placed the jurisdiction on this ground, See vol. 6 of *Papers, &c., on East*

1846.

REGINA v. SHAIK BOODIN.

India Affairs, pp. 1281, 85, 86, printed 1831. See also *Morton*, 207 to 212, and notes.

The affidavits show a case of false imprisonment by the military authorities, and by Mr. Hunter and the subordinate officers of the Nuggur Goal as ministerial to them.

As servants of the East India Company they are all personally subject to the jurisdiction of the Supreme Court for wrongs and trespasses. (See pp. 18 and 21 of the *Charter* 21 Geo. 3, c. 70, sect. 10 and 11, and the 53 Geo. 3, c. 155, sect. 109.)

All persons therefore against whom the writ is asked to go may now be sued in the Supreme Court for the trespass complained of.

Then *habeas corpus* will lie wherever action for false imprisonment will.

If it be shown that in another form of proceeding the Court must give damages for the false imprisonment, then it cannot refuse to issue the writ to release from that imprisonment.

Burdett v. *Abbott* (14 East), particularly pp. 149, 50, 51; also 161, 162, per LITTLEDALE, J. *Leonard Watson's case* (9 Ad. & Ellis, 795.)

The above constitutes in itself a complete case for the writ unless the decision of the Privy Council on Sir J. P. GRANT's petition (1 *Knapp's P. C. cases,*) debars the Court from issuing it.

The resolutions of the Privy Council in that case must be read by the circumstances before the Court, by the argument addressed to it, and also by the decision in *Calder v. Halkett*, (3 Moore's Privy Council Cases.)

The return made by the Nazir of the Tannah Court in the case of Bappoo Gunness was undoubtedly a good return, see it set out 1 *Knapp*, p. 11. It stated a conviction by a Court of competent jurisdiction, without anything being shewn to establish that the conviction or imprisonment was contrary to law. But the Judge refused to take judicial notice of the Court or its functions or laws, although there was nothing there to impeach the conviction.

1846.

REGINA v. SHAIK BOODIN.

This return would have satisfied the Queen's Bench, *Rex* v. *Suddis* (1 East.)

The argument, so far as it concerned this writ was directed to shew that the legislature had distinctly recognised the Provincial Courts. It was put forcibly by *Bosanquet* and *Spankie* that by the 21 Geo. 3, c. 70, sect. 24, no action would lie against an officer of a Provincial Court for acts done in such Court, and that if so the legality of the proceedings could not be questioned on a *habeas corpus*, see p. 43, 54, 1 *Knapp;* and the Privy Council in resolving that the Supreme Court had no power to discharge persons imprisoned under the authority of a Native court must be considered as having arrived at a conclusion in harmony with that argument.

The resolution does not declare that the writ may not go to a wrongdoer when a Native court exceeds its jurisdiction and orders imprisonment wholly without colour of law, that is not an imprisonment that can with any accuracy be termed an imprisonment "under the authority of a Native court."

That is not the case put by *Bosanquet* and *Spankie* as embraced within the 24th sect. of the 21 Geo. 3, c. 70, for *Calder* v. *Halkett* shews plainly that that section will not cover an act not within the jurisdiction of the provincial magistrate. *Regina* on the prosecution of *Shaw* v. *Ogilvy* (Morton, 181.)

A provincial magistrate may falsely imprison in two ways, either as an individual not professing to act officially, or he may clothe his act with the forms of office, but go beyond his jurisdiction or power.

In both cases he is liable to be sued and, if acting corruptly, indicted in the Supreme Court.

The Privy Council can never have meant to decide that in the one case, the writ of *habeas corpus* may go to him, but that when acting corruptly it may not. Their resolution must have reference to an imprisonment in respect of which the Judge ordering it, and the parties acting under it, could not under the 24th sect. of the 21 Geo. 3, c. 70, be sued in the Supreme Court, in other words to an imprisonment "under the lawful authority of a Native Court."

Suppose in the case of Bappoo Gunness that, instead of the return being objected to for not stating enough, it had shewn a clear case of false imprisonment, or that the party imprisoned had successfully impeached the truth of it, in such a case it is difficult to suppose that the Privy Council would have come to a resolution in the terms they did: certainly the argument founded on the 24th sect. of the 21 Geo. 3, c. 70, could not in such a case have been urged on the Court.

But the prisoner is not in fact driven to this argument, for no other court is referred to by it than the regularly constituted Judicial tribunals of the Mofussil from whose irregularities a due course of appeal is provided by law, and in fact the Privy Council have done no more than declare that the Supreme Court is not a court of error or coequal with the Suddr Adalut, and that it cannot review orders which that Court, on appeal, may declare legal and whose decisions on criminal matters are final to a greater extent than those of the Supreme Court itself.

If the decision of the Privy Council embraces the decisions of Native Courts martial it places the very lowest description of courts in the country above European Courts martial, above the provincial courts, and on footing with the two Supreme Courts. A Native Court martial has no claim to judicial respect. It has no judicial habits or knowledge. It is not a Mofussil Court. It assembles wherever required in the Mofussil or in Bombay. It is called together for the occasion, instructed in its law by an officer who then advises the commander-in-chief, and if they or he have committed a fatal error in misapplying the law, the Court martial could not afford remedy, for it is not in existence, and if no other court has jurisdiction over his imprisonment the subject is wholly without remedy.

To sustain such a view it must be conceded, that if a Native Court martial assembles in Bombay, and on a mistake of the law condemns a man to transportation, when the law for the offence awarded only dismissal from the service, however plain the prisoner may be able to make this appear, yet the

1846.

REGINA v. SHAIK BOODIN.

Court must refuse a writ of *habeas corpus,* and is bound to allow the sentence to be carried into effect under its very eyes.

To give a court of this nature such paramount jurisdiction, to set it above the law requires something in the shape of positive enactment. The separate system of the provincial courts of judicature has been distinctly recognised by act of Parliament, and British subjects residing at a distance of more than ten miles from the Presidency are made amenable to them, see particularly, 21 Geo. 3, c. 70, sect. 21, constituting the Governor General in council a Court of Record also, sect. 23, giving him power to frame regulations for the provincial courts, which regulations are to be sent home, and which the Crown reserves the power of disallowing or amending. Further provision for the purpose of insuring a proper knowledge and attention to these regulations is made by 37 Geo. 3, c. 142, sect. 8. Then the 53 Geo. 3, c. 155, sects. 107, and 113, recognises the Courts of Suddr Deewannee Adawlut, and Nizamut Adawlut as courts of the highest appellate jurisdiction, and the 109th sect. of the same act gives the provincial courts concurrent jurisdiction over Native servants of the Company with the Supreme Courts.

Courts so constituted and recognised are the courts referred to in the decision of the Privy Council embracing a complete, perfect, and separate system of judicature.

But Native Courts martial have never been placed on that footing.

The only legislation with respect to them is as late as the year 1813, 53 Geo. 3, c. 153, sect. 96.

Under this clause the Bombay Government has passed two Regulations, Reg. 22 of 1827, and Reg. 2 of 1829.

The act of Parliament has given the local Government no power to create courts that shall be above the law. The local Government has not attempted to do so, and if it had attempted to do so it is clear on first principles, that this Court's jurisdiction derived from Parliament and the Crown direct could not be hereby ousted any more than it would have been if the local Government had declared by Regulation that the Members of the Court martial should not be sued or indicted in the Supreme Court for false imprisonment. 1846. REGINA v. SHAIK BOODIN.

With reference to the suggestion of the Court that it is the right of a British subject to sue and be sued in the Supreme Court, and that a Native in the Mofussil has no such right, it is contended, that the very reverse is the case, and that it is the undoubted right of every Native in the country to have every wrong or trespass committed against him by the Executive tried and adjudicated upon by the Supreme Court. Therefore it is his right abstractedly to have the writ.

The privilege of suit in the Supreme Court is not the privilege of the defendant but of the plaintiff.

Vide acts above quoted. The right of the Native in the Mofussil to the protection of the court is quite as full as that of a British subject. A British subject imprisoned in the Mofussil by a Native, not personally subject to the jurisdiction of the Court, could no more obtain redress from the Court either by action for false imprisonment or *habeas corpus*, than a Native, nor has he any special privilege for suing an Executive officer in the interior reserved to him by law.

Le Messurier, A. G., *contrà*, shewed cause.

Cur. adv. vult.

1846. August 13.

PERRY, J. (*a*). The motion in this case was that a writ of *habeas corpus ad subjiciendum* should issue to Mr. Hunter, the

(*a*) The reason why so very elaborate a judgment was given, was that the prisoner who had been a native officer in authority at Poona, having been sentenced to a long imprisonment, and being possessed of considerable means, was about to bring actions against the commander-in-chief, and other members of the Court martial, in order to test the validity of the sentence; and as it was thought that these actions founded on Calder *v.* Halkett, decided in the Privy Council, proceeded on erroneous views of law, it was deemed expedient to go into the law fully at once in order to enable an immediate appeal to the Privy Council, if the decision should be disapproved of. The result was, no actions were brought.

1846.

REGINA v. SHAIK BOODIN.

Judge of Ahmednuggur, having as such Judge the charge of the gaol there; to his Nazir; to the commander-in-chief and to others; commanding them to bring up the body of Shaik Boodin, who has been convicted by a Native Court martial and sentenced to six years' imprisonment.

The affidavits on which the motion was founded, set forth that the Court martial had exceeded its jurisdiction, and therefore that the sentence was illegal, but as I entertained a strong opinion when the motion was first made that the third resolution (in Sir *J. P. Grant's case*) conclusively determined that this Court has no jurisdiction to issue writs of *habeas corpus* where parties were undergoing imprisonment under the sentence of a Native court, I declined to hear any discussion of the facts as to the legality or otherwise of the imprisonment, until the jurisdiction of the court over such sentence had been previously established.

I accordingly directed that the notice of motion should be served on the law officers of the Company, and as Mr. *Howard* was kind enough, at my suggestion, to draw up a very able precis of the arguments on which he relied in support of the Court's jurisdiction, the question came on for argument with the fullest preparation on all sides.

Arguments for jurisdiction of Supreme Court extending over native Courts martial.

The argument in support of the jurisdiction of this Court was briefly this. The Supreme Court has the same jurisdiction to issue writs of *habeas corpus* wherever wrongful imprisonment exists as the Queen's Bench, and as that Court may issue its writs into any of the Queen's dominions so also may this Court issue it into the Mofussil.

But as a sentence inflicting imprisonment by a court exceeding its jurisdiction is a wrong for which an action may be brought, the writ of *habeas corpus* necessarily lies to deliver the party from his imprisonment.

And as British subjects are exclusively liable to this Court for any actions for false imprisonment, or other subject-matter, the more appropriate remedy for the restoration of liberty, namely, the *habeas corpus* must be co-extensive with the right of action. For otherwise it might happen that a party might bring his action for an illegal sentence and imprison-

1846.

REGINA v. SHAIK BOODIN.

ment, recover heavy damages, and yet continue to lie in gaol without any power in the Court to deliver him.

The decision in Sir *J. P. Grant's case,* was explained in two ways.

First, it must be viewed with reference to the special circumstances of the case. For the Tanna Court, whose sentence was there under review, had full jurisdiction over the subject-matter, and had not in any way exceeded it.

Secondly, even if such decision prevents this Court from reviewing the judgments of Native Courts of the Company Native Courts martial do not fall within that category.

The Mofussil Courts are recognised by Parliament, decisions in them are subject to appeal, and a perfectly separate jurisdiction is sanctioned by the Imperial Legislature.

But Courts martial stand on a very inferior basis, the only legislation with respect to them is as late as the year 1813; and they are courts whose necessary composition requires infinitely greater control on the part of a supervising tribunal, than the civil Courts of the Mofussil which are furnished with permanent and fixed Judges. And as Native Courts martial are not amenable to the superintendence of the Sudr Adalut as the Native Courts civil are, the Supreme Court is the only tribunal in which remedy can be obtained for any wrong done in the former by a British subject.

The analogy of a Native Court martial with an English Court martial was also forcibly put, and the undoubted liability of the members of the latter to the Queen's Courts for any excess of jurisdiction was instanced as a case completely in point.

Sir J. P. Grant's case, an answer to above arguments.

The main answer to the above argument at the Bar was the decision in Sir *J. P. Grant's case*; and it was also contended that although an action of trespass for false imprisonment might possibly lie, it did not at all follow that the writ of *habeas corpus* would issue.

At the conclusion of the argument I retained the opinion I had originally formed against the jurisdiction of the Court, for it appeared to me that the decision in the Privy Council was completely in point, and I was not at all disposed to

1846.

REGINA v. SHAIK BOODIN.

admit the postulate on which the whole of Mr. *Howard's* argument was built, namely, that an action would lie against a Mofussil Judge for an erroneous judgment. But as I understood that Sir HENRY ROPER's mind had wavered when the case was originally brought before him, and as various nice questions were involved, such as the extent of the jurisdiction of this Court, the responsibility of Judges for misdecision, and the true legal basis and character of the Native courts, I thought it best not to deliver judgment off-hand, but to investigate thoroughly the above doctrines before I decided finally the particular case before me.

Question, whether Supreme Court ever had jurisdiction over Mofussil Courts not doubtful.

Upon the broad general question as to whether it was intended that the Supreme Court should entertain any jurisdiction over the Native courts of the Mofussil, I confess that it has always appeared to me a very plain matter. For notwithstanding the great learning and industry which have been expended in former times in arguing for the jurisdiction, and notwithstanding the ambiguous, and as it is now generally admitted, the very loose language in which the Acts of Parliament, and charters of justice, establishing the Supreme Courts in India, have been couched, I think it is quite evident, upon the face of them, that the Legislature never contemplated giving to these Courts any controlling authority over the Mofussil tribunals. The loose and careless language, however, of which I have spoken, was quite sufficient to enable different legal conclusions to be drawn by men to whose opinions I pay the highest deference, and which should necessarily lead me to distrust my own views. But the authoritative exposition by the Privy Council in Sir *John Grant's case* of the meaning of the charters, shows conclusively that what appears *primâ facie* as the intention of the Legislature is in point of fact the true construction. Now the purport of the decision in that case being that this Court has no power to issue writs of *habeas corpus* to bring up persons imprisoned by Native courts, because the Court has no power to discharge such persons so imprisoned, it follows conclusively that the distinction attempted between a lawful and an unlawful imprisonment is baseless, and that in both

1846.

REGINA v. SHAIK BOODIN.

cases the power is denied to us of issuing the writ. Again, as the principle of the decision is founded on the wholly different systems of law which prevail in the Mofussil and the Presidency I am unable to draw any distinction, for reasons which I will state more fully presently, between Native Courts martial, and Native Courts civil; they are both comprised under the general term Native Courts, and the immunity from our jurisdiction required for the one would seem at least equally requisite for the other.

If the authorities stood here, therefore, it would be sufficient to say that this case is governed by the decision of the Privy Council on Sir *John Peter Grant's petition.*

Decision in *Sir J. P. Grant's case* somewhat shaken by *Calder* v. *Halkett.*

But in the more recent decision of *Calder* v. *Halkett,* also in the Privy Council, Mr. Baron PARKE appears to have laid down some doctrines which re-open the whole question. The action there was brought by a European against Mr. Halkett, who was a magistrate and Judge of the Foujdary, or Criminal Court of Nuddeah, in Bengal, and the cause of complaint was that the plaintiff being an Englishman, and therefore not subject to the jurisdiction of the Mofussil Court, had been arrested by the Judge's orders, on a charge of assault, and had been detained in custody, on such charge for two days.

On the trial of the cause in the Supreme Court at Calcutta, the plaintiff recovered a verdict for Rs. 500 damages, but on consideration of the law affecting the case, the Court afterwards held that the action did not lie, in consequence of the 21 Geo. 3, c. 70, s. 24, which enacts,

"That no action for wrong or injury shall lie in the Supreme Court, against any person whatsoever, exercising a judicial office in the County Courts for any judgment, decree or order of the said Court, nor against any person for any act done by or in virtue of the order of the said Court."

This decision went home to the Privy Council on appeal, and although they did not exactly overrule the decision of the Court below, for they confirmed it upon what would seem a subtler web of reasoning than is usually adopted in the Privy Council on appeals from the colonies, according to what we

1846.

REGINA v. SHAIK BOODIN.

learn from Lord KENYON, in *Rex* v. *Suddis* (1 East Rep.), still they certainly seemed to have overruled the reasoning on which such experienced Indian Judges as Sir EDWARD RYAN and his brethren proceeded.

The Privy Council laid down that the true meaning of the statute is to protect Judges of the Native Courts for things done within their jurisdiction erroneously or irregularly, but leaving them liable for things done wholly without jurisdiction. The result of this principle would have been to give Mr. Calder a cause of action for which indeed he had already recovered Rs. 500 in the Court below, but the Privy Council held that it did not distinctly appear on the evidence before them that the Judge knew the plaintiff to be an Englishman, and thus the appellant was cast on a question of fact, which had never come in question in the Court below where the facts were inquired into, and which in all probability never could have been a matter of question.

The latter point may indeed be considered to be the only point decided in the case, for although the passage before cited contains a strong expression of opinion by Mr. Baron PARKE, still on the safe rule, which prevails in English law, of considering every thing that falls from a Judge in the course of his decision, which is not absolutely essential to the point to be decided, *obiter dictum*, the exposition of the statute as above given is undoubtedly open to argument, and the question when it arises for decision will have to be treated as *res integra*.

If a Mofussil Judge may be sued in the Supreme Court for acting judicially where he has no jurisdiction;

Assuming, however, that the law thus stated as to the right of action against a Mofussil Judge is sound, Mr. *Howard* is enabled to build a powerful argument upon it, which it is not very easy to meet, and which in point of fact was not met at the Bar. For it was said in reply, that although an action for false imprisonment might lie, it did not by any means follow that a *habeas corpus* would issue, whereas the exact converse of the proposition is true, namely, that a *habeas corpus* will issue to put an end to a wrongful imprisonment in many cases where no action will lie. The case of Sir JOHN HOWELL, Recorder of London, is a marked instance of this. At a sessions at the Old Bailey he committed the jury to

jurisdiction may also exist over Native Courts martial.

1846.

REGINA v. SHAIK BOODIN.

Newgate because they found a verdict contrary to his direction, but upon *habeas corpus* the imprisonment was held to be illegal, and they were discharged. One of the jurors afterwards brought his action against the Recorder for damages, but it was held that the action did not lie, as the Recorder, though acting wrongfully, was acting as a Judge of Record.

The remedy for wrongful imprisonment by action for damages, however, is evidently so imperfect without the *habeas corpus*, that it seems to flow necessarily, both from general principles and the Judge's remarks in *Burdett* v. *Abbott*, that wherever the action lies the prerogative writ issues as an inseperable adjunct.

Powers of Supreme Court to issue writs of *habeas corpus*, &c.;

Much discussion took place at this branch of the argument respecting the powers of this Court to issue writs of *habeas corpus*, and the foundation of such power was placed, as it was also by Sir CHARLES GREY and Sir EDWARD RYAN, in their *Minute to the Board of Control* in 1831, on that clause of the charter, which gives the Judges the power of the Justice of the Court of Queen's Bench. It therefore became necessary to the argument to magnify the powers of the Queen's Bench, and it was strongly contended that it was competent to that Court to issue its writs to any part of British India. For this purpose the often quoted sentence of C. J. MONTAGUE, in James the First's time, was relied upon. "This writ is a prerogative writ, which concerns the king's justice to be administered to his subjects. For the king ought to have an account why any of his subjects are imprisoned, and it is agreeable to all persons and places."

likened to powers of Queen's Bench.

But Queen's Bench can only issue *habeas corpus* to jurisdictions governed by common law; and as to which it is the Court of Appeal.

That case also shows that it used to issue to Calais; and a recent decision in England has held that it would go to Jersey. Indeed Lord MANSFIELD, in *Rex* v. *Cowle*, laid down generally that the King's Bench can issue prerogative writs to every place under the subjection of the crown of England, to. "Ireland, the Isle of Man, the Plantations, Guernsey, and Jersey;" and he only makes one exception, *viz.*, as to "foreign dominions which belong to a prince who succeeds to the throne of England," such as Scotland and Hanover, which distinction, by the bye, ought to exclude the Channel Islands.

1846.

REGINA v. SHAIK BOODIN.

and contrary doctrine examined.

Now as I conceive much error prevails in the doctrines held on these subjects, and as, with the growing empire of Great Britain, very pernicious consequences may flow from these erroneous views, it is worth while to examine them somewhat closely; and on a careful review of the decided cases I think they will be found in no way to support the general proposition which Lord MANSFIELD laid down.

Habeas corpus to the Cinque Ports.

The question before C. J. MONTAGUE respected the issuing of a *habeas corpus* to one of the Cinque Ports to bring up a prisoner who had been lying in gaol there for nearly half a year, under an order of the Lord Warden, on a question arising out of a claim made by the Lord Warden himself to the possession of some wreck. The Court held that although the Cinque Ports were a special jurisdiction into which the ordinary writs of the king did not run, still that the prerogative writs ran everywhere within the kingdom, and the Chief Justice then pronounced the words which have been since cited as a universal proposition.

To Calais whilst an English settlement.

It is upon the same ground that the writ ran to Calais, for that place also was considered within the realm, and was governed by a Mayor's Court, and by English laws, as we learn from the 4th *Inst.*, p. 282. And it is remarkable with respect to India, that wherever it became requisite for the purposes of justice that the Queen's Bench should issue its writs to this country, special statutes were passed to grant the power needed. It would seem, therefore, that the principle to determine whether the Queen's Bench has jurisdiction to issue the writ or not is involved in the consideration whether the Court to which it is directed is subordinate or not. All Courts within the realm where the common law prevails—even the Privy Council itself—are subordinate to the Queen's Bench, and the prerogative writs necessarily belong to it, to keep all such Courts within their respective jurisdictions. But in countries where a different system of law prevails, where the Queen's justice is administered in other modes unknown to the common law, it is impossible to me to conceive on what legal footing a jurisdiction can be claimed for the Queen's Bench to review law proceedings of nations whose codes, whose languages, and whose names even must be often wholly unknown to them. 1846.

REGINA v. SEAIK BOODIN.

"The King's Bench," as it was put by *Norton, arguendo* in *Rex* v. *Cowle*," hath a general jurisdiction of all inferior jurisdictions in England," and therefore, as it appeared in that case that Berwick-on-Tweed was wholly governed by the English criminal law, and was not amenable to the Scotch Courts, Lord MANSFIELD's decision, as to the jurisdiction of the King's Bench to control the proceedings of the Berwick Criminal Court, seems quite conformable to the previous authorities, although the dictum embracing Ireland and the Plantations within the reach of *habeas corpus* has no case to support it, and there seems the strongest ground in principle why it should not be so.

To Berwick-on-Tweed.

When an empire grows to the magnitude of that which is now ruled over by her Majesty, embracing so many different nations, systems of judicature, and diversified law tribunals, it becomes of the greatest importance, in order to avoid an unseemly conflict of Courts, to draw the lines broadly which shall separate their jurisdictions from one another. No one ever thought of asserting a right in the Queen's Bench to issue writs into Scotland. Why not? Evidently because a different system of jurisdiction prevails there, the administration of which has been entrusted to other hands than those of the Queen's Judges at Westminster. A claim has been asserted that such prerogative writs should issue to Ireland, and with some show of reason, because the common law prevails there, and because formerly error used to lie from judgments in the Queen's Bench in Dublin to the Queen's Bench in Westminster Hall. But no such writ has ever in fact been held to issue to Ireland, and the claim, I believe, has been successfully resisted. The principle, therefore, which seems to have been present to the mind of all our earlier lawyers in the decided cases, is that which I have ventured to deduce above, namely, that the Court of Queen's Bench has only the jurisdiction to issue its writs to Courts inferior to itself, such Courts being within the realm of England.

But does not run to Scotland, or to colonies.

(See *Ventr.* 351.)

Whether to Ireland, *quære?*

I am aware that the late decision of the Queen's Bench

1846.

REGINA v. SHAIK BOODIN.

The writ running to Channel Islands an anomalous case.

in *Carus Wilson's case*, that the *habeas corpus ad subjiciendum* lies to the Channel Islands, militates with the above doctrine. But the question as to this writ issuing, and the principles on which it should issue, were not then fully discussed; and it seems to have been taken for granted, on the loose note in *Ventris*, of a *habeas corpus* issuing to Jersey to deliver up the body of one of the regicides in the time of Charles the Second, that the law was established on the point. Possibly, if the question had been thoroughly gone into, if the special clauses in the *habeas corpus* acts, allowing the writ to run in certain cases to the Channel Islands, had been pointed out, and if the admirable treatise on the jurisdiction of the King's Bench in *Hargrave's Law Tracts* had been brought to the notice of the Court, and which seems to have prevented, at the time of its publication, the Court of King's Bench from extending its jurisdiction over Wales, (see *Sampler* v. *Thomas*, 1 Wils.) the Queen's Bench might have decided, in conformity with the authority of *Blackstone*, that the common law writ of *habeas corpus* did not run there.

But accepting the doctrine in its full extent, that the prerogative writs do run to Jersey and Guernsey, it is impossible not to perceive that their case is wholly anomalous. In the early days of our history the laws of England and of the Norman isles were almost identical; and although no doubt, when the King of England was Duke of Normandy, the appeals from the Norman courts would lie, not to the *aula Regia*, and the Justiciary of England, but to the Duke's court and his Norman Justicier, who, as we learn from *Madox*, had the same power in Normandy as his contemporary Justicier possessed in England; still, when Normandy was lost, it is quite easy to conceive how the powers formerly exercised by the Norman Justiciary were quietly transferred to the Queen's Common Law Courts at Westminster. Indeed Normandy, as a feudal duchy, was so inferior in dignity and importance to the kingdom of England that we see, even before the loss of the former, but whilst the Duke's power was gradually succumbing to his encroaching neighbour in France, instances of the King's Courts at Westminster exercising jurisdiction over matters belonging properly to the Norman Courts. See *Hale's Hist. Com. Law*, p. 206, ed. 1794.

1846.

REGINA *v.* SHAIK BOODIN.

In either view, therefore, the case of the Channel Islands cannot be drawn in, any more than the other decided cases, to support the general proposition thrown out in argument by Lord MANSFIELD.

Jurisdiction of Supreme Court as based on powers of Queen's Bench fails.

The jurisdiction of our Court therefore must be based on other grounds than its supposed analogy to the supposed universality of the Queen's writs as issued by her Court of Queen's Bench. And it seems to me that a very simple rule presents itself for ascertaining whether our process issues or not, by merely reversing the order of the argumentation which has been usually employed.

Test to ascertain where jurisdiction of Supreme Court exists.

It has generally been assumed, as the fact is, that our process issues to every part of the Presidency, or perhaps further, and therefore it is often concluded that our jurisdiction over the persons within those limits is co-extensive. This appears to me to be vicious reasoning, as from the supposed existence of an accident it draws conclusions as to the existence of the principal. The rule, I think, is first of all to ascertain whether the personal jurisdiction is given by the Charter, &c., and then it may be safely assumed that all the process necessary for carrying out the efficiency of a Court of justice belongs to it in virtue of its constitution. The distinction has often occurred to me in cases of disputed jurisdiction, and I have never found it fail to present a clear, intelligible guide.

Admitted Supreme Court has jurisdiction over all Europeans in Mofussil for wrongs, &c.

The question, therefore, here comes round to what I consider the basis of Mr. *Howard's* argument, namely, the assumption that Judges of native Courts martial are within the jurisdiction of this Court for *bonâ fide* but erroneous judgments. In considering a proposition of this nature an Indian lawyer has a much more difficult task to perform than practitioners at home. There from the peculiar nature of the system, and the abundance of materials at hand, reasoning on a disputed law point is brought as nearly to a mechanical operation as possible. When a doubtful case arises, the pleader is able to refer to the immense repertory of decisions which the industrious reporters furnish forth year by year, and

And assumed that therefore it has jurisdiction for errors in judicial procedure:

but erroneously.

1846.

REGINA v. SHAIK BOODIN.

he is sure to find some precedent which fits his own case more or less exactly, the antagonist pleader is able to obtain a similar weapon, and when the question comes before the Court, the duty of the Judges is principally limited to the measuring, the weighing, and comparing the different circumstances in the conflicting cases.

And the system works admirably well, for if one case is like another in its leading circumstances, the decision in the first may well serve as a guide to the latter without any reference to the ultimate principles of jurisprudence.

Difficulty of applying English decisions to Indian facts pointed out.

But this course is by no means open to our Indian Courts, and a special pleader from Westminster Hall who would apply the last precedent on his file in all its rigour to a case arising in India, would often commit the grossest injustice. Nor is the reason of this difficult to ascertain, for in a case arising in this country, however similar many of its leading features may be to those of a reported case in England, there is always wanting that similarity of circumstances which pervades all English cases, arising from race, history, religion, and constitution, and which form the unnoticed but not the less well recognised substratum of every English decision.

But it may be asked is it then competent to an English Judge administering English law in India to dispose of every case that arises according to his mere discretion? God forbid!

A larger discretion must be exercised by Indian Judge, to be governed rather by the principle than by the letter of previous decisions.

The tyranny of the most cramped system of laws that ever was penned would be preferable to the tyranny of such an arbitrary discretion. What, then, is the rule to be propounded which shall keep the Court in a golden mean between these two evils? I humbly conceive it to be no other than an industrious searching out of the sound jurisprudential principle which lies at the bottom of all decision, and a firm application of such principle when found to the case in hand.

Principle as to the liability of Judge to action for erroneous decision discussed.

To apply this doctrine to the question now before us, what is the principle which, as it should seem, ought to govern in reference to the responsibility of Judges? A Judge, according to European systems, is a public servant who is called upon to pronounce often an immediate, always a

1846.

REGINA v. SHAIK BOODIN.

decided, judgment on the most complicated questions of fact, or the most embrangled points of law. But such is the imperfection of evidence by which facts are to be established, and of language in which laws are couched, that it is certain the finest mind ever organized will occasionally arrive at erroneous conclusions both on one and the other. In such cases the party against whom the misdecision is directed will often be much damnified. But if the judgment has been pronounced with *bona fides*, due care, and ordinary competence, it undoubtedly would seem to result from all legal principles that the party damaged should have no compensation against the innocent but erring magistrate. In the language of lawyers the party has sustained *damnum sine injuria*. If, on the other hand, the Judge has in any way abused his high office, if the least moral obliquity can be established against him, it seems equally fitting that he should be amenable to criminal justice, and to amends making towards the injured party. But the line here is not very easy to draw, for as in every decision the Judge is nearly sure to give offence to one side or the other, as the legal advisers who have been exclusively contemplating their clients one-sided statements, and their own arguments, will rarely be satisfied with the reasons which have overruled their own, and as the parties smarting under the judgment hostile to their fortunes will often give way to the tendency of human nature to ascribe the worst motives to acts militating against their interests, the facility to be given, or the check interposed, to proceedings against Judges for alleged misconduct in their office, becomes a matter for anxious inquiry, and will be found to vary much in different codes.

Difficulties of subject: how disposed of in civil law.

The principles above stated are to be found clearly laid down in what Lord Chancellor Lyndhurst lately called "that monument of human wisdom, the Roman law," *Ulpian* writes, "*Quo jure potestates a magistratu fiunt ad injuriarum actionem non pertinent,*" Dig. 47, 10, 13, s. 6," and although the *judices* were made responsible to the party pronounced against for an erroneous judgment ("*per imprudentiam,*") the Roman Judge as is well known was not a Judge, but a sort of

1846.

REGINA v. SHAIK BOODIN.

juryman, who was assigned by the prætor to determine questions of facts. See a passage of *Aul. Gell.* cited by *Heineccius, Aut. ad Inst.* 4, 5; Dig. 50, 13, 6.

Liability of Roman Judge for misconduct.

If, on the other hand, the Roman Judge made use of his office to wreak his malice on an enemy, then he became liable to the penalties of the law. The same *Ulpian* says, "*nec magistratibus licet aliquid injuriose facere, si quid igitur per injuriam fecerit magistratus vel quasi privatus vel fiducia magistratus injuriarum potest conveni.*"—Dig. 47, 10, 32.

Liability of barristers to action by civil law.

And *John Voet*, in his commentary on another passage of the Digest, examines the doctrine more at length, and contains some very valuable remarks on the extent of the privileges of barristers as well as of others engaged in Courts of law which it might be useful to cite, but to which from their length I am unable to do more than refer. *J. Voet ad Pand.* vol. 2, p. 988.

Provisions of English law on subject.

The old English laws contain the same doctrines, though with a curious modification. A Judge, in the days of the 1st William, might be fined for an erroneous judgment, unless he could swear that he did not know better, "*quod rectius judicare nescivit,*" or, in the Anglo Saxon, "*na righter ne couthe,*" but in all the feudal codes he was made punishable for misconduct in his office —See *Wilkins' Leges Anglo-Saxonicæ*, p. 77, note (*d*).

English Judge not liable for erroneous judgment;

Exactly the same principles as those of the Roman code and probably derived therefrom, exist in modern English law. An English Judge is not responsible for a *bonâ fide* but erroneous judgment, whether on a question of fact or of law;

for misconduct he is so.

he is responsible to some tribunal or other, if any moral imputation lies against him for his conduct in his office.

But municipal distinction between Judges of record and not of record.

But from very early days of our legal history a distinction has been drawn between the immunity to be afforded to superior and inferior Judges, or in the language of the law to Judges of Record and Judges not of Record. This distinction is to be satisfactorily explained on constitutional and historic grounds, and on those alone. In the feudal system under which our common law gradually formed itself, the whole country, as is well known, was cut up into an infinitude of

1846.

REGINA v. SHAIK BOODIN.

petty jurisdictions. The King held his Court, the Baron holding of him had his, and the petty Lords of Manors holding of the Baron had, each, his own Court, in which the sale of writs and of Justice formed a considerable item of the revenue which supported their state from the King downwards.

Judges not of record made responsible for erroneous judgment.

When, therefore, our early English Judges came to apply the doctrines of the Roman law, which had been promulgated in England, through the school founded at Oxford by Vacarius, and through the treatise of one of its scholars, Bracton, although it was laid down peremptorily in several cases that a Judge is not responsible for an erroneous judgment, still when the case of one of these feudal small cause Courts was brought before the twelve Judges, they held unanimously that the Judge of such a Court did not fall within the reason of the rule, and they determined that an "ignorant" judgment of one holding a manor Court was punishable with fine and imprisonment. *Vin. Abr.* Judges, *F. Jenk.* 162, *tit. B.* 243, C. See the 27th Ass. there cited, 2 *Hawk. P. C., B.* 2, c. 27, § 25.

The distinction between the immunity given to the two grades of Judges was afterwards embodied in the formula, "no action lies against a Judge of record, but it does against a Judge not of record."

The distinction originally significant;

This distinction was perfectly significant at the time it was framed, by its drawing a broad line between the petty Courts then existing (Courts, *viz.* which could hold pleas of debt under 40*s.*, but which could not hold plea of trespass, as they were incompetent to issue the process of arrest necessary to the commencement of such a suit), and the Superior Courts, where trained public servants were presiding, and where alone an authority, entitled to the denomination of Judge, existed.

And a very instructive case is to be found in 1 *Roll. Rep.* 92, which shews the train of reasoning that led the Judges in those early days to entertain this sort of jurisdiction over inferior Courts, for they argued if an erroneous judgment is given in an inferior Court of record, the record can be brought up and the error amended, but if the Court below

1846.

Regina v. Shaik Boodin.

has no records, unless we allow an action to be, there will be no remedy for the misdecision.

In process of time, however, the principle of the distinction was lost sight of, but the verbal formula being handed down from mouth to mouth, the liability, or otherwise, of a Judge to an action, for an erroneous judgment was supposed to subsist on some metaphysical difference between a Court of Record and a Court not of record, which no lawyer of the present day is able to define (*a*).

but has become unmeaning; and is exploded.

Thus, in *Beauvain* v. *Scott*, (3 Campb.), one of the greatest magistrates in our annals, Lord Stowell, had an action brought against him for what was said by one Judge,—Lord Eldon, to be an error of judgment, but which was denied to be so by two other Judges, Lord Ellenborough and Sir John Nicholl, and a verdict of 40*s*. damages passed against him, because he was said not to be a Judge of record. But the absurdity of this distinction was carried to the utmost, and, as I conceive, exploded for ever; when a similar action was attempted against the Lord Chancellor, because he, forsooth, also is not a Judge of record; *Dicas* v. *Lord Brougham*, (6 C. & P.)

Other reasons in England for making inferior Judges civilly liable for erroneous judgment.

There are other and constitutional grounds which have subjected another large class of Judges, *viz.*, the magistrates of England, to actions for mere errors of judgment. Considering how that body is composed—their great power, and their freedom from the ordinary responsibility of public Judges,—the check thus held over them by the Court of Queen's Bench is most salutary; and I should be sorry to see it one whit diminished; but the foundation of this check should be traced to its right source, *viz.*, to constitutional grounds, and to the peculiar character of the English magistracy, and the legal principle prevailing in our law on the subject should be carefully viewed apart.

Constitutional check over unpaid magistrates.

If any one will take the trouble to attend to the chronology of the cases establishing this jurisdiction over magistrates, he

(*a*) See the definition of Holt, C. J., in *Groenvelt* v. *Burwell*, denied by De Grey, C. J. in *Miller* v. *Scare*, but no other propounded in its place.

will find how often, in the early cases, up to the time of Elizabeth and later, the principle is recognised that a magistrate acting judicially is not responsible for error; acting ministerially, he was always considered to be so (*a*).

The constitutional tendency, however, to keep these magistrates within due bounds, and the gradual increase of summary powers committed to their hands, creating additional necessity for an efficient check, the result was that the jurisdiction over them arose gradually and unquestioned, and in what has been selected as the leading case on this subject, *Cripps* v. *Durden*, (1 Smith's Leading Cases), where the magistrate for an erroneous construction he had put upon an Act of Parliament, was held liable to an action, it was not even argued that he was acting as a Judge in the discharge of his duty, and to the best of his ability, but his general liability passed undisputed.

The celebrated judgment of *Richardson*, J. in *Britain* v.

(*a*) In 9 Ed. 4, it was held, action would not lie against a Judge for ill exercise of discretion, see *Jenk.* 162; Vin. Ab. *Justice of the Peace*, p. 16; same point in 9 Henry 6, see 1 Rol. Rep. 92. In 31 Eliz. action held to lie against a Justice (though doubted by one Judge) on the ground he was acting ministerially. *Green* v. *Bucklechurch*, Lev. 323; see Sid. 209, pl. 3. In the same year an action was held to lie against a Justice, but there malice was proved. *Windham* v. *Clare*, Cro. Eliz. 130.

In 43 Eliz. occurs the first case where an action was held to lie against a magistrate for an erroneous exercise of discretion, *Scavage* v. *Tatham*, Cro. Eliz. 829, but *quære* whether the act there was not ministerial only, see *per Holt*, 1 Salk. 396. Magistrates being thus made liable to actions for mere errors of judgment, the inconvenience of the decision was speedily felt by the number of causeless and litigious suits which were immediately commenced against magistrates by "evil disposed and contentious persons," and the first of a series of statutes for their protection was passed, 7 Jac. 1, c. 5. The true judicial rule is again returned to by HOLT, C. J. in 1 Salk. 396, "a Judge is not answerable either to the king or the party for mistakes or errors of his judgment," 6 Mod. 228, and see 1 *Hawk.* c. 72, ss. 5, 6; 2 *Hawk.* c. 1, s. 17. A series of cases, however, has established the jurisdiction over magistrates. *Billings* v. *Prinn*, Cowp.; *Dyer* v. *Missing*, Cowp. 1035; *Miller* v. *Scare*, Cowp. 884; 2 Wils. 250, n.; *Smith* v. *Dr. Bourcheir*; *Cripps* v. *Durden*, 1 Smith's Leading Cases, where all the subsequent cases are collected, and it is undoubted law now, that if magistrates acting judicially err in an exercise of jurisdiction by exceeding their powers, they are liable to an action.

1846.

REGINA v. SHAIK BOODIN.

Kinnaird, applies on all legal principles as much to an error of judgment on the obscure wording of a statute, as it does to a similar error on the obscure testimony of witnesses.

He lays down "if a magistrate acts *bonâ fide*, and comes to his conclusion as to matters of facts, according to the best of his judgment, it would be highly unjust if he were to have to defend himself in a civil action." (1 *Bro. & B.*)

And it is a very remarkable circumstance that whereas, in all the cases except one, where a Judge has been held responsible for an erroneous judgment of law, his immunity from action has never been insisted upon, yet wherever this legal principle of the non-liability of a Judge for an error in judgment has been brought forward solemnly in argument, the Court has decided in favour of the Judge. *Groenvelt* v. *Burwell*, (1 Lord Raymond, 454), *Ackerley* v. *Parkinson*, (4 M. & S.), which must be taken to overrule what I should otherwise consider a disgrace to our law, the case before cited of *Beauvain* v. *Sir William Scott*, (1 Campb.), *Dicas* v. *Lord Brougham*, (6 C. & P.), *Garrett* v. *Farrund*, (6 B. & C.), and the excepted case which I have referred to, *Miller* v. *Seares*, (Cowp.), which is really the leading case as to the responsibility of inferior Judges, and from which most of the modern doctrines are drawn, is in itself not law, as it was solemnly overruled after full discussion in *Boswell* v. *Impey*, (1 B. & C. 163.)

On principle, English Judge is not liable to action, but municipal reasons have created a large exception to rule.

Thus, we find that a clear legal principle exists in the English law conformable to what might be supposed *a priori* to be the sound rule, and conformable also to that which exists in other codes. But this rule has been much broken in upon by decisions, having local and municipal objects distinctly in view. And, as will always be found to be the case, when a broad principle is departed from for some limited and specific object, the attempt to reconcile the rule, with its exception, is clogged with difficulties, and a number of artificial distinctions have been attempted to be drawn, which are found on examination to furnish forth no general principle. *Terry* v. *Huntingdon*, (Hardres), seems to be the first case which sought to lay down the distinction between the responsibility of

1846.

REGINA v. SHAIK BOODIN.

a Judge acting erroneously on a subject-matter within his jurisdiction, and acting wholly without jurisdiction, and how successful it has proved as a guide to future cases on the same subject; I will leave with those to determine who have gone through the decisions so carefully as I have.

Such being the law of England as to the responsibility of Judges, for an erroneous judgment, we are called upon to apply it to the case of Judges of a Native Court. And the unmeaning jargon of a Court of record and a Court not of record is prayed in aid to guide our decision.

Question now, whether rule or exception should be applied to native Courts.

I do not think that this doctrine was much urged at the Bar here, but it seems to have formed the principal staple of the argument addressed to the Privy Council in *Calder* v. *Halkett*. But how, I may ask, is this technical common law notion at all capable of being applied to a wholly different system of judicature?

If a Scotch or a French Judge happened to be in England, and to be sued for an erroneous judgment he might have given against some Englishman, it is impossible that the decision could turn upon the foreign Court, being one of record or not; for the phrase would be unmeaning in the one code, and untranslateable into the language of the other The technical distinction, therefore, by which exceptions have been grafted on the general rule in England being inapplicable to this country, and the conditions which gave birth to such distinction being here unknown, it appears to me to follow irresistibly, that the broad general rule is the only one we have to follow. But that even on the technical reasons which would be urged in England, a Foujdarry or Zillah Judge having unlimited jurisdiction over millions of inhabitants, with the exception of one half-dozen Englishmen, is much more analogous to a Judge of Oyer and Terminer, though, in point of fact, exceeding even him in powers, than to any of the petty Judges, who, by the English law, are responsible in civil suits.

Native Courts entitled to same immunity as Courts of record in England.

But finally, in order to dispose of this branch of the subject, and to distinguish the decision in *Calder* v. *Halkett* from the present case, on the supposition that all the doctrines,

1846.

REGINA v. SHAIK BOODIN.

there laid down are sound law, I may observe that, although as it seems to me the safer and sounder decision would be to give a Zillah Judge the same protection in the exercise of his office, as a Superior Judge in England possesses; still this immunity may exist to its full extent wherever his general jurisdiction prevails, and that it is only broken in upon when he assumes to hold a jurisdiction over Englishmen, in respect to whom the Legislature has hitherto been chary in giving powers of legislation.

But native Courts martial are alleged to be peculiarly under control of Supreme Court.

The argument however principally used at the Bar on this head was in respect of a distinction which is supposed to exist between the Civil Courts and Courts martial in the Mofussil. Here again an analogy is relied upon derived from English constitutional principles, which are applied to institutions wholly dissimilar in their origin, their essence, and their operation.

Reasons, why English Courts martial are under Queen's Bench.

In constitutional England it is deemed one of the birthrights of an Englishman, obtained for him by *Magna Charta* and a series of subsequent statutes, that he shall only be subjected to the penalties of the law on the "*judicium parium*," or trial by jury. This legal privilege was frequently invaded in the arbitrary times of the Tudors and the Stuarts, and especially in the instances of martial law as then exercised; but the Petition of Right, in Charles the First's reign, gave a fresh sanction to the principle laid down in *Magna Charta*, and placed martial law on a definite legal basis. The preamble of the Mutiny Act, which is passed from year to year, clearly records the great constitutional doctrine which I have before noted, in these terms,—"whereas no man can be prejudged of life, or limb, or subjected in time of peace to any kind of punishment within the realm by martial law, or in any other manner than by judgment of his peers, and according to the known and established laws of this realm;" and then having laid down the principle it proceeds to make temporary provision for the preservation of discipline in the army, and enacts the various clauses forming the code of martial law to which the British army is subject.

But no one is pedant enough to suppose that *Magna Charta*

1846.

REGINA v. SHAIK BOODIN.

and the *Petition of Right*, are applicable to the Hindu and Mussulman inhabitants of British India; and no jurist, who is acquainted with the history of this country, can fail to perceive what the true legal character of the Indian Governments was to which the East India Company, by conquest, succeeded. Every native Government of which we have any knowledge, whether Hindu, Mussulman, or Sikh, has been a pure despotism, sometimes well, generally ill, administered, with various checks no doubt in operation, arising from religious obligations, or caste and priestly influences, such as all despotisms have been more or less subjected to, but still despotisms to which the maxim of the Roman lawyers was as applicable as to that of their own emperors, "*Quod principi placet legis vigorem habet;*" and indeed the essential meaning of a despotism involves this proposition.

But Magna Charta and the Petition of Right does not apply to Hindus in the Mofussil.

The distinction therefore between a Civil Court and a Military Court under such a Government is untenable, for each depends entirely on the orders of the sovereign. A despotic monarch had the power when each emergency arose to take such steps, and to institute such proceedings towards bringing the criminal to justice, as seemed to him the most fit. And he did so. Whatever he ordered was the law; and a question such as has been now made could not possibly arise under a Native Government. And that is the exact legal character at the present moment of those countries in India under our rule, into which the regulations have not been introduced.

The Government of India always despotic.

No distinction between a Court civil and a Court martial.

But I have said that to these despotic Governments the East India Company succeeded by conquest. The fact is unquestionable, though as to various parts of India it would not be very easy to point out the precise moment when the sovereignty passed from the Mogul into the hands of the Company. But this is not an unexampled occurrence in history, the transfer of the kingdom of France to the Carlovingian dynasty, and of the Rajah of Satara's rule to the Peishwah and his successors, will at once suggest themselves as analogous cases.

1846.

REGINA v. SHAIK BOODIN.

The English Government possesses all the same powers as its predecessors, except when it has altered them by law.

But what is the rule of English law, as to the institutions which prevail in a conquered country? The rule is that they continue on the same footing as before the conquest; constitutional, if previously constitutional; despotic, if previously despotic, until altered at the will of the conqueror.

Now as the country in which the proceedings under this Court martial took place was a country conquered by the East India Company within the last thirty years, and a country ruled by despotic institutions, that is to say by the will of the prince, it follows that the Courts now existing in the country either exist on the same basis as heretofore, or they exist in virtue of some expression of will, some voluntary limitations of power, which the Government have imposed on themselves; but in either case they are the Native Courts of the country, and therefore *quacumque via data*, the decision of the Privy Council withdraws them from our supervision.

This train of reasoning has not been adverted to by the counsel for the prisoner, and the establishment of the Civil Courts, as well as of Military Courts in the Mofussil, is supposed to rest on Parliamentary recognition, the former in the statutes 13 Geo. 3, c. 65, 21 Geo. 3, c. 70, 37 Geo. 3, c. 142, the latter in an act so late as the year 1813. But that this is an unsound view, is manifest at once from this consideration, that if the statute 53 Geo. 3 was the first authority for holding Courts martial over native troops, hundreds of natives must have been murdered during the previous 150 years, wherein the Company were obliged to maintain military discipline.

Important question discussed.

The great importance of obtaining correct views upon a subject like this makes it necessary for me to go deeper into it than I could have otherwise desired.

Acts of sovereignty in Company traced to legal basis.

Every one is able to perceive that the East India Company, in point of fact, has exercised all the essentials of sovereignty over the different territories it has acquired, either by conquest or otherwise, since the moment of acquisition. Every one must also see that the necessity for such exercise of sovereign powers was imperative and irresistible. But it has never yet been very clearly ascertained how the power *de facto* is to be supported by authority *de jure;* the acquisition of vast kingdom, by a corporation of merchants is a new fact in the history of the world; the relations of subjection and sovereignty ensuing thereupon between the conquered country, the corporation, and the metropolis, were never very nicely analysed or understood, and the argument became more complicated by a number of apparently clashing, or imperfectly worded, acts of Parliament, passed at a great distance from the scene, and very often in ignorance of the true facts of the case.

But in truth, a sound legal basis is afforded to the East India Company in one of their early charters for all the acts of sovereignty they have exercised, and I only account for such accomplished Jurists as Sir CHARLES GREY and Sir EDWARD RYAN having omitted to notice it in their investigation of the subject, from the fact of the charter being very rare and not to be met with in the ordinary printed collections.

Printed papers, vol. 6, 1831, *ubi sup.*

The charter I speak of is that granting the Island of Bombay to the Company, which it does by way of feudal principality, and it gives them all the necessary rights of sovereignty, even to the power of making war, which could be held by a feudal prince acknowledging a superior lord. The charter also extends the same rights and the same sovereign powers to any other territories within the limits of their charter which they might subsequently acquire, and the feudal tenure is made complete by directing the whole to be held of the Crown as of the Manor of East Greenwich.

Ample powers of sovereignty granted by charter of Car. 2.

There then we find powers granted, ready to come into operation whenever the occasion called for them, and it is well to remark how essentially necessary these powers were when the tide of British conquest overwhelmed the greater part of India.

The battle of Plassey threw a territory containing thirty millions of inhabitants into the hands of the Company. Those territories were ruled over by the Mussulman law, which, as is well known, deals largely in its criminal code in the *lex talionis*, and in other punishments which we deem barbarous. Moreover, this Mussulman law was administered as to its civil as well as to its criminal provisions, even where Hindus were defendants.

1846.

REGINA v. SHAIK BOODIN.

Exercised by the legislation of Clive, Warren Hastings, &c.

Judicial establishments organized;

These laws, Lord Clive, Warren Hastings, and the local Government of Bengal altered most largely long before any Parliamentary legislation took place on the subject. In 1769, judicial officers were appointed by the Company; in 1772, Warren Hastings framed regulations for the Dewanny or Civil Courts, and the Foujdarry, or Criminal Courts, and appointed Judges to each, and in the same year he passed enactments creating new crimes, with new punishments, such as against Dacoity, &c., whereas the first statute that can be taken to have conferred any legislative authority on the Company was not passed till the year after, namely, 1773.

without authority of Parliament;

And various acts of Government remodelling the judicial establishments are to be traced down to the year 1780, when Sir ELIJAH IMPEY drew up the Code of Regulations, which, as observed by the Select Committee of the House of Commons, "constitute the principal foundation of the rules now in force," but probably these latter regulations were framed in pursuance of the act passed in the same year, 21 Geo. 3, c. 70, and not in virtue of the sovereign powers previously exercised by the Company. Still what confirms my argument that these necessary sovereign powers of Legislation, &c. were duly as well as actually exercised by the Company in the territories lately come into their hands, is the fact that the Legislature itself, with the knowledge of what had been done by the Company recognised the existence of such powers and confirmed them.

but with due authority of law.

This important clause, which singularly enough has not been printed in the recent collection of statutes published by the East India Company, is the 7th sect. of the 13 Geo. 3, c. 63, and the concluding words after appointing a Governor and four councillors, in whom the whole civil and military Government of the Presidency, and the Government of the Kingdoms of Bengal, Bahar, and Orissa is vested, are as follows: "In like manner to all intents and purposes whatsoever, as the same now are, or at any time heretofore might have been exercised by the President and Council, or select committee in the said kingdoms." And it is satisfactory to be able to add, that a select committee of the House of Commons on the affairs of the East India Company, in 1813, takes precisely the same view with myself as to the effect and meaning of this clause. (See *5th Report of the Select Committe in* 1813, p. 40).

Explanation of the limited powers of legislation subsequently given by Parliament.

But the same statute (s. 36,) confers powers on the Governor General in Council to make rules, ordinances, and regulations for the good government of the settlement, enforceable by fines, and a statute twenty-seven years later (39 & 40 Geo. 3,) extended the sanction to moderate corporal punishment by public or private whipping! The evident inadequacy of such limited powers of punishment where the government was granted of what was called erroneously, three kingdoms (being in fact three large provinces of one kingdom) is however so startling as to provoke a smile, until the proper explanation is afforded.

Mere copy of the usual clause giving power to make by-laws; and founded on jealousy to allow a private corporation to have any greater power over their fellow subjects.

These clauses evidently relate to an entirely different subject-matter and to a different class of persons, they are such, and in exactly the same terms, as have been conferred for centuries past on other corporations, giving them power to fine and moderately punish the servants of the corporation, (being their fellow-subjects,) who might be employed by them.

And the contrast is remarkable how, in recognising the powers of the Company to govern the kingdoms they had acquired, the British Parliament with that constitutional regard for the liberties of English subjects, which runs through all our institutions, took care that no further infringement upon these liberties should be made than was absolutely necessary.

The conclusion is that the Company under royal Charter confirmed by Act of Parliament had absolute power granted to them to govern the countries they might acquire, and to continue or change the system of the jurisdictions there existing at their pleasure. But that as to English subjects their powers over them were restrained within the same constitutional limits, as in the case of corporations in England.

Conclusion, large powers given over

A deduction from the same principles enables a satisfactory explanation to be given to a clause in the Charter Act of

1846.

REGINA v. SHAIK BOODIN.

1813, which was relied on at the Bar, as showing that the Company's intrinsic power to hold Native Courts martial was very doubtful.

native subjects, limited powers over English fellow citizens.

The 53 Geo. 3, c. 155, s. 96, recites, "Whereas doubts have been entertained whether the several governments of the said Company have sufficient *power in all cases* to make laws and regulations and articles of war, &c., &c.," for native soldiers, and the Act then proceeds to confer the necessary powers. It is now easy to see in what case considerable doubts might exist. At the Presidencies, English law, with all its constitutional privileges in favour of the liberty of the subject, prevails, and a great question might have been made, how any one, under the protection of English law, could be brought before a criminal tribunal unknown to that law except under the sanction of an Act of Parliament. The Parliamentary enactment was therefore necessary to set the question at rest.

Mofussil judicature not founded on enactments of Parliament.

It appears to me, therefore, to result quite clearly from the above inquiries that the Mofussil system of judicature stands upon a basis altogether independent (except in the case of British subjects) of the common or statute law, and that it is quite as much a foreign system of law, as that administered in Scotland. It is true that the Judges of the Mofussil Courts are themselves liable to the jurisdiction of this Court for wrongs committed by them, and for breaches of contract, &c., and such causes of action are to be determined by the personal law, which every Englishman carries about with him in India. But this personal law is not participated in by the natives amongst whom they are thrown, and cannot in any way affect the character of the Courts over which they may preside as judges, or the law which regulates the rights of the natives who may sue therein.

Their system, like the Scotch, is foreign law,

In the Code of English law, an institute of a peculiar character exists by which parties injured by the erroneous judgment of certain inferior Courts are enabled to obtain damages from the Judge and from those ministers who act under his orders. But in what mode is a similar right of action conveyed to the Hindu inhabitant of the Mofussil and

and their proceedings not subordinate to Court of English common law.

1846.

REGINA v. SHAIK BOODIN.

such a right must spring from a positive law, but no such remedy against a Judge acting *bonâ fide* is to be found in the Hindoo or Mussulman Codes, and no clause in any act of Parliament contains anything on the subject. The fact, however, of the Judges of the Mofussil Courts being amenable to a different code of laws from that of the suitors over whom they preside, gives rise to a curious question on the conflict of laws, which has never yet arisen in any other system of jurisprudence, and for which, therefore, no precedent occurs,—are the wrongs for which such Judges are liable to a civil action, wrongs defined and created by the Native law, or wrongs defined and created by the English law? It has been seen that by the English law imprisonment under an erroneous judgment gives birth, in some cases, to a cause of action, and is in some sense a wrong, still, if that which is called a wrong, is not one by the Hindoo or Mussulman law, it is difficult to see how the Hindoo or Mussulman can avail himself of the law which exists in the country of his Judge, and which bears there a wholly local and specific character. However, there is clearly much ambiguity on the point and logical deduction might possibly draw results wholly at variance with the intention of the Legislature, which desired to subject individual acts of wrong by British subjects to the control of the Supreme Courts, but did not desire to place under them the whole of a separate and independent system of judicature.

Curious question on conflict of laws, arising out of *status* of English Mofussil Judge.

It was a fit knot, therefore, for the Legislature to untie, and, in my opinion, they have done so by the enactment before cited of 21 Geo. 3, c. 70, and which lays down the true principles, which I have striven at such length to show are the true principles of our law, and of sound jurisprudence; *viz.*—First, Responsibility of Judges for any misconduct;—Secondly, Non-responsibility for mere error of judgment.

True principles of judicial responsibility laid down by 21 Geo. 3, c. 70.

I do not wish to conceal my opinion that in certain cases appeals to this Court from the Mofussil tribunals might be useful, and the Judges here certainly have time for more judicial business than they perform, but without a full legislative view and sanction of all the duties to be so performed

Supreme Court might, perhaps, sit usefully in appeal from the Mofussil; but the jurisdiction should be given by

1846.

REGINA v. SHAIK BOODIN.

Legislature, not assumed by the Judges.

by this Court as a Court of Appeal, I am fully convinced that any interference by the Supreme Court with Mofussil decisions would be quite as mischievous, or even more so than if the Court of Queen's Bench were to sit in review of all the cases from the Scotch Courts. I would also add that the arguments urged in this case as to the absence of any legal tribunal, where the sentences of Native Courts martial can be reviewed, however illegal that sentence may be, would seem to shew that the attention of Government should be called to the point, as it should, possibly to many others connected with forming a more perfect system of judicature in India. But having made this remark, I ought not to conclude without stating, that although the whole of the above reasoning proceeds on the assumption that the sentence of the Court martial now complained of is illegal, I have not the least reason to believe it to be so. I have purposely abstained from reading the affidavits in which the supposed flaw is pointed out. And all I know of it is that the counsel on one side assert its existence, whilst the counsel on the other side just as strenuously deny it.

If there is no Court for correcting the misdecisions of native Courts martial, attention of Legis lature should be called to it.

I regret exceedingly to have been obliged to occupy such space as I have done, but having ventured to controvert certain doctrines of the highest names in our law, of Lord MANSFIELD, and of Mr. Baron PARKE, it would have been extreme arrogance to have done so without showing, what it only needs local information and humble industry to be able to shew, that they do not correspond with the principles of our law as laid down in our ancient books, when applied to a country like India. The importance of having such doctrines settled, and of aiding the endeavours of the British Legislature to substitute the government of law, for the arbitrary ever changing and unknown rule which prevails where the law is doubtful and obscure, has been a sufficient stimulus to me to contribute towards such result by making this long inquiry.

The object of this long inquiry, to enable a fixed rule of law to be established instead of arbitrary fluctuating decisions.

The result of the present motion is that it must be discharged.

JANORDHUN RAMCHUNDER
v.
EXECUTORS OF DHAKJEE DADAJEE.

1847.
May 6.

[*Coram* PERRY, J.]

Discrepancies of law and equity in the treatment of executors as to costs discussed.

THE points arising in this case as to the liability of executors to costs are fully discussed in the following judgment.

PERRY, J.—In this case the plaintiff has obtained a judgment against the executors of Dhakjee Dadajee, which in terms warrants him to obtain his debt and costs out of the assets of the testator, if the defendants have so much, but if not, then the costs out of the defendant's own goods. In substance, however, the judgment establishes a personal claim on the executors for the whole debt and costs, in the event of there being no assets of the testator available. But as Dhakjee Dadajee's estate was in the course of administration on the equity side of this Court, the defendants applied for an injunction to prevent the plaintiffs from taking out execution, and thereby obtaining full payment of his debt to the injury of the other creditors. This application was opposed on the ground, that by the course of defence the defendants had adopted in their action, they had made themselves personally liable to the plaintiff's claim, and on the authority of *Lee* v. *Park*, (1 Keen), and another case, the injunction was granted to restrain execution against the estate of Dhakjee only, leaving the plaintiff to pursue his remedy against the executors.

Upon this judgment a writ of execution against the goods of Dhakjee was directed to the sheriff, which he was directed to return *nulla bona*, and thereupon another writ of fi. fa. was issued out against the goods of the defendants, upon which, after some negotiation, the defendants paid the whole amount of debt and costs to the plaintiff.

1847.

JANORDHUN
v.
Executors of
DHAKJEE.

The defendants now seek to set aside this execution and have the money which they have paid refunded. There is no doubt whatever that the plaintiff has been wrong in the practice he has pursued. Three courses generally are open to a plaintiff who obtains judgment against an executor. He may issue execution against the goods of the testator, and procure the sheriff, if he can, to suggest a devastavit against the executor, and thereupon proceed against the latter personally; or he may issue out a *scire fieri* inquiry; or he may bring debt upon the judgment, suggesting a devastavit. But the first course is obsolete, as I do not find any instance of it within the last 150 years; the second course is inapplicable to this country; and I only recollect one instance of it even in England, when it was treated as an antiquated proceeding, *Palmer* v. *Waller*, (1 C. & M.:) the third course, therefore, is the only one now in practice. But the plaintiff has adopted none of these courses, and the only question is, whether his departure from the forms prescribed by the law for attaching a personal liability on executors amounts to an irregularity or to a nullity; for if it be the former there is some ground to suppose that the conduct of the defendants amounts to a waiver.

It is not, however, necessary to consider that point, as I am clearly of opini on that the execution issued against the defendants personally is illegal, and, therefore, not to be cured by consent.

An executor is only liable to pay the debt of his testator upon a devastavit being established against him in fact. In all the three courses I have mentioned, this fact is established on record. If the sheriff take upon himself to assert this fact, and it turns out to be false, he is answerable in an action for a false return, as in *Rock* v. *Leighton*. In the two other modes, the fact of a devastavit may be traversed by pleading. But, by the course the plaintiff has adopted, this fact, this condition precedent to the defendant's liability, nowhere appears; it follows, therefore, that the execution against them is illegal.

The whole difficulty in this case arises from the decree pronounced on the equity side of this Court, and from the mistaken notions which have prevailed amongst equity lawyers as to the liability at law of executors, and as to the nature of the judgment against them; and I fear that this Court, by proceeding on such mistakes, has pronounced a decree which cannot be carried out. Equity lawyers have supposed that in certain cases an executor may make himself liable to a judgment *de bonis propriis*; and, therefore, when injunctions have been prayed, to prevent creditors from suing an insolvent estate, they have very consistently refused to protect the executors personally, when the only object of the Court was to protect the estate for the benefit of the creditors at large. Lord ELDON acknowledged that he had misunderstood what the effect of a judgment against executors was, but even in *Lord* v. *Wormleighton* he draws a broad distinction between the two judgments, usually pronounced against executors; (and the latest writer on Practice is equally incorrect, 3 *Daniel's Pract.* 299, 1st ed.); whereas, in point of fact, they are almost exactly the same in their operation, as is observed by Mr. *Williams, Exors.*, p. 1410; and the distinctions taken in equity are not warranted by the nature of the judgments at law, p. 1360.

The truth however is, there is no such thing as a judgment *de bonis propriis* at law, except where the action is brought against the executor personally on a devastavit; in all cases where he is sued simply as executor the judgment is against the testator's goods first of all; and it is only on his assets being found deficient, that the executor's liability arises.

The liability of an executor at law cannot be better stated than in the words of BULLER, J. "The creditor has no right to call on the executor but in respect of the effects which he has in his hands belonging to the deceased: by law, therefore, the creditor is to be paid out of those effects; and unless it appear that there are none such, the proper judgment is, that the debt shall be paid out of the effects in the hands of the executor." (3 *T. R.* 689.)

So long, therefore, as there are assets of the testator, the personal liability of the executor never arises at law; and although misconduct on the part of an executor may make

1847.

JANORDHUN *v.* Executors of DHAKJEE.

him personally liable in equity, and prevent him from setting up as a discharge disbursements which he may have made at law: or at all events, may only allow him to claim *pro ratâ* on the estate, as LORD ELDON intimates in *Clark* v. *Lord Ormonde*—the judgment at law never determines these facts, but proceeds merely on this simple ground: you have admitted by your pleadings that assets exist—you shall never be heard in a Court of law to assert the contrary; if, therefore, you fail to pay the debt out of such assets you must pay out of your own pocket. But *Vernon* v. *Thellusson* conclusively shews that if on such judgment the executor does pay out of his own resources, he may recompense himself out of the assets of his testator.

But the decree, such as was pronounced in this case, presupposes that there was an absolute personal liability on the part of the executor, for which no recourse could be had to the estate of the testator; and this is evidently so incorrect a conception of what the legal liability is, that it convinces me the decree was altogether erroneous.

I have gone into this case at length. because I am always desirous, when it is possible, to let the parties depart from the Court with due notions of what their rights are, of the grounds on which the decision has proceeded, and of the course which they ought to adopt for the future. It would have been sufficient to intimate that the judgment is against the plaintiff, because the practice adopted by his legal advisers has been erroneous. But it would be extremely unsatisfactory to leave the parties at sea, and to impose upon them the difficulty of ascertaining the correct practice, when even the law books afford false guides on the subject. I have therefore gone on to intimate a doubt whether the plaintiff can take any advantage by proceeding further.

Still I do not fail to perceive that the plaintiff is very probably damnified by a decree of this Court, which I now think erroneous, and although that decree was pronounced at the suggestion of the plaintiff's counsel, who was bound to bring all the law bearing on the subject before the Court, and if it had been so brought the decree would not have been pro-

1847.

JANORDHUN v. Executors of DHAKJEE.

nounced, I am clearly of opinion that the Court should take all the steps in its power to prevent any injury to the parties which may have accrued through any error to which the Court has been a party. I will therefore hear any suggestions that may be made on the subject; and, in the absence of any being offered, will make a proposal by which the judgment dictated by the charter, *viz.* one according to justice and right, may be delivered between the parties (*a*).

(*a*) The parties having assented, the Judge made a decree disposing of the case.

IN THE MATTER OF THE WILL OF

THUCKER CURRAMSEY SHAMJEE.

1843.

March 19.

1. Rule to be followed on the ecclesiastical side of the Supreme Court when conflicting decisions occur of the spiritual Courts, and the courts of common law in England.

2. The Court on its ecclesiastical side will entertain objections to an inventory, notwithstanding the decisions of the Queen's Bench that the spiritual Court has no jurisdiction over inventories.

3. The next of kin, notwithstanding that they dispute the validity of a will, have sufficient *locus standi* in the Ecclesiastical Court to dispute the sufficiency of the inventory exhibited by an executor.

A SUIT had been instituted by the next of kin in this case to set aside the will, and on an inventory being filed by the executors, the next of kin, on an affidavit suggesting omissions, called upon them to show cause why they should not file a further and better inventory.

The cause shown was that the next of kin had no *locus standi* in Court, for there was no jurisdiction over the executors, except by virtue of the will, which the next of kin denied to be valid. Secondly, the common law Courts held that the Ecclesiastical Courts had no jurisdiction at all over inventories.

Cur. adv. vult.

PERRY, J.—It has been objected on the part of the executors that the next of kin, taking nothing under the will, have no interest to entitle them to raise objections to the inventory; and that although a suit is pending to set the will

1843.

In the matter of THUCKER.

aside, the result of which might be to entitle the next of kin to the estate of the testator, still in that case the character of executor would be gone, in which character only they are under any obligation to furnish an inventory. But we disposed of this objection at the argument on the ground that the next of kin had a possible interest in the effects of the testator, and that that was sufficient to induce the Court to entertain his application. The cases on the subject in the books do not perhaps go quite so far as this decision, for they only decide that a contingent, or an equitable, or an apparent interest is sufficient, none of which perhaps can be said, strictly, to exist in the present case; but the principle laid down in the different cases fully, I think, bears out our decision, for it is this, that it is the duty of executors to exhibit an inventory, that it is very beneficial to all who are or who may be interested that he should do so, and that the Court therefore will lend its assistance to any one of the above classes to enforce its exhibition.

The second objection made in this case is more difficult to dispose of, and we accordingly took time to consider of it. It is contended, namely, that the Ecclesiastical Courts have no jurisdiction to entertain objections to an inventory, and that if they do so the Courts of common law will prohibit them; and the cases of *Catchside* v. *Rington*, (3 Burr.); *Henderson* v. *Trench* (5 M. & S.), and *Griffith* v. *Anthony*, (5 A. & E.), are undoubtedly strong to that point; on the other hand, it is alleged, that notwithstanding these decisions the Spiritual Courts still proceed to entertain objections to inventories, that the practice is very beneficial, and that we, sitting as a Spiritual Court, ought to follow their practice. It is clear, however, that this latter argument must be taken with some qualifications, for if we, whilst sitting on the ecclesiastical side, are bound by the practice of the Consistory Court in London, so also, whilst sitting as a Court of common law, we are at least equally strictly bound by the authority of the Courts at Westminster. If, therefore, we follow the precedent set us by the ecclesiastical Judges to-day, for such is their practice, we may to-morrow be called upon to put a stop to our proceedings on the authority of the cases in the Court of Queen's Bench. To avoid this absurdity, therefore, we must lay down clearly to which set of authorities we give in our adhesion; and if, on looking into the question, we see reason to believe that the jurisdiction contended for does exist in the Ecclesiastical Court, we must be prepared distinctly to overrule the cases I have cited; and to which may be added *Clinton* v. *Parker*, (8 Madd.); and, though not quite to the same point, *Bellamy* v. *Alden* (Noy, 78). When the question is put in this naked form, and when it is recollected that the decisions we are called upon to disregard proceed from such Judges as Lord HALE, Lord MANSFIELD, and Lord ELLENBOROUGH, I confess that it has been with much difficulty I have been able to bring myself to consider the point as open to inquiry.

I have however, carefully, looked into the question, and on the amplest consideration I am capable of giving to it, I think that it is our duty to pronounce for the jurisdiction of the Ecclesiastical Court; and that, upon the same principle that the ecclesiastical Judges have adopted, we ought not to regard the decisions of the Court of King's Bench as solemn adjudications of the point. If they were so, there can be no doubt that it is equally our duty, as it would have been that of Sir WILLIAM WYNN, and Sir JOHN NICHOLL, to pay deference to them; if they are not, I hope that it is not arrogating undue powers to ourselves, when we adopt the practice and feel ourselves governed by the arguments of those learned persons.

It is clear that up to the case of *Griffith* v. *Anthony*, (5 A. & E.), the Ecclesiastical Courts would have adopted the course which we are now following; for notwithstanding *Catchside* v. *Rington*, (3 Burr.), Sir WILLIAM WYNNE, in *Shackleton* v. *Lord Barrymore*, (2 Add. 329, cit.), after mature deliberation, decided in favour of the jurisdiction; and although *Catchside* v. *Rington* was followed up by *Henderson* v. *French*, (5 M. & S.), Sir JOHN NICHOLL equally disregarded the latter case in his very powerful judgment of *Telfred* v. *Morison*, (2 Add. 319). But it cannot be denied that the case of *Griffith* v. *Anthony*, (5 A. & E.), carries the common law authorities further than the two preceding decisions; for Sir J. NICHOLL expressly

1843.

In the matter of THUCKER.

decides *Telfred* v. *Morison,* on the ground that the Court of Queen's Bench had not fully disposed of the subject in *Henderson* v. *French,* whereas *Griffith* v. *Anthony* was argued with a view of bringing *Henderson* v. *French* under consideration, and the contrary practice to it in the Ecclesiastical Courts was cited, notwithstanding which however the Court of Queen's Bench upheld *Henderson* v. *French,* and even went further than the preceding cases in ousting ecclesiastical jurisdictions in such matters; for whereas Lord HALE, in *Clinton* v. *Parker,* had held that it was competent to a legatee, though not to a creditor, to falsify an inventory in the spiritual Court, Lord DENMAN denied such power to them both. It is to be observed however of *Griffith* v. *Anthony,* the argument of which I perfectly well remember, that the points which Sir JOHN NICHOLL remarked had never been brought to the notice of the Court, were not submitted to the Queen's Bench in that case. The counsel who argued for the ecclesiastical jurisdiction contented himself with reading a passage from Mr. *Williams's* book, and did not seem to be acquainted with *Telfred* v. *Morison;* and the decision passed so quickly, and was thought so unsatisfactory, that I remember adding a note to my report of it in *N. & P.*, to cite *Telfred* v. *Morison,* and in which I suggested that the spiritual Courts might still persist in their practice, on the ground that the question of the ancient jurisdiction, independent of the stat. Hen. 8, had not yet been solemnly discussed. It will be seen also that Mr. *V. Williams,* although the successful counsel in the case, is not altogether satisfied with the decision, for he observes on it in the last edition of his work on *Executors,* that it is supportable on another ground, irrespective of the principle in *Henderson* v. *French,* although this special ground was certainly not mentioned in the judgment of the Court.

For these reasons, *viz.* because I am of opinion that it has never yet been brought to the consideration of the Courts of common law that the jurisdiction of the spiritual Courts over inventories is long antecedent to the statute of Henry; because the jurisdiction of the latter, and the power to take oaths in such matters, is expressly reserved to them by the stat. *articuli cleri,* 13. 3. (see 2 *Inst.* 600); and because, in the words of

Sir J. NICHOLL, "it is of great convenience to creditors and legatees (for the same considerations apply to both) to obtain a *constat* of assets, before they engage here or elsewhere in perhaps expensive litigations for recovery of debts and legacies," I think that the jurisdiction, which has been exercised for some hundred years by the spiritual Courts over inventories, has not been put an end to, and that it is so useful a jurisdiction to suitors under the peculiar circumstances of this country as to induce us to be prone to support it as long as possible. I may add that, if we were to adopt a different conclusion, and were to consider the last decisions of the Queen's Bench *in rem*, we might present this anomaly,—that after refusing to entertain such jurisdiction in the spiritual Court, and so departing from the practice of the Courts in London, the question might come to be raised solemnly in the Courts at Westminster Hall, and then it is very probable that the powerful reasoning of Sir JOHN NICHOLL might prevail. We should thus neither act in pursuance with what is the practice of the Court who deals specially with these matters in England, nor with what might ultimately turn out to be the law, when the question was solemnly raised in the superior Courts. It is much better, therefore, to come to a conclusion which is on the safe side of offering benefit to suitors and hinderance to fraud, and which appears to have all the preponderance of reason and convenience in its favour.

1843.

Nov. 7.

LADHA KESSOW
v.
JEHANGHIR SHAPURJI.

[*Coram* ROPER, C. J., and PERRY, J.]

Held, by Supreme Court at Bombay that the Statutes of Limitations bind Hindus and Mussulmans; although the Supreme Court at Bengal held otherwise.

ASSUMPSIT for goods sold.

Plea, Statute of Limitations. Demurrer.

Dickinson contended that the statute only applied to British subjects. By the charter of justice and 21 Geo. 3, c. 70, s. 17, the contracts of Natives are to be determined by their own laws and usages; and he stated that the Supreme Court at Calcutta had held that the statute did not apply to Natives, *sed*

PER CURIAM. The words of the charter do not apply to this defendant, who is a Parsí, and therefore to be governed by English law. But even if both parties were Hindus, the decision would be the same, because the Statute of Limitations does not constitute a portion of the contract, but forms a portion of the law of procedure; and the parties who sue in a Court must submit to its rules of procedure, however different they may be from those of the country where the contract was made; *Story's Conflict of Laws;* 3 *Burge; Huber* v. *Steiner*, (2 New. Cas.)

Judgment for plaintiff.

HER HIGHNESS RUCKMABAI
v.
LULLABHAI MOTICHUND.

1850.

August 31.

[*Coram* Roper, C. J., and Perry, J.]

Where a party carried on business in a shop at Bombay by means of a gomashter or agent, but personally resided in Malwa, out of the Company's territories, *held* not to be a resident "beyond seas," so as to come within the exception in the Statutes of Limitations.

Trover for 200 chests of opium.

Plea, Statute of Limitations.

Replication, that at the time the cause of action accrued the plaintiff was residing without the territories subject to the East India Company, and without the jurisdiction of the Court, to wit, at Rutlam in Malwa, and that the plaintiff did not, from the time when, &c. until within six years, &c., come within the said territories or the said jurisdiction.

Rejoinder, that the plaintiff was a Hindu, and at the time when, &c., and up to, &c., and still doth carry on business or trade in a shop at Bombay, and during all that time was and is an inhabitant of Bombay, though personally resident at Malwa aforesaid.

Demurrer.

Howard argued the demurrer for the plaintiff, and contended that, if the Statute of Limitations was to be applied to India, the exceptions in the statutes must be also applied; and therefore, as the plaintiff was not personally an inhabitant of Bombay, she must be construed to be "beyond the seas."

Dickinson, contrà, contended that the true way to give effect to the act and to its meaning would be to hold that a person carrying on trade at Bombay by his agents was an *inhabitant*, and therefore bound to bring his action within six years; and of this opinion was the Court.

1850.

Ruckmabai v. Motichund.

This decision having been appealed against, the Judges transmitted to the clerk of the council under the rule of the Privy Council, the following reasons for the decision.

In compliance with the regulations of the Privy Council, we beg to subjoin the reasons which governed the Court in overruling the demurrer to the third plea in this case.

The Supreme Court at Bombay, having for some years past held that the Statutes of Limitations (21 Jac. 2, c. 16; 4 & 5 Anne, c. 16), apply to Bombay and to Hindus, as well as to Europeans, on the ground of such laws being laws affecting procedure, and not affecting the contract (see *Story's Conflict of Laws*, p. 483, Edinburgh), the point argued before us was, whether the plaintiff not residing personally within the jurisdiction of the Supreme Court of Bombay, was not to be considered as being "beyond the seas" at the time of the cause of action accruing, and of its being commenced.

Rutlam is one of the petty Rajput Rajahships of Malwa, adjoining the Bombay Presidency, and tributary to Sindia, under the guarantee of the British Government. The plaintiff, who by her title, is probably connected with the ruling family in Rutlam, appears by the record to keep a money shop in Bombay, under an assumed name, which is a custom very prevalent amongst monied Natives of rank in most parts of India.

We thought that the expression "beyond the seas," which can only be applied *çy pres* in India, did not include a place situated like Rutlam, and the case of *King* v. *Walker* (1 W. Bl. 286), clearly shews that the being without the jurisdiction of the Court, is not equivalent to the above expression.

We also thought that the carrying on a business or trade in the island of Bombay, amounted to a constructive presence in the island, so as to exclude the expression in the statute, even if Rutlam were to be considered as coming within the expression "beyond the seas;" and we conceived that the like conclusion would be arrived at by the Courts of Westminster Hall, if one of the great banking houses in London, such as Coutts' or Hammersley's, which are known to have been occasionally represented by a single individual, were to claim the right of

1850.

RUCKMABAI v. MOTICHUND.

bringing an action of assumpsit twenty years after the contract had been made, on the ground that that individual had been during the period "beyond the seas."

(Signed) E. PERRY.
W. YARDLEY.

31st *August*, 1850 (*a*).

(*a*) This case has been twice argued in appeal before the Privy Council, but no decision has yet been given. Jan. 1853.

END OF PART III.

PART IV.

MISCELLANEOUS.

1843.

Sept. 3.

JOHN DOE, on the demise of THE EAST INDIA COMPANY, *v.* HIRABAI.

[*Coram* ROPER C. J., and PERRY, J.]

1. Right of the East India Company to waste lands in Bombay.
2. Amount of notice required to a yearly occupant of Government land.
3. Rights of old occupiers of cultivated lands in India.
4. Rights acquired by long possession against Government.
5. Meaning of the terms pensâo, foras, in Bombay.

THE *Advocate General*, *Cochrane*, and *Herrick*, for plaintiff. *Howard* and *Dickinson*, for defendant.

Ejectment.

The question raised in this case had been previously before the Court in August term, 1842, when a trial of four days occurred as to the title of the defendant to some plots of ground at Colabah. She had bought up these plots from some cultivators, and had formal English conveyances made to her by them, and on registry in the collector's books, the rent was raised upon her considerably. She then attempted to build on the *locus in quo*, but the Company being desirous to preserve their title to the land, gave her notice to quit, and sent parties to take possession. She brought trespass *quare clausum fregit*, to which the defendants pleaded *lib. ten.* and the plaintiffs replied a lease for a year.

The Court upon the whole case thought that the tenure existing between the Government and defendant was a yearly tenancy, and therefore that the Company could not eject without six months' notice, and accordingly Hirabai had a verdict.

1843.

Doe d. E. I. Company v. Hirabai.

Six months' notice having been now given, this ejectment was brought.

Howard, for the defence, now contended that there was no tenancy at all between the parties, that the amount paid by the defendant was not rent, but land revenue, and contended that so long as the assessment was paid, no power existed in the Company to turn her out of possession, and he relied on Regulations XVII., XIX. of 1827.

Roper, C. J., at the close of the argument, gave judgment for the plaintiffs; but unfortunately no note is forthcoming of his argument.

1843. Sept. 3.

Perry, J. (*a*).—I quite agree with his Lordship, that the plaintiff is entitled to recover in this ejectment.

So many important questions have been started in the discussion of this case, and decisions relating to the tenure of land in Bombay, are interesting to such a large class of persons that I could have desired to prepare my judgment in writing, in order to limit my conclusions precisely to the sole point before the Court. But as I consider that point to be a very simple one, and in fact to raise no doubts at all when once it is distinctly stated, I have no hesitation in expressing my opinion upon it off hand. The question raised to which I desire to limit my observations, is as to the title of the East India Company to the waste lands of Bombay, and as to their power to dispose of them.

Title of Company to waste lands in Bombay the question in cause.

Much discussion has been raised during the argument as to the title to land throughout India generally, and Lord Lyndhurst's opinion in *Freeman* v. *Fairlie*, has been cited to shew that the proprietors of land (meaning thereby Zemin-

(*a*) At the request of the counsel in the cause, the note taken at the bar of this judgment was subsequently revised, and put into its present shape.

1843.

Doe d. E. I. Company v. Hirabai.

The question as to Government rights in land generally not before the Court.

dars) have an absolute ownership and dominion of the soil, although on the same side the opinion of the Court of Directors in 1815 (*a*) was also cited, laying down that the Zemindars had no such ownership, but that an hereditary indefeasible right existed in the ryots or cultivators. With respect to this much-agitated question, I would merely say that it does not come on the tapis at all now, for the celebrated dispute which has been raised relates to cultivated lands only, whilst that which we are now considering is the right to waste lands. From time immemorial in India the lands round villages have been subject to the plough, and have descended from occupier to occupier in endless succession, and as to such lands only the various questions touching hereditary right have arisen. But with respect to another great portion of land, amounting to at least one-half even in the most fertile districts according to Mr. *Mill*, and which, though, perhaps, equally fertile, still from the universal habits of the natives to congregate in villages around their temple and their tank, has never been brought into cultivation at all, no question has ever been raised as to any independent rights adverse to those of the Government. I will show, directly, that the very Regulation XVII., on which so much stress has been laid on behalf of the defendant, distinctly points out the power of Government to dispose of such waste lands in any way it pleases.

Government claims to waste lands denied by defendant.

The question, then, being as to the right to waste lands, I am distinctly of opinion that it is vested in the East India Company, and this not only with respect to the waste lands in Bombay, but also as to all the uncultivated lands in the Presidency. For it must be observed, that the construction we are called upon by the defendant to put upon Regulation XVII., equally limits the powers of the Government over lands in the Mofussil as over lands in Bombay.

The property admitted to exist in Government.

Now, I do not think it is expressly controverted that the Government does possess the fee simple in such lands in Bombay, and indeed it is admitted that if the Government officers had carefully preserved their rights by granting out

(*a*) From a Blue Book published by the Court.

1843.

Doe d. E. I. Company v. Hirabai.

leases for a certain period, in such case the land with whatever improvements had been erected upon it would return, according to the well-established law, into the hands of Government at the expiration of the term. But if so much admission be made, it seems to me necessarily to follow that the same right of proprietorship, which enabled a conveyance for a term of years to be granted out, must also admit of a grant being made for any shorter period. What, then, is there in the case to shew that the Government have precluded themselves from exercising the ordinary rights of ownership belonging to all other owners? To answer this, I will recapitulate shortly the facts which have come out in the trial.

Evidence as to occupation of waste lands in Bombay.

The result of the evidence on my mind is, that at some period between forty and fifty years ago, the land in question was a waste rocky ground, which then was brought into cultivation for the first time. The parties who occupied different plots of ground were of the humblest description, principally Coolies (*a*), and paid one or two rupees each for their occupation, which, until very lately, appears to be all that the ground was worth. I fix upon the period of forty or fifty years, from one or two circumstances, which, though minute, are sufficient to carry conviction to my mind. One of them is the fact spoken to by an early witness, when he states that, being a boy in 1803, he recollects his mother, who was a coloured woman, beginning to occupy the ground, and that she did so, because she saw other persons going to the ground and doing likewise. Another circumstance is, that an old man about the same period bought from another cultivator the right of occupation of the hill for Rs. 20, and that he then laid out Rs. 150 in clearing away the rocks, to prepare it for cultivation, showing thereby that it was then first made available as garden ground. I have no doubt, then, upon the

(*a*) This word so much used in Anglo Indian writings denotes the humblest exerciser of labour: it is usually derived from the Turkish word signifying "a porter," but in western India it is more probably derived from *Koli*, or Cooley, the name of the aboriginal race who are found in the Concan, in Gujarat, and indeed under the name of Koles, &c. over a much wider surface in India.

1843.

Doe d. E. I. Company v. Hirabai.

The *locus in quo* first occupied fifty years ago.

evidence, that about that time the ground first began to be occupied, and that immediately upon occupation, a small rent was paid to the Government for the scanty vegetables which could be obtained during the few months of the monsoon. It is also in evidence, that these cultivators have sold amongst themselves, for small sums of Rs.15 or Rs. 20, the right to occupy the ground; but this no more appears to me to denote an indefeasible right in the soil, than the same insignificant sales we have occasionally heard of in England, where one sweeper of a crossing sells his occupation right to another. And, indeed, I think it most distinctly appears, when these cultivators were called upon to make a more formal sale to a different class of purchasers, namely, to the defendant and her sons, that they evinced clearly their consciousness and their fears, that they were doing that which they had no right to do.

Loss to Government by culpability of their officers.

I also gather from the evidence that a great portion of land in Bombay had, through the apathy and negligence of former collectors, and perhaps through the dishonesty of Native clerks in the Government offices become wholly lost to the Government, and it seems that the attention of the present collector has been called to the matter, and that he has devised measures to prevent further encroachments being made. Just in the same way the Crown lands in England were diverted from their true destination by the negligence of Government, and we learn from *Blackstone* that when judicious steps were finally adopted to prevent any further encroachments, the remedy came too late for almost every valuable possession of the Crown had been alienated. Such, also, in great part, may be the case in Bombay, notwithstanding the endeavours of Mr. Grant, the collector, to prevent any more land slipping through his fingers, as it had done with his predecessors in office. Still the fact seems quite notorious that through apathy on one side and encroachments on the other, the Government has lost a great portion of its lands. But because it has been neglectful of its interests in a great many instances, it does not at all follow that it is incumbent on Government, or its officers, to continue to be so, when so barefaced an attempt as that made by

Fraudulent conduct of defendant's family.

the defendant is being committed before their eyes. For I quite agree with his Lordship that the conduct of the defendant's family has been fraudulent throughout, and that these purchases from the cultivators of that which they knew they had no right to sell, these payments only half made, and made as it seems to me merely because the case was to be brought on for trial, more than double the sums paid being also inserted as the consideration, and these solemn forms of conveyance, drawn out in English by some lawyer's clerk, all these serve to convince me that the whole was a scheme concocted to get the land out of the cultivators, to steal a march on the Government, and to deceive this Court when this written evidence at some distant time should be brought before it. Finally, it appears that the rents have been raised, during the last few years, upon some of these cultivators, and upon the defendant herself, and that several of the cultivators had been removed from their occupations from time to time to make way for Government buildings. Now, these being the facts, the Government being admitted to be the proprietors of the land, and this Court having at the previous trial held (very favourably for the cultivators I think) that these persons were tenants from year to year, what is there to prevent the Government, like any other proprietor of the soil, from ejecting tenants who are attempting to set up an adverse title? The proposition contended for by the defence is, that those payments which have been made by the occupiers do not constitute rent, but revenue, that they are not paid to the Government as proprietors of land, but exacted from the cultivators as their contribution to the State; and, therefore, that from the fact of these payments no inference as to the relationship of landlord and tenant can be drawn. But this distinction between rent and revenue, where the lands are admitted to belong to Government is often a faint one. Rent may be said not to exist anywhere in India in the scientific sense in which a former Chief Justice of this Court (Sir Edward West) and Mr. *Malthus* have defined it; but the monopoly price which a sole proprietor is enabled to exact for land is not improperly termed rent in the legal sense of the

Argued that the payments to Government by defendant not rent but revenue.

1843.

Doe d. E. I. Company v. Hirabai.

Distinction between rent and revenue sometimes nominal only.

word, and if that proprietor is the Government, it is also revenue, although the proposition is not true conversely; that is, all rent is revenue when it is received by the Government, though all revenue derived from land may not be rent. But the decision of the Lord Chancellor and the arguments of Master *Stephen* respecting a Bengal Pottah in *Freeman* v. *Fairlie* are brought to bear to prove that the reservations of money in the receipts which the collector gave to these cultivators are mere assessment and not rent. But the Pottah in Bengal cannot be brought into analogy with these receipts, it is found distinctly in that case that when Government granted out or sold its waste lands, it did so by way of Pottah reserving a money payment, and it is also expressly stated that the reservation contained in these Pottahs could not be increased. Here we have not the slightest evidence of any intention of Government to make a grant, or of any belief by the cultivator that a grant had been made, but the contrary, and we know from the Regulations, and the facts, that the rent could be increased.

Bombay regulations relied on;

The main argument of Mr. *Howard*, however, is founded on Regulations XVII. and XIX., and he contends that as Government have prescribed the mode in which the land revenue shall be raised, and as they have only given the collector power to sell the lands in case the assessment shall be in arrear, they have impliedly parted with the power (if they ever possessed it) of turning out tenants upon a six months' notice. He also contends that as the clause in Regulation XIX. sect. 4, enables the collector to sell the interest of the cultivator in his land, it is a legislative recognition that the cultivator possesses a vendible interest in the land. But first of all it appears to me quite clear that the clauses in Regulation XVII. which he refers to, do not relate to waste lands at all. They all refer to the cultivated lands which I have spoken of at the beginning of my judgment, they define who is to be considered the occupant, how his interest may be disposed of, and they give very stringent powers to the collector and revenue officers to sell the lands. When uncultivated lands are spoken of, a different set of powers is

but they relate to cultivated lands only.

given, and they are provided for in Regulation XVII., sect. 7. That section it is true is not made applicable to similar lands in Bombay, but if there are such lands in the island, and if no special legislation has been passed respecting them, it follows that the Government may dispose of them at its free-will just like any other proprietor of the land. Suppose, then, that instead of the Government being entitled to the waste lands, there were a lord of the manor here, and there is a trace in Mr. *Warden's Report on Land Tenures in Bombay* (a), of some such manorial rights at the time of the Portuguese cession, and suppose also that the evidence in the present case were given of payments of rent to such lord of the manor, how could this Court possibly decide that the occupiers were entitled to hold over against him. But if the right in question flows naturally out of the rights of property, the Government is entitled to the same legal protection as any other proprietor. The argument drawn from the clause in Section 4, of Regulation XIX. which speaks of the lands of the cultivator being saleable appears to me to involve the fallacy *quod dictum de uno dictum de omnibus!* In many cases undoubtedly the cultivator or occupant possesses an interest in the soil, he did so at the time of the Regulations in 1827; he did so, when Mr. *Warden* reported to Government in 1814; he did so long before when the Portuguese ceded their island. In the capitulation made to Ensign Cook there is a provision in respect of the accustomed *Foras*, which, perhaps, is equivalent to the celebrated Spanish word *Fueros* we hear so much of in modern times, or it may mean the rent reserved for outlying grounds, for lands lying *fora* the demesne lands. Then there is the fixed sum called pension or *pensao* of the Portuguese corresponding, I suppose, with the word *pensio* which denoted in middle ages a settled sum paid for land, for I find it used by *Bracton* in respect of the King's tenants in ancient demesne, who, he says, "*a gleba amoveri non possunt quamdiu solvere possunt debitas pensiones.*" These ascertained or asserted interests in the soil, therefore, being known to exist, the collector under section 4, is enabled to sell them for arrears of revenue; but it no more proves that every culti-

Cultivators in India often possess an indefeasable right in the land,

which is recognised by the regulations.

(a) Printed in *Transactions of Bombay Geographical Society*, Vol. I.

1843.

Doe d. E. I. Company v. Hirabai.

vator must possess an interest in the soil, than an enactment that his beasts of the plough might be sold would prove that every cultivator possessed bullocks.

But a mere squatter in India gains no title to the land.

But the restrictions which Mr. *Howard* would seek to impose on the power of the Government to deal with their waste lands, lead inevitably to the conclusion that directly a cultivator has placed himself on a piece of vacant ground, and has paid Government a money payment, for which his name is entered in the village or revenue records, from that moment he has acquired an indefeasible right in the soil, from which he cannot be ejected so long as he pays this assessment. This proposition is the undoubted logical result of the arguments which have been brought forward in behalf of the defendant, and it has been very candidly adopted as the position by which the defendant's case must stand or fall. It is said that this tenure may be of a startling character to an English lawyer, but that it is well known in India, and consonant to the habits and manners of the people. The proposition appears to me to be much more startling to any one acquainted with Indian tenures and manners than to an English lawyer. The latter, on arriving in this country, must be prepared to meet with divers varied relations as to land from those he has been accustomed to in his own country; but an Indian revenue officer would, I think, indeed be astonished to hear such a claim set up for the ryots with respect to common or waste lands. And it is only necessary to say that not the slightest evidence has been brought forward that any such extraordinary tenure has ever been supposed to exist in any part of India.

Argued, most landlords in Bombay have no better title.

But another forcible argument has been urged, which undoubtedly demands an answer. For it has been asked if the Court decides for the plaintiffs, where is the line to be drawn? and whether it does not follow that all the ancient possessors of land in Bombay, who with their ancestors may have occupied for hundreds of years, may not also be turned out at a six months' notice, if they are unable to produce any sanad (*a*) for the original occupation? I should indeed pause if any such construction were likely to follow on our decision. It is very possible that some of the houses in the fort alluded to by

(*a*) Grant in writing.

Mr. *Howard* may have been originally built on Government ground; but where a proprietor, and, *a fortiori*, a Government has stood by for a long period, and witnessed large capital invested in his soil, it is impossible to suppose that any Court of law or equity would take such land from its ancient possessor. But all such cases are wholly unlike the one under consideration; here the occupant has not vested fixed capital in the soil, the Government has not connived at her encroachments, but has done all in its power to prevent a title being gained; here no expectations were created that Government interference would not take place; and the only tangible ground on which the defendant can rest her case is in the existence of that supposed right of the cultivator, which I have already stated to be, in my opinion, equally novel and preposterous.

Rights may be acquired against Government as against others by long possession.

But defendant's possession recent, and permissive.

I therefore think that the verdict must be for the plaintiff; and that any other decision would be wholly at variance with those rights which the laws of India, equally with the laws of all other civilized communities, concur in conferring upon the proprietors of land.

Conclusion. Company proprietor of waste lands.

HOUGH *v.* LECKIE AND OTHERS.

1848. June 30.

[*Coram* Sir E. PERRY, C. J.]

Tenure of houses built on land of the East India Company in Bombay.

Semble, where a grant to occupy land in India is made by Government in general terms, on payment of the ordinary assessment, the presumption is that it is a grant in perpetuity, although the assessment may be raised from time to time, but where the Government enters into a special contract, the terms of the contract must be looked at to ascertain whether the Government is dealing as landlord, or as a Government having reference to the assessment.

Thus, when Government granted permission to W. to build in Bombay, and a valuable house was built in consequence, but a question arising as to the extent of property in the house, Government having subsequently granted, and W. having accepted, a lease for nine years, *held*, that W. at the expiration of such lease became tenant from year to year.

MAJOR GENERAL WADDINGTON by his will, dated 16th November, 1813, after certain bequests to his wife, his son Henry, and his daughter Mrs. Hough, proceeded as follows:

1848.

HOUGH v. LECKIE and Others.

The house I have lived in (No. 1) upwards of twenty years to be entirely at the disposal of my wife Diana, during her life, or until she marries again; then to go to my son Henry, but not to be sold or alienated from the family in any way whatever."

General Waddington died in 1814, and the widow remained in possession of the house till her death in 1841, when it was taken possession of by her daughter Mrs. Hough.

Henry Waddington, the son, died in 1818, leaving a widow and an infant daughter Lilias, and by his will he devised all his property to his wife for life, remainder to his daughter.

Lilias Waddington died in 1819, and her mother afterwards intermarried with G. Thompson, by whom she had two sons, and died.

The reversion to the house in question having thus vested in Lilias Waddington, the question arose whether at her death it vested in her mother as next of kin, or in Mrs. Hough as heiress of Lilias Waddington her neice, or of General Waddington, her father.

On a petition in this suit, which had been filed soon after the death of General Waddington, to obtain a construction of the will, it was referred to the Master by consent to inquire what was the tenure of the house described as No. 1, and in which of the parties it was vested.

It appeared in evidence that the house in question had been built by General Waddington on waste ground of the Honorable Company at Colabah in the year 1786.

In 1796, it seemed that the Government had instituted inquiries as to several houses which had been built at Colabah, as they alleged, "without any permission or authority whatever,".........."as it never was the intention of Government that houses of a permanent construction should be built on the island of Colabah, which was a place of cantonment for the troops."

In consequence of such inquiries the houses so built were classified, and by regulations of the Governor in Council, in 1793, the proprietors were informed that they must not ask higher rents than the rents allowed by Government for officer's quarters, as specified for each class, and that if they did not conform to such regulations their houses would be pulled down. Two houses which General Waddington had built (including the house now in dispute) were accordingly classified as military quarters.

In 1799, General Waddington remonstrated on his houses being thus treated, and forwarded to Government the copies of the documents, &c. in his possession for leave for building on Old Woman's Island.

In 1805, he again addressed Government on the subject, apparently in consequence of the military authorities having continued to treat his houses as military quarters; and he offered to sell or let them to Government.

Mr. Warden, Secretary to Government, replied as follows:

"Sir,

"I am directed by the Honorable the Governor in Council to acknowledge the receipt of your letter of the 29th March last, and to intimate that your houses do not appear to have been built under circumstances that exempt them from their being subject to the conditions of houses set down as military quarters; yet considering the length of time you have occupied these premises, and the expense you must have been at in their improvement, the Governor in Council is willing to acquiesce in the essential object of your present application by granting you a lease of the ground now in your occupancy, subject to the payment of such an assessment as the collector of Bombay may prepare under the sanction of the Governor in Council, which will virtually and definitively exempt and secure your premises from being subjected hereafter to be converted into military quarters.

I have, &c.

6th *June*, 1805. FRANCIS WARDEN.

Orders were thereupon issued to the collector of land revenue, who thereupon gave the following instrument to General Waddington:

"In compliance with the orders of the Honorable the Governor in Council under the 14th February, 1806, I, Peter Le Messurier, collector of the Honorable Company's rent and

1848.

HOUGH v LECKIE and Others.

revenue, do in virtue thereof let out to General Waddington, on behalf of the said Company, a spot of ground situate, &c., on condition of his paying annually for the term of nine years, commencing from the above date, (at the end of which period this grant or lease is to be returned into this office, either to be renewed or otherwise as the Honorable the Governor in Council might deem proper), on account of the said Company, to their collector for the time being Rs. 216, calculated at 11 reas per square yard, being the usual rate of quit and ground rent.

"14th *Feb.* 1806."

This document was produced by the executors of General Waddington, into whose hands all his papers had come.

The Master reported that the estate of General Waddington in the premises, was a yearly tenancy up to 1806, and that in that year he accepted a lease from the Company for nine years, at the expiration of which lease, the tenancy became a yearly holding, and that nothing had occurred since that period to change as between the Company and the tenant the nature of the tenure, but that having regard to the circumstances that the land held of the East India Company in Bombay on similar tenure is permitted to be enjoyed with all the certainty of the continuance of an actual lease for years, the interest which the executors of General Waddington had in the house and premises, must be regarded as a valuable chattel interest, though of an indeterminate duration available as part of his personal assets.

Exceptions were filed to this report:

Dickinson, in support of the exceptions.

First. General Waddington's estate in the house up to 1806, was the ordinary estate which every one holds under a grant from government. Such estate is a grant in perpetuity. Companys' officers, in their reports to government, always seek to make out such holdings to be merely precarious or permissive, but it is too late now to contend for such doctrine. There are numerous instances where government has bought back such estates from the owner at the value of the fee simple, and *Freeman* v. *Fairlie* (1 Moore, Priv. Coun. Rep.) is conclusive, that the fee passes under such a grant.

Second. Such an estate being vested in General Waddington, his acceptance of the lease of 1806 could not divest it. There was no consideration for it. But it is not in fact a lease. Mr. Le Messurier, the collector, calls it a grant lease. And, as in the case of the Pottahs in Bengal, strict conveyancing language is not required in these documents. The intention of the government was to grant an estate in perpetuity to General Waddington, and the true construction of the instrument is, that the term of nine years there mentioned is only a pledge by government that they will not raise the assessment during that period. The Master ought, therefore, to have found that this was an estate in perpetuity, or an equitable fee, which therefore passed to the heir.

Third. General Waddington always treated this as an estate in fee. By his will he expressly directs that it should never be alienated from his blood. The next of kin therefore, who are now claiming, and who are legatees under the will, are bound either by estoppel, or by election, or by evidence, from disputing the freehold character of this house, whatever may be the true nature of it as between the East India Company and the tenant.

The Master, when he talks of the tenure having all the certainty of continuance of an actual lease for years is unintelligible. And he corroborates his views by referring to property held *on similar tenure*, but he had no evidence of any similar tenures before him.

Howard, contrà. The language of the Master may be slightly inaccurate, but his conclusions are sound. Whatever may have been the terms of the grant to General Waddington in 1786, and there is no evidence at all of them, although it is clear that the documents were in General Waddington's possession, still the grant and acceptance of the lease in 1806 clearly defines what the terms of the relation were between General Waddington and the East India Company. That being so, no length of time, no explanation of the lease being

1848.

Hough v. Leckie and Others.

renewable, no actual value inherent in the term, will change the nature of the relation. *Clayton* v. *Attorney General*, (Cooper, Cas. temp. Cottenham, 97).

In point of fact, all the land held of the Company, on which a yearly rent is paid, is held on a tenure from year to year, and the argument of the Advocate General in the case of *East India Company* v. *Hirabai* (*a*), which was tried in this Court in 1846, is irresistible, that when once the relation of landlord and tenant is proved to have been created, no lapse of time will change the relation, so long as the rent is paid.

As to the doctrine of election or estoppel, no authority has been cited, and it is untenable.

[Perry, C. J.—If a testator leaves his freeholds to A., and his leaseholds to B., the legatees may surely discuss in a Court of Justice, whether an estate in Dale is leasehold or freehold. In this case, the testator leaves the house to his son, without expressing where it is to go after the son's death, except by intimating that it was not to be sold, which was a limitation he had no power to affix. On the son's death, therefore, the devolution of the property turns entirely on its legal character, and the construction of a Court of law is inevitable, if any question arises].

Dickinson, in reply. If this estate, at the termination of the lease of 1806, became a tenancy from year to year, then Mrs. Waddington, by continuing to be occupant till her death in 1841, and Mrs. Hough, her daughter, by continuing in occupation since, has acquired title to the term, and to whatever equities may accompany it.

Cur. adv. vult.

1848.

June 30.

Perry, C. J.—The question in this case respects the title to a house in Colaba, which (passing over a life estate to Mr. Waddington) in 1818, vested in Lilias Diana Waddington, an infant, and which, at her death, passed to her mother, Mrs. Thompson, if it was a chattel interest, or to Mrs. Hough, her aunt, if it was freehold.

(*a*) *Ante*, p. 480.

1848.

HOUGH v. LECKIE and Others.

The house in question was built by General Waddington in 1786, on land belonging to the East India Company; and it would seem, at first sight, as if the question were now raised, which has been so often approached in this Court, but on which no solemn decision has been given, as to the true legal relation existing between the East India Company and the occupant of valuable house property built on their land; but as it has not been found necessary to decide this point hitherto, so it is unnecessary to decide it now. I may observe, however, with reference to the much-disputed question of the soil in India, that the notion of an ownership in fee is not at all a familiar one in the minds of Asiatics, in the sense in which Europeans trace the relation so as to determine between the conflicting rights of individuals. The notions which are present to native minds are, the right of possession of the soil as evidenced by ancient usage and the right to revenue, which the Sovereign, or those claiming under him, are deemed to be entitled to.

Long disputed question as to the title of valuable house property built on Government land; not necessary to decide it.

Grants of such revenue, assignments of a portion of it, authority to collect it, or exaction of it by conquest or usurpation, account for the various parties who are found all over India, receiving what is equivalent to rent in Europe, such as Enamdars, Talookdars, Zemindars, Grassias, holders of the Chouth, and occasionally, in Bombay and its neighbourhood, Fazendars. English ideas of law have occasionally been applied to these receivers of revenue; and a class of them, the Zemindars, were held by the Regulations of 1793 (which were implicitly followed by Lord LYNDHURST in *Freeman* v. *Fairlie*), to be the owners of the land in fee simple; but what is now generally admitted to be an erroneous application of an English law notion, caused the historian Niebuhr to observe, "that Lord CORNWALLIS's scheme was one of the most unfortunate, but best intended plans that ever ruined a country." It results from these notions, that usually throughout India, when a permission to occupy or cultivate land, without specifying any terms, is granted by Government, a right in perpetuity is thereby supposed to be conferred on the grantee, subject only to such payment of revenue as the Government may choose

Question as to Indian land tenures has been complicated by applying English law notions.

Indian notions simple; right of Government to assessment; right of occupier to possess.

1848.

HOUGH v. LECKIE and Others.

And have been introduced into Bombay.

to exact. And, as native agency is, and must be, extensively employed in an Indian Government, it is not surprising, that the same doctrines should have introduced themselves into Bombay as are seen to prevail extensively in the interior. The consequence is, that the clear distinction which exists between rent and revenue is usually lost sight of, and the Government, for the most part, acting by their native agents, treats the sums obtained from the occupants of the land as revenue only.

But in Bombay Government have a feudal tenure of the lands: and ordinary rights of landlord.

In the island of Bombay however, whatever may be the case elsewhere, there appears to be no doubt that all the soil of the island, which was not in private hands at the time of the cession, vested in the East India Company. The island belonged to a European power, with whom the feudal laws as to landed property prevailed, and the Company also hold the island by feudal tenure from the Crown.

Rights of landlord and of Government often confounded.

Now it is obvious, that when the Government of Bombay deals with such lands they may either make grants of the land in perpetuity, for the purpose of obtaining assessment or *jumma*, just as the Indian Governments have been accustomed to do from time immemorial, in which case, according to *Freeman* v. *Fairlie*, a perpetuity or freehold would pass; or they may deal with their land as any other landlord may do, and grant it out for short or long terms, or on any other condition they are able to impose. An attentive consideration to this distinction appears to me to enable every case of this kind to be disposed of. In the present case, for example, we have no evidence of the terms on which the Government granted General Waddington permission to build, but we find that, in 1793, the Government complained that his houses, with several others in Colaba, had been built by usurpation within a military cantonment; and Government informed him and other proprietors that they must submit to have their houses classified, and rents allotted to them corresponding with the rents which officers were allowed from Government, or that their houses would be pulled down.

How distinction to be drawn.

Facts in this case.

General Waddington remonstrated against these regulations, but his houses were classified under them as military quarters till March 1805. On that date the Secretary to Government, in consequence of a renewed claim by General Waddington, that his houses should be erased from the list of houses set down as military quarters, intimated to him, that without acceding to his claim, the Government, in consideration of the length of time he had occupied, and the money he had laid out on the premises, would acquiesce in the essential object of his application, by granting him a lease of the ground now in his occupation.

And on the 14th February, 1806, the collector of Bombay delivered to General Waddington an instrument, in substance as follows:—"In compliance with the orders of Government, I, Peter Le Messurier, collector, &c., do, in virtue thereof, let out to General Waddington, on behalf of the Honorable Company, a spot of ground situated, &c., on condition of his paying annually, for the term of nine years, commencing from, &c.; at the end of which period this grant or lease is to be returned into this office, either to be renewed or otherwise, as the Honorable the Governor in Council may deem proper, on account of the said Company, for Rs. 216, calculated at 11 reas per square yard, being the usual rate of quit and ground rent." If this instrument is a valid lease, then *cadit quæstio,* and it would be analogous to the pottah granted to Mr. Vansittart, which is mentioned in *Freeman* v. *Fairlie.* The interest in the term passed to Mrs. Waddington at the general's death, in 1814, as devisee for life. On the expiration of the lease, in 1815, Mrs. Waddington continued to hold, as tenant from year to year, with whatever equitable right to renewal might accompany the term; and at her death, in 1841, the interest in the term vested in the devisee in remainder under General Waddington's will, the representative of whom at the present day is Spencer Compton, as administrator of Mrs. Thompson. I can see no reason for doubting that this is a valid lease; it is curt and inartificial in form, but the forms of conveyancing never have been in use or required in the East. The letter of Mr. Secretary Warden, in 1805, states clearly, that it was the intention of Government to grant a lease, and this is the instrument granted in consequence. Up

1848.

HOUGH v. LECKIE and Others.

Conclusion, in this case Government has granted lease, and dealt as landlord.

to that time the title of General Waddington was disputed; and the fact of this lease being found among his muniments appears to me to prove distinctly that it was accepted by him.

I was pressed, however to declare what the equitable title of the tenant, from year to year, on such a lease might be; for that, if it amounted to a perpetual right to renewal, it might enure as an equitable fee, so as in some way to entitle the heir. I do not think that I am bound to do so, or that the Court is in a condition to pronounce upon the equity, without the East India Company being before it. This is an exception to the Master's report, who has found that the tenure of the house in question is by a yearly holding, and as I agree with him in that conclusion, it is sufficient to overrule the exceptions.

It ought to be added, that the Recorder's Court, in 1822, arrived at the same conclusion with respect to the title to this house which I have now formed; but there is some doubt whether the question was properly in issue at that period.

Under the circumstances, no order as to costs.

1848.

March 9.

DOE DEM. DORABJI DADI SANTUK *v.* THE BISHOP OF BOMBAY

FAZENDARY CASE.

[*Coram* PERRY, C. J., and YARDLEY, J.]

Fazenda tenure in Bombay. *Held*, that a Fazendar who had no other title to shew to the land than the receipt of a small quit rent, was not entitled to eject the tenant on the latter's pulling down his house, and rebuilding without permission, *dissentiente* YARDLEY, J.

EJECTMENT for a portion of vacant ground at Sonapur, which had been formerly occupied by a house bought by the

1848.

Doe d. Dorabji v. Bishop of Bombay.

Bishop of Bombay for religious purposes in 1843, for the sum of Rs. 1250, and which his Lordship had pulled down for the purpose of rebuilding premises connected with the London Mission.

The lessor of the plaintiff was the fazendar(*a*) of the soil whereupon the house in question, with two others, stood, and had purchased his fazendary right in 1838 for Rs. 601.

Upon the Bishop proceeding to rebuild without having obtained the permission of the lessor of the plaintiff as fazendar, the latter claimed a right to eject him, and accordingly brought this action.

At the first trial, before Perry, C. J., *Le Messurier*, A. G., launched his case as an ordinary one of landlord and tenant, and contented himself with proving that the owner of the house in question had always paid the fazendar Rs. 8 per annum.

Howard, contrà, contended that the receipt of a small quit rent did not prove any thing more than the title to such rent; per Holroyd, J. (*Gow*, 473); and observed that this was an attempt made by the fazendar to set up an absolute title to the land, which had often been made, but which had been universally denied in this Court by all the Judges of the Supreme Court, ever since he had practised in it.

Le Messurier, A. G., replied.

Perry, C. J.—My experience, since I have sat here, certainly is in accordance with what Mr. *Howard* states. I had always understood from Sir H. Roper, C. J., that the fazendar's claim could not be supported, and I acted upon it no longer ago than last Term, when I decided against the fazendar in an action of ejectment. The defendant, therefore, must have a verdict.

Le Messurier, A. G., subsequently moved for a rule for a

(*a*) For meaning of this term, see *post*, p. 505.

1848.

Doe d. Dorabji v. Bishop of Bombay.

new trial, on the ground that the course of decisions cited was a surprise upon him, that he could not ascertain that any solemn decision had ever been given, that the tenure between fazendars and tenants was most important, and that if there were any custom it would be well to ascertain what it was, and what mode existed for enforcing it.

On these grounds a rule was granted, and the cause came on for trial before Perry, C. J., and Yardley, J., in the November Term, 1847.

The points urged on either side are so fully stated in the following judgments, that it is unnecessary to give the arguments of counsel.

Cur. adv. vult.

1848. March 9.

Perry, C. J.—This action of ejectment has been brought to recover a portion of vacant ground, called Fazendary land, on which two houses were situated in 1843, and which the Bishop of Bombay then purchased for the sum of Rs. 1250, subject to the payment of Rs. 8 per annum to a person called the Fazendar, who is the lessor of the plaintiff.

The Bishop pulled down these two houses, with a view to erecting a school or other building connected with some religious society, and the fazendar, who purchased in the year 1838 for Rs. 601 what may be called the fazendarship of the oart or close in which these two, with two other, houses stood, is now seeking to eject the Bishop, on the ground that he has no right to rebuild after he has received notice to quit from the fazendar.

The action was originally tried before me in June Term last, when a verdict was found for the defendant; but for reasons which I will state presently I granted leave for a new trial, which took place before my learned brother and myself in November Term last, and in which we have now to give our verdict.

Court not unanimous.

I regret exceedingly to state that this verdict will not be unanimous, but that after earnest, repeated, and anxious attempts to ascertain the one true solution of a difficult case,

1848.

Doe d. Dorabji v. Bishop of Bombay.

we have not been able to concur, and must, therefore, respectively give effect to the conclusions which our reason dictates.

This unfortunate, but occasionally inevitable, result, where two independent minds have to deal with a question in which many disputed facts, some artificial reasoning, and a few nice propositions of law occur, has led me of course to examine my own reasonings with more than usual distrust; and as I cannot but feel that the principal responsibility of an erroneous judgment lies with me, I think it right to state certain principles which I have kept in view during the discussion as those which ought, as I conceive, to be present to my mind in an inquiry of this nature.

The defendant in this case happens to be a European of distinguished rank, but the question in the case is one of almost exclusively native interest, as it affects the entire relation which exists between the occupants of houses in this island and the persons called Fazendars, and possibly no other European in the place except his Lordship has any interest in such a point. Now in all such cases it appears to me, from the language used in divers acts of Parliament and in our Charter of Justice, that it is the bounden duty of the Judges to observe the ancient usages and customs of the inhabitants as much as possible. Wherever usages and customs exist, innocent in themselves, or at all events not detrimental to the public interests, the Judges should be astute to discover a legal basis for them, and so to carry out in a legitimate manner those principles of order and conventional rules which the community had insensibly adopted for themselves.

Usages and customs of Natives a guide to legal decision.

When states of fact occur to which analogous conditions in European life may present themselves to the mind of an English lawyer, the latter should be cautious in applying the rule of English law applicable in England, unless he is satisfied that the analogy is complete; and, in all cases he should be studious to ascertain whether the phenomena of human life which come before him are not much more readily to be traced to an Indian origin, and to be explained by Asiatic notions and habits than by principles of European civilization.

English analogies to be applied cautiously.

1848.

Doe d. Dorabji v. Bishop of Bombay.

It appears to me that it has been owing to the careful application of these principles to the Asiatic communities at each Presidency that the introduction of English law has been attended with so little difficulty, and has worked on the whole so beneficially. Nothing, I think, will be found more marked than the reluctance of English Judges on the Indian Bench to introduce English law doctrines which clash with the prevalent notions of the community, and I trace the operation of this feeling in every case I meet with where it could legitimately have play.

Cautious dealing of Indian Judges in applying English law: and wise exercise of discretion.

It results no doubt from this doctrine that Indian Judges are invested with a wider discretionary power in the application of what may be called *municipal* English law, than English Judges possess, or ought to possess at home. But the true correction of any possible evil that might flow from this source consists in the obligation which I conceive is incumbent upon the Judges to follow humbly the steps of their predecessors in every case in which a solemn decision has been pronounced upon questions which do not depend on principles of universal jurisprudence.

By applying these canons to the present case I find but one conclusion open to me. The lessor of the plaintiff to succeed in this ejectment must make out that a Bombay fazendar, the origin of whose title is not shown, and who can prove no contract between himself and the occupant of the house, may eject that occupant whose title is founded on similar ancient usage, and on that alone, on the latter pulling the house down for the purpose of rebuilding it.

Duty to follow previous decisions.

Larger rights were claimed by the Advocate General for fazendars in the course of the argument, and some of the fazendar witnesses did the like; but it is not necessary to put the claim of the lessor of the plaintiff higher on the present occasion than I have stated them.

Now to contradict such claim it appears to me that the decisions of this Court are so uniform, continuous, and precise for as long a period as we can trace them back that the question really is not open to discussion.

During the seven years that I have sat on the Bench there

1848.

Doe d. Dorabji v. Bishop of Bombay.

is no question of Native usages which has come more frequently before this Court, and whether incidentally or directly on the question arising (and I have had repeated personal experience in both forms) I have acted upon the law as handed down to me in denying such a right to exist.

The late Chief Justice Roper, who had a much more extensive experience of the business in this Court for the twenty years preceding his departure than any person in the country, laid down the same law from time to time, and often declared in Court that the question had been immutably settled by the decisions of the various Judges he had known. And the case cited by Mr. *Howard* at the bar of *Doe* on the demise of *Bhawoo Narronjee* v. *Mariam Bebee*, and others which was tried in 1827, and which lasted three days was a most solemn adjudication of the question, now attempted to be put in issue, as any one who will take the trouble to read the evidence on the files of our Court may easily satisfy himself.

It is true that in a case in Sir *Herbert Compton's Note Book*, which I brought to the attention of the Advocate General, there is an entry of a cause, *Doe* on the demise of *Changeah Govind* v. *Bomonjee Bazonjee*, (which defendant was a witness in the present case) and which was called on before him for trial in November, 1832, but referred by him to arbitration, and to which the Chief Justice appended this marginal note :—

"This case was said to involve a question of fazendar tenure—respecting which there has been much dispute in Bombay—no satisfactory decision, and little if any authentic information. It was to have been asserted by the defendant that the chawl which had been formerly built on the ground in dispute, and which had belonged to the party under whom the lessor of the plaintiff claimed (and which had been burnt down in 1826-7) the land reverted to the fazendar!"

Mr. Advocate General contends from this note that at all events the question was not settled in 1832, but without laying any stress on the note of admiration with which Sir H. Compton concludes his memorandum as any indication

1848.

Doe d. Dorabji v. Bishop of Bombay.

of his opinion, or on the fact that the arbitrators decided against the fazendar's claim, it is sufficient to state that at this time Sir H. Compton had only been ten months in Bombay, that he was sitting alone on the Bench, that no cases were cited, and no discussion at all took place at the Bar.

The point in dispute in this cause settled by decisions.

I repeat, therefore, my conviction, that so far as the decisions of this Court can settle a question, such as is now before us, this question has been settled, and that even if we had the power it would be most injurious to re-open it.

But if question *res integra*, evidence calls for decision against fazendars.

Fazendary tenure discussed.

But even if the case were *res integra*, I should come to exactly the same conclusion upon the evidence as a juror having some local knowledge of the circumstances and of the island, as my learned predecessors have done upon similar testimony. The origin of the relation between fazendars and householders, where the possession is ancient, and no proofs of a contract are forthcoming, is altogether unknown. Whether the fazendars were the original owners of the soil, or mere cultivators and farmers holding of other persons, such as the Jesuits, and religious houses, once existing in Bombay; whether the house occupiers have encroached upon the fazendars, and have turned their permissive right to occupy into an indefeasible, right on certain conditions like the copyholders and tenants of the Northern manors in England; or, whether the fazendars have encroached upon the Government, and usurped the right to claim the Government assessment from the tenants, it is by no means easy to say. I believe that occasionally the one state of facts has occurred, occasionally the other. From what we know of the state of the island at the time of the cession, it was occupied by only a few thousand souls, 10,000 according to Dr. Fryer who visited the island in 1671, and who then found the population much increased by a mixture of people from the neighbouring countries, most of them fugitives and vagabonds. The soil of the island, except in the portions built over in the Native town, Mahim, and Mazagon was swampy, or covered by the sea in the low portion of the island, or barren uncultivated ridges in the remainder.

1848.

Doe d. Dorabji v. Bishop of Bombay.

Judging from analogy in the other parts of India, such uncultivated ground would belong to Government, not to private individuals. The term fazenda is not significant in any oriental tongue, and is plainly derivable from the Portuguese word fazendeiro, which, in *Vieyra's Dictionary* is Englished "a cultivator, a tiller, a husbandman," and never seems to be used to designate a proprietor; and it does not appear that the Portuguese law contains any trace of a tenure similar to that called fazendary in Bombay. The system therefore, in all probability, has grown up in this island during the last 200 years by much usurpation on either side; and as in all cases of usurpation, which by long efflux of time has given birth to a right, the extent of the respective rights which have arisen must be measured by the actual usage which has taken place. This short remark disposes of the great body of evidence in the case.

Meaning of *fazendar*.

The lessor of the plaintiff called a cloud of fazendar witnesses, principally Parsees, and all, with one or two exceptions, belonging to the humbler walks of life. These witnesses were of course interested to place the claims of fazendars as high as they could, and being thus deeply interested they made no impression on my mind whatever, except where their testimony was corroborated by facts known to the Court or by antecedent probability. But amid all the anomalous and rambling evidence which they gave, the most of which was referrible to their opinion of what fazendars could do, or to their own practice of what *they* had done with certain poor people, such as Coolies (*a*) and milkwomen, not capable of resisting aggression, not one of them was able to adduce an instance in which a fazendar had exerted the right which they all said he possesses, of turning out the occupant of a substantial house which had been enjoyed time immemorially. With one other remark, which may serve to explain portions of the evidence, I will dismiss this part of the case.

True meaning of *fazendary* land.

The true meaning of the expression fazendary land is, land not belonging to Government. The classification has its origin entirely in the mode in which the Government assessment is

(*a*) See *ante*.

1848.

Doe d. Dorabji v. Bishop of Bombay.

made. A different rate of tax, pension, or assessment, is applicable to Government land and to fazendary land, and the accounts are kept distinct. But in this distinction the Government have not sought, nor have they been interested, to define what the rights of the private parties holding fazendary lands are. And thus a fazendar occupying and tilling land himself, and paying a fixed rent to Government; or one making contracts with tenants to occupy the fazendary land on terms to be agreed between them; or one merely receiving a certain fixed sum by virtue of ancient usage, are all fazendars in the eye of Government, and in the popular language of the Bazar.

But in these three persons we perceive three different characters, with wholly different legal relations attachable to them, and for the most part equivalent to our English notions of a tenant in fee simple holding of a superior lord by rent service, a landlord demising at rack rent, and a party seized of an ancient rent issuing out of the land. But as this ambiguity is contained in the word fazendar, we must be cautious how we apply general propositions to the term.

Reasons for granting new trial.

There is another point which it is necessary to mention. It may be asked how, with this strong impression that the main right which the fazendar puts forward, and which he must establish in order to succeed, is not open to discussion, I allowed a new trial to take place? I can only say, that if I had anticipated that any such discussion was to arise, I should almost as soon have thought of granting an issue to try the validity of the charter granting Bombay to the East India Company. I granted the rule when I was sitting alone, because I had been long of opinion that although the fazendar did not possess the right which he was setting up in this case, it was possible that he might establish some claim to a fine, relief, or small increase of what has been generally called in this Court quit rent, in certain contingencies. If such right were established I thought that there were plenty of analogous cases in our old books to show that the right might be peaceably enforced by this Court.

Certain claims made by fazendars, the legality of

The counsel for the defendant, however, denies that fazendars possess any such right, and attributes the practice, which undoubtedly occurs in late years of increasing the quit rent,

1848.

Doe d. Dorabji v. Bishop of Bombay.

(an example of which occurred in the present case), and of demanding shawls, &c., by way of fine, to the necessity which the municipal acts introduced in R. R. O., 20 of 1812, and which has been countenanced by the Building Act, of a householder's obtaining the fazendar's certificate when he wants to rebuild. It is sufficient to say now that when a case is brought before the Court raising such a demand on the part of the fazendar, I see quite sufficient authority in the cases collected in *Viner's Abr.*, *Copyhold*, and elsewhere, for assisting the fazendar to his remedy for that which he may establish; but as the Court is not unanimous we can do nothing on this occasion.

which required a decision of the Court.

The only other portion of the Advocate General's argument which I need notice is the eloquent judgment of Lord Chancellor Brougham, in the case of *The Duchy of Lancaster*, in *Cooper's Reports*, and which seems much relied on. I think it wholly inapplicable, for these two reasons,—first, in that case it was admitted on all hands that the Dukes of Lancaster were the owners of the soil *in fee simple;* secondly, contracts between the Duchy and the tenants were proved to exist, and they were specific, unambiguous, and in writing.

This is the train of reasoning which has led me to the conclusion that the verdict must be entered for the defendant. I have already mentioned the deep regret which I feel at my learned colleague not being able to concur in this decision; and I will only add, that great as that regret is, I should have regretted still more if I had been compelled to arrive at a different conclusion, as I feel convinced that such a decision in this case would have had the effect of transferring a large portion of the house property in Bombay from one set of proprietors to another.

Yardley, J.—This is an action of ejectment to recover a piece of land situate in Chuncy Oart, without the Fort of Bombay.

The piece of land came into the possession of the defendant, by purchase, in the year 1843.

At that time, and for many years previously, there was a house and also a bungalow standing on the land. Since the

1848.

Doe d. Dorabji v. Bishop of Bombay.

purchase, by the defendant, the house and bungalow have been pulled down, and there are now no buildings at all standing upon the land.

The lessor of the plaintiff is what is termed "the Fazendar" of the land in question, and claims a right as such fazendar, to recover possession, now that the buildings which formerly stood upon it have been pulled down, and, accordingly, duly served the defendant with notice to quit. The defendant contends that he has a right to erect other buildings on the land, and to hold it in perpetuity upon continuing to pay to the fazendar the yearly rent which was paid by the former owners of the houses which have been removed, or that, at the most, the lessor of the plaintiff can only demand a reasonable increase in the rent, or a reasonable fine for permission to rebuild, and has no right to resume possession of the land. It must be admitted, the origin and extent of the rights of the fazendars are involved in much obscurity, and, I presume, the means of dispelling that obscurity do not exist, or they would have been used upon the present trial.

It appears, however, that the word "fazendar," in the Portuguese language, means a "farmer," and that all the land in the island of Bombay, whether built upon or not, consists either of what is called "fazendary land," or of "Government land;" but it is doubtful whether this distinction, so far as it implies a diversity of tenure, be a sound one. For the fazendary land pays a "pension" or tax to the Government, as well as the Government land, and I have observed in the course of this trial, that in every instance in which reference has been made to an immediate landlord, other than the Government, he has been termed the fazendar, and though at the time of the cession of Bombay to the Crown of England, and for some time afterwards, the term may have implied a peculiarity of tenure, I incline to think that, at the present day, it implies no more in common parlance, than that the individual so designated is the immediate landlord of the person who actually occupies the land, and the fact, that the piece of land which the plaintiff seeks to recover, is called "fazendary ground," does not further assist us in ascertaining the relative rights of the person entitled to receive the rent payable in respect of the land; that is to say, the plaintiff, on the one hand, and of the person who represents those who were the owners of the buildings, which, until recently, stood on the land, that is to say, the defendant, on the other hand; and that the judgment of the Court ought to be just the same as it would have been, if the ejectment had been brought to recover any other piece of land, which had never been called "Fazendary Ground" at all, and the same evidence had been adduced as in the present case.

Having thus endeavoured to disencumber the case from the difficulty arising from the use of a term, the meaning of which is not clearly defined, I will proceed to a consideration of the facts, presented in evidence, so far as I think them material.

It appears that in the year 1805, one Hormusjee Dhunjee, a Parsee, who was called as a witness for the plaintiff, purchased the house, which, until lately, stood upon the land in question from one Bhasker Purshotumjee for Rs. 650. In the conveyance (No. 1.), it is described as "all that" messuage or dwelling-house, situate without "the town walls in the" Oart of Runajee Bhunjee, and assessed No. —, bounded, &c. (subject to the payment of the yearly ground-rent to the owner of the said Oart), "To hold the said messuage, &c., unto the said Bhasker Purshotumjee," (the vendor's name being here used, by mistake, instead of the purchaser's), "his heirs, executors, administrators, and assigns, as his *and their own goods and chattels*, from henceforth for ever." Now, it is observable, that in this deed, which is the earliest document in evidence in the cause, the rent payable to the owner of the Oart or Garden, in which the house stood, is called a ground rent. We shall find that, in subsequent deeds executed after the disputes as to the rights of the owners of the ground had arisen, it is called a "quit ground rent." It is also to be observed, that the house is treated as a moveable chattel, and, indeed, it does not appear to be disputed that when a house is built by any one on land belonging to another person in this island, in the absence of any agreement to the contrary, the structure, however substantial, is considered as something

1848.

Doe d. Dorabji v. Bishop of Bombay.

altogether distinct from the land on which it stands, and removable at the expiration of the tenancy, something like the erections for the purposes of trade in England. It also appears from the evidence of Hormusjee Dhunjee, that Bhasker Purshotumjee paid the rent of Rs. 6 a year; but that on the transfer to Hormusjee, the rent was increased to Rs. 8, the "fazendar" being unwilling otherwise that the house should be transferred.

Five or six years after the purchase, Hormusjee was desirous of adding a bungalow to the house, and, in consideration of a present, obtained the fazendar's permission to do so. The fazendars, at that time, were two Hindoo brothers, Wisswanath and Cassinath. By indorsement on the purchase-deed, Hormusjee gave the house to Bagor Begum, who is also called Begum Beebee. The rent of Rs. 8 a year was paid to the owner of the ground up to 1838, when the lessor of the plaintiff purchased the ground (see description of parcels in deed A). Soon after the lessor of the plaintiff had purchased the ground, Hormusjee, being desirous of rebuilding the house, applied to him for permission to do so; but he being desirous of adding the ground on which the house stood to some adjacent premises occupied by himself, refused such permission, and Hormusjee, acting, I suppose, on behalf of the Begum, as well as himself, not being able to obtain permission to rebuild, sold the "house, bungalow, and all" which, he says, were situated in one compound (inclosure), and formed one building, and the same were, by indenture, dated 10th December, 1839, conveyance (see parcels in deed No. 2,) to Nowrojee Furdonjee Vacha (Andaroo), subject to the payment of the "quit-ground rent" to the fazendar. By endorsement on that deed, dated 22nd September, 1842, the executors of Nowrojee Furdonjee Vacha transferred the said property (see translation of Guzerattee, indorsement No. 3), to Dorabjee Ruttonjee, Parsee, broker, who, by deed, dated 26th January, 1843, conveyed it to the defendant, the Lord Bishop of Bombay; and this is, I believe, the first conveyance which, in terms affects to transfer the "land or ground belonging to the house." Since the conveyance to the Bishop, the house and other buildings have been pulled down, and a trench has been dug preparatory to the erection of new edifices. The lessor of the plaintiff, however, as the proprietor or fazendar of the ground, disputes the right of the defendant, either to build upon it, or to hold it as ground, and has brought this ejectment to recover possession of it.

On behalf of the plaintiff it is contended, first, that the payment of rent by the holders of the houses raises a presumption that they were merely tenants from year to year, and that the landlord has consequently a right to determine their tenancy at any time upon giving them half a year's notice to quit; or, secondly, that according to a general understanding which has acquired the force of a custom in this island, the term which the owners of the houses have in the land on which the houses stand is to be measured by the duration of the houses themselves, and that the tenant has no right to make such repairs as amount to a rénovation of the house, and still less to rebuild a house which has been pulled down, without the license of the fazendar, which he may either grant or withhold at his pleasure.

I think it impossible to infer from the evidence that those whom the defendant represents were merely tenants from year to year. The smallness of the amount paid in proportion to the value of the premises, the almost uniform amount of the rent, which has only been raised once in forty years, and the conduct of the parties themselves; the sale of the premises by the owners of the structure on the one hand, and the forbearance of the fazendar to obtain possession until the houses had been pulled down, although he required the land for his own use, on the other hand, forbid any such conclusion.

The second, and the main point for consideration is, whether the fazendar (as he is called) has established his right to recover the ground now that the houses have been removed. A great many witnesses have been called to prove this part of the case. As their evidence has been taken down for the use of both sides by the officer of the Court, it is needless to recapitulate it here. To my mind it is clear, from the acts of the parties themselves, without reference to the other testimony in the case, that the

1848.

Doe d. Dorabji v. Bishop of Bombay.

owners of the superstructure had not an interest in fee simple in the land on which it stood, and that the rent paid was in truth what, in the most ancient of the documents it is called—"a ground rent," and not a quit rent, as it is called in one of the more modern conveyances executed since these disputes arose, nor a fee farm rent, nor a chief rent, all of which have been suggested.

The single instance of the amount having been altered is, in my opinion, sufficient to prove that it does not fall within any of these latter descriptions of rent; in addition to which we have the recognition by the owner of the house of the landlord's right to "a present," in consideration of an addition made to the house originally standing on the land, and also of his right altogether to withhold his assent to the rebuilding of the house, a claim acquiesced in by the tenant at a time when it was manifestly his interest to oppose it if he had thought he had any grounds for doing so.

And now having drawn the inference that the rent paid was a ground rent, it is necessary to determine the difficult question—what was the interest or term of the tenant in the land on which the houses stood? We have already seen that the structures themselves belonged to the tenant, and he was at liberty to pull them down and carry them away whensoever he pleased; a right which has in fact been exercised by the defendant. Where a house has been standing for several generations it is of course impossible to shew the precise terms of the agreement under which it was built, unless they are preserved by a written instrument; and the most we can do is to draw an inference from the act of the parties interested, with the assistance of evidence of the general understanding (if such there be) in the neighbourhood as to the rights of parties under similar circumstances, and we have had a great body of evidence in this case, tending to shew that a general understanding, which has acquired the force of a custom, has been established in Bombay, that the fazendar has a right, in the language of most of the witnesses, "to be satisfied," by a payment of money, a present of shawls, turbans, or other valuables, or an increase of rent, for his consent to the substantial

1848.

DOE d. DORABJI v. Bishop o BOMBAY

repairing or rebuilding of the houses standing upon his land. That the tenants must "agree with the fazendar," and indeed it is not disputed that he is entitled to something on these occasions; but the great question in dispute is this,—What is the alternative if the tenants cannot agree with the fazendar, or if he chooses to withhold his consent to rebuild, and *the houses are pulled down* by the owner of them? The witnesses for the plaintiff say that he has a right to resume the possession of the ground. It has been suggested that this Court is to determine the reasonable amount of fine or gratuity to be given to the fazendar for his consent. I own it appears to me that this would be rather to legislate for, than to decide between, the parties. The inducement to the fazendar to consent to rebuilding has never been fixed or determinate. It has depended upon a variety of circumstances, the value of the site, the quality of the house, the value of the privilege to the tenant, the terms of intimacy between the parties, even the temper and disposition of the fazendar; it has sometimes been a present of shawls, turbans, or money; sometimes an increase of rent; all which tends to show that it is purely a matter of contract between the parties, which it would no longer be if the Court were to hold that the fazendar should be compelled to take what was awarded to him without having himself a voice in the matter. Considerable difficulties may arise from holding that the term of the tenant in the land is commensurate with the duration of the house; but I think there is much greater difficulty upon this evidence in coming to any other conclusion. We find from the evidence that there are abundant instances of landlords resuming possession of the ground upon which slightly built, or, as they are called, "cadjan"(*a*) houses had stood, upon those houses having been pulled down. In the case of more substantial houses the instances of the ground becoming vacant would of course be more rare, and it would be unreasonable to expect much evidence of the exercise of the right within the memory of persons now living. The houses are of a much more substantial

(*a*) Cadjans are the leaves of the brab palm or palmyra (borassus flabelliformis), and are much used for roofing and side walls in Bombay.

1848.

Doe d. Dorabji v. Bishop of Bombay.

character than they were formerly, and the owners of them, if they desired to keep possession of the site, would naturally make terms for rebuilding with the owner of the ground before the house fell down; and it would almost invariably be to the interest of the owner of the ground to accede to moderate terms, and to receive an increase of rent in respect of a well-built house, rather than to continue to receive a smaller rent in respect of a house which, although dilapidated, might stand for generations. I confess that, with my notions on these subjects formed in a country where a totally different state of things exists, I was somewhat startled at the novelty of the proposition, that the interest of the owner of the house in the land was commensurate with the duration of the house; but I find that even at this day an arrangement somewhat similar is not uncommon. I may instance the bungalows on the esplanade, many of which belong to private individuals, and are commodious and even elegant residences, but they are, by the permission of Government, built upon ground which is public property. Some of them are removed each year before the summer monsoon, and perhaps rebuilt when the rains are over. So perhaps, originally, the ancient houses standing upon what is called fazendary ground, were, by the like license of the fazendars, erected, and an annual acknowledgment exacted, for the purpose both of remunerating the fazendar for the use of his ground, and of preventing the setting up of any such claim to the fee simple of the ground as is made by the defendant in this case.

As the prosperity of the island increased, with wealth and civilization were introduced the luxuries of life, the houses became of a more substantial character till they reached that degree of comfort and convenience which those who dwell in them now enjoy. But no one would expend a large sum of money in building a house if the owner of the ground could at any time compel him to remove the house, and thus an understanding, which has perhaps acquired the force of a custom, gradually obtained, not, be it observed, for the benefit of the owners of the house, that his possession of the land should not be disturbed so long as the house continued fit for

1848.

Doe d. Dorabji v. Bishop of Bombay.

habitation; but the landowner, as it appears to me, no more alienated the land itself than the Government does at the present day by allowing persons to build upon the esplanade. This inference, I admit, partakes of the nature of conjecture; but it is the most reasonable solution that occurs to my mind of the difficulties of the present case, and I do not think it would, if established as a legal conclusion, practically affect the interests in any material degree of the owners of the houses on this island. True it is that the value of building ground in some parts of the island has enormously increased but that affords no stronger argument against the claim of the land-owners here than it would in London against the Duke of Bedford, or the Marquis of Westminster, if either of them were seeking to recover a portion of his estates in Bloomsbury or Pimlico. I am of opinion that the interest of the defendant in the land was in respect of the houses which stood upon it, and that the houses having been removed that interest has ceased, that the lessor of the plaintiff Dorabji Dady Suntook has, consequently, established his right to recover the piece of ground in question from the Lord Bishop of Bombay. This opinion I express with unfeigned diffidence, for I understand that this Court has on more occasions than one arrived at a different conclusion in cases of a similar description, and I would that this were an instance in which I could, with the profound respect I feel for them, bow to the decisions of the able and experienced Judges who have so held, and it is especially very painful to my feelings to be obliged now to differ from his Lordship the Chief Justice, who has bestowed great attention on the subject, and my confidence in the soundness of my own conclusions is greatly shaken in this and all other instances in which I have the misfortune so to differ from him. If this had been purely a question of law, I should, of course, have held myself bound, by the previous decisions of the Court until they had been reversed by a superior tribunal; but as we are called upon to draw an inference from the facts proved on this trial, and from those facts alone, I could only give expression to the conclusion to which my mind has been irresistibly, though perhaps erro-

1848.

Doe d. Dorabji v. Bishop of Bombay.

neously led. I have the satisfaction of knowing that if I am wrong, the judgment of the Court will be right, and as it is the avowed intention of the lessor of the plaintiff to carry this case by appeal to the Privy Council, the question will, I hope, be finally set at rest by the judgment of the higher Court. Judgment for defendant.

1852.

Sept. 25.

Ex parte BALARAM. (*a*)

[*Coram* Sir E. Perry, C. J.]

Where the wife of a Hindu convert refused to live with her husband, on the ground of his conversion to Christianity, a Judge at Madras, on *habeas corpus*, ordered her to be delivered up to her husband. But in a similar case at Bombay, on its appearing by the affidavit on application for the writ of *habeas corpus*, that the wife had left the house of her husband voluntarily, on the ground of his having abandoned the usages of the Hindu religion, and that she was living with her relations under no restraint, the Court refused to issue the writ.

One Balaram Ganpat, a Hindu of the Shenwi cast, having ceased to join in the various ceremonies of the Hindu religion, his wife in consequence left his house in March last, and took up her abode with her mother. On the 16th September last, Balaram, the husband, was admitted to Christian baptism, and on the 23rd September, he applied to Perry, C. J., sitting in Chambers, for a *habeas corpus* to bring up the body of his wife, on the following affidavit:—

"I, Balaram Gunpat, of Bombay, a Hindu, of the Shenwi caste by birth, and a Christian by faith, make oath and say, that in or about the Christian year one thousand eight hundred and forty-three, I, then being of the age of thirteen years, and professing the Hindu religion, was married to Pootlabaee, then of the age of seven years or thereabouts. That in the year one thousand eight hundred and fifty the said Pootlabaee, having arrived at womanhood, came to live with me, and did live with me as my wife for a period of about eighteen months, up to about the month of March last, when, on my refusing to conform to and join in the various ceremonies of the Hindu religion, she, at the advice and instigation of her relations, left my house, and went to live with her mother, Keekeebaee, a widow, at the house of her grandfather, Bappu

(*a*) See *ante*, p. 91, *et sqq*., and note (*a*), p. 107, as to a conflict of decisions in the Supreme Courts of India on the important subject of the custody of children, and the difficult questions arising out of conversion to Christianity. The case in the text, having occurred after the previous cases were in type, has been necessarily inserted out of its proper place.

Bhaee Soorut Khur, where she has remained ever since, and is now. And I further say, that some time ago, after very long and mature consideration of the grave importance of the step I was about to take, I determined on renouncing the Hindu religion and embracing the Christian Faith; and on the sixteenth day of September instant, I was admitted by baptism, received at the hands of the Reverend W. S. Price, a clergyman of the Church Missionary Society, a member of the Church of England. And I further say that since my renunciation of the Hindu religion, my said wife Pootlabaee has remained closely shut up with her mother in the house of the said Bappu Bhaee; and that I have never been able to gain admission to her presence, or speak with her. And I further say that I am much attached to my said wife, and that, during the period hereinbefore mentioned, in which we lived together as husband and wife, she evinced great affection for me, and we lived very happily together. And I further say that I am very desirous of again enjoying the society of my said wife, and a resumption of my marital rights, and I believe if I were enabled to see and reason with her, I might be able to overcome any religious scruples she may at present entertain in acceding to my wishes.

BALARAM GUNPAT.

"Sworn at Bombay aforesaid, this twenty-third day of September, 1852. Before me, W. BROOKFIELD, *Commissioner*."

The Chief Justice, however, directed the application to be made in open Court, and accordingly on this day, after the grand jury had been charged, the application was renewed by

Dickinson, who, on the above affidavit, contended that he was entitled to the writ as a matter of course.

Sir E. PERRY, C. J.—No illegal imprisonment is shewn, and, therefore, as a matter of course, your application must be refused, unless you have any authorities to support it.

Dickinson then relied strongly on the case of Mrs. *Cochrane*, (8 Dowl. Pr. Cases), in which COLERIDGE, J. ordered the wife to return to her husband. Moreover, the case of *Lutchmee*

1852.

Ex parte BALARAM.

v. *Ummall*, reported in the *Bombay Oriental Christian Spectator* (*a*), decided by Sir WM. BURTON, at Madras, is expressly in point. In that case the wife, it had at first been sworn, was willing to return to her husband who had become a convert, but was prevented from doing so by her relations; it would seem, however, that, in fact, she was unwilling to rejoin her husband. But the learned Judge refused to let her wishes be consulted, and held that it was her duty, and that the law would compel her, to return to her husband.

[The following is an extract from the report of Sir W. BARTON's Judgment. "A Court in England very recently determined, in the case of a woman who left her husband by a sort of stratagem, that she should return to him, and enforced the right of the husband. The Court even acknowledged the husband's right to lay a restriction on the personal liberty of his wife. A wife's virtue is safe only in her husband's keeping; there is her proper place. No one need apprehend ill usage for this young woman. I order and direct her to return to her husband. What may be the influence he may exercise over her, the Court has nothing to do with: no doubt she must have been much influenced by her relatives with whom she had lived the last two months. I will not ask what may be her own wishes in the matter: even should she tell me she has no desire to go, I should be obliged to say that she must return to her husband. The law will protect her in her husband's house, and directs that she should be restored to him."

"Listen to me! young woman," said the Judge, addressing the girl, "listen to me as a father. Open your eyes to your own good. You are a married woman, and your husband is bound to protect you as long as you live. The law has decided that he should do so, and that you shall return to him and again enjoy his society. You have been long deprived of this society and of the happiness of your married state, but you shall be deprived no longer. You are quite safe from ill usage: every one will save you from that. You are simply restored to your husband from whom you have been separated."

(*a*) July, 1851.

1852.

Ex parte BALABAM.

"The judgment of the Court then was," says the *Athenæum*, "that the wife be restored to her husband." His Lordship ordered the wife (she is a mere girl of fifteen years of age, and not particularly prepossessing in appearance) to walk over to Streenevassa, who was seated on the other side of the Court.

"She refused to do so, twitching herself, in the way, no doubt many of our readers have seen young girls do when offended, but she positively refused to stir an inch. Streenavassa was told to take her hand and lead her into his Lordship's room; but no, the hand was not to be obtained. Sir WILLIAM spoke to and entreated her to hear him as she would a father; he advised her, in the most soothing language he could use, to return to the man to whom she had been married for nine months. To all appearance this tender regard for her welfare had not the slightest effect, and it was at last found necessary to have her carried by one of the European constables to his Lordship's room. The aunt and father of the girl now commenced proceedings; the old woman screeching and yelling, tearing her hair, and making ineffectual attempts to reach her child; it took all the force of two or three men to hold her back. The aunt would not be pacified. She rushed down the stairs of the Court, threw herself on the pavement, beating her head, pulling her tongue, and going through all the demonstrations of the most frantic grief."(*a*)]

Sir E. PERRY, C. J., on the learned counsel concluding his argument, pronounced judgment as follows:—

When this application was made to me the day before yesterday in Chambers, the affidavit of the husband for the production of his wife, was merely handed to me by my clerk, and it was expected that I should issue a fiat for the writ as a mere matter of course. When I read the affiavit, however, and discovered that the wife was aged sixteen years and upwards, that she was not detained by any one in custody, but that she was living with her own family, apart from her husband, and refused to return to him because he had become a convert to

(*a*) *Oriental Christian Spectator*, July 1851, p. 265.

1852.

Ex parte BALARAM.

Christianity, I saw at once that no ground for a writ of *habeas corpus* existed. I accordingly commenced an indorsement on the affidavit to the effect, 'that the proper mode for the husband to obtain the restitution of conjugal rights was by a regular suit, and not by the summary process of *habeas corpus.*' When I recollected, however, the keen excitement which prevails on this subject, and the liability to misconception which exists, when an adverse decision is pronounced without giving reasons, I erased the indorsement, and stated that the application was so novel in principle that it ought to be made in open Court.

Having now heard the learned counsel, it might be sufficient to repeat the substance of my indorsement, namely, that in a case circumstanced like the present, where no illegal imprisonment is even charged to exist, the husband must be left to assert the rights which he conceives belongs to him, in a regular suit, wherein the wife may have a full opportunity of stating her case. In deference, however, to a counsel of the eminence of Mr. *Dickinson*, who appears to think that he is entitled to succeed in this application, I suppose I must give my reasons at length for refusing this writ. It is the more necessary to do so, because not only is the writ of *habeas corpus* incomparably the most important institute in English law as the preservative of our rights and liberties, and therefore it is essential that clear ideas should prevail on the subject, but also because considerable conflict amongst the Supreme Courts of India has occurred, and I cannot help perceiving that a want of familiarity with first principles connected with the writ exists largely in our European Society, and is traceable occasionally even to the Bar. Thus, on the very last occasion, when I granted the writ to bring up the body of a Hindu child, who it was sworn was illegally imprisoned in a European house, and who was about to be baptized immediately against the wishes of her family I granted the writ returnable 'immediaté,' and yet I heard it suggested at the Bar, in some degree as a matter of surprise, that I had adopted an unusual course in requiring this instant obedience to the writ.

Conflict of Courts in India as to the writ of *habeas corpus.*

1852.

Ex parte BALARAM.

The principles which govern the issue of a writ of *habeas corpus* I conceive to be extremely clear and simple, and by the application of them to various much contested cases which have come before this Court, the Judges have been able to pursue one uniform line of conduct. As a general rule, the writ issues whenever a party is shown on affidavit presented to the Court or a Judge, to be illegally imprisoned or confined *against his will.* So considerable an element do these latter words form, that the Courts at Westminster Hall, as a matter of practice, refuse to grant the writ unless an affidavit from the party himself complaining of the confinement is produced. But occasionally the confinement is so close that the imprisoned party is unable to make an affidavit, and when this fact appears to the satisfaction of the Court, the rule requiring such an affidavit is necessarily relaxed, as is shown by the case of the negro woman, called the Hottentot Venus, who was exhibited in London as a show,—and also, I think, in the celebrated case of the Canadian State Prisoners. I have stated what I conceive to be the general rule, but there is an exception to it which, when duly considered, makes the rule more forcible. It is the case of parent and child. The law in this case does not regard or take notice of the will of the child as opposed to the will of the father. On the wisest principles, it maintains the authority of paternal dominion, and does not allow any party to step in and interfere with the lawful custody which every father is entitled to maintain over his offspring.

Principles on which the writ issues.

Illegal imprisonment.

By the application of these principles, the Court has been enabled to administer the law on the subject with an equal hand. I will recall to the recollection of the Bar, two cases which occurred in 1843, in both of which strong passions and excitement existed on the part of the Native community, and perhaps no less vehement feelings on the part of the zealous body of missionaries who were assisting their Christian converts to assert their supposed rights and claims. In the first of these cases a Parsi had embraced Christianity (*a*), and his family refused to give up to him an infant child of the age of five years, on the ground of his having lost all rights to it by his

Examples at Bombay.

(*a*) See *ante*, p. 91, *Reg.* v. *Shapurji*.

1852.

Ex parte BALARAM.

conversion. An application was made to this Court for a writ of *habeas corpus*, which was immediately granted. There was immense excitement amongst the Parsi community. Various schemes were adopted to avoid obedience to the writ; and a settlement was even made on the child so as to avert the jurisdiction of the common law, and to raise a complicated question of guardianship in a Court of equity. But the Court firmly maintained the rights of the father, and laid down broadly in answer to very vigorous arguments at the Bar, that, whatever the religious faith of the father might be, he was entitled to the custody of his own child. Later in the same year a case very similar in principle, but the converse in facts, occurred(*a*). A Hindu father applied for the custody of his child, who was aged twelve years. It appeared that the elder brother of the boy had recently become a convert to Christianity, that the boy in question was inclined to take the same course, and that both were living in a missionary family, where they had made themselves outcasts by partaking of food not lawful to Hindus. The argument urged at the Bar was, that this boy was not illegally imprisoned, that he was old enough to choose for himself, and that he preferred to live with the missionaries. The Court was also strongly pressed to examine the boy as to his progress in theology, and as to his own views and wishes. A strong case in point was decided at Calcutta, in which the Supreme Court appear to have delivered up a Hindu boy to Dr. Duff in preference to the father, on the lad preferring to go back to the reverend and able teacher by whom he had been educated.

Case at Calcutta.

The Judges, however, consisting of Sir HENRY ROPER and myself, maintained the authority of the father with equal stoutness to their decision in the former case; they entirely ignored the right of a child of this age (and they carefully guarded themselves from stating at what age parental authority ceases) to set up his own will against the will of his parent, and they protested against the unseemliness of a theological examination in open Court. The conflict of opinion which thus seemed to prevail between the Supreme Courts of Calcutta and Bombay I am inclined to think no

(*a*) See *ante*, p. 103, *Reg.* v. *Nesbitt*.

1852.

Ex parte BALARAM

longer exists; for if the report of a late decision in the newspapers in the case of *Brigadier Warren* can be relied upon, Sir LAWRENCE PEEL will be seen to have laid down, in equally strong terms with any that have been heard in this Court, the rights of a father to the custody of his unemancipated daughter, even though her own will would lead her elsewhere.

Now, on applying these principles to the present case, it will be seen that no illegal imprisonment exists here, nor is the relation of a wife to her husband the same as that of a child to its parent.

Case in England, distinguishable.

But Mr. *Dickinson* has brought two cases before the Court to-day which he conceives entitle him to the writ. The first is the case of Mrs. *Cochrane,* decided by Mr. Justice COLERIDGE in 1840. But, with submission to so able a logician as Mr. *Dickinson,* it appears to me to be completely distinguishable from the present case. The point decided there was, that the husband, in order to prevent his wife from eloping, had a right to imprison her in his own house, although the threatened elopement was not connected with any apprehended danger either to his honour or his property. The decision is founded upon some principles in our old law which appear to me to savour of a rather barbarous state of manners, as they confer upon the husband the "power of exercising dominion over his wife, and of keeping her, even by force, within the bounds of duty, and of beating her, though not in a violent or cruel manner." This law will not be heard with dissatisfaction by many of our native community, who fear that the introduction of English law and manners will result in making Asiatic females wholly insubordinate. The decision, however, appears to me sound to the extent to which it goes, though I think it approaches the very verge of those limits which sever the independent rights of the woman, as a member of society entitled to the protection of the law, from the rights of domestic dominion wisely vested in the husband.

But in that case the wife was clearly attempting to commit a breach of her most obvious duties. She had obtained a writ of *habeas corpus,* on the ground that she had been illegally

1852.

Ex parte BALARAM.

imprisoned, against her will, by her husband; but when the husband produced her in open Court, with the reasons why he had subjected her to this confinement, the Judge decided that the imprisonment was not illegal, and he restored her to the lawful custody of her husband. None of these circumstances occur in this case: the objections of the wife to rejoin her husband may possibly be found valid in law, but to compel her forcibly to go back, before the validity of those reasons can be inquired into, would be at once to subject her to all those consequences which a Hindu female is taught to believe contamination and pollution.

Case at Madras, disapproved of.

Another case, however, has been cited by the learned counsel,—the case of *Lutchmee*, decided by Sir WILLIAM BURTON at Madras in 1851, which I freely admit is not distinguishable from the present. I am bound to pay the greatest deference to a Court of co-ordinate jurisdiction like that of the Supreme Court of Madras, and I entertain unfeigned respect for the conscientious Judge who pronounced that decision; but having carefully perused all the proceedings which occurred in that case at the time of their occurrence, I consider the decision so entirely at variance with all the principles that had previously ruled in this Court, and so unsupported by any decision in our collections of jurisprudence, now ranging over more than three hundred years, that I feel unable to surrender the deliberate convictions which I have formed, after long and careful study of the authorities, in deference to a single decision.

Important question as to rights of Hindu wife, on her husband's conversion.

The husband, however, in this case is not prevented by my refusal of the summary process now asked for from asserting the usual rights of a husband to his wife's society. If ever the question is raised in a formal manner, it will appear that a point of the very gravest importance will have to be decided. In all these cases of conflicting personal rights, wherein social interests and different religious persuasions so strongly combine to call the most potent feelings of our nature into operation, and thus to cloud the judgment,—cases which have already often occurred, and which will again often occur, in Indian Courts of justice,—there is one simple clue for ascer-

1852.

Ex parte BALARAM.

taining what the dicates of justice require, which I always employ myself, and which may possibly be found useful to others. I always ask myself what the sound decision would appear to me to be if my own case had to be presented to a Hindu or Musalman Judge. There are millions of Christians in Europe living under Musalman sway, and in the vicissitudes characterising the present age it would not be at all an improbable occurrence that an Englishman and his wife should become domiciled in Turkey, and thereupon Turkish subjects. If then the Christian husband apostatized from his faith, and then availed himself of the privileges of the law belonging to Mahomedan husbands, I would ask what the legal condition of the Christian wife would become? If she fled from the harem, and the companions there imposed upon her, and sought refuge under her father's roof, would the decree of any Court, in which the immutable dictates of justice prevail, compel her forcibly to return to the house and arms of the man whom she loathed as a renegade? If no Christian tribunal could pronounce such a decree in the case of a Christian wife, it is obvious that a Court of justice set down in the midst of a Hindu community must pronounce a decision founded on the same broad views of justice in behalf of the equally conscientious scruples and repugnance of a Hindu female. But it is not incumbent on me to carry out this view of the case further.

Similar case put as to Christian wife.

The present application is refused.

THE ADVOCATE GENERAL ON THE RELATION OF SUNDAR JAGJIVAN AND OTHERS, *v.* DAMOTHAR AND KARSON MADOWJI.

1852. Feb. 18.

[*Coram* Sir E. Perry, C. J., and Sir W. Yardley, J.]

The Court refused to establish as a charity a residuary clause in a Gujráti will leaving the testator's estate to Daramkatê (translated charity account) on the ground that the Gujráti expression was not equivalent to the technical term charity, as defined in the Court of Chancery. Meaning of the term Dharm, or Dharmma, as used by the Hindus.

This was an information filed by *Le Messurier*, A. G., to establish a charity, on a clause in the will of one Ratonsi Dharsi, who died 11th March, 1842.

By the will in question, in the Gujrati language, which was made by the testator in 1837, whilst on a pilgrimage to Benares, he enumerated, as is usual with Hindus, the whole of his property, moveable and immoveable, and, after making certain bequests to temples, to images of the gods, and to his Maharajah or spiritual head, and after ordering certain feasts and presents to be given to the Mahajans, (*a*) and to the eighty-four tribes of Brahmans, he bequeathed the residue of his estate to his wife and his sister-in-law for life; and "in the event of the death of these two persons, whatever goods of mine there may be, these are to be placed to the account of charity, (daramkate), and things are to be so done that my name may remain after me."

Demurrer for want of equity.

Howard, for the demurrer, contended that, although by a long course of decisions in the English law recognised, but deplored, in *Moggridge* v. *Thackwell*, (7 Ves.), the Court of Chancery would establish this will if it were an English will, and the words used had been "charity account;" still these decisions were not applicable to Hindu wills, and to the course of succession amongst Hindus, which is to be governed by Hindu law.

(*a*) Maháȷans are the leading merchants or heads of the commercial community.

1852.

The ADVOCATE GENERAL v. DAMOTHAR.

Further, by the Hindu law of Western India, a Hindu is not able to make a will; and although the power has been tacitly admitted by this Court, there has been no solemn decision establishing the power, nor is a decision of the Court able to alter the Hindu law, as laid down in their books of authority.

Le Messurier, A. G., and *Dickinson, contrà.* It being admitted that if this were an English will the Court would establish the charity, why should any different principle be applied to this case? The testator was animated by precisely the same motives of rendering some great service to the public, and of continuing his name to posterity, as have actuated testators in England, whose wills have been established, and, therefore, for the public good, exactly the same construction should be applied. If the charity shall be established it will be for the Court to declare, after a reference to the Master, what sort of public establishment, whether a school or hospital, shall be instituted, but the interests of the public ought to be maintained.

Cur. adv. vult.

On this day the judgment of the Court was delivered by

Sir E. PERRY, C. J.—This is an information filed by the Advocate General to establish a charity under a general clause in the will of one Ratonsi Dharsi, who died in 1842. By that will, which is in the Gujrati language, after making several specific bequests to temples, and having directed that the Brahmans and Mahajans (leading merchants of his cast) should be feasted, he leaves his property to his widow for her life, and in case of his leaving no child, he disposes of the residue, at her death, as follows:—"Whatever goods of mine there may be these are to be placed to the account of charity; and (things) are to be so done that my name may remain after me."

It appears, by the information, that the defendants who claim as next of kin have taken possession of the residue, and

1852.

The Advocate General v. Damothar.

it is not disputed that the next of kin are entitled so to do; unless the English law, which gives a very large operation to charitable bequests, will carry out this clause in favour of charity, which, from its vagueness and uncertainty, it would not have done in favour of an individual, or in favour of any other general object not within the rule of the Court of Chancery.

It appears, by the authorities which were fully brought before us in the argument, that from a very early period subsequent to 43 Eliz., the Court of Chancery has taken great liberties in expounding wills in favour of charity, so as frequently to make wills for the testator wholly different from those intended by himself. It is equally clear, that in the wisdom of subsequent times it has been deemed that the Courts of equity have gone too far; and, indeed, a statute has been passed (9 Geo. 2, c. 36) for the purpose of preventing the public mischief of large improvident alienations or dispositions, made by languishing and dying persons or others, to uses called charitable uses, to take place after their deaths, to the disinherison of their lawful heirs!

And the law now appears to be that, although the course of decisions makes it imperative to give effect to a general clause in behalf of charity so as to exclude the heirs, if the words used in the bequest are not equivalent to the term charity in its technical legal sense, the bequest will be rejected as uncertain, and the next of kin will take. Thus a bequest to the Bishop of Durham, for all such objects of benevolence and liberality as he should approve of, was held not to be a bequest for *charitable* purposes. So where a testator directed that the residue of his estate should be "given in private charity," it was held that "private charity" was a convertible term with "benevolence," and was not equivalent with the technical term *charity*, to which an exceptional effect in the law had been attributed. These decisions, in which a subtle distinction was relied on to withdraw the cases from the operation of an anomalous rule not approved of in principle, are illustrations of the desire of the Judges not to carry the rule a bit farther than they were obliged by precedent, and the practice corresponds with the wise maxim of the Roman law, "*jus singulare ad consequentia non producitur.*"

This being the state of the law, the inquiry in a case of this kind, as was observed in *Morice* v. *The Bishop of Durham*, is a question rather of philology than of law. It is admitted that, if this were the case of an Englishman and of an English will, the terms used, "Charity Account," would entitle the Advocate General to a decree; but the will is in Gujrati; and it is quite clear that the Gujrati merchant who made the will had no reference to the technical meaning of that term, or even to the more extended meaning which it bears amongst Christian writers. A great master of language, Sir WILLIAM GRANT, said: "That word (charity), in its widest sense, denotes all the good affections men ought to bear towards each other: in its most restricted and common sense, relief of the poor. In neither of these senses is it employed in this Court Here its signification is derived chiefly from the statute of Elizabeth. Those purposes are considered charitable which that statute enumerates, or which by analogies are deemed within its spirit and intendment; and to some such purpose every bequest to charity generally shall be applied. But it is clear liberality and benevolence can find numberless objects not included in that statute in the largest construction of it." 9 *Ves.* 405.

The question, therefore, in this case is whether the word used by the testator is equivalent with *charity*; if it is larger, or different, then, as in the case just cited, the bequest is void, and the next of kin inherit. The word used by the testator is "Dharamkhaté," a compound substantive, from the Sanscrit Dharmma, and a Gujrati word signifying a mercantile account. In the Gujrati Dictionary, edited by one of the interpreters of this Court this word is Englished: "1. A charitable establishment; a benevolent institution. 2. Account opened under the head of charities." But this Dictionary does not profess to give more than a colloquial rendering of the Gujrati for every day use. The inquiry turns upon the meaning of the much used, thoroughly Hindu, word *Dharmma*, as to which we may say the European, who knows it well, has obtained a

1852.

The Advocate General v. Damothar.

tolerably deep insight into Hindu life and thought, for the idea of it appears to enter into almost every action of life. Eleven different meanings are given to the term in the Sanscrit Dictionary of *Horace Wilson*, but the first appears to give the more general spirit and meaning of the term as we meet with it in daily life, *viz.*, "Virtue, moral and religious merit according to the law and the Védas." From all we can learn on the subject, we are satisfied that the term used by the testator is not equivalent to the term *charity*, as defined in the Courts of equity; that it implies the performance of acts considered meritorious in the Hindu religion, many of which could by no latitude of construction be brought within the term *charity;* and therefore that the English cases which turn upon the employment of the English word "charity," or of words pointing out a disposition held to be charitable, do not govern the present case. We may observe that a similar decision appears to have been come to by the Supreme Court at Calcutta in two cases cited from *Fulton's Reports*, where the Court would not give effect to the bequests on account of their vagueness; and it is clear that the term translated "pious acts to procure me future bliss," in one of those cases, is a Hindu expression of exactly the same import as the Hindu expression used in the present will.

Another objection was made by the next of kin to the residuary bequest, *viz.*, that all cases of Hindu succession are to be determined by Hindu law, and that by the law of Western India Hindus are not competent to make wills, or, at all events, are not able to disinherit their heirs, except in cases allowed by the Hindu Shasters. But we think that this question is too important, and that the argument was too cursorily raised, to allow us to treat it as calling for any expression of opinion on the present occasion; for so long back as the present Judges have any knowledge of the course of decision in this Court, Hindu wills have been looked upon as valid testamentary documents, and if it is ever sought to shake this doctrine of the Court, the whole question must be raised formally, and after full notice, so as to enable the decision of a Court of appeal to be obtained upon it.

1852.

The Advocate General v. Damothar.

On the assumption, then, that this will is valid, but for the reasons before given, we think that the attempt made by the relators to obtain the residue from the next of kin, on the ground that it was bequeathed to a public charity under the statute of Elizabeth, must fail, and that this information must be dismissed.

1852.

March 25.

DOE DEM. M'KENZIE AND OTHERS *v.* PESTONJI DADABHAI.

[*Coram* Sir Erskine Perry, C. J.]

English law has been introduced into Bombay, but not the forms of English conveyancing, and all that is required to pass land is a simple writing, not under seal, expressive of the intentions of the parties.

A grant by the Bombay Government in the form of a certificate, putting the family of a shipbuilder, in recompence for services performed to the nation, into possession of certain rice lands, which grant was subsequently confirmed by the Court of Directors to the family and their descendants, is a complete grant in fee, and does not render the estate inalienable.

Quære, the exact legal ground on which the supercession of Portuguese law as to lands, and the introduction of English law was effected.

Ejectment to recover the Lalbagh estate belonging to Messrs. Dadabhai and Muncherji Pestonji, and which, on their becoming insolvent in 1850, had been assigned by them to the lessors of the plaintiff for the benefit of their creditors.

The action was defended by the son of Dadabhai Pestonji, on the ground that the estate was inalienable; and to raise the point intended to be argued, the case was tried on admissions.

Dickinson for the plaintiffs.

Jenkins for the defendant.

Cur. adv. vult.

Sir Erskine Perry, C. J. now delivered judgment.

This is an action of ejectment brought by the trustees of Dadabhai Pestonji to recover the Lal Bagh estate in the

1852.

Doe d. M'Kenzie v. Pestonji.

island of Bombay, which is claimed by the family of the Pestonjis to be inalienable, being a grant from Government for services performed.

The case has been tried upon admissions, and all that is necessary to be stated for raising the point in dispute is as follows.

The family of Lowji, the shipbuilder, by whom in 1735 the art of shipbuilding was introduced into Bombay, having in the opinion of several heads of departments rendered essential services to Government, in the year 1783 obtained the following from the Bombay authorities:—

"This is to certify that Vice Admiral Sir Edward Hughes, K. B., and commander-in-chief of his Majesty's ships and vessels in the East Indies, having by letter under date the 10th March, 1783, pointed out the great services rendered the nation at large, and the United East India Company, by Manockjee Lowjee and Bomanjee Lowjee, the two master builders at this Presidency; and having also strongly recommended to us to confer on them a certain portion of ground on this land, which will yield annually forty morahs of toca batty (*a*); this is to certify that the said Manocjee Lowjee and Bomanjee Lowjee have accordingly been put in possession of certain *batty* (*a*) grounds in the district of Parell, with their *foras* (*b*) and *purteneas* (*b*) of the side grounds, which will yield the above quantity of toca batty: and that they are to be kept in possession of the same, without molestation until the pleasure of the Honorable the Court of Directors is known. —Given under our hands in Bombay Castle, this 29th day of December, 1783."

By a letter from the Honorable Court, dated 28th April, 1795, that is nearly twelve years afterwards, the above grant was confirmed in the following terms:—

"Observing by your advices of 30th September, 1783, and 10th February, 1784, that you were induced to issue the beforementioned grant to the two master builders and their

(*a*) *i. e.* Rice lands.

(*b*) Portuguese words signifying outlying or waste lands.

sons, at the earnest recommendation of the late Sir Edward Hughes, as a reward for the essential and important services they have rendered the nation, and the Company in particular, in refitting his Majesty's squadrons; and as we ourselves have borne frequent testimony of their merits, we hereby ratify and confirm the said grant, with a due proportion of *foras* and *purteneas,* to their family and descendants."

Under the grant in question, the family became possessed of a large quantity of land, principally waste, and of little value at that period; but which, with the growth of population and wealth in the island, has now become very valuable.

In the year 1823, the estate thus granted was in the possession of the descendants of the original grantees, but the family having ramified into various branches, they agreed to divide the estate amongst them, and the portion called the Lal Bagh fell to the lot of Dadabhai and Mancherji Pestonji, who from that period have had exclusive possession. In 1850 these gentlemen mortgaged the Lal Bagh estate for Rs. 60,000, and subsequently in the same year, having become insolvent, they conveyed the estate in trust to the lessors of the plaintiff for the benefit of their creditors.

The son of Dadabhai Pestonji now contests the right of the father to grant any more than a life interest in the property.

The argument which is set up in behalf of the inalienability of this property is twofold:—1. It is said that when the Crown grants lands in tail with reversion to itself for services performed, the reversion cannot be barred, as it can in any other case, so as to exclude the Crown's right. 2. By a regulation of the Bombay Government,—XVII. of 1827, ch. 9,—lands granted in jaghire may be resumed at the pleasure of Government. On the analogy of these two rules it is contended that the grant of the Lal Bagh estate must be considered not as a grant in fee, but a grant for the benefit of this family only, and therefore inalienable.

But the answer to these arguments is obvious. The grant in question does not create an estate tail, and the reversion is not reserved to the Crown; any inferences therefore deducible from the technical rules relating to English convey-

1852.

Doe d. M'Kenzie v. Pestonji.

ancing, or to the rights of the prerogative, are inapplicable. Although English law has been introduced into this island to the supercession of the Portuguese feudal law, which appears to have prevailed at the period of the cession, (and it may not be very easy to define the exact juridical mode by which the change was effected,) the forms of English conveyancing have never been in use, and the oldest practitioners have never heard of a fine or recovery. Land therefore passes from hand to hand with all the simplicity of a transaction not fettered by forms; and all that we see in Courts of justice on such occasions is a simple writing, not under seal, expressive of the intention of the parties. It is the duty of the Court to put a construction upon such instruments when brought before it; and in the present case, on looking to what the Court of Directors call the grant by the Bombay Government, and to their own confirmation of it, I feel no doubt that the effect of those documents was to give the grantees a complete estate in fee of the lands so granted.

With respect to the arguments derived from the power of the Government to resume jaghire lands at pleasure, I need only observe that, though such appears to be law in the Mofussil, it is not so in Bombay.

I took time to consider my judgment, not from any doubts as to what the decision ought to be, but because a very long report of a case before the Privy Council in 1838, from the short-hand writer's notes, was brought before me, in which it was stated that their Lordships had inquired fully into the nature of Enam Grants by Indian Governments; but on reading the case, I do not find that it bears any application whatever to the present.

Judgment for the plaintiff.

DOE DEM. HOWARD AND OTHERS
v.
PESTONJI MANOCKJI.

1852.
Feb. 26.

[*Coram* Sir E. PERRY, C. J., and Sir W. YARDLEY, J.]

Where two Parsi brothers erected a fire temple on their estate, and by a document which they recorded in a solemn meeting of their community, declared that they erected this temple, and placed the sacred fire within it, in commemoration of their deceased father, but that it should always be subject to the authority of themselves and their heirs, and that all the members of the Zoroastrian community were at liberty to have their religious ceremonies performed therein without any obstruction on their part;

Held, that this document contained no grant of the temple to the Parsi community, but that the entire ownership remained in the Parsi brothers, and would pass to their assignees in case of insolvency.

Held, also, that evidence of custom amongst the Parsis as to their mode of consecrating fire temples, and thereby rendering the land on which they stood inalienable, was not admissible, as no custom of any particular sect can alter the tenures of land, so as to be binding on the community.

THIS was an action of ejectment brought by the trustees of Dadabhai and Muncherji Pestonji against the defendant as representative of the Parsí community, and by consent of the parties the following special case was stated for the opinion of the Court.

Case.

Dadabhai Pestonji and Muncherji Pestonji were Parsís residing and trading in Bombay, and were, previously to 1834, jointly possessed of an estate of freehold of inheritance of a considerable extent of ground, on part of which a dwelling-house had been erected, with a pleasure garden and compound attached, surrounded by a wall, situate at Parell, and called The Lall Bagh, where they resided with their families. In or previously to the year 1834 they erected a Fire Temple in a part of the garden at the back of their said dwelling-house. This building with the outhouses and appurtenances covered 2387 square yards of ground or thereabouts, which building *was duly consecrated,* and the sacred fire placed on a Pyrea, according to the rites and ceremonies enjoined by the Zoroastrian religion; and the said building was set apart *as a*

1852.

Doe d. Howard v. Pestonji.

place of charity, on or about the 18th day of August, 1834, in the presence of the leading members of the Parsi Punchayet and of the community assembled within the precincts of the Temple. In the presence of the public assembly the said Dadabhai and Muncherji Pestonji caused the following document, bearing their signature, to be read and promulgated,—a document which is in the words and figures following, that is to say:

"By the aid of Dadar Hormazd (God Almighty) the just, who assists every righteous undertaking, and under the guidance of Huzrut Zurtosht Asfuntman Anoshcherwan, the servants Vahadia Dadabhai Pestonji and Muncherji Pestonji respectfully announce to the whole of the Zoroastrian community that, agreeably to our desire and in conformity to the precepts of the pure Mazdeeashnee faith, we, having constructed and finished this Durehmeher (Fire Temple) in our garden at Parell, sacred to the memory of our late patron Wadajee Seth Pestonji Bomanji, have this day placed the sacred fire (Aderan) therein in commemoration of the deceased; [this Durehmeher (Fire Temple) shall always be subject to the authority of ourselves and our heirs]; *and all the members of the Zoroastrian community are at liberty to have their religious ceremonies performed in this Durehmeher* (Fire Temple) *without any obstruction on our part.* But the priests officiating in this Durehmeher shall be subject to the authority of ourselves and our heirs in all respects. This we the servants represent in writing to this assembly. Moreover we the servants have subscribed Rs. 1001 in figures one thousand and one to the memory of the deceased, in aid of the fund raised by the Punchayet for the relief of the blind and disabled.

"The 20th day of the 11th month Shahanshahee, year of Yezdijird 1203. 16th August, 1834, A.D.

"Written by Wadia Dadabhai Pestonji.

"Written by Wadia Muncherji Pestonji."

This document was then transmitted to and placed with the records of the Parsi Punchayet by the managing member

1852.

DOE d. HOWARD v. PESTONJI.

thereof. On this occasion the Parsí Punchayet, in order to mark their sense of the obligation conferred on the Parsí community by Dadabhai and Muncherji Pestonji, directed Khursetji Manockji, shroff, to present a pair of shawls to Wadia Dadabhai and one shawl to Wadia Muncherji on behalf of the community: this was accordingly done in the presence of the said assembly. An account of what took place at this meeting, together with a true copy of the said document, was thereupon published in the Guzerattee papers for the information of the public. Although the said Dadabhai and Muncherji Pestonji regulated the management of the said temple as far as regarded the payment of the priests' wages and the employment of competent persons to superintend the performance of the religious rites therein up to the date of their stopping payment as hereinafter mentioned, the Temple has ever since its dedication been free of access to Parsís of both sects, whether Kudmees or Shayanshaee, who possessed a right to have their religious rites and ceremonies performed in the said Agiary or Fire Temple, without any objection on the part of the said Dadabhai and Muncherji Pestonji. The sacred fire has been kept up day and night in the said temple to the present time, and all the Parsís residing at Parell use the temple for the performance of their rites and ceremonies, and the Parsí priests who officiate in the temple reside therein or in the adjoining buildings.

The Fire Temple is situated in a small compound (*a*) altogether detached from the compound in which the Lall Bagh House is situated, as appears from the annexed plan. It is accessible from the high road through the entrance leading to Lall Bagh, which entrance has no gate, and therefore cannot be closed, and it is also accessible through another entrance on one side of the Lall Bagh compound, the doors of which entrance are and have always been kept open for the admission of all persons professing the Zoroastrian religion. The temple is accessible without going through the front gate of the inner compound of the Lall Bagh, which gate was kept open or

(*a*) Corruption from *campagna*, the Portuguese for country house, but used in India to denote the enclosed land or garden in which a house stands.

1852.

Doe d. Howard v. Pestonji.

shut according to the pleasure of Dadabhai and Muncherji Pestonji, and which might be kept open or shut according to the pleasure of the plaintiffs. The entrance to the said Agiary or Fire Temple being thus separate from the main entrance to the Lall Bagh, its continuance as a public temple would not, it is contended by the defendant, inconvenince the plaintiffs or injure the value of the Lall Bagh property. It is contended, on the contrary, by the plaintiffs, that its continuance as a public temple would greatly injure the Lall Bagh property.

In the year 1850 the said Dadabhai Pestonji and Muncherji Pestonji borrowed Rs. 60,000 from Messrs. Ritchie, Stewart, and Company, and in order to secure the repayment thereof they executed a regular deed of release and conveyance, dated the 7th day of November, 1850, and thereby conveyed to Alexander Henry Campbell, Esq., and his heirs and assigns, the said dwelling-house, garden, and land called Lall Bagh in fee, subject to redemption on payment of Rs. 60,000 and interest, and giving the mortgagee a power of sale in case of non-payment. Neither during the negociation nor at any time afterwards was it intimated by Dadabhai Pestonji and Muncherji Pestonji that any part of the land or buildings at the Lall Bagh had been dedicated as a Fire Temple, or otherwise alienated or charged by them; but the said Alexander Henry Campbell believed that the Lall Bagh estate was conveyed to him fully and unreservedly, subject only to redemption on payment of the mortgage money and interest. Such mortgage was made without the knowledge of the members of the Parsí Punchayet.

Dadabhai Pestonji and Muncherji Pestonji stopped payment on the 30th day of December, 1850, and on that day executed a deed, conveying and assigning all their estate and effects, including their equity of redemption in the said Lall Bagh estate, to the lessors of the plaintiff.

The said Alexander Henry Campbell, on the 4th of October, 1851, in exercise of the power of sale reserved under the said mortgage deed, put up the said Lall Bagh estate to sale by auction; on which occasion Mr. Henry Richardson attended, and on behalf of the Parsí Punchayet protested against the

sale of the Fire Temple. The property was purchased by the lessors of the plaintiff for Rs. 42,000, and by a deed dated the 15th day of November, 1851, and made between the said Alexander Henry Campbell of the one part, and the lessors of the plaintiff of the other part, the said Lall Bagh estate has been conveyed to the lessors of the plaintiff in fee free from the said mortgage.

The parties are to be at liberty to refer to the said several deeds and papers hereinbefore mentioned.

The question for the opinion of the Court is, whether the defendant, on behalf of the Parsí community, is entitled to the said building called the Agiary, or Fire Temple, and the ground on which it stands, and to exclude the lessors of the plaintiff from the same.

If the Court shall be of opinion in the affirmative, a verdict shall be entered for the defendant; if in the negative, then a verdict is to be entered for the plaintiffs.

Jenkins and *Holland*, for the defendant, contended that the above instrument operated as a grant of the temple to the Parsí community, or, at all events, it amounted to a dedication to them for the purpose of performing their religious rites; and it was suggested that the universal feeling among the Parsís was that a temple devoted to religious purposes could not be used in any other manner.

Dickinson, contrà. Language is used in this case suggesting very false analogies: *consecration*, for example, and *charity purposes.* A Fire Temple of the Parsís has exactly the same legal character attached to it as the chapel of a dissenting community in England, and no other. It is clear that the Pestonjis retained the property of this temple in themselves, just as an English proprietor might do who built a chapel for his own use in his park, to which he allowed his neighbours access. Even if this instrument amounts to a license by Dadabhai Pestonji to attend the temple, there was nothing to prevent him from changing his mind next day and employing the temple for some other purpose.

1852.

Doe d. Howard v. Pestonji.

Jenkins replied.

Perry, C. J.—As the decision which we arrived at on Friday last, with respect to the Parsí Fire Temple, involves a question of considerable interest, not only to the Parsís, but to the Native community generally, I have thought it desirable to place the grounds of our decision in writing.

The case presented on the part of the Parsís was that, by what had occurred between the brothers Pestonji and the Punchayet, either a grant of the temple had been made to the latter, or, at all events, a dedication to the Parsí community of the use of the temple for the religious ceremonies peculiar to that community. But on considering the terms of the instrument of the 16th August, 1834, on which the question turns, it is quite clear that Dadabhai and Muncherji Pestonji intended to retain the property of the temple in themselves and their heirs for ever, and that no words are to be found which can be tortured into an expression of any intention to make a grant to the Punchayet. The instrument, therefore, cannot be supported as a grant; and the question submitted to the Court, whether the Parsí community is entitled to the said temple, and to exclude the lessors of the plaintiff, must on this short ground be answered in the negative. For it is unnecessary to consider the effect of a dedication, as that can have no operation in the case, even supposing, as we are inclined to think, that by this instrument the Pestonjis gave full permission to the Parsís to use this Fire Temple, because they have imposed no legal obligation on themselves and heirs to maintain and repair the temple; and the fact of dedication to a particular use implies that the ownership remains with the grantor.

But it was also argued before us that the question raised in this case was possibly couched in too general language, and that the real point desired to be submitted was that, after the solemn ceremony which had occurred, the building had become devoted to the religious purposes of the Parsís, was thereby placed as it were *extra commercium*, and was in fact inalienable.

We may readily admit, on the facts stated in this case, that the Pestonjis intended in 1834 to dedicate the Fire Temple in their own demesnes to the memory of their late father, to which all the members of the Zoroastrian faith should have liberty of access, and that they intended also that the property in this temple and the right of patronage should remain in themselves and in their heirs for ever. They, no doubt, also fully intended that the temple should never be used for any other purpose. A very large question is raised on these facts as to the power of any individual to attach a peculiar character to land, so as to prevent posterity from using it in any manner that may seem good to them; but in this particular case a narrower view may dispose of the question. It is sufficient to say that the law looks with great jealousy on any attempts to fetter the transmission of property; it is a common weakness with mankind to think themselves able to dictate to their successors a better mode of enjoying the property they leave behind them than those successors would have found out for themselves; accordingly, the law in most civilized countries has interposed to prevent individuals from imposing shackles on the enjoyment of property after their decease. The right to do so is altogether an artificial right, and its exercise depends on an exact conformity with the particular provisions of the law. We are clearly of opinion that by the course adopted by the Pestonjis they have performed no act, and incurred no obligation, which the English law recognises, by which they denuded themselves of the full right of ownership to this temple and to the land on which it stands; and as these gentlemen have become insolvent, such right of course passes, with all other rights of property, to their assignees or trustees. I may add, as I did at the argument, how very strongly public policy is in accordance with the conclusion at which we have arrived. It is no doubt offensive to any religious community to see the temple in which the sacred offices of their religion have been performed become desecrated to profane purposes; and this painful feeling has been experienced frequently by many of the religious denominations in England, whose places of worship, in the vicissitudes

Power in natives of India to grant lands in perpetuity?

Policy of law to maintain alienability of land.

1852.

Doe d. Howard v. Pestonji.

of human affairs, have fallen into the hands of new owners. On the other hand, it is an evil of very limited extent; if the religious community in question is sufficiently numerous, the property which is sacred in their eyes will always be deemed more valuable by them than by any common purchaser in the market, and a very moderate portion of zeal on their part will enable them to retain the property. If, on the contrary, they form but an insignificant and decaying fraction of the community, every consideration shews that the interests of the great majority should not be sacrificed to them.

Consecration of land, whence derived.

Perhaps a word ought to be added on a term that is to be found in the case, and that seems to be relied on, *viz.* that the building had been *duly consecrated.* Consecration is a term which has come to us from the Roman law. It was a solemn ceremony adopted in the days of Polytheism by which temples were devoted to the gods; it was imitated by the early Roman emperors who embraced the Christian religion; and it has been continued by the churches of Rome and of England. It is sufficient to say of it, that by the Roman law it could not be performed without the intervention of the government authorities, and that by the English law it not only requires the interposition of the Bishop, but also the creation of an endowment, that is, the grant of property in fee to maintain the object which the consecration has in view. Nothing of this kind has occurred in the present case.

Judgment, therefore, must be entered for the plaintiffs.

Yardley, J.—The question which it was intended, on behalf of the Parsí community, to submit to us for our consideration was, whether, by the document of the 16th August, 1834, Dadabhai and Muncherji Pestonji had divested themselves of that portion of the Lall Bagh property on which the Fire Temple stands, and had irrevocably devoted it to the use of the Zoroastrian community for the performance of their religious ceremonies. The instrument relied upon by the defendant is one of considerable solemnity of expression, and I may say at the outset that I have no doubt that, at the time it was executed, it was the intention of Dadabhai and Mun-

cherji Pestonji to set aside that portion of their property to be used exclusively for religious purposes, and to admit to a participation therein such members of the Parsí community as might wish to have their ceremonies performed there: a pious resolve, binding, no doubt, on their own consciences, but not involving such an obligation as it is the business of Courts of justice to enforce; for I am clearly of opinion that they had no intention to make a grant of any portion of their land away from themselves and their heirs, either to the Parsí community generally, or to any one or more persons in trust for them. There are no words of conveyance, and there are no persons named or even described as grantees, to say nothing of the large reservations to the brothers and their heirs. It was faintly suggested in argument that the instrument was something in the nature of a covenant to stand seised of the Fire Temple to the use of the Parsís generally, but I do not think much stress was, or could be, laid on that suggestion; for, without adverting to the extremely technical doctrine as to the consideration necessary to "raise an use" by such means, it is difficult to see here who could enforce the performance of such a covenant. The question then is, what is the legal effect of the document of 1834, as to the right of all Parsís to use the temple? I am of opinion that the utmost effect, in that respect, which can in law be attributed to it is that of a mere license revocable at the pleasure of the grantors, and, consequently, that no estate or interest in the temple passed out of Dadabhai and Muncherji Pestonji, or to any one else whomsoever; and that therefore, as the ground on which the temple stands was part of the Lall Bagh estate, it so continues to this day, and passed with the rest of it to the lessors of the plaintiff.

It is not necessary to the decision of this case to enter upon the consideration of the questions relating to alienation in mortmain, whether or not all or any of the numerous statutes passed in the middle ages to restrain such alienations are applicable to this country; whether before Magna Charta the license of the Crown as *ultimus haeres* was necessary to enable land to be held in mortmain, and if so, whether such doctrine

1852.

Doe d. Howard v. Pestonji.

is applicable to this country; with a variety of other questions involving much legal and antiquarian research and discussion of interest and importance. It may hereafter become necessary to enter upon such inquiries, and I am desirous not to commit myself to any opinion upon the questions involved in them until I shall have had the advantage of the learning and industry which will be doubtless brought to bear on the subject when the occasion arises.

The following motion was then made, of which a report is abstracted from the *Bombay Gazette*.

In the same case Mr. *Jenkins*, who on Friday last appeared in behalf of the Parsí Punchayet, moved this day for a rehearing. He stated that on the day of trial he laboured under a very serious misconception, in not having made more particular reference to the customs of the Parsís and their usages regarding Fire Temples. The decision of the Court had caused great anxiety among the followers of the Zoroastrian faith, as all the Fire Temples on the island were held under grants similar to that involved in the present litigation. The learned counsel supported his application by putting in affidavits from the following parties:—Pestonji Manockji, the secretary to the Parsí Punchayet, who stated that the recent decision of the Court had caused great anxiety among Zoroastrians, adding that, if the verdict were carried out, it would be the first occasion on which the sacred fire would be removed from a temple once consecrated. Messrs. D. and M. Pestonji, the grantors, certified that by the document of 1834 they intended to divest themselves of all ownership in the ground or edifice, only retaining control over the priests and servants attached to the temple. They considered that the solemnities of the consecration had rendered the alienation irrevocable. And an affidavit from Mr. Burns, the solicitor, set forth that a number of the priests and leading men of the Parsí community were desirous of giving information as to their usages respecting Fire Temples.

1852.

Doe d. Howard v. Pestonji.

The Chief Justice observed that he was very glad that both himself and his learned brother had put the grounds of the decision just given in writing. He was aware that that decision must have been of great interest, not only to Parsís, but to all classes of the native community who universally viewed with pain the desecration of any religious edifice. Application was now made to grant a new trial, but in the first place there was a technical objection against complying with it. When parties came forward, knowing how the case on each side stood, and submitted their disputes for trial, it was obviously against all right procedure to grant the losing party a rehearing in order that a new class of evidence should be taken. However, supposing that the case were one of such importance as to warrant the Court in departing from this rule, yet would that circumstance warrant the whole matter being opened afresh merely in order that evidence of the nature described by Mr. *Jenkins* should be brought forward? His Lordship was of opinion that the Court could not listen to such evidence. The Parsís had established themselves in this island only within the last 150 years, and it was not till very lately that they had risen to their present position; and it could not be allowed that any particular usages of theirs should fetter the soil of a country into which they had introduced themselves so recently. What the defendants would wish to shew is, that land could, by the customs of their sect, be rendered useless as land; but the law would not permit such evidence to be entertained. The Parsís, no doubt, made a great point of what Messrs. D. and M. Pestonji's intentions were, but in a matter of this kind the question was not to ascertain any party's intentions, but whether the law of the land would allow such a conveyance as the brothers wished to make. The mode adopted by them was founded on no institution of law, and the Court could not therefore recognise what they described as a dedication for ever. If the Court departed from this strict reading of the law, the consequences would be very injurious. Parsís temples might in time be erected in every Parsí compound; and were that race to decay or be reduced, the remaining inhabitants would be

1852.

Doe d. Howard v. Pestonji.

obliged to live in the midst of so much useless land. Therefore it was that the policy of repressing such alienations was so binding. His Lordship concluded by observing that the case was now sufficiently ripe to be forwarded to the Privy Council, and that although the value of the property in dispute would not warrant an appeal, there were other circumstances which would, affecting as they did so many solemn interests.

Mr. *Jenkins* hoped that the sacred fire at present deposited in the temple would not be profaned.

Mr. *Dickenson* observed, that if the defendants chose, they might remove the fire: there were a thousand ways to prevent desecration.

The Chief Justice remarked that there was no reason for apprehending that the lessors of the plaintiffs would be guilty of any rashness in respect to the temple.

Mr. *Jenkins*' application was refused.—*Bombay Gazette*, Feb. 27, 1852.

REGINA v. BHIMA DOSA AND NINE OTHERS.

1843.
Sept. 30.

THE BUNDER GANG.

[*Coram* PERRY, J.]

A joint stock partnership for receiving stolen goods consisting of thirty or forty persons, carried on for many years at Bombay with success.

On an indictment against a gang for receiving a bale of long cloth, knowing it to have been stolen, the proof was that thefts of merchandize had been committed daily from the ships in the harbour, and carried to the warehouses of the defendants for sale, the defendants held a daily auction for ready money, and their books, which were in other respects regularly kept, with periodical division of profits among the partners, shewed that the goods were not obtained by purchase; an accomplice having sworn that the bale of cloth in the indictment had been received by him in the harbour like other stolen goods, and had been sent to the warehouse for sale as usual; but there being no proof as to which of the partners received the bale at the warehouse; an objection made that no proof of a joint receiving had been given, which was necessary by English law, held, that if a conspiracy existed for the purpose of receiving and selling stolen goods, the receipt by one partner was a receipt by all, and that whether such a conspiracy did exist was a question for the jury.

THE successful perpetration of offences against property carried on for a series of years, and to a very large extent, as displayed in the following case, gives a remarkable picture of Indian crime, of the power of confederacy amongst natives, of the corruption of subordinate officials, and though last not least, of the ignorance by Europeans of what is going on around them from the unwillingness or apathy, or, at all events, the failure of the natives to give information to Government authorities of offences, by which many of them must have been injured.

The case is also remarkable as an example of the inapplicability of the letter of the law of English decisions to states of facts wholly different in their kind from any that come before English Courts of justice.

From the evidence given at the trial in this and subsequent cases, it appeared that a partnership consisting of more than forty persons, had existed for many years in Bombay, for the purpose of receiving goods stolen from merchant ships in the harbour. There being no loading dock in Bombay, the ships receive all their cargoes from different quays or bunders (*a*),

(*a*) Persian word for quay.

1843.

REGINA v BHIMA and Others.

which are carried off to them in small boats, and therefore if the Custom House officers and subordinates employed at the bunders could be bribed, a considerable facility existed for committing depredations. A system had been accordingly organised by the gang in question of considerable refinement, by which for many years they had been able to drive a most successful trade, represented by one of the accomplices as producing a profit of six or seven laks a year (60,000*l.* or 70,000*l.*), though this is probably an exaggerated statement. One of the most remarkable features in the case was, that although it was clearly proved that the gang had existed for years, although its existence and means of livelihood were notorious in the Bazaar, not a single complaint had ever been lodged at the Police Office (*a*).

The gang possessed warehouses, cargo boats, canoes, &c., and each day systematically distributed members of their body to the different quays, from which boats were sent off to the different ships loading in the harbour; the plunder obtained in the course of the day was sent to the partnership warehouses, and every morning a regular auction was held, at which the goods were sold at the ordinary market rates.

Division of profits was made with scrupulous honesty amongst the different partners (forty-three in number), and two shares were reserved for charity (*b*)!

The leading members of the gang also carried on separate trades of their own, and by their punctuality in dealing, were of course able to adduce strong evidence as to their respectability at the trial.

These facts were at length brought to the notice of the authorities, by the information of one of the accomplices, who having been accused (apparently with truth) by his partners of robbing *them*, had been fined by them 60*l.*, and thus was led to betray them. On this information the magistrates

(*a*) In the case of English and large native shippers this may be easily accounted for All they would hear of the loss would be by complaints of short deliveries from England many months afterwards, and the difficulty then of ascertaining where the loss should fall, would usually prevent any very minute inquiry being made.

(*b*) *Dharmma*, see *ante*, pp. 529, 530.

issued their warrant, and succeeded in securing the partnership books (nineteen in number), and took possession of nine warehouses full of merchandize, but to which no one made any claim.

The books were kept as regularly as those of any other partnership, day-book or journal, ledger, &c., and the only differences from ordinary books were 1st, that the daily profit was each day posted up in the ledger, and thence distributed to each partner's account, and 2nd, that no entries of disbursements for purchases appeared; each parcel of goods received, being entered with the letters M. V. C., &c., which, another book shewed, denoted the Bunders, Mandavi, Vasid, Carnac, &c.

At the trial in the particular case, which was an indictment for receiving a bale of goods belonging to some person unknown, knowing the same to have been stolen, the evidence of the accomplice, after describing the general operations of the gang, stated, as to the particular bale of goods in question, that about four months before he had been sent to the bunder as usual with orders, and that he had gone out in his canoe into the harbour, where he was accosted by another party connected with the gang, who was coming towards them in a cargo boat from a vessel in the harbour; this party placed a bale of long cloth in the canoe, and the accomplice returned with it to the quay. The bale contained fifty pieces of cloth, and the witness stated that usually they tore off the wrapper whilst in the canoe, and threw it into the sea, and thus they were enabled to take the pieces on shore with less fear of detection. On arriving at the quay, he sent the bale to the warehouse by porters belonging to the gang; but these porters were not called, and there was no direct proof of the bale having been sold, or of what partners were present at the warehouse when it was delivered; but an entry appeared in the defendant's books of a bale containing fifty pieces having been received at that period.

At the close of the case for the prosecution,

Cochrane and *Crawford*, for the prisoners, contended most

1843.

REGINA v. BHIMA and Others.

vigorously, that as this was an indictment for jointly receiving stolen goods, the prisoners could not be legally convicted, unless they actually received the goods jointly, and that whatsoever conspiracy, guilty partnership, or guilty knowledge might have existed amongst them, that was not sufficient to sustain such an indictmant as this, and they relied on *Messingham's case*, (Ryan & Moody, 257). They further argued that there was no proof of the receipt of any *stolen* goods at all.

PERRY, J.—In the case cited, a man and his mother were indicted for jointly receiving some pork knowing it to have been stolen, but it appeared in evidence that the son received the pork in the absence of his mother, and the Judges held that this did not sustain a charge for a joint receipt. But if a gang conspire to carry on a regular trade for the sale of stolen goods, then the receipt by one partner in the course of the trade is a receipt by all; and if this evidence is not admissible, the absurdity would follow that it would not be possible to prove a fact in a Court of justice on evidence that out of a Court of justice no living being could doubt.

Whether such a conspiracy did in fact exist in this case is a question for the jury.

Cochrane then addressed the jury.

Verdict, guilty; and the prisoners were sentenced respectively to ten and fourteen years' transportation.

REGINA *v.* ALU PARU.

1845.
May 29th.

[*Coram* ROPER, C. J. and PERRY, J.]

Admiralty side.

After conviction for felony it is discretionary with the Court to grant a copy of the indictment, and it will not be granted where the intention is to pick out technical errors.

Leave to appeal to the Privy Council refused on the same grounds.

Semble, the Legislative Council of India has power to legislate as to offences on the high seas committed by persons subject to their jurisdiction, per PERRY, J.,

On appeal to Privy Council, it was held that the power to grant or withhold liberty to appeal in criminal cases was vested absolutely in the Supreme Courts.

THE prisoner had been tried before PERRY, J., in October, 1844, and convicted for being an accessory before the fact, to the wilful burning on the high seas of the ship Belvidere, by which several insurance offices in Bombay had been defrauded.

The indictment was framed on Legislative Act XXXI., of 1838, s. 24.

At the trial it appeared that a conspiracy had been formed by Stephenson, the master of the ship, the prisoner, and one Ranmal Lacka, to make heavy insurances on cargo to be forwarded to China, and to burn the ship in the course of the outward voyage. Insurances were made in consequence on opium, and other valuable commodities, and the better to carry out the fraud, some hundred chests of opium were laden on board the Belvidere, whilst in Bombay harbour, but were secretly transhipped before the vessel sailed. On the outward voyage, the master, Stephenson, was proved to have wilfully burnt the ship.

It was contended at the trial that the Court had no jurisdiction, for that the offence being committed by Stephenson on the high seas, the Legislative Council had no authority to legislate for offences there committed, and that if there was no jurisdiction over the principal, there was none also over the accessory. PERRY, J., overruled the objection, and the prisoner was found guilty and sentenced to ten years' transportation.

On a subsequent day, *Howard* moved that the record of the conviction be sent home with a recommendation of pardon, and he again argued the point taken at the trial, and con-

1845. | REGINA v. ALU PARU.

tended that although the right of appeal in felonies in criminal cases is discretionary in England, still, if a *primâ facie* good objection is taken, the Court would grant leave to appeal.

Cur. adv. vult.

1844. | October 9.

PERRY, J.—This is an application on the part of the two wives of Alu Paru, who was convicted of felony nearly nine months ago, and transported to Singapore, that the Clerk of the Crown should furnish their attorney with an office copy of the indictment. The application is made on the part of the attorney, who states that he has laid cases before two advocates, and he swears that he believes the said Alu Paru to have been illegally tried and convicted, and that the illegality would appear on the records of the said trial and conviction if they were forthcoming.

Application for copy of indictment after judgment in order to take technical objections.

No grounds are stated for this belief, no legal objection so far as I recollect was taken to the indictment at the trial, and it is impossible to help suspecting that the motion is the result of a mere afterthought, in pursuance of the efforts of a wealthy criminal to leave no stone unturned by which he may be rescued from the hand of justice.

Still, if the law allows the friends of the prisoner the advantage they are now seeking, it is no answer to point out the great public inconveniences which might arise from it.

The counsel for the applicants founds his claim on an old statute of Edw. 3, which ordains that all subjects may have recourse to the judicial records of the Court in any matter wherein they are interested ("*que les touche in ascun manner*") This statute is not printed in the statutes at large, but is to be found in the preface to the Third Report, and an examined copy of it from the roll was produced at Lord Preston's trial. On that occasion the prisoners claimed their right to have a copy of the indictment, and referred to this statute as an authority for giving it to them, the Judges, however, C. J. HOLT and C. J. POLLEXFEN, expressly refused the application, and this in terms which, I think, affords a direct precedent in this case.

POLLEXFEN, C. J., after stating that the statute had reference to such records only as parties might require to make out their evidences to their estates, goes on thus, "But to have a copy of an indictment, thereby to be enabled to consult with counsel how to make exceptions to that indictment, is a thing that has been denied in all ages, by all the Judges that ever were;" and HOLT, C. J., said, "It is a settled point at law, and as plain as any whatsoever, that no copy of an indictment ought to be allowed to a prisoner in felony or treason." 12 *Howell*, 159.

No right in prisoners to have such copy.

And it is to be noted, that the refusal to grant a copy of the indictment was not only made before, but also after the trial, for one of the prisoners after the verdict was pronounced applied for a copy that he might be enabled to assign errors upon it, but the Court refused, stating that there was no instance of any record of an indictment being shown to a prisoner; and the wisdom of the refusal of the record is perhaps not ill shown by that case, as the error which the prisoner wished to assign was, that the Latin word for boat (*cymba*) was spelt with an *s* instead of a *c*. The law thus laid down has been the rule up to the present day, and the learned counsel who moved has not been able to cite a single precedent for the application he is making.

The nearest authority in his favour is that of *The King* v. *Justices of Middlesex* (5 B. & Adol.), where the Court issued a mandamus to the justices to make up a record of the proceedings of the trial of a prisoner at a lapsed sessions, but it will be seen by the report of the case in 2 *Nev. & Man.* 113, that the Court refused to order the justices to give a copy of the record. The decision therefore merely shews that the Queen's Bench will order the justices of a Court of Record to do their duty by recording the proceedings which have taken place before them. Another authority is *The King* v. *Brangan*, (1 Leach, 32,) where WILLES, C. J., refused the prisoner (who had been acquitted) a copy of the indictment on the ground that, by the laws of the realm, "every prisoner upon his acquittal had an undoubted right to a copy of the record of such acquit-

1844.

REGINA v. ALU PARU.

tal;" notwithstanding this strong language, however, the rule of the Judges to the contrary in the 16 Car. 2, which is given in *Kielway*, and which was republished in 1739, appears to have governed the law in this respect, and therefore the Chief Justice's observations cannot be said to have overruled it, although its validity has certainly been the subject of remark by text writers: see Mr. Serjt. Coleridge's note in his edition of *Blackstone*, and the late edition of *Russell on Crimes and Misdemeanors.*

Appeals after verdict in criminal cases on technical grounds not favoured by English law.

But the overpowering argument against the prisoner's application is, its entire novelty. Rich criminals have been before now convicted, but no instance can be adduced of their having been able, after conviction, to obtain a copy of the record so as to allow it to run the gauntlet of the Profession; and the rationale of this practice is very easily stated; after a conviction upon the merits in criminal cases, the English law does not favour appeals on technical grounds. Indictments for felony all pursue well known forms, and use language, every word of which has its precise signification and well-defined place. At the trial the prisoner and his counsel may have the indictment read so slowly that he may well take note whether any substantial defect, or even any technical objection, occurs or not; if no such defect can then be pointed out, the time is gone by for insisting on clerical errors or mispleading. For this reason it is, and also on account of the great public inconvenience that would ensue, that the liberty to appeal in cases of felony is not *ex debito justitiæ,* but *ex gratia.*

In *Dr. Groenvelt's case,* (1 Lord Raym. 252), Lord HOLT lays down that "a man cannot have a copy of a record of treason or felony without the leave of the Attorney General."

In misdemeanors which are more of a civil nature, the Attorney General's fiat for appeal is obtainable as a matter of course, but it is not so in felony; and I remember perfectly well the point being raised in Westminster Hall, and the refusal of Sir *John Campbell,* when Attorney General, to grant his fiat for an appeal in a case of felony, where he thought the objection proceeded on mere technical grounds.

1844.

REGINA v. ALU PARU.

I think therefore that justice does not require this application to be acceded to; public policy is against it, and no authority has been brought forward in its favour.

On application to the full Court for leave to appeal under the Charter, the Court took time to consider, and this day delivered judgment. ROPER, C. J., stated his reasons for refusing the appeal (*a*).

1848.

June 24th.

PERRY, J.—I also think that the leave to appeal against the conviction in this case should be refused, and this upon two grounds; first, because the objection taken, being wholly technical and unconnected with the substantial justice of the case, is not one of those to which the Court should accede within the true meaning of the Charter of Justice; and, secondly, because, even upon strict law, the objection is untenable.

Upon analysis of the arguments urged in behalf of the prisoner, they will be found to amount to this, that the words "against the form of the statute" are not inserted in the indictment. For it is quite obvious that Stephenson might have been indicted for this offence under the 9 Geo. 4, c. 74, according to the argument of Mr. *Howard*, or under 7 Wm. 4 & 1 Vict. c. 89; in either of which cases, the words I have mentioned would have been sufficient. This being so, and supposing the objection to be a good one, I cannot conceive that it is one to which the Court ought to give way, urged as it is now for the first time, nine months after the trial and after the sentence of transportation has been carried into effect, provided, that is to say, that the Court has any discretion to exercise upon the matter.

Supreme Court has absolute power to refuse or grant an appeal in criminal cases.

Decisions have been referred to in England to show that a similar defect is fatal in arrest of judgment, but it is most important to observe that our Charter of Justice has not allowed to criminals a writ of error, nor even the right to appeal absolutely as in civil cases, but has given this Court *full and absolute power and authority* to allow and deny such appeal as it shall think fit.

It is very easy to understand why the writ of error was not

(*a*) Unfortunately no note has been preserved of the Chief Justice's judgment.

1848.

Regina v. Alu Paru.

given in criminal cases, and why such a large discretion should be attributed to the Judges to allow or admit the appeal. The extreme technicality which has disfigured our criminal law has brought down upon it much obloquy, from its evident tendency to defeat the main interests of justice.

The most distinguished Judge, perhaps, who ever adorned the English Bench wrote nearly 200 years ago as follows: "Many times gross murders, burglaries, robberies, and other heinous and crying offences escape by these unseemly niceties, to the reproach of the law, to the shame of the Government, to the encouragement of villainy, and to the dishonour of God;" 1 *Hale P. C.* A writer of high authority of the present day re-echoes the same complaint. "It is to be regretted," says Mr. *Starkie,* "that the Courts, in listening to trivial errors, have so frequently sacrificed the great end of justice to a mistaken and misplaced humanity, precarious in its application, since it extends without distinction to all degrees of guilt, and mischievous in its consequences;" 1 *Starkie's Crim. Plead.* 353. When the strong minded men who aided Sir Elijah Impey to draw the charter of the Supreme Court, Lord Thurlow, Lord Loughborough, Chief Justice De Grey, and Lord Bathurst,—men distinguished both as statesmen as well as lawyers,—were considering the provisions relating to criminal law, it is not likely that they would willingly inflict on the Indian community a mass of technicalities, the painful inheritance of centuries, which had been found so signally to favour crime at home. What was desired by them, no doubt, was to promote justice to the utmost by discountenancing appeals on frivolous technical grounds, and to allow them only when the substantial merits of the case were involved. This object was accomplished, in my opinion, by their refusal to give a writ of error in criminal cases, and by clogging the right to appeal with the discretionary power before mentioned which is confided to the Court. We know that, in civil appeals, the principle is always acted on by the Privy Council of regarding substance only, and not form; and with respect to criminal matters, we have it from the highest authority that the same principle is kept in view and substantial objections only are attended to in that tribunal.

Statesmen, who framed the charter of Supreme Court, did not intend to apply technicalities of English law to India.

1848.

REGINA
v.
ALU PARU.

In *Rex* v. *Suddis*, Lord KENYON said, "On appeals to the Privy Council from our colonies no formal objections are attended to if the substance of the matter, or the *corpus delicti*, sufficiently appear to enable them to get at the truth and justice of the case." And in the case then before him, the Court of King's Bench, though a Court of strict law, disregarded a technical objection to a decision of a Court of Gibralter, which undoubtedly would have prevailed if the proceedings had come up from an English tribunal.

Danger in colonial Courts attempting to dispense justice on technical pleadings.

It seems to me impossible that any other rule could exist with regard to the due execution of justice in colonial Courts. Legal practitioners in the Supreme Courts in India are called upon to draw pleadings according to four very different and all very technical systems. Each of these is cultivated as a science by a special branch of the Profession at home, but even there, we have seen in a recent case where the highest talent which the Bar could afford was available, how difficult it is, it may be even said how impossible, to draw criminal pleadings, which shall stand the fire of the host of Professional men who may be arrayed against it, when the pecuniary means are sufficient to call their services into the field (*a*). But if the law pleadings of colonial Courts are to be tested by the same golden scales which are occasionally applied in England, if at any length of time after conviction our indictments may be overhauled to discover whether any "then" or "there" has been omitted, or other similar error is apparent, I think I may safely say that crime will enjoy an immunity from punishment which it is somewhat painful to contemplate.

I therefore think that the decisions on writs of error in England do not govern the point now under discussion, namely, whether the Judges are at liberty to exercise a discretion in refusing an appeal on an objection like the present. I think further, that where the petition for leave to appeal is founded on a mere technicality unconnected with the guilt or innocence of the party, the question comes before us as *res integra*, and is to be disposed of on broad principles, and finally, I think it would be a most dangerous precedent to

(*a*) *Regina* v. *O'Connell*.

1848.

REGINA v. ALU PARU.

set to our successors if we were to allow an appeal in the present case on the objection which I have before stated.

But even supposing this Court had no discretionary power in the case, and that we are bound to allow the appeal if a writ of error would lie, I am clearly of opinion that the objection propounded is not maintainable. The main argument of the counsel for Alu Paru is, that the late Charter Act does not give the Governor General authority to legislate for offences committed on the high seas, but only for those committed within the territories of the East India Company, or of an allied state. The argument was not put quite so broadly as this, because it was conceded that there might be a power of legislating as to natives of India whilst on the high seas, but as this concession was demurred to by the other counsel for the petition, and is, in point of fact, fatal to the validity of the reasoning, it must be taken that the broad proposition was enounced as I have stated it.

Jurisdiction of Supreme Court over offences at sea.

The question turns on the true interpretation of sect. 43 of the late Charter Act. By that clause the most ample powers of legislation are given, power to repeal all existing laws, whether acts of Parliament or local regulations, and power to enact others in their stead, and the restrictions as to what acts shall not be passed, are carefully and distinctly specified. They are four in number, first, that no provision in the Charter Act shall be repealed; second, that no provision in the Mutiny Acts shall be repealed; third, that no provision of any future act affecting the Company or the inhabitants of India shall be repealed; fourth, that no act of Parliament or unwritten law respecting the constitutional relations between the Company or the inhabitants of India, and the sovereign authority of the Crown and Parliament shall be in any way varied or repealed.

Powers of legislation given to the Legislative Council of India.

All these provisions are manifestly inserted on the broad ground, that it was necessary in the delegation of so important an element of the sovereign authority as the power of legislation, to preserve the paramount rights and powers of the sovereign legislature intact. But the expression of these reservations clearly establishes in my mind that all other powers of legislation not reached by them are included in the general words of the clause. The particular words relied upon to shew that the Governor General in council has no power to legislate for persons on the high seas are these; "The Governor General in council shall have power to make laws *for all persons,* whether British or native, foreigners or others, and for all Courts of justice, whether established by his Majesty's charters or otherwise, and the jurisdiction thereof, and for all places and things whatsoever, *within and throughout the whole and every part of the said territories.*"

Distinction in construction of laws, applying to *persons*, or to *things*.

It is contended that these latter words apply to the persons who are to be legislated for, as well as to the places and things with which they are immediately collocated. But the express distinction which is made in the act between persons and things lies deeply seated, I apprehend, in the principles of legislation, and corresponds with the distinction well known to jurists between personal and real statutes.

The laws of a country prohibiting crime are personal laws, and render the persons of that country amenable to its criminal jurisdiction wherever the crime may have been committed. A real statute on the other hand, a statute affecting the *res* or thing, only has operation where the *res* is locally situated.

It is only by accident connected with the peculiar nature of English procedure, that offences committed by Englishmen on the high seas, or in *partibus transmarinis,* are not cognizable by the common law, and that they have required special legislation to reach them. At every period of our history, a murder, or a robbery, must have been a crime which society was interested to punish, whether it was committed at sea or on land; but by the common law the trial of all offences must take place on the spot where they occurred, by a jury belonging to that locality. If then a crime occurred in a place from which no jury could issue, as on the high seas, the common law became impotent to afford a remedy. But still the criminal did not escape, and other tribunals known to the ancient law were open for the trial of the offender.

The constable and marshal had jurisdiction independent of special statutes over all offences committed on land out of the

1848.

REGINA v. ALU PARU.

realm. The latter point was solemnly determined by the Judges in the mysterious case of Doughty, who was executed by Sir Francis Drake on an island in South America. And I would here just note that the late biographer of the great circumnavigator, has strangely overlooked the criminal proceedings which vere instituted against Drake on his return to England (*a*). Old law books were probably much out of the course of Mr. Barrow's reading, but if he had fallen in with Lord Coke, (3 Inst. 48, 1 Inst. 74, *a*,) Mr. Hargrave's note, and Hutton, 3, he would have seen that Doughty's friends did not fail to stir the matter in the criminal courts, and that it was only through the interposition of the Queen that it was allowed to drop. There are other instances of the Court of constable and marshal sitting to try crimes committed out of the British dominions, and although this Court has now fallen into desuetude, these instances are quite sufficient to prove my proposition, that the criminal laws of the land, without any express provision to that effect, are binding on persons subject to that law in whatever part of the world they may transport themselves to (*b*). A complete confirmation of this may be found in the laws of other nations. In the Code Penal of France, for instance, the law denouncing the crime of malicious burning merely states the offence and the punishment, without the least reference to the locality where the crime may be committed. Art. 432 expresses in one paragraph, that the burning of a dwelling-house, ship, boat, or warehouse, used or serving for habitation, shall subject the offender to the punishment of death, and it is quite clear that such a personal statute binds the persons subject to the French law equally on sea and on shore.

Crimes committed by Englishmen out of the realm are cognizable by Courts in England.

The inference from the above reasoning is, that the unlimited delegation of authority to legislate for all persons, carries with it the inherent power to pass all such personal statutes as are requisite for the good government of a great country.

But can it be contended for a moment that it is not essential

(*a*) See Barrow's Life of Drake.

(*b*) See in confirmation *Rex* v. *Sawyers*, Russ. & Ry. Cr. Ca., a trial for a murder committed in Portugal.

Necessity for legislation over the high seas by the Government of India.

to a government like that of India, to be able to prevent excesses and enormities committed on its coasts, or on the uninhabited and barbarous islands in the Indian Seas.

Suppose that the fishermen on this coast were discovered to be engaged in a series of fraudulent transactions half a mile from the shore, can it be that under the clause which enables the Governor General in council to legislate "for all persons, whether British or Native" no power exists to regulate fisheries? or suppose that under the new trade which has sprung up of transporting coolies to the Mauritius, a set of unprincipled men were to find their way to the commands of the carrying ships, and a repetition of the horrors of the middle passage were to occur, is it possible that the Government of this country is unable to introduce any laws to restrain such practices? It may be said that in all such cases the remedy is to be sought by applying to the Imperial Legislature, but the answer is that Parliament, from its distance, from its multiplicity of business, from its necessary unacquaintance with local details, felt itself wholly incompetent to deal with such matters of internal Government, and for these reasons has delegated this portion of its authority to the Governor General in council.

I think, therefore, it is quite clear that it was not the intention of Parliament to restrict the powers of the legislative council to *persons* merely within the territories of India.

Who the persons are to whom their powers of extra territorial jurisdiction extends is another question, and one which may call for nice legal interpretation in certain cases.

It is pretty apparent that the same rule of construction might not apply if the person were a foreigner, as if he were an Englishman or a Native, for as the imperial legislature does not possess the power of passing personal statutes for foreigners *extra territorium*, of course it could delegate no such power to the legislative council.

But we have not to dispose of such a case now, and have only to consider whether Stephenson was such a person to whom the clause in question extends. But Stephenson was described in this indictment as every other British subject

1848.

REGINA
v.
ALU PARU.

who is brought to the criminal bar for trial; no special clause in the indictment to bring such a prisoner within our jurisdiction, is ever inserted in Admiralty cases, and our Admiralty jurisdiction being co-extensive with any such jurisdiction at home, as the Chief Justice has conclusively shewn, no special averment I conceive was necessary. In *Æneas Macdonald's case,* (Foster's C. L.) the prisoner, who was indicted for high treason, set up that he was a native of France, but the Court held that the presumption in all cases of this kind is against the prisoner, and "the proof of his birth out of the King's dominions, when the prisoner putteth his defence on that issue, lieth upon him."

Yet the indictment in that case did not aver, any more than the indictment in this, that the prisoner was a native of Great Britain.

By the evidence at the trial in this case, Stephenson was shewn to have been an inhabitant of Bombay for many weeks, if not months, previous to the concocting of this offence, and after the burning of the ship he returned here voluntarily, and again remained many weeks, and indeed was then tried for an offence committed within the harbour of Bombay; if then he is not to be considered as one of those British persons over whom the Governor General in council has the power of legislating, there seems scarcely any one to whom the clause can apply, as we know that the majority of the English, although they may pass the greater part of their lives in this country, are still held not to have their domicile in India.

English residents in India are not domiciled there.

I think, therefore, that the words are quite sufficient to carry out the intention, which I conceive to be abundantly apparent on the face of the act, to enable the Governor General in council to provide for offences committed on the high seas by a person like Stephenson. But, as the argument relied on has proceeded on what are supposed to be some specially restrictive words, I think it right to point out that there are other words in the clause which give this authority specifically.

The clause in question enables the Governor General to legislate for the Supreme Courts, and for *the jurisdiction thereof,* but this Court had already jurisdiction over the high seas, the high seas therefore are brought within the range, over which the Governor General in council is expressly authorized to make laws.

This argument by itself appears to me to be conclusive, but I have thought it right in a case where such very important interests are conceived, and where so much of our past criminal procedure is implicated, not to rest the case on what may be mere fortuitous expressions, but to grapple boldly with the question as to what is the manifest intention and object of the Legislature.

Conflict of jurisdictions over offences at sea occasionally inevitable.

There is only one other argument that I think it necessary to notice. It is considered a fatal objection to the legislative council having jurisdiction over the high seas, that a man might thereby be subjected to two different punishments, and that it would depend on the mere chance of the Court to which he was first brought, which of the two punishments he should receive.

But this is no objection at all; it is inherent in the subject-matter; the high seas, being a place subject to the common jurisdiction of nations, have always given rise to the same difficulty. Parliament itself has perceived it, in the case of the legislative authority they have given to India.

By the Mutiny Act for the Indian Navy, which was made under the authority of Parliament, offences on the high seas may be disposed of by Court martial, but such offences may also be dealt with, and have a different rate of punishment assigned, by this Court sitting on its Admiralty side. The act has foreseen this, and provided for it, by enacting that there shall not be two trials for the same offence.

A conflict of laws between two parts of the same dominions is no doubt an evil, but it is occasionally inevitable. Such conflict existed between England and India, when the former country repealed the English Act relating to malicious burning, 7 & 8 Geo. 4, c. 30, and the Irish Act, 9 Geo. 4, c. 56, but omitted to repeal the Indian Act. The 7 Wm. 4, & 1 Vict. c. 89, repealing these acts, was passed in consequence of the recommendation of the Criminal Law Commis-

1848.

REGINA
v.
ALU PARU.

sioners, who advised that a lesser punishment than death should be awarded in certain offences not directed against life or limb. But as the Indian Act was not repealed, a man brought before the Supreme Court might still have suffered death for an offence like that committed by Stephenson. Whereas, if he had been tried in England, he could only have been sentenced to transportation.

Course adopted by Parliament to avoid conflict of jurisdiction.

Such conflict, no doubt, is unseemly, and inconvenient, but it is the lesser of two evils, for if Parliament had assumed to repeal the Indian Act, the consequence would have been that a man might have been sentenced to death, and executed by a judgment of the Supreme Court in India, under a law which no longer existed, although that fact was not known in India. An occasional conflict of laws, therefore, being wholly inevitable when two distinct sources of law are allowed to co-exist with respect to the same subject-matter, it must be left to the wisdom of the two legislatures to make this conflict as short and as unimportant as possible.

This, in my opinion, has been completely achieved by the course taken by Parliament and the legislative council. The former would not interpose its authority in a locality wherein it had permitted another legislative body to operate, and the latter at the earliest moment took up the task, which the imperial legislature had left to it, of repealing the clauses in the 9 Geo. 4, c. 74, which clashed with the new English statute and enacted similar positive clauses in their Act, No. 31 o 1838.

In my view, therefore, the law as to both countries is now perfectly harmonious, and the conflict upon which the learned counsel has built part of his argument is wholly imaginary (*a*)

Petition dismissed.

Note.—Alu Paru, the prisoner in the above case, was a Kojah merchant of great wealth, and at the time of his apprehension was said to be worth 80,000*l*. An amusing account of him

(*a*) See this case on appeal, 5 Moore, Priv. Coun. Cas. 206, where it was held that the Supreme Courts have the absolute power to refuse an appeal in criminal cases, and the appeal was accordingly dismissed.

whilst undergoing his sentence at Sincapore, will be found in *Lieut. Marriott's Voyage in the Pacific, &c.*

Stephenson, the accomplice of Alu Paru, had been previously indicted for fraudulently transhipping opium before the voyage commenced, and substituting rubbish in its place, but on the trial, the evidence being somewhat weak, he was acquitted, and forthwith a grand dinner was given him by his brother captains in the port. When the subsequent evidence came to light, which led to the apprehension of Alu Paru, a diligent search after Stephenson was made throughout England and the colonies, but in vain.

Mode of dealing by Indian Governments with small Indian Potentates.

On information being given to the magistrates by an accomplice against Alu Paru, the latter fled from Bombay, and after some time it was discovered that he had taken refuge in the capital of an adjoining chieftain, the Habschi (*a*) of Jinjira, with whom he was living on terms of great amity. This chief, who is the descendant of the Admiral who commanded the fleet while the Mussalman dynasty of Bijapur was in power, has preserved his little port through all the vicissitudes, which the subsequent Government of the Péshwah, and its *bouleversement* by the English brought about, and from his insignificance has grown up into an independent power, his old masters having disappeared from the scene, and the new lords of the ascendant never having thought it worth while to take any notice of him. As no treaty therefore for extradition, or anything else, was in existence between the British Government and this Potentate (of perhaps 300*l.* a year) the question arose, how a law-respecting people like the English could obtain such an arch offender as this Kojah merchant from his Court. The difficulty was solved by the Bombay Government sending down a steam frigate with the chief magistrate on board, and *a request* to deliver up the criminal; it is needless to add that his Abyssinian Highness at once complied, and few will question that this breach of Vatel and Grotius was justified by the circumstances.

(*a*) Habschi is the name applied by Hindus to the natives of Abyssinia (*Habesch*); from which country the Adil Shahi dynasty of Bijapur obtained their admirals.

THE ADVOCATE GENERAL
v.
RICHMOND.

1845.

Nov. 28th.

[*Coram* Roper, C. J , and Perry, J.]

The goods of felons convicted in Bombay belong to the Crown, per Roper, C. J., to the Company, per Perry, J. Canons for construing the acts relating to India suggested. Broad distinction between acts relating to the Company as a trading corporation, and as a governing power. In the last Charter Act the interests of the Imperial Legislature and of the Company are treated as identical.

This was a special case, which was brought for the purpose of ascertaining whether the Crown or the East India Company was entitled to the escheats of felons' goods.

The prisoner, Alu Paru, (see last case), being possessed of large property, *inter alia*, of shares in the Oriental Bank, it became a question to whom this property escheated.

The *Advocate General*, for the Company, founded the right of the Company on the clause in the Charter of Justice, but more especially on the charter of Car. 2, granting the island of Bombay to the Company, and by which all *jura regalia* were granted, and therefore felons' goods; *Com. Dig.* "*Forfeiture.*" Bombay was made a proprietary Government, and the right of making laws was conceded, and therefore forfeitures passed to the grantees.

Cochrane for the Crown. Whatever the power and the rights of the Company might be under the charter of Charles 2, its rights now rest wholly on the late Charter Act. If the first charter gave the power of legislation, the statute has taken it away, therefore if forfeitures are incident to legislative authority, they are also gone. The term forfeitures in the charter does not include felons' goods, which must have express words to pass them.

Cur. adv. vult.

Roper, C. J., thought that express words were required

to convey the grant of felons' goods, and cited *Rex* v. *Mayor of Dover* (1 C., M. & R.; Sir W. Jones, 349, and Com. Dig. G. 7, Grant).

1845.

The Advocate General v. Richmond.

1845. Nov. 22.

PERRY, J.—The question to be decidedb etween the Crown and the East India Company, depends upon a very careful examination of the different charters and acts of Parliament which have been granted and passed with respect to British India during the last 240 years; and I would just observe, that if this question is to go home on appeal, there are not the materials stated on the face of the special case upon which a proper judgment can be pronounced.

Conflict of title to felon's goods between Crown and Company.

The only fact stated in the case is, that Alu Paru was convicted in this Court of felony, at the October sessions of 1844, and the question is then put whether the forfeiture consequent upon his conviction belongs to the Crown or the East India Company.

The point taken by itself is not a very material one, for the relations between the British Government and the Company have now become so intimate, that nothing like adverse interests can be seen to exist; and the consequence, perhaps, was, that the argument did not present such a vigorous battling as if the question had arisen between two hostile parties. In point of fact, however, some very important questions are more or less remotely involved in the decision.

Importance of charter granting Bombay to E. I. Company.

The construction of the charter granting Bombay to the Company comes mainly into question, and, as upon the due construction of the charter (*a*), which has been unaccountably overlooked in most discussions of this nature, the only solid basis can be found for many of the most important functions of government, and of jurisdiction, which have been exercised not only in Bombay but in India generally, too much attention cannot be paid to its provisions, I have gone more minutely into the case than the discussion at the Bar would have necessitated.

To form a decision on the rights and authorities of the East India Company, I have already mentioned that charters and

(*a*) See *ante*, p. 61, *Perozeboye's Case*.

1845.

The Advocate General v. Richmond.

acts for a long period of years (since 1601 in fact) must be consulted. Now these are not to be had in any printed collection, some of them are not to be found in Bombay at all, and others (most important ones) are only visible in a worm-eaten and defaced copy belonging to the Advocate General. I question, therefore, whether this Court can be altogether sure of its having sufficient materials before it, when questions of this nature arise. It will be found, however, I presume to think, that the following canons of construction may be safely laid down as useful guides on any inquiry of the sort.

Canons for determining rights and powers of E. I. Company.

1. No question can be decided with respect to the general powers and authorities of the East India Company upon any isolated clause of an act of Parliament or charter, but the whole must be taken together in order to elicit the intention of the legislature.

Mercantile and political character to be discriminated.

2. For nearly 200 years past two different characters have been recognised (though not very distinctly perhaps) in the East India Company, the one as a trading corporation, the other as a governing power; upon every disputed clause therefore respecting their authority, the question must be first ascertained to which character it is referable, and although upon those clauses in support of the monopoly a limited construction may have to be put, all those provisions which confer powers of Government must, as in favour of the subject, be construed liberally (*a*).

The Legislature sometimes hostile to Company; but in last Charter Act, interests of Company and Legislature identified.

3. The policy of the Crown and the legislature having varied at several times with respect to the Company, at one time granting large powers, at another restricting them; but the late Charter Acts having, to a great measure, identified the interests of the two Governments, the key to the construction of all previous acts and charters is to be found in the policy of the last act.

The first rule is almost self-evident to every legal mind, but it requires to be reinforced in order to keep in sight the necessity of making rather a painful research through a number of documents not very easily procurable.

An exemplification of the second rule may be seen in the

(*a*) As to this broad distinction, see *ante*, p. 356, 357.

1845.

The ADVOCATE GENERAL v. RICHMOND.

power to make bye-laws, punishable with fine and amerciament, which is to be found in so many of the charters commencing with 43 Eliz., and which seems to have formed a precedent for the celebrated clause in 13 Geo. 3, enabling the Governor General in Council to make rules, ordinances, and regulations in like manner, and which the 39 & 40 Geo. 3, c. 79, further enforced, by authorizing public or private whipping (*a*). Now, undoubtedly, this clause in its origin referred to the Company as a trading corporation.

The words in which it is couched in the Charter of Elizabeth, are exactly the same as are to be found in other charters of that day to other corporations of traders. And afterwards, when the East India Company acquired territories, and exercised the rights of Government under the powers granted by the Charter of Charles 2 (to be mentioned hereafter), although such rights of Government are confirmed by subsequent charters, still the clause as to bye-laws with fines and amerciaments, copying the language of the original charter, likewise appears.

Instances of this may be found in the Charter of 10 Wm. 3, granted in pursuance of the 9 & 10 Wm. 3, and in the indenture tripartite to which Queen Anne was a party.

Legal basis of high acts of Government in India.

The only possible solution, therefore, of these two clauses as they are found in the same charters, appears to me to be, that whilst the powers of Government contained in one clause, enabled so much to be done which has been done, and which necessarily required to be done, for instance, the exercise of all governmental powers including, judicial authority, the appointment of Judges and application of English civil and criminal codes to the inhabitants of Bombay, exertion of similar powers in the Mofussil involving the abrogation of the Mussulman criminal law with respect to Hindus, and the restoration, that is to say, the enactment, of Hindu criminal law in its place; whilst all these things were done, I say, and legally done on this basis, the only operation which can be

(*a*) See *ante*, p. 463, *Shaik Boodin's Case*.

1845.

The Advocate General v. Richmond.

attributed to the clause as to bye-laws, must be with respect to that subject-matter for which it was originally introduced, *viz.* solely in respect of the trading interests of the corporation.

With respect to the third canon, it appears to me quite evident, that the last Charter Act (3 & 4 Wm. 4, c. 83) no longer denotes anything like distrust of the Company, or a desire to impart powers with a niggard hand, but that it now recognises the Company fully as a Government exercising all its great functions in trust for, and in harmonious subordination to, the Imperial Legislature, and that, therefore, the Act requires the liberal construction which I have suggested.

Felon's goods not granted to Company by charter of justice.

On the argument at the Bar in the present case, the Advocate General based the right of the Company to forfeitures on the Charter of Charles 2, granting Bombay to the original East India Company, and also on the last Charter Act. He very properly rejects the clause in our Charter of Justice, and the similar preceding clauses, which give fines, amerciaments, forfeitures, &c., to the Company. For, although the word forfeiture in legal strictness denotes the *bona et catalla felonum* more strictly perhaps than anything else, according to *Rex* v. *Dover* (1 C., M. & R.), and in *Tomes* v. *Etherington* (1 Saund.), the word in an Act of Parliament was argued to comprise felons' goods, yet it is clear from the context of our charter, that the word there does not refer to felonies at all, but that all that is granted only relates to contempts, misdemeanors, and offences of that nature. And if a more specific meaning is required for the word "forfeiture," it is easily found in many preceding charters, where the goods and ships of interlopers are declared to be forfeited, one-half of which is to be to the Crown, and one-half to the Company.

The Company, however, found their claim on the extensive grant contained in Charles II.'s Charter, by which "all and singular the royalties, revenues, rents, customs, castles, forts, buildings and fortifications, privileges, franchises, pre-eminences and hereditaments whatsoever," are granted by the King "in as ample a manner" as we ourselves now have, and enjoy the same, by virtue of the grant of the King of Portugal, with a saving only of the faith and allegiance due to the royal power and sovereignty, and to be held in free socage as of the Manor of East Greenwich, on payment of the annual sum of 10*l.* in gold. The charter further grants all the warlike stores belonging to the Crown on the island, enabling the Company to entertain troops, and to make laws for the good government of the island, and the same to revoke at pleasure, and to enforce them by pains and punishments, extending to life and member. It further enables them to appoint governors and other servants, who may exercise judicial authority, and authorizing them to make war in self-defence, and to exercise martial law. And all these powers they are to exercise in any other place in the East Indies, which they shall at any time hereafter purchase or lawfully acquire.

But *jura regalia* granted by Charles II.

The Advocate General contends that this is an absolute grant of the Government and all the revenues of Bombay, exactly in the manner that a feudal principality was wont to be granted, and that it resembles the grants of the Proprietary Governments of the plantations of America, where also the power of making laws was imparted, and where it is suggested the forfeitures attaching on convictions passed to the grantee. And he further contends that as one branch of the royal revenue in feudal states consisted of the profits arising from Courts of justice, such as fines, forfeitures of recognizances, and amerciaments, 1 *Bl.* 289; and another branch of "forfeitures," strictly so called, *foris facta*, 1 *Bl.* 299; these two royalties or branches of revenue have passed under the grant.

The answer given to this is, that the goods of felons cannot pass in the King's grant under general words. And the text books, *Comyn*, &c., are cited to this effect. On referring to the cases collected in 2 *Roll. Abr.* "*Prerogative*," it is true that there are a number of decisions where a limited and restricted construction has been put upon grants of the Crown, possibly in some cases going against the manifest intention of the grantor. But it is impossible to help perceiving that these

1845.

The Advocate General v. Richmond.

cases between the Crown and individuals, bear but a very remote analogy to the present case. It has been an undeviating rule of construction with Courts of justice in all such cases to protect the interests of the Crown, and to lean against all improvident grants. The revenues of the Crown belonging to it for the support of the royal dignity, every grant of a portion to individuals in fee tended *pro tanto* to the injury of the public service. Moreover, in such cases the specific grant was only of specific portions of the royal revenue, it was, therefore, by no strained construction that a grant of part was held to convey no more than what it actually expressed in terms.

But there is no decision that I am aware of, which has held that a grant of all the royal revenues in a particular liberty or district, where the intention evidently was to grant all such revenues, and where all public charges were to be borne by the grantee, requires all the particular items of revenue to be specified.

Grant of *jura regalia* comprises forfeitures of felon's goods.

On the contrary, the cases relating to grants of *jura regalia* are expressly in point. In 2 *Dyer*, 281, 8 b., it was held that the grantee of *jura regalia* was entitled to the forfeitures for treason, which, by a statute passed subsequent to the grant, were expressly declared to belong to the King. But this case still leaves open the question, perhaps, what *jura regalia* consist of; and it may be argued that the grant of a county palatine possibly expressed "forfeitures." *Jura regalia* are defined by *Cowell*, citing *Spelman*, to be "*Jura omnia ad fiscum spectantia;*" and by *Ducange*, as, "*jura regia quæ ab imperatoribus vel regibus interdum ecclesiasticis aliisque personis conceduntur;*" and he cites several instances, by which *regalia* are shewn to comprise matters of revenue, such as toll, portage, seignorage, "*et alia si qua sunt similia.*"

But fortunately, we are not left in doubt as to what the grant of a county palatine actually expressed; for Lord Coke sets out the grant itself of the Duchy of Lancaster to John of Gaunt (4 *Inst.* c. 36); he also gives the words of the grant by William the Conqueror of the county of Chester; and by these it will appear, that the same general words are used in those charters as in the Charter of Bombay; and the only difference is in favour of Bombay; for, the Charter to the Company contains much larger sovereign powers than were ever supposed to pass to the grantee of a county palatine.

Another objection made on the part of the Crown is, that, if the charter passed these forfeitures, there was no necessity for the subsequent limited grant of fines, &c., which occurs in our Charter of Justice, and elsewhere, and which it is admitted do not convey the forfeitures in question. This objection appears to me the more formidable one of the two to the claim of the Company, for it certainly would seem on the occasion of the first *special* grant of such fines, &c., that neither the Crown nor the Company believed that the latter were entitled to the forfeitures now under discussion.

The history of the clause is this; from the time of the Charter of Charles 2, in 1669 to 1726, the Company governed this island under the provisions therein contained.

Introduction of English law into Bombay; the fact clear, the legal mode doubtful.

The English law prevailed; by what means introduced, whether by a lost order of Council during the time the island belonged to the Crown, or by a law made under the common seal of the Court, under the powers of their Charter, or more probably, by its being the only law known to those who were in authority in the island, for there is not the least vestige of Portuguese law or Courts at any time after the cession by the King of Portugal; but in whichever of these ways introduced, there is no doubt that English law was the law of the place (*a*). During this period, the Company's servants exercised all judicial authority, and the Crown did not interfere in any way with the administration of justice, except by granting the Company additional powers to erect an Admiralty Court for offences and matters having place on the high seas. It is stated in some of the histories also, that, during this period, forfeitures for offences committed by the Jesuits brought large

(*a*) See Sir Josias Child's indignant exclamation against English law, as given in 1 Mill, 112, citing Captain Hamilton's New Account of India, clearly shewing that English law was the *lex loci* at Bombay.

1845.

The Advocate General v. Richmond.

landed estates into the possession of the Company (*a*). And in the trial for treason against Rama Comattee in 1726, a record of which is in the secretary's office, the indictment is drawn according to English law, and is laid *contra pacem* of the Company. A conclusion, which, though it is said to have been laughed at in this Court, I apprehend to be quite right, where a grant of separate jurisdiction has been made by the Crown. See 1 *Bl.* 118 (*b*).

Establishment of Courts of the Crown in Bombay, 1726.

Such was the internal government of this island up to 1726; but in that year the Crown, upon the petition of the Company, setting forth that the Company, by a strict and equal distribution of justice (which the charter recognised) had encouraged large numbers of people to establish themselves in their different settlements; but that there was great want in all the said places of a competent and proper power and authority for the more speedy and effectual administering of justice, established Courts at each of the Presidencies, called the Mayor's Court, with civil and criminal jurisdiction.

In the following year, George 2 granted another Charter to the Company, in which, after reciting the last charter granted by his royal predecessor, and that in virtue of such grants and the authorities thereby given, "sundry fines, amerciaments, forfeitures, penalties, and sums of money may have arisen, been ordered, charged, set or imposed, in and by the said respective Courts, to which we, our heirs, and successors are, and may be entitled by virtue of our royal prerogative:" and reciting, also, that the Company had petitioned for a grant of all such fines, &c., his Majesty proceeds to grant them to the Company, though in more limited terms than the previous recital would have implied, for the restriction before mentioned is here introduced, confining them to "any contempts, misdemeanors, or offences whatsoever."

Now it is to be observed of this grant, that if the true effect of the charter of 26th March, 1669, is to vest all the royalties

(*a*) See Mr. Warden's Report to Government in 1812.

(*b*) The stat. 27 Hen. 8, c. 24, only applying to franchises "within the realm," *i. e.* to England and Wales; and the marches of the same."

and revenues in Bombay in the East Indian Company just as in the grant of a county palatine, the ignorance or forgetfulness of the grantees that such was the case would not tend to revest them in the Crown. The grant might be good for further confirmation, it might have been applied for *ex majori cautela*, and indeed there may be subject-matters on which the clause in question might well operate. It has been before shewn that previous charters had ordered goods and ships of interlopers to be confiscated, and half of the forfeitures were directed to go to the Crown; so, penal acts of Parliament applicable to India might expressly give the penalties to the King; in all such cases the clause might have been beneficially operative to the Company. It is impossible to argue, therefore, that the existence of this clause in our Charter denotes that no larger grant had been made by any previous charter.

The objection, however, may perhaps be put more forcibly, or in a different shape, by conceding that the Charter of Charles, and the subsequent charters granting like powers of government (for the first charter, being granted to the old Company, was surrendered in 1709) did in fact grant the revenues and forfeitures proceeding from Courts of justice, but that the petition of the Company for the establishment of the King's Courts operated as a surrender of their previous franchises, and the emoluments attached thereto. Several instances are given in the *Abbot of Strata Marcella's case* (9 Rep. 256), of franchises and liberties which had been granted by the King, being reunited to the Crown by escheat, surrender, or otherwise. And, if in this case this establishment of the King's Courts had been attended with any charge to the Crown, I think there would have been very good ground to contend that the petition of the Company did, in fact, operate as a surrender of this portion of their franchises.

All the charges of judicial establishments fall on Company, the benefits arising from the forfeitures should belong to them also.

I think, however, that the mere fact of the establishment of royal Courts cannot be held to have this effect, the whole charges of the royal Courts of justice in India have always fallen, in common with the other charges of Government (and it has always been the intention to make them fall) on the Company. Even in unforeseen and extraordinary cases, this

1845.

The Advocate General v. Richmond.

policy has been carried out; when, for instance, the *Ecclesiastical Registrar* of the Supreme Court of Madras died insolvent, leaving a deficiency due to suitors and others of upwards of 50,000*l.*, upon the report of the Judge that there was no fund applicable to the discharge of these balances, the 11 Geo. 4 & 1 Wm. 4, c. 75, was passed, throwing the payment upon the Honorable Company.

When, therefore, we find that such has been the policy of the legislature, when we see in the Charter of Charles a valid legal foundation for the claim of the Company to all the revenues of the territories they might acquire in India, and when in the last Charter Act, the 1st and 2d section confirm and vest in the Company "all the territorial acquisitions and revenues mentioned in 53 Geo. 3," and "all the lands, hereditaments and revenues of the Company," and "all rights to fines, penalties, and forfeitures, and other emoluments whatsoever, in trust for his Majesty for the service of the Government of India," I cannot doubt that the true construction on the whole matter is, that the petty branch of revenue now under consideration has, with all other branches of revenue arising in India, vested in the Company absolutely during the continuance of the present charter.

I think, therefore, that a verdict should be entered for the defendant on the *ex officio* information, and for the Company in the other action.

Sir Henry Roper, C. J., however, was of opinion that a grant of felons' goods was required to be made in express terms in order to bar the right of the Crown.

Judgment accordingly for the Crown (*a*).

(*a*) The case was carried home on appeal, but the interests between the Crown and the Company being so much blended under the present charter, it has not been deemed necessary to bring on the case for argument. I have never heard what became of the property of Alu Paru, which was stated to be 80,000*l.*

THE QUEEN

v.

ESSUB IBRAHIM AND BABA FAQUIRA.

1845. October 1.

[*Coram* PERRY, J.]

Crown side.

The common law jurisdiction of the Court on its Crown side includes the harbour of Bombay.

The extent of the port of Bombay has been defined by the Regulations.

THESE prisoners were tried for the murder of two girls of the town and a lad, whom they had induced to go off with them in a boat to some ships in the harbour, under pretence that the girls had been sent for by some of the officers. The girls had, as usual, put on ornaments to the value of many hundred rupees, and it appeared by the testimony of one of the boatmen, that as soon as the prisoners had rowed about half a mile from the shore, they knocked their victims on the head with the rullocks of their boat, and threw them overboard. The corpses were not found, and the prisoners were soon after apprehended on the coast with the jewels of the unfortunate girls in their possession.

The jury found the prisoners guilty, and the Judge was just about to pronounce sentence, when

Dickinson, who had conducted the defence, suggested that the prisoners should have been indicted on the Admiralty side, PERRY, J., thereupon ordered the point to be argued before the full Court, when it appearing satisfactorily that the harbour was within the common law jurisdiction of the Court, the objection was overruled, and the prisoners were executed.

The following is a note of the judgment of Mr. Justice PERRY:—

1845.

The Queen v. Essub.

Perry, J.—The ordinary jurisdiction of the Court on its criminal side, comprehends "the island of Bombay and the limits thereof;" but the port of Bombay has always been annexed to the possession of the island, and indeed the island itself was formerly of no value except for the port annexed to it. The port, in fact, has always been appurtenant to the island, and the grant from Charles 2, makes use of the terms "the port and island of Bombay." If such a harbour as that of Bombay existed in England, it undoubtedly would be held to be within the body of the surrounding county, or if there were different counties on each side, as is the case with the Severn, one-half would be held to be within one county, one within the other; and the same rule holds as to the Thames, (3 *Inst.*)

The port then being appurtenant, and within the limits of Bombay, the question is, how far the limits extend; this may be a question of fact or a question of law, but it has been settled by law, for the regulations which the Bombay Government were enabled to make under 47 Geo. 3, have determined these limits and regulations, and Reg. xi. of 1810; Reg. i. of 1820, and Reg. i. of 1821, clearly show that the spot where these murders were committed, was within the limits of the harbour.

IN THE MATTER OF THE LAST WILL OF BHIMJI CALLIANJI.

1845.
Jan. 1[illegible]

[*Coram* PERRY, J.]

The Cour[illegible] grant libe[illegible] appeal ag[illegible] an order d[illegible] missing a caveat.

PROBATE of the will had been applied for, against which a caveat had been entered, but, on argument, the caveat was dismissed.

Cochrane now moved for liberty to appeal against the order dismissing the caveat.

Dickinson, contrà. No appeal lies for the dismissal of a caveat. The effect of a caveat in the Spiritual Court is to prevent the Judge from granting probate to a will for three months, (*Jacobs' Law Dictionary, ad voc.*); but the Common Law Courts do not regard a caveat at all. And this appeal is purely frivolous.

Cur. adv. vult.

PERRY, J.—The right of appeal is so essential for the maintenance of the uniformity of the law in its administration by inferior Courts that I think it is our bounden duty to give every facility to it, and that the only limitation, which we should seek to place upon its exercise, should have reference to those cases where it is resorted to as a means of vexation or delay. According to the Canon Law, as cited by Lynwood, "*discussio appellationis an sit justa vel injusta, frivola vel non frivola, non spectat ad judicem a quo appellatur, sed ad judicem ad quem*" (*a*), and although, by the clause in our charter, power is given to this Court to deal with frivolous appeals, and a petition for leave to appeal is necessary, I am much inclined to doubt

(*a*) See 1 Add. R. 21, *in not.*

1845.

In the goods of BHIMJI.

whether the Court has any power to refuse the subject that right to appeal which is given absolutely in terms in the commencement of the appeal clause, provided, that is to say, that the conditions imposed as restrictions on that right are fully complied with by him.

The objections to this appeal are, that the decision did not affect any matter of property, and that it was not given in a *civil cause.*

But, as to the first, we have the authority of the Privy Council, in *Nathoobhoy Ramdass* v. *Mooljee Madowdass,* that he right of "appeal is not *confined* to cases in which some right or duty is finally decided," and in the Ecclesiastical Courts we know that appeals have always lain upon interlocutory matters, technically called grievances.

And as to the expression *civil* cause, I think it is quite clear that the ambiguous word *civil* is used in that passage of the charter in opposition to *criminal,* and that it embraces every decision upon civil rights and liabilities, so far as they can be distinguished from decisions in Crown cases.

I have laid these views before the Chief Justice, and he thinks "there can be no doubt as to the party being entitled to appeal, but to obviate objections," (he suggests, as I had before suggested), "that the appeal should be against both the dismissal of the caveat and the order for administration, the latter being consequent upon the former."

INDEX.

THE END.